Climate Change and Energy Transition

The series aims to provide a collection of books covering all relevant topics on climate change and energy transition. It starts from a global perspective and pays special attention to the interdisciplinary nature of this area. The objective of this series is to provide a full range of coverage on theoretical, empirical, and policy-relevant research addressing climate-driven energy transition problems. It aims to present contents at different levels and target broad categories of readers including policymakers, researchers, and also the general public. By covering the most recent advances in this area, the series seeks to provide a toolbox of relevant information, a platform for knowledge sharing, and also a forum for debates on relevant topics.

Fei Wu · Dayong Zhang · Qiang Ji
Editors

Climate Finance

Supporting a Sustainable Energy Transition

ISETS
INTERNATIONAL SOCIETY FOR
ENERGY TRANSITION STUDIES

Springer

Editors
Fei Wu
Southwestern University of Finance and Economics
Chengdu, China

Dayong Zhang
Southwestern University of Finance and Economics
Chengdu, China

Qiang Ji
Institutes of Science and Development
Chinese Academy of Sciences
Beijing, China

ISSN 2731-9903 ISSN 2731-9911 (electronic)
Climate Change and Energy Transition
ISBN 978-981-97-3307-1 ISBN 978-981-97-3308-8 (eBook)
https://doi.org/10.1007/978-981-97-3308-8

This Springer imprint is published by the registered company Springer Nature Singapore Pte Ltd.
The registered company address is: 152 Beach Road, #21-01/04 Gateway East, Singapore 189721, Singapore

Contents

The Emerging Field of Climate Finance: Theory, Practice, and Frontiers

Fei Wu, Dayong Zhang, and Qiang Ji

Abstract Against the backdrop of global efforts to actively address the challenges of climate change, the development of climate finance, covering both investing and financing, has become an international consensus. Academically, climate finance has emerged as a burgeoning interdisciplinary field exploring the connection between climate change and financial activities, giving rise to climate finance theory. This chapter systematically introduces the conceptual issues of climate finance, reviews the latest research development in the field of climate finance through a bibliometric approach, and discusses the theoretical frontiers and application scenarios for the future development of the climate finance discipline. China's experiences in climate finance are introduced to showcase the importance of a comprehensive approach that combines fund support, academic research, and industry collaboration.

Keywords Climate finance · Emerging fields · Theory and practice · Cutting-edge topics

1 Introduction

Over the past century, climate change has emerged as an ever-growing threat to humanity, casting a shadow over the delicate balance of our global environment. The unmistakable signs of this phenomenon manifest in the increasing frequency and intensity of natural disasters and extreme weather events, each leaving an indelible

F. Wu (✉) · D. Zhang
Research Institute of Economics and Management, Southwestern University of Finance and Economics, 555 Liutai Avenue, Chengdu 611130, China
e-mail: wufei@swufe.edu.cn

Q. Ji
Institutes of Science and Development, Chinese Academy of Sciences, Beijing 100190, China

School of Public Policy and Management, University of Chinese Academy of Sciences, Beijing 100049, China

F. Wu et al. (eds.), *Climate Finance*, Climate Change and Energy Transition,
https://doi.org/10.1007/978-981-97-3308-8_1

mark on diverse regions across the globe. What was once considered sporadic occurrences have become unsettlingly regular, challenging the resilience of communities and ecosystems worldwide and surpassing the expectations of even the most vigilant observers.

In response to this escalating crisis, the international community, cognizant of the urgency and gravity of the situation, took a historic step with the establishment of the United Nations Framework Convention on Climate Change (UNFCCC). This pivotal moment marked a collective acknowledgment of the need for coordinated global action to address the multifaceted challenges posed by a changing climate. Since its inception, the UNFCCC has become the cornerstone of international efforts, providing a platform for nations to come together, share insights, and forge agreements in the pursuit of sustainable solutions.

Built upon multiple rounds of intense international negotiations, countries around the world have gradually coalesced into a consensus, recognizing the imperative to confront the climate crisis as a long-term development strategy. This consensus reflects a shared understanding that the impacts of climate change extend beyond geographical boundaries and societal structures, affecting the very fabric of our interconnected world. As a result, nations have committed to collaborative endeavours aimed at mitigating the causes of climate change, adapting to its inevitable consequences, and fostering global resilience to safeguard the well-being of current and future generations.

Notwithstanding, global actions to address climate change and climate crisis remain slow, and the situation regarding climate change has become even more dire. The Sixth Assessment Report of the United Nations Intergovernmental Panel on Climate Change (IPCC) points out that climate change is expanding globally at a faster pace. Unless rapid and substantial actions are taken to reduce greenhouse gas emissions worldwide, it will be difficult to achieve the goal of limiting global temperature rise to 2 °C and striving to keep it within 1.5 °C. It is estimated that by 2030, the direct damage costs to health due to climate change will be approximately 2–4 billion US dollars annually (World Health Organization 2021). The impact of global climate change is leading to significant changes in the entire Earth's ecosystem, threatening the security of human economic and social systems and even directly affected the survival of some nations (Dell et al. 2012).

The demands to address the climate crisis and pursue sustainable development are pressing. However, achieving established climate goals is extremely challenging, requiring concerted efforts across borders and facing significant risks and challenges. One crucial constraint is the contradiction between investment needs and financing constraints. Whether it is through energy conservation, emissions reduction and carbon sequestration to mitigate climate change, or proactive adaptation to climate change, substantial financial investments are required. According to the World Bank's 2019 estimates, the world will need \$90 trillion in climate-related investments over the next 15 years. Boehm et al. (2021) estimate that by 2030, the annual climate finance flows will reach \$5 trillion to limit global warming to 1.5 °C. Looking at the developed economies, the European Commission estimates show that to achieve EU's zero net greenhouse gas emissions by 2050, investments in energy and infrastructure, which are mainly provided by the private sector, will need to rise from 2 to 2.8% of EU's gross domestic product (GDP).[1] Similar estimates are made for future spending on decarbonizing power generation in the United States (Hong et al. 2020).

In terms of developing economies, the United Nations Environment Programme (UNEP)'s 2022 Adaption Gap Report (UNEP 2022) estimates that the annual climate adaptation costs for developing countries will rise from $70 billion in 2020 to as high as $140–300 billion by 2030. China as the world's largest emitter of greenhouse gases faces tremendous pressure to reduce emissions. This necessitates increased climate investment and financing, supported by corresponding theoretical frameworks. According to the 2021 report by China's Climate Policy Initiative titled "Unlocking the Potential of Climate Finance in China," domestic climate-related investments currently account for only 4% of the entire financial system. To meet China's climate commitments, the country will require an annual investment of 9.5 trillion yuan (approximately 1.5 trillion US dollars) over the next decade.

Climate finance plays a pivotal role in supporting and accelerating the transition to a low-carbon and resilient global economy. The growth of domestic climate investment and financing reflects a commitment to addressing climate change at the national level. Coordinated progress in emission reduction goals and financial systems is essential for ensuring that climate finance aligns with broader climate objectives. This involves integrating climate considerations into financial regulations, risk assessments, and investment strategies. By aligning financial systems with emission reduction goals, countries can create an enabling environment for sustainable finance and ensure that capital is directed toward climate-friendly projects. Countries worldwide are increasingly recognizing the economic, environmental, and social benefits of sustainable practices. Governments, businesses, and financial institutions are collaborating to channel funds into projects and initiatives that contribute to emission reduction, climate resilience, and the overall sustainability agenda.

As nations strive to meet their climate commitments and transition toward sustainability, understanding the complexities of climate finance becomes essential. The rapid development of domestic climate investment and financing, along with coordinated progress in emission reduction goals and the financial system, highlights the increasing importance of establishing and advancing comprehensive climate finance theories. These theories should encompass various aspects, including financial instruments, risk management strategies, and innovative funding mechanisms. Comprehensive theories can guide policymakers, financial institutions, and investors in making informed decisions that contribute to effective climate action.

Financing momentum, channels, and risks have become new challenges for the global climate change response. The outbreak of the global COVID-19 pandemic has added additional complexity to the landscape of climate finance. The economic recession triggered by the pandemic has intensified international climate finance pressures. Governments worldwide are grappling with the need to address both the immediate challenges posed by the pandemic and the long-term imperative of combating

[1] EU's 2050 Climate Plan Sees Benefits of Up to 2% of GDP, Euractiv, 28 November 2018.

climate change. The pandemic has disrupted financing momentum, altered channels for climate investments, and introduced new risks to the global climate change response. Despite the challenges, the post-pandemic recovery presents an opportunity for a "green recovery." Governments and financial institutions can prioritize investments in sustainable and resilient infrastructure, clean energy projects, and climate adaptation initiatives. This approach not only addresses immediate economic needs but also contributes to long-term climate goals.

In the face of the increasing global demand for climate investment and financing, climate finance, as an emerging interdisciplinary academic field, has attracted widespread attention from scholars worldwide (Stroebel and Wurgler 2021). Climate finance, as a newly emerging discipline, extends beyond the basic question of funding sources for climate-related initiatives. It encompasses a wide array of issues with profound social significance and urgent practical needs. The research in climate finance operates on multiple levels, addressing macro-scale systemic challenges and micro-level intricacies within organizations. The goal is to develop comprehensive theoretical frameworks, methodologies, and practical toolkits that can guide decision-makers, corporations, and investors in navigating the complexities of climate-related investments. Here are key aspects that highlight the breadth and depth of climate finance research.

At a macro level, climate finance research deals with overarching challenges related to system design and market development. This involves creating and optimizing financial systems and structures that can effectively channel funds towards climate-friendly projects. It also encompasses the development of markets for climate-related financial instruments, fostering liquidity and transparency to attract a diverse range of investors. At the micro level, climate finance research delves into corporate investment and internal governance issues. Corporations play a pivotal role in climate action, and understanding their investment strategies, risk assessments, and internal governance mechanisms is crucial. This micro-level analysis helps identify best practices, assess the effectiveness of climate-related investments, and explore ways to integrate sustainable practices into corporate governance.

From a theoretical standpoint, climate finance research aims to contribute to the development of frameworks and methodologies specific to investment and financing for addressing the climate crisis. This involves exploring new financial instruments, risk assessment models, and valuation methods tailored to the unique characteristics of climate-related projects. Developing robust theoretical foundations is essential for guiding practitioners and policymakers in making informed decisions.

Climate finance research also has a practical orientation, seeking to provide toolkits for decision-makers. These toolkits include resources for enhancing risk supervision and institutional development. Decision-makers, whether in government or the private sector, can benefit from practical guidance on integrating climate considerations into financial decision-making processes. This includes assessing climate-related risks, identifying investment opportunities, and incorporating sustainability into overall institutional development. Notably, investors play a critical role in driving climate finance. Research in this field aims to offer guidance and services for investors to mitigate risks associated with low-carbon investment.

This involves developing strategies for evaluating the climate resilience of investment portfolios, understanding the potential impacts of climate change on assets, and incorporating sustainable practices into investment decisions.

In summary, the research in climate finance is a multidimensional and interdisciplinary endeavour. It operates at different scales, from the systemic design of financial markets to the internal governance structures of individual corporations. It balances theoretical exploration with practical applications, aiming to equip decision-makers and investors with the knowledge and tools needed to navigate the challenges and opportunities presented by the climate crisis. As the urgency of climate action grows, the insights generated by climate finance research become increasingly critical for steering the global economy toward a sustainable and resilient future.

This chapter systematically examines the research field of climate finance, considering the environmental context that gave rise to climate finance theories and taking into account the needs and challenges faced by various countries such as China in achieving their decarbonization goals. It starts from the fundamental conceptual definitions and unique characteristics of this discipline and reviews the latest developments in relevant fields. This chapter comprehensively reflects on the interdisciplinary nature of climate finance research, with the aim of promoting the construction of theoretical frameworks in climate finance. It further provides a concise overview of the development trajectory of climate finance in China, highlighting its distinctive features in both theoretical research and practical activities. The case of China is hoped to be generalizable in a broader global context. Finally, the chapter discusses the theoretical frontiers and application scenarios for the future development of the climate finance discipline.

2 Climate Finance: Definition and Attributes

Defining climate finance is a crucial step in understanding the trajectory and significance of research in this field. The UNFCCC provides a comprehensive definition of climate finance, serving as a foundational framework for researchers, policymakers, and practitioners. According to the UNFCCC, climate finance is defined as: "Local, national, or transnational financing—drawn from public, private, and alternative sources of financing—that seeks to support mitigation and adaptation actions that will address climate change."[2]

This definition encapsulates several key elements. It implies that climate finance encompasses a broad spectrum of financing mechanisms that can operate at the local, national, or transnational levels. This acknowledges the multi-dimensional nature of climate change and the need for financial support across different geographical scales. Second, climate finance draws from a variety of sources, including public, private, and alternative financing. Public sources may involve funding from governments or international institutions, private sources could include investments from

[2] https://unfccc.int/topics/introduction-to-climate-finance.

businesses or individuals, and alternative sources might involve innovative financial instruments or mechanisms designed to mobilize climate-related funding. Third, the primary purpose of climate finance is to support both mitigation and adaptation actions. Mitigation actions aim to reduce or prevent the emission of greenhouse gases, addressing the root causes of climate change. Adaptation actions, on the other hand, seek to enhance resilience and reduce vulnerability to the impacts of climate change, acknowledging that some level of climate change is already inevitable. Fourth, the transnational nature of climate finance recognizes the global nature of climate change. It implies that financial support may flow across borders to address climate challenges collectively. This highlights the shared responsibility of the international community in mobilizing resources to combat climate change.

As climate finance research progresses, scholars and practitioners explore various aspects of this definition. While the term "climate finance" captures the broader financial support for climate-related actions, some scholars may be more acquainted with specific terms such as "green finance" and "carbon finance." Each of these terms highlights different aspects of the broader climate finance landscape and has specific implications for sustainable development and environmental conservation.

Green finance encompasses a series of financial activities conducted to advance environmental governance and promote the clean and efficient utilization of resources. It encompasses a range of financial instruments and mechanisms aimed at supporting projects with positive environmental impacts. These may include renewable energy projects, energy efficiency initiatives, sustainable infrastructure development, and other ventures that align with environmental and climate objectives. Green finance plays a crucial role in redirecting capital towards environmentally friendly and sustainable practices.

Carbon finance, as an innovative financing activity, specifically addresses the trading of carbon credits or offsets as a means of mitigating greenhouse gas emissions. It involves the financial valuation of emission reductions achieved through projects or activities that reduce or sequester carbon dioxide. Carbon finance mechanisms, such as financial derivatives trading, cap-and-trade systems or voluntary offset markets, create financial incentives for entities to adopt cleaner technologies and reduce their carbon footprint. These mechanisms aim to facilitate the transition to a low-carbon economy by assigning economic value to emission reductions.

Within the scope of financial activities, green finance has the broadest scope, followed by climate finance, with carbon finance having the narrowest scope. Although in practice, all these concepts aim to improve the environment and address the challenges of climate change, theoretically, climate finance possesses its own uniqueness and a more rigorous academic characteristic. This can be understood by borrowing from the definition in economics. For instance, climate economics is a well-defined interdisciplinary field with a clear theoretical framework and complete structure. Green economics, on the other hand, is more of a concept rather than a discipline. Similarly, green finance emphasizes the broader use of financial activities to address environmental issues, while climate finance focuses specifically on financial activities related to climate change. By reviewing the development of the international climate finance system, a framework has already taken shape, with national entities and international organizations being key players. This framework plays a vital role in global climate investment and financing processes (Zhang et al. 2019; Watson and Schalatek 2020).

The global nature of the climate crisis necessitates an international perspective when addressing climate finance. Climate change affects all countries, albeit to varying degrees, and collaboration on an international scale is essential to effectively combat its impacts. Consequently, the academic discourse and practical application of the climate finance system inherently possess an international attribute. The principles and standards developed in this context are designed to be universally applicable across countries and regions. The UNFCCC serves as a foundational international instrument in this regard. In its early articulations, the UNFCCC established that climate financing aims to achieve several key objectives, including the reduction of greenhouse gas emissions, the decrease of vulnerability of human and ecosystem systems to adverse climate impacts, and the enhancement of their capacity to resist climate-related risks. These objectives underline the comprehensive and global nature of climate finance, emphasizing the need for international cooperation to address climate challenges effectively.

Over the years, as nations and stakeholders have engaged in practical efforts to implement climate finance, basic standards and a foundation for international cooperation in this field have been established. These standards encompass various aspects, including transparency, accountability, and the alignment of financial flows with climate goals. Multilateral initiatives and financial mechanisms, such as the Green Climate Fund, have been developed to facilitate the mobilization of climate finance on a global scale. However, despite the existence of these international standards and cooperative frameworks, the current emphasis, both at the national and international levels, often revolves around policy formulation related to climate investment and financing. Practical activities, such as the development and implementation of climate-related projects, are at the forefront of current efforts. From a disciplinary perspective, there is a notable focus on the practical application of climate finance principles, while a universal definition is missing.

This chapter posits that climate finance is an emerging interdisciplinary field, which studies the relationship between climate change and financial activities. Climate finance fully integrates the critical attributes and essential characteristics of climate with traditional financial theories, researching the impact of climate change on asset pricing, investment and financing, financial risks, financial policies, and a series of financial issues. From the perspective of disciplinary development, climate finance holds significant practical significance and theoretical value.

2.1 Climate Finance: A Complex Giant System

In essence, climate finance refers to all financial activities conducted globally to address the climate crisis and achieve sustainable development. It constitutes a complex giant system encompassing multiple dimensions (see Fig. 1). The research

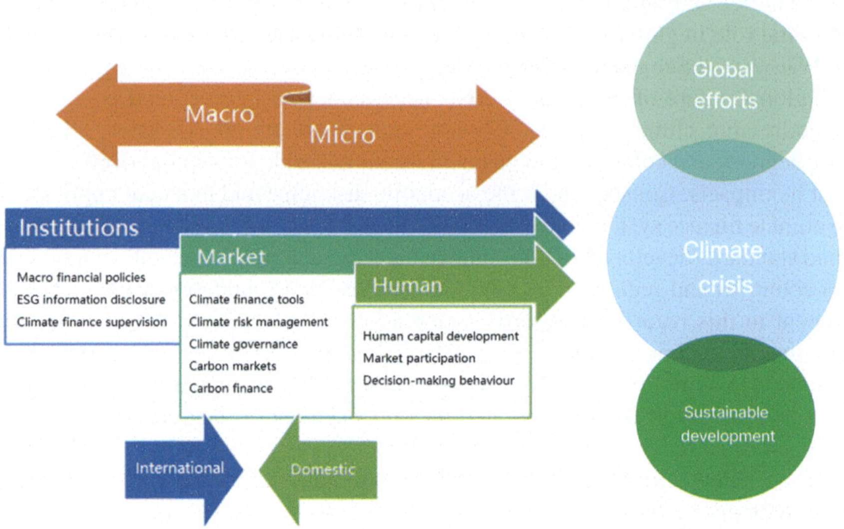

Fig. 1 Climate finance: a complex giant system with multiple dimensions

in climate finance investigates the situations of both individual countries and the international community. It seeks to provide evidence and toolkits to support both domestic sustainable development in response to the climate crisis and international cooperation in climate finance. Meanwhile, both macro and micro levels are considered. It involves research at the institutional, market, and human levels. At the institutional level, issues such as macro financial policies, ESG (Environment, Social and Governance) information disclosure, and climate finance supervision all fall into the scope of climate finance research. At the market level, climate finance includes the examination and evaluation of climate finance tools, climate risk management and governance, carbon markets and carbon finance, etc. At the human level, climate finance covers topics related to human capital development, market participation, and decision-making behaviour.

2.1.1 Inclusivity

First, the research perspective on climate finance is inherently broad and externally inclusive due to the global and public good nature of climate change. Several key aspects contribute to this inclusivity, shaping the theoretical frameworks and interdisciplinary nature of climate finance research. Climate change is a global challenge that transcends national borders. The impacts of climate change, such as rising temperatures, extreme weather events, and sea-level rise, have consequences that extend far beyond the borders of individual countries. The externality of climate change implies that its effects are not confined to those directly responsible for emitting greenhouse gases. As a result, addressing climate change requires collective global efforts, and climate finance becomes a tool for international collaboration in mitigating and adapting to its impacts. On the other hand, climate, like the environment, possesses the characteristics of a public good. This means that its benefits, such as a stable climate and healthy ecosystems, are non-excludable and non-rivalrous. Everyone shares the same atmosphere and climate system, and actions taken by one country or entity to address climate change can have positive externalities for others. The public good nature of climate emphasizes the importance of considering broader societal and global interests when designing theoretical frameworks for climate finance.

The term "inclusive" in the context of climate finance draws from development economics, particularly the concept of "inclusive growth." Introduced by the Asian Development Bank in 2007, inclusive growth emphasizes people-cantered, harmonious development among individuals, society, and nature. Applying this concept to climate finance means considering the diverse stakeholders involved in climate-related actions. These stakeholders include governments, international organizations, private sector entities, civil society, and affected communities, indigenous groups, and vulnerable populations. The diversity of stakeholders underscores the complexity of climate finance, requiring an inclusive approach to address the differing needs, priorities, and capacities of these entities, and to realize equitable participation and benefits distribution in the pursuit of sustainable and climate-resilient development.

Therefore, the inclusivity of climate finance research stems from the recognition that climate change is a global challenge with externalities that affect societies worldwide. The public good nature of the climate and the principles of inclusive growth emphasize the importance of considering the diverse interests and stakeholders involved in climate-related actions. An inclusive approach in developing the theoretical frameworks and methodologies for climate finance is essential for addressing the complexities of a global issue that requires collaborative and comprehensive solutions.

2.1.2 Macro and Micro Systems

The research scale in climate finance is characterized by its organic integration of macro and micro systems. After experiencing three centuries of the industrial revolution, the harm caused by climate change is not only manifested in physical disasters but also permeate various dimensions of the economy and society. Climate change influences ecological chains, disrupts supply chains, and poses risks to financial systems. Beyond the immediate environmental consequences, climate change affects the stability and resilience of economies, posing risks to industries, infrastructure, and livelihoods. The repercussions extend to the broader socio-economic system, impacting employment, income distribution, and overall societal well-being. The socio-economic impact of the climate crisis is vast and immeasurable. The interconnectedness of environmental and economic systems necessitates a comprehensive approach that addresses both the causes and consequences of climate change.

This dual-scale perspective is thus essential for comprehensively understanding and addressing the complex challenges posed by the climate crisis.

Climate finance research at the macro level involves a top-down approach, focusing on broad regulatory frameworks, policy interventions, and market structures. Given the systemic and global nature of climate change, macro-level research aims to design and implement regulatory measures that can effectively guide financial systems and markets toward sustainable and climate-resilient practices. This includes the development of international standards, climate-related financial regulations, and policy incentives to channel investments into environmentally friendly projects. In short, macro-level research essentially explores ways to align financial systems with climate goals, develop sustainable investment frameworks, and create incentives for low-carbon activities.

Simultaneously, climate finance research delves into the micro level, adopting a bottom-up approach that examines the intricacies of risk management and market behaviour. On the micro level, research focuses on understanding how businesses and financial institutions adapt to climate risks, integrate environmental considerations into decision-making, and contribute to the development of sustainable markets. This micro-level perspective recognizes that individual entities, such as businesses, financial institutions, and investors, play crucial roles in shaping the trajectory of climate finance.

The organic combination of macro and micro systems in climate finance research is essential for developing holistic solutions to the challenges posed by climate change. This dual-scale perspective recognizes the interplay between overarching regulatory structures and the nuanced decision-making of individual entities. By addressing both macro and micro aspects, climate finance research aims to contribute to the creation of resilient, sustainable, and climate-friendly financial systems that can effectively respond to the multifaceted impacts of the climate crisis.

2.1.3 Institution, Market and Human

From a research level perspective, climate finance operates across three key dimensions: institution, market, and human. Each of these levels plays a critical role in shaping the trajectory of climate finance, reflecting the interconnectedness of policies, market dynamics, and human behaviour.

The development of climate finance is closely related to the macro policies and institutions of a country. The institutional level of climate finance research is therefore concerned with the macro policies and structures that guide and govern financial systems within a country. The case of China provides a good example of the transition from traditional economic growth models to a more sustainable and environmentally conscious approach. Historically, China pursued rapid economic growth that, at times, led to significant consumption of fossil energy and environmental degradation. However, recognizing the environmental challenges and the need for sustainable development, China has shifted its focus towards high-quality and sustainable economic growth. This transition places green development at the forefront of China's economic agenda. Green development emphasizes environmentally friendly and sustainable practices that prioritize the preservation of natural resources. To support this shift, the government has set key objectives to build a green financial system, emphasizing the integration of environmental considerations into financial policies and practices. This system aims to channel funds towards projects and initiatives that promote green development, including investments in renewable energy, energy efficiency, pollution control, and ecological conservation. The guiding ideologies related to climate investment and financing system construction, as outlined by the Chinese government, are pivotal in shaping the development of China's climate finance system. Regulatory measures, policy frameworks, and institutional structures are integral components of the top-level design, influencing how climate finance operates within a given jurisdiction.

The core of climate finance lies in market construction. At the market level, research focuses on developing climate investment and financing tools, innovating climate financial derivatives, constructing carbon financial markets, improving climate risk management, and enhancing climate governance. A well-functioning market is essential for translating policy guidance into effective and liquid financial mechanisms. It stimulates the active participation of private capital and facilitates the flow of funds toward sustainable and climate-resilient projects. The market level represents the practical implementation and operationalization of climate finance within the broader financial ecosystem.

The human level encompasses the behaviours and decisions of individuals within the climate finance ecosystem. Both investment decisions and market supervision rely on human capital. Understanding and influencing human behaviour are essential aspects of climate finance research, shaping how financial actors respond to climate-related risks and opportunities. Decision-makers, investors, and the public collectively form a crucial link in the success of climate finance initiatives. The behaviours of these stakeholders influence the allocation of funds, the adoption of sustainable practices, and the overall effectiveness of climate finance strategies. Specifically, researchers examine the decision-making processes of individuals and institutions involved in climate finance, exploring factors that influence their choices, risk perceptions, and motivations. The behaviour of investors, ranging from institutional investors to individual investors, is another key focus. Research in this area explores how investors integrate climate considerations into their portfolios, assess climate risks, and engage in sustainable investment practices. Research further explores how to enhance public understanding of climate-related financial issues and encourage environmentally conscious choices, as public perception, awareness, and demand for sustainable finance products are integral to the success of climate finance.

The three levels of climate finance research—institutional, market, and human—work in concert to shape the development and effectiveness of climate finance systems. The success of climate finance initiatives depends on the alignment of macro policies, the functionality of financial markets, and the informed and sustainable behaviours of individuals and institutions. A comprehensive approach that addresses these interconnected levels is essential for building resilient, adaptive, and sustainable climate finance systems that contribute to global climate goals.

2.2 *Climate Finance: An Interdisciplinary Field*

2.2.1 Interdisciplinary Development of Climate Finance

Climate finance, as an interdisciplinary field, stands at the intersection of various academic disciplines, borrowing theories and knowledge from diverse domains to address the complex challenges posed by climate change (see Fig. 2). The interdisciplinary development of climate finance reflects the need to draw insights and methodologies from various fields. An inclusive approach to disciplinary development ensures that climate finance research integrates perspectives from economics, finance, environmental science, policy studies, and other relevant fields.

One of the foundational pillars supporting climate finance research is rooted in finance theories and practices. Drawing inspiration from asset pricing, corporate finance, and international financial markets, researchers in this field utilize established theoretical frameworks to analyze the dynamics of financial instruments and markets within the context of climate-related investments. This approach helps in understanding how financial mechanisms can be structured to incentivize sustainable practices and efficiently allocate resources. In addition to theoretical underpinnings, climate finance research incorporates technical methods derived from models and techniques in finance. These tools provide quantitative insights into risk assessment,

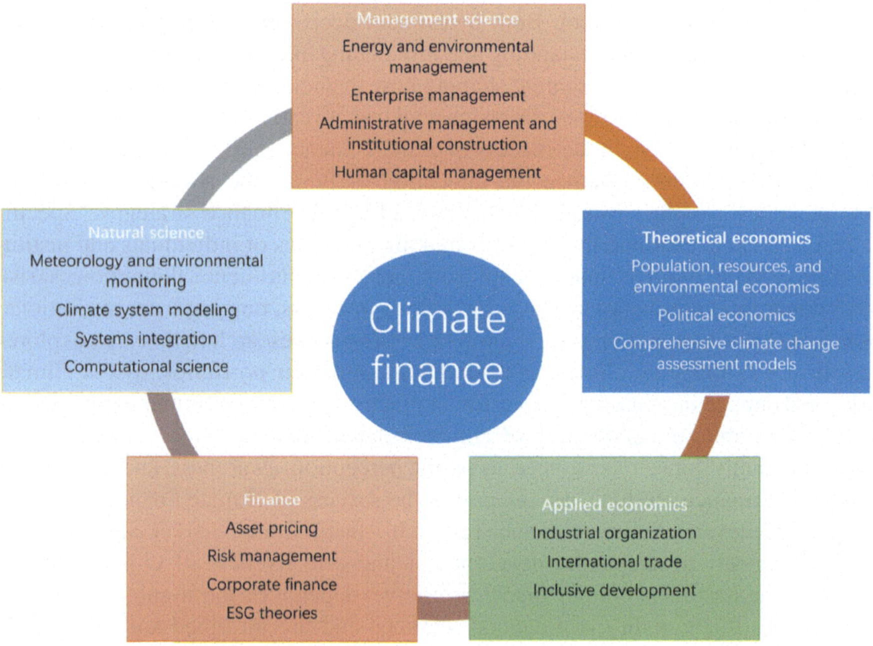

Fig. 2 Climate finance: an interdisciplinary subject

return expectations, and the overall performance of climate-related financial instruments. By adapting and extending traditional financial models, researchers can assess the impact of climate risks and uncertainties on investment portfolios, facilitating the development of resilient and adaptive financial strategies.

On the other hand, the forward-looking nature of climate finance research necessitates a robust integration of fine-grained data, big data analytics, and intelligent tools from the natural sciences. Climate scientists and environmental researchers contribute essential data and insights, enabling finance professionals to make informed decisions that account for the long-term implications of climate change. This collaboration between finance and natural sciences ensures that climate finance strategies are grounded in a comprehensive understanding of the environmental challenges they seek to address.

Furthermore, the design of effective climate finance frameworks requires insights from management science. This involves understanding organizational structures, decision-making processes, and the strategic management of resources within the context of climate-related initiatives. Additionally, theoretical support from economics provides the foundation for developing models that assess the economic viability and societal impacts of climate finance interventions.

Additionally, the imperative to transition energy systems and address the global climate crisis underscores the pivotal role of knowledge from the fields of energy and environmental management in the realm of climate finance. The intricate relationship between energy production, consumption, and environmental impact necessitates a deep understanding of these dynamics to formulate effective financial strategies that promote sustainability. Within the context of climate finance research, insights from energy management are crucial for evaluating the financial implications of transitioning to cleaner and more sustainable energy sources. Researchers and practitioners need to navigate the complexities of energy markets, understand the economic viability of renewable energy projects, and assess the financial risks and returns associated with different energy transition scenarios. This integration of energy management knowledge ensures that climate finance initiatives align with the broader goals of decarbonization and sustainable energy development.

Environmental management expertise is equally vital for climate finance, as it provides a framework for evaluating the environmental impact of financial decisions and investments. This includes assessing the ecological footprint of projects, considering biodiversity conservation, and accounting for the broader environmental externalities associated with different investment choices. The incorporation of environmental management principles into climate finance ensures that financial decisions not only contribute to climate mitigation but also promote overall environmental stewardship.

In this regard, relevant knowledge from the natural sciences is of significant importance for climate finance research. For example, satellite remote sensing technology emerges as a powerful tool in climate finance research to monitor and assess various environmental indicators critical to climate change, with a particular focus on carbon emissions. By utilizing satellite remote sensing, researchers can dynamically supervise changes in carbon emissions, enabling real-time monitoring and evaluation of the effectiveness of climate finance interventions. Furthermore, it facilitates the effective pricing of carbon assets by providing transparent and verifiable data on emissions levels, contributing to the development of robust carbon markets.

2.2.2 Challenges in Disciplinary Development of Climate Finance

The construction of the climate capital market represents a formidable challenge, and a critical aspect of this challenge lies in the absence of clear theoretical guidance on how to mobilize substantial amounts of capital, attract increased participation from the private sector, and ensure the effectiveness of climate investments. The complexity of aligning financial markets with climate goals requires innovative and robust theoretical frameworks that currently face significant gaps and uncertainties.

Raising large amounts of capital for climate finance initiatives necessitates the development of strategies that appeal to a diverse range of investors. Traditional financial markets may lack the mechanisms and incentives to adequately channel funds toward sustainable and climate-resilient projects. Bridging this gap requires the creation of new financial instruments, innovative risk-sharing mechanisms, and policy frameworks that align financial incentives with environmental and social objectives. Attracting private capital to participate in climate finance is another hurdle that requires attention. Private sector engagement is crucial for scaling up climate investments, and yet, barriers such as perceived risks, uncertainties, and the absence of standardized metrics for evaluating climate impact can impede private investors. Clear theoretical guidance is essential to create an environment that encourages private capital to flow into climate-friendly projects and initiatives. Ensuring the effectiveness of climate investments is a multifaceted challenge that involves not only mobilizing capital but also deploying it strategically to achieve tangible and sustainable outcomes. The lack of well-defined theoretical models can impede the development of investment strategies that balance financial returns with long-term environmental and social benefits. The integration of climate impact assessments, robust risk management practices, and adaptive financial instruments requires theoretical frameworks that are currently underdeveloped.

In addition to theoretical challenges, the shortage of professionals with interdisciplinary expertise in both climate and finance poses a significant obstacle. The successful construction and improvement of the climate capital market demand a workforce equipped with a nuanced understanding of climate science, financial markets, risk management, and sustainable investment practices. The scarcity of individuals with this interdisciplinary skill set hampers the effective functioning of the entire complex system. Addressing these human resource constraints requires targeted efforts to cultivate a workforce that can bridge the gap between climate and finance. Educational programs, training initiatives, and professional development opportunities can play a pivotal role in nurturing a cadre of experts capable of navigating the intersection of climate science and financial markets.

2.2.3 From Local to Global

The international dimension of climate finance adds layers of complexity to the relationship between financial activities within a country and its climate conditions. Recognizing the interconnected nature of climate change and the global economy, it becomes essential for financial activities related to climate considerations to transcend domestic boundaries. This entails not only assessing the status quo of domestic financial systems and market development but also taking into account the dynamics of the international environment and the evolving trends and characteristics of the global climate finance system.

In the context of global initiatives, the strategic deployment of the 19th Central Committee of the Communist Party of China, as exemplified by the promotion of a new development pattern with domestic circulation as the mainstay and the reinforcement of domestic and foreign markets, reflects a recognition of the need for an integrated approach to economic development. This approach aligns with the interconnected nature of climate issues and the understanding that effective climate finance strategies must consider both domestic and international factors. The concept of "dual circulation" acknowledges that a country's economic development is influenced not only by internal factors but also by its interactions with the global economy. In the context of climate finance, this dual circulation policy framework emphasizes the importance of international relations and politics. Climate change is a global challenge that requires collaborative efforts and shared responsibilities across nations. Therefore, international cooperation and diplomatic relations play a crucial role in shaping climate finance theories and practices.

Constructing a robust global climate finance system necessitates collaboration, broader consensus, and improvements in rules, regulations, supervision, and guiding policies across all countries. The complexity of climate change and the need for significant financial resources to address it underscore the importance of creating a coherent and well-coordinated international framework. This involves aligning policies, regulations, and financial mechanisms to facilitate the flow of climate finance across borders, ensuring that investments are directed where they are most needed and can have the most significant impact on mitigating and adapting to climate change.

Additionally, addressing climate change through finance requires consideration of geopolitical dynamics and international relations. Negotiating and establishing global agreements on climate finance involve navigating political landscapes, fostering cooperation, and building trust among nations. The success of international climate finance initiatives relies on the ability to navigate and overcome geopolitical challenges to create a supportive environment for sustainable and equitable development.

In summary, the interdisciplinary nature of climate finance sets it apart from many existing disciplines, emphasizing the need for a specialized and cohesive field to address the complexities associated with financing initiatives aimed at mitigating and adapting to climate change. The theoretical foundations of climate finance are crucial for guiding practical interventions and decision-making processes. As the field continues to evolve, there is a need for well-established frameworks that can inform the design of financial instruments, risk management strategies, and policy interventions. Theoretical advancements are necessary to address the evolving dynamics of climate finance, considering factors such as technological innovations, changes in global geopolitics, and emerging environmental challenges. The international attribute of climate finance emphasizes the need to go beyond domestic considerations and take into account the broader global context. International relations, politics, and collaboration are integral components of climate finance theories and practices. The construction of a global climate finance system requires concerted efforts to enhance cooperation, build consensus, and improve regulatory frameworks on an international scale.

3 The Development Trajectory of Climate Finance Research

3.1 Overview of Publications on Climate Finance

To summarize the publications on climate finance topics, the study of Zhang et al. (2023) reviews the latest research progress in the field of climate finance through a bibliometric analysis approach. The authors first use the term climate finance as the keywords to search for published articles indexed in the Social Sciences Citation Index (SSCI) within the fields of economics, business, or finance. Through co-occurrence analysis of keywords in these articles, we attempt to comprehensively and objectively capture the research directions and research contents in the field of climate finance, so as to provide an overview of the development trajectory of climate finance theory. The publications included here covers the period from 1 January 1980 to 17 October 2021, incorporating a total of 3,239 articles.

Figure 3 displays the annual publication count of climate finance literature based on Zhang et al. (2023). The earliest publication dates back to 1988, and until 2008, research in the climate finance field remained limited. After 2008, there was an exponential growth in related publications, increasing from 41 to 413 articles in 2020, marking a tenfold increase. As of 17 October 2021, there were 396 publications for that year. These articles were published across 410 different journals, indicating the diversification of climate finance research across various subfields. Table 1 lists the top 10 journals based on the volume of published articles on climate finance. *Energy Policy* ranks first with 546 articles, followed by *Ecological Economics* with 250 articles and then *Energy Economics* with 160 articles.

Zhang et al. (2023) then conduct co-occurrence analysis of keywords to identify and analyze the hot topics and main directions in climate finance research. Specifically, Zhang et al. (2023) set a one-year time slice for the literature data and extract the top 50 keywords with the highest citation frequency for each time slice. Figure 4 presents the co-occurrence network, consisting of 499 keyword nodes and 1,453 connections. Larger nodes indicate higher co-occurrence frequencies,

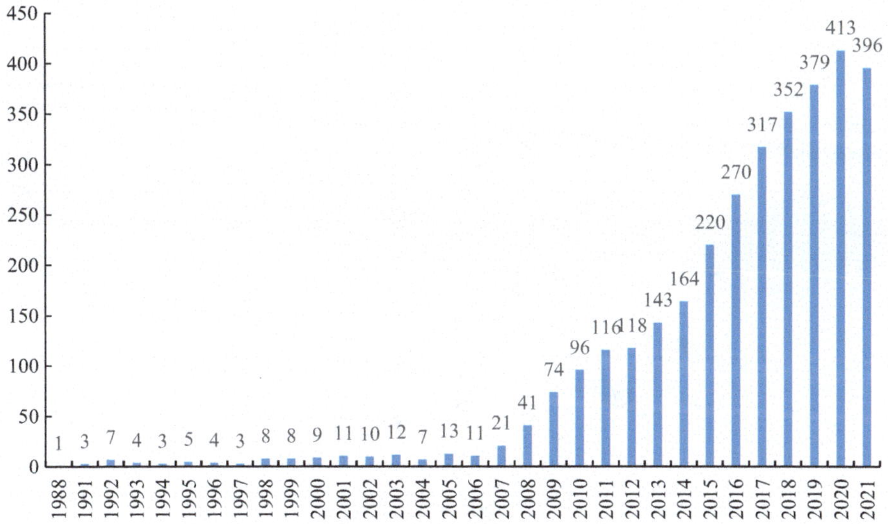

Fig. 3 Annual number of climate finance publications from 1988 to 2021. (*Source* Zhang et al. (2023))

Table 1 Top 10 journals by volume of published articles on climate finance

Ranking	Journal	Number of published articles
1	Energy Policy	546
2	Ecological Economics	250
3	Energy Economics	160
4	Environmental Resource Economics	104
5	World Development	91
6	Forest Policy and Economics	74
7	Journal of Environmental Economics and Management	71
8	Business Strategy and the Environment	58
9	Journal of Business Ethics	54
10	Technological Forecasting and Social Change	53

Source Zhang et al. (2023)

the number of connections represents the co-occurrence frequency between two keywords, and thicker connections indicate stronger relationships. Keywords with a frequency exceeding 120 are displayed in the graph.

Based on this analysis, Table 2 further extracts the top 20 important keywords. The results show that terms such as climate change, energy, impact, policy, and emission have the highest frequencies. In terms of published time, keywords such as agriculture, value, finance, determinant, and policy appeared rather late during the studied period. These findings indicate the diverse and complex nature of climate

Fig. 4 Keywords co-occurrence atlas of climate finance from 1988 to 2021. *Note* In this figure, time slice is set as one year; there are 499 nodes and 1453 connections; density is 0.0117; the rule of connection is minimum spanning tree (*Source* Zhang et al. (2023))

finance research, encompassing topics such as energy, greenhouse gas emissions, policy, pricing, risk, technology, innovation, and the interrelationships among various factors within the climate and financial systems. The research in this field covers not only individual behaviours such as investment and consumption but also corporate and industry-led activities related to energy consumption, greenhouse gas emissions, and technological innovations, as well as political negotiations and collaborations at the national level.

3.2 Main Research Directions

Based on the information provided by keyword co-occurrence, existing research in climate finance can be broadly categorized into three directions: climate consciousness, asset pricing and risk management under climate change, and climate-related fiscal, financial, and monetary policies (Zhang et al. 2023). Research on climate consciousness primarily focuses on studying the awakening and practical behaviour

Table 2 Top 20 high-frequency keywords from 1988 to 2021

Ranking	Frequency	Keywords	Earliest appearance	Ranking	Frequency	Keywords	Earliest appearance
1	635	Climate change	1998	11	164	Cost	1998
2	429	Energy	1993	12	160	Market	1992
3	401	Impact	1997	13	160	Growth	1998
4	352	Policy	2001	14	159	Consumption	1997
5	349	Emission	1996	15	140	Innovation	1996
6	282	Risk	1999	16	127	Technology	1992
7	265	Economics	1995	17	127	Determinant	2000
8	256	Country	1993	18	112	Finance	2000
9	191	Performance	1995	19	110	Agriculture	2005
10	187	Management	1993	20	109	Value	2003

Note The information in the table is up to 17 October 2021. *Source* Zhang et al. (2023)

of individuals related to awareness on climate change, mainly from an ethical perspective. Research on asset pricing and risk management under climate change emphasizes the study of market economic behaviour related to climate change. Research on climate-related fiscal, financial and monetary policies aims to analyze and compare different categories of policy tools for mitigating the effects of climate change.

3.2.1 Climate Consciousness

Climate consciousness refers to people's cognitive level of climate change and climate protection. It is also the awareness of individuals to constantly adjust their economic activities and social behaviour to consciously mitigate climate change. It includes both cognitive and practical aspects.

At the cognitive level, concepts such as green consumption and green investment have gained widespread acceptance, and sustainable practices have been incorporated into individual entrepreneurial activities (Hasan and Du 2023; Zhu et al. 2020). Compared to individuals' bounded rationality, institutional investors, companies, industries, and markets exhibit deeper and more value-oriented climate consciousness. Addoum et al. (2021) find that extreme temperature shocks within a quarter do not immediately trigger reactions from analysts and investors but can impact end-of-quarter profit forecasts for many industries. Busch and Hoffmann (2007) argue that companies' risk exposure depends on their reliance on carbon-based materials and carbon intensity, which financial markets have begun to incorporate into valuations. Krueger et al. (2020) similarly demonstrate that climate risks can have financial impacts on portfolio companies, and institutional investors are aware of these effects. Rajnoha et al. (2017) find that many companies have transformed traditional performance measurement systems into strategic and sustainable performance measurement systems, emphasizing the shift away from short-term consumption and production patterns.

At the practical level, existing literature primarily focuses on decarbonization challenges, particularly in the areas of carbon emissions trading mechanisms, investment and financing related to clean energy and renewable energy, and the allocation of international climate adaptation aid (Zhang et al. 2021). Concerning carbon emissions trading, a well-designed and reasonable carbon emissions trading system is undoubtedly an ideal choice for the decarbonization practices of the industrial and financial sectors, but the complexity of its design process is widely criticized by researchers. It is pointed out that the complexity of the development path of carbon finance is determined by various legal frameworks at the international level (Tu 2012). Spash (2010) argue that the intricate design issues of carbon emissions trading markets have surpassed the negative impacts of climate change itself.

Regarding investment and financing related to clean energy and renewable energy, Ji and Zhang (2019) point out that low-carbon technology research and development not only has high risks, uncertain returns, and strong spillover effects. This type of technology also usually possesses the characteristics of public goods. In the absence of financing incentives, social capital is reluctant to invest in such initiatives. Currently, international climate finance mechanisms, policy support, and financial institution participation are the main financing channels for clean energy and renewable energy development projects. Ji and Zhang (2019) illustrate this reality in their research, emphasizing that investment and financing issues significantly constrain China's energy revolution, and financial development can contribute up to 42.42% of the overall growth in renewable energy.

In terms of the allocation of international climate adaptation aid, developed countries advocate providing aid to developing countries, with priority given to "especially vulnerable" nations. Betzold and Weiler (2017) quantitatively analyze data on bilateral adaptation aid from the Organization for Economic Cooperation and Development (OECD) and find that vulnerability indicators are crucial for adaptation aid distribution. Countries greatly affected by extreme weather events or rising sea levels receive more aid both per capita and in total. However, some literature also documents donors using aid as a diplomatic tool to promote their political and economic goals (Weiler et al. 2018). Weiler et al. (2018) find that donors only partially consider climate change vulnerability; instead, they reward good governance countries with adaptation aid to promote their own economic interests.

3.2.2 Asset Pricing and Risk Management Under Climate Change

Climate risk-related asset pricing covers a wide range of asset classes, including real estate, stocks, and fixed-income securities (Giglio et al. 2021). Murfin and Spiegel (2020) explore the relationship between sea level rise risks and residential real estate prices, and find limited price effect. Baldauf et al. (2020) argue that housing prices reflect differences in people's beliefs about climate change. Similarly, Bernstein et al. (2019) and Eichholtz et al. (2019) find that communities concerned about global warming and sophisticated investors are key drivers for capitalizing sea level rise risks into housing prices. According to the efficient market hypothesis, publicly traded stocks reflect all current and publicly available information, and changes in stock returns after environmental events imply that the market has priced the impact of these events on the net present value of companies (Klassen and McLaughlin 1996; Hong et al. 2019). While Keele and DeHart (2011) find no evidence of positive cumulative abnormal stock returns for listed companies after announcing environmental actions, they still believe that measures to reduce greenhouse gas emissions may indicate a company's long-term profitability and attractiveness to investors. This viewpoint is supported by the empirical results of Ziegler et al. (2011). They focus on companies that disclose or do not disclose climate risk mitigation measures and find that constructing portfolios by buying stocks of the former and selling stocks of the latter result in more valuable portfolios over time.

Climate governance practices have generated a series of new financial products, such as catastrophe insurance, green bonds, and carbon emission permits (Hong et al. 2020; Baker et al. 2018). Pricing these new financial products is a major challenge in the field of climate finance with respect to asset pricing. Painter (2020) finds that countries more likely to be affected by climate change have to pay higher underwriting fees and initial yields when issuing long-term green municipal bonds compared to counties less likely to be affected. On the other hand, emission trading systems have a global impact and attention, and a stable carbon emission price is considered a core mechanism for achieving the long-term emission reduction goal of "zero emissions" globally. The carbon emission quota price reflects the opportunity cost of selecting effective emission reduction measures (Schleich et al. 2006). Taking the European Union's Emissions Trading System as an example, Ehrhart et al. (2005) find in a game model that banning of saving carbon emission quotas would lead to inefficient adjustments, namely, there was insufficient investment in emission reduction technology, resulting in a low quota price during 2005–2007, while in 2008–2009, there were stricter upper limits on quota prices and excessive emission reduction investment. Daskalakis et al. (2009) similarly find that banning saving carbon emission quotas would have a significant impact on futures pricing.

Reasonable financial asset pricing should reflect not only intrinsic value but also risk premiums. While risk is generally proportional to returns, people always expect to control risks to maximize returns, and this is no exception when facing climate-related risks. Existing literature on climate risk management primarily focuses on losses and damage associated with climate risks and the latent risks of climate management financial products. In addressing losses caused by climate risks, studies focusing on individuals and families find that climate risk management often evolves into a funding problem in many cases. For example, Collier et al. (2009) find that although weather indices can provide a safety net and price signals related to weather risks for vulnerable families, increased weather risks and the impact of climate change can raise insurance prices, surpassing the affordability of vulnerable families. Tian and Chen (2014) study farmers' climate adaptation capacity and highlight the importance of financial capital in combating climate risks and mitigating related losses. Financial products and businesses serving climate management present significant opportunities but also entail risks, such as international price fluctuations, exchange rate risk, and the synergistic interactions and complex correlations among multiple risk factors. Du et al. (2014) summarize the characteristics and content of policy risks, credit risks, operational risks, market risks, liquidity risks, and project risks in carbon finance transactions.

3.2.3 Climate-Related Fiscal, Financial and Monetary Policies

Global climate risks cannot be resolved solely through market mechanisms, where policy agreements should play a complementary role (Stiglitz 2019). Existing literature discusses a range of possible fiscal, financial, and monetary policies in this regard. Fiscal policy tools can be divided into price policies (taxation, subsidies), expenditure and investment policies, and public safety policies. In terms of price policies, it is widely believed that designing appropriate carbon pricing policies is crucial for slowing down climate change (Gren et al. 2012; Kaufmann and Hines 2018; Lin and Jia 2019). However, the actual effects vary. Farid et al. (2016) demonstrate that carbon pricing can reduce emissions and generate substantial fiscal revenue. Fay et al. (2015), on the other hand, find that price policies cannot induce the expected changes in the absence of low-carbon alternatives. Regarding expenditure and investment policies, infrastructure investment policies can lock in the types of energy used in the long term, therefore affecting climate change (Strand et al. 2014).

In terms of public safety policies, Owen et al. (2018) argue that the public sector's support for donations, equity, debt, and new forms of crowdfunding financing can help address the funding gap for low-carbon innovation in enterprises. In summary, fiscal policy tools attempt to internalize the externality of climate risks through the use of taxation and public investment. However, these tools may not be sufficient. The low-carbon transition of the economy and society requires joint efforts from both private and public investments to support relative price movements in energy structure and the transformation of the production structure.

The much-needed private investments can exactly be stimulated by financial policy tools to support green production, infrastructure, and research and development. Studies have generally shown that financial markets have underpriced climate risks (Addoum et al. 2021; Hong et al. 2019). This results in subsidizing investments in assets with high climate risks, whilst hampering the reallocation of capital to low-carbon investment projects. Scholars advocate increasing transparency in disclosing climate risks and correcting mispricing of climate risks in various ways, such as establishing specialized institutions for climate data collection, validation, and dissemination (Battiston 2019), standardizing or even mandating disclosure of climate-related information (Bebbington and Larrinaga-González 2008), and incorporating climate-related risks into the macroprudential supervision scope of central banks and regulatory authorities (Dietz et al. 2016).

Compared to correcting mispricing, supporting the development of the green securities market can more directly stimulate private investments. Flammer (2020) find that independent third-party certification improves the market trading performance of green securities, thus encouraging the development of green security certification systems. Additionally, some literature suggests using financial regulatory tools directly to promote climate financing. For example, Tooze (2019) proposes introducing "green support" and "brown penalty" elements in capital requirements, encouraging banks to increase green investments and reduce carbon-intensive investments. Aglietta and Espagne (2016) call for an international requirement to introduce a minimum quantity of "green" asset on banks' balance sheets.

Monetary policy has traditionally maintained a prudent approach, but some scholars argue that it should also play a role in maintaining a stable climate. Monnin (2018) emphasizes the correction of the weights of climate risks, meaning that central banks should ensure that climate risks are appropriately reflected in their asset portfolios. This shift can not only mitigate the climate risks faced by central banks but also set an example to reduce the relative market value of carbon-intensive assets and encourage investors to reallocate their capital into low-carbon industries. Furthermore, Van Lerven and Ryan-Collins (2017) and Olovsson (2018) advocate for green quantitative easing policies to support the purchase of low-carbon assets and completely abandon carbon-intensive assets. However, the purchasing targets of central banks in some countries are limited to government bonds or bonds issued by government agencies, making green quantitative easing policies not always feasible. To address this issue, many studies suggest that central banks should focus on reducing the relative capital costs of low-carbon industries. Proposed solutions in this regard include purchasing low-carbon bonds from national or multilateral development banks, using balance sheets to provide collateral, and revising forward-looking guidance policies (Campiglio 2016; Campiglio et al. 2018).

4 Funding Support of Climate Finance Research

4.1 Global Funding Support

Research on climate finance around the world receives funding support from various sources, reflecting the global recognition of the importance of addressing climate change. The funding landscape for climate finance research is diverse and involves contributions from public and private sectors, international organizations, philanthropic foundations, and research institutions.

4.1.1 National Governments

National governments play a pivotal role in supporting climate finance research by allocating funds through agencies responsible for environmental and climate-related initiatives. This commitment reflects the recognition of the pressing need to understand, mitigate, and adapt to the impacts of climate change, as well as to develop sustainable financial mechanisms. Governments may also collaborate with international organizations, bilateral partners, and multilateral agencies to collectively pool resources and address climate finance challenges. International cooperation between governments often involves funding collaborative research efforts on climate finance. Funding may be channelled into joint research projects that benefit from shared expertise and diverse perspectives.

Government-funded research provides valuable insights that can inform the development of evidence-based policies. Research outcomes may lead to policy recommendations aimed at creating an enabling environment for sustainable finance and climate resilience. Government-funded climate finance research is often aligned with national climate policies and commitments. Governments may prioritize research areas that directly contribute to achieving climate goals outlined in national plans or international agreements. These funds are also allocated to stimulate innovation and the development of new technologies that enhance climate finance practices. This could include research on financial instruments, risk assessment models, and technology solutions that support sustainable finance. Here, national agencies play a crucial role in prioritizing research topics based on the country's unique climate challenges and vulnerabilities. Funding may be directed towards studies that assess the impacts of climate change on specific sectors, identify adaptation strategies, or evaluate the effectiveness of climate finance mechanisms.

4.1.2 Multilateral Institutions

Multilateral institutions exert considerable influence in the realm of climate finance, providing crucial financial support for research and initiatives aimed at addressing climate change challenges. The involvement of institutions like the United Nations (UN), World Bank, International Monetary Fund (IMF), and regional development banks signifies a collaborative and coordinated global effort to mobilize resources and expertise. Multilateral institutions pioneer innovative financing mechanisms to address climate-related challenges through initiatives like the Global Environment Facility (GEF), which supports projects focused on biodiversity, climate change, and sustainable development.

Among them, the United Nations, through its various specialized agencies, plays a central role in coordinating international efforts to combat climate change. The UNFCCC and its annual Conference of the Parties (COP) meetings serve as platforms for discussions and negotiations on climate finance strategies. The Green Climate Fund (GCF) is a specialized international fund established to assist developing countries in their climate change mitigation and adaptation efforts. It serves as a major financial mechanism under the UNFCCC. The GCF not only provides funding for climate-related projects but also allocates resources for research initiatives that enhance the understanding of effective climate finance practices.

The World Bank is another key player in climate finance, supporting a wide range of projects that promote low-carbon development, climate resilience, and sustainable practices. It channels funds toward climate finance research that informs policy decisions and project development. The World Bank's financial and technical assistance extends to both mitigation and adaptation initiatives. While the IMF's primary mandate is economic stability and monetary cooperation, it recognizes the interconnectedness between economic stability and climate change. The IMF provides policy advice and technical assistance to member countries, including support for developing climate finance frameworks that align with broader economic goals. Regional development banks, such as the Asian Development Bank (ADB), African Development Bank (AfDB), and Inter-American Development Bank (IDB), play region-specific roles in climate finance. They contribute by financing projects that enhance climate resilience, promote sustainable development, and support research initiatives tailored to regional challenges.

4.1.3 Private Sectors

Private sector engagement in climate finance research is a critical component of the broader effort to address climate change. Private companies, driven by a commitment to sustainability, clean energy, and responsible business practices, play a significant role in funding and supporting research initiatives. Additionally, philanthropic organizations contribute to the landscape by providing grants and forming partnerships. Private sector companies and philanthropic organizations contribute significantly to the funding and advancement of climate finance research. Their involvement reflects a growing awareness of the private sector's role in driving sustainable financial practices and fostering a global transition to a low-carbon economy.

Private companies involved in sustainable finance, clean energy, and environmental consulting recognize the importance of staying informed about climate finance trends and strategies. As part of their commitment to environmental responsibility, these companies may allocate resources to fund research projects that contribute to the advancement of sustainable financial practices. Private companies may directly invest in climate finance research projects that align with their business interests and sustainability goals. Some may integrate climate-related research into their CSR (Corporate Social Responsibility) initiatives, which involve a commitment to contribute positively to society, and funding research on sustainable finance practices aligns with companies' efforts to mitigate environmental impact and promote responsible business conduct. Those in technology and innovation sectors may invest in research that develops new tools, technologies, or methodologies for climate finance. These innovations contribute to more effective and efficient financial solutions for addressing climate challenges. The direct investment can take the form of financial contributions, in-kind support, or collaboration with research institutions. Private companies may also form partnerships with research institutions to foster a symbiotic relationship. Companies benefit from the latest research insights, while research institutions gain access to real-world data and industry expertise. This partnership approach ensures that research remains relevant and applicable to practical business scenarios.

Philanthropic foundations, such as the Bill and Melinda Gates Foundation, the Rockefeller Foundation, and the Hewlett Foundation, recognize the transformative impact of climate finance on global sustainability. They allocate funds to support research projects that explore innovative financial solutions, address climate-related challenges, and contribute to long-term environmental resilience. Researchers and institutions can apply for grants to conduct studies that advance knowledge in the field and contribute to evidence-based policymaking. Some philanthropic organizations engage in impact investing, directing financial resources toward projects and initiatives that generate positive environmental and social outcomes. This includes investing in climate finance research that has the potential to influence policy, financial markets, and sustainable development practices. Their support for climate finance research extends beyond funding, encompassing efforts to raise awareness, influence policy decisions, and promote international collaboration.

4.1.4 Academia

Universities, research centres, and think tanks play a significant role in advancing the understanding of climate finance through academic research. They actively seek grants and research funding from diverse sources to conduct studies that contribute valuable insights to the complex intersection of finance and climate change. Additionally, collaborative research projects, involving partnerships with other academic institutions and stakeholders, enhance the depth and impact of the research.

Climate finance research often demands an interdisciplinary approach, drawing on expertise from finance, economics, environmental science, and other relevant fields. Universities and research centres are well-positioned to facilitate interdisciplinary collaborations, bringing together researchers with diverse backgrounds to tackle the multifaceted challenges of climate finance. Academic institutions contribute to the dissemination of knowledge by publishing research findings in academic journals, reports, and other scholarly outlets. This not only advances the understanding of climate finance within the academic community but also provides valuable resources for policymakers, practitioners, and the general public. Student researchers are often involved in research on climate finance and gain hands-on experience and exposure to real-world challenges. This involvement fosters the development of the next generation of professionals who are well-versed in the complexities of climate finance.

Collaborative projects provide a platform for knowledge exchange between academia, industry, and government agencies. Researchers gain access to real-world data and challenges, while industry partners benefit from cutting-edge academic insights. Collaborative projects often include mechanisms for assessing the impact of research on industry practices, policy decisions, and societal outcomes. This ensures that the research contributes tangibly to the advancement of climate finance and sustainable development goals. First, universities and research centres can influence policy discussions by conducting research that informs evidence-based policymaking. Engaging with policymakers and government agencies ensures that research outcomes are considered in the formulation of climate finance policies at local, national, and international levels. Second, collaborations between academic institutions and private sector entities further enhance the practical relevance of climate finance research. Public–private partnerships bring together academic expertise with industry insights, ensuring that research outcomes address real-world challenges faced by businesses and financial institutions. Also, collaboration with industry stakeholders, such as financial institutions, energy companies, and environmental organizations, ensures that research is aligned with industry needs. This engagement facilitates the development of practical solutions that can be implemented within the financial sector.

It should also be noted that collaborative research projects often extend beyond national borders, involving partnerships between academic institutions from different countries. International collaboration allows for a broader perspective, considering regional variations in climate impacts and financial systems.

4.1.5 Research Networks

Global and regional networks dedicated to climate research play a vital role in coordinating and funding efforts related to climate finance. One of the most prominent examples is the IPCC, which serves as a leading international body for assessing and synthesizing climate science.

The IPCC is a global scientific body established by the UN to provide comprehensive assessments of climate change science, impacts, adaptation, and mitigation. While the IPCC's primary focus is on climate science, it recognizes the critical importance of understanding and addressing the financial aspects of climate change. The IPCC periodically releases Assessment Reports that bring together contributions from thousands of scientists worldwide. These reports include sections on the economic and financial implications of climate change, providing policymakers with insights into the complex interplay between climate science and finance. The IPCC involves experts with diverse backgrounds, including finance, economics, and policy analysis. This interdisciplinary approach ensures that the financial dimensions of climate change are thoroughly examined, contributing to a more holistic understanding. The IPCC also serves as a coordinating body that facilitates collaboration between scientists, policymakers, and stakeholders. It advocates for evidence-based decision-making and provides a platform for discussing the financial mechanisms needed to address climate challenges.

On the other hand, various regional organizations dedicated to climate research and action may coordinate and fund research efforts specific to their geographical areas. These organizations bring together experts, policymakers, and stakeholders to address climate challenges that are regionally relevant. Regional networks often fund research initiatives that focus on climate finance solutions tailored to the unique challenges faced by specific regions. This may include studies on the financial implications of regional climate impacts, adaptation strategies, and sustainable finance practices. Regional networks also contribute to capacity-building efforts by supporting research institutions and experts within their regions. This ensures that there is a pool of skilled professionals equipped to address the intersection of climate and finance.

Collaborative global initiatives, beyond the IPCC, may bring together researchers and stakeholders from various regions to address overarching climate challenges. These initiatives often involve the coordination and funding of research projects that span multiple countries and continents. Global climate research networks facilitate the sharing of data, research findings, and best practices among countries and regions. This knowledge transfer enhances the collective understanding of climate finance and promotes the adoption of effective strategies worldwide. By coordinating research efforts on a global scale, these networks contribute to the harmonization of climate policies and financial mechanisms. This is essential for creating a cohesive and collaborative international approach to climate finance.

4.2 Funding Support in China

In recent years, various levels of project management institutions in China, such as the National Natural Science Foundation, the National Office for Philosophy and Social Sciences Planning, and the Ministry of Education, have begun to focus on research work in the field of climate finance. Preliminary statistics show that since 2010, the National Natural Science Foundation, focusing on basic research, has funded over a hundred climate finance-related projects in areas such as financial engineering, financial economics, resource management and policy, environmental and ecological management, and more. National Social Science Foundation projects, which address major practical and hot issues in China's economic and social development, have covered over two hundred topics related to climate finance within disciplines like management, applied economics, theoretical economics, and statistics. In the past decade, an average of more than 30 projects are approved each year in the field of climate finance as national-level projects represented by the National Natural Science Foundation and the National Social Science Foundation, with a steady upward trend. Especially in the last five years, topics related to climate finance have gained increasing popularity among funding applicants, with more scholars pondering how to use financial tools to address the crisis of climate change and contribute to the green, low-carbon transition of the society and economy.

Looking at the types of funded projects, initiatives in the field of climate finance range from conventional projects such as general projects and young scholar projects (encouraging exploration by young scholars) to comprehensive projects reflecting government guidance, including emergency, key, and major projects. For instance, against the backdrop of China's economic development entering a new normal, the National Natural Science Foundation introduced the major project "Key Management

Scientific Issues and Policy Research in Green Transition and Low-Carbon Development" in 2016; two emergency projects, namely "The Impact of the United States' Withdrawal from the Paris Agreement on Global Climate Governance and China's Response Strategies" and "Preventing and Resolving Financial Risks", in 2017 and 2018; and a special project "Major Fundamental Scientific Issues and Strategies for Achieving National Carbon Neutrality" in 2021. These guidance projects, rooted in the new development concept of "innovation, coordination, greenness, openness, and sharing" and starting from new turning points in response to global climate change, explore new issues related to climate finance. These issues include climate technology transfer mechanisms, funding mechanisms, market mechanisms, and more.

Furthermore, in the field of climate finance and its related areas, a group of outstanding young talents has grown rapidly. More than ten scholars focusing on directions such as "Energy Economics and Climate Policies", "Carbon Emission Reduction Impact Mechanisms and Policies", and "Energy Finance" have been supported by the National Distinguished Young Scientists Fund and the National Excellent Young Scientists Fund, which are influential and prestigious funding sources recognizing and supporting exceptional young scientists in China. The rapid growth of young talents supported by prestigious national funds signifies a promising future for climate finance research in China. These scholars, focusing on crucial directions within the field, are poised to make lasting contributions to our understanding of climate-related challenges and the development of sustainable financial solutions. Their work not only advances academic knowledge but also has practical implications for shaping policies and practices that address the urgent issues of climate change.

The research content of funded projects in the field of climate finance is extensive, covering various research directions including climate change and financial asset pricing, climate finance risk management, and climate change and financial policies. The interdisciplinary nature of these projects is evident. Most research related to climate change and financial asset pricing focuses on energy prices and environmental asset prices, such as natural gas pricing mechanisms and the determination of carbon quota trading prices. In terms of climate finance risk management, more attention has been given to financial risks associated with natural disasters and natural assets, including the improvement of insurance systems for natural disasters and risk measurements for carbon markets or carbon finance. Research related to climate change and financial policies encompasses the formulation of climate finance policies and the establishment of carbon emission trading markets.

In China, investment and financing activities related to climate change require theoretical support and efficient tools tailored to provide solutions to investment and financing practice. This means that project management institutions need to increase research funding in the field of climate finance, promote the development of climate finance theories in China and provide guidance to practical activities.

5 Academic Communities and Platforms for Climate Finance

5.1 Global Academic Communities and Platforms

Academic communities and platforms for climate finance play a crucial role in fostering research, knowledge exchange, and collaboration among scholars, policy-makers, and practitioners dedicated to addressing climate change challenges. These communities provide forums for discussing innovative ideas, sharing research findings, and influencing policy decisions. Here are some notable examples of global academic communities and platforms for climate finance:

As mentioned above, the IPCC is a leading international body that assesses scientific information related to climate change. While its primary focus is on climate science, it includes sections on economic and financial aspects, making it a valuable resource for researchers and policymakers interested in climate finance.

The Global Research Alliance for Sustainable Finance and Investment (GRASFI) is an international network that brings together researchers and academics focusing on sustainable finance. It provides a platform for collaboration, knowledge sharing, and the development of research initiatives related to climate finance and sustainable investment.

Based in Bangladesh, the International Centre for Climate Change and Development (ICCCAD) is a research and academic centre that focuses on climate change and sustainable development. It conducts research, provides training, and engages in policy advocacy, including issues related to climate finance.

The Global Risk Institute (GRI) is a research organization that focuses on understanding and managing risks in the financial sector. It conducts research on climate finance, exploring the risks and opportunities associated with climate-related investments and financial decision-making.

The Climate Finance Leadership Initiative (CFLI) is a global initiative that brings together leaders from the public and private sectors to mobilize private capital for climate solutions. While not exclusively academic, it engages with financial leaders, policymakers, and academics to drive innovations in climate finance.

The Centre for International Climate and Environmental Research—Oslo (CICERO) is a research institution based in Norway that focuses on interdisciplinary climate research. It engages in research related to climate finance, including the evaluation of financial mechanisms and policy instruments for climate change mitigation and adaptation.

The Climate Policy Initiative (CPI) is a research organization that provides analysis and expertise on climate finance and policy. It produces reports, conducts research, and engages with policymakers and stakeholders to enhance understanding and effectiveness in the field of climate finance.

The International Institute for Sustainable Development (IISD) is an independent think tank that focuses on sustainable development. It conducts research on climate finance, including tracking financial flows, analyzing policies, and providing insights into the effectiveness of climate finance mechanisms.

The Green Finance Institute (GFI) is based in the United Kingdom and is a collaborative initiative that brings together academia, finance professionals, and policymakers to accelerate the transition to a green and sustainable economy. It engages in research and knowledge exchange on topics related to green and climate finance.

The UNEP Inquiry explores how to align the financial system with sustainable development. While not exclusively focused on climate finance, it addresses broader issues related to the integration of environmental considerations into financial decision-making.

The Network for Greening the Financial System (NGFS) is a global network of central banks and financial supervisors that explores ways to integrate climate-related risks into financial governance and decision-making. While primarily focused on regulatory aspects, it contributes to the academic understanding of the financial implications of climate change.

These academic communities and platforms contribute significantly to the advancement of knowledge, research, and policy development in the field of climate finance. They provide spaces for collaboration, facilitate interdisciplinary research, and contribute to the ongoing global efforts to address the challenges posed by climate change through informed financial decision-making.

5.2 *Academic Communities and Platforms in China*

As addressing climate change becomes a globally concerted effort, scholars from China's financial industry, domestic universities, and research institutions are actively strengthening academic exchanges and collaborations. In addition to dedicated centres and institutes, collaborative research networks involving scholars and researchers from various institutions further enhance academic exchanges in climate finance. These networks may take forms of academic platforms or alliances, joint research projects, conferences, and publications, aiming to foster a collaborative and interdisciplinary approach to addressing climate change through financial mechanisms. Here are some examples of well-known climate finance platforms in China:

The Green Finance Committee of China Society for Finance and Banking. Established in 2015, it was mainly initiated by state-owned commercial banks, investment banks, insurance companies, securities and other financial institutions. It aims to promote innovation of green investment and financing products and services, and actively advocate the concept of green finance.

The China Energy Finance Network, established in 2017, is composed of eight domestic research teams specialized in energy finance. By adopting an organizational structure of a small core and a large network, it has attracted scholars and researchers from more than ten countries to join.

The China University Green Finance Research Alliance, established in 2018, was initiated by Fudan University and more than ten green finance research institutions from other Chinese universities, aiming to better address and resolve issues in the development of green finance.

The Climate Investment and Finance Association of Chinese Society for Environmental Sciences, established in 2019, was jointly established by China's Ministry of Ecology and Environment, the People's Bank of China, the China Banking and Insurance Regulatory Commission, the National Development and Reform Commission, and the Ministry of Finance. It seeks to harness the role of markets to optimize resource allocation and accelerate the development of climate investment and financing.

The Guangdong-Hong Kong-Macao Greater Bay Area Green Finance Alliance, established in 2020 under the guidance of the Green Finance Committee primarily serves the green finance cooperation among Guangdong, Hong Kong, and Macao, aiming to achieve breakthroughs in cross-border green asset transactions.

The ISETS Energy Finance Network of the China Society of Optimization, Overall Planning and Economical Mathematics, established in 2021, is the first academic organization in China named "Climate Finance." It focuses on major international frontier issues in the field of climate finance. It aims to nurture a leading expert team and cultivate top research talents specialized in climate finance and green finance. It has organized, jointly with China Energy Finance Network, a series of high-level international academic conferences on energy and climate finance. The conference series is widely considered as a flagship in the field of climate finance in China and has attracted growing international attention. Since 2020, it has been listed in each year's "Important Academic Conference Guide" issued by the China Association for Science and Technology.

These academic platforms collectively contribute to the knowledge base, policy discourse, and practical applications of climate finance in China. Their activities encompass research, education, and knowledge dissemination, fostering a vibrant academic community dedicated to addressing the complex challenges posed by climate change within the financial context.

6 Climate Investment and Financing Activities

6.1 Climate Investment and Financing Around the World

Climate investment and financing activities around the world are critical components of global efforts to address climate change, transition to sustainable energy systems, and build climate resilience. These activities encompass a wide range of financial mechanisms, investments, and initiatives aimed at mitigating greenhouse gas emissions, adapting to the impacts of climate change, and promoting sustainable development.

6.1.1 Funding Allocation

Climate-related investments are directed to the following fields. First, significant investments are directed towards the development and expansion of renewable energy sources, including solar and wind energy projects. Countries and businesses are increasingly adopting renewable energy sources to reduce reliance on fossil fuels and decrease carbon emissions. On the other hand, investments in energy storage technologies, such as batteries, are growing to enhance the stability and reliability of renewable energy systems, making them more suitable for widespread use. Financing is also directed towards energy efficiency measures in buildings, including retrofitting projects that improve energy performance and reduce overall consumption. Industrial upgrades also involve investments in improving energy efficiency, reducing emissions, and promoting cleaner production methods. Furthermore, funding is allocated to projects that enhance the resilience of critical infrastructure, such as transportation, water, and telecommunications systems, to withstand the impacts of climate change, including extreme weather events. Climate financing activities also support projects that address climate-related challenges in agriculture, forestry, and water resource management, promoting sustainable practices and adaptation strategies.

6.1.2 Green Bonds

Climate-related projects are increasingly financed green bonds. The issuance of green bonds has grown significantly, with governments, municipalities, and corporations raising funds for climate and environmentally friendly projects. Green bonds have become a popular financial instrument for raising funds dedicated to projects that promote environmental sustainability and climate action. The increasing financing of climate-related projects through green bonds reflects a growing recognition of the role financial markets can play in addressing environmental challenges. Green bonds are also a prime example of impact investing, attracting a broad spectrum of investors, including institutional investors, asset managers, and individual investors, who actively seek opportunities to generate positive environmental and social outcomes alongside financial returns and prioritize investments that contribute to sustainable development goals and address climate challenges.

Another notable trend in the global financial market is that financial institutions are increasingly incorporating ESG screening into investment decisions, directing capital towards businesses and projects that align with sustainable and climate-conscious practices. Green bonds, being specifically designed for environmentally friendly projects, align seamlessly with ESG criteria, making them a preferred choice for financial institutions adopting sustainable investment practices. As financial institutions increasingly integrate ESG considerations, green bonds offer a means of diversifying investment portfolios. This diversification contributes to managing risk by incorporating assets that are aligned with long-term sustainability trends.

6.1.3 International Financial Mechanisms

Besides green bonds, international financial mechanisms have been established to address climate change challenges and support developing countries in their efforts to mitigate and adapt to the impacts of climate change. The GCF and the Climate Investment Funds (CIF) are two prominent funds for such purposes. The GCF, established in 2010 under the UNFCCC, serves as a key financial instrument to assist developing countries in their climate actions. The primary objective of GCF is to mobilize funds at a global scale and channel them to support developing countries in their climate initiatives, covering both climate mitigation and adaptation efforts. It funds a wide range of projects, including those related to renewable energy, energy efficiency, climate resilience, sustainable agriculture, and ecosystem conservation. Meanwhile, the GCF operates as a multilateral institution, involving contributions from both developed and developing countries. It fosters collaboration among governments, private sector entities, and civil society to mobilize financial resources and implement effective climate projects.

The CIF represents a collaborative effort involving multiple multilateral development banks, including the World Bank, the African Development Bank, and the Asian Development Bank. Launched in 2008, the CIF comprises several funding windows, each with a specific focus. These include the Clean Technology Fund (CTF), the Forest Investment Program (FIP), the Pilot Program for Climate Resilience (PPCR), the Scaling Up Renewable Energy Program (SREP), and the Strategic Climate Fund (SCF). The CTF focuses on supporting the deployment of clean technologies, the FIP addresses deforestation and forest degradation, the PPCR targets climate resilience, and the SREP promotes renewable energy projects. These funding windows collectively aim to reduce greenhouse gas emissions and enhance climate resilience in developing countries. The CIF uses public funds to attract additional private investments, recognizing the importance of mobilizing private capital for achieving climate goals.

6.1.4 Carbon Markets and Carbon Trading

The development of carbon markets and carbon trading has gained significant momentum in recent years as part of global efforts to address climate change. These market-based approaches play a crucial role in incentivizing emissions reduction and promoting the transition to a low-carbon economy.

Emissions Trading Systems (ETS), also known as cap-and-trade systems, are market-based mechanisms designed to limit greenhouse gas emissions. Participating countries or regions set an overall cap on emissions and allocate or sell emission allowances to entities within the system. Emission allowances represent the right to emit a specific quantity of greenhouse gases. Companies subject to the ETS can buy and sell these allowances based on their emission needs and reduction capabilities. ETS provides a financial incentive for companies to reduce their emissions. Entities that reduce emissions below their allocated allowances can sell excess allowances to those struggling to meet their emission targets, creating a market-driven mechanism for emissions reduction. Emission trading also encourages the adoption of cleaner technologies and practices. Companies are motivated to invest in technologies that reduce their carbon footprint, making it economically favourable to transition to low-carbon alternatives. Emission trading systems are implemented at both national and regional levels. For example, the European Union Emissions Trading System (EU ETS) is one of the largest and most established systems, covering various sectors and member countries.

Voluntary carbon markets, on the other hand, operate independently of regulatory requirements and allow companies and individuals to voluntarily offset their carbon emissions. Participants in voluntary markets buy these credits to offset their own emissions, effectively neutralizing their carbon footprint. Voluntary carbon projects span various categories, including reforestation and afforestation initiatives, renewable energy projects, methane capture from landfills, and energy efficiency projects. The credits generated contribute to sustainable development and environmental conservation. Many companies participate in voluntary carbon markets as part of their CSR initiatives. Offsetting carbon emissions through these markets can enhance a company's sustainability profile and demonstrate a commitment to environmental stewardship. The voluntary carbon market has become a global phenomenon, with participants from various sectors and regions. Carbon offsetting allows businesses and individuals to take direct action to mitigate climate change impacts, irrespective of regulatory requirements. To ensure the credibility and transparency of voluntary carbon credits, various certification standards and organizations exist. These standards, such as the Gold Standard and the Verified Carbon Standard, provide guidelines for project development, monitoring, and verification.

6.2 Climate Investment and Financing in China

In October 2020, the Ministry of Ecology and Environment, the National Development and Reform Commission, the People's Bank of China, the China Banking and Insurance Regulatory Commission, and the China Securities Regulatory Commission jointly issued the "Guidance on Promoting Climate Change Investment and Financing," which clearly states that China needs to accelerate the construction of a climate investment and financing policy system and relevant standards, and strive to channel resources such as funds, talents, and technology into the field of climate investment and financing. On 27 December 2021, nine ministries, including the Ministry of Ecology and Environment, jointly issued the "Climate Investment and Finance Pilot Work Plan", which clearly guides and promotes more funds to be invested in activities related to climate change mitigation and adaptation.

In terms of domestic investment and financing practices, China's green finance market has continued to expand, with increasing innovation in products and services. According to data from the China Banking and Insurance Regulatory Commission, as of the end of September 2021, the balance of green loans of 21 major banks in

China reached 14.08 trillion yuan, and the overall quality of green loan assets is good, with a non-performing loan ratio below 0.7% in the past five years.

Green bonds are the second-largest carrier of China's green finance, second only to green loans in scale. According to the People's Bank of China, as of the end of 2020, China had issued approximately 1.2 trillion yuan of green bonds, ranking second in the world, only after the United States. In the first half of 2021, 198 new labelled green bonds were issued in China, and innovative types of green bonds such as "carbon–neutral bonds," "green rural revitalization bonds," and "sustainability-linked bonds" were introduced.

The estimates by China International Capital Corporation Limited highlight the substantial financial requirements for China to achieve its ambitious net-zero emissions goal. The need for 140 trillion yuan in debt financing over the next 40 years underscores the scale of investment and financial resources required for the country's transition to a sustainable and low-carbon economy.

Despite the substantial financing needs, China's green bonds currently account for less than 1% in the domestic debt market, which is valued at 18 trillion US dollars. This indicates that the issuance of green bonds is not yet proportionate to the overall debt market. China faces challenges related to the issuance of green bonds, including concerns about issuance costs, expected returns, and the motivations of investors. To overcome these challenges and boost the green bond market, more comprehensive policy support will be crucial. This support may include regulatory frameworks that incentivize green investments, clearer standards for green projects, and financial incentives for issuers and investors engaged in sustainable financing.

On the other hand, China has made significant strides in the development of carbon markets and ETS as part of its commitment to address climate change and reduce greenhouse gas emissions. The country has implemented various pilot programs and initiated national-level efforts to establish a comprehensive and robust carbon market. China initiated pilot carbon markets in several provinces and cities as a precursor to a national ETS. These pilot programs were launched to test different trading mechanisms, assess market dynamics, and gather insights to inform the development of a national system. The pilot carbon markets therefore provided valuable lessons that were used to refine and improve the design of the national ETS. This iterative process allowed authorities to address challenges and enhance the effectiveness of the market.

In December 2017, China officially launched its national Emission Trading System, covering key industries such as power generation, iron and steel, chemicals, and cement. The national ETS is a crucial component of China's strategy to achieve its climate goals outlined in the Paris Agreement. The national ETS initially focused on the power sector, which is responsible for a significant portion of China's carbon emissions. Over time, the coverage is expected to expand to include more sectors, gradually encompassing a larger portion of the economy.

China's ETS adopts a cap-and-trade approach, where a cap is set on the total allowable emissions, and companies are allocated a certain number of permits. Companies that exceed their allowances can buy additional permits from those with surplus allowances, creating a market for emissions trading. Meanwhile, China has encouraged the participation of financial institutions in the carbon market to facilitate liquidity and market efficiency. This involvement includes the development of financial products related to carbon trading and the establishment of carbon funds.

China's efforts to develop a national carbon market and emission trading system represent a significant commitment to addressing climate change. The development of the carbon market aligns with China's commitment to peak carbon emissions by 2030 and achieve carbon neutrality by 2060. The establishment of the ETS reflects China's recognition of the importance of market-based mechanisms in achieving its climate goals and fostering a more sustainable and low-carbon economy. The success of China's carbon market will not only contribute to domestic emissions reduction but also serve as a model for other countries working toward similar objectives.

7 Frontier Directions and Application Scenarios of Climate Finance

Climate change has been a problem faced by human society for many years. However, it is only in recent years that scholars in the financial and economic fields have gradually turned to study financial issues related to climate risks. Significant progress has been made in areas such as climate risk measurement, climate risk management in financial systems, and climate risk governance. This section presents eight research prospects from three dimensions: the theoretical framework of climate finance, climate financial risk management, and international cooperation mechanisms for climate innovation. These prospects provide a concise summary of the current frontier directions and application scenarios of climate finance.

7.1 Theoretical Framework of Global Climate Governance

The complexity of the climate finance system and the evolving impact of climate change on financial institutions necessitate the development of a comprehensive and robust theoretical framework. As of now, the understanding of the interplay between climate change and the financial system is largely derived from practical experience, and existing theoretical paradigms are not fully mature. To establish a comprehensive climate finance theoretical framework, it is crucial to address the role of theoretical guidance in practice and clarify the following key points.

First, it should be global in scope. Climate change is not a problem limited to one country, and its governance requires global action. Existing studies show that the impact of climate shocks on individual nations' financial institutions often has a contagious effect, potentially triggering more severe chain reactions in the global financial system. Therefore, it is necessary to establish a global climate finance governance framework. A theoretical framework for climate finance should also be globally oriented, acknowledging the interconnectedness of financial systems across borders.

Second, the climate finance theoretical framework should be systematic. The impact of climate change is not limited to the evolution of ecological systems. It also affects various aspects of the entire social, economic, and financial systems. Constructing a theoretical framework for climate finance requires the introduction of the principles and methods of complex systems to explore the interconnections and feedback mechanisms among the climate system, social systems, and financial systems. Especially, it should systematically characterize the mechanisms, patterns, transmission paths, and impact intensities of the long-term and short-term effects of climate change on the financial system. The theoretical framework for climate finance can draw inspiration from the complex systems theory of climate economics. This involves understanding the intricate relationships and feedback loops between different components of the climate system and their interactions with social and financial systems. Complex systems theory provides a toolset for modeling and simulating the dynamic and interconnected nature of climate finance.

Third, the climate finance theoretical framework is inherently interdisciplinary. Climate finance itself is an interdisciplinary field, and constructing the theoretical framework of climate finance requires the integration of theories from natural sciences, finance, economics, management, and other related fields. A unified theoretical framework should comprehensively consider the uncertainties associated with natural, social, financial, and economic factors. This interdisciplinary approach enables a more holistic understanding of the dynamic impacts of ecological systems on financial activities. Establishing a universally applicable theoretical framework enables the development of a methodological system for climate finance. This system encompasses research methodologies, modeling approaches, and analytical tools that can be employed to study the impact of climate change on financial activities. A standardized methodological system contributes to the creation of a new scientific field dedicated to understanding and addressing the intersection of climate and finance.

Climate finance operates in a context of significant uncertainty, encompassing climate-related risks and the unpredictability of financial markets. The development of a theoretical framework for climate finance is imperative for guiding research, informing policy decisions, and addressing the challenges posed by climate change on the financial system. By adopting a global, systematic, and interdisciplinary approach, researchers can create a comprehensive theoretical foundation that contributes to the establishment of climate finance as a distinct and impactful scientific field.

7.2 Climate Finance Risk Management

In climate-related investment and financing activities, the challenges of climate change risks to the financial system and the relevant responses are the primary concerns of regulatory authorities. This constitutes the core focus of research in the field of climate finance. Due to the complex interactions and uncertainties in the Earth and human systems, quantifying climate finance risks is challenging. This section discusses relevant research on climate finance risk management from three aspects: measurement of climate risks, identification of climate finance risks, and ESG investment strategies.

7.2.1 Measuring Climate Risks

There are two categories of climate risks: physical risks and transition risks. Physical risks reflect the economic harms and financial losses caused by extreme weather events and natural disasters related to climate change. For example, coastal real estate and public infrastructure in low-lying areas face physical risks due to rising sea levels, and global temperature rise poses long-term risks to human health and food production. Transition risks arise from uncertainties in asset values when countries undergo economic transition to reduce greenhouse gas emissions. This risk is particularly prominent in the energy sector and may lead to economic losses and stranded assets for high greenhouse gas-emitting enterprises.

Effectively mitigating the adverse impacts of climate risks requires a scientific and systematic approach to measure and assess these risks. Various countries and regions have made progress in formulating measurement frameworks for climate risks, aiming to enhance understanding, inform decision-making, and guide investments in resilience and adaptation. Notably, initiatives by global institutions, such as the World Bank and the European Union (EU), exemplify efforts to develop robust frameworks for climate risk assessment.

In 2016, the World Bank introduced the "Environmental and Social Framework" (ESF) as a comprehensive approach to addressing environmental and social risks and impacts in its projects. While initially designed to assess a broad spectrum of risks, the ESF includes specific provisions for evaluating potential physical and transition risks associated with climate change. The ESF considers the direct impacts of climate change on the environment and societies, including factors such as extreme weather events, sea-level rise, and changes in temperature and precipitation patterns. It aims to assess how these physical risks might affect the success and sustainability of World Bank projects. Recognizing the importance of transitioning to a low-carbon economy, the ESF also assesses risks associated with societal shifts, policy changes, and market dynamics related to climate action. This includes evaluating how projects may be affected by changes in regulations, market demand for sustainable practices, and technological advancements.

The European Union has taken steps to measure and address climate risks through its climate risk assessment tool. This tool focuses on evaluating environmental risks at both macro and international levels, contributing to the flow of funds toward projects that support the transition to a low-carbon economy. At the macro-level, the tool assesses climate risks by considering the potential impacts on sectors, industries, and economic stability. This macro-level analysis helps policymakers and financial institutions understand the systemic implications of climate risks on the broader economy. Recognizing the transboundary nature of climate risks, the EU's tool also incorporates an international dimension. This enables the assessment of risks that may affect cross-border investments, trade relationships, and global financial stability.

However, the existing research on characterizing both physical and transition risks in the context of climate finance faces certain limitations. These limitations include a one-sided focus on individual risks and a lack of consideration for the intricate coupling relationships among various risk factors. This may lead to underestimation of risks. Additionally, recognizing the dynamic and spatially dependent nature of physical risks and the multifaceted nature of transition risks, researchers are exploring innovative methods and technologies to construct comprehensive climate risk systems and databases. Here are some key considerations in this exploration.

First, current research often analyzes physical and transition risks in isolation, overlooking the interconnectedness between these two categories. Recognizing that physical risks can influence and be influenced by transition risks (and vice versa), there is a growing need for research that explores the coupling relationships among various risk factors. Integrated models that consider the interplay between physical and transition risks can provide a more accurate representation of the overall climate risk landscape.

Moreover, physical risks associated with climate change are dynamic and spatially dependent, meaning they vary over time and across geographical locations. Characterizing these risks requires the incorporation of temporal and spatial elements in research frameworks. Advanced modeling techniques, data analytics, and satellite-based remote sensing technologies, which can provide real-time, high-resolution data on physical changes in the environment and land-use, can be used to capture the evolving nature of physical risks and their spatial distribution.

Transition risks, on the other hand, are related to macro policies, technological progress, investor sentiment, and business innovation models. Constructing reliable transition risk indices demands comprehensive and heterogeneous data sources. Natural language processing algorithms can be applied to extract meaningful information from vast and diverse textual datasets, including policy documents, news articles, and financial reports. Transition risks manifest over various time scales and themes. Researchers need to explore methods to construct transition risk indices that account for different temporal perspectives and thematic focuses. This involves capturing short-term policy changes, long-term technological shifts, and sector-specific transition risks. Robust and adaptable methodologies are required to create indices that accurately reflect the exposure of assets to transition risks.

Addressing the complexities of climate risk requires interdisciplinary collaboration. Bringing together experts from fields such as climatology, finance, economics, data science, and environmental science can foster innovative approaches and comprehensive understanding. Collaborative efforts are essential for advancing research methodologies and developing practical tools for climate risk management. Meanwhile, building a comprehensive climate risk system and database is a critical component for climate asset pricing and risk management in climate finance. This system should incorporate a wide range of physical and transition risk factors, providing a unified platform for researchers, investors, and policymakers.

The database should facilitate the analysis and assessment of climate risks across different sectors, regions, and time horizons.

7.2.2 Identification of Climate Finance Risks

Due to the nonlinearity, profound uncertainty, and endogeneity of climate risks, it is not suitable to employ traditional methods in climate economics or risk-based pricing models in finance to study them. Mispricing climate risks may lead to volatility in asset prices, harm financial stability and give rise to systemic risks. An important research direction in climate finance is to analyze the relationship between climate risks and financial stability and to find appropriate financial tools to hedge climate-related risks. Current research on the relationship between climate risks and financial stability mainly includes the following directions.

First, the complexity and interconnectedness of climate risks necessitate advanced modelling approaches that can capture potential feedback loops and provide quantitative estimates of their impacts on the macroeconomy and financial systems. Researchers have adopted sophisticated models, such as stock-flow consistent models and agent-based models, to enhance the understanding of climate risks and their interactions with economic and financial variables. The stock-flow consistent (SFC) models capture the dynamic interactions between different economic sectors and financial flows. These models are particularly well-suited for analyzing the complex feedback loops that may arise from climate risks. By integrating climate-related variables into SFC models, researchers can simulate the impact of physical and transition risks on key economic indicators, such as GDP, investment, and employment. Agent-based models (ABMs) are used to simulate the behaviour of individual agents, such as households, firms, and financial institutions, within a complex system. In the context of climate finance, ABMs enable researchers to explore how agents respond to climate risks and policy interventions. This approach is valuable for studying the heterogeneous nature of risk exposures across different entities and understanding how individual decisions aggregate to macroeconomic outcomes.

Additionally, these models allow for the assessment of the impacts of climate policies, both independently and in conjunction with fiscal, monetary, and financial policies. Recognizing the interdependencies among fiscal, monetary, financial, and climate policies, researchers model the interactions to evaluate their collective impact on individual countries' financial systems. This holistic approach enables a comprehensive understanding of how policy measures can influence climate-related risks and financial stability. Some research extends its focus to analyze financial risks related to climate change in the context of the COVID-19 pandemic. This involves assessing how the economic fallout from the pandemic intersects with and amplifies existing climate-related risks. Researchers explore policy designs that align with climate goals while addressing the challenges posed by the pandemic.

The second research direction involves internalizing climate change considerations into financial valuation and portfolio risk management. This area of study aims to understand how incorporating climate-related factors into financial decision-making processes can lead to more informed and resilient investment strategies. This involves assessing whether and how traditional financial valuation models incorporate climate-related risks and opportunities. Understanding the integration of climate considerations into valuation is crucial for identifying potential financial benefits and risks associated with climate-related investments. The research explores the effectiveness of green financial tools, such as green bonds, green credit, and carbon taxes, in delivering significant financial benefits to their issuers. This includes examining the market reception and financial performance of entities employing these tools. For instance, studies may evaluate whether issuing green bonds contributes to lower borrowing costs or whether companies adopting sustainable practices experience enhanced financial performance.

Researchers are also interested in studying the impact of climate change risks on asset pricing across different markets, including stocks, bonds, and commodities. This involves understanding how climate-related risks, such as physical risks and transition risks, affect the pricing of financial assets. By incorporating climate factors into asset pricing models, researchers aim to provide insights into the valuation dynamics of various financial instruments. In summary, the second research direction emphasizes the internalization of climate change considerations in financial valuation and portfolio risk management by assessing the financial benefits of green financial tools, understanding the impact of climate change risks on asset pricing, and identifying strategies for climate-resilient investing. The findings from this research contribute to the development of sustainable finance practices and inform investment decisions in a changing climate.

The third research focus is on the management of climate risks within the financial sector. This is a complex and evolving challenge, and there is currently no universally accepted methodology. Institutional investors employ various methods to address climate risks, and these approaches continue to be refined as the understanding of the interplay between climate and finance deepens.

Some key methods used by institutional investors for climate risk management include: (1) carbon footprint analysis, where institutional investors analyze and seek to reduce the carbon footprint of companies in their portfolios by assessing the greenhouse gas emissions associated with a company's activities and products. By understanding and managing the carbon footprint, investors aim to align their portfolios with climate-related goals and reduce exposure to carbon-intensive assets; (2) Stranded asset risk analysis, which involves evaluating the potential risks associated with assets that may become economically unviable due to climate-related factors. This could include fossil fuel reserves that may lose value as the world transitions to cleaner energy sources. Investors assess the vulnerability of their portfolios to stranded asset risks and adjust their investments accordingly; (3) Valuation models incorporating climate risks, where investors utilize company valuation models that incorporate climate risks. This entails integrating climate-related factors, such as physical and transition risks, into traditional financial valuation models. By factoring in climate risks, investors aim to make more informed decisions about the true value and potential risks associated with their investments; (4) Third-party ESG ratings provided by third-party agencies are widely used by investors to evaluate the sustainability and ethical practices of companies. ESG ratings often include assessments of a company's climate-related initiatives, disclosure practices, and overall environmental impact. Investors rely on these ratings to guide their investment decisions; (5) Green finance tools used by institutional investors, such as green bonds and other sustainable financial instruments. These tools channel funds toward environmentally friendly projects and companies, allowing investors to support sustainable initiatives while managing climate-related risks.

Future research is expected to explore the mechanisms, degree, patterns, channels, and scenarios of risk contagion from climate to the financial system. Understanding how climate risks can propagate through financial markets and institutions is crucial for developing effective risk management strategies. Urgent calls are made for the creation of global standards for climate finance risks. Establishing standardized frameworks for risk monitoring, scenario analysis, forecasting, and early warning systems is essential to provide guidance to the global financial sector. This includes developing common metrics and methodologies for assessing and reporting climate-related risks. Regulatory bodies play a key role in shaping the environment for climate risk management. Standardized approaches can assist regulators in ensuring that financial institutions are adequately addressing and disclosing climate-related risks.

In summary, institutional investors are employing a range of methods to manage climate risks in their portfolios. Future research and industry efforts are directed toward refining methodologies, understanding risk contagion mechanisms, and establishing global standards for climate finance risks. The development of standardized frameworks is crucial for guiding both investors and regulatory bodies in effectively addressing the challenges posed by climate change in the financial sector.

7.2.3 ESG Investment Strategies

ESG has become a pivotal framework for assessing the sustainability and ethical practices of companies, influencing investment decisions, and promoting responsible corporate behaviour. The ESG framework comprises three main aspects: ESG disclosure standards, ESG ratings and corporate performance evaluations, and investment guidance based on ESG evaluations.

Among these aspect, ESG disclosure standards are considered a foundational cornerstone for achieving sustainability goals, including the "dual-carbon" goal. These standards provide a framework for companies to transparently report their environmental impact, social initiatives, and governance practices. The Global Reporting Initiative, established by the Global Reporting Initiative Organization in 2000, is the most widely adopted ESG disclosure standard globally. Used by companies in over 60 countries, the Global Reporting Initiative provides a comprehensive and internationally recognized set of guidelines for reporting on ESG performance. It covers various aspects, including environmental impact, social responsibility, and governance practices. In addition to the Global Reporting Initiative, other standards play a role in shaping ESG disclosure. The Sustainability Accounting Standards Board

(SASB) and ISO 26000 are notable examples. SASB focuses on industry-specific standards to help companies disclose financially material sustainability information, while ISO 26000 provides guidance on social responsibility.

ESG disclosure standards can be influenced by specific national-level factors, such as political and cultural systems. Different countries may adopt or adapt international standards to align with their political environments and societal expectations. The development of ESG disclosure rules is also influenced by the national regulatory frameworks of each country. Differences in legal and regulatory environments may lead to variations in the stringency and focus of ESG disclosure requirements. Some countries or regions, such as the United States and the European Union, have formulated relatively mature ESG disclosure rules in their capital markets. These rules are designed to enhance transparency, accountability, and comparability of ESG information disclosed by companies.

The second aspect, ESG ratings and corporate performance evaluations, involves assessing how well companies adhere to ESG principles. Ratings agencies and research organizations evaluate companies based on their ESG practices, providing investors and stakeholders with a quantifiable measure of sustainability and ethical performance. ESG ratings have a significant impact on investor decisions. Investors increasingly consider ESG factors when making investment choices, as higher ESG ratings are often associated with better long-term financial performance and reduced risks. ESG ratings are increasingly integrated into traditional financial analysis to provide a more comprehensive view of a company's overall performance. This integration enables investors to make informed decisions that align with both financial objectives and sustainability goals.

The third aspect, investment guidance based on ESG evaluations, directs capital toward companies that prioritize sustainability and responsible practices. Investors, including asset managers and institutional funds, use ESG considerations to create portfolios that align with environmental and social values. ESG evaluations guide positive impact investing, where investors seek financial returns while making a positive contribution to society and the environment. This approach aligns with the growing demand for investments that address global challenges, including climate change, social inequality, and corporate governance issues.

While the ESG framework has gained prominence in guiding sustainable investments, challenges persist within the current ESG disclosure and rating frameworks. These challenges include the limited effectiveness of existing frameworks in fully guiding investments and issues related to selective disclosure and "greenwashing." First, the current ESG disclosure and rating frameworks may not fully guide investment decisions. Investors face challenges in comprehensively assessing the ESG performance of companies, and the existing frameworks may not capture all material ESG factors that could impact financial performance. Second, companies often have the option to voluntarily disclose ESG information, leading to issues of selective disclosure. This can result in an incomplete or biased representation of a company's sustainability practices, hindering investors' ability to make fully informed decisions. The third issue is related to greenwashing concerns, which refer to the practice of conveying a false impression or providing misleading information about a company's environmental practices. Some companies may strategically present themselves as more environmentally responsible than they truly are, potentially leading investors to make decisions based on inaccurate information.

Future research is expected to address these challenges and enhance the role of ESG in investment decision-making. Research will focus on developing methodologies and tools to discern genuine ESG information from selective or misleading disclosures. This involves enhancing the verification and validation processes for reported ESG metrics and practices. Efforts will be directed towards establishing a standardized ESG disclosure and rating system. Standardization aims to create consistency in reporting, making it easier for investors to compare ESG performance across companies and industries.

Research also needs to seek to enhance and upgrade quantitative management and analysis tools for ESG investments. This includes the development of advanced data analytics, machine learning, and artificial intelligence techniques to extract valuable insights from large sets of ESG data. The development of optimal portfolio strategies based on ESG information will be a key research area. This involves exploring how ESG considerations can be integrated into traditional portfolio management to achieve both financial and sustainability objectives.

7.3 *International Cooperation Mechanisms for Climate Innovation*

According to cooperation theory, the mechanisms for international climate governance are designed to address climate change through a combination of multilateral, bilateral, and transnational cooperation. The international climate finance system, as a crucial component of international climate governance, incorporates three major types of funds: multilateral climate funds, bilateral climate funds, and national or regional funds.

Multilateral climate funds involve contributions from multiple countries and are managed collectively to support climate-related projects and initiatives globally. Examples include the GCF and the GEF. Bilateral climate funds are established by countries through direct agreements between two nations. These funds allow for targeted collaboration between specific partners, tailoring climate finance to the needs and priorities of the involved countries. Countries or regions may establish their own funds to address climate issues within their borders. These funds are often designed to align with national or regional climate goals and strategies.

Despite collective efforts, challenges persist in the practical implementation of international cooperation on climate issues. First, Countries exhibit varying levels of progress in addressing climate change. Economic, political, and developmental disparities contribute to differences in the ability and willingness of nations to undertake climate action. Second, despite collective actions and commitments in multilateral meetings and international agreements, there has not been a universal consensus on a common and effective approach to tackling climate change. Divergent national interests and priorities contribute to challenges in forging a unified strategy. Countries often have distinct policy and regulatory frameworks, making it challenging to create standardized approaches to climate governance. Harmonizing diverse national strategies becomes a complex task. A third challenge arises from the practical implementation of international cooperation on climate issues. There are difficulties in coordinating diverse national policies, mobilizing sufficient financial resources, and ensuring the equitable distribution of responsibilities and benefits.

Regarding international cooperation mechanisms for climate innovation, several aspects are worth exploring. These involve addressing institutional complexity, conflicts of interest among countries, and developing effective global strategies for climate change mitigation and adaptation.

First, improving international cooperation mechanisms for climate innovation requires navigating the institutional complexity and conflicts of interest among different countries, which contributes to identifying effective global strategies for both mitigation (reducing emissions) and adaptation (adjusting to the impacts of climate change). Establishing core technology cooperation groups at the international level can facilitate collaboration on key climate technologies. These groups can bring together countries with shared interests and expertise to advance innovation in critical areas such as renewable energy, carbon capture, and climate-resilient infrastructure. Existing initiatives, such as the "Belt and Road," can serve as platforms for cross-border climate-related collaborations. Integrating climate considerations into large-scale infrastructure projects and international economic cooperation initiatives enhances the impact of these endeavours on climate resilience.

Second, it is necessary to explore how central banks and financial regulatory agencies of various countries can adopt collaborative mechanisms. By coordinating regulatory measures, these institutions can guide financial institutions in addressing funding gaps for climate-related projects, promote the construction of diversified climate investment and financing governance systems, and design innovative financial instruments and products that attract private sector investments and align with sustainable development goals. Central banks and financial regulatory agencies can use financial policies to prevent and mitigate the impact of climate risks on financial stability. This includes incorporating climate risk assessments into financial regulations and encouraging the integration of climate considerations into investment decisions.

Third, recognizing the interconnected nature of global challenges, it is crucial to connect climate issues with other international concerns, such as biodiversity conservation and marine ecosystem management. International cooperation should not be limited to climate change alone. Adopting a comprehensive sustainable development perspective promotes synergies and coordinated efforts across multiple fields. By connecting climate issues with broader sustainability goals, a more comprehensive approach can be achieved, which fosters coordinated innovation and development across various domains through international collaboration.

In summary, improving international cooperation mechanisms for climate innovation involves addressing institutional complexities, leveraging international initiatives, enhancing financial collaboration, and adopting a comprehensive sustainable development perspective. Through cross-sectoral integration and collaborative efforts, countries can achieve coordinated innovation and development in climate change and related fields on a global scale.

8 Conclusions

This chapter introduces the conceptual issues of climate finance, its background and development, and reviews frontier research in this emerging field. Against the backdrop of global efforts to actively address the challenges of climate change, the development of climate finance, covering both investing and financing, has become an international consensus. Under the framework of climate change, climate finance has emerged as a burgeoning interdisciplinary field that explores the connection between climate change and financial activities, giving rise to climate finance theory. This chapter systematically reviews the concept and implications of climate finance and the latest research developments in the field of climate finance through a bibliometric approach.

Both theoretical and practical developments in the field of climate finance have evolved significantly worldwide, with various countries adopting diverse approaches to fund support, academic organization construction, and industry investment and financing activities. This chapter reviews the theoretical and practical developments of climate finance worldwide, with China as an example. China, as the world's largest emitter of greenhouse gases, has been actively addressing climate change through various initiatives. The country has made substantial progress in the development of renewable energy projects, emission reduction strategies, and sustainable infrastructure. China's experiences in climate finance showcase the importance of a comprehensive approach that combines fund support, academic research, and industry collaboration. Examining China's experiences in this context can offer valuable insights into the broader landscape of climate finance.

Finally, this chapter discusses the theoretical frontiers and application scenarios for the future development of the climate finance discipline. In the post-pandemic era, the resurgence of anti-globalization sentiment brings new uncertainties to climate change policies in countries worldwide. Financial solutions are becoming increasingly prominent in global climate governance, as the need for funding for global green development will be enormous. Incorporating climate factors into risk management frameworks and effectively enhancing the climate risk management of financial systems is a prevailing trend and a crucial scientific challenge that governments around the world urgently need to address.

Currently, major frontier issues related to climate governance and its practical needs include the construction of a theoretical framework for climate finance, climate asset pricing, ESG investments and practice, climate financial innovation, and the financialization of climate policies, all of which remain unresolved. The top-level design and planning for the development of climate finance also lack a scientific basis, calling for more exploration and breakthroughs at the theoretical level. Therefore, to better leverage the role of finance in addressing climate change, new theoretical support is required. Traditional finance theories alone may not fully solve these issues. Instead, an integration of multidisciplinary fields, including economic science (energy economics, climate economics, etc.), management science, natural science, and more, is essential. Climate finance as a new interdisciplinary discipline will play an increasingly important role in supporting global green finance actions and climate governance.

References

Addoum J M, Ng D T, Ortiz-Bobea A. 2021. Temperature shocks and industry earnings news. SSRN, https://ssrn.com/abstract=3480695 or https://doi.org/10.2139/ssrn.3480695

Aglietta M, Espagne É. 2016. Climate and finance systemic risks, more than an analogy?: The climate fragility hypothesis. CEPII, Centre d'etudes prospectives et d'informations internationales.

Baker M, Bergstresser D, Serafeim G, Wurgler J. 2018. Financing the response to climate change: The pricing and ownership of US green bonds. National Bureau of Economic Research working paper 25194.

24. Baldauf M, Garlappi L, Yannelis C. 2020. Does climate change affect real estate prices? Only if you believe in it. The Review of Financial Studies, 33(3): 1256–1295.

48. Battiston S. The importance of being forward-looking: Managing financial stability in the face of climate risk. Financial Stability Review, 2019 (23): 39–48.

49. Bebbington J, Larrinaga-González C. 2008. Carbon trading: Accounting and reporting issues. European Accounting Review, 17(4): 697–717.

25. Bernstein A, Gustafson M T, Lewis R. 2019. Disaster on the horizon: The price effect of sea level rise. Journal of Financial Economics, 134(2): 253–272.

20. Betzold C, Weiler F. 2017. Allocation of aid for adaptation to climate change: Do vulnerable countries receive more support? International Environmental Agreements: Politics, Law and Economics, 17(1): 17–36.

Boehm S, Lebling K, Levin K, Fekete H, Jaeger J, Waite R, Nilsson A, Thwaites J, Wilson R, Geiges A, Schumer C. 2021. State of Climate Action 2021: Systems Transformations Required to Limit Global Warming to 1.5 C. World Resources Institute. https://www.wri.org/research/state-climate-action-2021

13. Busch T, Hoffmann V H. 2007. Emerging carbon constraints for corporate risk management. Ecological Economics, 62(3-4): 518–528.

57. Campiglio E. 2016. Beyond carbon pricing: The role of banking and monetary policy in financing the transition to a low-carbon economy. Ecological Economics, 121: 220–230.

58. Campiglio E, Dafermos Y, Monnin P, Ryan-Collins J, Schotten G, Tanaka M. 2018. Climate change challenges for central banks and financial regulators. Nature Climate Change, 8(6): 462–468.

37. Collier B, Skees J, Barnett B. 2009. Weather index insurance and climate change: Opportunities and challenges in lower income countries. The Geneva Papers on Risk and Insurance-Issues and Practice, 34(3): 401–424.

36. Daskalakis G, Psychoyios D, Markellos R N. 2009. Modeling CO2 emission allowance prices and derivatives: Evidence from the European trading scheme. Journal of Banking and Finance, 33(7): 1230–1241.

2. Dell M, Jones B F, Olken B A. 2012. Temperature shocks and economic growth: Evidence from the last half century. American Economic Journal: Macroeconomics, 4(3): 66–95.

50. Dietz S, Bowen A, Dixon C. Gradwell P. 2016. Climate value at risk'of global financial assets. Nature Climate Change, 6(7): 676–679.

39. Du L, Wang L, Zhang Y. 2014. Risk during carbon finance transaction: measuring and control. Economic Management, 36(04): 106–116. (in Chinese)

35. Ehrhart K M, Hoppe C, Schleich J, Seifert, S. 2005. The role of auctions and forward markets in the EU ETS: Counterbalancing the cost-inefficiencies of combining generous allocation with a ban on banking. Climate Policy, 5(1): 31–46.

26. Eichholtz P, Steiner E, Yönder E. 2019. Where, when, and how do sophisticated investors respond to flood risk? Available at SSRN 3206257, 2019.

Farid M M, Keen M M, Papaioannou M M G, Parry IW, Pattillo MC, Ter-Martirosyan A. 2016. After Paris: Fiscal, macroeconomic and financial implications of global climate change[M]. International Monetary Fund.

Fay M, Hallegatte S, Vogt-Schilb A, Rozenberg J, Narloch U, Kerr T. 2015. Decarbonizing development: Three steps to a zero-carbon future[M]. World Bank Publications.

51. Flammer C. 2020. Green bonds: effectiveness and implications for public policy. Environmental and Energy Policy and the Economy, 1(1): 95–128.

22. Giglio S, Kelly B, Stroebel J. 2021. Climate finance. Annual Review of Financial Economics, 13(1): 15–36.

41. Gren M, Carlsson M, Elofsson K, Munnich, M. 2012. Stochastic carbon sinks for combating carbon dioxide emissions in the EU. Energy Economics, 34(5): 1523–1531.

10. Hasan M M, Du F. 2023. Nexus between green financial development, green technological innovation and environmental regulation in China. Renewable Energy, 204:218–228.

28. Hong H, Li F W, Xu J. 2019. Climate risks and market efficiency. Journal of Econometrics, 208(1): 265–281.

4. Hong, H, Karolyi, G A, Scheinkman, J A. 2020. Climate finance. The Review of Financial Studies, 33(3), 1011–1023.

19. Ji Q, Zhang D. 2019. How much does financial development contribute to renewable energy growth and upgrading of energy structure in China? Energy Policy, 128: 114–124.

42. Kaufmann R K, Hines E. 2018. The effects of combined-cycle generation and hydraulic fracturing on the price for coal, oil, and natural gas: Implications for carbon taxes. Energy Policy, 118: 603–611.

29. Keele D M, DeHart S. 2011. Partners of USEPA climate leaders: An event study on stock performance. Business Strategy and the Environment, 20(8): 485–497.

27. Klassen R D, McLaughlin C P. 1996. The impact of environmental management on firm performance. Management science, 42(8): 1199–1214.

14. Krueger P, Sautner Z, Starks L T. 2020. The importance of climate risks for institutional investors. The Review of Financial Studies, 33(3): 1067–1111.

Van Lerven F, Ryan-Collins J. 2017. Central banks, climate change and the transition to a low carbon economy: A policy briefing. New Economics Foundation. 2017.

43. Lin B, Jia Z. 2019. Impacts of carbon price level in carbon emission trading market. Applied Energy, 239: 157–170.

Monnin P. 2018. Central banks should reflect climate risks in monetary policy operations. SUERF Policy Note, Issue, 2018 (41).

23. Murfin J, Spiegel M. 2020. Is the risk of sea level rise capitalized in residential real estate? The Review of Financial Studies, 33(3): 1217–1255.

56. Olovsson C. 2018. Is climate change relevant for central banks? Sveriges Riksbank Economic Commentaries, 13:1–8.

47. Owen R, Brennan G, Lyon F. 2018. Enabling investment for the transition to a low carbon economy: Government policy to finance early stage green innovation. Current Opinion in Environmental Sustainability, 31: 137–145.

33. Painter M. 2020. An inconvenient cost: The effects of climate change on municipal bonds. Journal of Financial Economics, 135(2): 468–482.
15. Rajnoha R, Lesnikova P, Krajčík V. 2017. Influence of business performance measurement systems and corporate sustainability concept to overall business performance: "Save the planet and keep your performance". Economics and Management, 20(1): 111–128.
34. Schleich J, Ehrhart K M, Hoppe C, Seifert, S. 2006. Banning banking in EU emissions trading? Energy Policy, 34(1): 112–120.
18. Spash C L. 2010. The brave new world of carbon trading. New Political Economy, 15(2): 169–195.
40. Stiglitz J E. 2019. Addressing climate change through price and non-price interventions. European Economic Review, 119:594–612.
46. Strand J, Miller S, Siddiqui S. 2014. Long-run carbon emission implications of energy-intensive infrastructure investments with a retrofit option. Energy Economics, 46: 308–317.
6. Stroebel J, Wurgler J. 2021. What do you think about climate finance?. Journal of Financial Economics, 142(2): 487–498.
38. Tian S, Chen J. 2014. Farmers' adaptation to climate change within the sustainable livelihood framework. China Pollution, Resources and Environment, 24(05): 31–37. (in Chinese)
52. Tooze A. 2019. Why central banks need to step up on global warming. Foreign Policy, 2019, 20.
Tu Y. 2012. Legal reshaping of carbon finance. Social Sciences in China, 2012(03): 95–113+207. (in Chinese)
UNEP. 2022. Adaptation Gap Report 2022. UN Environment Programme. https://www.unep.org/resources/adaptation-gap-report-2022
Watson C, Schalatek L. 2020. Climate Finance Regional Briefing: Middle East and North Africa. Climate Finance Fundamentals.
21. Weiler F, Klöck C, Dornan M. 2018. Vulnerability, good governance, or donor interests? The allocation of aid for climate change adaptation. World Development, 104: 65–77.
World Health Organization. Climate change and health. 2021. https://www.who.int/news-room/fact-sheets/detail/climate-change-and-health
7. Zhang D, Zhang Z, Managi S. 2019. A bibliometric analysis on green finance: Current status, development, and future directions. Finance Research Letters, 29: 425–430.
16. Zhang Z, Peng B, Xie W, Liao H, Tang B, Zhao X, Wu Li. 2021. Scientific research issues in the field of energy transition and management. Journal of Management Sciences in China,24(08), 147–153. (in Chinese)
9. Zhang D, Zhang Y, Wang Y, Wang Q, Ji, Q. 2023. The discipline connotation, Chinese practices, and research hotspots of climate finance. Journal of Management Sciences, 26(8), 1–15. (In Chinese)
11. Zhu W, Yao N, Guo Q, Wang F. 2020. Public risk perception and willingness to mitigate climate change: city smog as an example. Environmental geochemistry and health, 42:881–893.
30. Ziegler A, Busch T, Hoffmann V H. 2011. Disclosed corporate responses to climate change and stock performance: An international empirical analysis. Energy Economics, 33(6): 1283–1294.

Global Climate Finance Architecture: Institutional Development

Yajie Chen, Fei Wu, and Dayong Zhang

Abstract Climate change poses a challenge for all countries globally. Consequently, climate finance inherently possesses an international dimension. Establishing a robust global climate finance architecture can facilitate technology transfer, knowledge exchange, and financial support flows to assist developing countries in addressing climate change. This chapter discusses the fundamental principles underpinning the development of a global climate finance architecture. It examines the evolution of climate finance mechanisms derived from successive global climate negotiation conferences, alongside an exploration of the current global climate finance architecture, encompassing multilateral, bilateral, and national/regional mechanisms. This chapter seeks to underscore the significance and challenges associated with multilateral, North–South, and public–private cooperation. It is important to note that the global climate finance architecture is an ongoing process of refinement and development, necessitating an acknowledgment of the international climate finance system from a dynamic and evolving perspective.

Keywords Climate change · Climate finance architecture · Climate finance mechanisms

1 Characteristics of Global Climate Finance Architecture

Climate finance plays a pivotal role as a financial mechanism intricately linked to the overarching issue of global climate change (Long et al. 2022). The United Nations Framework Convention on Climate Change (UNFCCC) provides a comprehensive definition, characterizing climate finance as "local, national, or transnational financing drawn from public, private, and alternative sources of financing that seeks to support mitigation and adaptation actions that will address climate change" (Hong et al. 2020). This definition underscores the diverse and inclusive nature of climate

Y. Chen · F. Wu · D. Zhang (✉)
Research Institute of Economics and Management, Southwestern University of Finance and Economics, 555 Liutai Avenue, Chengdu 611130, China
e-mail: dzhang@swufe.edu.cn

F. Wu et al. (eds.), *Climate Finance*, Climate Change and Energy Transition,
https://doi.org/10.1007/978-981-97-3308-8_2

finance, encompassing various funding sources and aiming to support a range of actions directed at both mitigating and adapting to climate change.

In essence, climate finance reflects and responds to specific characteristics of climate change. The multifaceted nature of climate change, marked by features such as publicity and quasi-publicity, temporality, spatiality, and distinctiveness, necessitates a structured and globally coordinated approach. These characteristics highlight the public nature of the issue, its interconnectedness across different geographical locations and timeframes, and the unique challenges it poses. As such, the establishment of a global climate finance architecture becomes imperative for effectively addressing the multifaceted challenges presented by climate change.

The concept of a global climate finance architecture encompasses a strategic framework that facilitates the efficient allocation of financial resources for climate-related initiatives worldwide. This architecture serves as a mechanism to streamline and coordinate efforts, ensuring that funding from various sources is directed towards impactful mitigation and adaptation projects. By recognizing the inherent complexities and distinct characteristics of climate change, a well-designed global climate finance architecture becomes an essential tool in mobilizing resources and promoting collective action to address the global challenges posed by climate change.

1.1 Publicity and Quasi-publicity

Climate governance, recognized as a global "public good" (Khan and Munira 2021), extends benefits beyond specific countries or regions, rendering it non-exclusive in consumption. However, this non-exclusivity introduces the risk of "free-riding," wherein certain countries or entities reap the advantages of climate actions initiated by others without contributing. In this context, private capital often avoids substantial, long-term, and low-return investments, underscoring the need for public capital to step in and invest in both mitigating and adapting to climate change. The characteristics of the public and quasi-public aspects of climate governance lay the foundation for similar attributes in climate finance.

The concept of publicity in climate finance aligns with its inherent focus on serving the public interest. Its primary objectives involve addressing climate change, mitigating environmental degradation, and fostering sustainable development for the collective benefit of society and the environment. These goals resonate with broader societal and global objectives rather than individual or private interests.

Moreover, climate finance frequently relies on funding from governmental sources, international organizations, philanthropic foundations, or public institutions. These funds are strategically directed towards achieving social and environmental sustainability goals, emphasizing the publicity of climate finance. Commonly provided in the form of subsidies, grants, or direct investments, this funding aims to support initiatives that contribute to the common good.

While climate finance predominantly exhibits a strong public orientation, it also operates in a quasi-public manner. This involves engaging in partnerships or collaborations with private entities, leveraging their expertise, resources, and innovative approaches to achieve climate goals. These collaborations often take the form of public–private partnerships, where private sector involvement complements public initiatives, thereby driving sustainable climate actions and investment. In such cases, the quasi-public nature of climate finance combines elements of both public and private sectors to enhance its overall impact and effectiveness.

1.2 Temporality

The temporality of climate finance revolves around the time-related considerations inherent in funding initiatives addressing climate change. The Paris Agreement sets a clear target for the end of this century, emphasizing the need to limit the global average temperature rise to 2 °C relative to the industrial level, with efforts to further restrict it to 1.5 °C. To attain these objectives, substantial funds must be mobilized within a finite timeframe.

Recent data from the World Bank (October 2019) underscores the imminent need for global infrastructure investment over the next 15 years, projecting an estimated investment requirement of approximately $90 trillion by 2030. The United Nations Environment Programme (UNEP) released the "2021 Adaptation Gap Report: The Storm Ahead" during the United Nations Climate Change Conference (COP26), revealing that developing countries alone face adaptation costs ranging from $140 billion to $300 billion annually before 2030, potentially escalating to $280 billion to $500 billion per year by 2050. China, as outlined in the Climate Policy Initiative's report on "China's Potential for Scaling up Climate Finance," invested $640 billion in domestic climate finance between 2017 and 2018, with a forecast indicating an annual investment requirement of $14 trillion in the coming decade.

In light of the direct consequences of climate change on society, evidenced by emerging impacts such as extreme weather events, rising sea levels, ecosystem destruction, and global food safety concerns (Zscheischler et al. 2018), urgent actions are imperative. Enhancing infrastructure and resilience to mitigate and adapt to climate change become pressing needs. The urgency of the climate governance challenge shapes the temporal characteristics of climate finance. The execution of green infrastructure, clean energy projects, and sustainable development strategies demands substantial financial resources, necessitating prompt initiation and investment in these projects.

1.3 Spatiality

Greenhouse gases emitted anywhere on Earth exert the same temperature rise effect on the global atmosphere, their characteristics dictating their widespread distribution and influence. Regardless of their origin, these gases can traverse the globe upon entering the atmosphere, underscoring the universality of the greenhouse effect. Given this lack of geographical constraints, individual countries or regions cannot singularly resolve the global climate problem. Moreover, the ramifications of climate change-induced extreme weather events may lead to global population migration, exacerbating social instability on a global scale. Financial risks stemming from climate change are similarly pervasive, with climate-related events causing losses and disasters potentially impacting a country's financial system, thereby affecting global financial markets (Barnett et al. 2020). The intricate interconnections within financial markets and among financial institutions mean that a financial crisis in one country can reverberate and trigger instability in the international financial system.

Confronting the challenge of climate change necessitates collective action by countries worldwide. The international community must collaborate to establish global emission reduction targets and policies that effectively address the impacts of climate change. This entails the active participation, cooperation, and mutual assistance of countries globally, fostering the development and dissemination of green technologies and the exchange of environmental experiences and resources.

The global scope of climate governance inherently dictates the spatiality of climate finance. Climate issues transcend national borders (Benzie and Persson 2019), demanding global financial support and investment to effectively address the challenges posed by climate change. Climate finance must be sourced globally to support national projects and programs related to emission reduction, climate change adaptation, renewable energy sources, energy efficiency, and more. International cooperation and joint investment are not only critical for achieving climate goals but also serve as the cornerstone for building a foundation conducive to sustainable development.

1.4 Cross-Country Disparities

Historically, developed countries have been the primary contributors to global greenhouse gas emissions since the Industrial Revolution. The extensive industrial production and energy consumption during this period significantly increased emissions, particularly carbon dioxide, fostering modern society's prosperity and economic development. These emissions, however, have had far-reaching consequences, contributing significantly to severe climate change issues globally. In contrast, less developed countries made relatively minor contributions to global greenhouse gas emissions during the early stages of industrialization, with smaller roles in industrialization and economic growth. Nevertheless, with the acceleration of globalization, certain emerging economies have witnessed increased industrialization and urbanization, resulting in a surge in greenhouse gas emissions. Recognizing these historical differences in contributions and the varying stages of development, it becomes imperative to incorporate principles of differentiation in the allocation of climate funds.

Presently, developed countries possess stronger economic and technological capabilities, enabling them to proactively and effectively address climate change through mitigation and adaptation measures. These countries have more resources available for initiatives such as promoting clean energy technologies, enhancing urban planning, and establishing flood control and disaster management systems. Conversely, developing countries often grapple with challenges such as financial constraints and limited technology, making it difficult for them to effectively mitigate and adapt to climate change while being more vulnerable. In light of this, developed countries should bear the primary economic responsibility and provide increased climate finance to support the efforts of less developed countries in addressing climate change.

Considering these characteristics, the establishment of a robust global climate finance architecture emerges as the linchpin in promoting international cooperation in the climate field. This architecture has evolved since the 1990s, forming multilateral and bilateral fund mechanisms within and outside the UNFCCC framework, with ongoing improvements. Aligned with the principle of "common but differentiated responsibilities and respective capabilities" established in the Convention, developed countries commit to providing financial support to developing country parties for achieving the Convention's objectives. The Paris Agreement reiterates these obligations while introducing a mechanism encouraging voluntary contributions from all parties. Developed country parties should consider the needs and priorities of developing country parties, continuing to lead in mobilizing climate funds from various sources. Public funds, particularly supporting state-driven strategies, play a crucial role, representing an advancement over previous efforts in climate funding mobilization.

2 Development of Global Negotiation for Climate Change

Global negotiations for climate change have indeed placed significant emphasis on the crucial aspect of climate finance. This emphasis has been a central theme in discussions within the United Nations Climate Change Conferences, where funding mechanisms play a pivotal role in addressing the multifaceted challenges associated with climate change mitigation and adaptation. The international community recognized early on that financial support is essential for developing countries to effectively respond to climate change, as they often lack the resources and capacity to implement necessary measures.

The journey towards a comprehensive climate finance framework began with the International Climate Convention Negotiations in 1991, marking the genesis of international efforts to address climate change collectively. Subsequent milestones in this trajectory include the establishment of key intergovernmental institutional arrangements guided by the UNFCCC, the Kyoto Protocol, and the Paris Agreement. The UNFCCC, adopted in 1992, laid the foundation for international cooperation to combat climate change. The Kyoto Protocol, adopted in 1997, introduced market-based mechanisms and financial instruments to facilitate emission reduction efforts. The Paris Agreement, a landmark accord reached in 2015, further elevated the importance of climate finance by establishing a goal to mobilize $100 billion annually by 2020 to address the needs of developing countries.

Despite the achievements, challenges persist in meeting the financial commitments outlined in these agreements. There are ongoing debates about the adequacy of funding, the effectiveness of existing mechanisms, and the need for additional resources to address the evolving challenges of climate change. The negotiation process, spanning over several decades, has been marked by complexity and challenges, reflecting the diverse interests and priorities of nations. However, amid the difficulties, there have been historic achievements in international climate cooperation, particularly in the realm of climate finance. The establishment and activation of climate funding mechanisms represent significant milestones that underscore the global commitment to supporting developing countries in their climate change endeavors.

The global negotiation process for addressing climate change is dynamic and involves various stages, each playing a crucial role in shaping international efforts to combat the impacts of climate change. Figure 1 visually depicts the process of global climate negotiations and highlights the key meetings that have been instrumental in shaping international efforts to combat climate change. The negotiations involve a complex interplay of ideas, commitments, and decisions, culminating in the continuous evolution of strategies and actions to address the challenges posed by climate change on a global scale.

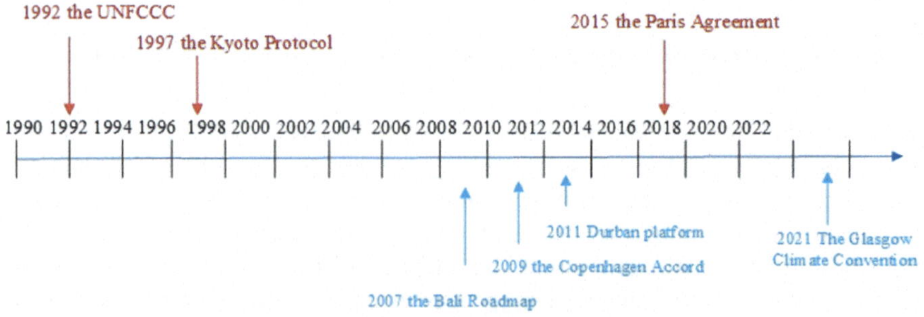

Fig. 1 Global climate negotiation process and important meetings

The timeline is marked by ongoing negotiations, assessments, and updates, reflecting the evolving nature of the climate challenge. Here are the key stages in the process of global negotiation for climate change.

2.1 The First Stage: 1991–1994

The period from 1991 to 1994 represents the first stage of global negotiations on climate change, laying the groundwork for the subsequent evolution of international efforts to address this pressing issue. It is a crucial period that saw the establishment of the UNFCCC and the formal recognition of key principles, including common but differentiated responsibilities. This stage set the tone for subsequent negotiations and actions, shaping the international response to the challenges posed by climate change.

The late 1980s and early 1990s witnessed a growing recognition of the environmental and economic implications of climate change. Scientific evidence, particularly the findings of the Intergovernmental Panel on Climate Change (IPCC), underscored the need for concerted global action. Against this backdrop, the first stage of negotiations gained momentum with the establishment of the Intergovernmental Negotiating Committee for a Framework Convention on Climate Change (INC/FCCC) in 1991. This committee brought together representatives from countries worldwide to lay the foundation for an international treaty.

The pinnacle of this stage was the United Nations Conference on Environment and Development (UNCED), also known as the Earth Summit, held in Rio de Janeiro in 1992. The UNFCCC was adopted during this summit, marking a significant milestone in international efforts to combat climate change. The UNFCCC then officially entered into force on 21 March 1994, marking the beginning of a new era in global cooperation to address climate change. The UNFCCC acknowledged the principle of common but differentiated responsibilities, emphasizing that all nations share a common responsibility to address climate change while recognizing the differing capacities and historical contributions of developed and developing countries.

The Convention laid out key principles, including the objective to stabilize greenhouse gas concentrations in the atmosphere, the recognition of the vulnerability of developing countries, and the importance of financial and technological support for their climate actions. Developed countries were urged to take the lead in reducing emissions and providing financial assistance to developing nations, reflecting the concept of historical responsibility and the need for equity in addressing climate change.

The Convention provided a framework for subsequent negotiations and actions to curb emissions and enhance resilience. Post-Rio, countries engaged in ongoing negotiations to elaborate on the provisions of the UNFCCC and to define the modalities for its implementation. The period following the adoption of the UNFCCC saw efforts to establish concrete commitments and timelines for action. Negotiations focused on developing a framework for the formulation of national strategies to mitigate climate change and adapt to its impacts. These negotiations included discussions on issues such as reporting and verification of emissions, financial contributions, and technology transfer. The ongoing negotiations and elaborations since the UNFCCC's adoption have continued to refine and strengthen the global framework for addressing climate change.

2.2 The Second Stage: 1995–2005

The second stage of global negotiations from 1995 to 2005 was characterized by the negotiation and adoption of the Kyoto Protocol, representing a significant step forward in international efforts to address climate change. The protocol's entry into force in 2005 marked the beginning of the first commitment period, shaping the landscape of climate action and setting the stage for subsequent negotiations under the UNFCCC. The Kyoto Protocol's achievements and challenges pave the way for ongoing efforts to strengthen global climate agreements and address the evolving challenges of climate change mitigation.

The first significant development in this stage occurred at the third Conference of the Parties (COP3) to the UNFCCC in Kyoto, Japan, in 1997. During this conference, the international community negotiated the Kyoto Protocol, which would become the first implementation agreement following the adoption of the UNFCCC. The Kyoto Protocol aimed to establish legally binding emission reduction targets for developed countries, setting specific goals for the reduction of greenhouse gas emissions. The negotiations clarified the principle of common but differentiated responsibilities, acknowledging the historical responsibility of developed nations for the majority of historical emissions. The Kyoto Protocol officially entered into force on 16 February 2005, marking a historic moment in international climate negotiations. This milestone reflected the commitment of the global community to taking concrete actions to address climate change and marked the first time that legally binding emission reduction targets were established for a group of countries.

The Kyoto Protocol introduced the concept of differentiated targets for developed countries. These targets were phased, with the first commitment period set from 2008 to 2012. During this period, developed countries collectively committed to reducing their emissions by an average of 5.2% below 1990 levels. It also established mechanisms such as emissions trading, the Clean Development Mechanism (CDM), and Joint Implementation (JI) to enhance flexibility and promote cost-effective emission reductions. The Kyoto Protocol's first commitment period represented a period of active implementation. Participating developed countries worked to meet their assigned emission reduction targets through a combination of domestic policies and international cooperation mechanisms. However, the Kyoto Protocol faced challenges, including the absence of legally binding commitments for developing countries and the withdrawal of the United States, a major emitter, from the protocol. These limitations underscored the complexity of achieving a comprehensive and inclusive global climate agreement.

2.3 The Third Stage: 2007–2010

The third stage of global climate negotiations from 2007 to 2010 was marked by the adoption of the Bali Roadmap, which initiated the process of negotiating a successor to the Kyoto Protocol. The subsequent Copenhagen Accord and the definition of emission responsibilities and action targets in the following years laid the groundwork for the post-2012 international climate system. This stage was a pivotal period that shaped the direction of international climate negotiations and set the stage for the ambitious agreements that would follow, including the historic Paris Agreement in 2015.

The Bali Roadmap was a significant outcome of the UN Climate Change Conference held in Bali, Indonesia, in 2007. It marked a turning point in international climate negotiations by initiating the process to negotiate the successor to the Kyoto Protocol for the post-2012 period. The roadmap acknowledged the need for enhanced global efforts to address climate change and set the stage for negotiations on a comprehensive international climate agreement. The period following the adoption of the Bali Roadmap involved intense negotiations to shape the international climate system beyond the Kyoto Protocol's initial commitments. Countries engaged in discussions on emission reduction targets, financing mechanisms, adaptation strategies, and the inclusion of all major emitters in the agreement.

The Copenhagen Accord emerged from the 15th Conference of the Parties (COP15) held in Copenhagen in 2009. While the conference did not result in a legally binding agreement, the accord represented a political commitment to limit global temperature increases and provided a framework for countries to submit their emission reduction targets and actions voluntarily. The accord marked a significant step in global climate negotiations, as it included commitments from both developed and major developing countries, signaling a move towards a more inclusive and comprehensive approach to addressing climate change.

Over the next two years, the negotiations continued, culminating in the definition of emission responsibilities and action targets for all parties. This process was formalized through the decisions of the Conference of the Parties (COP), outlining the post-2012 international climate system. These decisions set the foundation for countries to submit their Intended Nationally Determined Contributions (INDCs), specifying their emission reduction targets and actions, in the lead-up to the Paris Agreement. The decisions made during this period established the structure and framework for the post-2012 international climate system, defining the roles and responsibilities of all parties, both developed and developing. This period was crucial in setting the stage for the Paris Agreement, which would be negotiated in the subsequent years and ultimately adopted in 2015.

2.4 The Fourth Stage: 2011–2015

The fourth stage of global climate negotiations from 2011 to 2015 witnessed a paradigm shift with the adoption of the Paris Agreement. The Durban Platform negotiations and the move towards a collaborative, nationally determined approach marked a departure from the traditional North–South divide, setting the stage for a more inclusive and flexible framework for addressing climate change on a global scale. The Paris Agreement's emphasis on voluntary contributions and the ongoing implementation efforts reflect a dynamic and evolving approach to international climate governance.

The Conference of the Parties (COP) in Durban, South Africa, in 2011, authorized the opening of the "Durban Platform" negotiation process. This marked a pivotal moment as countries agreed to develop a new international climate agreement applicable to all parties, to be adopted in 2015 and implemented from 2020 onward. The Durban Platform negotiations aimed to overcome the distinction between developed and developing countries that had characterized previous climate agreements, emphasizing a more inclusive and collaborative approach to climate action.

The negotiations under the Durban Platform focused on shaping the post-2020 international climate system. This process sought to build on the achievements and lessons learned from earlier agreements, including the Kyoto Protocol and the Copenhagen Accord. The "top-down" logic of action, as established by the Obama administration during the negotiations of the Copenhagen Accord in 2009, continued to influence the approach to climate negotiations during this period. This approach emphasized a collective, rather than a differentiated, response to climate change.

The pinnacle of this stage was the adoption of the Paris Agreement at the 21st Conference of the Parties (COP21) in Paris in 2015. The Paris Agreement represented a historic shift in global climate governance, moving away from the North–South divide and emphasizing a universal and collaborative framework for climate action. The agreement introduced the concept of "nationally determined contributions" (NDCs), whereby each country determines its own contribution to climate action based on its domestic circumstances and capacities. Unlike previous agreements, the Paris Agreement did not impose specific emission reduction targets on countries. Instead, it encouraged voluntary commitments that reflected the varying capabilities and circumstances of nations.

While the Paris Agreement does not impose legally binding emission reduction targets, it establishes a robust framework with legally binding elements. This includes the obligation for countries to regularly submit and update their NDCs and to participate in a global stocktake to assess collective progress. The Paris Agreement established a new global climate governance paradigm characterized by collaborative action among multiple countries. The emphasis on nationally determined contributions recognizes the sovereignty of nations while fostering a collective commitment to addressing the global challenge of climate change. The period following the adoption of the Paris Agreement has been characterized by ongoing efforts to implement the commitments made by countries in their NDCs. This includes the mobilization of climate finance, technology transfer, and capacity-building support to assist developing countries in their climate actions.

2.5 *The Fifth Stage: 2016–Present*

During this period, the international climate governance process has experienced the negative the change of government in the United States and Brazil, and has struggled to move forward. The Paris Agreement, which came into force in 2016, emphasized the need for financial support from developed to developing countries. It set a goal of mobilizing $100 billion annually by 2020 to aid developing nations in climate change adaptation and mitigation. In 2018, The Conference of the Parties (COP24) held in Katowice, Poland, was crucial in setting the stage for countries to implement and follow through on their commitments under the Paris Agreement. It highlighted the importance of collaborative efforts, transparency, and increased ambition in combating climate change on a global scale. It also strengthened the global action on climate change to make further arrangements.

The fifth stage of global climate negotiations from 2016 to the present has been marked by challenges, including changes in government leadership and the need for accelerated action to address the climate crisis. The Paris Agreement's implementation, COP24 in Katowice, and ongoing international efforts underscore the continued commitment to collaborative action and the imperative to strengthen global responses to climate change challenges. The period remains dynamic, with countries working towards fulfilling their commitments and navigating evolving global dynamics in the context of climate governance.

The Paris Agreement officially came into force in 2016, marking a new phase in global climate governance. The agreement emphasizes the importance of financial support from developed to developing countries to facilitate climate change adaptation and mitigation efforts. Developed countries committed to mobilizing $100 billion annually by 2020 to support developing nations in their climate actions. However, achieving this financial target has been a challenge, and progress has been closely monitored in subsequent climate conferences.

The Conference of the Parties (COP24) in Katowice, Poland, in 2018, played a crucial role in setting the stage for the implementation of the Paris Agreement. The conference focused on finalizing the rulebook for the agreement, specifying guidelines for transparency, reporting, and accountability. COP24 emphasized the importance of collaborative efforts, transparency, and increased ambition in combating climate change on a global scale. It highlighted the need for countries to enhance their commitments to align with the goals of limiting global temperature increases and strengthening adaptation efforts.

One significant issue during this period has been the change in government leadership, particularly in the United States and Brazil. The decision by the United States to withdraw from the Paris Agreement under the Trump administration in 2017 had a notable impact on international climate efforts. Brazil, under President Jair Bolsonaro, also faced criticism for environmental policies that could impact efforts to address climate change.

The period from 2018 to the present has witnessed ongoing efforts to strengthen global action on climate change and make further arrangements to address emerging challenges. The urgency of the climate crisis has spurred discussions on raising ambition and accelerating efforts to achieve the goals set forth in the Paris Agreement. The international community has continued to respond to climate change challenges through various initiatives, partnerships, and agreements. Increased attention has been given to issues such as climate finance, technology transfer, capacity building, and addressing loss and damage associated with the impacts of climate change. The annual COP meetings continue to serve as crucial platforms for countries to assess progress, negotiate new agreements, and strengthen global collaboration on climate action. Discussions focus on issues such as updating NDCs, enhancing adaptation efforts, and mobilizing financial resources to support developing nations. Despite challenges, there has been a renewed commitment to addressing climate change globally. The increased recognition of the climate crisis and the need for urgent action has led to enhanced awareness, advocacy, and collaborative efforts across sectors and borders.

3 Negotiation Structures Within the UNFCCC Framework

The evolution of the institutional framework for addressing climate change is marked by significant milestones in key international agreements. The Convention in 1992, the Kyoto Protocol in 1997, and the Paris Agreement in 2015 have collectively shaped the global response to the pressing challenges of climate change. The transition of this institutional framework is visually represented in Fig. 2, illustrating the dynamic and interconnected nature of global climate negotiations over the years.

This framework encompasses various governing bodies, each playing a unique role in orchestrating international efforts. As the primary decision-making body, Conference of the Parties on Climate Change (COP) convenes annually to assess and guide the implementation of climate-related agreements; Conference of the Parties Serving as the Meeting of the Parties to the Kyoto Protocol (CMP) oversees the implementation of the Kyoto Protocol, focusing on commitments to reduce greenhouse gas emissions; Conference of the Parties Serving as the Meeting of the Parties to the Paris Agreement (CMA) is responsible for overseeing the implementation of the Paris Agreement, a pivotal accord that outlines commitments to combat climate change.

COP, CMP and CMA are convened annually at different locations. These gatherings serve two primary objectives. First, the conferences aim to assess and review the implementation progress of the Convention, the Kyoto Protocol, and the Paris Agreement, respectively. This involves evaluating the actions and commitments made by

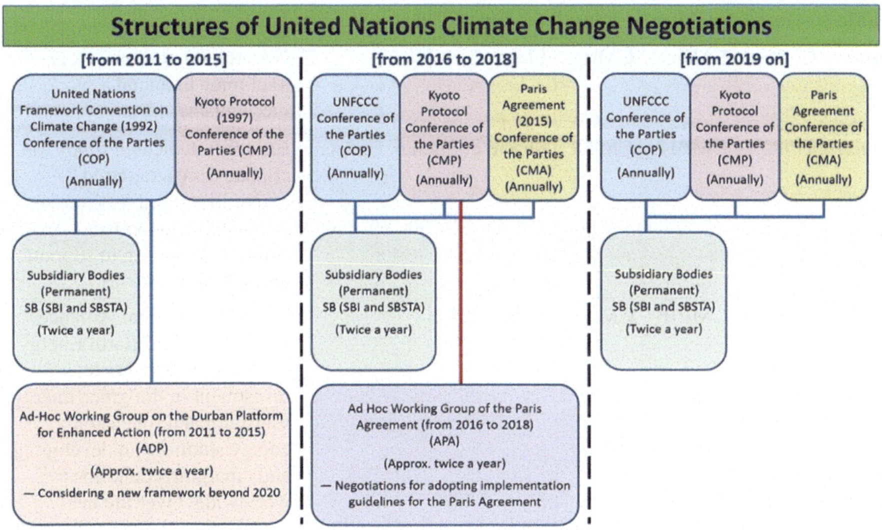

Fig. 2 Transition of the UN negotiation framework. *Source* https://www.mofa.go.jp/

member countries to address climate change. Another crucial aspect of these conferences is to adopt decisions related to the further development and implementation of the three instruments. These decisions guide future actions and policies, shaping the global response to climate change. Throughout the years of COP, CMP, and CMA negotiations, a global Climate Funding Mechanism has evolved. This mechanism plays a vital role in supporting climate-related projects and initiatives. The funding mechanism has been shaped through ongoing discussions and agreements during the annual conferences. Table 1 lists the COP/CMP/CMA Meetings and specific outcomes related to climate finance.

Additionally, two permanent bodies, the Subsidiary Body for Scientific and Technological Advice (SBSTA) and the Subsidiary Body for Implementation (SBI), provide essential support. SBSTA offers scientific and technological guidance related to the UNFCCC, Kyoto Protocol, and Paris Agreement. SBI evaluates the effective implementation of climate frameworks, ensuring that commitments translate into tangible actions.

The Ad Hoc Working Group of the Paris Agreement (APA) emerged as a subsidiary body dedicated to facilitating the entry into force of the Paris Agreement. APA played a crucial role in preparing for the initial meeting of CMA and was tasked with discussing and establishing guidelines for the Paris Agreement's implementation. APA successfully concluded its functions with the closure of CMA1-3 in December 2018.

The Ad-Hoc Working Group on the Durban Platform for Enhanced Action (ADP) served a distinct purpose, addressing two primary objectives. First, it discussed the

Table 1 The COP/CMP/CMA meetings and specific outcomes related to climate finance

Year	COP	CMP	CMA	Place	Negotiation outcome (related to climate financial mechanism)
2022	COP27	CMP17	CMA4	Sharm el-Sheikh, Egypt	Establish dedicated funds for climate disasters; Hold corporations and institutions accountable; Mobilize additional funding to support developing countries
2021	COP26	CMP16	CMA3	Glasgow, UK	Launch the Global Alliance for Humans and Earth Energy (GEAPP) to accelerate investment in the green energy transition and renewable energy solutions in developing and emerging economies worldwide. Over the next decade, the alliance will aim to raise a total of $100 billion through both public and private financing channels
2015	COP21	CMP11		Paris	Adopt the Paris Agreement; countries are allowed to define their own contributions to carbon reduction, while binding states parties with procedural obligations
2013	COP19	CMP9		Warsaw, Poland	Adopt the decisions, including furthering the Durban Platform, the Green Climate Fund and long-term financing, REDD+ Warsaw Framework, the Warsaw International Mechanism, and others
2011	COP17	CMP7		Durban, South Africa	Implement the second commitment period of the Kyoto Protocol and launch the Green Climate Fund
2010	COP16	CMP6		Cancun, Mexico	Adopt the Cancun Agreement; Establish the Green Climate Fund

(continued)

Table 1 (continued)

Year	COP	CMP	CMA	Place	Negotiation outcome (related to climate financial mechanism)
2009	COP15	CMP5		In Copenhagen, Denmark	The Copenhagen Accord establishes four mechanisms: reducing emissions from deforestation in developing countries, including the Forest Protection Mechanism (REDD-plus); a high-level committee under the Conference of the Parties on how to implement the funding provisions; the Copenhagen Green Climate Fund; and a technology transfer mechanism
2008	COP14	CMP4		Poznan, Poland	Decide to launch the "adaptation fund"
2007	COP13	CMP3		Bali, Indonesia	Adopt the Bali Roadmap. Four key elements are identified, including mitigation, adaptation, funding and technology
2006	COP12	CMP2		Nairobi, Kenya	Reach dozens of decisions, including the Nairobi Work Plan; Make important progress in managing the adaptation Fund
2005	COP11	CMP1		Montreal, Canada	Adopt the Montreal Roadmap; Reach more than 40 important decisions, including launching the second phase of greenhouse gas emission reduction negotiations after 2012
1997	COP3			Kyoto, Japan	Adopt the Kyoto protocol
1995	COP1			Berlin, Germany	Adopt the decision of the joint implementation of the convention by industrialized and developing countries

Source https://unfccc.int/process/bodies/supreme-bodies/conference-of-the-parties-cop

Table 2 Climate finance funds and initiatives

Dedicated climate finance funds and initiatives	Implementing/closed climate funds and initiatives
ACT—Accelerating Coal Transition program	ADB—Asian Development Bank
ACCF—Africa Climate Change Fund	AFD—Agence Francaise de Developpement
AF—Adaptation Fund	AfDB—African Development Bank
AREI—African Renewable Energy Initiative	BEIS—Department for Business, Energy & Industrial Strategy
ASAP—Adaptation for Smallholder Agriculture Programme	BMZ—Bundeministerium fur Wirtschaftliche Zusammenarbeit und Entwicklung
CAFI—Central African Forest Initiative	CBFF—Congo Basin Forest Fund
CBFF—Congo Basin Forest Fund	CIDA—Canadian International Development Agency
CDM—Clean Development Mechanism	DEFRA—Department for Environment, Food and Rural Affairs
CIF—Climate Investment Fund	DFAT—Department of Foreign Affairs and Trade
CTF—Clean Technology Fund	DFC—United States International Development Finance Corporation
FCPF—Forest Carbon Partnership Facility	EBRD—European Bank for Reconstruction and Development
FIP—Forest Investment Program	EIB—European Investment Bank
GCCA—Global Climate Change Alliance	FAO—Food and Agriculture Organisation of the United Nations
GCCI—Global Climate Change Initiative	FCDD—Foreign, Commonwealth and Development Office
GCPF—Global Climate Partnership Fund	FFEM—Fonds Francais pour l'Environnement Mondial
GEF—Global Environment Facility	GIZ—Deutsche Gesellschaft fur Internationale Zusammenarbeit GmbH
GEEREF—Global Energy Efficiency and Renewable Energy Fund	IDB—Inter-American Development Bank
ICF—International Climate Fund	IFAD—International Fund for Agricultural Development
IKI—Internationale Klimaschutzinitiative	JBIC—Japan Bank of International Cooperation
JI—Joint Implementation	JICA—Japan International Cooperation Agency
LDCF—Least Developed Countries Fund	KfW—Kreditanstalt fur Wiederaufbau
MDG-F—MDG Achievement Fund	MDG-F—Millennium Development Goals Achievement Fund
NAMA Facility—Mitigation Action Facility	MIES—Mission Interministérielle de l'Effet de Serre
NICFI—Norway's International Climate Forest Initiative	MOFA—Ministry of Foreign Affairs
PMR—Partnership for Market Readiness	NMFA—Ministry of Foreign Affairs
PPCR—Pilot Program on Climate Resilience	NORAD—Norwegian Agency for Development Cooperation
REM—REDD+ Early Movers	UNDP—United Nations Development Programme
SCCF—Special Climate Change Fund	UNEP—United Nations Environment Programme
SCF—Strategic Climate Fund	USAID—United States Agency for International Development
SREP—Scaling Up Renewable Energy Program	WB—World Bank
UN-REDD—United Nations Collaborative Programme on Reducing Emissions from Deforestation and Forest Degradation	

Source https://climatefundsupdate.org/

framework applicable to all nations from 2020. Second, it aimed to enhance mitigation ambition by 2020. The ADP completed its mandate during COP21 in 2015, coinciding with the adoption of the Paris Agreement.

4 Development and Formation of Climate Finance Mechanisms

4.1 The UNFCCC in 1992

The Convention, negotiated by the United Nations Intergovernmental Negotiating Committee, was finalized on 22 May 1992, and officially adopted on 4 June 1992, during the United Nations Conference on Environment and Development (Earth Summit) in Rio de Janeiro, Brazil. It marked the world's inaugural international convention dedicated to the comprehensive regulation of greenhouse gas emissions, particularly carbon dioxide, with the goal of mitigating the adverse impacts of global climate warming on human economies and societies. While the convention serves as a fundamental framework for international collaboration on global climate change issues, it lacks legal binding force and specific action plans.

The primary objective of the Convention is to stabilize the concentration of greenhouse gases in the atmosphere at levels that prevent dangerous anthropogenic interference with the climate system. It emphasizes achieving this objective within a defined timeframe, allowing ecosystems to naturally adapt to climate change, safeguarding food production, and fostering sustainable economic development. The Convention categorizes the world into two groups: industrialized countries, recognized as primarily responsible for anthropogenic greenhouse gas emissions (commonly known as Annex I countries), and developing countries, whose emissions are expected to rise in the future (commonly known as non-Annex I countries).

All parties to the Convention are mandated to compile inventories of their national greenhouse gas emissions and sinks,[1] commit to formulating national strategies for adaptation and mitigation of climate change, and integrate climate change considerations into their social, economic, and environmental policies. Additionally, they are required to promote sustainable management, energy efficiency, and enhance the functionality of greenhouse gas sinks, including forests and various terrestrial, coastal, and marine ecosystems.

To support developing countries in implementing the Convention and addressing climate change, the Convention has established financial mechanisms, such as the Global Environment Facility (GEF), which provides grants or concessional loans. In 1998, the Fourth Conference of the Parties to the Convention designated GEF as its permanent funding mechanism, subject to review every four years. The financial

[1] "Sinks" means any process, activity, or mechanism of removing a greenhouse gas, aerosol, or greenhouse gas precursors from the atmosphere.

mechanism is accountable to the Conference of the Parties, which determines climate change policy, priority areas of planning, and criteria for funding. The Conference regularly offers policy guidance to the funding mechanism.

4.2 The Kyoto Protocol in 1997

The Kyoto Protocol stands as the world's pioneering international legislation designed to regulate greenhouse gas emissions among nations. During the third Conference of the Parties to the Convention in December 1997 in Kyoto, Japan, representatives from 149 countries and regions adopted the protocol with the objective of restricting greenhouse gas emissions from developed countries to mitigate global warming. The primary aim is to stabilize the concentration of greenhouse gases in the atmosphere at a suitable level to prevent drastic climate change that could harm humanity. To safeguard against the threat of climate warming, the Kyoto Protocol mandates that developed countries must reduce their greenhouse gas emissions by 5.2% compared to the 1990 level.

Aligned with the "common but differentiated responsibilities" principle outlined in the Convention, developing countries are not obligated by legally enforceable greenhouse gas limitations. Developed country parties to the Protocol are mandated to assist developing nations in undertaking greenhouse gas reduction projects through financial support or technological assistance.

To achieve emission reduction targets, the Kyoto Protocol established three flexible compliance mechanisms: Joint Implementation (JI), Clean Development Mechanism (CDM), and Emissions Trading (ET). These mechanisms afford developed countries flexibility in meeting emission reduction tasks through avenues such as carbon trading markets, while enabling developing countries to receive technological and financial support from developed countries to collaborate on and achieve emission reduction goals.

JI, established under Article 6 of the Kyoto Protocol, is a project-based cooperation mechanism among Annex I countries (developed countries). It involves cooperation between Annex I countries through technology and financial investment to implement specific projects that achieve greenhouse gas emission reductions or absorptions (measured as Emission Reduction Units, ERUs), transferred to the investing country as a means to fulfil their obligations under the Protocol. The trading subjects are Annex I country parties, and the trading object is the ERUs.

CDM, established under Article 12 of the Kyoto Protocol, is a flexible mechanism for cooperation between developed and developing countries. It allows the transfer and acquisition of credits for project-level emission reductions between Annex I (developed) and non-Annex I (developing) parties, enabling greenhouse gas emission reduction projects in developing countries.

ET, established under Article 17 of the Kyoto Protocol, is one of the flexible mechanisms designed to assist Annex I in meeting their greenhouse gas emission reduction targets. It enables countries to buy and sell emission allowances within their set limits. For example, if a country exceeds its emission reduction targets, it can sell its surplus allowances to another country needing additional allowances to meet its target. This mechanism encourages cost-effective emission reductions adaptable to market conditions, facilitating compliance with emission reduction commitments. ET serves as a cooperative mechanism among countries listed in Annex I established in the Protocol.

4.3 The Copenhagen Accord in 2009

The Copenhagen Accord, forged during the 2009 United Nations Climate Change Conference (COP15) in Copenhagen, represented a pivotal initiative to address global climate change and advance mitigation efforts. It served as a critical endeavor to bring together nations in a collaborative effort that extended beyond the provisions of the Kyoto Protocol. The Accord achieved a broad consensus on key global issues, encompassing long-term goals, financial and technical support, and transparency.

One of the significant achievements of the Copenhagen Accord was its acknowledgment of the scientific imperative to limit global warming to no more than 2 °C. This was established as a long-term goal for cooperative global action. The Accord also reached consensus on the transparency of emission reduction obligations for developed countries and the mitigation actions required from developing countries.

Despite its commendable efforts, the Copenhagen Accord faced criticism for its non-legally binding nature. It relied on voluntary commitments, lacked specific emission reduction targets, and did not engage all nations in its formulation. These shortcomings sparked concerns about its effectiveness and enforceability. However, it is crucial to recognize that the Accord laid the foundation for future international climate negotiations, paving the way for continued discussions on global climate action.

During the negotiations, the Copenhagen Green Climate Fund was established to support "projects, plans, policies, and other activities related to palliative action in developing countries." This fund recognized the critical role of reducing emissions resulting from deforestation and forest degradation, emphasizing the need to strengthen the role of forests in mitigating greenhouse gas emissions. Additionally, the Accord established a forest protection mechanism known as Reducing Emissions from Deforestation and Forest Degradation-plus (REDD+), acknowledging the importance of addressing issues related to forests in the context of climate change.

While the Copenhagen Accord had its limitations, its contributions in framing discussions around global climate action, fostering international collaboration, and emphasizing the significance of forest protection were crucial steps in the ongoing efforts to combat climate change on a global scale.

4.4 The Paris Agreement in 2015

On 12 December 2015, the highly anticipated Paris Climate Change Conference concluded, marking the culmination of negotiations initiated in Durban in 2011. The conference delivered a series of significant outcomes focused on the Paris Agreement, a landmark document that addressed a spectrum of crucial aspects in global climate governance. Covering long-term objectives, mitigation, adaptation, loss and damage, finance, technology, capacity building, transparency, and global stocktaking, the Paris Agreement ushered in a new era in international efforts to combat climate change.

As the second legally binding climate agreement operating under the UNFCCC, the Paris Agreement built upon the foundation laid by the Kyoto Protocol. Its primary objective is to cap the global average temperature increase to below 2 °C above pre-industrial levels, with an aspirational target of striving for a limit within 1.5 °C. The Paris Agreement represents a groundbreaking advancement in global climate governance, encapsulated in four key aspects.

First, the agreement made substantial progress in redefining and expanding the scope of climate finance. Alongside mitigation and adaptation targets, the Paris Agreement identifies "making capital flows into the path of greenhouse gas emissions and climate adaptation development" as one of its three major goals. Second, the agreement establishes a unique system that combines a "bottom-up" approach to setting action targets with a "top-down" framework comprising accounting, transparency, and compliance rules. This dual approach encourages proactive engagement among countries while ensuring a common platform for dialogue, tracking progress, and promoting comprehensive participation. Third, the agreement introduces an upgraded review mechanism centered on a global stocktaking every five years. This mechanism ensures coherence between actions and objectives, addressing issues related to insufficient "independent contributions" and challenges in achieving temperature control targets. Starting in 2023, global progress in climate actions will be reviewed comprehensively every five years. Forth, the agreement introduces the ambitious "1.5 °C temperature control target" into the goal of global climate governance. This target reflects the unprecedented intensity of climate governance efforts and outlines, for the first time, a "pathway to align financial flows with low greenhouse gas emissions and climate-resilient development." This directive points to the necessary direction to achieve global mitigation and adaptation goals.

The Paris Agreement represents a transformative shift in the global approach to climate change, emphasizing collective action, financial commitments, transparency, and an ambitious temperature control target. It sets the stage for ongoing international cooperation and periodic reviews to ensure progress toward a sustainable and resilient future.

4.5 The Glasgow Climate Convention in 2021

In December 2021, the Glasgow Climate Change Conference marked a significant milestone in advancing the global climate agenda, particularly in the realm of funding. The Glasgow Climate Agreement acknowledged a critical shortfall in meeting the commitment to raise $100 billion annually by 2020 for developing countries. It emphasized the imperative of achieving this funding target by 2025 and underscored the continued need for financing to realize the goals outlined in the Paris Agreement. The conference initiated discussions on post-2025 financing goals, recognizing the evolving landscape of climate finance needs. To ensure sustained focus on the financing objective, the "Long-Term Finance agenda" was extended until 2027.

A noteworthy development at the conference was the agreement for parties to submit a progress report on the $100 billion. This commitment aimed to amplify the voices of developing countries, fostering transparency, and reinforcing trust in the global climate governance process. The inclusion of this reporting mechanism represents a significant step towards greater accountability and accountability in meeting financial commitments.

Beyond the governmental level, the Glasgow Financial Alliance for Net Zero (GFANZ) emerged as a groundbreaking initiative involving over 450 of the world's largest banks, pension funds, asset owners, asset managers, banks, and insurance companies. This alliance, collectively holding about $130 trillion in assets (equivalent to 40% of global financial assets), is committed to utilizing science-based guidelines. These guidelines guide efforts to achieve net-zero carbon emissions by mid-century, with participating entities required to establish medium-term targets by 2030. The formation of GFANZ underscores the critical role of the financial sector in steering the global economy towards sustainability.

In tandem with GFANZ, the Global Energy Alliance for People and Planet (GEAPP) was launched. GEAPP aims to accelerate investment in the green energy transition and renewable energy solutions in developing and emerging economies across the globe. Over the next decade, the alliance has set an ambitious target to raise a total of $100 billion through a combination of public and private financing. The focus areas of the alliance include addressing critical issues such as providing stable and reliable renewable energy for a billion people, avoiding and preventing 4 billion tons of carbon emissions, and creating, enabling, or improving access to 150 million job opportunities. This initiative signifies a comprehensive and multifaceted approach to addressing both environmental and social aspects of sustainable development.

The outcomes of the Glasgow Climate Change Conference reflect a renewed commitment to addressing the financial aspects of climate action, with an emphasis on transparency, accountability, and leveraging the substantial influence of the financial sector to drive the transition to a sustainable and resilient global economy. The initiatives undertaken, such as GFANZ and GEAPP, signal a collective effort to align financial flows with climate goals and accelerate the transition towards a more sustainable future.

5 Multiple-Level Climate Finance Mechanisms

The landscape of global climate finance is complex, characterized by a dynamic and evolving structure. Financial resources for climate action flow through a myriad of channels, involving multilateral mechanisms within and outside the UNFCCC Financial Mechanism, bilateral and regional initiatives, as well as national climate change funds in recipient countries (Watson et al. 2022). At the national level, these funds play a crucial role in aligning the interests of contributors with the priorities of the local communities they aim to benefit, often by receiving contributions from multiple countries.

Figure 3 provides an overview of the global architecture, with a particular focus on public climate financing mechanisms. These mechanisms encompass a spectrum of funding options, ranging from grants and concessional loans to guarantees and private equity. Each mechanism operates with distinct governance structures, modalities, and objectives.

The diversity of these financing mechanisms reflects the multifaceted nature of climate challenges and the need for tailored approaches to address them effectively. The proliferation of various finance mechanisms, each with its unique features, poses challenges in coordinating access and monitoring (Browne 2022). Coordinating efforts to access funds efficiently and ensuring transparent monitoring of financial

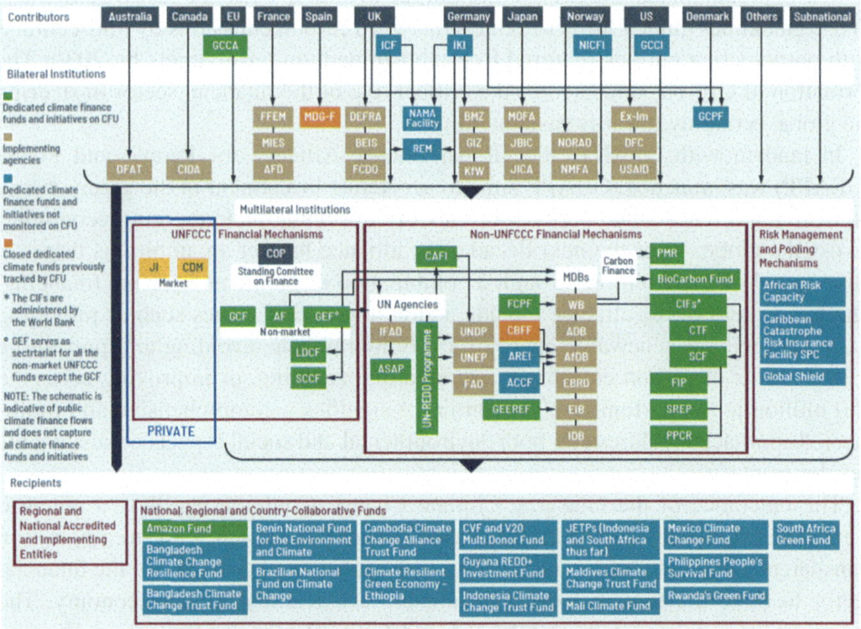

Fig. 3 Global climate finance architecture. *Source* https://climatefundsupdate.org/

flows are critical aspects of effective climate finance. The complexity of the financial architecture requires enhanced coordination mechanisms to streamline access for countries and organizations engaged in climate-related projects. Additionally, robust monitoring frameworks are essential to track the utilization of funds, assess the impact of investments, and ensure accountability in achieving climate-related goals.

5.1 *Multilateral Climate Funds and Initiatives*

Multilateral funds and initiatives constitute international institutions formed and governed by the collaboration of three or more countries, where the membership includes not only developed nations contributing funds but also developing countries accessing financial support. These mechanisms are designed with the overarching objective of eradicating poverty and fostering sustainable development on a global scale. Unlike some donor-led structures, multilateral mechanisms prioritize inclusivity, giving developing countries and their governments a more significant voice and representation in decision-making processes. The participation of both donor and recipient countries in these mechanisms reflects a cooperative approach to addressing global challenges. The pooling of resources and expertise enables a more comprehensive response to issues such as poverty alleviation, environmental conservation, and the promotion of sustainable development.

Several major multilateral funds and initiatives operate within and outside the UNFCCC Financial Mechanism, exemplifying the diverse areas of focus and collaborative efforts on the global stage. Some notable examples of multilateral funds and initiatives are shown here, with information sourced from their official websites.

5.1.1 Multilateral Funds and Initiatives Within UNFCCC

Green Climate Fund (GCF)

As part of the UNFCCC Financial Mechanism, the GCF stands out as a key multilateral fund. In 2010, the Cancun Conference adopted a resolution establishing the GCF as the operational body of the financial mechanism for contracting party agreements. It was established to support the efforts of developing countries in mitigating and adapting to climate change. The GCF's purpose is to support climate change mitigation programs, projects, policies, and other activities in developing countries. Headquartered in South Korea, it is overseen by a board of 24 members representing various countries, operating under the guidance of the UNFCCC. The GCF plays a crucial role in channeling financial resources to projects that address the impacts of climate change, especially in vulnerable communities. The fund allocates resources to support projects and programs that promote low-emission and climate-resilient initiatives in developing countries. Notably, it focuses on addressing the specific needs of societies vulnerable to climate change, with particular attention to the Least Developed Countries (LDCs), Small Island Developing Countries (SIDs), and African States.

As of November 2020, the GCF had partnered with 103 implementing entities for project delivery, marking an increase of eight since 2019. During this period, the fund approved USD 7.2 billion for 159 projects. In the 27th virtual meeting of the GCF Board in mid-November 2020, 16 project proposals, totaling USD 1.01 billion in GCF resources, received approval. Despite the challenges presented by the Covid-19 pandemic, the GCF demonstrated resilience by allocating over USD 2.2 billion for 37 projects, programs, readiness, and preparatory support within its initial replenishment period (GCF-1, covering 2020–2023). This underscores the fund's commitment to advancing climate-related initiatives and overcoming obstacles to sustainable development.

The Adaptation Fund (AF)

Established in 2001, the AF functions as a financial mechanism within the UNFCCC and its Kyoto Protocol (KP), with a dedicated focus on financing concrete adaptation initiatives and programs in developing countries that are parties to the KP. The Adaptation Fund is overseen by the Adaptation Fund Board (AFB), which comprises 16 members and 16 alternate members, convening at least twice annually. The primary objective of the AF is to provide funding for specific adaptation projects and plans in developing countries that are particularly susceptible to the adverse impacts of climate change, with a particular emphasis on Kyoto Protocol parties. The areas of focus for AF programs include food security, agriculture, water management, and disaster risk reduction. The initiatives encompass the management of water resources, land, agriculture, health, and infrastructure in fragile ecosystems, as well as the enhancement of disease and vector monitoring affected by climate change. Additionally, the AF prioritizes capacity building, covering institutional readiness for preventive measures, planning, and disaster management related to climate change.

Funding sources for the Adaptation Fund are diverse and include a portion of revenues generated by Clean Development Mechanism (CDM) project activities, as well as voluntary commitments from contributing governments, non-governmental entities, and individual contributors. Notably, it receives 2% of the Certified Emission Reductions (CERs) issued for each CDM project activity. As of 30 June 2022, the cumulative revenue of the AF Trust Fund comprises $211.8 million from certified emission reduction (CER) monetization, $982 million from donations, and $41.26 million from investment income derived from the trust fund's balance. This financial structure underscores the fund's commitment to mobilizing resources from various channels to support adaptation efforts in vulnerable regions.

The Global Environment Fund (GEF)

Established in 1991, the GEF operates as a financial mechanism supporting several international conventions, including the Minamata Convention on Mercury, the

Stockholm Convention on Persistent Organic Pollutants, the United Nations Convention on Biological Diversity, and the United Nations Convention to Combat Desertification. The World Bank serves as the trustee for the GEF, overseeing the management and utilization of the funds, assets, and earnings held in trust. The GEF focuses on providing grants and concessional funding to support projects that address global environmental issues.

The core objective of the GEF is to safeguard the global environment and promote environmental health and sustainable development. It concentrates on five major areas: biodiversity loss, chemicals and waste, climate change, international waters, and land degradation. Employing an integrated approach, the GEF strives to advance sustainable food systems, enhance effective forest management, and create resilient urban landscapes. The GEF also plays a pivotal role as an innovator and catalyst, fostering multi-stakeholder alliances to protect threatened land and sea ecosystems, develop greener cities, improve food security, promote clean energy, and contribute to a more prosperous and resilient world, securing an additional $5.20 for every $1 investment.

Contributions to the GEF Trust Fund have been made by both developed and developing countries, with 40 donor countries contributing since its inception. Currently, the GEF has established partnerships with international agencies, civil society organizations, and the private sector across 183 countries. Over the past three decades, the GEF has disbursed over $23 billion and mobilized an additional $129 billion in co-financing for more than 5,000 national and regional projects. This underscores the GEF's substantial impact in addressing global environmental challenges and catalyzing resources for sustainable development initiatives worldwide.

The Least Developed Country Fund (LDCF)

Established during the 7th Conference of the Parties (COP7) in 2001, the LDCF was created to address the adaptive needs of the least developed countries (LDCs). Its primary focus is on financing the development and implementation of the National Adaptation Program of Actions (NAPAs). LDCs actively engage in sectors such as water, agriculture, food security, health, disaster risk management and prevention, infrastructure, and fragile ecosystems, making the LDCF the largest portfolio of adaptation projects of its kind. The Global Environment Facility (GEF) serves as a dedicated trust to manage the LDCF and serves as the foundation for program resources.

Tailored to meet the specific needs of the 51 LDCs particularly vulnerable to the adverse effects of climate change, the LDCF prioritizes supporting the development and implementation of NAPAs. These state-driven strategies identify urgent adaptation needs and aim to diminish vulnerability and enhance resilience through innovative technology transfer for climate change adaptation. The LDCF strives to systematically integrate climate change adaptation and resilience for substantial impact, fostering conducive environments for effective and comprehensive climate change adaptation measures.

The LDCF concentrates its efforts on pivotal sectors crucial for livelihoods and national progress, including water, agriculture, food security, health, disaster risk management and prevention, and infrastructure. As of November 2020, approximately half of the LDCF projects actively contributed to reducing land degradation and managing biodiversity. As of the same date, the fund had garnered contributions totaling $1.6 billion. Key contributors include Australia, Austria, Belgium, Canada, the Czech Republic, Denmark, Finland, France, Germany, Hungary, Iceland, Ireland, Italy, Japan, Luxembourg, the Netherlands, New Zealand, Norway, Portugal, Romania, Spain, Sweden, Switzerland, the United Kingdom, and the United States. This underscores the international collaboration and commitment to supporting LDCs in adapting to the challenges posed by climate change.

The Special Climate Change Fund (SCCF)

The SCCF, established in 2001, addresses the specific needs of developing countries in adapting to the impacts of and enhancing resilience to climate change within the framework of the UNFCCC. Managed by the Global Environment Facility (GEF) as a dedicated trust, the SCCF focuses on covering the incremental costs of interventions for climate change adaptation relative to the developmental baseline.

The primary thrust of SCCF funding is directed towards supporting adaptation initiatives in developing countries. Additionally, the SCCF allocates funds for technology transfer and mitigation measures in specific sectors. Aligned with the Global Environment Facility's strategy, the SCCF has three strategic objectives: diminishing vulnerability and enhancing resilience through innovation and technology transfer for climate change adaptation; systematically integrating climate change adaptation and resilience to achieve substantial impact; fostering an environment conducive to effective and comprehensive climate change adaptation measures.

As of November 2020, the cumulative pledges to the SCCF amounted to approximately $375 million. Donors to the fund include Belgium, Canada, Denmark, Finland, Germany, Ireland, Italy, the Netherlands, Norway, Portugal, Spain, Sweden, Switzerland, the United Kingdom, and the United States. Contributions from these donor countries are classified as Official Development Assistance.

5.1.2 Multilateral Funds and Initiatives Outside UNFCCC

The Climate Investment Fund (CIF)

The CIF represents a well-established governance model operating independently of the Convention framework. Inaugurated in 2018, it is a collaborative initiative with joint funding from 14 developed countries spanning nine European nations, two North American countries, and three countries in the Asia–Pacific region, with the funds held in trust by the World Bank. The resources mobilized by CIF serve to empower governments, civil society, indigenous groups, the private sector, and multilateral development banks. CIF's comprehensive approach encompasses four major projects: the Clean Technology Fund (CTF), the Pilot Program for Climate Resilience (PPCR), the Forest Investment Project (FIP), and the Scaling Up Renewable Energy Program in Low Income Countries (SREP). The overarching goal is to significantly bolster climate change mitigation and adaptation efforts across 48 countries.

Among the projects, the CTF stands out as one of the two multilateral funds operating within the CIF framework. CTF focuses on facilitating expanded financing for the demonstration, deployment, and transfer of low-carbon technologies. It extends low-interest loans to middle-income countries, supporting the demonstration, development, and transfer of technologies in clean energy, energy efficiency, and sustainable transportation. CTF plays a pioneering role in funding promising renewable energy technologies, such as concentrated solar power. It collaborates with institutions including the African Development Bank, the Asian Development Bank, the European Bank for Reconstruction and Development, the Inter-American Development Bank, and the World Bank Group.

The objectives of CTF are multifaceted. It aims to provide positive incentives for low-carbon development and greenhouse gas emission reduction through investments from both the public and private sectors. CTF funds projects integrated into national plans and strategies, fostering development and expediting the dissemination and transfer of clean technologies. The fund seeks to achieve shared environmental and social benefits, demonstrate the potential of low-carbon technologies in promoting sustainable development and achieving the Millennium Development Goals, and support international cooperation on climate change. Additionally, CTF leverages the expertise of multilateral development banks to mobilize new and additional resources, including official and preferential funding. The fund places a strong emphasis on sharing lessons learned from the challenges of addressing climate change.

Established in 2008, the PPCR was designed to provide strategic funding for national development programs geared towards climate resilience. The program is guided by four primary objectives: piloting and demonstrating approaches for the seamless integration of climate risk and resilience into development policies and strategies; enhancing national capacity to incorporate climate adaptation into development planning; expanding and leveraging climate adaptation investments in conjunction with other ongoing initiatives; and disseminating valuable lessons at the national, regional, and global levels.

As of November 2020, the PPCR's fund capital stands at $1.1 billion. The program has supported a range of activities spanning sustainable agriculture, hydrometeorology, climate information services, coastal zone management, resilient infrastructure, and adaptation finance. Notable contributors to the PPCR include Australia, Canada, Denmark, Norway, Germany, Spain, Japan, the United Kingdom, and the United States.

Established in 2008, the FIP operates within the framework of the CIF and is subject to the "sunset clause," which outlines the CIF's closure upon the establishment of a new financial framework within the UNFCCC regime. However, the execution of this clause has faced multiple suspensions and was indefinitely postponed in 2019. Consequently, donors and recipients continue to operate within the existing framework until further developments transpire.

The FIP is specifically crafted to support developing countries in their efforts to Reduce Emissions from Deforestation and Forest Degradation (REDD) and advance sustainable forest management. The program's primary objectives include instigating and promoting transformative changes in forest-related policies and practices in developing countries, advocating for the use of additional financial resources for REDD, implementing replicable models to enhance understanding of forest-related investments and policies, and providing valuable experience and feedback. The initiative aims to benefit approximately 31 million hectares of forest landscape through improved management. Donors contributing to the FIP include Australia, Denmark, Japan, Norway, Spain, Sweden, the United Kingdom, and the United States. Currently, the FIP is active in 23 countries, including Bangladesh, Brazil, Burkina Faso, Cambodia, Cameroon, Republic of Congo, Ivory Coast, Democratic Republic of Congo, Ecuador, Ghana, Guatemala, Guyana, Honduras, Indonesia, Lao People's Democratic Republic, Mexico, Mozambique, Nepal, Peru, Rwanda, Tunisia, Uganda, and Zambia.

Established in 2008 as well, the SREP is designed to showcase the economic, social, and environmental feasibility of low-carbon development in the energy sectors of low-income countries. With five main objectives, SREP aims to assist the low-carbon transition in these countries by developing their renewable energy potential, emphasize the economic, social, and environmental benefits of renewable energy programs, support private sector investments aligned with SREP objectives, promote financing of renewable energy projects from multiple sources, and facilitate knowledge sharing and the exchange of international experiences and lessons. SREP's specific targets include generating over 3 million MWh per year of renewable energy, improving access to energy for over 140,000 businesses and 17.3 million people, and reducing 2.5 million tons of greenhouse gas emissions per year. Donors supporting SREP include Australia, Denmark, South Korea, the Netherlands, Norway, Spain, Sweden, Switzerland, Japan, the United Kingdom, and the United States.

The Central African Forest Initiative (CAFI)

The CAFI, established in 2015 on the margins of the United Nations General Assembly, is a partnership initiative designed to address both the global climate and biodiversity crises. Functioning as both a Trust Fund providing direct investments on the ground and a political negotiation platform, CAFI aims to drive high-level policy dialogue. The primary objectives of CAFI include supporting the development and implementation of National Investment Frameworks (NIFs) endorsed at the highest levels by national institutions with cross-sectoral mandates. The initiative allocates funds in accordance with the NIFs and the achievement of specific policy and programmatic milestones outlined in Letters of Intent. Additionally, CAFI aims to stimulate coordination among donors, align bilateral aid with partner countries based on the NIFs, and advocate for inclusive engagement of stakeholders.

As a partnership initiative, CAFI's Union of donors comprises Belgium, the EU, France, Germany, the Netherlands, Norway, Sweden, the Republic of Korea, and the United Kingdom (currently holding the presidency). The six partner countries involved in CAFI are the Central African Republic, the Democratic Republic of the Congo (DRC), the Republic of Cameroon, the Republic of Congo, the Republic of Equatorial Guinea and the Republic of Gabon. The initiative also involves the

Executive Organization and South-South partners. CAFI's unique structure allows for a collaborative and comprehensive approach to addressing the challenges posed by climate change and biodiversity loss in the Central African region.

The Adaptation for Smallholder Agriculture Program (ASAP)

The ASAP was established in 2001 and serves as the flagship program of the International Fund for Agricultural Development (IFAD) dedicated to providing climate and environmental finance to small farmers. Since its commencement in 2012, the program has secured $300 million in funding and has offered financial support and assistance to 8 million vulnerable smallholders across 43 countries in two phases, known as ASAP 1 and ASAP 2. Currently, a forthcoming phase, the Enhanced Adaptation for Smallholder Agriculture Program (ASAP+), is under development.

ASAP+ aims to further channel climate and environmental funding to smallholders, expand climate change adaptation within rural development plans, and integrate climate adaptation into the broader focus of IFAD. This next phase reflects a commitment to addressing the impacts of climate change on smallholder agriculture and fostering sustainable development in vulnerable communities.

Key donors supporting ASAP include the Government of Canada, the Korea International Cooperation, the Finnish Ministry of Foreign Affairs, the Belgian Development Organization, the Norwegian Ministry of Foreign Affairs, the Dutch Ministry of Foreign Affairs, the Swedish government, the Swiss Development Agency, the British Aid Organization (UK Aid), among others. These contributions play a crucial role in advancing the program's objectives and supporting smallholders in adapting to climate change while promoting sustainable agricultural practices.

The Forest Carbon Partnership Facility (FCPF)

The FCPF, initiated in June 2008 and funded by the World Bank, represents a collaborative effort involving governments and non-governmental entities. This facility comprises two distinct funding mechanisms: the Readiness Fund and the Carbon Fund, with the overarching goal of supporting countries in their efforts related to Reducing Emissions from Deforestation and Forest Degradation (REDD+). The primary objectives of the FCPF include providing financial and technical assistance to eligible countries to advance their REDD+ initiatives, specifically targeting emission reductions resulting from deforestation and/or forest degradation. Additionally, the FCPF aims to enhance the capacity of recipient nations to engage in potential future incentive systems that yield positive outcomes for REDD+, fostering sustainability.

The Readiness Fund within the FCPF is supported by contributions from entities such as the European Commission, Australia, Canada, Denmark, Finland, France, Germany, Italy, Japan, Netherlands, Norway, Spain, Switzerland, the UK, and the USA. This fund is geared towards preparing countries for effective participation in REDD+ initiatives.

On the other hand, the Carbon Fund within FCPF receives contributions from the European Commission, Australia, Canada, France, Germany, Norway, Switzerland, the UK, the USA, BP Technology Ventures Inc., and The Nature Conservancy. This fund is designed to pilot a payment system based on emissions reduction performance in REDD+ activities, ensuring fair benefit distribution and encouraging broader positive incentives for REDD+ at a larger scale.

All financial contributions to the FCPF, whether to the Readiness Fund or Carbon Fund, are recognized as official development assistance (ODA). The FCPF also serves as a platform for experimenting within the REDD+ framework to preserve biodiversity, improve the livelihoods of local communities, and share knowledge gained through the development and execution of FCPF initiatives with associated readiness and emissions reduction proposals.

The Global Energy Efficiency and Renewable Energy Fund (GEEREF)

The GEEREF was established in 2008 as a response to the growing need for increased energy efficiency and renewable energy development in developing countries. The European Commission played a pivotal role in its creation by allocating €80 million to initiate GEEREF, with the overarching objective of mitigating global warming. The management of GEEREF is entrusted to the European Investment Bank (EIB).

The core mission of GEEREF is to catalyze private enterprise involvement in projects that enhance energy efficiency and promote the use of renewable energy, particularly in smaller-scale environmental protection initiatives. By focusing on projects with a value of less than €10 million, which are often overlooked by commercial investment institutions and larger financial bodies, GEEREF addresses a critical gap in funding for environmentally sustainable endeavors. One of GEEREF's primary goals is to accelerate the development and transfer of environmentally friendly products and technologies to developing and least developed countries. By doing so, the fund seeks to facilitate access to reliable sources of clean energy for the populations of these countries.

Managed by the European Investment Bank, GEEREF has actively operated in emerging markets across Africa, Asia, and Latin America. As of the end of 2019, GEEREF has successfully built and managed a diverse portfolio of 15 funds, with 14 of these funds remaining active. Through its strategic investments, GEEREF contributes to the global effort to combat climate change by promoting sustainable energy solutions and supporting environmentally responsible initiatives in developing regions.

The United Nations-Reducing Emissions from Deforestation and Forest Degradation (UN-REDD)

The UN-REDD Program, launched in 2008, represents a collaborative effort by three key UN agencies: the United Nations Environment Program (UNEP), the United Nations Development Program (UNDP), and the Food and Agriculture Organization of the United Nations (FAO). At the core of the program's governance structure is the UN-REDD Program Policy Board, which assumes leadership responsibilities by setting the strategic direction and determining financial allocations. This Board convenes annually and maintains equal representation from both developed and developing countries.

The UN-REDD Program is guided by a set of ambitious outcomes designed to address critical challenges related to deforestation, forest degradation, and climate change. These outcomes include achieving emissions reductions from forest-based activities, mobilizing substantial funds amounting to $5 billion from carbon markets and other mechanisms, encouraging more than 15 countries to significantly enhance their nationally determined forest contributions in the 2020–2050 cycle, and fostering a global campaign for transformative nature-based solutions to expedite climate action.

The overarching aim of the UN-REDD Program is to reduce carbon emissions, enhance forest carbon reserves, and promote sustainable national development. As of November 2020, the program has garnered a total source of funds amounting to approximately $325 million. The primary contributors to the UN-REDD Program include Norway, the European Union, Denmark, Spain, Japan, Luxembourg, and Switzerland. Through its comprehensive approach, the UN-REDD Program plays a pivotal role in advancing global efforts to combat deforestation, mitigate climate change, and foster sustainable development.

The Partnership for Market Readiness (PMR)

The PMR was established in 2010, serving as a collaborative effort between developed and developing countries and operating under the management of the World Bank. Originally conceived as a platform to assist developing nations in building capacity within their carbon markets, the PMR has evolved over the years to adapt to changing global circumstances.

Initially, the PMR focused on preparing markets for the anticipated growth of global carbon markets. However, its scope has expanded to encompass a broader and more flexible approach. The PMR now provides grants and technical support for initiatives that leverage market tools to address climate change mitigation.

The primary objectives of the PMR include offering grants to countries to develop components related to market readiness, experimenting with and conceptualizing new market instruments, establishing a platform for the exchange of experiences and information on market readiness to foster south-south cooperation and innovation, and developing and disseminating a knowledge base on market instruments applicable to specific countries.

As of November 2020, the cumulative pledges to the PMR Fund amount to approximately $130 million. A total of 11 contributors, including countries such as Australia, Denmark, the European Union, Germany, Japan, the Netherlands, Norway, Spain, Switzerland, the United Kingdom, and the United States, have played a crucial role in supporting the PMR's initiatives. Through its activities, the PMR continues to contribute to enhancing the readiness and effectiveness of carbon markets in addressing climate change on a global scale.

The Biocarbon Fund

The Biocarbon Fund, established in 2004 and expanded in 2007 for its first two phases, stands as a noteworthy initiative with a combined commitment of $90 million. Functioning as a public–private partnership under the management of the World Bank, the primary focus of this project revolves around biodiversity conservation, improving water services, and fostering societal and institutional reciprocity.

This unique collaborative effort engages participants from both governmental and public sectors as well as private sector entities. The public sector contributors include Spain, Luxembourg, Canada, Italy, Ireland, and France, showcasing a diverse group of nations committed to environmental and sustainable development goals. On the private sector front, the Biocarbon Fund has garnered support from eleven entities spanning Japan, Spain, Switzerland, and France. The private sector participants in the Biocarbon Fund are drawn from a range of industries, underscoring the diverse and inclusive nature of this environmental initiative. Among these industries are oil and gas, utilities, food and beverage, steel, chemicals and pharmaceuticals, and agriculture. The inclusion of such a broad spectrum of industries reflects a collective acknowledgment of the role that diverse sectors can play in addressing environmental challenges.

One of the key mechanisms employed by the Biocarbon Fund is the allocation of emission reductions. These reductions are purchased on behalf of the fund's participants, with the subsequent transfer of these reductions to each participant based on their proportional financial engagement within the fund. This financial engagement model ensures that participants are not only contributing to the fund but also reaping the benefits of emission reduction efforts in alignment with their commitment levels.

By facilitating collaboration between governments, private enterprises, and international organizations, the Biocarbon Fund exemplifies a holistic approach to addressing environmental challenges. Its emphasis on biodiversity conservation and improvement of water services demonstrates a commitment to comprehensive and sustainable development. As the Biocarbon Fund continues to evolve and potentially enter new phases, it serves as a model for effective public–private partnerships in the pursuit of environmental conservation and climate action.

5.1.3 Sizes of the Multilateral Climate Funds

Based on the Climate Funds Update statistics, Tables 3, 4 and 5 provide a comprehensive overview of various multilateral climate funds, sorted by fund, contributor and recipient, respectively. As of 2022, the GCF holds the distinction of being the largest multilateral climate fund globally. Its significance lies in its role as a key financial mechanism aimed at supporting developing countries in their efforts to mitigate and adapt to climate change. In terms of individual country engagement, the data highlight the United Kingdom as a leading participant. The UK has demonstrated its commitment to addressing climate change by making substantial commitments and deposits into climate funds. These financial contributions from the UK play a crucial role in supporting global initiatives aimed at climate mitigation and adaptation.

Simultaneously, when considering recipient nations, India emerges as a significant beneficiary of climate funds. The country has become the largest recipient of donations, signifying the recognition of its vulnerabilities to climate change and the importance of supporting its efforts to build resilience and undertake sustainable development practices.

Table 3 Multilateral climate funds sorted by fund (amount in million dollars)

Fund name	Promise amount	Storage amount	Approved amount	Spending amount	Number of approved projects
GCF IRM	10,322.03	8,310.83	5,134.65	2,376.51	458
GCF	10,001.04	7,164.26	6,523.56	666.11	233
CTF	7,901.56	7,901.56	5,752.77	1,806.22	170
LDCF	2,075.02	1,830.31	1,428.99	530.22	312
GCCA	1,652.83	1,652.83	891.36	540.14	107
AF	1,423.92	1,243.35	996.65	588.88	296
Amazon fund	1,288.23	1,288.23	679.74	586.12	102
PPCR	1,155.79	1,155.79	1,029.43	734.7	116
GEF-5	1,152.41	1,147.92	825.88	485.87	233
GEF-6	1,117.16	1,109.43	902.55	207.04	238
GEF-4	1,082.98	1,082.98	930.68	930.68	227
FCPF-CF	874.5	874.5	–	–	0
GEF-8	852.71	852.71	5.45	–	1
CAFI	794.77	572.06	308.43	272.58	26
SREP	779.34	779.34	680.57	131.43	95
FIP	752.56	752.56	688.09	276.14	59
GEF-7	728.38	728.38	1,725.14	–	243
FCPF-RF	469.99	469.99	314.34	291.11	46
UN-REDD	389.8	355.48	353.08	338.03	39
ASAP	382.1	331.97	299.7	223.82	45
SCCF	380.64	373.98	284.91	180.66	73
BioCarbon Fund ISFL	350.9	237.63	71	–	5
GEEREF	281.5	275.5	223.59	89.07	19
CBFF	186.02	164.65	83.11	58.91	37
Partnership for Market Readiness	131.5	129.8	82.36	64.37	42
ASAP+	93.48	62.96	–	–	0
MDG Achievement Fund	89.5	89.5	89.52	89.52	18
ICCTF	26.17	16.7	–	–	0

Note Data are obtained from https://climatefundsupdate.org/data-dashboard, as of February 2023, sorted by the promised amount

Table 4 Multilateral climate funds sorted by donor (amount in million dollars)

Donor	Promised amount	Storage amount	Donor	Promised amount	Storage amount	Donor	Promised amount	Storage amount
Britain	7631.86	6786.74	Central Africa, Caribbean and Pacific Region (Intra Africa Caribbean and Pacific, ACP) projects	46.91	46.91	The Indonesian budget for revenue and expenditure	5.15	2.14
America	6971.25	4942.55	Five EU member states	46.91	46.91	The nature conservancy	5	5
Germany	6343.94	5709.33	European development fund	44.85	44.85	BP technology venture capital investment	5	5
Japan	4978.45	4207.2	EU	42.99	41.69	The Slovak Republic	4.32	3.69
Norway	3817.33	3523.14	Wallonia, Belgium	35.61	35.95	Poland	4.29	4.11
France	3555.18	3481.43	The Flanders district of Belgium	32.82	32.82	Flanders	2.38	2.38
Sweden	2270.46	2215.5	New Zealand	31.47	30.87	Estonia	2.24	2.24
Canada	1992.62	1987.55	Mexico	26.4	26.4	The Republic of Ivory Coast	2.14	2.14
Italy	872.97	585.29	China	25.28	25.28	Turkey	1.94	1.94
Holland	776.65	689.56	Russia	21.81	14.15	Cyprus	1.82	1.82
The Global Cargo and Challenge Program	763.71	763.71	India	16.86	16.86	Paris	1.34	1.34
Spain	696.62	662.03	The Capital Region of Brussels, Belgium	15.37	15.31	Malta	1.1	1.04

(continued)

Table 4 (continued)

Donor	Promised amount	Storage amount	Donor	Promised amount	Storage amount	Donor	Promised amount	Storage amount
revenue from investments	649.75	649.75	Portugal	13.82	11.99	Vietnam	1	1
Switzerland	604.11	545.45	Czech Republic	13.82	13.82	Panama	1	1
Denmark	590.11	529.88	Pakistan	11.36	11.36	Indonesia	0.77	0.5
Belgium	559.4	478.97	Quebec, Canada	10.18	10.18	Qatar	0.5	0.5
Australia	539.74	539.74	Slovenia	9.57	9.51	The Qatar Development Fund	0.5	0.5
European Commission	442.83	297.13	Greece	8.8	7.04	Latvia	0.47	0.47
Finland	426.52	361.83	South Africa	8.47	8.47	Romania	0.31	0.31
ENRT P Plan	330.39	380.39	Petrobras	7.71	7.71	Chile	0.3	0.3
Korea	321.51	159.65	Brazil	7.49	3.96	Liechtenstein	0.21	0.2
Austria	266.37	232.23	Monaco	6.75	5.73	Bulgaria	0.21	0.21
Certified emission reduction sales	211.8	211.8	Hungary	6.36	6.32	Lithuania	0.13	0.13
Ireland	118.54	114.38	Nigeria	6.31	5.35	The United Nations fund	0.07	0.07
Private sector investors (from North America, Europe and Australia)	112	112	Iceland	6.17	3.86	Corporación Andina de Fomento (CAF)	0.06	0.06
Luxembourg	111.44	93.26	Columbia	6	0.8	Mongolia	0.05	0.05

(continued)

Table 4 (continued)

Donor	Promised amount	Storage amount	Donor	Promised amount	Storage amount	Donor	Promised amount	Storage amount
11th EDF intra ACP allocation	88.76	88.76	Peru	6	0	The People's Republic of Bangladesh	0.05	0.05
EC Rapid Start-Up Funds (EC Fast Start Funding)	84.1	84.1						

Note Data are obtained from https://climatefundsupdate.org/data-dashboard, as of February 2023, sorted by the promised amount

Table 5 Multilateral climate funds sorted by recipient (amount in million dollars)

Country	Approved grant	Amount paid	Country	Approved grant	Amount paid	Country	Approved grant	Amount paid
India	1679.87	730.26	The Kingdom of Bhutan	124.72	59.38965	Micronesia	39.31	10.37104
Brazil	1158.22	774.5737	Sri Lanka	122.21	65.69841	Angola	35.15	13.44002
Indonesia	956.17	409.6121	Bolivia	115.55	84.5158	Uzbekistan	34.98	16.30693
The People's Republic of Bangladesh	653.56	182.4602	Gambia	106.18	54.5414	Dominica	34.55	13.54378
South Africa	647.74	142.8525	Nigeria	104.31	50.01884	Somalia	33.26	8.804562
Mexico	561.72	374.4811	Guatemala	102.36	25.50166	Belize	32.91	19.65259
China	531.75	320.1	Cote d'Ivoire	100.7	37.76092	Cameroon	31.35	12.9059
Turkey	506.9	171.99	Benin	99.19	30.05	Panama	30.93	29.31586
Egypt	473.42	276.1841	Timor-Leste	97.72	35.91747	Nauru (Island)	30.55	27.04
Mongolia	462.75	60.02227	Cuba	97.71	31.3133	South Sudan	28.41	1
Vietnam	435.92	121.4768	Congo	94.84	22.24139	Central African Republic	28.23	8.31
Columbia	417.83	145.7529	Armenia	93.52	32.30216	Moldova	27.32	16.12332
Ukraine	397.31	78.69	Georgia	92.99	29.24723	Uruguay	27.06	22.37276
Ethiopia	390.53	96.99774	Comoros	89.85	40.99581	Dominican Republic	26.73	21.60763
Costa Rica	372.48	78.08409	Lesotho	83.68	35.9994	Eritrea	24.33	6.879495
Congo	368.89	283.56	Salvador	82.62	43.77	Trinidad and Tobago	23.96	6.556758
Nepal	325.31	116.6685	Malawi	82.33	41.09305	Lebanon	23.93	14.22408

(continued)

Table 5 (continued)

Country	Approved grant	Amount paid	Country	Approved grant	Amount paid	Country	Approved grant	Amount paid
Tanzania	319.36	56.59305	Madagascar	82.2	38.28	The West Bank and the Gaza Strip	22.97	2.76
Chile	294.5	143.7039	Kyrgyzstan	79.75	18.49844	Suriname Republic	22.32	21.94838
Morocco	293.11	175.4829	Burma	77.49	33.6827	Iraq	21.93	6.000319
Cambodia	259.68	144.4715	Mauritania	75.53	38.87999	Cape Verde	20.94	16.73
Argentina	246.27	169.664	Barbados	75.27	20.91	Guyana	20.09	17.38954
Burkina Faso	239.06	72.57275	Namibia	73.35	42.88	Turkmenistan	18.97	6.497828
Zambia	236.52	117.1031	Mauritius	69.37	33.22199	The Cook Islands	18.34	13.84006
Kazakhstan	227.92	140.6598	Afghanistan	68.55	24.69707	St. Vincent and the Grenadines	17.96	17.68978
Mozambique	227.85	157.5991	Papua New Guinea	66.95	43.19018	Azerbaijan	17.24	8.577142
Rwanda	224.71	74.18432	Chad	66.41	20.77154	Seychelles	16.32	15.6
The Niger	223.39	142.8134	Djibouti	66.38	42.64	Belarus	16.28	7.85
Ecuador	205.64	80.92	Tonga	61.25	48.41387	Serbia	14.97	5.443267
Ghana	203.82	89.3717	Kiribati	60.47	18.27226	Equatorial Guinea	13.07	3.163121
The Philippines	182.64	35.79433	Jamaica	60.26	38.84334	Montenegro	11.38	7.896766
Mali	182.36	74.01811	Togo	59.06	27.06169	Bahamas	11.32	2.83
Pakistan	177.76	59.80621	Guinea-Bissau	58.06	14.225	Albania	10.88	3.77
Senegal	176.93	53.41166	Tuvalu	57.69	38.42875	Syrian Arab Republic	10.88	7.667275

(continued)

Table 5 (continued)

Country	Approved grant	Amount paid	Country	Approved grant	Amount paid	Country	Approved grant	Amount paid
Uganda	166.61	79.74985	Mauritius	57.57	33.77976	Iran	9.87	9.836995
Tadzhikistan	165.84	95.78594	Jordan	57.54	29.36099	Macedonia	9.38	8.448176
Honduras	165.36	36.69376	Sierra Leone	54.82	22.06	St Kitts and Nevis	7.96	0.630681
Kenya	164.85	61.29464	Antigua and Barbuda	54.11	17.46542	Romania	7.32	7.32
Thailand	160.71	25.95747	Gabon	52.48	40.13221	Algeria	5.57	0.12
Maldives	152.01	68.78	Fiji	51.61	39.74706	Niue	3.95	0.69489
Peru	146.62	62.79608	Saint Lucia	51.47	20.23783	Venezuela	3.64	3.64
Solomon Is	142.15	110.5886	Zimbabwe	50.34	19.45658	Bahrain island	2.32	0.91
Libya	138.56	51.66358	Marshall Is	48.21	33.09	Palau	2.32	1.37
Haiti	137.51	44.18825	Yemen	48.12	6.92301	Oman	2.1	1.15
Paraguay	134.51	68.6437	Tunisia	47.81	17.19099	Swaziland	2	1.96588
Vanuatu	133.97	40.06377	Sao Tome and Principe	45.9	16.11534	Slovak Republic	0.93	0.93
Sudan	131.23	62.24838	Guinea	45.83	12.87242	Eswatini	0.86	0
Russia	129.49	71.24	Burundi	43.96	18.73	Kuwait	0.85	0.85
Samoa	129.29	91.92	Malaysia	43.63	23.98833	Democratic People's Republic of Korea	0.75	0
Laos	127.27	70.60017	Botswana	41.77	4.08088	Saudi Arabia	0.35	0.35
Nicaragua	125.97	35.92347	Bosnia and Herzegovina	39.67	17.9	Libya	0.3	0.227934

Note Data are obtained from https://climatefundsupdate.org/data-dashboard, as of February 2023, sorted by approved grant amount. The year of approval starts in 2003. Global, regional or multinational recipients are not included

5.2 Bilateral Climate Funds and Initiatives

Bilateral climate funds and initiatives are financial mechanisms established between two individual countries or entities, aiming to address climate change challenges and support projects that mitigate its impacts or facilitate adaptation. These funds are allocated and managed by one country or organization to assist initiatives, projects, or aid in developing countries or emerging markets. The objectives and allocation of these funds are typically outlined through agreements or partnerships between contributing and recipient countries/entities, focusing on mutual goals for climate action and sustainable development. Here are details about two major bilateral climate funds and initiatives, with information sourced from their official websites.

The Global Climate Partnership Fund (GCPF)

The GCPF, founded in 2009 with the initiative of the German Federal Ministry for the Environment, Nature Conservation, Nuclear Safety, and KfW, Germany's Development Bank, represents a collaborative effort involving Germany, the United Kingdom, and Denmark. With a primary focus on advancing renewable energy and energy efficiency, the fund stands as a beacon for public–private sector partnerships in the pursuit of sustainable development.

GCPF adopts a multifaceted approach to investment, primarily channeling its resources through local financial institutions while also engaging in direct investments. This strategy ensures that projects benefit from local expertise and knowledge, contributing to the fund's mission of fostering sustainable and impactful initiatives. The fund's funding initiatives are directed towards a diverse range of projects, with a particular emphasis on small and medium enterprises (SMEs) and private households. By targeting these sectors, GCPF aims to address energy consumption at the grassroots level, making a tangible impact on communities and businesses. The fund's commitment to inclusivity and accessibility is evident in its support for projects that aim to achieve a minimum 20% reduction in greenhouse gas emissions. This reduction is realized through a combination of energy efficiency measures and the promotion of renewable energy generation projects.

GCPF's dedication to reducing greenhouse gas emissions aligns with broader global climate goals, contributing to the mitigation of climate change impacts. By investing in projects that enhance energy efficiency and promote the use of renewable resources, the fund not only facilitates environmental sustainability but also stimulates economic development at the local level.

The International Climate Fund (ICF)

Initiated by the UK government in 2008, the ICF stands as a pivotal instrument dedicated to assisting developing countries in their transition toward low-carbon and climate-resilient development. This initiative underscores the UK's commitment to addressing global climate challenges and supporting nations in building sustainable, resilient economies. The UK government's financial commitment to the ICF has been substantial, with a pledge of £5.8 billion for the period between 2016 and

2021. In a notable move signaling heightened dedication, in 2019, the UK government announced a doubling of investments, reaching an impressive £11.6 billion for the subsequent period from 2021 to 2026. This augmented financial commitment underscores the UK's recognition of the urgency and scale of the climate crisis, emphasizing the need for robust support to foster global climate action.

The UK's contribution to the ICF extends beyond direct funding, as the country allocates a significant portion of its financial resources through dedicated multilateral funds. These include prominent entities such as the Green Climate Fund and the BRICs Bank, reflecting a strategic approach to leveraging collaborative platforms for maximum impact. By engaging with these multilateral institutions, the UK seeks to amplify the reach and effectiveness of its climate finance initiatives on a global scale.

Since its inception, the ICF has played a crucial role in supporting a diverse array of projects across more than 70 countries. With over 300 projects under its umbrella, the fund has made substantial contributions to initiatives promoting sustainable development, climate resilience, and emission reduction strategies. The broad geographic reach and scope of supported projects highlight the ICF's commitment to addressing climate challenges on a global scale.

Funding sources for the ICF include key government departments, demonstrating a coordinated and cross-sectoral approach. These include the Department for International Development (now part of the Foreign, Commonwealth and Development Office), the Department for Business, Energy and Industrial Strategy, and the Department for Environment, Food and Rural Affairs. This collaborative effort reflects the comprehensive and integrated nature of the UK government's strategy in addressing climate change through the ICF.

In essence, the International Climate Fund exemplifies the UK's leadership in global climate finance, contributing significantly to international efforts aimed at fostering sustainable development and building climate resilience in developing nations. Through strategic financial commitments and partnerships with key multilateral institutions, the ICF remains a critical tool in the global fight against climate change.

The Internationalen Klimaschutzinitiative (IKI)

The IKI in Germany stands as a cornerstone of the country's commitment to international climate financing. Established as a crucial instrument, the IKI has played a pivotal role in advancing Germany's efforts to address global climate challenges. As of 2022, the IKI has been implemented through a collaborative effort involving key ministries, namely the Federal Ministry for Economic Affairs and Climate Action, the Federal Ministry for the Environment, Nature Conservation, Nuclear Safety, and Consumer Protection, as well as the Federal Foreign Office. This multi-ministry collaboration underscores the comprehensive and integrated approach that Germany employs in its international climate initiatives.

The IKI focuses on providing support to developing and emerging countries, aligning with their Nationally Determined Contributions (NDCs) outlined in the Paris Agreement. By doing so, the IKI facilitates the implementation of measures that help these nations adapt to the impacts of climate change, protect and restore natural carbon sinks, and address environmental, economic, and social considerations. One of the notable aspects of the IKI is its commitment to not only climate action but also biodiversity conservation. The initiative actively aids partner countries in achieving the objectives set forth by the Convention on Biological Diversity. This dual focus on climate and biodiversity underscores the interconnected nature of environmental challenges and the need for comprehensive, cross-cutting solutions.

Since its inception, the IKI has made significant strides in supporting climate and biodiversity projects on a global scale. The initiative has approved over 950 projects in more than 150 countries worldwide, showcasing its extensive reach and impact. The total funding allocated for these projects from 2008 to 2022 amounts to nearly €6 billion, demonstrating Germany's substantial financial commitment to addressing climate change and biodiversity loss on the global stage. The IKI serves as a flagship program in Germany's portfolio of international climate and environmental initiatives. Through its collaborative and multi-ministerial approach, the IKI has become a key player in advancing sustainable development and contributing to the global goals outlined in international agreements such as the Paris Agreement and the Convention on Biological Diversity.

The Mitigation Action Facility (NAMA Facility)

The NAMA Facility, a collaborative initiative involving the UK, Germany, Denmark, and the European Community, evolved from the NAMA Fund in 2023. This transformation marks a strategic step forward in the joint efforts of these nations to address climate change and promote sustainable development. The initiative was spearheaded by key entities, including the German Federal Ministry for Economic Affairs and Climate Action, the UK Department for Business, Energy and Industrial Strategy, the Danish Ministry of Climate, Energy and Utilities for Net Zero, the Danish Ministry of Foreign Affairs, and the European Children's Investment Fund Foundation.

The fundamental purpose of the NAMA Facility is to provide crucial technical support and climate financing for mitigation projects. These projects are strategically designed to decarbonize pivotal sectors of the economy and society, with a particular emphasis on energy, transportation, and industry. By focusing on these critical areas, the NAMA Facility aims to address key sources of greenhouse gas emissions and contribute significantly to achieving climate targets. The technical support offered by the NAMA Facility plays a pivotal role in ensuring the successful implementation of mitigation projects. This support may encompass a range of activities, from feasibility studies and technology assessments to capacity building and knowledge transfer. By leveraging the expertise and resources of the involved nations and organizations, the NAMA Facility enhances the effectiveness of climate action initiatives.

In addition to technical support, the NAMA Facility provides climate financing, recognizing the financial requirements associated with implementing large-scale mitigation projects. This funding is instrumental in overcoming barriers to the adoption of sustainable practices and technologies, fostering innovation, and driving the transition towards a low-carbon and resilient future.

The NAMA Facility's focus on energy, transportation, and industry underscores a commitment to tackling emissions at their source. These sectors are often significant contributors to greenhouse gas emissions, and efforts to decarbonize them are critical for achieving broader climate goals. By concentrating on these key areas, the NAMA Facility aligns its objectives with global priorities for mitigating climate change. The NAMA Facility represents a collaborative and forward-looking initiative by the UK, Germany, Denmark, and the European Community. Through its evolution from the NAMA Fund and with the support of key ministries and foundations, the NAMA Facility stands as a testament to the commitment of these entities to drive positive change in the fight against climate change.

The Norway's International Climate Forest Initiative (NICFI)

The NICFI, established in 2008, stands as a testament to Norway's commitment to addressing critical global challenges related to climate change, biodiversity loss, and sustainable development. The primary focus of NICFI is on reducing tropical forest loss, recognizing the pivotal role that forests play in achieving climate stability, preserving biodiversity, and fostering sustainable development. The management of NICFI is a collaborative effort between the Norwegian Ministry of Climate and Environment and the Norwegian Agency for Development Cooperation. This collaborative governance structure ensures a coordinated and effective approach to the initiative's objectives, leveraging both environmental and developmental perspectives.

Partner countries of the NICFI span a diverse range of regions, reflecting the global nature of the challenges addressed by the initiative. These partner countries include Brazil, Colombia, the Congo Basin, Ecuador, Ethiopia, Indonesia, Guyana, Liberia, and Peru. By engaging with countries across different continents, NICFI embraces a holistic approach to tropical forest conservation, recognizing the unique environmental contexts and challenges faced by each nation.

The financial commitment of partner countries is a key element of NICFI's impact. Collectively, these countries pledge an impressive $350 million annually. This funding is mobilized through a combination of bilateral partnerships, multilateral channels, and engagement with civil society. The diverse sources of funding highlight the collaborative and inclusive nature of NICFI's approach, recognizing the importance of partnerships at various levels to achieve meaningful results. Notably, countries such as Brazil, Indonesia, Tanzania, and Guyana have played a significant role in contributing to activities related to REDD+. These activities involve efforts to reduce carbon emissions by preventing deforestation and promoting sustainable forest management practices. The active participation of these countries underscores their commitment to environmental conservation and sustainable land use.

5.3 National, Regional and National Cooperation Funds

The establishment of national climate funds by developing countries reflects a proactive approach to financing domestic initiatives aimed at mitigating and adapting to climate change. These funds serve as vital channels for mobilizing resources, coordinating efforts, and consolidating control over climate finance within the respective nations. The goal is to enhance the effectiveness and efficiency of climate action by integrating projects with similar objectives, albeit operating under different governance structures. These national climate funds play a crucial role in aligning disparate climate initiatives and projects under a unified framework. By doing so, they promote synergy and coherence in the pursuit of common climate goals, avoiding duplication of efforts and streamlining resource allocation. This integration is particularly important for countries that may have various climate funds operating independently, each with its own set of governance and responsibility arrangements.

Funding sources for these national climate funds are diverse and may include contributions from international financial institutions, domestic budget allocations, and the involvement of the domestic private sector. International financial institutions, such as the World Bank, regional development banks, and climate finance mechanisms like the GCF, often provide financial support to developing countries' national climate funds. Additionally, governments may allocate funds from their domestic budgets to bolster climate initiatives, recognizing the importance of national commitment to addressing climate challenges. The involvement of the domestic private sector further enhances the sustainability and impact of these funds, fostering collaboration between government and industry in the pursuit of climate goals.

While the specific structure and mechanisms of national climate funds may vary from country to country, they share the common objective of facilitating robust and coordinated climate action. Here are some examples of national climate funds for developing countries, based on information from their official websites.

China Clean Development Mechanism Fund

In August 2006, the State Council of China approved the establishment of the China Clean Development Mechanism Fund and its Management Center, commonly referred to as the Clean Fund. Operational commencement took place in November 2007, and a significant milestone occurred on 14 September 2010, when the Ministry of Finance, along with seven other ministries, issued the "Administrative Measures for the China Clean Development Mechanism Fund." This marked the comprehensive initiation of the fund's operations. Subsequent to economic and social development progress, revisions were made to these measures. On 28 June 2022, following State Council approval, the Ministry of Finance and seven other ministries announced the revised "Administrative Measures for the China Clean Development Mechanism Fund."

Established with national authorization, the Clean Fund operates in a market-oriented manner, representing the first national-level fund in China and among developing countries dedicated to addressing climate change. It stands as a significant achievement in China's international cooperation on climate change, functioning as an innovative national mechanism to address climate change and contributing to China's sustainable development through its involvement in the CDM under the United Nations' Kyoto Protocol.

The primary objectives of the Clean Fund are to support green and low-carbon activities related to national carbon peaking, carbon neutrality, climate change response, pollution prevention, and ecological conservation. It aims to foster high-quality economic and social development, with a particular emphasis on supporting emission reduction activities in emerging industries, technological advancements in emissions reduction, and market-driven emission reduction initiatives. The Clean Fund's diverse sources of funding include income from the transfer of greenhouse gas emission reduction credits obtained through CDM projects, operational revenues, donations from domestic and foreign institutions, organizations, and individuals, as well as other sources.

In its role, the Clean Fund allocates a specific amount of funding to support various project activities, including policy research and academic endeavors related to carbon peaking, carbon neutrality, and climate change. It also supports international cooperation and exchange activities, training initiatives aimed at enhancing capabilities for carbon peaking, carbon neutrality, and climate change response, public awareness campaigns, educational activities, and other projects aligned with the fund's overarching objectives.

Bangladesh Climate Change Resilience Fund

In September 2008, Bangladesh took a significant step in addressing the challenges posed by climate change by launching its first Climate Change Strategy and Action Plan. The initiative was unveiled at the UK-Bangladesh Climate Change Conference in London, underscoring the country's commitment to formulating a medium-to-long-term plan aimed at enhancing climate resilience and promoting low-carbon, sustainable growth. Subsequently, the plan underwent an update in 2009 to ensure its continued relevance and effectiveness. To further implement and support the objectives outlined in its climate change strategy, the Bangladeshi government, along with development partners and the World Bank, signed a pivotal agreement in May 2010. This agreement marked the establishment of the Bangladesh Climate Change Adaptation Fund, signaling a collaborative effort to address the multifaceted impacts of climate change in the country.

The primary objective of the Bangladesh Climate Change Adaptation Fund is to support the implementation of Bangladesh's comprehensive climate change strategy and actions. The fund focuses on several key areas, including food security, social safety and health, comprehensive disaster management, climate-resilient infrastructure development, research and knowledge management, mitigation, low-carbon development, and capacity building.

One of the distinctive features of the fund lies in its diverse sources of financial support. Contributions come from donor countries and international entities committed to aiding Bangladesh in its climate change endeavors. Notable contributors include Denmark, the European Union, Sweden, the United Kingdom, Switzerland, the Australian Agency for International Development, and the United States Agency for International Development. This collaborative funding approach reflects the global recognition of Bangladesh's vulnerability to climate change and the importance of international cooperation in building resilience.

The Bangladesh Climate Change Adaptation Fund operates as a vital mechanism for translating climate change strategy into actionable projects and initiatives. By addressing critical areas such as food security, disaster management, and infrastructure development, the fund aims to enhance the country's capacity to adapt to climate challenges while fostering sustainable and low-carbon growth. Bangladesh's initiatives, from the formulation of a climate change strategy to the establishment of the adaptation fund, exemplify the country's commitment to proactively addressing the impacts of climate change. The collaborative approach involving international partners further underscores the importance of collective efforts in building climate resilience and promoting sustainable development on a global scale.

Brazilian National Fund on Climate Change

In December 2009, President Luiz Inácio Lula da Silva approved Law No. 12,014, establishing the Brazilian National Fund on Climate Change. This significant legal framework aimed to ensure the availability of financial resources for projects and actions addressing and adapting to the impacts of climate change in Brazil. The creation of the fund reflected the country's commitment to proactive climate action and sustainable development. As outlined in the legal provisions, the management of the Brazilian National Fund on Climate Change involves a committee comprising representatives from the federal government and various sectors of society. This inclusive approach ensures that decisions regarding fund allocation and project selection consider diverse perspectives and expertise.

The fund operates through two main modalities: loans and non-reimbursable contributions. The utilization of loans allows for the mobilization of financial resources, while non-reimbursable contributions facilitate the implementation of projects without the obligation of repayment. This dual approach provides flexibility in financing mechanisms to address a wide range of climate change-related initiatives. A specific allocation of the fund, as mandated by Law No. 9,478, designates 10% for the renovation of oil production facilities. Additionally, 6% is earmarked for establishing new funds. These allocations underscore the integrated approach to climate action, recognizing the need to address environmental sustainability alongside economic considerations.

The funding sources for the Brazilian National Fund on Climate Change are diverse, reflecting a comprehensive approach to resource mobilization. These sources include the national budget, donations from domestic and international public and private institutions, as well as loans. The involvement of various stakeholders and financial instruments enhances the fund's resilience and capacity to support a wide array of climate-related projects. To ensure financial oversight and accountability, the Brazilian Development Bank for Economic and Social Development serves as the designated financial oversight entity for the fund. This entity plays a crucial role in monitoring fund disbursements, evaluating project outcomes, and maintaining transparency in financial management.

Indonesia Climate Change Trust Fund

The Indonesia Climate Change Trust Fund is a critical component of Indonesia's commitment to implementing the Jakarta Commitment, a comprehensive initiative aimed at achieving inclusive economic growth and enhancing climate resilience. This trust fund is strategically designed to strengthen the government's effectiveness and leadership in managing climate events, reflecting Indonesia's proactive stance in addressing the complex challenges posed by climate change.

Comprising two distinct funds, the Indonesia Climate Change Trust Fund demonstrates a multifaceted approach to climate action. The first is the Innovation Fund sourced from development partners and other contributors. Its primary objective is to channel funds towards climate change adaptation activities that provide socio-economic benefits. Unlike traditional investment funds, the Innovation Fund focuses on projects that may not offer direct financial returns but contribute significantly to building climate resilience and fostering inclusive economic growth. This fund underscores Indonesia's commitment to innovative solutions that address both environmental and social dimensions of climate change.

The other is the Reform Fund. Coordinated and managed in collaboration with the Ministry of Finance, the Reform Fund takes a more diverse financing approach. It plans to utilize domestic funds, loans, and other types of financing to invest in projects specifically focused on low-carbon economies and climate-resilient development. Unlike the Innovation Fund, the Reform Fund aims to generate direct income, emphasizing sustainable and financially viable initiatives. This dual-focus on economic sustainability and climate resilience aligns with Indonesia's broader goals of achieving a low-carbon, resilient economy.

6 Challenges and Implications

There are several challenges persisting in the global climate finance architecture.

First, the persistent funding gap in global climate finance is a significant challenge, despite the notable increase in its volume. Estimates from various sources consistently emphasize that the current level of investment is insufficient to meet the demands of climate-related initiatives. The "Global Climate Finance Report 2021" by the International Climate Initiative provides crucial insights into this ongoing issue. While there has been an encouraging surge in climate investment, surpassing $600 billion in the 2019/2020 period, the momentum has encountered a slowdown in fund flows. The COVID-19 pandemic is identified as a potential influencing factor, disrupting financial flows and diverting attention and resources to immediate public health and economic concerns. Despite this record-high investment, the annual flow of climate funding saw a modest growth of only 10% between 2017/2018 and 2019/

2020. This growth rate is significantly lower than the preceding period, which experienced a growth rate exceeding 24%. This deceleration raises concerns about the ability to mobilize the necessary resources to address the escalating climate crisis effectively.

The disparity between the achieved funding levels and the estimated annual needs is stark. Conservative estimates suggest that $4.5–5 trillion annually is required to adequately confront climate challenges. This stark contrast highlights the substantial shortfall in current financing levels and underscores the urgency of ramping up efforts to secure the necessary financial resources. Looking forward, achieving the internationally agreed-upon climate targets by 2030 demands a transformative shift in the scale of climate financing. To bridge this gap and adequately address the climate crisis, there is a pressing need for a substantial annual increase of at least 590% in climate financing. This ambitious target reflects the magnitude of the climate challenge and the necessity for a rapid and significant mobilization of financial resources to implement effective mitigation and adaptation measures.

Second, the commitments made by developed countries to provide climate finance to developing nations, particularly the landmark pledge of $100 billion annually at the 2009 United Nations Climate Change Conference in Copenhagen, have encountered significant challenges in realization and effective implementation. One major source of contention revolves around disagreements regarding the nature of the funding. Key points of contention include whether the financial support should be "provided" or "mobilized," whether it should be categorized as "public" or "public and private," and whether it should be "new and additional" beyond the traditional Official Development Assistance (ODA). These distinctions are critical as they shape the character and sources of the funds, influencing the transparency, accountability, and effectiveness of the financial contributions. The lack of specific agreements on the allocation of the $100 billion has hindered the ideal implementation of these commitments. The absence of clarity on fundamental aspects, coupled with differing interpretations and expectations, has led to challenges in tracking, disbursing, and ensuring the intended impact of the pledged financial support.

The Paris Agreement, adopted in 2015, sought to address these challenges by reaffirming the $100 billion commitment. According to the agreement, developed countries committed to mobilizing at least this amount annually in financial support to developing countries after 2020. However, even with this reaffirmation, challenges persist in ensuring the efficient and equitable distribution of these funds. Efforts to operationalize the commitment under the Paris Agreement have been met with ongoing complexities. Disagreements persist on issues such as the pace at which the funding should increase, the balance between adaptation and mitigation efforts, and the mechanisms for tracking and reporting the financial contributions. Furthermore, the distinction between "new and additional" funding beyond traditional ODA remains a contentious point. Developing countries emphasize the need for genuinely additional resources to address the unique challenges posed by climate change, while developed nations may view the existing financial mechanisms, including ODA, as part of their contribution.

Third, the effectiveness of climate finance in addressing the challenges of climate change requires substantial improvement. Climate change plans and strategies in recipient countries often suffer from confusion and inefficiency. This is particularly evident at multiple levels, including national, sub-national, local, and sectoral levels. The lack of clear coordination and alignment among these different levels hampers the coherent implementation of climate actions. Achieving effective climate action necessitates strong vertical coordination among various actors, ensuring a seamless transition of plans and strategies from national to local levels. It is crucial to foster collaboration and cooperation among governmental entities, non-governmental organizations, and local communities to ensure ownership of climate actions and effective utilization of climate finance.

Tracking adaptation funding also faces significant challenges, especially in defining resilience-related activities under Official Development Assistance (ODA) as adaptation. This ambiguity can lead to challenges in appropriately allocating funds to projects that contribute to building resilience and adapting to the impacts of climate change. Moreover, the measurement and evaluation of the impacts of adaptation funding are still in early stages. The lack of internationally standardized methods, data, and baselines makes it difficult to assess the effectiveness of adaptation interventions comprehensively. This poses challenges in understanding the real-world outcomes and benefits of funded projects. Quantifying the effectiveness of adaptation interventions remains a complex task. The interconnected and dynamic nature of climate change impacts, coupled with varying local contexts, makes it challenging to establish clear cause-and-effect relationships between funded projects and their outcomes. Overall, there is a critical need to enhance the efficiency and effectiveness of climate finance.

Effectively addressing the challenges and issues within the global climate finance architecture necessitates a concerted effort involving various stakeholders. Here are key aspects that can contribute to overcoming these challenges. First, climate change is a global issue that requires collaborative efforts. Enhanced international cooperation is crucial for mobilizing resources, sharing best practices, and fostering a collective commitment to addressing climate challenges. Countries, both developed and developing, need to collaborate on financial and technological transfers to ensure a more equitable and effective response. Second, clear and transparent commitments are essential for realizing climate finance goals. Developed countries, in particular, must honor and fulfill their pledges. Clarity in commitment terms, including definitions of funding sources and types, can contribute to effective implementation.

Third, strengthening coordination mechanisms at both national and international levels is vital. This involves fostering collaboration among various government departments, agencies, and international organizations. Coordinated efforts can streamline processes, avoid duplication, and ensure that climate finance is directed to the most impactful projects. Forth, transparency is crucial for building trust among stakeholders and ensuring accountability in the allocation and utilization of climate finance. Transparent processes in decision-making, fund distribution, and project selection contribute to more effective and equitable outcomes.

Fifth, developing and adopting standardized methodologies for assessing the impact of climate finance interventions is essential. This includes robust frameworks for evaluating both mitigation and adaptation projects, ensuring that funds are effectively contributing to climate resilience and sustainable development. Improved methodologies can provide a basis for informed decision-making and help refine future strategies. Furthermore, embracing innovation in financial instruments and adapting approaches to evolving circumstances can enhance the effectiveness of climate finance. This involves exploring new financing mechanisms, leveraging private sector involvement, and staying adaptable in response to emerging challenges, such as those posed by the COVID-19 pandemic.

In conclusion, addressing the challenges and issues within the global climate finance architecture requires a holistic and collaborative approach. Through international cooperation, clear commitments, improved coordination, transparency, and innovative methodologies, the global community can work together to ensure that climate finance plays a pivotal role in building a sustainable, resilient, and low-carbon future.

References

Barnett M, Brock W, Hansen L P. 2020. Pricing Uncertainty Induced by Climate Change. The Review of Financial Studies, 33(3), 1024-1066.

Benzie M, Persson Å. 2019. Governing borderless climate risks: moving beyond the territorial framing of adaptation. International Environmental Agreements: Politics, Law and Economics, 19(4), 369-393.

Browne K E. 2022. Rethinking governance in international climate finance: Structural change and alternative approaches. WIREs Climate Change, 13(5), e795.

Hong H, Karolyi G A, Scheinkman J A. 2020. Climate Finance. The Review of Financial Studies, 33(3), 1011-1023.

Khan M R, Munira S. 2021. Climate change adaptation as a global public good: implications for financing. Climatic Change, 167(3), 50.

Long S, Lucey B, Kumar S, Zhang D, Zhang Z. 2022. Climate finance: What we know and what we should know? Journal of Climate Finance, 1, 100005.

Watson C, Schalatek L, Evéquoz A. 2022. The global climate finance architecture. Climate Funds Update. https://climatefundsupdate.org/wp-content/uploads/2023/03/CFF2-2023-ENG-Global-Architecture.pdf

Zscheischler J, Westra S, Van Den Hurk B J, Seneviratne S I, Ward P J, Pitman A, AghaKouchak A, Bresch D N, Leonard M, Wahl T, Zhang X. 2018. Future climate risk from compound events. Nature Climate Change, 8(6), 469-477.

Climate-Driven Financial Innovations: Green Financial Tools

Xiangyang Zhai, Qiang Ji, and Fei Wu

Abstract This chapter reviews the development and status quo in the markets of several financial tools increasingly adopted to combat climate change. Financial institutions are increasingly offering sustainable loans tied to specific environmental performance targets and to incentivize borrowers to adopt sustainable practices. The market for green bonds has also experienced significant growth. The emergence and development of ESG (Environmental, Social, and Governance) bonds reflect investors' increasing demand for greater transparency regarding the sustainability practices of companies. The insurance sector has developed fast worldwide to enable diversification to meet climate-related insurance demands. These trends in the development of climate financial tools reflect a growing recognition of the urgent need to address climate change and promote sustainable practices.

Keywords Climate finance · Green finance · Financial innovation · Green finance tools

1 Background

The development of green financial tools is intricately linked to the broader evolution of the green financial system. The inception of the concept of green finance can be traced back to the greening transformation of traditional financial businesses. Although the term "green finance" emerged in the 1990s, its roots can be found in

---

X. Zhai · Q. Ji
Institutes of Science and Development, Chinese Academy of Sciences, Beijing 100190, China

School of Public Policy and Management, University of Chinese Academy of Sciences, Beijing 100049, China

F. Wu (✉)
Research Institute of Economics and Management, Southwestern University of Finance and Economics, 555 Liutai Avenue, Chengdu 611130, China
e-mail: wufei@swufe.edu.cn

F. Wu et al. (eds.), *Climate Finance*, Climate Change and Energy Transition,
https://doi.org/10.1007/978-981-97-3308-8_3

the post-World War II era. Following a period of rapid economic growth in the post-World War II era, developed countries began confronting environmental challenges in the 1960s and 1970s. Issues such as environmental pollution and resource scarcity became apparent, prompting public protests in Europe and the United States. Wasteful use of natural resources and the environmental impact of production and operations became significant concerns.

As public awareness of environmental issues grew, there was a shift in consumer values towards green protection. Consumers began making choices that favored environmentally friendly products. This shift influenced businesses to produce and provide goods and services with a lower environmental footprint. The demand for sustainable and eco-friendly products started to shape the market landscape. Improved environmental laws and regulations played a crucial role in this evolution. As governments implemented stricter environmental standards, investors began recognizing that a company's environmental performance could impact its financial performance (Guo et al. 2023). It became evident that environmental issues posed financial risks to companies, ranging from regulatory fines to reputational damage (Ma et al. 2022).

At this juncture, the concepts of "greenness" and "low carbon" started to permeate various economic sectors, including the financial industry. The realization that sustainable practices could enhance financial stability and performance led to the integration of green finance principles. Such integration of green concepts into the financial sector involved a paradigm shift. Financial institutions began to explore ways to align their operations with environmental goals, both to mitigate risks and capitalize on emerging opportunities. Green financial tools, such as green bonds, sustainability-linked loans, and environmental risk assessments, emerged as a response to the growing demand for financial instruments aligned with environmental values (Zhang and Ji 2022). Over the years, green finance has evolved into a global phenomenon. The development of green financial tools is not only driven by regulatory pressures but also by a recognition of the long-term economic benefits of sustainability.

In the 1970s, as environmental concerns gained prominence globally, the German government took a groundbreaking step by establishing the world's first policy-oriented environmental bank, known as the "Ecology Bank," in 1974. The Ecology Bank was conceived as a response to the environmental challenges that emerged in the wake of rapid industrialization. Germany, facing issues such as pollution and resource depletion, recognized the need for targeted financial support to incentivize environmentally friendly projects. One of the primary functions of the Ecology Bank was to offer preferential loans to projects that faced challenges in securing funds through traditional channels. By providing financial incentives and support, the bank aimed to encourage the development of initiatives that prioritized environmental sustainability. This initiative made it a pioneer in what would later be recognized as green credit business and marked a significant milestone in the development of green finance. It laid the foundation for policies and institutions aimed at fostering environmentally sustainable practices.

Inspired by the success of the German model, countries worldwide began to recognize the potential of transforming traditional businesses into environmentally sustainable enterprises. The establishment of ecology banks in other nations became a global trend, with many countries seeking to replicate the German experience (Wang et al. 2020). These institutions were designed to act as effective platforms for supporting the growth of green industries by providing targeted financial support. The establishment of ecology banks around the world reflected a broader international commitment to addressing environmental challenges through financial means. These banks became instrumental in fostering a shift towards sustainable practices by channeling funds to projects that promoted eco-friendly technologies, renewable energy, and resource efficiency.

Today, facing global climate risks, green finance plays a critical role in funding environmentally sustainable projects, mitigating climate risks, and fostering a financial system that aligns with broader environmental objectives (Chang et al. 2021). In the backdrop of ongoing international trade tensions, green finance has emerged as a rare consensus within the global financial community. The recognition that financial development must align with the goal of achieving global net-zero carbon emissions has become a shared perspective, driven by the imperative of promoting long-term sustainable economic development. The growing consensus on green finance reflects a fundamental shift in priorities and a collective acknowledgment of the need to address environmental challenges through financial means.

The urgency of addressing climate change and achieving net-zero carbon emissions has gained prominence on the global stage. As countries grapple with trade tensions and economic uncertainties, the consensus on green finance provides a unifying framework that transcends geopolitical differences. The evolution of international cooperation in the field of green finance reflects a maturation of global attitudes towards environmental responsibility. Initially led by a few developed countries, the initiation and implementation of green finance measures have expanded to include universal participation on a global scale. Recognizing the interconnectedness of environmental challenges, countries are increasingly working together to share best practices, establish common standards, and create a conducive global environment for green financial initiatives. Emerging economies, developing nations, and international organizations are actively engaging in the dialogue and contributing to the development of green finance mechanisms that suit diverse economic contexts.

The universal participation in green finance is evident in collaborative efforts, such as the establishment of international funds, joint research initiatives, and the sharing of knowledge and expertise. Multilateral institutions, such as the United Nations and the World Bank, play a pivotal role in facilitating cooperation and fostering a global environment conducive to green finance. In 1992, the United Nations Conference on Environment and Development formulated and adopted the "Agenda 21" with sustainable development as its guiding principle. The "Kyoto Protocol," adopted in 1997, represented a landmark effort to address climate change on a global scale. While its primary focus was on reducing greenhouse gas emissions, its impact extended beyond environmental considerations. The Kyoto Protocol heightened global awareness of the urgent need for coordinated efforts to combat climate change. This awareness, in turn, influenced the financial sector by emphasizing the importance of integrating environmental considerations into investment decisions.

A significant milestone in the global promotion of green finance concepts was the introduction of the "Equator Principles" in 2002. These principles were developed by financial institutions in collaboration with environmental and social non-governmental organizations. The Equator Principles are a set of corporate loan principles that require financial institutions to conduct comprehensive assessments of the potential environmental and social impacts of a project before investing in it. The Equator Principles promote responsible lending by financial institutions, emphasizing the need for a thorough evaluation of the environmental and social impacts of projects. The signing of the Equator Principles elevated the practice of green finance to new heights. As of July 2022, 134 financial institutions from 38 countries have adopted the Equator Principles, including Citibank, Barclays, Dutch Bank, HSBC, and nine domestic banks in China.

In 2016, green finance was first included as a topic in the G20 summit, leading to the establishment of the G20 Green Finance Study Group. The inclusion of green finance as a key topic in the G20 agenda signaled a shift in global priorities, emphasizing the importance of aligning financial practices with environmental objectives. In the wake of the G20 summit, the outcomes and discussions influenced policy directions in more than 30 countries worldwide, leading to widespread adoption of green finance policies. In 2021, the G20 Sustainable Finance Study Group was reinstated. This move reinforced the importance of sustainable finance within the G20 agenda and highlighted the continued commitment of major economies to advance global green economic development, boosting confidence in global green economic development and encouraging more countries to participate in the field of green finance.

This chapter aims to provide a comprehensive overview of the concepts, development, and diverse array of financial tools within the field of green finance. By shedding light on the transformative potential of these tools, the chapter encourages a deeper understanding of their role in addressing climate change and promoting sustainable development. The fast development of financial technology and the financial market has enabled the diversification of funding sources for green projects. As we delve into the various instruments and mechanisms, it becomes evident that innovative financial solutions are playing a crucial role in addressing the challenges posed by climate change and promoting sustainable development. Furthermore, the evolving landscape of green finance underscores the importance of adapting financial strategies to meet the dynamic needs of environmentally focused initiatives. This chapter aims to provide an overview of the evolving trends and strategies within the realm of green finance, shedding light on the transformative potential of financial tools in fostering a more sustainable and resilient future.

2 Categories of Climate Financial Tools

The definition of green financial tools has yet to achieve consensus, and many scholars often consider them as climate financial instruments. From a narrow perspective, green financial tools focus on evaluating the quality of environmental management and the impact during life cycles to identify key green industries and technologies. In a broader sense, they target the entire green financial system with the aim of establishing a sustainable financial system to facilitate economic transformation or maintain economic stability and growth, as proposed by the Greening China's Financial System research group of the State Council Development Research Center of China in 2016.

To address environmental issues such as climate change, the credit market, securities market, and insurance market actively develop green financial products to achieve integration of finance and the green economy. Green financial tools primarily serve three functions: resource allocation, risk management, and market pricing. The resource allocation function guides and leverages financial resources toward green and low-carbon areas through the innovative use of green financial tools. The risk management function involves developing green insurance, green derivatives, and other financial instruments to mitigate the physical and transition risks posed by climate change to the financial system. The market pricing function directs more funds to support green and low-carbon areas through the pricing and market price discovery functions of different products.

Common green financial tools include green credit in the credit market, green bonds and Environmental, Social, and Governance (ESG) indices in the securities market, as well as green insurance in the insurance market (Long et al. 2022).

3 Green Credit

In the credit market, green credit refers to credit products and services provided to support economic activities aimed at environmental improvement, addressing climate change, and promoting efficient use of resources (Gilchrist et al. 2021; Akomea-Frimpong et al. 2022). Specifically, this involves banks incorporating environmental information about projects and related companies as evaluation criteria into their review mechanisms during the loan approval process.

In 1974, the establishment of the German Ecological Bank is considered the origin of green credit. Subsequently, many banks worldwide followed Germany's example, establishing "ecological banks" and driving the rapid development of green credit, as mentioned earlier in this chapter. The implementation of the "Equator Principles" in 2003 was a milestone for the credit market and the entire banking industry. It clarified and specified the previously vague environmental and social standards in project financing, leading to a basic uniformity in environmental and social standards across the banking industry. This was conducive to regulating the credit market, fostering a positive cycle, and improving the ethical standards of the entire banking industry. For individual banks, following the "Equator Principles" is advantageous for gaining or maintaining a good reputation, protecting market share, ensuring good corporate governance, and more accurately assessing financial risks, thereby reducing political risks for their projects. For society as a whole, the adoption of "Equator Principles" facilitates the implementation of strategies for sustainable environmental and social development, making Equator Banks act as agents for protecting the environment and society.

In addition to the "Equator Principles," the international community has initiated various initiatives such as the "UN Global Compact," "UNEP Finance Initiative," "Carbon Disclosure Project," "Global Reporting Initiative," "UN Principles for Responsible Investment," and "Climate Principles." Banks around the world have signed and committed to complying with these initiatives. Mainstream banks have also established internal environmental management systems and effective incentive and constraint mechanisms based on the ISO 14000 series environmental management standards drafted by the International Organization for Standardization (ISO) Technical Committee 209.

Driven by the aforementioned international rules and efforts, banks in the credit market are shifting their strategies and solutions towards sustainable development. More and more financial institutions are directing their resources and lending capacity towards curbing ecological degradation and promoting consumer practices and decisions that support sustainable development. The major challenge faced by banks is how to develop effective and meaningful solutions based on market conditions to address various environmental issues, including climate change, deforestation, air quality issues, and biodiversity reduction, while identifying and obtaining new business opportunities beneficial to their customers. Some successful examples of green credit products provided by commercial banks in the international credit market are shown in Tables 3.1.

The development of green credit in the Chinese banking sector is worth introducing and discussing. The Chinese government is committed to sustainable development and has rapidly promoted green credit in China (Lv et al. 2021). From 1995 to 2012, China's green credit-related policies underwent initial exploration. During this period, the government mainly adjusted industrial structure and strengthened environmental protection by issuing "differentiated" credit policies. The People's Bank of China took the lead in issuing the "Notice on Implementing Credit Policies and Strengthening Environmental Protection" in 1995, which, for the first time, highlights environmental protection and pollution control as important considerations for bank loans.

In July 2007, the National Environmental Protection Agency (the former government agency of the Ministry of Ecology and Environment of China), the People's Bank of China, and the China Banking Regulatory Commission jointly released the "Opinions on Implementing Environmental Protection Policies and Regulations to Prevent Credit Risks." This document requires financial institutions to make compliance with environmental laws a prerequisite for loan approval. For newly built projects without environmental impact assessment approval, financial institutions are

Table 3.1 Green credit products for climate financing provided by commercial banks worldwide

Loan type	Example
Project financing	The energy from waste project provides up to 25 years of loan support, requiring only the signing of a waste disposal contract with the local government and a commitment to supporting the disposal of waste outside the scope of the contract
Green credit card	It provides cardholders with discounts and lower borrowing rates for purchasing green products and services. 50 percent of the profit generated by the green credit card business is used for carbon emission reduction projects worldwide
Transportation loan	The Small Business Administration Express Loan provides fast approval and unsecured loans with preferential terms to truck companies, supporting their investment in fuel-saving technology and helping them purchase Smart Way upgrade kits with fuel-saving rate of 15%
Auto loans	The Clean Air Auto Loan offers preferential interest rates to all low-emission car models
Commercial building loan	It provides a 0.125% loan discount to commercial or multi-purpose residential units in green projects
Home equity loan	It signs a joint marketing agreement with Sharp Electric Company to provide convenient financing to customers who purchase civilian solar technology
Housing mortgage loan	Structured Energy Efficient Mortgage (EEM) incorporates energy-saving indicators such as electricity saving into the credit scoring system of loan applicants
	The Eco-Home Loan provides free household energy assessments and carbon dioxide offset services for all home purchase transactions. In 2005 alone, it successfully offset 50,000 tons of carbon dioxide emissions

prohibited from providing any form of credit support. The document also stipulates that for existing projects subject to penalties by environmental authorities for excessive emissions, lack of emission permits, or failure to complete scheduled remediation tasks, financial institutions should strictly restrict loans when reviewing working capital loan applications of affiliated enterprises. This document places comprehensive and foundational requirements on the green credit business of commercial banks in China.

In February 2012, the China Banking Regulatory Commission issued the "Green Credit Guidelines," further requiring Chinese banking financial institutions to engage in green credit. Financial institutions are urged to vigorously promote energy conservation, emission reduction, and environmental protection; advance green credit from a strategic perspective; enhance support for the green economy, low-carbon economy, and circular economy; guard against environmental and social risks; optimize credit structures to better serve the real economy. This "Guidelines" marks the accelerated development of the green credit system for China's commercial banks. To improve the green credit policy system and development framework, the Chinese government successively introduced documents such as the "Opinions on Green Credit Work," "Overall Plan for Ecological Civilization System Reform," "Comprehensive

Work Plan for Energy Conservation and Emission Reduction in the 13th Five-Year Plan," "Notice on Submitting Green Credit Statistical Information," and "Notice on Conducting Performance Evaluation of Green Credit for Deposit-taking Financial Institutions in the Banking Industry." Under government promotion and policy guidance, financial institutions in China, including banks, have vigorously developed green credit and achieved notable accomplishments.

Some green credit products in the Chinese market are developed in collaboration with international financial institutions. For example, the Ministry of Finance of China and KfW (Kreditanstalt für Wiederaufbau), the German development bank, signed a loan agreement, where Chinese banks act as intermediaries. Under the China-Germany cooperation in international climate protection, energy efficiency/renewable energy loans are provided. The China Export–Import Bank acts as the intermediary. In 2012, KfW provided 42 million euros for a new phase of green intermediate credit projects. This funding is specifically used to support energy-saving and emission reduction projects of small and medium-sized enterprises in China. The intermediary banks are the Chinese commercial banks CITIC Bank and Chang'an Bank.

Green credit products for climate financing provided by commercial banks in China are quite diversified. Here are a few examples. Commercial banks provide loans to enterprises to support fixed asset investments in energy-saving and emission reduction projects, such as the streetlight renovation project in Chang'an town, Dongguan city, which was financed by a special buyer's credit line provided by Industrial Bank for equipment purchase. Bank loans are also granted to support the operation and working capital turnover of energy-saving and emission reduction projects, and the construction and operation of energy management projects based on contracts. In the latter case, borrower companies use the shared energy-saving benefits as the main repayment source, pledging future revenue rights of the project or using other collateral methods. In terms of carbon asset pledge credit, the Qingyuan Hydropower Limited in Minhou County, Fuzhou city, was granted by Industrial Bank the first carbon asset pledge loan in China. Another type of loan is the pollution discharge right pledge credit, where an enterprise pledged the initial emission right of 30.91 tons of chemical oxygen demand per year to Industrial Bank to apply for a loan, resolving the issue of its financial constraints.

4 Green Bonds

In the securities market, green bonds are defined as securities issued through a legal process, with the raised funds dedicated exclusively to supporting green industries, green projects, or environmentally friendly economic activities that meet specified conditions, and repayment of bond principal and interest will be made according to the agreed terms (Bhutta et al. 2022). In a narrower sense, green bonds refer to "labeled green bonds" that have undergone regulatory green certification and bear a green label. Besides labeled green bonds, there are a certain scale of "non-labeled green bonds" in the market, which are bonds not specifically labeled but effectively channel funds towards green industries. Together, these labeled and non-labeled bonds constitute bonds directed towards the green sector, known as "green bonds."

The concept of "green bonds" was first introduced by the European Investment Bank and the World Bank in 2007. In the same year, the European Investment Bank issued the world's first climate awareness bond, using the raised funds to provide loans for renewable energy or energy efficiency projects, achieving a combination of bond investment value and environmentally friendly corporate value. The first truly labeled green bond on a global scale was issued by the World Bank in 2008, explicitly stating that the funds raised must be exclusively used for green projects addressing global greenhouse effects. Subsequently, more institutions joined the development of green bonds.

As certain energy-saving and environmentally friendly technologies have matured, larger-scale bond investments are made possible. From a regulatory perspective, new financial regulations (such as "Basel III") may lead to more projects being financed from the capital market or project financing market. Furthermore, changes in asset allocation strategies have increased the demand for green or climate-related bonds among certain investors who seek investment opportunities with long-term fixed income, such as pension funds and insurance companies. Institutional investors are incorporating sustainability indicators into their asset portfolios, which have expanded from equity of listed companies to other asset classes. This in turn provides opportunities for the development of green bonds and climate bonds.

Compared to developed countries, the green bond market in China is in an early stage and there is great potential of future development. At the end of 2015, the People's Bank of China and the National Development and Reform Commission officially issued the "Green Bond Issuance Guidelines." Since then, the development of green bonds in China has exhibited rapid momentum. Benefiting from the continuous deepening of policies related to carbon peaking and carbon neutrality since 2021, as well as related policy preferences, China's green bond market has experienced a leap in development. In 2022, the issuance of labeled green bonds in and outside China amounted to $155 billion (approximately CNY 1 trillion), a year-on-year increase of 35 percent. Among them, the issuance volume of green bonds that meet the Climate Bonds Initiative (CBI) definition (i.e., labeled green bonds from China included in the CBI Green Bond Database) reached $85.4 billion (CNY 575.2 billion), ranking first globally. Meanwhile, the majority of China's green bonds will mature by 2025, and the growth potential of the issuance scale is considerable.

The issuance institutions of green bonds in the international market are relatively diversified, mainly including government agencies, international institutions, multilateral financial institutions, and investment banks. Meanwhile, companies engaged in green and low-carbon businesses issue green or climate bonds in the form of corporate bonds or private placements. This section categorizes green bond products based on the issuer. Depending on the issuer, issuance venue, and regulatory body, green bonds typically include green financial bonds, green corporate bonds, green company bonds, green debt financing instruments, and green asset-backed securities, among others. Green financial bonds are securities issued by financial institution entities in accordance with the law, raising funds to support green industries or projects and repaying principal and interest as agreed. Green corporate bonds are bonds issued by eligible domestic companies following regulations, with raised funds primarily used to support green industries or projects. Green company bonds are bonds issued by eligible green enterprises engaged in energy conservation, environmental protection, sustainable development, and climate change adaptation, with funds raised mandatorily directed towards green industrial projects. Green debt financing Instruments are financing tools issued by non-financial enterprises in the interbank market, with funds raised specifically allocated to financing green projects related to energy conservation, pollution prevention, resource conservation, and recycling. Green asset-backed securities are structured green financial products where raised funds are used for the construction, operation, acquisition, or repayment of bank loans related to green industrial projects. This involves securitizing fee income or rights or credits from the original equity holder, or packaging credit assets in accordance with the green industry support catalog to raise funds.

Green bonds issued by governments or multilateral banks

Green bonds issued by governments or multilateral banks can either be asset-backed securities linked to specific green infrastructure projects or mass-market bonds with a sovereign bond style, where the proceeds are allocated among various green projects (such as those issued by the World Bank).

In December 2007, the World Bank issued the first green low-carbon bonds, targeting small and scattered investment institutions in the Netherlands, Belgium, and Luxembourg. The bonds carried a floating interest rate of no less than 3%, with specific interest rate fluctuations linked to a series of market development indices. In June and September 2008, low-carbon bonds totaling USD 31.5 million, tied to Certified Emission Reductions (CERs), were issued for a five-year term by the World Bank. The initial stage featured a fixed interest rate, while the later stage's interest was tied to the futures market price of CERs and the issuance volume of certain CERs. In November 2008, bonds with a total value of SEK 2.7 billion (approximately USD 350 million) were issued by the World Bank through the Swedish Bank (SEB) to support the development of low-carbon projects in a low-carbon economy. An additional SEK 150 million was issued in February 2009. The bonds were issued with an interest rate of 3.15%, which is 0.25% higher than the Swedish government's national bonds. Major purchasers included the Swedish National Pension Fund and the United States Joint Pension Fund. In December 2009, a four-year bond with an annual interest rate of 2%, totaling USD 130 million, was issued by the World Bank in collaboration with SEB and Credit Suisse, with an additional USD 50 million bond issued in January 2010. Purchasers of these bonds included the California State Teachers' Retirement System, Swedish life insurance companies, and the Swedish National Pension Fund.

The European Investment Bank also has issued a series of green/climate bonds. In 2007, the first five-year zero-interest "Climate Awareness Bond" with a total value of 600 million euros was issued. The funds raised from the bond were primarily used for the European Investment Bank's investments in renewable energy and energy efficiency projects. In 2009, the second "Climate Awareness Bond" was issued in

Switzerland. The bond was mainly managed by Swed Bank, and the funds raised were also dedicated to the construction of energy-efficient and new energy projects. Unlike the first "Climate Awareness Bond," the second series of bonds had a combination of fixed and floating interest rates. The total value was 2.25 billion Swedish Kronor, with 1.7 billion Swedish Kronor having a fixed interest rate of 2.95%, and the remaining 5.5 million Swedish Kronor having a quarterly floating interest rate (3-month Stibor + 10 bps).

In the US, the US Department of the Treasury issued $2.2 billion worth of "Clean Renewable Energy Bonds" (CREBs) in 2009 to support various renewable energy initiatives. In the same year, the US government implemented a measure to stimulate economic development at the local level by issuing high-interest bonds known as "Build America Bonds." The funds raised from these bonds were primarily used for green energy projects, with interest rates reaching as high as around 35%. Additionally, the US government issued a type of bond called "Property Assessed Clean Energy Bonds" (PACE bonds) to support the application of clean and renewable energy in residential and commercial buildings. However, the issuance of these bonds was somewhat negatively impacted by policy conflicts. The Federal Home Loan Banks (Federal Home Loans Agency) stipulated that households benefiting from PACE bond loans were ineligible for home loan insurance, significantly constraining the development of PACE bonds.

In China, on 22 December 2015, the People's Bank of China introduced green financial bond products, encouraging financial institutions to issue green financial bonds, officially launching the Chinese green bond market. On 7 September 2023, the London branch of Bank of China successfully issued a 3-year, $600 million overseas green bond. This bond represents the first green bond from a Chinese financial institution where all funds raised are dedicated to European projects. It is also the largest single-scale Chinese green bond in the European region since 2023.

Green bonds issued by companies

The issuance of corporate green bonds is a quite novel practice. Some examples of the green bonds issued by companies are shown in Table 3.2, sorted from high to low by the issuance volume.

Structured green bond products

In addition to bonds issued by supra-national or governmental entities, other fixed-income products, such as structured and securitized products, use structured note mechanisms to benchmark their returns against the yields of inflation or other significant derivatives. They are likely to become a part of private sector financing, given investors' familiarity with underlying assets.

In 2008, Crédit Agricole introduced the first "synthetic green bond," known as the Environment Optimizer/Top Green Bond. Essentially, this is a synthetic fund related to the Lyxor Dynamic Environment Fund. As a synthetic product created through financial engineering using zero-coupon bonds, it pays face value upon maturity. This structure exposes investors to environmental risks while protecting the invested capital.

Table 3.2 Green bonds issued by companies

Year	Bond type	Issuance volume (in $100 million)	Bond information
2009–2012	Certified energy Efficiency bonds project	3200	Initially, taxation was imposed on credit-enhanced bonds for energy efficiency (EE), but after 2010, it was changed to direct subsidies for the bonds
2009–2010	Clean renewable Energy bonds project	2400	Taxation for credit-enhanced bonds related to renewable energy (RE)
2008–2010	Green bonds	1896.7	With a maturity period of 2 to 10 years, financing for climate change initiatives
2007–2010	Climate awareness bonds	1630	With a maturity period of 3 to 8 years, investment in both RE and EE
2010	Clean energy bonds	705	With a maturity period of 3.5 to 7 years, investment in renewable energy projects and infrastructure construction
2006	Wind power asset securitization	676	With a 20-year term, targeting a portfolio of wind power companies in Germany and France, issued through an SPV. Initially rated BBB and BB+, downgraded to BB and B in 2010 due to insufficient wind power
2010	Water governance bonds	645	With a maturity period of 2 to 3 years, used for improving water quality, management, and irrigation
2010	Wind power project bonds	580	With a 25-year term, used for constructing a three GW wind farm, rated Ba3 by Moody's
2003	Wind power asset securitization	370	BBB rated, secured by cash flow from seven US wind power projects
2006	Renewable energy bonds	300.8	With a 3-year term, financing for wind farms in the US and Europe
2010	Solar project bonds	260	Issued in two tranches with a total term of 18 years, secured by a 44 MW solar park's electricity generation. Partially guaranteed by the Italian export credit agency SACE
2011	Clean energy bonds	193	Targeting Japanese investors, financing for climate change projects in the Norwegian municipal sector

In Europe, there is a growing focus on financing gaps for achieving renewable energy goals, where institutional investors entering the bond market and developing innovative structured products could be a breakthrough. Taking the wind energy industry as an example, wind energy projects have shifted from relying primarily on bank funding to securitization in recent years. In 2010, Italian solar company Montalto di Castro successfully issued the first publicly rated bonds for a solar project. These bonds are asset-backed, with a majority of their buyers being institutional investors. Notably, they are fully guaranteed by the Italian export credit agency SACE, making them more like secured mortgage bonds than asset-backed securities. The unguaranteed portion was entirely sold through the European Investment Bank. This financial structure may represent a new model for renewable energy financing, signaling a significant new source of liquidity for the renewable energy market.

The CRC Breeze Bond is a notable innovation in the field of climate bonds. In 2006, CRC Hedge Fund's energy fund acquired 430 MW of wind power facilities in Germany and France with funding provided by a bank. CRC then sold the project to a Special Purpose Vehicle (SPV) named "CRC Breeze Finance," which issued €470 million in asset-backed securities. This marked the first time an international renewable energy project was financed directly by the securities market. The bond's structure ensures that the revenue generated by the wind power plant can cover the interest and principal payments of the bond. This wind power plant converts kinetic energy from the wind into electrical energy, and the revenue from selling the generated electricity is used to repay the long-term debt of CRC Breeze Finance, with CRC receiving the remaining revenues. Even if the wind is not as strong as usual or the operational and maintenance costs exceed previous estimates, there are still sufficient funds to pay bondholders. These revenues are relatively stable, making them suitable for fixed-income investors.

The CRC Breeze Bond was the first batch of green asset-backed securities (ABS) issued by a Special Purpose Vehicle (SPV), marking the first time the international capital market was used on a large scale to support renewable energy. Following the CRC Breeze Bond, there were two more wind energy-supported bonds: the Alta Wind Bond worth $580 million and the Shephard's Flat Bond worth $525 million. However, these bonds were downgraded in 2010, mainly due to the volatility of wind supply, caused by historically low wind levels over the past four years. In fact, this low level was significantly below historical averages. It is expected that in the coming years, the financing structure of wind energy asset securities will continue to evolve into multi-tranche transactions, reflecting the changing possibilities of wind energy from conservative to aggressive.

5 Green Equity

The concept of "green equity" was initially proposed jointly by Swedbank and the Centre for International Climate and Environmental Research in Norway. It suggests that companies labeled as green should derive over 50 percent of their turnover deriving from green activities. This concept was widely applied in the European market in 2020. In May 2020, the Swedish real estate company K2A introduced a green equity framework, with Swedbank serving as its "structuring advisor" and CICERO providing third-party independent assessments. K2A was the first company in the world to apply this methodology. Subsequently, Swedbank provided advisory services for several companies, assisting them in designing green equity frameworks and promoting the concept of "green equity" in the market.

In June 2021, Nasdaq introduced the "green equity" label in Europe. Nasdaq's green equity label includes two types of designation: Green Equity Designation and Green Equity Transition Designation. The former aims to identify companies where over 50 percent of its turnover comes from activities considered green, while the latter is designed to recognize companies committed to green transformation, with over 50 percent of its investments directed towards the green activities. In the same month, NX Filtration, a filtering technology supplier assessed by CICERO, went public on the Amsterdam Stock Exchange. In February of the same year, German e-commerce company Rebelle debuted on Nasdaq Nordic, marking the first green stock IPO on Nasdaq. Four companies received Nasdaq green equity designations in the first quarter of the year. In November 2021, Citicore Energy REIT Corp., a Philippine real estate investment trust focusing on renewable energy, obtained CICERO's green equity certification and went public on the Philippine Stock Exchange in February, becoming the first green stock IPO in Asia. In recent years, "green equity" has made progress globally, but due to the lack of unified standards for the concept and equity assessment, they are still in the early stages of development.

In the current stock market, green equity indices are the primary focus. Green equity indices are centered on the concept of sustainable development and index the stock prices of listed companies in the environmental sector and those with low-carbon businesses. These indices are used for portfolio investment by investors and environmental performance assessment. To generate these indices, ESE performance analysis is conducted for component companies in certain mature stock indices, based on ESG theme screening or assigning different weights to ESG aspects. The sample selection and weight allocation aim to reflect the opportunities and risks faced by issuers in economic activities that seek to improve the environment, address climate change, and efficiently use resources.

There are several prominent examples of green equity price indices worldwide. For instance, the S&P Global Environment Index includes 30 of the world's largest environmentally-focused publicly traded companies, spanning clean energy, timber, environmental services, and waste management industries. The stock index is known as the Climate Change and Environmental Index (by Dutch Bank). This index covers eight branches of the environmental industry, with no more than 30 component stocks in total. Adjustments are made semi-annually based on the market value changes of each branch industry, aiming to fully reflect the actual growth of each branch industry.

The Sustainability Index is an indicator measuring changes in the sustainable development status of companies. Its compilation is fundamentally similar to other stock market indices, with the key difference lying in the selection of sample stocks. The sustainable development index comprehensively considers economic, social, and environmental aspects when selecting listed companies. In the process of compiling the sustainable development stock index, there are two types of methods for screening listed companies: positive indicator screening and negative indicator screening. Companies selected through positive indicator screening are considered leaders in sustainable development practices and are typically evaluated based on specific criteria assessing positive behaviors in economic, ethical, social, and environmental aspects. In contrast, the negative (exclusion) screening method excludes companies engaged in specific activities such as gambling and weapons manufacturing. The purpose of exclusion is to avoid including companies in the sample stocks that are severely environmentally polluting, unethical, or unfriendly to society. The selection of these criteria forms the basis for determining the sustainable development stock index.

Another well-known green stock index is the Dow Jones Sustainability index (DJSI). The establishment of this index is aimed at tracking the financial performance of leading sustainable development companies. All indices in the DJSI series follow the same corporate sustainable development evaluation system and respective standards. It includes the following subindices: Global Index, European Index, and North American Index. The Global Index comprises a composite index and five subsets, with the component stocks of the subsets excluding companies generating revenue from brewing, tobacco, gambling, weapons, or all of the aforementioned industries. This index series was first published on September 8, 1999. The European Index, known as the Dow Jones STOXX Sustainability Index (DJSI STOXX), includes a pan-European index, a Eurozone index, and two subsets. The component stocks of the subsets exclude companies generating revenue from brewing, tobacco, gambling, weapons, or all of the aforementioned industries. This index series was first published on October 15, 2001. The North American Index includes the Dow Jones Sustainability North America Index (DJSI North America) and the Dow Jones Sustainability United States Index (DJSI United States), along with two subsets. These subsets also do not include companies generating revenue from brewing, tobacco, gambling, weapons, or all of the aforementioned industries. This index series was first published on September 23, 2005.

In China, the practice related to green equity is primarily based on green equity indices. Currently, green equity indices in China mainly include climate benchmark indices and green theme indices. Climate benchmark indices typically use "dual carbon" strategies or international net-zero emission targets as the basic framework for sample selection. They achieve index carbon neutrality or net-zero emission goals by over- or under-weighting securities of listed companies based on different carbon emissions and climate transition performance. Green theme indices focus on specific thematic industries, selecting securities in sectors such as environmental protection, energy conservation, clean energy, green transportation, and green construction as index investment targets.

In September 2021, the Central Committee of the Communist Party of China and the State Council issued the "Opinions on Deepening the Reform of the Ecological Protection Compensation System," proposing to develop financing instruments for various types of resource and environmental rights, such as water rights, pollution rights, and carbon emission rights, and to establish green equity indices. In recent years, domestic index institutions in China have also been committed to increasing the supply of green indices, forming a green index system consisting of multiple subdivisions, including climate transition, low-carbon environmental protection, ESG, etc.

In the Chinese market, two green stock indices are worth mentioning. The first is the China Low Carbon Index. The index was jointly launched by the Beijing

Environmental Exchange and the Clean Technology Investment Fund Vantage Point Partner in June 2010. The other one is the CSI 300 Carbon Neutrality Index. This index, with the objective of reducing carbon emission intensity, was first introduced by China Securities Index Co., Ltd. on 7 March 2022. The compilation rules for the CSI 300 Carbon Neutrality Index involve excluding listed companies rated as B or below in the CSI ESG Rating from the sample stocks of the CSI 300 Index. The index weights are then adjusted based on the industry and the company's carbon neutrality contribution. The distribution is skewed towards green sectors and companies with significant carbon neutrality contributions, aiming to progressively reduce the index's carbon emission intensity year by year. Moreover, the carbon emission intensity of the CSI 300 Carbon Neutrality Index is reduced by over 20% compared to the CSI 300 Index.

6 Green Funds

Green funds, with the goal of promoting green development and improving the ecological environment, refer to public funds or other investment funds that invest in businesses and projects generating environmental benefits or engaged in environmentally related activities. Based on different investment targets, green funds can be divided into green industry investment funds and green securities investment funds. The former focus on investing in equity or green industrial projects, while the latter invest in green bonds and stocks of green enterprises.

In the United States, Japan, and Western Europe, green investment funds have developed early and experienced significant growth. However, due to differences in market development levels, green investment funds take different forms across countries. In the United States and some countries in Western Europe, non-governmental organizations and institutional investors are the main issuers of green investment funds, while in Japan, companies play a major role (Aruga and Bolt 2023). Initially, the United States did not establish dedicated green investment funds, incorporating ecological investments only within SRI (Socially Responsible Investing) funds. Since the launch of the first green investment fund, Calvert Balanced Portfolio A, more green investment funds have been introduced to the market, bringing positive economic and ecological benefits. In Western Europe, green investment funds belong to the third generation of socially responsible investment products. Before 1989, there were only 18 green investment funds in Western Europe, with 13 in the United Kingdom, totaling less than 1 billion euros in assets and accounting for less than 1 percent of SRI.

In recent years, with the increasing severity of climate change issues, the Green Climate Fund (GCF) was established at the 16th Conference of the Parties (COP16) to the United Nations Framework Convention on Climate Change held in Cancun, Mexico in 2010. The Green Climate Fund, the world's largest climate fund, is a critical element of the historic Paris Agreement, and is dedicated to addressing climate change by investing in low-emission and climate-adaptive development projects in developing countries. As the financial mechanism of the Convention, the Green Climate Fund will contribute funds to achieving the goal of keeping global temperature rise below 2 degrees Celsius, as pledged by countries in the Paris Agreement. According to previous resolutions, developed countries were supposed to contribute $30 billion as fast-start finance for the Green Climate Fund between 2010 and 2012 and provide $100 billion annually from 2013 to 2020 to help developing countries actively address climate change.

After two years of preparation and site selection, the Green Climate Fund was officially established and launched on 4 December 2013, in Songdo International City, South Korea. In comparison to other climate funds that primarily rely on public sector financing, the Green Climate Fund's most significant feature is increasing its sources of funds from the private sector. This not only alleviates the financial pressure on developed countries but also expands funding sources and scale, accelerating the fundraising process. For this purpose, the Green Climate Fund Secretariat has specifically established a Private Sector Facility to enhance the efficiency and flexibility of fund operations.

In 2019, the Green Climate Fund approved a $63 million forest project designed by the Food and Agriculture Organization and the Chilean government. The project aims to restore and protect approximately 25,000 hectares of native forests in five regions of the country. It seeks to reduce 1.1 million tons of greenhouse gas emissions, plant at least 7,000 hectares of trees, and sustainably manage and protect over 17,000 hectares of forests. The project includes areas affected by recent fires, covering over 4,000 hectares of land. It contributes to the restoration of evergreen tree species in the region, including native Chilean species such as oaks and Lenga beech.

One requirement for receiving funding from the Green Climate Fund is that the benefits of resource allocation should be shared among different genders, indigenous people, and vulnerable groups, to ensure positive social and environmental impacts. Therefore, over 57,000 people, including indigenous community members, are involved in activities such as afforestation, restoration, and sustainable management through this project. In 2023, the Green Climate Fund has committed to investing $12.8 billion. The goal is to achieve sustainable production of crops such as cocoa, palm oil, soybeans, and rubber in 11 countries, including Côte d'Ivoire, Zambia, Liberia, Gabon, the Democratic Republic of the Congo, and Cameroon, without reducing forest cover.

On the other hand, there exist ESG theme funds in the green fund market, which are a type of investment fund that uses environmental, social, and governance factors as investment criteria. The three ESG factors, Environmental, Social, and Governance, are considered crucial indicators for assessing a company's overall performance. The primary objective of ESG funds is to select companies that excel in environmental protection, social responsibility, and corporate governance for investment while avoiding those that may have negative impacts on society or the environment. This investment approach not only contributes to promoting sustainability but also helps reduce investment risks and enhance long-term investment returns.

In China, green funds mainly invest in green enterprises or industries, with equity investment funds being the primary form. Although it started later, the development momentum is strong. In 2001, Qingyun Venture Capital Investment Management Co., Ltd. was established, and in 2002, the company founded the first international investment fund in China's environmental protection industry, focusing on areas such as new energy, environmental protection, energy conservation, new materials, comprehensive resource utilization, and carbon reduction. In February 2011, the first green investment fund investing in the securities market, the Xingquan Green Investment Stock-type Securities Investment Fund, was officially launched. The fund focuses on green technology industries or companies, including clean energy and environmental protection industries, as well as companies in traditional industries that actively fulfill environmental responsibilities, are committed to transitioning to green industries, or contribute to the development of green-related industries.

In recent years, China's green funds have shown tremendous market explosiveness, and green funds have experienced significant development in the country. In 2021, the number of registered companies related to Chinese green funds increased from six in 2010 to 52. In terms of green private equity funds, as of the end of the third quarter of 2021, there were 800 private equity funds in China focusing on green, sustainable, ESG (Environmental, Social, and Governance), and other green directions, with total assets under management of CNY 370 billion. By the end of 2021, there were over 500 private equity funds related to green ecology, low-carbon environmental protection, environmental governance, clean energy, and other green areas, with total assets under management exceeding CNY 200 billion. In terms of green public funds, starting from the second half of 2021, more than 50 companies, including E Fund Management, Penghua Fund Management, Funde Sino Life Asset Management, Huaxia Fund Management, Huitianfu Fund Management, Industrial and Commercial Bank of China (ICBC) Credit Suisse Fund Management, China Construction Bank Fund Management, and Invesco Great Wall Fund Management, began to increase their green investment layout. As of the end of the third quarter of 2021, the number of public and private funds focusing on green, sustainable, and ESG approached 1,000 in China, with a combined scale of managed assets over CNY 790 billion, representing a 36 percent growth compared to the end of 2020. Among them, there were over 190 public funds, with total assets under management of over CNY 410 billion. Table 3.3 shows some ESG theme funds issued in China in 2022.

7 Green Insurance

Facing significant risks from climate change, the global insurance industry has undergone a shift in its approach to addressing climate change, transitioning from a negative avoidance stance to proactive measures, aiming to transform climate change risks into opportunities (Wang et al. 2017). Historically, the insurance industry has played a leading role in managing risks related to disasters such as fires and earthquakes.

Table 3.3 ESG theme funds in China issued in 2022

Fund name	Date of issuance	Type of fund	Fund scale (CNY)
Zhonghang Ruihua ESG annual open-end bond initiated securities investment fund	16 March 2022	Bond fund	999, 999, 000
Invesco great wall ESG quantitative stock initiated securities investment fund	6 June 6 2022	Equity fund	144, 569, 111.6
Huaxia ESG sustainable investment one-year holding period hybrid securities investment fund	9 March 2022	Hybrid fund	194, 929, 147.7
Orient red ESG sustainable investment hybrid securities investment fund	2 March 2022	Hybrid fund	434, 947, 942.4
Da Cheng ESG responsible investment hybrid initiated securities investment fund	24 June 2022	Hybrid fund	359, 516, 214.9
Huaxia CSI 300 ESG benchmark traded open-end index securities investment fund	24 February 2022	Equity fund	291, 083, 347
Funde China securities 500 ESG benchmark traded open-end index securities investment fund	28 July 2022	Equity fund	229, 486, 619
Yingda CSI ESG120 strategy index securities investment fund	15 March 2022	Equity fund	28, 034, 070.18
China resources Yuanda ESG theme hybrid securities investment fund	23 June 2022	Hybrid fund	504, 809.12

Source CSMAR database

Presently, insurance companies are increasingly likely to create methods and products for preventing losses, mitigating climate-related damages for clients, governments, and the companies themselves, while simultaneously reducing greenhouse gas emissions.

Insurance entities, including insurance companies, reinsurance companies, insurance brokerage firms, insurance agency companies, brokers, and agents, are increasingly focusing on climate change and implementing corresponding action plans. Currently, over 140 institutions globally have signed the "Principles for Sustainable Insurance," including insurance companies representing over 25% of the total global premiums and managing assets worth $14 trillion. The Principles for Sustainable Insurance have been incorporated into the Dow Jones Sustainability Index and the FTSE4Good Social Responsibility Index as part of industry standards.

More insurance institutions are actively participating in climate change initiatives, involving the development of climate emergency products and services, raising public awareness, quantifying and disclosing climate risks, and advocating for the inclusion of climate factors in investment decisions. The ultimate goal of these activities is to reduce losses caused by climate-related reasons for clients and minimize industry risks. For example, RMS has established the first Cat prediction model by incorporating climate change factors into insurance actuarial models. Insurance brokerage company MMC has formulated the "Climate Change White Paper," signed relevant contracts with clients, and developed new products. Reinsurance companies such as Swiss Re, Munich Re, and General Reinsurance have also adopted climate change action plans. The operations related to quantifying and managing climate change risks and mitigating losses from climate disasters through the market are well-established.

Other market entities in the insurance industry, such as investors, government departments, and consumers, provide external driving forces for the insurance industry to actively address climate change. Currently, investors are increasingly focusing on climate change. For instance, investment company INCR, with assets totaling $3 trillion, has joined the Carbon Disclosure Project (CDP) and sent letters to the world's 30 largest insurance companies, requesting improved disclosure of climate change information. A Mercer survey shows that 58% of institutional investors consider climate change as a very important or quite important economic term, with an expectation that it will become even more important within the next five years. Additionally, government departments and consumers are showing increased concern about climate change, strongly supporting regulatory policies by governments, thereby exerting pressure on the insurance market.

Currently, various insurance institutions worldwide have launched 1,148 initiatives and projects to address climate change. These projects have generated nearly $2 trillion in revenue for the industry, constituting 44% of the total industry revenue. Furthermore, at least 130 insurance products have been introduced to the market, encouraging people to use efficient energy in their daily lives and businesses. For example, the innovative environmental product "Pay-as-You-Drive" car insurance policies have gained popularity. The coverage under this scheme is not a fixed amount but is calculated based on the mileage driven by the policyholder. This pricing method has led to an 8% reduction in the total miles driven in the United States, a 4% reduction in fuel consumption, and an annual reduction of $50 billion to $60 billion in economic losses from car accidents and traffic congestion.

Globally, 26 insurance companies have stated that the insurance projects they have introduced have achieved carbon neutrality. For instance, Tokyo Marine & Nichido Fire Insurance Co., Ltd., based in India, has been implementing an environmental insurance project dedicated to restoring mangrove forests in India and Southeast Asian countries since 1999. The project is close to achieving its goal of restoring 8,200 hectares of mangroves. The restoration of these mangroves has effectively reduced losses from coastal storms and increased the world's carbon sequestration content.

7.1 Green Insurance Products

Green insurance, also referred to as environmental liability insurance, covers the insured's compensation or governance responsibilities for environmental damage they are legally obligated to bear. Typically, the insurance coverage is limited to economic losses resulting from sudden events such as natural disasters or accidents, causing bodily injury, property damage, or other economic losses. Currently, "green insurance" business conducted by insurance companies in developed Western countries mainly includes two types. The first category is Environmental Damage Liability Insurance for General Enterprises, which encompasses various businesses such as waste treatment, disposal, storage, landfill, and incineration companies, real estate companies, warehousing and transportation companies, diverse manufacturing industries, natural resource development companies involved in mining, petroleum, and natural gas, engineering and construction companies, medical institutions, and public management organizations. These enterprises or institutions have the potential to generate various pollutants during their operations, leading to environmental infringement incidents. The second category is the Environmental Insurance for Professional Environmental Consultancy, Design, Engineering, and Service Companies.

Specifically, green insurance can be divided into the following types:

Environmental impairment liability insurance and own-site cleanup liability insurance

Environmental Impairment Liability Insurance (EIL), also known as Pollution Legal Liability Insurance in the United States, pertains to compensation liability incurred by the insured for personal injury and property damage to third parties caused by environmental pollution. The insurance company assumes the responsibility to pay insurance benefits. This type of environmental liability insurance does not cover all environmental damage risks but is specifically associated with personal injury and property damage to third parties.

Own-site Cleanup Liability Insurance pertains to the insured's responsibility for pollution on self-owned sites, where the insured is legally obligated to remediate pollution and incurs costs for such remediation. The insurance company assumes the responsibility to pay insurance benefits based on the compensation limit specified in the insurance contract. This type of insurance widely applies in the United States.

Occurrence-based liability insurance and claims-based liability insurance

In the case of Occurrence-based Liability Insurance, regardless of when a claim is filed, as long as the loss occurs during the policy's effective period, the insurance company should bear the responsibility to pay insurance benefits. To limit their liability exposure, insurance companies typically specify in the insurance contract the maximum duration within which the insured must notify the company of a claim.

Claims-based Liability Insurance refers to events for which claims are made during the policy's effective period but occur after the retroactive date specified in the insurance contract. The insurance company is responsible for paying insurance benefits. Due to the high-risk nature of "green insurance," insurers providing claims-based liability insurance usually assume smaller risks than those providing occurrence-based liability insurance. Therefore, modern "green insurance" has evolved from occurrence-based liability insurance to claims-based liability insurance.

Mandatory liability insurance and voluntary liability insurance

Mandatory Liability Insurance, also known as statutory liability insurance, is a type of liability insurance that must be taken out as mandated by law. Many countries around the world enforce mandatory liability insurance for "green insurance," such as the United States, Sweden, Germany, etc., for handling damages that may arise from the handling and disposal of toxic substances and waste.

Voluntary Liability Insurance refers to liability insurance where the policyholder and the insurance institution voluntarily, on an equal and mutually beneficial basis, negotiate and enter into the insurance contract. Whether to insure is entirely decided by the potential polluter who may cause environmental pollution. For example, France has implemented voluntary liability insurance for environmental damage.

Through insurance instruments, risks faced by industries vulnerable to the impacts of climate change can be transferred, serving the economic compensation function and contributing to disaster reduction and prevention. Additionally, the insurance industry can promote the application of technology and products, especially in periods when clean technologies are not yet mature.

7.2 *Climate Insurance Tools*

In terms of climate insurance tools, agricultural insurance, weather index insurance, and catastrophe insurance are relatively mature and important risk mitigation tools employed by the international insurance industry in the field of climate change (Bucheli et al. 2021).

Agricultural insurance

Agricultural insurance is a type of property insurance designed to provide protection for economic losses suffered by agricultural producers during the process of engaging in crop cultivation and livestock farming, caused by natural disasters and unforeseen accidents. In many developing countries, the development of agricultural insurance is intertwined with the goal of reducing the poverty population. On the one hand, it stabilizes premium income, and on the other hand, it reduces potential loss risks. For example, the African Risk Transfer Insurance Agency (HARITA) promotes climate risk mitigation and crop insurance in five regions in northern Ethiopia. This insurance scheme is underwritten by local insurance companies with international reinsurers, using rainfall indices to trigger compensation. It compensates farmers who cultivate the three major food crops in case of losses due to drought. Cash shortage is a major reason people do not participate in insurance plans. The uniqueness of this plan lies in allowing farmers to offset premiums by engaging in climate change mitigation activities, such as tree planting, in their local areas. This "work reward" mechanism allows farmers to benefit even without paying premiums. Cash-paying farmers can also participate in this plan, driving market development.

Four insurance companies in China have made outstanding contributions to the development of agricultural insurance in the country. Currently, more than 270 varieties of crops are covered by national agricultural insurance, spanning various fields. According to data released by the China Banking and Insurance Regulatory Commission, the original premium income of agricultural insurance reached CNY 58.3 billion from January to September 2019, providing risk coverage of CNY 3.6 trillion. The scale of agricultural insurance business in China has consistently ranked first in Asia, making it one of the most active agricultural insurance markets globally.

Weather index insurance

In China, the development of weather index insurance started to gain attention only in very recent years. In April 2008, the Ministry of Agriculture in China launched the "Weather Index Agricultural Insurance for vulnerable rural areas" project, in collaboration with the International Fund for Agricultural Development and the United Nations World Food Programme. Weather index insurance has entered the research and development stage in many regions. Examples include the typhoon disaster meteorological index insurance project in Fujian province, the rice agricultural meteorological index insurance project in Zhejiang province, and the apple meteorological index insurance project in Shaanxi province. A few companies have attempted to operate weather index insurance. In 2011, Swiss Reinsurance Company collaborated with Dinghe Property Insurance Co., Ltd. to provide the first domestic precipitation-based power generation index insurance scheme for Guangdong Meizhen Hydropower Co., Ltd. The scheme helped hydropower enterprises partially transfer risks arising from weather changes, alleviating the enormous losses caused by drought in local areas. Some more examples of weather index insurance are show in Table 3.4, including those for economic crops, cereal crops, livestock, and aquaculture sectors and compiled based on publicly available information.

In Africa, with the assistance of the World Bank and the World Food Programme, Malawi initiated a pilot project for weather insurance. The insurance pilot provided loans to 1,000 farmers, enabling them to purchase drought insurance based on weather indices. By bundling insurance and loans, the project not only improved the creditworthiness of insured farmers but also increased their agricultural productivity.

In the northern and central highland regions of Bolivia, four provinces participated in an insurance plan that combined risk reduction with index insurance mechanisms. The index in this scheme is based on the production levels of reference fields in the region with similar geographic environments in terms of temperature, precipitation, humidity, soil type, etc. The farmer with the highest technical level in a group is selected as the technical advisor for other farmers, helping them reduce risks and increase yields. The land of the advising farmer serves as the reference field. Losses can be assessed based on the yield of the reference field, distinguishing between

Table 3.4 Examples of weather index insurance in China

Insurance product	Year	Weather	Area	Company
Economic crops				
Western sweet melon rainfall intensity index insurance	2007	Precipitation	Shanghai	Anxin Agricultural Insurance
Nanfeng honey orange low-temperature freezing index insurance	2011	Low temperature	Jiangxi	PICC Property and Casualty Company Limited
Tobacco meteorological index insurance	2012	Precipitation, low temperature	Fujian	China Life Insurance
Open field cultivation of green leafy vegetables index insurance	2014	High temperature, precipitation	Shanghai	Anxin Agricultural Insurance
Crops planting frost meteorological index insurance	2014	Low temperature	Heilongjiang	Sunshine Mutual Insurance
Rubber wind disaster index insurance	2015	Typhoon	Hainan	PICC Property and Casualty Company Limited
Loquat low-temperature index insurance	2016	Low temperature	Zhejiang	Pacific Insurance
Apple planting precipitation index insurance	2017	Precipitation	Shandong	Pacific Insurance
Drought weather index	2018	Drought	Gansu	Tian'an Property Insurance
Fruit meteorological index insurance	2019	Low temperature, heavy precipitation	Guangdong	Sunshine Mutual Insurance
Asparagus precipitation weather index	2019	Precipitation	Henan	Zhongyuan Agricultural Insurance
Tea oil weather index insurance	2019	Drought, low temperature, freezing	Hunan	PICC Property and Casualty Company Limited
Honeysuckle Meteorological Index Insurance	2020	Low temperature, high temperature, precipitation	Hebei	PICC Property and Casualty Company Limited
Cotton high-temperature meteorological index insurance	2020	High temperature	Xinjiang	Pacific Insurance

(continued)

Table 3.4 (continued)

Insurance product	Year	Weather	Area	Company
Lemon weather index insurance	2020	Precipitation, high temperature	Chongqing	Ancheng Insurance
Tea comprehensive insurance meteorological index	2021	Low temperature, high temperature, heat damage, drought	Zhejiang	PICC Property and Casualty Company Limited
Cereal crops				
Rice planting weather index insurance	2009	Precipitation, high temperature	Anhui	Guoyuan Agricultural Insurance
Wheat planting weather index insurance	2010	Precipitation, high temperature	Anhui	Guoyuan Agricultural Insurance
Corn drought meteorological index insurance	2014	Precipitation	Shanxi	China Coal Insurance
	2014	Precipitation	Liaoning	
	2015	Precipitation	Beijing	
Corn planting meteorological index comprehensive insurance	2015	Precipitation, wind speed, temperature	Shanxi	China Coal Insurance
Rice high-temperature heat weather index insurance	2011	High temperature	Anhui	Wuhu Agricultural Insurance
	2016	High temperature	Hube	PICC Property and Casualty Company Limited
Miscellaneous grains (millet) weather index comprehensive insurance	2017	Precipitation, temperature, wind speed	Shanxi	China Coal Insurance
Corn meteorological index catastrophe insurance	2019	Precipitation, temperature, wind speed	Jilin	Anhua Agricultural Insurance
Millet weather index insurance	2019	Wind speed, precipitation	Henan	Zhongyuan Agricultural Insurance
Wheat hot wind meteorological index	2020	Hot wind	Henan	Pacific Insurance
Livestock and aquaculture				
Zhangzidao group wind power index insurance	2013	Wind power	Dalian, Shandong	PICC Property and Casualty Company Limited
Beekeeping meteorological index insurance	2014	Precipitation, temperature	Beijing	Anxin Agricultural Insurance

(continued)

Table 3.4 (continued)

Insurance product	Year	Weather	Area	Company
Chinese mitten crab temperature index insurance	2014	High temperature	Jiangsu	Pacific Insurance
Scallop farming wind disaster index insurance	2015	Wind speed	Shandong	Pacific Property Insurance
Sea cucumber farming temperature index insurance	2015	Temperature	Shandong	Pacific Property Insurance
Tibetan sheep and yak snowfall meteorological index insurance	2017	Snowfall	Qinghai	Pacific Insurance, Anxin Agricultural Insurance
Aquaculture typhoon index insurance	2017	Typhoon	Fujian	China Life Property and Casualty Insurance
Crayfish farming weather index insurance	2017	Low temperature, heavy precipitation	Hubei	PICC Property and Casualty Company Limited
	2019		Henan	Zhongyuan Agricultural Insurance
	2019		Hunan	China United Property Insurance Company Limited
Cattle and sheep weather index insurance	2019	Snowfall, drought	Inner Mongolia	PICC Property and Casualty Company Limited
Eel meteorological index	2020	Precipitation, wind speed, temperature	Guangdong	Sunshine Mutual Insurance

those caused by environmental factors and those within the farmers' controllable range. If losses are due to environmental factors, insurance claims are triggered.

Catastrophe insurance and derivatives

"Catastrophe" refers to natural events that cause significant destruction and losses to people's lives and property, with severe impacts on a region's or a country's economy and society. Mainly including earthquakes, fires, hurricanes, floods, hailstorms, freezes, snow disasters, tsunamis, volcanic eruptions, etc. Catastrophe insurance is designed to cover these major disasters. Due to the enormous losses and sudden occurrence of catastrophes, insurance companies may face challenges in having sufficient funds to settle claims promptly. Therefore, while obtaining catastrophe insurance coverage is not difficult, managing claims effectively in the event of a disaster becomes a crucial issue.

Before the development of the insurance industry, many countries used subsidies for affected populations when catastrophes occurred. With the advancement of the insurance industry, some countries have shifted the burden of subsidies to the insurance sector or made it mandatory for customers to purchase catastrophe insurance when buying property insurance. However, governments do not unconditionally subsidize or enforce measures on the insurance industry. Instead, they adopt a tiered subsidy approach, providing different levels of subsidies based on the loss amounts caused by catastrophe insurance.

To alleviate the substantial payout pressure of catastrophe insurance, many countries' governments or private entities have established reinsurance companies. These companies provide reinsurance for catastrophe insurance of insurance companies, even engaging in second-level reinsurance. This way, when a disaster occurs, a portion of the risk is transferred to reinsurance companies, reducing the pressure on insurance companies. However, some insurance companies, due to a "gambling mentality," may resist having their interests shared with reinsurance companies, thereby diminishing their profits when significant natural disasters do not occur. Therefore, when engaging in reinsurance, government-mandated measures are necessary, such as enacting relevant laws to specify the limits of reinsurance for catastrophe insurance, ensuring adequate risk sharing when a catastrophe occurs.

Derivatives of catastrophe insurance can transfer its risks to the capital market. However, the introduction of derivatives requires the implementation of a mature capital market at the national or regional level to absorb the market turbulence caused by catastrophes and bear significant losses. These derivatives mainly include catastrophe bonds, catastrophe futures, catastrophe options, catastrophe equity puts, and catastrophe risk swaps.

Currently, the development of catastrophe insurance in many developing countries is in its early stages. To take China as an example, since the establishment of catastrophe insurance as a system by the state, pilot explorations of catastrophe insurance have been diversified and tailored to local conditions. These pilot programs include multi-peril catastrophe insurance represented in Shenzhen city, catastrophe index insurance in Guangdong Province, and earthquake catastrophe insurance for urban and rural residential properties in Yunnan and Sichuan provinces. Table 3.5 lists some examples of China's catastrophe insurance pilot programs, compiled based on publicly available information.

7.3 Innovations in Green Insurance Products

The development of key areas such as green transportation, green architecture, green low-carbon technology, and ecological carbon sinks is crucial to the progress of green transition. In response to the risks in these areas, the insurance industry is innovating products and services, attempting to leverage its professional advantages in insurance protection and risk management. It aims to safeguard green travel, empower green architecture, support the promotion of green low-carbon technology, enhance the

Table 3.5 Examples of China's catastrophe insurance pilot programs

Time	Area	Insurance program
June 2014	Shenzhen city	The first catastrophe insurance pilot program adopts a "co-insurance body" underwriting model. The municipal finance fully funds the purchase of catastrophe insurance annually, ensuring that all natural persons within the administrative region of Shenzhen receive disaster relief insurance services after a catastrophe
May 2015	Sichuan province	The first provincial-level catastrophe insurance pilot program in the country is initiated by Sichuan Province. Residents independently purchase insurance, with subsidies from various levels of government finance
August 2015	Dali prefecture, Yun-nan province	It follows a policy earthquake index insurance model, representing China's first index-type catastrophe insurance system and the first pilot for earthquake insurance for rural houses
June 2016	Zhangjiakou city	It adopts a public catastrophe insurance system model where the government fully funds it. This model combines personal injury, housing loss, and property loss, forming a public catastrophe insurance system
July 2016	Guangdong province	It pioneers the model of catastrophe index insurance, with the government serving as both the policyholder and the insured, using parameters such as continuous rainfall and typhoon intensity as the basis for compensation payments
August 2016	Heilongjiang province	The agricultural finance catastrophe index insurance model introduces a new approach in China for the government to collaborate with commercial insurance and reinsurance companies to address agricultural financial risks arising from natural disasters. It is the first innovative agricultural index insurance scheme utilizing satellite remote sensing technology and meteorological monitoring technology
July 2017	Hunan province	Adopting a public catastrophe insurance system model, the premiums are centrally arranged by fiscal planning, fully funded by the finances at the provincial, municipal, and county levels
June 2017	Hainan province	The policy-driven agricultural insurance selects 2–3 cities and counties to conduct catastrophe insurance pilot programs, exploring the establishment of a catastrophe risk diversification mechanism
August 2017	Chongqing city	Adopting a public catastrophe insurance system model, the government fully funds the purchase and acts as both the policyholder and the insured, to bear the responsibility of providing assistance, as required by law, in the event of a catastrophe

(continued)

Table 3.5 (continued)

Time	Area	Insurance program
May 2018	Shanghai city	Employing a government-led, commercially operated model, the government acts as the policyholder for catastrophe insurance. The district government pays the catastrophe insurance premiums through fiscal payment methods
April 2019	Hubei province	This policy-driven catastrophe insurance in Wuhan, Shiyan, Huanggang, and Enshi cities is against torrential rain and flooding. The government fully purchases insurance for residents in the jurisdiction, providing basic economic compensation for related personal injuries and property losses. Traditional claim models are tested in Shiyan, Huanggang, and Enshi cities, while the index model is used in the Wuhan city
January 2020	Ningxia Hui autonomous region	A public catastrophe insurance system model is employed, where the government fully funds the purchase of catastrophe insurance, achieving full personnel coverage. The surplus from insurance premiums is fully allocated to the catastrophe risk special reserve account, managed and supervised by designated departments appointed by the city government
July 2020	Wuhan city	Using the catastrophe index insurance model, it establishes a combination of "catastrophe insurance + agricultural insurance" as a fiscal policy insurance package. The government finances the purchase, with compensation directly deposited into the designated fiscal account based on the disaster situation, allowing fiscal coordination
June 2022	Henan province	Conducting unified insurance at the provincial level for cities under its jurisdiction, using both the actual claims model and the index model. Premiums are borne by city and county finances, with specific ratios determined by the pilot provincial city

capacity of ecological carbon sinks, and contribute to nature-based solutions (NbS) to propel the transformation towards a green society.

In terms of green low-carbon technology, there are various types of insurance covering technology research and development, intellectual property rights, and product quality. The development of insurance products in this regard is relatively mature. However, in areas such as green travel, green architecture, and ecological carbon sinks, the innovative application of insurance products and services is currently in a partial, decentralized pilot exploration stage. It has not fully realized its risk protection role, and an effective commercial model has not yet been established.

Green transportation insurance

Green travel refers to a mode of transportation that conserves energy, enhances energy efficiency, reduces pollution, promotes health, and emphasizes efficiency. It includes low-carbon travel behaviors such as taking public transportation, cycling, walking, carpooling, and environmentally friendly driving. To encourage the public to prioritize green travel methods such as public transportation, walking, and cycling, reduce the number of private cars on the road, and enhance the overall level of green travel, insurance companies, in collaboration with car manufacturers, have upgraded and launched innovative green products. For example, Usage-Based Insurance (UBI), also known as User Behavior Insurance, is considered a form of green insurance. UBI car insurance determines the amount of insurance premiums based on the driver's actual driving time, location, mileage, and specific driving behaviors. To obtain greater premium discounts, vehicle owners may reduce the frequency of vehicle usage, subsequently reducing carbon dioxide emissions and potentially alleviating environmental pollution issues. The technological foundation of the UBI car insurance pricing model includes the Internet of Vehicles, smartphones, and connected devices such as On-Board Diagnostics (OBD), which stands for "On-Board Diagnostics System" and serves as the communication interface for in-car monitoring systems.

Since its introduction in the United States in 1998, UBI car insurance has matured internationally, with over 300 insurance companies globally offering UBI products. Italy has the highest penetration rate of UBI, exceeding 15%. While the UBI penetration rate in the United States is lower than Italy, its UBI premium scale ranks first globally, with over half of its insurance companies providing UBI products and services. UBI car insurance is still in its early stages of development in China. With the support of policy dividends and technological empowerment, major domestic insurers have been piloting UBI. However, due to the lack of a mature pricing model and insufficient functionality of OBD, monitoring information and data analysis struggle to achieve a certain level of precision. China Taiping Insurance has introduced UBI car insurance from the United States and is currently undergoing large-scale internal testing, reportedly meeting the conditions for market launch and actively applying for regulatory approval. As UBI car insurance continues to be applied in the international market, coupled with the continuous maturity of China's Internet of Vehicles technology and the successive introduction of regulatory policies, UBI car insurance is expected to usher in new development opportunities in China.

In addition, China is also experimenting with a small-scale "parking reduces premiums" initiative. This insurance leverages technology to upgrade traditional car insurance products by segmenting vehicle "usage" and "parking" on a daily basis, increasing the precision of risk calculation. In 2013, Shenzhen launched the "Love Shenzhen, Use Less, Travel Green " initiative, allowing vehicle owners who declare continuous parking for more than 30 days to extend their car insurance contract period. In 2017, both "CheChe Car Insurance" and "Anxin Insurance" introduced a "parking refund" product, allowing vehicle owners to receive a refund based on the number of "days" when not driving.

Green building insurance

Green building refers to a new type of construction that can save energy, improve resource utilization, provide a safe and efficient environment for humans, and enable mutual adaptation and integration between people, the environment, and the building. Green building insurance, as an innovative type of green insurance, can provide risk protection for various aspects of the green building industry, including buildings, products, equipment, and professional liability of personnel. It not only effectively promotes the healthy development of green buildings from the perspective of market regulation but also ensures that the performance of buildings meets people's needs for safety, comfort, and health. Furthermore, it provides assurance for operational maintenance after the delivery of construction projects, enhancing people's recognition of green building and energy-efficient construction.

Green building insurance originated in the United States and is currently mature in international markets. The mainstream international green building insurance products are mainly divided into two categories: green building property insurance and green building professional liability insurance. Green building property insurance covers green building assets, facilities, materials, and equipment, while green building professional liability insurance focuses on the professional liability risks of various green building professionals. The United States exhibits a diverse range of green building property insurance products. Fireman's Fund Insurance Company was the world's first provider of green building insurance, offering GreenGard green building property insurance since 2006 and providing risk protection for commercial buildings in the United States. In addition to GreenGard, Fireman's Fund Insurance Company's main green building products include residential green building insurance, green building upgrade property insurance, and industry-specific green building property insurance (for the education industry, church buildings, etc.). In 2010, the Insurance Services Office (ISO) introduced standard model clauses, making the green building insurance model mainstream in the insurance industry. Compared to green building property insurance, green building professional liability insurance started slightly later. In April 2009, Argo Insurance Brokers developed green building professional liability insurance, reaching an agreement with CNA Insurance to provide a 5% premium discount to members of the U.S. Green Building Council (including architects, engineers, consultants, and professional designers), with a maximum coverage of $1 million per policy. If coverage exceeds this limit, new underwriters are required, along with additional supplementary insurance contracts.

Green building insurance started relatively late in China and is currently in the early stages of development. In recent years, China has continuously introduced policies to promote the development of low-carbon building insurance. This includes encouraging and supporting insurance institutions to innovate green insurance products and services as a key initiative. In 2019, the Ministry of Housing and Urban–Rural Development of China issued the "Green Building Evaluation Standard" GB/T 50,378, which included scoring requirements for building-related insurance, including potential defects insurance for construction projects and green building performance insurance. This acknowledged the role of insurance mechanisms in the green building industry. In April 2020, the China Building Energy Conservation Association released a pilot plan for green building quality and performance insurance. The goal is to break through the responsibility risks of urban building quality management and government management through exploration, pilot projects, demonstrations, and leadership, achieving a win–win development for the government and the insurance industry. In April 2021, the Beijing Municipal Planning and Natural Resources Commission issued the "Review and Scoring Standards for High Standard Residential Construction Plans," where "insuring green building performance liability insurance and introducing risk control mechanisms" can earn additional points in the building quality scoring. This puts green building performance insurance at the forefront of land acquisition, ensuring the introduction of risk control services throughout the entire process. In 2022, the Ministry of Housing and Urban–Rural Development of China issued the "14th Five-Year Plan for Building Energy Conservation and Green Building Development," proposing specific indicators for the development of building energy conservation and green buildings during the 14th Five-Year Plan period.

Clean technology insurance

Clean technology refers to all carbon reduction or zero-carbon technical means that can adapt to the needs of low-carbon economic development, reduce greenhouse gas emissions, and prevent climate warming. It involves various sectors such as electricity, transportation, construction, metallurgy, chemical industry, petrochemicals, as well as the development of new technologies in renewable energy, new energy, clean and efficient utilization of coal, carbon dioxide capture and storage, and other areas that control greenhouse gas emissions. Due to the lack of market validation for these technologies, various risk transfer methods need to be explored. Currently, a relatively innovative practice in the field of clean technology insurance is a series of insurance products launched by Munich Reinsurance Group for clean energy technologies.

Munich Re's clean technology insurance products cover various factors that may affect the effectiveness of clean energy projects, such as performance insurance for solar modules, various potential loss insurance for wind farms, performance insurance for various products (such as lithium-ion batteries, concentrated solar power generation, LEDs, heat-insulating glass, etc.), and water level insurance for hydropower plants. These insurance products can exempt equipment manufacturers and developers of clean technology from measurable and predictable losses caused by product performance or objective conditions.

In 2011, Munich Re provided a performance guarantee solution for photovoltaic components of the Swedish photovoltaic manufacturer Eco Supplies Solar AB. In cases where their photovoltaic components fail to achieve the expected output power, compensation payments are provided for a period of 25 years. The agreement also guarantees that the output power of solar modules will reach 90% in the first 10 years and 80% in the remaining 15 years. In December 2012, Yingli Green Energy signed a "Component Quality Guarantee Insurance Agreement" with a professional insurance company under Munich Re, covering Yingli polycrystalline silicon components sold from 1 October 2012 to 30 September 2013.

Forestry carbon offset insurance

Forests are the largest terrestrial ecological carbon sink resources, possessing high economic value and a mature industry chain. They are a key focus of insurance protection in the realm of green resources. With the rapid advancement of global carbon emission trading, forestry carbon offsets, as a cost-effective means to offset corporate carbon emissions, are highly favored in the voluntary emission reduction trading market.

Forestry carbon offset projects often have long output cycles, unstable short-term income, and are highly susceptible to the impact of natural disasters and pests, bringing significant uncertainty to their output and income. Insurance mechanisms can be an effective risk management method for addressing the uncertainties faced by forestry carbon offsets. Insurance institutions around the world are focusing on the functions of forest carbon offsets, and actively exploring and developing innovative products. These innovative designs have provided new paths for realizing the value of ecological products. Three products are introduced in this section, including forestry carbon offset index insurance, forestry carbon offset price insurance, and forest carbon sequestration insurance.

The first type, forestry carbon offset index insurance, bases compensation on the measurement of carbon offset losses. It quantifies the forest carbon sequestration loss index caused by specified disasters such as fire, frost, mudslides, and landslides, as agreed in the contract. When the loss reaches the threshold stipulated in the insurance contract, it is considered an insurance incident. Compensation from forestry carbon offset index insurance can be used for post-disaster forest carbon offset resource assistance, carbon source removal, forest resource cultivation, ecological protection, and restoration-related expenses. For example, in March 2021, PICC Property and Casualty Company Limited signed the first "carbon offset loan" in China with Shunchang State Forest Farm in Fujian Province. This is a bank loan-type forest fire insurance providing CNY 21 million in risk protection for carbon offset forests. The "Carbon offset loan" is not only the first financing project that uses forestry carbon offsets as collateral in Fujian province, but also the first case of repurchase agreement with future carbon offset products as the underlying in China.

The second product, forestry carbon offset price insurance, is developed for forestry carbon offset trading projects. It can effectively prevent carbon offset forest planting enterprises from being affected by extreme price fluctuations, stabilize forestry carbon offset trading income, and thereby protect the surplus value, ecological and environmental value. It also covers the losses during carbon offset recovery and costs of carbon sequestration capacity restoration and protects carbon emission trading value generated by forestry. In May 2021, PICC Property and Casualty Company Limited introduced forestry carbon offset price insurance, signing an agreement with Shunchang County State Forest Farm in Nanping City, Fujian Province. During the insurance period, when the market price of forestry carbon offset projects fluctuates, causing the actual price of insured carbon offsets to fall below the target price, PICC P&C will compensate according to the contract.

The last product, forest carbon sequestration insurance, refers to insurance that provides economic compensation for the reduction in carbon absorption caused by natural disasters and accidents throughout the entire growth process of trees, including natural forests, timber forests, protective forests, economic forests, and other trees capable of absorbing carbon dioxide. For example, China Life Property & Casualty Insurance Fujian Branch has innovatively developed a forest carbon sequestration insurance product. This product uses satellite remote sensing technology combined with carbon offset theoretical methodology to establish a model for measuring forestry damage and calculating reduction in carbon sequestration capacity. In April 2021, the first policy was issued in Xinluo district, Longyan City, Fujian Province. The annual premium for this policy is CNY 1.2 million. When the cumulative loss area of the forest reaches 232 acres within one year, it is considered an insurance incident, triggering a minimum claim of CNY 1 million, with a maximum compensation of CNY 20 million.

Carbon trading credit insurance and CDM/JI project insurance

Carbon trading credit insurance, in a broad sense, is a guarantee-type insurance where an insurance company provides economic compensation according to the contract when one party in a transaction cannot complete the transaction, resulting in damages to the rights holder.

Specifically for CDM (Clean Development Mechanism)/JI (Joint Implementation) projects, carbon offset project insurance is mainly divided into two categories: (1) insurance for buyers in carbon offset trading contracts, providing compensation if the seller fails to deliver the required CERs (Certified Emission Reductions) or if there is a sudden change in carbon trading policies and laws, causing the buyer to not receive the agreed quantity of CERs at the end of the contract; (2) insurance for companies developing CDM/JI projects, i.e., sellers of CERs/ERUs (Emission Reduction Units), providing compensation when CDM/JI projects fail to achieve expected benefits or incur unexpected losses due to policy changes.

Internationally, large insurance companies such as American International Group (AIG) and Zurich Insurance have undertaken insurance for CDM/JI projects. For example, Zurich Insurance provided a policy insurance for a power company in India, offering protection against the risk of not obtaining CERs as specified in the agreement due to significant changes in CDM policies. With this guarantee, investors provided $10.65 million in funding for the construction of a biomass power plant. The electricity generated by the power plant will be purchased by the local state-owned power company and guaranteed by the Ministry of Finance. The original internal rate of return for this biomass power plant was 8%, but with the additional income from carbon reduction credits, the internal rate of return increased to 12%, attracting investments in energy-saving and emission reduction. The project was successfully developed.

8 Conclusions

The trend in the development of climate financial tools in the financial market reflects a growing recognition of the urgent need to address climate change and promote sustainable practices. Climate-related risk assessment has been increasingly integrated into the decision-making processes of financial institutions and investors. Tools such as climate stress testing and scenario analysis are being employed to evaluate the potential impacts of climate change on investment portfolios. On the other hand, from the Chinese cases, it can be clearly observed that regulatory initiatives of the government and regulatory bodies have played a vital role in introducing frameworks and standards to guide the development of climate financial tools. Under the policy guidance and the efforts made by the government, the regulatory environment keeps improving and is effectively shaping the financial industry's response to climate change and encouraging the adoption of sustainable finance practices.

This chapter reviews the development and status quo in the markets of several financial tools increasingly adopted to combat climate change. The first notable trend is that the financial institutions, such as commercial banks, are increasingly offering sustainable loans tied to specific environmental performance targets. These loans incentivize borrowers to adopt sustainable practices and are often linked to reduced interest rates based on the achievement of predefined sustainability goals. Second, the market of green bonds has experienced significant growth. Issuers, ranging from governments to corporations, use the proceeds to fund environmentally friendly projects. The market has expanded to include variations like ESG (Environmental, Social, and Governance) bonds, to reflect investors' increasing demand of greater transparency regarding the sustainability practices of companies.

Third, the insurance sector has developed fast worldwide to enable a diversification to meet climate-related insurance demands. With the rise in climate-related events, there is an increased interest and need in climate-linked insurance products. These insurance tools have significantly helped to mitigate the financial risks associated with extreme weather events, providing a mechanism to transfer and manage climate-related risks. Furthermore, carbon markets, including cap-and-trade systems and carbon offset mechanisms, have drawn increasing attention and gained traction. These tools allow entities to buy and sell carbon credits, fostering emissions reductions and supporting the transition to a low-carbon economy.

Besides the financial tools introduced in this chapter, it should be noted that the financial tools and technology to support the combat against climate change have been evolving. Financial derivatives related to climate variables are emerging. These instruments enable market participants to hedge against climate-related risks, such as fluctuations in renewable energy production or agricultural output. Innovation in climate-tracking technologies, such as blockchain and satellite imaging, are being employed to enhance transparency and traceability in climate finance. These innovations contribute to more accurate measurement and reporting of the environmental impact of financial activities. Overall, the trend in the development of climate financial tools indicates a growing alignment of financial markets with global efforts to combat climate change and achieve sustainable development goals. As awareness and urgency regarding climate issues continue to rise, it is likely that further innovations and initiatives will emerge in the realm of green and climate finance.

References

Akomea-Frimpong I, Adeabah D, Ofosu D, Tenakwah E J. 2022. A review of studies on green finance of banks, research gaps and future directions. Journal of Sustainable Finance & Investment, 12(4), 1241-1264.

Aruga K, Bolt T. 2023. Identifying factors affecting the preference for green bonds: A Japanese case study. Journal of Climate Finance, 5, 100021.

Bhutta U S, Tariq A, Farrukh M, Raza A, Iqbal M K. 2022. Green bonds for sustainable development: Review of literature on development and impact of green bonds. Technological Forecasting and Social Change, 175, 121378.

Bucheli J, Dalhaus T, Finger R. 2021. The optimal drought index for designing weather index insurance. European Review of Agricultural Economics, 48(3), 573-597.

Chang Y, Ji Q, Zhang D. 2021. Green finance and energy policy: Obstacles, opportunities, and options.

Gilchrist D, Yu J, Zhong R. 2021. The limits of green finance: A survey of literature in the context of green bonds and green loans. Sustainability, 13(2), 478.

Guo K, Luan L, Zhang D, Ji Q. 2023. Does climate risk affect the performance of companies in China?. Applied Economics Letters, 1–7.

Long S, Lucey B, Kumar S, Zhang D, Zhang Z. 2022. Climate finance: What we know and what we should know?. Journal of Climate Finance, 1, 100005.

Lv C, Bian B, Lee C C, He Z. 2021. Regional gap and the trend of green finance development in China. Energy Economics, 102, 105476.

Ma R, Ji Q, Zhai P, Yang R. 2022. Environmental violations, refinancing risk, and the corporate bond cost in China. Journal of International Financial Management & Accounting, 33(3), 480-504.

Wang C, Nie P Y, Peng D H, Li Z H. 2017. Green insurance subsidy for promoting clean production innovation. Journal of cleaner production, 148, 111-117.

Wang Y, Zhang D, Ji Q, Shi X. 2020. Regional renewable energy development in China: A multidimensional assessment. Renewable and Sustainable Energy Reviews, 124, 109797.

Zhang D, Ji Q. 2022. Review of the development of energy finance. Applications in Energy Finance: The Energy Sector, Economic Activity, Financial Markets and the Environment, 3–24.

Measuring Climate Risks and Impacts

Xiangyang Zhai, Qiang Ji, and Fei Wu

Abstract This chapter introduces the concept, categories and impacts of climate risks at the macro- and microeconomic levels, aiming to provide readers with an overall understanding of this critical topic. By establishing a conceptual framework, we seek to equip readers with the necessary foundation to navigate the subsequent discussions in this book. This chapter therefore sets the stage for a more profound exploration of climate risks in the subsequent contents of this book. Armed with the insights gained here, readers will embark on a more informed and enlightened journey through the complex terrain of climate challenges, thereby contributing to a collective understanding that is essential for informed decision-making and proactive adaptation in the face of an evolving climate landscape.

Keywords Climate risk · Climate physical risk · Climate transition risk

1 Introduction

Climate change is a prominent issue facing the present era. Addressing climate change has become one of the most heated topics, as the various problems caused by climate change have significant impacts globally. Changes in weather patterns threaten food production, and the rising sea levels increase the risk of catastrophic floods. Even if mitigation measures are successful, the negative impacts of climate change are expected to persist for decades. Such a serious climate situation calls for scientific and effective measures taken in a timely manner. Otherwise, adapting to

X. Zhai · Q. Ji
Institutes of Science and Development, Chinese Academy of Sciences, Beijing 100190, China

School of Public Policy and Management, University of Chinese Academy of Sciences, Beijing 100049, China

F. Wu (✉)
Research Institute of Economics and Management, Southwestern University of Finance and Economics, Chengdu 611130, China
e-mail: wufei@swufe.edu.cn

F. Wu et al. (eds.), *Climate Finance*, Climate Change and Energy Transition,
https://doi.org/10.1007/978-981-97-3308-8_4

life under the influence of climate change will become more difficult, accompanied by higher living costs.

Understanding climate risks and the economic impacts they cause is a crucial starting point to combat climate change. Existing major climate indicators tend to emphasize the increasing frequency and intensity of ongoing climate change, extreme weather events, and the significant losses and damages they cause, which affect humanity, the economy, and society to varying degrees. This chapter starts with an introduction of the concepts and categories of climate risks to help the readers establish a preliminary understanding of them. It then discusses commonly used climate risk measurements at the national, regional, and enterprise levels. Following this, it elaborates on the impacts of climate risks on economies at both macro and micro levels. At the macro level, the potential impact of climate risks is discussed within a framework encompassing the real economy, agricultural economy, and financial markets, while at the micro level it mainly involves the impact on micro-entities, including enterprises, financial institutions, households, labour force, and governments.

This chapter seeks to help readers acquire an understanding of how climate risks reverberate throughout the economy, influencing sectors, businesses, and financial systems, as well as how they tend to affect individuals, firms, regulators, and governments. The chapter emphasizes the significance of adopting a comprehensive perspective when gauging climate-related risks. From macroeconomic considerations to sector-specific analyses, the narratives outlined provide a comprehensive understanding of the potential consequences of climate change. This knowledge is helpful for decision-makers in both public and private sectors, aiding them to formulate strategies that factor in the complexities posed by climate-related risks.

Furthermore, the chapter addresses the dynamic nature of climate risks, acknowledging the evolving landscape of climate change and its potential ramifications. Readers will gain a general understanding of how to navigate this ever-changing terrain, allowing for adaptive and resilient responses to the challenges posed by a shifting climate. This chapter hopes to serve as a useful resource for those seeking a comprehensive grasp of measuring and interpreting climate-related risks. Whether assessing the macroeconomic impact or drilling down into sector-specific vulnerabilities, the discussions presented assist stakeholders to make informed decisions in the face of an increasingly uncertain climate landscape.

2 Definition and Characteristics of Climate Risk

2.1 Definition of Climate Risk

The escalating challenges posed by climate change to various regions around the world in recent years impact not only the environment but also economic stability. In February 2021, Texas faced an unprecedented severe cold wave, leading to a catastrophic failure of the state's power grid. The consequences were particularly severe for Brazos Electric Power Cooperative, the largest power company in the state, which declared bankruptcy. The cascading effects of the power outage resulted in widespread disruption, affecting businesses, households, and essential services. The economic losses incurred, totaling up to $195 billion, underscored the vulnerability of critical infrastructure to extreme weather events.

Moving to March, Sydney, Australia experienced devastating floods, causing substantial economic damage. Incomplete statistics from the Insurance Council of Australia estimated losses exceeding AUD 600 million. The flooding not only disrupted local communities but also emphasized the interconnectedness of climate events and their economic repercussions. Such incidents have broader implications for urban planning, infrastructure resilience, and insurance systems, necessitating a comprehensive approach to managing climate risks. In May, the northwest coast of India faced the impact of Cyclone Tauktae, a powerful storm causing direct economic losses amounting to several billion dollars. The cyclone highlighted the vulnerability of coastal regions to extreme weather events and underscored the need for robust disaster preparedness and response mechanisms. As climate change intensifies, the frequency and intensity of such storms are expected to increase, further emphasizing the imperative for adaptive strategies at both regional and global levels.

These events collectively emphasize the growing significance of climate risks to long-term economic stability. Climate risks usually refer to a broad range of uncertainties arising from various climate-related factors, such as extreme weather events, natural disasters, global warming, and the societal transition to sustainable development. These risks have far-reaching implications for economic and financial activities (Guo et al. 2023a), prompting increased attention and consideration in policy-making processes worldwide.

To the best of our knowledge, there has not been a universally agreed-upon, specific, and comprehensive definition of "climate risk" by major regulatory bodies. However, the recognition of the uncertainties induced by climate change and the consequences of climate-related risks has gained prominence in discussions and policymaking forums. One notable initiative addressing climate-related financial risks is the Task Force on Climate-related Financial Disclosures (TCFD). Established in 2015 by the Financial Stability Board (FSB), the TCFD aims to develop a framework that facilitates the disclosure of information related to the financial impacts of climate-related risks and opportunities (TCFD 2017). The TCFD framework is designed around four key thematic areas: Governance, which involves the disclosure of how the organization's governance processes integrate climate-related risks and opportunities; Strategy, that organizations are encouraged to disclose the actual and potential impacts of climate-related risks and opportunities on their businesses, strategy, and financial planning; Risk Management, which focuses on the disclosure of the processes used by organizations to identify, assess, and manage climate-related risks; Metrics and Targets, that organizations are prompted to disclose the metrics and targets used to assess and manage relevant climate-related risks and opportunities.

The TCFD framework provides a structured approach for organizations to enhance transparency and enable stakeholders, including investors, to make informed decisions by considering climate-related factors. It acknowledges that effective climate risk disclosure is essential for robust financial decision-making in the face of a changing climate. This growing emphasis on climate risk disclosure reflects a broader trend towards integrating environmental, social, and governance (ESG) considerations into corporate and financial decision-making. As climate change continues to present complex challenges, frameworks like TCFD play a crucial role in promoting transparency, accountability, and proactive management of climate-related risks across various sectors of the economy. It signals a broader shift towards recognizing the interconnectedness between climate issues and financial stability, encouraging a more sustainable and resilient approach to economic activities.

Similar considerations have been put forth by international organizations such as the Basel Committee on Banking Supervision, a global regulatory body that provides guidelines and recommendations for banking supervision, for the banking sector (BCBS 2021). It has emphasized that climate risks are not limited to environmental concerns but encompass a spectrum of challenges that can affect the safety and stability of individual banking institutions and, consequently, the broader banking system. Climate risks, as outlined by the Basel Committee, can be categorized into two primary dimensions: physical risks related to the direct impacts of climate change on assets and operations of banking institutions, and transition risks arising from the shift to a low-carbon economy and associated policy and market changes, impacting the safety and stability of individual banking institutions and thus having a more widespread effect on the banking system (BCBS 2021).

The frameworks provided by organizations like the Basel Committee highlight a crucial evolution in the understanding of climate risks. It goes beyond the recognition of environmental challenges and positions climate risks as a source of financial risk. In other words, changes in climate conditions and associated policies can directly or indirectly influence financial risks, reflected as dynamics in credit risk and operational risk in financial markets. This recognition underscores the need for financial institutions to incorporate climate risk considerations into their risk management frameworks. It also emphasizes the importance of understanding and disclosing the potential financial impacts of climate-related risks. As climate change continues to unfold, these frameworks contribute to a broader understanding of the interconnectedness between environmental sustainability, financial stability, and the resilience of the global financial system. The integration of climate risk considerations into financial regulation reflects a proactive response to the evolving challenges posed by a changing climate and the imperative to build a sustainable and resilient financial sector.

2.2 Characteristics of Climate Risk

Compared to other types of economic risks, there are several special characteristics of climate risks.

First, the highly uncertain nature of climate change distinguishes it from more traditional financial risks. In contrast to credit or market risks, climate change introduces a heightened level of uncertainty that complicates the prediction of its impact on both human ecology and economic activities. While more traditional financial risks are often based on historical data and statistical models, climate change involves dynamic, complex, interconnected systems with intricate interactions between various environmental factors, making it challenging to precisely anticipate its consequences. The uncertainty associated with climate change extends to its impacts on human ecology, encompassing ecosystems, biodiversity, and overall environmental health. Changes in temperature, extreme weather events, sea level rise, and shifts in precipitation patterns can have cascading effects on ecosystems, posing challenges for the adaptation and survival of various species. Furthermore, these ecological shifts can have indirect consequences on human societies, affecting agriculture, water resources, and overall community resilience. Economic activities are also profoundly influenced by the uncertain nature of climate change. Sectors such as agriculture, energy, and insurance, among others, may face disruptions and challenges due to changing climate patterns and increased frequency of extreme weather events. The uncertainty surrounding the timing and magnitude of these impacts makes it difficult for businesses and policymakers to formulate precise strategies for climate risk management, introducing a need for adaptive and resilient approaches in both ecological and economic contexts, as well as proactive measures, sustainable practices, and collaborative efforts to mitigate and adapt to the evolving challenges posed by climate change.

Second, the consideration of longer time spans and long-term impacts is a fundamental distinction when comparing the analysis of climate risks to more traditional credit and market risks. The typical approach to credit risk assessment involves predicting impacts for relatively short periods, usually one or a few years at most. Similarly, market risk predictions often operate within even shorter timeframes, frequently forecasting impacts within a single day or up to 10 days. However, the assessment of climate risks demands a broader temporal perspective, extending far beyond the relatively brief windows common in credit and market risk analyses. Climate risks necessitate predictions and evaluations over more extended periods, ranging from 5 to 10 years, and in many cases, even spanning hundreds of years. This extended time horizon is crucial for understanding the cumulative and evolving nature of climate change and its potential repercussions on various sectors and ecosystems. The longer time span associated with climate risks is primarily attributed to the persistent and gradual nature of climate change processes. Climate-related impacts unfold over extended periods as greenhouse gas concentrations accumulate in the atmosphere, leading to shifts in temperature, sea levels, and weather patterns. Additionally, the manifestation of certain climate-related risks, such as the melting of ice caps or changes in ocean currents, can have far-reaching consequences that unfold over decades or even centuries. This extended time perspective presents unique challenges for risk assessment methodologies. Predicting climate risks requires considering not only short-term fluctuations but also the cumulative effects of gradual changes and the potential for tipping points that may alter the trajectory of climate impacts. Moreover, the long-term nature of climate risks underscores the importance of incorporating sustainable and adaptive strategies into decision-making processes.

Third, the inherent uncertainty of climate risks stems from the intricate feedback loops within the Earth's climate system, the potential for nonlinear and abrupt changes, and the influence of human actions on a global scale. The non-linearity inherent in climate change introduces a crucial dimension to the understanding of climate risks. Unlike linear processes where changes occur in a predictable and proportional manner, climate change exhibits non-linear characteristics, meaning that the impacts may not follow a straightforward trajectory. This non-linearity suggests that climate risks are subject to varying degrees of change over time, and the consequences can escalate significantly when certain critical thresholds are surpassed, as critical thresholds represent tipping points in the climate system, beyond which the dynamics can shift rapidly and dramatically. Once these thresholds are exceeded, the severity and scope of climate risk impacts may undergo abrupt and sometimes irreversible changes. These tipping points can manifest in different aspects of the climate system, such as temperature levels, ice melt rates, or feedback mechanisms. The non-linearity adds complexity to risk assessments and planning, as traditional linear models may not adequately capture the dynamics of a changing climate.

Fourth, the global and systemic nature of climate change risks distinguishes them from many traditional financial risks. Climate change is not confined by geographic borders, and its impacts reverberate across various interconnected systems, including society, the economy, and the financial sector. This global scope introduces a level of complexity that goes beyond localized or sector-specific challenges and underscores the potential for systemic and cascading effects. Driven by the interconnected nature of the Earth's climate system, climate issues such as greenhouse gas emissions, rising temperatures, and shifts in weather patterns affect regions around the world. As a result, the risks associated with climate change have a global reach, impacting countries, communities, and ecosystems on a planetary scale. Climate risks are also intimately linked with societal dynamics. Changes in climate patterns can lead to disruptions in food and water availability, displacement of populations due to extreme weather events, and impacts on public health. These interconnected social dimensions amplify the challenges posed by climate change, as they require coordinated and global efforts to address issues like migration, resource scarcity, and societal resilience. The global economy is intricately connected with climate-dependent sectors such as agriculture, energy, and infrastructure. Climate-related events, such as hurricanes, floods, or droughts, can disrupt supply chains, damage infrastructure, and affect the overall productivity of economies. Furthermore, the financial system is not immune to the far-reaching impacts of climate change. Investments in sectors vulnerable to climate risks, such as fossil fuels or real estate in flood-prone areas, can face devaluation. Insurance companies may encounter increased claims due to more frequent and severe weather events. The interconnectedness of financial institutions means that climate-related shocks in one part of the world can have cascading effects on the entire financial system.

Hence, the considerable impact of climate risks stems from the elevated level of uncertainty, extended time spans with long-term consequences, non-linear dynamics, and the global, systemic nature of these risks. Together, these factors underscore the substantial threat climate risks pose to macroeconomic conditions and financial institutions. Addressing global and systemic climate risks requires coordinated efforts at the international level, involving governments, businesses, financial institutions, and communities. The interconnectedness of these risks emphasizes the importance of adopting a holistic and collaborative approach to building resilience, promoting sustainable practices, and mitigating the far-reaching consequences of climate change on a global scale.

3 Categories of Climate Risk

Climate risk is often understood in two main categories: physical risks and transition risks (Chen et al. 2022a).

3.1 *Climate Physical Risks*

Climate physical risk refers to the likelihood of adverse consequences resulting from various climate-related natural disasters and events, including extreme weather conditions, rising sea levels, changes in temperature patterns, ecological environmental pollution accidents, and depletion or scarcity of natural resources (Chen et al. 2022a). Among these, natural disasters including floods, typhoons, blizzards, droughts, and wildfires occur relatively more frequently and therefore have a more direct and significant impact on human production and life.

Numerous international institutions have extensively examined the correlation between natural disasters and the resulting losses. A prevailing consensus suggests that, in comparison to historical trends, the frequency and severity of extreme natural disasters have increased due to global warming and climate deterioration. An illustrative example is the analysis conducted by the International Monetary Fund, which examines global total losses and insurance losses from natural disasters spanning 1980 to 2018. The findings reveal a doubling of insurance claims attributed to natural disaster losses by 2018 when contrasted with the 1980s. Further substantiating this trend, BlackRock integrated the hurricane model of the Rhodium Group with its Commercial Mortgage-Backed Securities (CMBS) database, comprising approximately 60,000 commercial properties. The results indicate a 137% increase in the median risk of any of these properties being impacted by a Category 4 or 5 hurricane since 1980. Consequently, over an extended period, losses incurred from climate physical risks exhibit a discernible upward trajectory.

The World Economic Forum, in its Global Risks Report of 2020, highlights a noteworthy shift wherein the top five global risks for the ensuing decade are exclusively linked to environmental and climate concerns for the first time (World Economic Forum 2020). Notably, extreme weather events and natural disasters associated with climate physical risk ranked first and third, respectively (World Economic Forum 2020). A subsequent research report from the World Economic Forum in early 2021 reaffirmed that environmental and climate risks persist as the foremost concerns for human society in the coming decade, in terms of both probability and impact. Among these risks, those linked to extreme weather events retain the foremost position and warrant heightened priority (World Economic Forum 2021).

3.2 Climate Transition Risks

Climate transition risk refers to the economic or financial risks that arise from changes in policies to address climate change, technological innovations, shifts in market sentiment, and changes in consumer preferences (Chen et al. 2022a). For example, the impact of clean energy on traditional coal and oil companies, and the increase in operating costs for carbon-intensive companies due to carbon taxes, are considered transition risks (Acharya et al. 2023). It is evident that the sources of transition risk mainly involve human factors such as policies, technologies, and ideologies that undergo changes in response to climate change and environmental challenges.

During the transition process, economies are confronted primarily with the challenge of replacing "high-carbon" assets with "low-carbon" alternatives. The premature phase-out of "high-carbon" assets still within their effective lifespan results in their classification as stranded assets, presenting a significant problem. The Network for Greening the Financial System (NGFS), comprising central banks and regulatory authorities, has posited that transition risk primarily manifests as market risk and credit risk through the stranding of assets (NGFS 2019). Notably, stranded assets stemming from carbon-intensive industries not only impact their immediate upstream and downstream sectors but also have a ripple effect on companies associated with these assets. The reevaluation of the market value of stranded assets holds the potential to influence the balance sheets of financial institutions, consequently impinging on the ability of carbon-intensive industries to secure financing within the financial system. Given the crossholdings and mutual investments between financial institutions and carbon-intensive sectors, risks are amplified through a "cyclical feedback" transmission path, leading to a "climate Minsky moment" and triggering systemic financial risks (Oguntuase 2020).

The NGFS (Network for Greening the Financial System) released a set of reference scenarios in June 2020 to guide financial institutions in assessing climate-related risks. These scenarios, including the orderly transition, disorderly transition, and greenhouse world, help organizations evaluate their resilience under different potential future conditions (NGFS 2019). The scenarios provide a structured framework for risk management and stress testing exercises, enabling financial institutions to identify vulnerabilities, plan for contingencies, and make informed strategic decisions in the face of climate-related uncertainties (Acharya et al. 2023; Monasterolo et al. 2023).

In terms of orderly transition, an orderly transition envisions a smooth and well-managed shift towards a low-carbon economy. This scenario involves the adoption of effective and timely policies, technological advancements, and international cooperation to mitigate climate change. In an orderly transition, financial markets and institutions are better positioned to adapt to changes, with a reduced likelihood of abrupt shocks or disruptions. In contrast, a disorderly transition refers to a scenario in which the shift to a low-carbon economy is abrupt, uncoordinated, and marked by unexpected policy changes. This may result in market volatility, asset value fluctuations, and increased uncertainty for financial institutions. Disorderly transitions can pose significant challenges for risk management and may lead to financial instability if not appropriately addressed. The term "greenhouse world" describes an outcome resulting from a lack of policy adoption and concerted global efforts to address climate change. In this scenario, insufficient measures lead to a natural temperature increase of 4–5 °C. Such a situation implies severe and widespread environmental consequences, including more frequent and intense extreme weather events. Financial institutions operating in a greenhouse world would face heightened risks due to the physical impacts of climate change and the lack of preparedness.

By delineating these categories, the NGFS aims to facilitate a more comprehensive understanding of the diverse challenges associated with the transition to a sustainable future. This nuanced approach recognizes that the nature of the transition itself can significantly impact the financial landscape, influencing factors such as asset valuations, regulatory environments, and overall market stability. As financial institutions increasingly integrate climate risk considerations into their operations, the use of well-defined scenarios becomes a crucial tool for navigating the complex landscape of transition risks and ensuring the long-term resilience of the global financial system.

3.3 Relationship Between Physical Risk and Transition Risk

The distinction between climate physical risk and climate transition risk provides valuable insights into the complex dynamics of climate change and its impact on various sectors, including finance. These two types of risks embody different aspects of the challenges associated with climate change and represent contrasting approaches to addressing them.

Climate physical risk encompasses the costs and consequences of the passive acceptance or inadequate response to climate change. This risk is associated with the direct impacts of climate change on physical assets, operations, and infrastructure. As global temperatures rise, the frequency and severity of natural disasters, such as hurricanes, floods, and wildfires, may increase. The expense of dealing with these events and the damages they cause constitutes climate physical risk. It is widely acknowledged that an inability to effectively curb the continuous rise in global temperatures may lead to more frequent, severe, and destructive natural disasters, establishing a positive correlation between warming and physical risk.

In contrast, climate transition risk represents the costs and challenges associated with proactive efforts to actively address and mitigate climate change. This risk arises from the transition to a low-carbon economy, changes in regulatory frameworks, and shifts in market dynamics. Organizations and industries that are heavily dependent on fossil fuels or other high-emission activities may face challenges in adapting to new policies, technologies, and market expectations. However, successfully navigating this transition can lead to more sustainable and resilient business practices. Transition risk therefore emerges as a mechanism to mitigate the hazards associated with temperature increases, revealing a negative correlation with warming.

Hence, from a theoretical standpoint, a trade-off exists between climate physical risk and transition risk. The trade-off arises from the fact that actively addressing climate change through mitigation and adaptation measures can help mitigate the physical risks associated with temperature increases. In other words, there is a negative correlation between the efforts to address climate change (transition risk) and the severity of climate-induced damages (physical risk). Research conducted by the UK insurance company AVIVA, using a climate risk assessment model developed by Carbon Delta, supports this theoretical perspective. The findings based on examining the impact of climate transition risk and physical risk on its held assets suggest that in scenarios with higher temperature increases (e.g., 3 °C and 4 °C), more than 95 percent the impact on AVIVA's assets originated from physical risk. Conversely, in scenarios with lower temperature increases (e.g., 1.5 °C and 2 °C), the influence of transition risk and physical risk was approximately equal.

For businesses and financial institutions, understanding this trade-off is essential for effective risk management and strategic planning. It emphasizes the need for a balanced and comprehensive approach that considers both the physical impacts of climate change and the measures taken to transition to a more sustainable and resilient future. As the global community increasingly recognizes the urgency of addressing climate change, this trade-off perspective provides a valuable framework for decision-makers across various sectors.

4 Climate Risk Assessment

Climate risk assessment serves as a prevalent method for evaluating the potential impacts and risks of climate change on specific regions, industries, or organizations. The quantification and prediction of climate risks play a vital role in enabling governments, businesses, and other stakeholders to gain a comprehensive understanding and effectively manage climate-related challenges. Various models are commonly employed for climate risk assessment, including climate risk assessment models, climate risk index models, climate risk scenario models, financial climate risk models, supply chain and business continuity models, as well as social vulnerability and adaptability models. These tools typically necessitate a substantial amount of data, specialized knowledge, and computational capabilities for effective utilization. Climate scientists, government agencies, research institutions, and businesses frequently deploy these models to enhance their insights into climate risks.

Given the variances in methodologies and procedural steps across different levels of assessment, this section focuses on introducing the content and model tools employed for risk assessment at the national, regional, and enterprise levels.

4.1 At the National Level

At the national level, climate risk assessment is typically extensive and comprehensive, aiming to evaluate the impact of climate change on the entire country. It primarily includes measurements of physical risks and transition risks. Common model tools for climate risk assessment at the national level are also employed.

For national-level physical risk assessment, the first approach is Comprehensive Climate Impact Assessment. This measurement involves collecting and analyzing historical meteorological and climate data by relevant national agencies to understand climate change trends within the country. It assesses potential physical risks the country may face, including extreme climate events (such as floods, droughts, storms), sea-level rise, land degradation, etc. Further analysis examines the impact of physical risks on the ecological environment and various aspects of the national economy. The second approach is Greenhouse Gas Emission Measurement. In line with the imperative to construct a low-carbon society and implement green development concepts, measuring and assessing a country's emissions of greenhouse gases, such as carbon dioxide, methane, and nitrogen oxides, becomes increasingly important. This measurement aims to identify emission sources, including energy production, industrial processes, and land-use changes. It involves a comparison of emissions with international commitments and agreements, such as the Paris Agreement, and an analysis of trends in greenhouse gas emissions within the country.

In terms of measuring the national level transition risk, the first dimension is Energy and Resource Analysis. This assessment initiates by evaluating the country's energy structure, including the utilization of both fossil fuels and renewable energy sources. It identifies the prevailing energy consumption landscape and usage trends and analyzes potential avenues for enhancing energy efficiency and promoting the adoption of renewable energy. Building upon this analysis, the assessment delves into the supply and demand dynamics of energy and resources. It determines the developmental trajectory of energy transition and conducts an evaluation of the economic benefits or losses associated with a nationwide energy transition. This comprehensive analysis facilitates informed decision-making during the energy transition process. The second dimension is Policy and Regulation Assessment. The transitional process often introduces uncertainties in policies and regulations, posing inherent risks. This facet of the assessment involves a meticulous analysis of climate policies and regulations, including aspects like carbon pricing, emission targets, and renewable energy policies. The evaluation extends to understanding the impact of these policies and regulations on various facets of the country, spanning the economy, energy sector, environment, and society at large. This aids in identifying challenges and opportunities within policies, staying abreast of changes and developments across diverse domains, and making timely adjustments.

The third dimension, Climate Financing and Economic Risk Assessment, represents a comprehensive analysis that delves into the financial implications of climate-related risks on both the private and public sectors. This multifaceted examination is crucial for understanding the potential economic impacts of climate change and for developing strategies to enhance financial resilience. Taking China as an example, this dimension becomes particularly significant due to its unique national conditions, including state ownership of key energy resources like coal and oil. The national-level assessment of climate transition risks therefore requires a thorough examination of climate financing risks, including the exposure of financial institutions and investors to high-carbon industries, the financial viability of investments in sectors that may be adversely affected by the transition to a low-carbon economy, as well as state-owned enterprises involved in these sectors. It also considers the potential for stranded assets and asset devaluation due to changes in market dynamics or regulatory frameworks. Furthermore, the assessment goes beyond the immediate financial implications and rigorously analyzes the broader impact of climate-related risks on the national economy. This encompasses evaluating the effects on employment, industrial structure, and fiscal conditions. For instance, a shift away from high-carbon industries may lead to job displacement and require strategies for reskilling and retraining the workforce. It also necessitates a careful examination of the overall economic structure and potential fiscal challenges associated with the transition. The Climate Financing and Economic Risk Assessment, therefore, provides a holistic view of the financial landscape in the face of climate change, emphasizing the interconnectedness between financial, economic, and environmental considerations.

4.2 At the Regional Level

Conducting climate risk assessment at the regional level involves considering more specific and localized factors to evaluate the impact of climate change on specific areas. Similar to the national level assessment, at this level, the assessment includes measurement of both physical and transition risks.

In addressing climate physical risks, one approach involves the collection and analysis of meteorological and climate data within a specific region. This encompasses diverse parameters such as rainfall, temperature, wind speed, and more. By identifying climate change trends over the past few decades, this approach aims to evaluate the likelihood of extreme weather events like floods, droughts, hurricanes, and others occurring within the designated region. An alternative strategy integrates Geographic Information System (GIS) technology, utilizing spatial analysis to identify potential climate risks. For instance, it may assess coastal erosion induced by sea-level rise or flood risks arising from increased rainfall. Through this approach, risk maps are generated, providing a visual representation of areas and infrastructure under threat. On the other hand, Ecosystem and Resource Assessment primarily focuses on evaluating the impact of climate change on regional ecosystems and biodiversity. This comprehensive assessment spans diverse ecosystems, including forests, wetlands, and oceans. The analysis investigates the potential threats these impacts pose to resource supply and the availability of water resources. By examining the intricate interplay between climate change and ecosystems, this assessment sheds light on the vulnerabilities and challenges faced by regional biodiversity and vital resources.

In the measurement of transition risk, the following methodologies are employed. The first approach is Asset Vulnerability Assessment. This assessment concentrates on a specific evaluation of the vulnerability of various asset types within the region, including real estate, agriculture, infrastructure, and more. By assessing which assets are more susceptible to climate change risks and gauging their level of exposure, vulnerabilities are identified. The second approach is Social and Economic Impact Assessment. The assessment of social and economic impacts involves comprehending the potential effects of climate risks on employment, health, poverty rates, and other societal and economic facets within the region. Vulnerability assessments of social groups are conducted to pinpoint which groups are more likely to be affected by climate risks. The third method is Development of Adaptation Strategies. The development of adaptive strategies is instrumental in mitigating climate risks within the region. This may involve enhancing water resource management, constructing flood defenses, adjusting agricultural planting seasons, and other tailored measures. Comprehensive risk management plans, incorporating both emergency response measures and long-term climate change adaptation strategies, are formulated based on regional variations in climate risk characteristics. In summary, these methods can be customized according to specific regional conditions to better understand and manage climate risks. This enhances the region's climate resilience and helps mitigate the potential impacts of climate change.

4.3 At the Enterprise Level

Climate risk assessment at the enterprise level aims to evaluate the potential impact of climate change on business operations and strategies. Certain aspects from the national and regional levels are also applicable at the enterprise level. This includes content related to both physical risk measurement and transition risk measurement, along with commonly used model tools at the enterprise level.

The first aspect of enterprise-level physical risk measurement is Climate Risk Identification. Similar to the identification method at the regional level, this involves collecting meteorological and climate data to comprehend climate trends and assess the likelihood of extreme events in the location where the enterprise operates. Alternatively, GIS data can be used to identify potential physical risks, such as floods, hurricanes, and coastal erosion. The second aspect is Greenhouse Gas Emission Measurement and Management. In comparison to national-level greenhouse gas measurement methods, the assessment at the enterprise level adopts a more granular approach. It primarily evaluates the greenhouse gas emissions of enterprises based on classification standards for direct and indirect emissions (e.g., supply chain emissions). This enables the development of tailored greenhouse gas management strategies specific to the enterprise. At the enterprise level, these measurements and assessments play a pivotal role in enhancing the understanding of climate risks and formulating strategies to mitigate their impact on business operations. The granularity of these assessments allows for more precise and targeted risk management, contributing to the overall resilience of the enterprise in the face of a changing climate.

For enterprise-level transition risk measurement, there are three major strategies. The first is Energy and Resource Management. Similar to the national-level energy resource analysis, this method primarily analyzes the enterprise's energy usage to identify opportunities for improving energy efficiency and incorporating renewable energy. It facilitates the judicious allocation of fossil and renewable energy during the transition process, thereby reducing economic risks associated with resource utilization. The second strategy is Climate Policy Tracking. Enterprises must proactively track and comprehend climate policies and regulations relevant to their operations. Analyzing the potential impacts of these policies on business and financial conditions is essential. This involves mitigating risks associated with climate policy uncertainties and ensuring steadfast compliance with regulations. Energy-related enterprises, in particular, should vigilantly monitor the release of climate-related policies. The third strategy is Opportunity Assessment. Given that climate-related risks can impact the financial and strategic aspects of enterprises, including asset depreciation, supply chain disruptions, and increased insurance costs, opportunity assessment becomes crucial. This involves identifying operational risks and losses that enterprises may encounter while concurrently analyzing the potential for new market demands, innovative products, and business opportunities arising from climate change. The last strategy is Adaptation Strategy Development. Enterprises are required to formulate adaptation measures and emergency plans as integral components of climate risk management strategies, seamlessly integrating them into the overall enterprise strategy. Additionally, reporting climate risks and response measures to stakeholders enhances internal and external awareness of climate risks, fostering transparency and collaboration.

At the enterprise level, these comprehensive strategies not only serve to mitigate climate-related risks but also position businesses to harness potential opportunities emerging from the evolving climate landscape. The proactive approach to energy and resource management, policy tracking, opportunity assessment, and adaptation strategy development contributes to the overall resilience and sustainability of enterprises in the face of a changing climate.

5 Climate Risk and Macroeconomy

As previously mentioned, climate risk exerts a far-reaching and profound impact on the macroeconomy, influencing various facets such as the real economy, agricultural sector, and financial markets.

5.1 *Real Economy*

Climate change, water scarcity, degradation of natural capital, natural disasters, and air, water, and soil pollution are among the factors with direct negative impacts on the real economy. Climate change, in particular, amplifies the frequency of natural disasters, resulting in diminished production capacity, heightened costs, labor shortages, premature obsolescence of fixed assets, structural damage, and decreased business demand. Physical risks can be broadly categorized into two groups based on their effects and impact timelines. One group involves risks with relatively short-term occurrences but substantial impacts on the real economy, causing significant economic losses, such as floods and hurricanes. The other group comprises risks that evolve gradually, with less pronounced short-term effects but considerable long-term constraints on economic growth potential and output capacity, significantly affecting the real economy. These risks, marked by broad impact and large scope, include phenomena like global warming and rising sea levels driven by greenhouse gas emissions. From an industry standpoint, physical risks will notably affect sectors such as real estate, oil and natural gas, agriculture, forestry, electricity, and healthcare.

Factors such as policy adjustments, technological replacements, and shifts in consumer preferences lead to increased greenhouse gas emission pricing, changes in market demand and structure, resulting in heightened production costs, reduced profits, and elevated default risks for businesses. For instance, under intensified regulatory scrutiny, high-pollution-emitting companies may face environmental penalties and increased costs for purchasing emissions quotas, contributing to elevated operating costs, dwindling profits, and diminished valuations. Likewise, the ongoing introduction of clean energy policies exerts transformation pressures on traditional energy sources like coal and oil, as well as their downstream and related industries. The upgrading of equipment necessitates new technologies and machinery, contributing to increased costs for technology research and development and the acquisition of new equipment.

The widespread acceptance of the new development concept has ushered in green, environmentally friendly, and low-carbon practices as new consumption patterns. Consumers increasingly favor low-carbon and eco-friendly products in their daily consumption, leading to a gradual decline in demand for traditional high-energy-consuming products. This shift impacts the sales, operating income, and profits of traditional industries. From an industry perspective, transition risk significantly affects sectors grappling with excess capacity, such as coal, cement, steel, and smelting (Zhou et al. 2023).

5.2 Agricultural Economy

The development of the agricultural economy faces constraints from various factors, with climate risks emerging as the most direct and substantial negative influence. Particularly, as global climate change intensifies and climate risks continue to escalate, the economic repercussions are garnering increased attention.

First, escalating climate risks will directly impact the agricultural economy. Agriculture relies on natural forces such as biology, solar energy, soil, and climate in production activities. In essence, climate conditions are direct input factors for agricultural production. Therefore, climate change will directly affect the agricultural economy, including both crop cultivation and animal husbandry. For crop cultivation, heightened climate risks will elevate the likelihood of crop spike sterility and reduce assimilate accumulation, leading to decreased crop yields and losses in the agricultural economy. In animal husbandry, increased climate risks will impact the development and reproduction of livestock, resulting in a reduction in livestock and related product output. Hence, rising climate risks will directly and adversely affect the growth and reproduction of crops and livestock.

Second, heightened climate risks will increase the probability and severity of associated natural disasters, negatively impacting the agricultural economy. Results from disaster economics models indicate that climate change augments the mean, variance, and correlation of the risk distribution of natural disasters, thereby increasing the probability and extent of losses. Empirical studies also reveal a significant positive correlation between global warming and the probability and severity of natural disasters such as droughts and floods. In terms of the impact on the economy, neoclassical growth models point out that natural disasters directly damage output, leading to negative economic impacts. For the agricultural economy, natural disasters cause direct harm to crops and livestock, resulting in substantial losses.

Climate risks and related natural disasters may influence the input of agricultural production factors, causing adverse effects on the agricultural economy. According to neoclassical economic growth theory, in addition to directly causing output losses, climate risks and related natural disasters will adversely affect land use, capital stock, labor quantity, and efficiency. This, in turn, increases the marginal cost of agricultural production, negatively affecting the development of the agricultural economy. For instance, rising climate risks may reduce water resources, directly impacting agricultural production and negatively affecting the storage of agricultural products.

Furthermore, increased climate risks may diminish the efficiency of labor, with evidence suggesting a decrease in labor hours in industries, including agriculture, significantly affected by climate risks. The decline in labor efficiency in the manufacturing industry due to increased climate risks results in losses amounting to 3.5%-4.73% of total manufacturing output. Although there is currently no specific study analyzing the impact of climate risks on agricultural labor efficiency, agriculture is a vital part of the economy. From the conclusions of existing related studies, it can be inferred that rising climate risks will reduce agricultural labor efficiency, ultimately affecting agricultural output.

Additionally, it is crucial to note that the impact of climate risks on the development of the agricultural economy is heterogeneous across regions. The heterogeneous impact of climate risks on the development of the agricultural economy emphasizes the importance of considering regional disparities and vulnerabilities. This variability stems from a combination of socioeconomic factors and geographical characteristics that distinguish regions, influencing their ability to adapt and respond to climate challenges. In regions characterized by lower per capita income levels, several challenges exacerbate the impact of climate risks on the agricultural economy. One critical aspect is the relatively inadequate infrastructure for agriculture, forestry, and water resources. Limited financial resources hinder investments in modern technologies, irrigation systems, and resilient agricultural practices that can mitigate the adverse effects of climate change. As a result, these regions may face heightened vulnerabilities and reduced adaptive capacity, amplifying the negative consequences of climate risks on agricultural productivity. Furthermore, awareness and the ability to cope with climate risks are often constrained in lower-income regions. Limited access to information, education, and technology impedes the development and implementation of effective adaptation strategies. Farmers and local communities may lack the knowledge and resources needed to adopt climate-resilient farming techniques or invest in sustainable land and water management practices. This, in turn, intensifies the impact of climate risks on agricultural livelihoods and food security in these regions. Conversely, the geographical distribution of lower-income regions, often situated in warmer areas, exposes them to a higher susceptibility to the negative impacts of climate risks. Warmer climates may contribute to the exacerbation of heat stress, water scarcity, and the prevalence of pests and diseases, all of which can significantly affect crop yields and livestock production. The combination of economic constraints and climatic conditions creates a compounding effect, making these regions more vulnerable to the multifaceted challenges posed by climate change.

5.3 *Financial Markets*

The impact of climate risk on financial markets can be analyzed by examining its effects on the banking, insurance, and securities markets.

5.3.1 The Banking Industry

The influence of climate change on the banking industry is mainly observed in aspects including credit risk, market risk, operational risk, and legal risk.

Credit risk

In terms of credit risk, climate-related financial risks have the potential to directly or indirectly devalue collateral assets, impair borrowers' debt repayment capacity, increase default probability and default losses, consequently heightening credit risk. Credit risk manifests in two key aspects. Firstly, the physical risks arising from climate change place an increased financial burden on businesses, elevating the banking sector's risk exposure. For instance, the heightened frequency and intensity of floods and storms concurrently raise the likelihood of properties, both residential and commercial, in flood-prone areas being submerged. Second, the accelerated depreciation of assets due to chronic climate change amplifies expectations of future losses. As highlighted in the "Bulletin of Marine Ecology and Environment Status of China in 2018," 37.6% of the 471 monitored cities in China experienced acid rain, predominantly in the region east of the Yun-Gui Plateau and south of the Yangtze River (MEEC 2018). Prolonged exposure to acid rain can expedite the corrosion of structures like bridges and buildings, potentially necessitating the repricing or even discounted sale of asset prices. If these physical assets serve as collateral for loans, it may escalate the risk of default losses when borrowers are unable to meet loan repayments. Consequently, natural disasters resulting from climate change, by affecting product sales, diminishing business revenue, impacting profit margins, cash flow, and repayment capabilities, pose risks of damage, destruction, or loss to physical assets used as collateral. This increased vulnerability raises the likelihood of defaults, contributing to an elevation in credit risk for banks.

In the real estate industry, the reliance on real assets, particularly properties, as collateral for bank loans introduces significant challenges to the mitigation of project loan risks. This reliance amplifies the default loss rate, especially in the face of extreme weather events that pose a constant threat. The potential for losses or complete destruction of real assets during such events translates into substantial economic setbacks for asset owners. The aftermath of extreme weather events not only impacts the physical integrity of real assets but also creates a ripple effect in the financial realm. These events undermine the repayment capacity and willingness of asset owners who serve as borrowers. The resulting economic strain on asset owners contributes to an elevated probability and loss rate of defaults for banks, impacting the overall stability of the financial system.

Moreover, in the credit business, banks may extend loans to enterprises with high pollution, high emissions, and traditional business models. These enterprises face transformation risks triggered by shifts in environmental protection policies. The consequences of these policy changes include business interruptions, declining revenues, and devaluation of assets, collectively making the repayment of loans challenging for these entities. Illustrating with the coal industry, the transition to a low-carbon economy curtails the demand for fossil fuels, leaving some fossil fuels with proven reserves untapped and transforming them into stranded assets. Research indicates that, under China's nationally determined contributions scenario, the stranded assets of the Chinese coal-fired power industry are anticipated to reach a staggering

$90 billion by 2030. The current financial landscape of coal-fired power companies is characterized by a debt-to-equity ratio ranging between 60 and 80%, with a substantial portion of this debt originating from state-owned commercial banks. The potential implementation of government policies mandating the closure of coal-fired power plants poses a significant financial risk for lending banks, potentially leading to substantial losses. Beyond direct financial implications, the impact of low-carbon transformation extends to the broader supply chain. The shift towards low-carbon practices may elevate the operating costs of enterprises, particularly in industries heavily reliant on coal, such as cement and steel production. As emission reduction costs and carbon prices increase, the use of coal in manufacturing processes becomes more expensive. This not only diminishes the profitability of manufacturers but also raises costs for downstream enterprises and distributors, amplifying the likelihood of defaults within the supply chain.

This scenario highlights a dual challenge for banks: the exposure to heightened default risks due to the vulnerability of real assets to extreme weather events and the added risk associated with lending to enterprises facing environmental transformation challenges. As a result, banks must carefully assess and adapt their lending practices, considering the evolving landscape of environmental regulations and the potential impacts of climate-related events on the real assets securing their loans. This strategic evaluation is crucial for maintaining financial resilience and sustainability in the face of climate-induced uncertainties in the real estate sector and high emission sectors.

The interconnected nature of these challenges emphasizes the need for a comprehensive and strategic approach to navigate the complexities of transitioning industries. Lending institutions must proactively assess the potential risks associated with stranded assets, policy changes, and shifts in operating costs to safeguard their financial stability. Additionally, fostering collaboration with industry stakeholders and exploring innovative financial instruments can contribute to a more resilient financial system in the face of transformative changes brought about by the low-carbon transition.

Market risk

In terms of market risk, the impact of transitioning away from carbon-intensive industries resonates profoundly in the energy sector, causing substantial fluctuations in the prices of commodities, corporate bonds, stocks, and derivatives (Andersson 2023). The far-reaching consequences of climate change extend beyond mere market dynamics, including infrastructural vulnerabilities, economic deceleration, heightened unemployment, and inflationary pressures. These ramifications reverberate through the financial landscape, translating into credit rating downgrades for both national and local governments, increased sovereign risks, and exacerbated price volatility in national bonds. This, in turn, catalyzes the devaluation of government bonds held by banks, amplifying the challenges faced by financial institutions (Chen et al. 2022b).

The intricacies of this transitional phase are further compounded by significant adjustments in policy frameworks and changes in portfolio compositions

(Ren et al. 2023). Such changes can give rise to inconsistencies between investment portfolios and the anticipated trajectories of climate-related developments. As economies shift from high-pollution, high-emission models to more sustainable, low-carbon paradigms, banks find themselves navigating an environment characterized by heightened market risk. The specter of climate change further looms over financial institutions as it contributes to escalating input prices for energy, water, and insurance, thereby increasing the operational costs incurred by banks.

Weather events emerge as pivotal players in this intricate narrative, wielding the potential to induce drastic fluctuations in commodity prices and elevating the foreign exchange risk for banks. Take, for instance, the impact of drought—a phenomenon that not only curtails agricultural output but also amplifies the costs associated with restoring land productivity. This dual effect compounds the challenges faced by banks, as it not only undermines international competitiveness by diminishing the prices of agricultural products but also contributes to a reduction in exports. Should the influence of the agricultural sector on the trade balance outweigh that of other sectors, the outcome may manifest as trade deficits and consequent domestic real exchange rate depreciation. The interconnectedness of weather changes and commodity price dynamics creates a scenario where fluctuations in one country can trigger relative price changes in commodities, leading to increased macroeconomic variability. This, in turn, leads to greater exchange rate volatility, consequently expanding the market risk exposure of banks. In essence, the evolving climate landscape intertwines with market intricacies, necessitating a nuanced understanding and proactive risk management strategies for financial institutions navigating these challenging waters.

Operational risk

The ever-changing nature of weather conditions poses an array of operational risks to commercial banks, impacting internal processes, personnel, and systems, potentially leading to business interruptions and losses. Particularly, severe weather events can exert a significant toll on business continuity, affecting the very infrastructure that sustains the operational backbone of bank branches, offices, information networks, and other critical facilities. Adverse weather conditions, ranging from extreme temperatures to storms and flooding, can result in power outages and network interruptions, creating scenarios where data loss becomes a tangible operational risk.

Examining specific climatic trends, the "2019 China Climate Bulletin" shows that the national average temperature in 2019 was 0.79°C higher than the annual average, marking it as the fifth warmest year since 1951 (China Meteorological Administration 2019). The average precipitation was also 2.5% higher than the annual average. The intensification of the urban heat island effect further exacerbates challenges for banks, as the demand for cooling and drainage in bank buildings rises. The condition of related infrastructure directly influences the efficiency of banking services and operations. For example, climate-related operational risks affecting bank information data centers include rising temperatures, which can decrease the efficiency of IT hardware and increase component failure rates. Flooding poses a threat to equipment and may result in data loss, while storms can damage overhead cables, leading to business interruptions.

The operational risks associated with climate change extend beyond the immediate impact on physical infrastructure. Transformation risks stemming from climate change can expose banking institutions to reputation losses. For instance, banks engaged in credit operations that support businesses with high pollution and emission levels may draw heightened scrutiny from stakeholders and regulatory authorities during external audits and inspections. This increased scrutiny not only poses compliance challenges but also introduces reputational risks that can erode the standing of banking institutions in the eyes of customers, investors, and the public.

Banks are thus confronted with the imperative to fortify their resilience against these climate-induced operational risks. This involves not only bolstering physical infrastructure but also adopting adaptive measures and robust contingency plans to mitigate potential disruptions. As climate change continues to unfold, the proactive management of operational risks emerging from weather-related events becomes integral to the long-term sustainability and reputation of commercial banks.

Legal risk

This evolving landscape of climate-related legislation places a renewed focus on commercial banks, prompting them to reassess and manage legal risks associated with climate change. In response to the pressing challenges posed by climate change, China has taken significant steps to address the issue through the enactment of laws and regulations. Key examples among these initiatives are the "National Climate Change Plan (2014–2020)" and revisions to critical legislation such as the "Air Pollution Prevention and Control Law" and the "Energy Conservation Law." These legal frameworks represent an enhanced effort to strengthen climate change planning and enhance the construction of a judicial system capable of comprehensively addressing climate-related issues.

One such area of concern is liability risk, where banks may be held accountable for the consequences of climate change or face repercussions for failing to assume corresponding obligations. In cases where banks are deemed responsible, they may be obligated to pay compensation or fines. The growing awareness among investors regarding information disclosure further underscores the responsibility of banks to incorporate the impacts of climate change into routine investment information disclosures. Failure to do so may expose banks to legal lawsuits, as illustrated by the 2017 case involving the Commonwealth Bank of Australia (CBA). In this case, shareholders sued CBA, alleging insufficient disclosure of climate-related risks in the 2016 annual report, a violation of Australian corporate law. The shareholders argued that CBA should have disclosed climate change-related risks to investors, given its awareness or should-have-known status regarding the potential impact on entities with economic interests tied to CBA.

Beyond information disclosure, commercial banks providing consulting services to clients must navigate the intricacies of climate change impacts. However, there is a recognized issue of insufficient risk awareness within the consulting-type intermediary businesses of these banks in China. As professional advisers, banks bear the responsibility to consider the implications of climate change and provide advice on relevant and significant risks based on clients' actual situations, even when not explicitly requested. Neglecting to address climate change in consulting services may expose banks to serious and irreversible negative impacts on clients. Furthermore, such negligence could be construed as professional negligence, amplifying legal risks associated with consulting businesses.

In light of these legal considerations, commercial banks are compelled to proactively integrate climate-related risk assessments into their operations, demonstrating a commitment to legal compliance, responsible investment practices, and client-oriented risk management. As climate change continues to be a focal point of global concern, navigating the legal landscape becomes an essential component of sustainable and resilient banking practices in China and beyond.

5.3.2 The Insurance Industry

The relationship between the insurance industry and climate change is worth significant attention, given that the insurance sector plays a direct role in underwriting losses arising from a spectrum of risk events, with climate change at the forefront. More than a decade ago, scholars foresaw that climate change represented the foremost risk confronting the insurance industry, arguing that its impact would be substantial and far-reaching. The United Nations Environment Programme (UNEP) anticipates that by 2040, insurance payouts stemming from climate change could skyrocket to a staggering $1 trillion annually (Dlugolecki 2006). The attribution of responsibility for climate change within the context of insurance is poised to emerge as a major issue in climate policy and negotiations.

For a prolonged period, climate change and its associated risks were relegated to the periphery by the insurance industry and the broader financial sector, considered a distant and inconsequential concern. However, a paradigm shift has begun, spurred by three pivotal events that have altered this perception. First, in 2015, the Bank of England coined the term "Tragedy of the horizon" to describe the strategic challenge of climate change for the financial industry. This underscored the notion that waiting until climate change becomes a decisive issue for financial stability would be too late. Subsequently, the Bank of England has released multiple reports and statements, highlighting the urgency of addressing climate change and its implications for financial stability. Second, the establishment of the Green Finance Study Group (GFSG) of the Group of Twenty (G20) in January 2016 signaled the recognition of major national financial regulatory authorities toward climate change. Third, in June 2017, the Task Force on Climate-related Financial Disclosures (TCFD) of the Financial Stability Board introduced a framework on climate-related risks and opportunities in financial disclosures. This framework aims to provide clear, comparable, and consistent information, signaling the formation of global standards on climate change issues. The impact of climate change on the insurance industry is particularly evident in areas such as underwriting losses, investment losses, operating risks, premium pricing risk, interest rate risk, and liability risk.

As global standards solidify and awareness of climate-related risks grows, insurers find themselves at the forefront of adapting their practices. The industry is not only tasked with assessing the risks associated with climate change but also with innovating solutions and products that can withstand the evolving climate landscape. From reevaluating premium structures to devising comprehensive risk management strategies, the insurance sector is compelled to proactively engage with climate change, recognizing its transformative impact on the industry's dynamics and long-term sustainability.

Underwriting losses

Asset risk in the insurance industry primarily revolves around the potential challenges faced by users of insurance funds in meeting their contractual obligations. This risk is exacerbated by the threat of adverse changes in the creditworthiness of these users, leading to unforeseen losses for insurance companies. The occurrence of natural disasters further amplifies this risk, affecting the normal operations of companies invested in by insurance institutions. Such events can result in diminished corporate output, reduced profitability, heightened solvency pressure, and an increased likelihood of default, ultimately elevating the credit risk faced by insurance companies.

One specific facet of asset risk for insurance companies is underwriting losses, encompassing both direct and indirect losses. Direct underwriting losses, such as those stemming from global climate-related natural disasters, have exhibited a concerning trend. According to data from the NatCatSERVICE natural disaster research platform, the number of geophysical disasters such as earthquakes has remained relatively stable, while the number of climate-related natural disaster loss events has significantly increased. The annual average insurance losses from these events have surged from approximately \$4.5 billion in the 1980s to around \$13.6 billion from 2015 to 2018 (adjusted for inflation to the 2018 price level). The escalation of losses from weather-related disasters is attributed not only to expanded risk exposure due to economic growth and urbanization but also significantly to the impact of climate change. For instance, a rise in global temperatures by 1–2 °C is projected to substantially increase losses to US crops, requiring a significant surge of 22% to 57% in crop insurance rates to cover these losses. Moreover, climate change influences not just property insurance but also has broader implications, impacting human health and mortality rates. An analysis of panel data from various US states from 1968 to 2002 shows that for each additional day with an average temperature above 90 °F, the age-adjusted mortality rate increases by 0.11%. Based on this prediction, climate change is expected to increase the age-adjusted mortality rate by 3% by the year 2100.

Indirect underwriting losses add another layer to the complexity of asset risk. These losses manifest through "intermediary channels" and are often associated with climate-related risks. The 2011 floods in Thailand, for instance, resulted in \$45 billion in economic losses and \$12 billion in insurance payouts. A significant portion of these payouts was attributed to "second-order effects," such as disruptions in the supply chains of global manufacturing companies. Among them, the business interruption insurance of the insurer, Lohse, paid out $2.2 billion. Climate change can also impact food security, leading to increased payouts for insurance products in areas such as agriculture, trade logistics, terrorism, and political risks, resulting in additional indirect losses for insurance companies.

Investment losses

The second facet of the asset risk confronted by insurance companies is investment losses. Investment losses in the insurance industry are shaped by a complex interplay of factors, including the impact of climate change on global economic dynamics and the ongoing transition to a low-carbon economy. Understanding and managing these risks is crucial for insurance companies engaged in investment activities. According to a 2014 report from the Intergovernmental Panel on Climate Change (IPCC), the anticipated increase in global economic losses due to rising temperatures is a significant concern (IPCC (Intergovernmental Panel 2014). Real estate depreciation, in particular, is highlighted as having a substantial impact on insurance investments. In the short term, adverse weather events, increasing temperatures, and other climate-related factors can affect property values, leading to uncertainty and potential losses for investors heavily involved in these markets. They can further influence investor sentiment, giving rise to "sentiment shocks." These shocks may lead to irrational fluctuations in asset prices, potentially resulting in investment losses for insurance companies. Taking the automotive and related industries as another example, natural disasters such as heavy rain and mudslides can lead to the damage, destruction, or loss of vehicles. This directly impacts companies engaged in primary businesses such as transportation, causing substantial losses. Furthermore, climate risks extend beyond direct damage from natural disasters. They can induce price fluctuations in real estate markets, influence exchange rates, and contribute to a decline in market size and insurance demand in industries grappling with overcapacity.

For institutional investors like insurance companies, the concentration of asset allocation in traditional manufacturing industries and those with high pollution and energy consumption poses significant investment risks. The ongoing transformation or closure of companies in these sectors can have profound implications for their financial stability. For example, policies such as national subsidies for new energy vehicles and restrictions on the production and use of traditional energy vehicles contribute to the risk of generational transition and accelerated depreciation for traditional energy vehicle manufacturers. The risk of generational transition, wherein new technologies or energy sources replace existing ones, adds an additional layer of complexity. As the automotive industry shifts towards electric and sustainable alternatives, companies invested in traditional energy vehicles face not only the financial challenges of adapting to new technologies but also the risk of their existing assets losing significant value. The transition may render certain assets obsolete or, in extreme cases, turn them into "stranded assets."

This scenario poses a risk of significant depreciation or a transition to liabilities for high-carbon assets held by insurance companies, leading to financial losses. Notably, these assets constitute a substantial portion of the global equity and fixed-income markets, representing about one-third of total assets. As of 2015, the equity investments of European insurance companies and pension funds in non-financial institutions revealed a complex landscape. While the share of traditional energy industry assets was 8.72%, industries significantly impacted by climate policies (including traditional energy, traditional utilities, transport with high energy intensity, and real estate) accounted for a substantial 49.0%.

These factors collectively heighten investment risks and broad exposure of insurance companies to sectors that are particularly sensitive to climate-related developments and policies. The interconnectedness of climate risks with broader economic and policy shifts underscores the importance of insurance companies diversifying their investment portfolios. In navigating these challenges, insurance companies engaged in investment activities need to adopt strategies that account for both short-term fluctuations influenced by climate events and the long-term structural changes associated with the global transition to a low-carbon economy. Mitigating investment losses requires a proactive approach to portfolio management, risk assessment, and staying attuned to evolving market dynamics influenced by climate-related factors and the ongoing shift towards sustainability.

A strategic and forward-looking approach involves reducing overreliance on sectors vulnerable to climate-related disruptions and proactively seeking investments in industries aligned with sustainable and low-carbon practices. To mitigate market risks associated with climate change, insurance companies should engage in rigorous risk assessments, stress testing, and scenario planning to identify vulnerabilities in their portfolios and develop strategies to navigate the evolving landscape of climate-related challenges. Adopting sustainable investment practices and considering the long-term resilience of industries in the face of climate risks are essential steps for insurance companies aiming to safeguard their financial positions and contribute to a sustainable and stable investment landscape.

Operating risks

The third facet of asset risk for insurance companies lies in the impact of climate change on their operating models. The impact of climate change is not isolated but systemic, extending across various dimensions within the insurance industry. This systemic influence is evident through increased correlations between claims for different risk units, higher intensity of occurrence for specific risks during particular periods, and enhanced connections between different types of risks. One notable manifestation of this systemic impact is the doubling of occurrence rates for extreme El Niño and La Niña phenomena from the late twentieth century to the early twenty-first century. These climatic events have far-reaching consequences, affecting various regions and industries simultaneously. The increased frequency of such phenomena poses a challenge for insurance companies, as it amplifies the likelihood of multiple claims occurring concurrently, leading to higher payout obligations.

Physical risks associated with climate change can have direct implications for the value of certain assets, notably real estate. The potential for rising sea levels, increased frequency of severe weather events, and other climate-related factors directly affect the value and insurability of properties. This direct impact on assets is significant for insurance companies with substantial investments in real estate and underscores the importance of understanding and managing physical risks. Furthermore, the indirect impact of physical risks on the real economy can significantly influence various investment areas. Climate-related events, such as hurricanes, wildfires, and floods, can disrupt supply chains, hamper production, and lead to economic losses. These disruptions, in turn, affect the performance of investments across different sectors. For insurance companies, this interconnectedness necessitates a comprehensive approach to risk management that considers both direct and indirect effects on their investment portfolios.

The measurement of physical risks is becoming increasingly crucial for the balance sheet of insurance companies, particularly for life insurance firms striving to achieve long-term matching of assets and liabilities. Life insurance companies, which often have extended time horizons for their obligations, need to carefully assess and mitigate the impact of climate-related events on their investment portfolios. This involves not only understanding the direct exposure of assets to physical risks but also considering the broader economic implications and interconnectedness that can influence the performance of investments over the long term. The systemic nature of climate change impact underscores the need for insurance companies to adjust their operational models and adopt comprehensive risk management strategies. Assessing and addressing increased correlation between risks, higher intensity of specific risks, and the interconnectedness between different risk types are essential components in building resilience and ensuring the long-term sustainability of insurance operations in the face of a changing climate.

Moreover, the internal organization and personnel of an insurance company are not immune to the impacts of natural disasters resulting from climate change. Disruptions to operations, damage to infrastructure, and the well-being of employees can all contribute to solvency issues. These challenges may further hinder the insurance company's ability to make normal maturity payments, introducing an additional layer of financial strain.

Premium pricing risk

Premium pricing risk in the insurance industry is a multifaceted challenge that arises from the increased frequency and severity of claims prompted by climate-related and natural disaster events. This risk is not only borne by policyholders but also affects insurance companies themselves, leading to higher management and operational costs.

The foundation of premium pricing lies in a series of actuarial assumptions that are integral to an insurance company's ability to meet its financial obligations. The level of premium pricing serves as a concentrated reflection of the company's capacity to pay insurance claims and fulfill debt obligations. Climate change introduces a layer of uncertainty that can significantly impact the accuracy of actuarial assumptions, leading to pricing risk. Severe environmental events, such as hurricanes, wildfires, or floods, can result in substantial deviations between the actual occurrence of claims and the predetermined assumptions. This misalignment poses a considerable risk to insurance companies, as they may find themselves facing higher-than-expected claims, impacting their financial stability.

In extreme cases, this pricing risk can even threaten the continuity of an insurance company's business activities. Taking life insurance as an example, climate change can adversely affect policyholders' quality of life and the environment. This, in turn, may increase the incidence and mortality rates of diseases such as respiratory ailments. Such deviations from historical data used in actuarial calculations pose a compensation risk for insurance institutions beyond the initially estimated losses. The implications extend beyond immediate financial considerations, as the core function of life insurance—providing financial protection in the event of unexpected mortality—faces challenges in accurately pricing risk under changing environmental conditions.

In response to premium pricing risk, insurance companies must adapt their risk management strategies, incorporating a dynamic approach that accounts for the evolving nature of climate-related challenges. This includes regularly reassessing actuarial assumptions, enhancing disaster preparedness and response measures, and implementing strategies to ensure the resilience of internal organizational structures. By addressing these challenges, insurance companies can better navigate the uncertainties associated with climate change and uphold their commitment to policyholders while maintaining financial stability.

Interest rate risk

Interest rate risk is a critical consideration for insurance companies, reflecting the potential impact of inflation and interest rate fluctuations on the value of their assets and liabilities. This risk can lead to asset and liability mismatches, creating structural liquidity shortages that challenge the financial stability of insurance firms. In the context of natural disasters, such as earthquakes and tsunamis, central banks may implement measures, including adjusting interest rates, to address the broader economic impact of climate change. Changes in interest rates directly influence the valuation of both assets and liabilities held by insurance companies. In instances where interest rates are lowered, the values of both assets and liabilities increase. However, the increase in liability value may surpass the increase in asset value, contributing to a potential imbalance. During natural disasters and climate-related events, heightened risk awareness among policyholders often results in an increased demand for insurance coverage. This surge in demand can force insurance companies to purchase more assets to cover their liabilities, particularly as policyholders seek additional coverage. These purchased assets may have a higher value, contributing to an upward shift in the overall valuation of the insurance company's portfolio.

The interplay between interest rate changes and natural disasters creates a complex dynamic for insurance companies. Lower interest rates can lead to increased asset and liability values, while the heightened demand for insurance coverage during climate-related events necessitates additional asset purchases. This dual effect exacerbates interest rate risk, as the potential for asset and liability mismatches becomes more pronounced. To navigate interest rate risk in the context of climate-related events, insurance companies need to adopt proactive risk management strategies.

This includes regularly assessing and adjusting their investment portfolios to align with changing interest rate environments. Additionally, insurance companies should closely monitor the evolving landscape of climate-related risks, as the occurrence of natural disasters and shifts in policyholder behavior can have significant implications for their financial positions. By acknowledging the interconnectedness of interest rate risk and climate-related events, insurance companies can enhance their resilience to external shocks and contribute to the overall stability of the insurance industry. This entails a dynamic and adaptive approach to risk management that considers both macroeconomic factors and the specific challenges posed by climate change and natural disasters.

Liability risk

Liability risk in the context of climate change primarily revolves around the compensation sought from entities deemed responsible when individuals suffer losses due to the impacts of climate change. This risk is particularly significant in the liability insurance business and is closely tied to legislative and enforcement environments. In the event of a successful claim, where the party held responsible has liability insurance, a portion or the entirety of the costs incurred may be transferred to the insurance company. The sources of liability risk can be categorized into three types of responsibilities concerning climate change: mitigation failure, adaptation failure, and disclosure failure.

Claims under mitigation failure arise when the insured party is held responsible for physical losses caused by climate change. This could include scenarios where the actions or operations of a company contribute to or exacerbate climate-related events, resulting in harm to individuals or communities. Claims under adaptation failure stem from the inadequacy of the insured party in considering the impact of climate change risks in its actions or decisions. This could involve situations where businesses or entities fail to implement necessary measures to adapt to changing climate conditions, leading to adverse consequences for stakeholders. Claims under disclosure or compliance failure arise when the insured party fails to fully disclose information related to climate change or discloses information in a misleading manner. This may also involve non-compliance with regulations and supervision related to climate change, further exposing the entity to liability risks.

It is worth noting that climate change-related litigation is an emerging and evolving field, with few supported judgments at present. At this stage, the liability risk stemming from climate change for insurance companies is relatively small. However, as climate change continues to evolve and judicial practices develop, such litigation may gradually receive more support, becoming an increasingly important issue that the insurance industry cannot afford to overlook. The evolving nature of climate change-related liability risks emphasizes the importance of insurance companies staying abreast of legal developments, regulatory changes, and emerging judicial practices. This proactive approach enables insurers to adapt their risk management strategies, assess potential liabilities accurately, and ensure that their policies and coverage adequately address the evolving landscape of climate-related legal challenges. As the legal framework around climate change liability continues to develop, insurance companies will need to be vigilant and responsive to effectively navigate this complex and evolving risk landscape.

5.3.3 The Stock Market

The impact of climate risk on stock markets is intertwined with both physical and transition risks. Physical risk affects stock price volatility through the devaluation of assets, supply chain interruptions, and rising energy costs. Transition risk, on the other hand, affects stock price volatility through energy industry transformation, climate policy and regulations, investors' decision-making and pressure, and consumer preferences. As investors become increasingly aware of these risks and their potential financial implications, the stock prices of companies across various industries may experience heightened volatility in response to climate-related challenges and opportunities.

Asset devaluation

The phenomenon of asset devaluation is a significant consequence of extreme weather events, which are becoming increasingly frequent and severe due to climate change. Events such as floods, hurricanes, and wildfires pose direct threats to corporate assets, including physical infrastructure, real estate, and operational facilities. The aftermath of these events can result in a range of damages, from partial destruction to complete loss, leading to a decrease in the overall value of the affected assets.

The devaluation of assets due to climate-related events can have a direct and immediate impact on the stock prices of companies. Infrastructure, which forms a crucial component of many industries, is vulnerable to the impacts of extreme weather. The costs associated with repairing or replacing such damaged infrastructure contribute to the devaluation of assets. Similarly, real estate, whether commercial or residential, is particularly susceptible to climate-related damages. Properties in flood-prone areas, coastal regions, or areas prone to wildfires may experience reduced value after being affected by these events. The decline in property values can have a cascading effect on related industries, including construction and mortgage financing, impacting the stock prices of companies operating in these sectors. Furthermore, extreme weather events can disrupt normal business operations, leading to production halts and revenue losses. These operational disruptions, along with the costs associated with resuming business activities, contribute to reduced corporate profitability, further impacting stock prices.

The decrease in asset value and the anticipated financial challenges ahead can lead to a negative perception of the company's future earnings potential, prompting investors to readjust their portfolios. Additionally, the increased frequency and severity of extreme weather events contribute to a heightened risk profile for companies operating in climate-sensitive industries. Investors, being increasingly aware of these risks, may factor them into their decision-making processes, leading to a broader market reassessment of the valuation of companies within sectors vulnerable to climate-related damages. As climate change continues to escalate the frequency and intensity of these events, investors and stakeholders alike are placing greater emphasis on understanding and mitigating these risks to maintain long-term financial resilience.

Supply chain interruptions

Climate change-induced disruptions to the supply chain represent a critical risk for businesses across various industries. These disruptions can stem from a range of climate-related events, including droughts, wildfires, hurricanes, and other extreme weather conditions. Droughts, intensified by climate change, can significantly impact agricultural production. Reduced water availability can lead to lower crop yields, affecting industries reliant on these crops for raw materials. Companies in the food and beverage, textile, and biofuel sectors, for example, may experience shortages in critical inputs, resulting in production delays and increased costs. Wildfires can pose a threat to forests and other ecosystems, disrupting the availability of raw materials for industries such as forestry, paper production, and construction. Companies dependent on timber or other forest resources may face challenges in securing necessary inputs, leading to supply chain interruptions and potential stock price declines.

When climate-related events disrupt the supply chain, companies may face delays in production and, consequently, experience revenue losses. This can result in a reduction of quarterly earnings, leading investors to reassess the company's growth prospects and adjust their valuation accordingly. Due to shortage of inputs, supply chain interruptions often require companies to find alternative sources for raw materials or components, often at higher costs. The additional expenses associated with rerouting supply chains or securing alternative suppliers can impact profit margins and contribute to negative investor sentiment. Supply chain disruptions due to climate change can further impact a company's reputation and market perception. Investors may view such disruptions as a reflection of inadequate risk management practices, which can lead to a loss of trust and confidence. This, in turn, may trigger stock price declines as investors factor in the perceived risks associated with the company. The consequences of these disruptions extend beyond individual companies and industries, affecting the broader economy. Industries interconnected through supply chains may experience a domino effect, amplifying the economic consequences. Investors may respond by adjusting their portfolios to mitigate exposure to sectors vulnerable to climate-related supply chain risks.

As climate change continues to influence weather patterns and exacerbate extreme events, companies are increasingly recognizing the importance of building resilience into their supply chains. Investors, too, are factoring climate-related supply chain risks into their decision-making processes, emphasizing the need for companies to proactively address and disclose their strategies for managing these risks to maintain investor confidence and long-term financial stability.

Rising energy costs

Extreme weather events, intensified by climate change, can have ripple effects on energy prices, particularly fossil fuels like oil and natural gas. These fluctuations pose a considerable risk to companies that heavily rely on these energy sources for their operations. The interconnected nature of the global economy means that changes in energy prices can have widespread implications, affecting other commodities markets (Wang et al. 2024) and industries ranging from manufacturing to transportation (Zhang et al. 2020).

Extreme weather events, such as hurricanes, floods, or geopolitical tensions in oil-producing regions, can lead to disruptions in the supply of oil. These disruptions can result in decreased oil production, affecting global supply and subsequently leading to an increase in oil prices and greater price volatility. The damage caused by climate-related events to critical infrastructure, including oil refineries and pipelines, may impede the extraction, refining, and transportation of oil, contributing to supply constraints and upward pressure on oil prices. The surge in oil prices has direct implications for companies that heavily depend on fossil fuels, increasing their production costs while eroding profit margins. This decline in profitability can negatively impact a company's financial health and overall attractiveness to investors and, consequently, stock prices. Companies experiencing increased production costs due to higher energy prices may see adjustments to their earnings expectations. If these adjustments are downward, investors may respond by selling off shares, causing a decline in stock prices. The surge in energy price may also induce sectoral vulnerability. Entire sectors, such as transportation, manufacturing, and industries with high energy consumption, may face increased vulnerability to stock price volatility. Investors may adjust their portfolios based on expectations of reduced earnings and increased financial risks within these sectors. Persistent and severe fluctuations in energy prices can prompt companies to reconsider their long-term strategic plans. Investors, anticipating shifts toward more sustainable and resilient business models, may reallocate their investments, impacting the stock prices of companies slow to adapt.

Energy industry transformation

The global pursuit of greenhouse gas (GHG) reduction, driven by environmental concerns and the imperative to combat climate change, has profound implications for various industries. This shift can particularly impact traditional fossil fuel industries, such as coal and oil, while fostering the growth of renewable energy and clean technology sectors. The consequences of these transformations are reflected in the stock prices of relevant companies.

Governments worldwide are implementing regulations aimed at curbing emissions and transitioning to cleaner energy sources. Governments' commitments to GHG reduction targets may result in abrupt changes in regulations. This regulatory landscape poses challenges for traditional fossil fuel industries, including coal and oil, as they face increased compliance costs and potential constraints on their operations. Investors anticipating such policy shifts may adjust their portfolios and factor these regulatory pressures into their assessments, leading to adjustments in the stock prices of companies within these sectors. Meanwhile, the pursuit of GHG reduction goals is accompanied by a shift in market demand for cleaner alternatives. As governments and consumers prioritize cleaner energy sources, traditional fossil fuel industries may experience gradually declining demand for their products. Reduced market demand can adversely affect revenue streams and profitability, influencing the stock prices of companies operating in these sectors. Furthermore, investors in traditional fossil fuel industries face the risk of stranded assets. High carbon assets may become obsolete or economically nonviable due to the transition to a low-carbon economy. As the global community intensifies efforts to reduce GHG emissions, investments in industries associated with high carbon intensity may experience devaluation, impacting investor portfolios.

Investors, including institutional and individual investors, are increasingly favoring companies with strong ESG credentials. The growth of renewable energy and clean technology industries aligns with these preferences, attracting investment and potentially leading to higher stock prices for companies in these sectors. Meanwhile, advances in renewable energy and clean technology contribute to their increased competitiveness. The continuous innovation in solar, wind, and other clean technologies positions companies in these industries for growth. Investors seeking opportunities in sustainable and innovative sectors may drive stock prices higher for companies engaged in renewable energy and clean technology.

The pursuit of greenhouse gas reduction represents a significant driver of change in global markets. Traditional fossil fuel industries face challenges, including regulatory pressures and shifts in market dynamics, which can negatively impact their stock prices. Conversely, the growth of renewable energy and clean technology industries attracts investor interest, potentially leading to higher stock prices for companies in these sectors. Investors navigating the complexities of this transition must carefully consider the implications for their portfolios, recognizing both risks and opportunities associated with the global shift towards a more sustainable and low-carbon future.

Climate policies and regulations

The formulation and adjustment of climate policies directly shape the operating environment for businesses, with direct and indirect consequences for companies across various industries. Policies like carbon pricing and emission limits are key instruments in the global effort to mitigate climate change. The effects of these policies are far-reaching, influencing the operations, profitability, and market positions of businesses. Companies that align with the goals of climate policies, adapt their strategies, and embrace sustainable practices are better positioned to thrive in a rapidly evolving business landscape driven by the imperative to address climate change.

In terms of operational practice, climate policies often come with compliance requirements, such as emission reduction targets or carbon pricing mechanisms, and businesses emitting large amounts of greenhouse gases may face increased compliance costs as they invest in cleaner technologies, adopt energy-efficient practices, or purchase carbon credits to meet regulatory standards. Some industries may experience operational constraints due to climate policies. For instance, stringent emission limits may require significant changes in production processes or the adoption of alternative materials, therefore inducing higher operational costs. Stricter climate policies, on the other hand, incentivize businesses to adopt cleaner and more sustainable technologies. Companies that proactively invest in renewable energy, energy efficiency, and low-carbon technologies position themselves to comply with regulations and may benefit from reduced operational costs in the long run. Furthermore, carbon pricing mechanisms, such as carbon taxes or cap-and-trade systems, introduce a cost for emitting greenhouse gases. This cost directly influences a company's bottom line, impacting its profitability. Businesses that effectively manage and reduce their carbon footprint may fare better in a carbon-constrained market.

In terms of market position and competitiveness, climate policies change the market share of companies through shifting consumer and investor preferences. Companies perceived as environmentally responsible and compliant with climate regulations may gain increased market share and enjoy increased consumer and investor confidence. Conversely, businesses resistant to sustainability trends may face reputational risks and decreased market appeal. As climate policies often encourage supply chain resilience, companies that prioritize sustainable sourcing and resilient supply chains are better positioned to navigate regulatory changes, reduce risks associated with resource scarcity, and maintain consistent operations. At the sector level, climate policies can lead to shifts in sectoral dynamics. Industries with high carbon intensity may face challenges, while those contributing to a low-carbon economy may experience growth. Businesses anticipating and adapting to these shifts can strategically position themselves for long-term success and stabilize or push up stock prices.

Investors' pressure

An accelerating trend in the financial landscape is the growing recognition of climate risk by investors, particularly institutional investors. Investors are increasingly aware of the material impacts of climate change on businesses and portfolio resilience. Such awareness of potential risks associated with climate change, including regulatory changes, physical risks, and market shifts, is integrated into their risk assessments and investment strategies. Institutional investors, in particular, are emphasizing long-term sustainability. Companies that demonstrate a commitment to managing climate risks and opportunities are viewed as more resilient and better positioned for sustained success. This perspective is influencing the investment decisions of large funds and asset managers.

The ESG factors, with a specific focus on climate considerations, are becoming integral components of investment decision-making processes. In this context, the demand for standardized and consistent reporting of ESG metrics, including climate-related disclosures, has gained prominence. Transparency and accountability in climate reporting are critical factors that contribute to building investor trust and confidence in a company's management and governance practices. Initiatives like the TCFD have established guidelines for companies to disclose climate-related risks and opportunities. Investors increasingly rely on such disclosures to assess a company's preparedness for climate-related challenges. Companies that proactively disclose their carbon emissions, climate goals, and strategies for mitigating climate risks are viewed more favorably by investors, contributing to less sentiment-induced volatility in stock prices.

Conversely, companies that do not align with investors' sustainability requirements and lack transparency regarding climate-related risks and opportunities may face the risk of a decline in stock prices. Non-compliance with climate expectations may therefore limit a company's access to capital. Investors may be more inclined to allocate funds to businesses that align with their ESG goals, leaving non-compliant companies at a disadvantage when seeking financing or investment. Another negative impact of non-compliance with climate expectations is reputational damage. Negative perceptions regarding a company's climate practices can lead to consumer backlash and impact stock prices.

Consumer preferences

As the green transition proceeds, similar to environmentally sensitive investors, consumers are increasingly considering the ethical and sustainable practices of businesses when making purchasing decisions. Companies that do not align with this consumer trend may face the risk of a decline in market share, as consumer preferences shift towards brands that prioritize environmental sustainability and social responsibility.

Modern consumers are placing greater emphasis on ethical consumption. They seek products and services that align with their values, including environmental sustainability, fair labor practices, and social responsibility. Companies that can demonstrate a commitment to these principles are more likely to resonate with consumers. Consumers also expect transparency from the brands, including the environmental and social impacts of the entire supply chain. Companies that are transparent about their practices and accountable for their impact on the environment and society are likely to build trust with consumers and a positive brand image. Conversely, companies that neglect environmental and social responsibility may face reputational risks. In response to perceived ethical lapses, consumers may engage in boycotts or advocacy against companies they deem irresponsible. Such negative sentiments can be rapidly amplified by social media platforms, leading to declines in sales, market share and stock prices of the targeted companies.

Prioritizing sustainability, transparency, and ethical practices not only mitigates reputational risks but also positions companies to thrive in a market where consumer preferences are increasingly influenced by values beyond mere product features. As mentioned above, consumer concerns often align with and are shaped by regulatory trends related to environmental and social responsibility. Companies that proactively adapt to emerging regulations and industry standards may mitigate risks associated with non-compliance, therefore safeguarding their market position. Meanwhile, companies that prioritize ethical practices in their supply chains are better equipped to navigate evolving consumer expectations and regulatory landscapes. A resilient and sustainable supply chain can in turn contribute to maintaining market share in the face of changing consumer preferences. These factors jointly contribute to stock price stability.

5.3.4 The Bond Market

The bond market, a crucial component of the global financial system, is experiencing a growing impact from climate risk. Climate-related factors are influencing various aspects of the bond market, including bond issuance, pricing, credit quality, and investor preferences. As awareness of climate change and its financial implications grows, these factors are reshaping the dynamics of bond markets worldwide.

Bond issuance

Climate risk is reshaping the issuance dynamics of corporate and government bonds. As the financial industry continues to grapple with the implications of climate change, the integration of climate considerations into bond issuance practices is expected to become a pivotal aspect of sustainable and responsible finance. Specifically, the potential for higher financing costs, increased scrutiny on climate-related disclosures, and the evolving preferences of bond investors are driving issuers to adapt their strategies. Issuers that effectively navigate and disclose their climate risk management practices may enhance their appeal to investors in an environment where climate considerations are increasingly central to investment decisions.

Climate risk introduces an additional layer of perceived risk for bond investors. The concept of a "climate risk premium" is therefore emerging, where investors require higher interest rates to hold bonds from issuers with greater vulnerability to climate-related events. This risk premium reflects the added uncertainty and potential financial impact associated with climate risk (Zhang et al. 2023). Companies or governments with high exposure to climate-related hazards, such as extreme weather events or regulatory changes, may be viewed as riskier investments. Consequently, investors may demand higher yields to compensate for the perceived climate risk, leading to increased financing costs for issuers.

Bond issuers are also facing increasing pressure to provide comprehensive climate-related disclosures. As potential investors are seeking detailed information on how companies and governments assess, manage, and mitigate climate risk, bond issuers may need to disclose greenhouse gas emission data, climate risk management strategies, and the financial impacts of climate-related events to enhance transparency. On the other hand, the evolving regulatory landscape requires issuers to address climate risk and disclose climate-related information. Compliance with these regulations becomes essential for maintaining investor trust and satisfying regulatory expectations. Companies and governments are encouraged to adopt frameworks such as the TCFD initiatives to standardize and enhance the quality of climate-related disclosures, thereby assisting investors in making informed decisions. Failure to comply with emerging climate disclosure regulations may expose issuers to legal and reputational risks, potentially leading to negative perceptions among potential investors and reduced demand for these bonds.

Similar to other types of financial markets, there is growing emphasis on ESG considerations, including climate risk concerns, in the bond market. Bond investors, particularly institutional investors, are placing greater emphasis on ESG factors and tend to favor issuers that demonstrate robust climate risk management practices. In this regard, investors are increasingly showing a preference for sustainable bonds, including green bonds and social bonds, which finance environmentally or socially responsible projects. Therefore, issuers aligning their bond offerings with sustainability goals may find a receptive investor base.

To secure the effectiveness of bond issuance, issuers are proactively engaging in scenario analysis and climate stress testing to assess the resilience of their operations and financial performance under various climate-related scenarios. This information helps issuers and investors gauge the potential impacts of climate risk on the bond's performance. Insights from scenario analysis enable issuers to enhance their climate risk management strategies. Issuers with robust risk management practices are better positioned to communicate their preparedness to investors, potentially mitigating concerns and reducing the perceived risk associated with their bonds, therefore promoting bond issuance.

Bond pricing

Market awareness of climate risk is reshaping bond pricing and influencing portfolio management strategies. Investors are becoming more discerning, considering the climate resilience of bonds alongside traditional financial metrics. The incorporation of climate risk assessment into investment decisions reflects a broader shift towards sustainable and responsible investing, where environmental considerations play a critical role in changing the bond market landscape. Several key dynamics characterize the interplay between climate risk and bond pricing.

First, market awareness and perception of climate risk directly affects investor sentiment. If a bond is perceived to carry a higher climate risk, investors may view it as riskier than comparable bonds, leading to a decrease in demand and, consequently, a decrease in its market price, where the inverse relationship between bond prices and yields comes into play. As the market price of a bond decreases due to perceived climate risk, its yield—the return an investor receives relative to the bond's price—increases. Higher yields can be viewed as a climate risk premium representing the extra compensation required by investors to hold a bond that is exposed to climate-related hazards.

As climate risk assessment has become an integral part of portfolio management strategies by institutional investors and asset managers to align with broader ESG objectives, bond evaluation is not only based on their expected returns but also in the context of climate risk-adjusted returns. Climate risk assessment therefore adds a layer of complexity to this evaluation, influencing the risk-adjusted return calculations for each bond in a portfolio. Investors may adjust their bond portfolios to mitigate overall climate risk. Diversification strategies typically involve spreading investments across different bonds to reduce exposure to specific risks. Bonds from issuers with strong climate risk management practices may be favored in the portfolio to enhance resilience.

Similar to the issuance process of bonds, issuers are increasingly expected to provide detailed climate risk information, which can be used by potential investors who conduct enhanced due diligence to assess the climate resilience of bonds in their portfolios. Companies and governments that provide transparent and comprehensive climate risk reporting may be viewed more favorably by investors. Scenario analysis also aids in bond pricing and evaluation. Issuers and investors engage in scenario analysis to evaluate how different climate scenarios could impact the performance of bonds. This analytical approach assists investors in making informed decisions based on a deeper understanding of potential climate-related risks. Credit rating agencies are also incorporating climate risk into their assessments. A bond issuer's credit rating may be adjusted based on the perceived climate risk associated with its operations. Higher climate risk could lead to downgrades, affecting the market perception and pricing of the bond.

Credit quality

Climate risk has significant implications for the credit quality of bonds. As climate risk is increasingly becoming a quantifiable factor, credit rating agencies and investors are developing models that incorporate climate-related metrics, allowing for a more systematic assessment of the impact of climate risk on credit quality. The repercussions of climate-related events can lead to credit rating downgrades and an increased risk of debt default of the affected companies and governments. Investors are also increasingly scrutinizing the climate risk management capabilities of bond issuers, integrating it into their considerations of credit quality.

Companies and governments with high exposure to climate-related hazards, such as extreme weather events, rising sea levels, or regulatory changes, are vulnerable to significant damages (Guo et al. 2023b). Physical damages, business interruptions, or increased operational costs associated with climate events may strain the financial health of bond issuers, affecting their ability to meet debt obligations and elevating the risk of debt default. Companies in certain sectors, such as agriculture, energy, or coastal real estate, are particularly exposed to climate risk and may face more challenges in servicing their debt if their operations are significantly disrupted or if the economic viability of their activities is compromised due to climate-related factors. The assessment of these financial impacts of climate events contributes to the determination of credit ratings. In the aftermath of such events, credit rating agencies may reassess the creditworthiness of these issuers and potentially issue downgrades.

Investors are increasingly recognizing the importance of climate risk management in assessing credit quality. The ability of bond issuers to identify, mitigate, and adapt to climate risks is now a critical factor considered by investors when evaluating the likelihood of default and the overall creditworthiness of a bond. Meanwhile, investors are increasingly adopting forward-looking approaches, such as scenario analysis, to assess how different climate scenarios could impact the financial performance of bond issuers, to better evaluate the resilience of issuers to climate-related risks and make more informed decisions about the credit quality of bonds. Stress tests are also adopted in this context by issuers and investors to simulate the potential effects of extreme climate scenarios on the financial health of bond issuers. Stress testing helps identify vulnerabilities and assess the ability of issuers to withstand severe climate-related shocks without compromising credit quality.

Investor preferences

Climate risk is increasingly viewed as a component of the broader risk-return tradeoff by investors. While seeking attractive returns, investors are mindful of the potential risks associated with climate events that could affect the financial performance of their bond investments. The consideration of climate risk has become a significant factor in investment decision-making, influencing the choices investors make regarding the bonds they include in their portfolios. This shift in investor preferences has notable effects on liquidity, prices, and the overall dynamics of bond markets.

The increasing awareness of climate risk is reshaping investor preferences, particularly among institutional and ESG investors. Institutional and ESG investors are placing a heightened emphasis on ESG factors, with climate risk being a central component. Institutional investors, with their significant holdings and influence, play a pivotal role in shaping market dynamics. Their preferences and decisions regarding climate risk can have broad-reaching effects on the liquidity, pricing, and overall demand for bonds. Meanwhile, institutional investors often manage long-term portfolios such as pension funds, and recognize the long-term implications of climate risk. They are more inclined to consider the resilience of bonds to climate-related events and may prioritize investments in issuers with robust climate risk management practices.

On the other hand, investors, especially those with ESG mandates, are increasingly inclined to favor bonds that align with sustainability and climate transparency standards. Sustainable bonds, such as green bonds or social bonds, appeal to investors seeking to support environmentally and socially responsible projects, adding a positive impact dimension to their investment portfolios. These investors also tend to place a premium on transparency regarding climate risk. They seek detailed and comprehensive climate-related disclosures from bond issuers, wanting to understand the issuer's exposure, mitigation strategies, and the potential financial impacts of climate-related events. As mentioned above, the adoption of reporting standards, such as those recommended by the TCFD, has become a benchmark for climate transparency. Bond issuers adhering to these standards may find greater favor among investors concerned about the disclosure of climate-related information.

Investor preferences based on climate risk can lead to price adjustments in the bond market. Bonds from issuers with lower perceived climate risk may command higher prices, while those from higher-risk issuers may see price declines. These price adjustments reflect the market's assessment of the climate risk associated with different bonds. In summary, the consideration of climate risk is significantly influencing investor preferences and investment decisions. The demand for sustainability, climate transparency, and resilient investment options is reshaping the preferences in bond markets. As investors increasingly prioritize climate risk in their decision-making processes, the resulting shifts in demand and pricing dynamics are contributing to the broader integration of climate considerations into the financial markets.

Green and sustainable bond market

The increasing attention to climate risk and sustainability has given rise to the prominence of green and sustainable bond markets. These specialized bonds have gained traction as financial instruments that not only provide returns to investors but also contribute to financing projects with environmental and social responsibility objectives. These bonds therefore serve as a mechanism to address climate risk, promote sustainability, and generate positive environmental and social externality. The rise of green and sustainable bond markets reflects a broader shift in investor preferences towards responsible and impactful investing, driven by a growing awareness of climate-related challenges and a desire to channel investment towards projects that align with sustainability goals. The market presence of green and sustainable bonds has expanded globally, with a diverse range of entities, including governments, corporations, and municipalities, participating in these markets.

Green and sustainable bonds refer to financial instruments specifically designed to fund projects that promote environmental and social responsibility. Funds raised through these bonds are earmarked for initiatives such as renewable energy, energy efficiency, clean technology, sustainable agriculture, social housing, and other projects with positive impacts on the environment and society. These bonds align closely with ESG principles. They provide a structured way for investors to allocate capital to projects that adhere to sustainable and responsible practices, addressing climate change concerns and contributing to broader societal well-being. Investors, particularly those concerned about climate risk and sustainability, are increasingly inclined to invest in green and sustainable bonds as a targeted and transparent approach to channeling funds into ESG-related projects, which, in turn, can enhance the long-term value of their investment portfolios.

Among these bonds, one category is green bonds, including those explicitly dedicated to financing environmentally friendly projects, with proceeds allocated to initiatives like renewable energy installations, energy-efficient building projects, and sustainable water management, among others. The use of funds is typically certified by external entities to ensure compliance with green principles. The second type is social bonds, which focus on social responsibility, and finance projects that address social issues, including affordable housing, healthcare, education, and job creation. Similar to green bonds, social bonds undergo certification processes to verify the alignment of proceeds with predefined social goals. A more inclusive category is sustainability bonds that allocate funds to both environmental and social projects. This broader approach allows issuers to address a range of ESG objectives and attract investors with diverse sustainability interests.

There have been diverse factors supporting the rapid growth of green and sustainable bonds. First, financial innovation in bond structures is an important contributor. Issuers are exploring new structures, such as sustainability-linked bonds, which link financial terms to the achievement of predefined sustainability targets, encouraging ongoing commitment to sustainability goals. Second, to ensure transparency and credibility, green and sustainable bonds often undergo third-party certifications. The certification process conducted by independent entities to verify the alignment of the use of funds with predefined green or sustainable criteria helps build investor confidence and trust in the verified bonds. Third, the development of national and international green finance standards contributes to the establishment of clear guidelines for green and sustainable bond issuances, such as the Green Bond Principles (ICMA (The International Capital Market Association) 2021a) and the Sustainability Bond Guidelines (ICMA (The International Capital Market Association) 2021b). These standards contribute to the consistent and comparable reporting of green and sustainable bonds. The improved transparency and standardized information disclosure contribute to the development of green and sustainable bonds through streamlining market practices and facilitating potential investors to make informed decisions. Furthermore, governments and regulatory bodies worldwide are increasingly supporting green and sustainable finance through policy initiatives. Various countries have introduced incentives, tax benefits, or regulatory frameworks to encourage the issuance and investment in green and sustainable bonds, fostering a favorable environment for market growth.

6 Climate Risk and Microeconomy

Climate risk has multifaceted effects on microeconomic entities, primarily manifested at the levels of enterprises, financial institutions, households, and governments.

6.1 Enterprises

In the dynamic landscape of climate transition, marked by a shift towards sustainable practices and the mitigation of environmental impacts, there exist substantial market opportunities. However, these opportunities are accompanied by challenges and impacts that pose complexities for many enterprises. The impacts are multifaceted, predominantly emanating from shifts in policy frameworks, advancements in technology, and changes in market dynamics, all of which significantly influence businesses (Sautner et al. 2023).

6.1.1 Policy Risks

In terms of policy risks, the pursuit of global carbon reduction goals is driving governments and regulatory bodies worldwide to implement measures that encourage green and low-carbon transformations across diverse industries. This concerted effort will have profound implications for the production and operation of enterprises, with a particular emphasis on imposing significant pressure on businesses characterized by high emissions and high energy consumption. One notable policy approach is the implementation of carbon emission quota systems and the establishment of carbon emission trading mechanisms. These measures are designed to internalize the environmental costs associated with carbon emissions, creating economic incentives for businesses to reduce their carbon footprint.

However, for enterprises operating in sectors with high emissions, these policies can translate into increased operational costs, leading to reduced profits and, in some cases, financial losses. As the scope of carbon trading expands and standards become more stringent, the prices of carbon emission rights are likely to rise. This escalation in costs can intensify the financial pressure on enterprises involved in emission-intensive activities. Consequently, these businesses may find themselves compelled to accelerate their transition towards green and low-carbon development practices to remain economically viable.

Currently, many countries, especially developing countries such as China, are at the initial stages of exploring and implementing carbon reduction measures. The introduction of regional and sector-specific policies is anticipated to bring about a more rigorous regulatory environment. This heightened stringency in policy requirements poses an increased risk to enterprises, exposing them to more severe climate-related policy challenges. As regulatory frameworks evolve, businesses will need to adapt swiftly to comply with new standards and adopt a strategic and anticipatory approach. This involves closely monitoring regulatory developments, proactively adjusting business models to align with emerging standards, and investing in technologies, infrastructure, and operational adjustments that facilitate a transition toward sustainable and low-carbon practices. Embracing innovation and staying ahead of evolving policy landscapes, though costly in many cases, will be crucial for businesses seeking to not only mitigate policy-related risks but also thrive in an increasingly sustainable global economy.

6.1.2 Technological Risks

The low-carbon transition introduces a landscape of uncertainties for enterprises, particularly as they navigate the complexities of technological changes. Taking the transportation industry as a case in point, the reduction of emissions in land transportation primarily involves the development of new energy vehicles, electrification, and the utilization of green electricity. This transformative process is heavily influenced by a spectrum of emerging technologies, including clean energy sources, advanced battery technologies, energy storage solutions, and smart driving systems.

However, the trajectory of future technological advancements carries a substantial degree of uncertainty. The strategic choices made by enterprises in embracing or investing in specific technologies can significantly impact their competitive standing and industry leadership. Those who successfully control key core technologies stand to enhance their competitive advantage, potentially solidifying their position as industry leaders. On the flip side, enterprises that fail to invest in new technologies or lag behind in technological advancements may face the risk of obsolescence, elimination from the market, or unexpected financial losses. An illustrative example can be found in the experience of China's photovoltaic industry, which has undergone multiple rounds of industry reshuffling over its decades-long development. Companies within this sector faced challenges, with some going bankrupt and closing down due to the rapid updating and iteration of photovoltaic technology. Those unable to keep pace with technological advancements found themselves rendered obsolete, ultimately exiting the stage of industry history.

This underscores the critical importance for enterprises engaged in the low-carbon transition to remain vigilant, adaptive, and forward-thinking in their approach to technology. Investing in research and development, staying abreast of emerging technologies, accurately predicting and actively participating in the development and application of key innovations will be essential. The ability to effectively navigate technological uncertainties can not only safeguard an enterprise's competitiveness but also ensure its resilience in the face of dynamic shifts in the technological landscape induced by climate change.

6.1.3 Market Risks

Regarding market risks, the low-carbon transition is poised to reshape consumer preferences and investor priorities, creating both challenges and opportunities for businesses across various sectors. The shift toward environmentally sustainable practices may redirect financial investments away from high-emission industries, prompting a significant reallocation of funds. Investors are increasingly favoring assets associated with green and low-carbon initiatives, while divesting from carbon-intensive sectors such as fossil fuels. This shift can result in asset price fluctuations in industries and supply chain companies, potentially leading to the concept of "stranded assets" where certain assets lose value due to changes in market conditions.

On the consumer side, the younger generation's heightened awareness of climate change is influencing consumer behavior. A growing number of consumers are inclined to support climate-friendly and sustainable brands. The potential widespread adoption of "carbon labels" indicating a product's carbon footprint could further impact market dynamics. For instance, products with lower carbon footprints, like plant-based alternatives (for example, meat and dairy products), may gain market share at the expense of traditional counterparts, placing financial pressure on producers in high-emission sectors.

The impact of climate risks extends beyond tangible enterprises to financial institutions engaged in transactions with them. This dynamic therefore introduces risks to the broader financial system. Recognizing the systemic nature of these risks, governments and regulatory authorities globally are placing significant emphasis on climate-related financial risks. To address the potential systemic financial risks arising from climate change, several countries, including the UK, New Zealand, and Singapore, have implemented or proposed mandatory climate disclosure systems. These systems compel relevant enterprises, as well as financial institutions, to identify, manage, and mitigate climate-related risks. This regulatory trend underscores the importance of transparency and proactive risk management in the face of evolving climate dynamics.

In response to the significant threat posed by climate risk and the emerging regulatory landscape, enterprises and financial institutions are urged to proactively pay attention to, identify, and prevent transition risks. This involves not only complying with disclosure requirements but also integrating climate risk considerations into strategic planning, investment decisions, and overall risk management frameworks. To thrive in the evolving market landscape, businesses need to adapt to changing consumer preferences, anticipate investor priorities, and proactively manage market risks associated with the low-carbon transition. This entails embracing sustainable practices, innovating in product offerings, and aligning business strategies with the global shift towards a more sustainable and low-carbon economy.

6.2 Financial Institutions

Climate risk poses extensive and far-reaching effects on various financial institutions, encompassing banks, insurance companies, capital markets, and other financial entities. These impacts manifest predominantly in credit and pricing aspects, reshaping the landscape of financial risk management.

6.2.1 Credit Risk

Financial institutions, acting as pivotal intermediaries between residents, enterprises, and the broader economy, find themselves significantly influenced by the impacts of climate change. The credit mechanism, serving as the primary conduit for risk transmission among these stakeholders, plays a crucial role in shaping the macroeconomic financial landscape. The interconnectedness of financial institutions with residents and enterprises along the credit chain makes them susceptible to a range of climate-related risks. As the credit mechanism acts as a vital channel, risks associated with climate change are transmitted between financial institutions, residents, and enterprises. When financial institutions extend credit to individuals and businesses, they become intertwined with the economic activities of borrowers. This interconnectedness means that the repercussions of climate change, such as extreme weather events, can reverberate through the credit mechanism, leading to cascading effects on the financial sector.

Climate change can amplify the risk of defaults among borrowers. Residents and enterprises facing the impacts of climate-related events, such as floods, wildfires, or hurricanes, may experience disruptions to their income and operations. These disruptions, in turn, can lead to an increased likelihood of loan defaults. Financial institutions, holding these loans in their portfolios, face the challenge of managing a rising tide of non-performing assets, which can erode profitability and strain capital adequacy. The physical impacts of climate change can also contribute to the devaluation of collateral securing loans. For example, properties located in climate-vulnerable areas may experience a decline in value due to increased risks of damage or destruction. This collateral devaluation poses a dual challenge for financial institutions. Firstly, it affects the quality of assets on their balance sheets, potentially leading to valuation adjustments. Secondly, it diminishes the effectiveness of collateral in mitigating losses in the event of default. Financial institutions, particularly those heavily exposed to industries sensitive to climate risks, such as agriculture, real estate, or energy, face heightened credit risk exposure.

The aggregation of credit risks across the financial system can contribute to macroeconomic financial risks. If climate-related events lead to widespread defaults and collateral devaluation, the stability of the financial system as a whole may be at risk. Macrofinancial risks stemming from climate change have implications for economic growth, employment, and overall financial stability (Wu 2019). The interconnectedness of these sectors with climate-related factors means that financial institutions must assess and manage the evolving risks associated with their lending portfolios. This involves conducting comprehensive risk analyses, stress testing scenarios related to climate impacts, and implementing risk mitigation strategies. Additionally, enhancing transparency through disclosure of climate-related risks becomes essential for informed decision-making by financial institutions, investors, and regulators alike.

6.2.2 Mispricing Risk

The mispricing of climate risk by financial institutions has profound implications for financial stability, impacting the economic landscape through two main mechanisms.

The first mechanism is triggered when financial institutions' costs cannot be covered by their income. Financial institutions, particularly insurance companies, may underprice insurance products that are exposed to climate-related risks, such as extreme weather events (e.g., droughts, floods, storms). This mispricing can lead to a situation where the collected insurance premiums are insufficient to cover the costs incurred when a disaster occurs. In the aftermath of high-intensity or frequent climate-related events, insurance companies may face substantial payouts for insurance claims, exceeding the premiums collected. This imbalance can result in significant financial strain and operational risks for insurance companies. This issue tends to be particularly pronounced in the cases of property insurance and agricultural insurance.

Similarly, if banks fail to adequately consider climate risk, it can lead to the underpricing of loans or insufficient collateral requirements. In scenarios where customers default due to extreme weather events or if banks are held jointly responsible for contributing to climate damage, recovering costs becomes challenging. This, in turn, can lead to operational difficulties or even bankruptcy, posing considerable challenges to financial stability.

In the aftermath of climate-related disasters, whether affecting enterprises, financial institutions, or households, there is often an increased demand for liquidity. This heightened demand can stem from the need for capital replenishment, increased precautionary measures, or liquidity requirements to navigate the financial aftermath of the disaster. Financial institutions, including banks and insurance companies, may find themselves facing a surge in liquidity needs. If not managed effectively, this can lead to a liquidity crisis in the market. A liquidity crisis can disrupt the normal functioning of financial markets, creating a situation where entities struggle to meet their immediate financial obligations, further exacerbating financial instability and potentially triggering a systemic event.

From a risk contagion perspective, the consequences of mispricing climate risk also extend beyond individual institutions to the broader financial system. The interconnectedness of the financial system (Wu 2020) underscores the importance of addressing climate risk to maintain the resilience and stability of the broader economy. In the face of increasing climate-related events, the potential for simultaneous failures or financial distress across multiple institutions poses systemic risks. Financial stability becomes contingent on the ability of institutions to accurately assess and price climate risks, allocate capital appropriately, and implement effective risk management strategies. Proactive measures, including the aforementioned robust risk assessment frameworks, stress testing, and transparent disclosure of climate-related risks, are essential components of ensuring the financial sector's readiness for the challenges posed by climate change.

The second mechanism is triggered when loss of asset value occurs. Without due consideration for climate risk, financial institutions often overestimate the value of assets, leaving them susceptible to sudden and substantial declines in asset value. For instance, real estate situated in areas prone to extreme weather events, such as floods and tsunamis along rivers and coasts, may undergo abrupt destruction, rendering the properties worthless (Attoh et al. 2022). Similarly, as the global economy transitions to a low-carbon paradigm, the implementation of climate policies, advancements in energy technology, and other factors may lead to the sudden devaluation of large-scale fossil fuel assets or assets related to fossil fuels. These assets could become "stranded assets" as they lose economic viability.

If these damaged or stranded assets are held by non-financial sectors, the default rates of these sectors may surge, exposing the financial sector to increased credit risk. Additionally, the losses incurred by these non-financial sectors will be transmitted to the financial sector through the balance sheet, resulting in a decline in the value of financial assets held by financial institutions. Should these impaired or stranded assets be within the financial sector itself, the balance sheets of relevant financial institutions could deteriorate, potentially leading to disruptions in financial business operations and systemic functions. Interruptions in critical financial infrastructure or the operations of systemically important financial institutions (SIFIs) can significantly impact financial stability (Wu 2019).

While it is acknowledged that under the influence of climate change, asset values may also rise, particularly following natural disasters, such as when central banks stimulate the economy by lowering interest rates (Engle et al. 2020). This simultaneous increase in the value of both assets and liabilities for institutions like insurance companies might occur, with the rise in liability value being more pronounced. Nevertheless, regardless of whether asset values change positively or negatively due to the impact of climate change, these significant fluctuations introduce uncertainties and increase market risks and the potential for liquidity risks. Navigating these challenges necessitates a proactive and comprehensive approach to risk management within the financial sector. This involves integrating climate risk considerations into valuation models and implementing strategies to enhance resilience against the volatility induced by climate-related shifts in asset values.

6.3 Households and Labor Force

Climate change poses a substantial threat to the global labor force, impacting the health and well-being of workers and their families. The negative impact of climate change on households can be examined from an employment perspective, as the consequences of climate change extend beyond the workplace to various facets of residents' lives, including aspects such as health, personal safety, family wealth, lifestyle, and environmental awareness. These household factors can be reflected through employment indicators. On the other hand, employment is related to residents' income and security, directly determining the liquidity and debt-paying ability of the household sector. It therefore can be a key indicator reflecting the financial risk level of the household sector. Understanding the interconnectedness between climate change impacts, employment indicators, and the financial well-being of households is crucial for policymakers, businesses, and financial institutions. Supporting sustainable employment and enhancing income stability can contribute to enhancing overall resilience within the household sector to climate change.

6.3.1 Labor Force Reduction Due to Climate Change

The consequences of climate change contribute to a reduction in the labor force through several interconnected mechanisms. First, climate change-induced events make workers and their families face heightened risks to health and safety. Extreme weather events, rising temperatures, and changing disease patterns can result in injuries, illnesses, and even fatalities. Such health threats can temporarily or permanently incapacitate workers, preventing them from actively participating in the labor force. Second, workers may face temporary work disruptions due to disability, illness, or caregiving responsibilities stemming from climate-related events. For instance, in the aftermath of a natural disaster, workers may need to allocate time and resources to address immediate family needs, hindering their ability to engage in employment. In some cases, the severity of climate-related impacts may lead to permanent disabilities or long-term health issues, resulting in a lasting reduction in the labor force.

Third, climate change-induced poverty may lead to insufficient investment in health and human capital, which is particularly pronounced in vulnerable areas and communities. As households experience economic hardships, there is a consequential reduction in expenditures on essential aspects such as child nutrition, healthcare, and human capital development. Children growing up in households affected by climate-induced poverty and limited resources may experience lower educational attainment and reduced health outcomes. As these children enter the workforce, their productivity and working years may be compromised, contributing to a long-term reduction in the overall labor force, especially among high-skilled labor. The impact of climate change on poverty and human capital development thus exhibits intergenerational effects.

Fourth, climate change-induced factors, such as environmental degradation, resource scarcity, and changing economic conditions, can disproportionately affect high-skilled labor. High-skilled workers may face challenges related to disruptions in industries sensitive to climate risks or may be compelled to relocate due to environmental changes. These factors contribute to a reduction in the high-skilled labor force, impacting sectors that rely on specialized skills and expertise.

Addressing the reduction in the labor force due to climate change requires a multi-faceted approach. This includes implementing measures to enhance climate resilience, promoting sustainable employment practices, investing in education and healthcare infrastructure, and fostering economic policies that consider the long-term well-being of workers and their families. Proactive strategies aimed at mitigating the impact of climate change on the labor force are essential for building resilient and sustainable economies in the face of evolving environmental challenges.

6.3.2 Structural Unemployment

Climate change induces structural unemployment by necessitating significant adjustments in a country's industrial structure, energy systems, and transportation networks to effectively address environmental challenges. This transformative process involves the rapid elimination of inefficient and surplus capacities, particularly in industries that are energy-intensive and high-emission. The restructuring efforts, often driven by climate policies and environmental regulations, result in significant changes to the economic landscape, affecting both industries and the labor market.

There are several key factors contributing to structural unemployment in the context of climate change. The first is industrial restructuring. To align with climate change mitigation goals, countries may undergo a profound industrial restructuring. This entails a shift away from traditional, carbon-intensive industries toward cleaner and more sustainable alternatives. Industries that are heavily dependent on fossil fuels, emit high levels of greenhouse gases, or contribute significantly to environmental degradation may face stringent restrictions or even phase-outs, leading to surplus labor force and unemployment in these industries. The second factor is energy structure adjustment. Climate change mitigation efforts often involve transitioning to cleaner and renewable energy sources. As a result, industries reliant on fossil fuels or outdated energy technologies may experience a decline in demand, leading to a reduction in capacity and subsequent job losses. Conversely, the growth of green energy sectors may create new employment opportunities.

Third, efforts to combat climate change frequently include reforms to transportation systems. The promotion of electric vehicles, public transportation enhancements, and shifts toward sustainable urban planning can impact employment patterns within the transportation sector. Workers in industries related to traditional, high-emission transportation may experience job displacement. Furthermore, high-energy and high-emission industries, such as those involved in heavy manufacturing or certain types of resource extraction, may face strict regulatory measures. These restrictions can lead to a reduction in production capacity, rendering some workers unemployed due to the diminished demand for goods and services associated with these industries.

The transition to a low-carbon economy and industrial restructuring may result in a skills gap, as the demand for expertise in sustainable technologies and practices outpaces the availability of skilled workers. Retraining programs and educational initiatives become crucial in addressing this mismatch and facilitating the transition of workers from declining industries to emerging, environmentally sustainable sectors. Structural unemployment due to climate change can also exacerbate social and regional disparities. Certain communities or regions heavily dependent on industries facing restructuring may experience higher unemployment rates, while others benefit from the growth of green industries. Addressing these disparities requires targeted policies and investments in affected areas. To mitigate the impact of structural unemployment caused by climate change, policymakers and stakeholders must implement proactive measures. This includes developing comprehensive workforce transition programs, investing in education and skills development, fostering innovation in emerging green industries, and adopting policies that ensure a just and inclusive transition for affected workers and communities.

6.3.3 Frictional Unemployment

Frictional unemployment experiences an uptick in the context of intensified climate change and heightened public awareness of environmental protection. The growing demand for a sustainable and ecologically sound environment leads to various factors that contribute to voluntary job separations and increased worker mobility. As awareness of environmental issues increases, workers may be motivated by a sense of environmental responsibility to seek employment in industries aligned with sustainable practices. Individuals employed in high-energy, high-emission industries may voluntarily leave their jobs, contributing to frictional unemployment, as they actively choose roles in sectors that prioritize environmental conservation.

On the other hand, climate change can exacerbate local poverty, disrupt communities, and impact outdoor living conditions, compelling workers to change jobs and relocate. The consequences of climate change, such as extreme weather events, resource scarcity, and environmental degradation, can impact local economies. Workers in affected regions may experience economic hardships, prompting them to seek employment elsewhere. Climate change can also limit leisure opportunities and diminish the appeal of certain locations, adversely affecting outdoor recreation and local amenities. There are also increased uncertainties associated with climate change, including unpredictable weather patterns, natural disasters, and long-term environmental changes. Workers, facing adverse local conditions and increased uncertainty related to climate change, may choose to abandon their current jobs, and relocate to areas with better environmental prospects or improved economic conditions. This migration contributes to frictional unemployment as workers navigate new job markets.

Addressing frictional unemployment in the context of climate change requires a comprehensive approach. As workers may voluntarily leave their current roles to pursue careers dedicated to addressing environmental challenges, policymakers and businesses can play a role by investing in training programs that align with emerging green industries, fostering a supportive environment for workers seeking environmentally responsible employment, and implementing measures to reduce uncertainties associated with climate-related changes. As workers navigate transitions in response to environmental concerns, fostering adaptability and providing resources for skill development can contribute to a more resilient and sustainable workforce.

6.4 Governments

The impact of climate change on the government sector is substantial, and its effects are analyzed through the lens of government revenue and expenditure, both of which are intricately linked to the challenges posed by climate change.

From the revenue side, climate change can lead to reduced output levels, especially in sectors susceptible to climate-related risks such as agriculture, tourism, and infrastructure. When natural disasters strike, the government often implements relief policies to aid affected areas. However, these policies, while crucial for recovery, can result in a decline in government tax revenue as businesses and individuals face economic disruptions. From the expenditure side, governments bear the responsibility of providing assistance to residents, businesses, and financial institutions impacted by extreme weather events. This includes funding for emergency response efforts, evacuation procedures, and immediate relief measures. The financial burden on the government increases during such events. Following extreme weather events, governments must allocate funds for the reconstruction and rehabilitation of affected regions. Expenditures on rebuilding infrastructure, restoring utilities, and addressing long-term environmental consequences contribute to a significant rise in post-disaster expenditures.

The imbalance in government revenue and expenditure triggered by climate change poses macro-financial risks. Governments may face challenges in sustaining fiscal stability, managing budget deficits, and addressing the long-term financial implications of climate-related events. Governments may find it challenging to maintain a balanced budget, leading to increased debt levels or the reallocation of funds from other essential programs, potentially impacting overall economic stability. The need for increased expenditures in response to climate-related events may necessitate the reallocation of resources from other critical areas such as healthcare, education, or infrastructure development. This can have long-term implications for societal well-being and economic growth. Governments may face rising costs associated with implementing climate adaptation and mitigation strategies. Investments in resilient infrastructure, renewable energy projects, and sustainable practices are imperative but also contribute to the financial challenges faced by the public sector.

The revenue and expenditure mechanism of climate change-induced macro-financial risks reflects the broader economic consequences of climate-related challenges on government finances. Addressing these risks requires a comprehensive approach that includes proactive climate adaptation strategies, investment in resilient infrastructure, and the development of robust fiscal policies to navigate the evolving financial landscape shaped by climate change.

7 Conclusions

In this chapter, the focus is on elucidating the multifaceted nature of climate risks, spanning both macro and micro dimensions. The chapter serves as a comprehensive entry point for readers, providing a conceptual framework that is fundamental for comprehending the subsequent discussions within the book. By delving into the concept, categories, and impacts of climate risks, the objective is to arm readers with a foundational understanding that facilitates a nuanced exploration of this critical topic.

At the macroeconomic level, the chapter delves into the overarching implications of climate risks on a large scale, considering their effects on entire economies, industries, and global systems. It sheds light on how climate-related challenges can permeate and influence real economy, agricultural economic conditions, and dynamics in various financial markets. Understanding these macroeconomic dimensions is crucial for policymakers, business leaders, and global stakeholders as they grapple with the far-reaching consequences of climate change.

Simultaneously, from the microeconomic perspective, acknowledging the intricate ways in which climate risks manifest at the individual, community, and enterprise levels. By exploring the granular impacts of climate change on enterprise, financial institutions, households, and governments, the chapter underscores the necessity of recognizing diverse vulnerabilities and adapting strategies accordingly. This microeconomic lens is vital for individuals, businesses, and communities seeking to navigate the immediate and tangible consequences of a changing climate. The conceptual groundwork laid in this chapter acts as a guide, helping readers navigate the diverse and interconnected aspects of climate challenges discussed throughout the book.

References

Acharya V V, Berner R, Engle R, Jung H, Stroebel J, Zeng X, Zhao Y. 2023. Climate stress testing. Annual Review of Financial Economics, 15, 291-326.

Andersson, F. N. (2023). A scenario analysis of the potential effects of decarbonization on the profitability of energy-intensive and natural-resource based industries. Journal of Climate Finance, 2, 100008.

Attoh E M, de Bruin K, Goosen H, van Veldhoven F, Ludwig F, 2022. Making physical climate risk assessments relevant to the financial sector–Lessons learned from real estate cases in the Netherlands. Climate Risk Management, 37, 100447.

BCBS (Basel Committee on Banking Supervision). 2021. Climate-related financial risks - measurement methodologies. https://www.bis.org/bcbs/publ/d518.htm.

BCBS (Basel Committee on Banking Supervision). 2021. Climate-related risk drivers and their transmission channels. https://www.bis.org/bcbs/publ/d517.htm.

Chen Y, Zhang D, Wu F, Ji Q. 2022. Climate risks and foreign direct investment in developing countries: the role of national governance. Sustainability Science, 17(5), 1723-1740.

Chen Y, Zhang D, Ji Q, Wu F. 2022. Climate risks and foreign direct investment in developing countries: The role of national governance. Sustainability Science, 17, 1723–1740.

China Meteorological Administration. 2019. China Climate Bulletin of 2019.

Dlugolecki A. 2006. Adaptation and vulnerability to climate change: The role of the finance sector, United Nations Environment Programme, November.

Engle R F, Giglio S, Kelly B, Lee H, Stroebel J. 2020. Hedging climate change news. The Review of Financial Studies, 33(3), 1184-1216.

Guo K, Li Y, Zhang Y, Ji Q, Zhao W. 2023. How are climate risk shocks connected to agricultural markets? Journal of Commodity Markets, 32, 100367.

Guo K, Luan L, Zhang D, Ji Q. 2023. Does climate risk affect the performance of companies in China?. Applied Economics Letters, 1–7.

ICMA (The International Capital Market Association). 2021. Green Bond Principles. https://www.icmagroup.org/sustainable-finance/the-principles-guidelines-and-handbooks/green-bond-principles-gbp/.

ICMA (The International Capital Market Association). 2021. The Sustainability Bond Guidelines (SBG) 2021. https://www.icmagroup.org/sustainable-finance/the-principles-guidelines-and-handbooks/sustainability-bond-guidelines-sbg/.

IPCC (Intergovernmental Panel on Climate Change). 2014. AR5 Synthesis Report: Climate Change 2014. https://www.ipcc.ch/report/ar5/syr/.

MEEC (Ministry of Ecology and Envionment of China). 2018. Bulletin of Marine Ecology and Environment Status of China in 2018. https://english.mee.gov.cn/Resources/Reports/bomeaesoc/201911/P020191129369234962072.pdf.

Monasterolo I, Nieto M J, Schets E. 2023. Assessing the "Tragedy of the Horizons": Conceptual underpinnings of the NGFS scenarios and suggestions for improvement. SUERF Policy Brief No 602.

NGFS (Network for Greening the Financial System). 2019. Macroeconomic and financial stability implications of climate change, 2019: 1–48.

Oguntuase O J. 2020. Climate change, credit risk and financial stability. Banking and Finance; IntechOpen: London, UK, 75–90.

Ren X, Yan H, Gozgor G. 2023. Climate policy uncertainty and idiosyncratic volatility: Evidence from the non-financial listed hinese firms. Journal of Climate Finance, 5, 100026.

Sautner Z, Van Lent L, Vilkov G, Zhang R. 2023. Firm-level climate change exposure. The Journal of Finance, 78(3), 1449-1498.

TCFD (Task Force on Climate-related Financial Disclosures). 2017. on Climate-related Financial Disclosures.

Wang T, Wu F, Dickinson D, Zhao W. 2024. Energy price bubbles and extreme price movements: Evidence from China's coal market. Energy Economics, 129, 107253.

World Economic Forum. 2020. The Global Risks Report 2020. https://www.weforum.org/publications/the-global-risks-report-2020/.
World Economic Forum. 2021. The Global Risks Report 2021. https://www.weforum.org/publications/the-global-risks-report-2021/.
Wu F. 2019. Sectoral contributions to systemic risk in the Chinese stock market. Finance Research Letters, 31, 386-390.
Wu F. 2020. Stock market integration in East and Southeast Asia: The role of global factors. International Review of Financial Analysis, 67, 101416.
Zhang D, Li J, Ji Q. 2020. Access to credit and energy intensity of Chinese manufacturing firms. Energy Policy, 145, 111710.
Zhang Y, Li Y, Zhao W, Ji Q. 2023. Climate risk performance and returns integration of Chinese listed energy companies. Energy Economics, 107272.
Zhou F, Endendijk T, Botzen W W. 2023. A review of the financial sector impacts of risks associated with climate change. Annual Review of Resource Economics, 15, 233-256.

Climate Risks and Financial Markets

Fei Wu, Dayong Zhang, and Qiang Ji

Abstract This chapter discusses the impact of climate risks on the financial stability of Chinese banks, drawing on research conducted by Zhang et al. (2024). Despite the absence of formal inclusion of climate risks in the policy framework of Chinese authorities, there is a growing interest among financial regulators and central banks in this subject, attributed to China's extensive geographical reach, exposure to diverse climate challenges, and its explicit commitment to achieving carbon neutrality by 2060. The impact of green transition policy and the role of interbank competition are also discussed within the scope of Zhang et al. (2024), providing further policy implications to assist regulators in formulating effective measures to manage climate risks and uphold financial stability.

Keywords Climate risk · Financial markets · Non-performing loans · Transition policy · Regional commercial banks

1 Introduction

This chapter seeks to examine the significance of climate risk for the banking sector and explore potential responses from regulatory authorities, based on reviewing a recently published journal article by Zhang et al. (2024) focusing on a sample of Chinese commercial banks. The contemporary global landscape is marked by a disturbing surge in the frequency of extreme weather events, coupled with the relentless advance of anthropogenic-driven global warming. Climate change looms

F. Wu · D. Zhang
Research Institute of Economics and Management, Southwestern University of Finance and Economics, Chengdu 611130, China

Q. Ji (✉)
Institutes of Science and Development, Chinese Academy of Sciences, Beijing 100190, China
e-mail: jqwxnjq@163.com

School of Public Policy and Management, University of Chinese Academy of Sciences, Beijing 100049, China

F. Wu et al. (eds.), *Climate Finance*, Climate Change and Energy Transition,
https://doi.org/10.1007/978-981-97-3308-8_5

as a formidable and pervasive global threat to sustainable development (Zhenmin and Espinosa 2019). These intertwined phenomena have inflicted substantial socio-economic losses on a global scale, reverberating across diverse communities and ecosystems (Zhang and Managi 2020). The gravity of the climate challenge is starkly emphasized by the World Economic Forum's Global Risk Report for 2022, which identifies climate action failure, extreme weather events, and biodiversity loss as the top three most severe risks anticipated over the next decade.

This acknowledgment implies the profound and interconnected nature of the challenges posed by climate change, spanning economic, environmental, and social domains. The repercussions of climate change are not isolated events but rather systemic issues that demand comprehensive and urgent attention on a global scale. In response to this escalating crisis, the international community has rallied around the Paris Agreement, a landmark accord aimed at orchestrating a collective effort to mitigate climate change. The central goal of the agreement is to curtail global carbon emissions and achieve carbon neutrality by the mid-century. Despite these concerted efforts, the pace of global warming has proven to be more relentless than anticipated, as stated in the Sixth Assessment Report (AR6) by the Intergovernmental Panel on Climate Change (IPCC): "climate change is rapid and intensifying." This unambiguous statement stresses the urgency of the situation, signalling that the adverse impacts of climate change are not some distant, future concern but an immediate and intensifying challenge that requires immediate and robust action. The ramifications of climate change are not confined to specific regions; they manifest globally, affecting ecosystems, economies, and societies across continents.

As the understanding of climate change's real economic impacts deepens, there is a heightened awareness of the imperative to address the uncertainties arising from the dynamic interplay of climate shifts and associated policies (Chen et al. 2022). This awareness is particularly pivotal for the financial sector, where emerging evidence suggests that both physical climate risks (such as extreme weather events) and transitional climate risks (stemming from shifts toward a low-carbon economy) can significantly permeate financial institutions (Dafermos et al. 2018; Lee et al. 2022; Monasterolo 2020). This infiltration prompts growing concerns about climate-induced financial instability (Battiston et al. 2021; Reinders et al. 2023).

The financial sector, especially banking, stands at the forefront of this climate-induced paradigm shift. Urgent attention is required to comprehensively assess climate exposure within the banking industry (Battiston et al. 2017). The call for attention in the banking sector is not merely a theoretical proposition; it is a response to the tangible and evolving risks posed by climate change. These risks are multi-faceted, ranging from the direct impacts of climate-related disasters on loan portfolios to the potential devaluation of assets due to the transition to a low-carbon economy. The recognition that climate risks are not just environmental concerns but material financial risks has prompted financial institutions to reevaluate their risk management frameworks.

The recognition of the vulnerability of financial institutions to climate-related risks has led to a growing consensus on the need for proactive measures. Assessing climate exposure in the banking sector involves a nuanced understanding of how climate-related risks can affect loan portfolios, asset valuations, and overall financial stability. There is an increasing recommendation to integrate climate risk considerations into central bank policies as a strategic move to fortify and sustain financial stability (Campiglio et al. 2018). This reflects a strategic shift toward recognizing climate change as a systemic risk to the financial system. This proactive stance aims to ensure that financial institutions are well-prepared to navigate the challenges posed by climate change, safeguarding not only their own stability but also contributing to broader financial resilience.

The growing recognition of climate-induced financial risks has ushered in a new era for the financial sector. The intricate relationship between climate and finance unfolds on a dual axis, revealing a dynamic interplay that profoundly shapes both sectors. On one hand, the imperative of addressing climate change has given rise to the concept of climate finance (Hong et al. 2020; Long et al. 2022), where the financial sector assumes a pivotal role in channelling substantial investments towards climate mitigation and adaptation initiatives. Climate finance therefore serves as a linchpin in the global effort to combat climate change, acting as a catalyst for the necessary capital flows towards renewable energy projects, sustainable infrastructure, and other climate-resilient initiatives. Financial institutions play a crucial part in directing these investments, influencing the trajectory of climate action and sustainability on a global scale. This transformative role involves not only recognizing the environmental imperative but also understanding the financial opportunities embedded within the transition to a sustainable, low-carbon economy.

Conversely, the second facet of this interplay unveils the vulnerability of the financial system to climate-related shocks (Chenet et al. 2021). Natural disasters, intensified by climate change, can exact profound impacts on borrowers, leading to substantial losses and diminishing their ability to meet debt obligations. The work of Breitenstein et al. (2021) illustrates how environmental hazards can influence risk management within financial institutions. Moreover, the transition to a low-carbon economy, while essential for climate goals, introduces its own set of uncertainties across markets, rippling through the intricate web of financial institutions (Semieniuk et al. 2021). Policies aimed at facilitating this transition can introduce uncertainties that reverberate through investment portfolios, asset valuations, and overall financial stability. Dai and Zhang (2023) highlight the significant positive impact of climate policy uncertainty on the insolvency risks of commercial banks in China, emphasizing the tangible consequences that policy shifts can have on financial institutions.

This twofold interplay underscores the need for a nuanced and comprehensive approach to the intersection of climate and finance. Financial institutions not only serve as conduits for climate finance but must also navigate the risks emanating from climate-related shocks and policy uncertainties. The symbiotic relationship between climate and finance necessitates a strategic alignment of interests, policies, and risk management frameworks to ensure a resilient and sustainable future. Recognizing and addressing this interplay is not only an economic imperative but a foundational step towards building a financial system that is adaptive and robust in the face of an evolving climate landscape.

In the face of the complex challenges arising from the intersection of climate and finance, researchers have increasingly turned their attention to unravelling the intricate relationship and interactions between these two realms. The focal point of this exploration lies in understanding the role of climate risk and its integration into financial regulatory frameworks. This growing interest is particularly pronounced as climate-related risks become more tangible and their potential impact on financial stability more apparent. One significant manifestation of this recognition is the inclusion of climate risk in the policy initiatives of major central banks.

The Basel Committee on Banking Supervision (BCBS), a key international standard-setter for banking regulations, took a notable step in this direction. In June 2022, the BCBS issued a seminal report titled "Principles for the Effective Management and Supervision of Climate-related Financial Risks." This document marks a significant milestone in acknowledging and addressing the unique challenges posed by climate-related risks within the banking sector. It underscores the importance of integrating climate considerations into risk management practices and supervisory frameworks. Similarly, on 2 December 2022, the Board of Governors of the Federal Reserve System in the United States released guiding principles specifically designed for the management of climate-related financial risks within large financial institutions. These principles represent a strategic response to the evolving landscape of climate risks and aim to enhance the resilience of financial institutions in the face of both physical and transition risks associated with climate change.

In characterizing climate risk, Bolton et al. (2020) aptly coined the term "Green Swan," emphasizing the unprecedented and unpredictable nature of these challenges for bank regulators and supervisors. The Green Swan concept underscores the need for a paradigm shift in risk assessment and management, urging regulatory bodies to adapt swiftly to the novel challenges posed by climate change. In essence, the incorporation of climate risk into financial regulatory frameworks marks a pivotal moment in the evolution of financial governance. As climate-related risks continue to escalate, these initiatives not only reflect a proactive response to safeguard financial stability but also signal a transformative shift in how regulators and financial institutions perceive and address the profound interplay between climate and finance. The journey towards climate-resilient financial systems is underway, driven by a collective recognition of the imperative to navigate the Green Swan challenges of the current century.

The stark contrast in vulnerability to climate risk between advanced economies, such as the United States, and developing nations is a sobering reality that amplifies the global disparities in climate resilience (Chen et al. 2022). Developing nations, characterized by socio-economic challenges, often find themselves at the frontline of climate impacts, facing a higher susceptibility to extreme weather events, rising sea levels, and other climate-related risks. These vulnerabilities are exacerbated by factors such as limited resources, inadequate infrastructure, and high dependence on climate-sensitive sectors like agriculture. The financial systems in these nations are often intricately linked with sectors highly sensitive to climate variability, making them more susceptible to shocks induced by climate-related events. Compounding this vulnerability is the observation that the financial sectors of developing countries exhibit less resilience to the impacts of climate change (Chen et al. 2023a). The potential for significant economic losses, disruptions to supply chains, and increased pressure on public finances pose formidable challenges for these developing economies.

Despite these heightened vulnerabilities, there is often a lack of adequate preparations in developing countries to integrate climate risk into their banking regulatory frameworks. This discrepancy in readiness stems from a combination of factors, including limited financial and technical resources, competing developmental priorities, and, in some cases, a lack of awareness or understanding of the intricacies of climate-related financial risks. In many developing nations, the urgency of addressing immediate socio-economic challenges often takes precedence over long-term climate resilience planning. This prioritization is understandable, given the immediate needs for infrastructure development, poverty reduction, and social welfare. However, the consequences of not integrating climate risk into banking regulatory frameworks can be severe, with potential repercussions for financial stability, economic growth, and the well-being of the population.

Addressing this disparity requires a multi-faceted approach that combines international cooperation, capacity building, and tailored policy frameworks. Developed nations, international organizations, and financial institutions can play a pivotal role in providing support, both in terms of financial resources and expertise, to help developing countries enhance their resilience to climate-related financial risks. Furthermore, raising awareness and fostering a deeper understanding of the implications of climate change within the financial sector of developing nations is crucial. Building capacity within regulatory bodies, financial institutions, and the broader business community can empower these countries to develop robust risk management strategies that consider both immediate and long-term climate risks.

Examining China, a paradigmatic example of a developing nation with a pivotal and expansive banking industry critical to its economic progress (Zhang et al. 2016), unveils the profound challenges it faces from the escalating impacts of climate change. The nation grapples with an increasing frequency of natural disasters, leading to substantial economic losses (Chen et al. 2023b). This heightened vulnerability is especially significant given China's economic reliance on sectors sensitive to climate variability, such as agriculture and manufacturing. In response to the urgent global call for climate action, the Chinese government has made a landmark commitment to achieving carbon neutrality by the year 2060. This ambitious target signals a decisive shift toward a low-carbon economy and underscores the imperative for an accelerated transition to sustainable practices. However, this swift transition introduces heightened uncertainties that extend beyond the real sector, potentially reverberating into the financial industry and contributing to increased financial instability (Zhang et al. 2022). The accelerated low-carbon transition may trigger shifts in asset values, alter investment patterns, and introduce new risks that financial institutions need to navigate. The potential for stranded assets, regulatory changes, and disruptions in supply chains poses challenges within the banking industry. Despite the acknowledgement of these risks, concrete actions by the People's Bank of China, the country's central bank, have been relatively limited. Further evidence is necessary to provide policymakers with the requisite support to take decisive steps.

By reviewing the work by Zhang et al. (2024), this chapter involves an evaluation of both physical and transitional climate risks to gauge their potential impact on loan quality, measured by non-performing loans (NPLs), which is widely used as an indicator of bank risk-taking (Zhang et al. 2016). Based on analyzing a dataset of 591 banks across 201 prefectural cities in China from 2010 to 2019, Zhang et al. (2024) find the significant association between elevated levels of physical and transition climate risks and notably increased non-performing loans (NPLs). These results emphasize the substantial impact of climate risks on regional banks, contributing to financial instability by impairing loan quality.

The authors further find that exceedingly high temperatures primarily drive physical climate risk. Furthermore, rural banks exhibit heightened sensitivity to both forms of climate risk in comparison to their urban counterparts. Moreover, the authors employ a difference-in-difference (DID) regression analysis and validate that banks situated in green finance pilot zones demonstrate improved loan quality, which can be attributed to lower levels of transition climate risk in these designated areas. Additionally, this policy shift results in a decrease in the proportion of high-carbon loans. Their study also extends to identifying the role of regional institutional development in mitigating climate risk, revealing that heightened competition in the local banking sector can alleviate the adverse effects of climate impacts on loan quality.

The study of Zhang et al. (2024) makes noteworthy contributions to the existing literature in threefold. First, the authors construct measures of region-specific physical climate risk and bank-specific transition climate risk, which allows them to further evaluate their impacts on bank loan quality. Their findings offer crucial evidence that climate risks have the potential to introduce substantial vulnerabilities in the banking sector, posing a threat to the overall financial stability of the nation. Second, the authors demonstrate that the green finance policy reform in China contributes to enhancing financial stability by reducing banks' exposure to risks associated with the low-carbon transition and thereby improving loan quality. Third, this research contributes to the climate finance literature by emphasizing the imperative of addressing climate change and illustrating the intricacies linked to the low-carbon transition process, particularly from the standpoint of a large emerging market. These results furnish a robust basis for Chinese bank regulators to integrate climate risk considerations into their regulatory and supervisory frameworks.

Based on the article of Zhang et al. (2024), the remaining parts of this chapter are organized as follows: Sect. 2 introduces the construction of climate risk measurements, research design and contributions of Zhang et al. (2024); Sect. 3 provides details on the sources and attributes of the empirical data; Sect. 4 presents the empirical results of both the baseline regression analysis and several robustness tests; Sect. 5 discusses the impact and policy implications of the green finance reform in China; Sect. 6 includes further discussion on the role of competition in affecting the relationship between climate risks and bank loan quality; and the final section offers concluding remarks.

2 Research Design

2.1 Categories of Climate Risks

Climate risk, a focal point of discussion among scholars, regulators, and practitioners, has become an increasingly critical aspect of global discourse. While its significance is widely acknowledged, the definition of climate risk remains a contentious issue, reflecting the complex and multifaceted nature of the challenges posed by climate change. The United States Environmental Protection Agency (EPA) has contributed to the conceptualization of climate risk by categorizing it into two main components: physical risks and transition risks.

Physical risks pertain to the tangible and direct impacts of climate change on the environment and businesses. These risks manifest in the form of extreme weather events, sea-level rise, temperature changes, and other climate-related phenomena. Physical risks, exemplified by extreme weather events, have the potential to cause direct damage to assets, disrupt business operations, and result in losses for firms. This heightened risk increases the likelihood of default and diminishes loan quality (Klomp 2014). Moreover, firms with greater exposure to climate risk may face increased financing costs, leading to heightened financial distress (Javadi and Masum 2021). As demonstrated by Huang et al. (2022a), physical risks can contribute to poor financial performance and an elevated risk of default for firms, indirectly impacting banks.

Transition risks refer to the uncertainties and vulnerabilities associated with the global shift toward a lower-carbon economy. Transition risks therefore primarily stem from policies and efforts directed at mitigating climate change and reducing greenhouse gas emissions. As the world endeavors to move away from fossil fuels and adopt cleaner, more sustainable energy sources, businesses and industries face a range of challenges. These challenges include policy and regulatory changes, market dynamics, technological advancements, and shifts in consumer preferences.

While the impact of physical climate risk on bank loans is relatively straightforward, the mechanisms through which transition climate risks may affect bank loan quality are more intricate. The shift toward a low-carbon economy necessitates firms to invest in green technology, which is generally believed to be risky and with higher level of uncertainties. Additionally, more stringent climate policies, such as emissions trading, can impose additional costs on regulated firms, thus creating disadvantages to these firms (Löschel et al. 2019). The low-carbon transition can give rise to uncertainties that may reduce firms' operational performance or increase their risk exposure. These negative impacts can then transfer to banks in the form of heightened credit risk. On the other hand, transitional policies may confer benefits on specific industries, such as the low-carbon sector, therefore potentially favoring banks with greener portfolios in the transition process.

2.2 Selection of Banks

Physical climate risk is typically assessed at the regional or city level. In light of this, Zhang et al. (2024) associate this category of climate risk with regional commercial banks in China to evaluate its implications. The assessment of physical climate risk at the regional or city level provides a nuanced understanding of the potential challenges faced by businesses and financial institutions operating within specific geographical areas. This perspective recognizes the regional concentration of these banks, particularly their reliance on local businesses, and explores the potential vulnerabilities arising from climate influences at the regional level.

In China, regional commercial banks have emerged and experienced significant growth in recent years. Originally focused on serving local businesses, recent regulatory reforms have granted them the opportunity to expand their operations beyond regional boundaries. Despite this expanded scope, evidence suggests that their core business activities remain predominantly localized. This characteristic makes them uniquely susceptible to the impacts of regional climate variations (Zhang et al. 2018). These banks have grown to be increasingly influential within the country's banking sector following decades of reforms (Fu and Heffernan 2009). As per data from the China Banking and Insurance Regulatory Commission (CBIRC), regional commercial banks, including rural financial institutions, accounted for a substantial 85.8% in terms of numbers within China's commercial banking sector by mid-2022, as shown in Table 1. Despite their numerical strength, these banks exhibit distinctive characteristics that set them apart from larger state-owned commercial banks. Notably, regional commercial banks tend to have higher levels of non-performing loans, as illustrated in Fig. 1. This susceptibility to financial instabilities accentuates the importance of scrutinizing the impacts of climate change on these institutions.

Given the substantial presence of regional commercial banks and their unique vulnerabilities, understanding the implications of physical climate risk on these institutions becomes imperative for regulatory bodies. The heightened likelihood of financial instabilities, combined with the potential localized impacts of climate change, underscores the need for a comprehensive assessment. The study by Zhang et al. (2024) thus highlights the intersection of regional commercial banking, climate risk, and regulatory considerations in the Chinese context. The sample selection emphasizes the importance of acknowledging the localized nature of these banks' operations, their susceptibility to climate influences, and the subsequent regulatory implications. As climate change continues to impact different regions in distinct ways, such research provides valuable insights for both financial institutions and regulatory bodies striving to navigate the complexities of climate-related risks within the banking sector.

Table 1 Statistical information on regional commercial banks by the end of june 2022 (Zhang et al. 2024)

	Total assets (100 million RMB)	Share	Growth rate (%)
Bank institutions	3,972,514	N/A	10.9
Commercial banks	3,371,160	84.9%	11.7
Large commercial banks	1,664,212	41.9%	14.0
Join-stock banks	689,170	17.3%	7.5
City commercial banks	520,287	13.1%	11.5
Rural financial institutions	529,480	13.3%	9.8
Other financial institutions	569,364	14.3%	7.4

Data source CBIRC website (http://www.cbirc.gov.cn/cn/view/pages/ItemDetail.html?docId=1109300&itemId=954&generaltype=0)

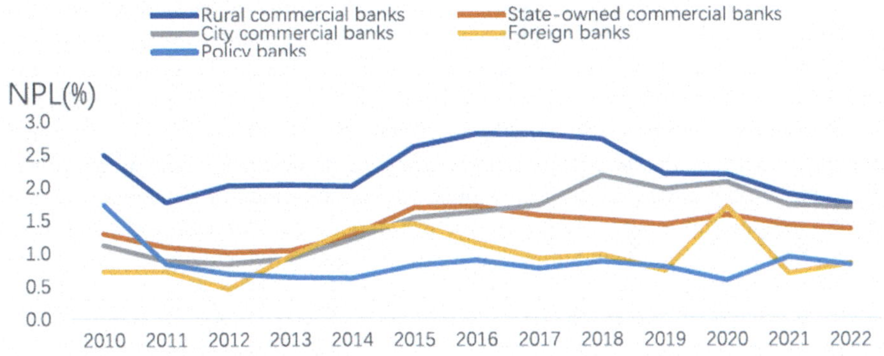

Fig. 1 Non-performing loans of the Chinese commercial banks: 2010–2022 (Zhang et al. 2024). *Data source* CSMAR database

2.3 *Measuring Climate Risks*

2.3.1 Measuring Climate Physical Risks

In academic research, scholars often employ measures tailored to the specific focus of their studies to gauge climate risks. For instance, Chen et al. (2022) investigate the impacts of climate risks on foreign direct investment in developing countries and climate risks are measured by centering on natural disasters and their consequential socioeconomic losses. In assessing the impacts of climate change on listed food companies, Hong et al. (2019) adopt the Palmer Drought Severity Index as a proxy for climate risk, while Zscheischler et al. (2018) propose using a combination of extreme weather events.

Several databases have been developed and utilized to assess climate physical risk, providing valuable tools for researchers, policymakers, and organizations seeking to understand and address the impacts of climate change. Germanwatch, for instance, regularly publishes the Global Climate Risk Index, offering a comprehensive assessment of climate-related risks on a global scale. This index relies on data related to weather-induced loss events and includes information spanning from the year 2000 onward. By analyzing the frequency and severity of weather-related disasters, the Global Climate Risk Index helps identify countries that are particularly vulnerable to climate impacts (Eckstein et al. 2021). The CRED/OFDA International Disaster Database, commonly known as EM-DAT, is another widely used resource for evaluating climate risk (Zhang and Managi 2020). This database records information on various types of disasters, including those related to climate, and spans a global scale. EM-DAT provides a historical perspective on disasters, aiding in the analysis of trends and patterns over time. An extension of EM-DAT, the Geocoded Disaster dataset (GDIS), offers spatial information on disasters across nearly 40,000 locations, enhancing the precision of risk assessments (Rosvold and Buhaug 2021).

Furthermore, the Notre Dame Global Adaptation Index, or ND-GAIN database, focuses on measuring climate physical risk by incorporating data on climate-related disasters. ND-GAIN provides a unique perspective by assessing a country's vulnerability and readiness to adapt to the impacts of climate change. This database offers insights into a nation's capacity to cope with and recover from climate-related events, contributing to a holistic understanding of climate risk (Chen et al. 2022). Extreme temperature serves as a crucial indicator for assessing climate risk. Escalating temperatures and global warming are often linked to various natural disasters, making extreme temperature a suitable metric for gauging the potential impact of climate change. Monitoring trends in temperature extremes can provide early warning signs of climate-related risks and guide adaptation strategies (Griffin et al. 2019). These databases collectively contribute to a comprehensive understanding of climate physical risk by offering diverse perspectives, historical context, and spatial information. Researchers and decision-makers can leverage these resources to identify regions and countries that are particularly susceptible to climate-related challenges.

Zhang et al. (2024) employ a robust methodology to gauge the level of physical climate risks, focusing specifically on extreme high and low temperatures. The study establishes temperature thresholds to define extreme conditions, providing a nuanced understanding of climate risks at the regional level. The authors adopt thresholds of 32°C for extreme high temperatures and −15°C for extreme low temperatures. The threshold of 32°C for extreme high temperatures aligns with the guidance provided by the World Meteorological Organization (WMO) for defining heatwaves. This threshold serves as a marker for exceptionally high temperatures that may have significant implications for various sectors, including agriculture, health, and infrastructure. The lower threshold of −15°C is in accordance with the Chinese authorities' adoption of this temperature level as the code yellow warning. This threshold signifies extremely cold conditions that may pose risks such as frostbite, freezing of water bodies, and disruptions to transportation and energy systems.

In a robustness check of their main results, Zhang et al. (2024) apply more stringent temperature thresholds to further assess the sensitivity of their findings. They adopt a higher threshold of 37°C for extreme high temperatures and a lower threshold of −

20°C for extreme low temperatures. This approach allows the researchers to explore the impact of even more extreme temperature conditions on physical climate risk.

To quantify extreme weather events, Zhang et al. count the number of days in a given year when temperatures exceed the established upper and lower thresholds for each prefectural city. The authors generate two distinct physical risk measures: "High" and "Low." The "High" measure reflects the risks associated with extremely hot weather (exceeding the upper threshold), while the "Low" measure represents risks arising from extremely cold weather (falling below the lower threshold). The "Total" measure is then calculated as the sum of "High" and "Low," providing an aggregated assessment of physical climate risks for a city in a given year. This comprehensive measure captures the combined impacts of both extremely hot and cold weather conditions.

By employing these well-defined temperature thresholds and measures, Zhang et al. (2024) offer a robust framework for assessing physical climate risks at the regional level. This methodology allows for a detailed examination of the diverse challenges posed by extreme temperature conditions and provides valuable insights for policymakers, businesses, and communities seeking to build resilience against the impacts of climate change. The inclusion of stricter thresholds in the robustness check enhances the reliability and applicability of the study's findings, contributing to a more comprehensive understanding of the potential risks associated with extreme temperatures.

2.3.2 Measuring Climate Transition Risks

Beyond the tangible risks associated with weather-related events, another layer of complexity in assessing climate risks arises from the actions and efforts of individuals and organizations to address and adapt to climate change. This transition risk introduces a set of challenges distinct from those associated with physical climate risks. One of the primary challenges in addressing transition risk lies in the absence of a universally accepted measure. The intricacy of transition risk assessment is acknowledged by various entities, including the US Environmental Protection Agency (EPA).

Quantitatively assessing transition risk is particularly challenging because direct measures are not always readily available. Unlike physical climate risks, for which specific indicators such as extreme temperatures or sea-level rise can be employed, transition risk lacks a standardized metric. While there has formed a global consensus to curtail carbon emissions and mitigate global warming (Lynas et al. 2021), the specific strategies to achieve these objectives remain ambiguous, leading to uncertainty during the transition to a low-carbon, sustainable future. As there has been an increasing number of countries committing to achieving carbon neutrality targets by mid-century, more robust policy interventions are expected to promote the development of low-carbon technologies for both production and consumption. These interventions may incur additional costs for firms, including expenses related to emissions trading schemes and stranded assets (Caldecott et al. 2016). Various uncertainties may arise during the transition process, stemming from the evolution of green technologies (Jung and Feng 2020), the changing legal environment (Park 2021), and shifts in investor beliefs (Krueger et al. 2020).

One significant source of uncertainty in this context is the formulation and evolution of transition policies, giving rise to the extensively studied concept of "climate policy uncertainty" (CPU) (Gavriilidis 2021; Guo et al. 2022). Climate policy uncertainty refers to the unpredictability and ambiguity surrounding the development and implementation of climate-related policies. This uncertainty arises from factors such as changes in political landscapes, varying policy priorities, and the dynamic nature of international agreements on climate action. The lack of clarity in policy direction can create challenges for businesses and investors trying to navigate the transition to a low-carbon economy. Guesmi et al. (2023), for instance, explicitly examine the interactions among climate risk (physical risk), CPU, and carbon emissions in the United States. Their findings support the use of carbon intensity of bank loans and pilot policies to capture transition risks. Some recent studies also explore the potential effects of climate policy uncertainty on various financial markets, including equity markets (Xu et al. 2023) and credit markets (Ren et al. 2022).

In the effort to understand and quantify climate policy uncertainty (CPU), many studies have turned to textual analysis of news channels as a valuable source of information. This approach allows researchers to gauge the sentiments, discussions, and trends related to climate policies and their potential impact on various sectors. Gavriilidis (2021) contributes to the field by constructing a dedicated climate policy uncertainty (CPU) index using textual analysis of news content from major US newspapers. Similarly, Guo et al. (2022) and Bouri et al. (2022) use proxies to gauge policy uncertainty and investigate its repercussions for financial markets. While textual analysis of news channels provides valuable insights, a drawback of these measures is that they are typically at the aggregate level. This means that they offer a high-level overview of the prevailing sentiments and discussions but may lack granularity at the sectoral or organizational level. Transition risk, being multifaceted, involves diverse impacts on different industries and businesses, and aggregate measures may not effectively capture these nuances. The reliance on news analysis as the sole measure of climate policy uncertainty may also be limited in capturing the entirety of transition risk.

The level of carbon emissions usually serves as a tangible and measurable indicator reflecting a company's or industry's contribution to greenhouse gas emissions. Carbon emission refers to the total amount of carbon dioxide or other greenhouse gases released into the atmosphere as a result of human activities. Transition uncertainties in the context of climate change often stem from efforts to address and mitigate greenhouse gas emissions. Essentially, higher emissions may signify a greater need for and difficulty in transitioning to more sustainable practices, thereby indicating heightened transition risk. Therefore, one might expect a correlation between higher emissions levels and increased uncertainty regarding the transition. This connection provides a basis for using the level of carbon emissions as a proxy for the level of transition risk, as demonstrated in studies such as Chen et al. (2022).

At the firm level, Bolton and Kacperczyk (2021) use total carbon emissions as a proxy for transition risk and document that higher carbon risk results in higher returns, a phenomenon referred to as the "carbon premium" in related studies, see for example, Bauer et al. (2023), Lemoine (2021), and Ramelli et al. (2021). This unexpected positive relationship suggests that investors may view companies with higher carbon risk as undervalued or potentially underrating the risks associated with carbon emissions.

While carbon emission is an absolute measure providing an overall quantitative assessment of the total greenhouse gas output associated with a specific activity, entity, region, or country, carbon intensity is a relative measure of the amount of carbon emissions associated with a unit of economic output or financial activity (such as Gross Domestic Product-GDP, energy production, or some other relevant parameter). Carbon intensity is typically measured as a ratio, such as grams or kilograms of CO_2e per unit of GDP or per unit of energy produced. This measurement allows for a more nuanced evaluation of the environmental impact of activities, as it considers the efficiency or productivity of resource use and provides a normalized assessment. Monitoring carbon intensity provides insights into the environmental impact of investments and loans, allowing stakeholders to assess the alignment of financial activities with climate goals. The use of the carbon intensity of bank loans, as highlighted by Guesmi et al. (2023), is indicative of the financial sector's exposure to transition risks.

Built on the rationale that banks holding substantial carbon-intensive portfolios are susceptible to heightened transition risk, and vice versa, Zhang et al. (2024) suggest formulating a measure grounded in borrowers' carbon intensity (Nguyen et al. 2023) to gauge bank-specific transition risk. Li and Pan (2022) adopt a similar approach in constructing a climate transition risk measure for a sample composed of Chinese commercial banks. To measure the level of transition risk of commercial banks in China, Li and Pan (2022) consider the loan structure of these banks and employ the level of carbon emissions in each industry to construct the climate transition index. Their approach of adopting carbon emissions as a proxy for transition risk basically aligns with the idea of Zhang et al. (2024). However, this method assumes that the carbon exposure of a bank is directly proportional to its loan exposure to different sectors, and the accuracy of using sectoral emissions weighted by a bank's loan share remains a questionable issue. Moreover, Li and Pan (2022)'s reliance on total emissions, as opposed to emissions intensity, raises considerations about the scalability of banks. Total emissions may be influenced by the sheer size and scale of a bank's operations. Therefore, the metric may not necessarily reflect the environmental efficiency or impact of the bank's lending activities. Using intensity measures may offer a more normalized assessment, accounting for the scale of operations.

To address this concern, Zhang et al. (2024) propose an improved measure, $TranR_{jt}$, to gauge a bank j's transition risk in its loan portfolio at a given point of time t. It is calculated as the summation of each sector's carbon intensity multiplied by the bank's actual loans to that sector, and then scaled by the bank's total assets. The logic is to first find the total outstanding carbon intensity for a bank's loan portfolio and then scale this total carbon intensity by the bank's assets. The first component, carbon intensity of each sector, represents the emissions produced per unit of economic output or loans in that sector and quantifies the environmental impact associated with the activities funded by the bank in each sector. The sconed component, bank's loans to each sector, accounts for the actual exposure of the bank to each sector by considering the amount of loans extended to businesses or projects within that sector, reflecting the scale of the bank's involvement in different sectors. Finally, scaling the transition risk by the bank's total assets addresses the concern related to the size of the bank. Larger banks naturally have more extensive loan portfolios and may have a higher total carbon content due to their larger volume of loans. Scaling by total assets helps in normalizing the transition risk, allowing for a fairer comparison between banks of different sizes.

Similar to Li and Pan (2022), Zhang et al. (2024) take natural logarithm of this measure $TranR_{jt}$ in their empirical analysis. Seven sectors are included in the study of Zhang et al. (2024): Agriculture, forestry, livestock and fishing (AFLF); Mining; Manufacturing; Electric, heating, gas, and water supply (EHGW); Construction; Wholesale, retail trade, and food (WRF); and Transportation, storage and postal services (TSP).

2.4 The Impact of Transition Policies

Going beyond the investigation of the impacts of climate risks on the loan quality of Chinese regional commercial banks, Zhang et al. (2024) undertake a more in-depth exploration of the role of transition policies, attempting to identify a causal relationship and offer policy recommendations. As argued above, Zhang et al. (2024) conjecture that transition policies can indirectly influence firms, subsequently prompting banks to react. To verify it, Zhang et al. (2024) employ a crucial green finance reform policy announced in August 2016 and implemented in 2017 as a quasi-natural experiment to evaluate how such a transition policy tends to impact banks' loan quality and their loan structure (Liu and Wang 2023).

This policy reform was led by the Ministry of Finance in China and several government agencies participated in it. The core mechanism of the policy involved the creation of pilot zones to serve as experimental regions for testing and promoting green finance practices. Initially, eight cities across five provinces were designated as pilot zones, including Huzhou and Quzhou in Zhejiang, Ganjiang in Jiangxi, Guangzhou in Guangdong, Guian in Guizhou, and Hami, Changji, and Kelamayi in Xinjiang. The policy underwent expansions in subsequent years. In 2019, two additional pilot regions were established in Gansu, and in 2022, Chongqing became another pilot region. These expansions reflected the ongoing commitment to testing and implementing green finance practices across diverse geographic and economic contexts.

The establishment of these pilot zones marks a significant stride for China in advancing institutional development toward low-carbon transition. This initiative not only aligns with broader environmental goals but also introduces a range of benefits for firms, financial institutions, and the economy as a whole. The pilot zones serve as experimental regions where innovative policies and practices are tested, contributing to the overall transition to a more sustainable and low-carbon economy. The establishment of green finance pilot zones streamlines firms' access to green loans. By designating specific regions for testing and implementing green finance practices, the policy aims to create an environment where businesses are incentivized to adopt more sustainable practices and can easily access financial resources to support these initiatives. The concentration of green finance activities in pilot zones promotes institutional agglomeration. This clustering effect can lead to the sharing of best practices, knowledge transfer, and the development of specialized expertise in green finance within these regions. It fosters collaboration among financial institutions, businesses, and regulatory bodies with a shared focus on sustainability. The establishment of green finance pilot zones can also have positive fiscal implications. As businesses within these zones adopt green practices, there is a potential for increased economic activity and innovation, contributing to job creation and revenue generation. Fiscal stimulation is a key aspect of encouraging the adoption of sustainable practices at both the corporate and regional levels. Furthermore, the pilot zones provide a structured environment for testing and refining supervision mechanisms related to green finance. Regulatory bodies have the opportunity to observe and assess the effectiveness of policies, identify challenges, and develop strategies for scaling successful initiatives. This iterative process contributes to the continuous improvement of supervision and regulatory frameworks.

Evaluations of the effects of these pilot zones have generally yielded positive results. For instance, Yan et al. (2022) use this reform as a quasi-natural experiment to assess its impact on corporate investment efficiency and find that the reform enhances efficiency while contributing to reducing agency problems. Huang et al. (2022b) and others document a significant causal effect of this green finance reform on green innovation. Drawn on these favorable findings, Zhang et al. (2024) conjecture that the green finance pilot zone policy can enhance the loan quality of banks that operate within these zones through mitigating transition risk. Banks may adjust their loan portfolios toward low-carbon-intensive sectors in alignment with the reform's principles.

3 Data and Variable Selection

The dataset utilized in the study of Zhang et al. (2024) covers the period from 2010 to 2019, excluding earlier data to mitigate the influence of the 2008 global financial crisis and more recent data to avoid the influence of the COVID-19 pandemic. The selection of such a sample period therefore minimizes the impacts on economy and financial markets associated with these systemic events (Zhang et al. 2020). Bank information in this study is obtained from the WIND database. After excluding banks with less than two years of information, a total of 591 regional commercial banks are included in their empirical analysis. This dataset comprises 122 city commercial

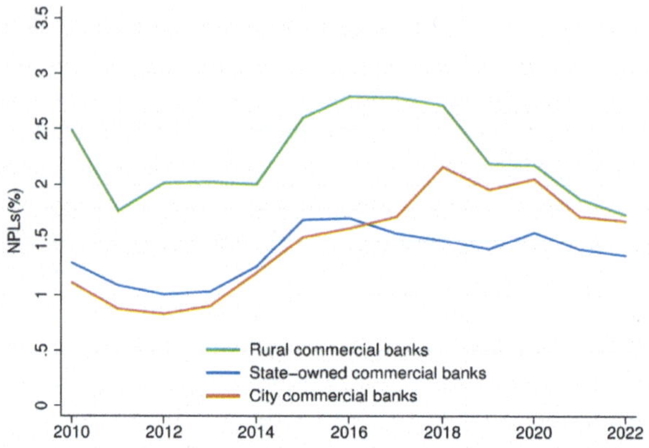

Fig. 2 Non-performing loans for different types of banks in China (2010–2022) (Zhang et al. 2024)

banks and 469 rural commercial banks, including rural credit unions, located in 201 prefectural cities or municipalities, with a total of 3,461 observations. However, due to unavailability of sectoral loan information for some banks, the total number of observations is reduced to 1,512 for transition risk analysis.

The dependent variable in the empirical analysis of Zhang et al. (2024) is the non-performing loans (NPL ratio) of the banks in the sample. Data of the bank NPLs are obtained from the WIND database. Non-performing loans (NPLs) are commonly used in the literature to measure the loan quality of banks and their associated credit risks (for example, Zhang et al. (2016)). The average value of NPLs in the sample banks is 2.037%, indicating that it was not a serious problem. However, the highest value exceeds 10% in the sample, raising concerns about potential instability. In addition to the average value, Fig. 2 plots the NPLs for the three groups of banks, showing that rural commercial banks have higher NPL levels relative to the other types of banks over the entire sample period. There is a rising trend in NPLs for city commercial banks, with the level approaching that of rural commercial banks at the end of the sample period, which raises significant concerns for regulators. The average loan deposit ratio for these regional commercial banks is 65.273%.

For the key independent variables, Zhang et al. (2024) first introduce regional (city-level) physical risks, denoted as *PhyR*. The data used for calculating *PhyR* are collected from the National Centers for Environmental Information (NCEI) at the US National Oceanic and Atmospheric Administration (NOAA). For the construction of *PhyR*, Zhang et al. (2024) first generate two physical risk measures, "High" and "Low", respectively counting the days exceeding the upper threshold and below the lower threshold for a city within a given year. *PhyR* is then calculated as the sum of "High" and "Low," providing an aggregated assessment of physical climate risks for a that city in the given year.

Figure 3 plots each year's extreme weather days for the provincial capital cities and four municipalities between 2010 and 2019, which are positioned roughly in accordance with their actual geographical locations. For each year's extreme weather days represented by the vertical bar in Fig. 3, extreme cold days are marked by blue, while extreme hot days by red. It can be observed that physical climate risks exhibit clear geographical patterns. Regions in Southern China are more affected by extreme hot weather, while Northern cities are more likely to be affected by extreme cold weather. Among all the sample cities, Changchun city in Jilin province has the highest number of days in both extreme temperatures (102 days) and extreme cold temperatures (92 days). Zhaoqing city and Meizhou city in Guangdong province have the highest number of hot days (100 days).

Next, Zhang et al. (2024) construct the measure of transition climate risk for each commercial bank in the sample, denoted as *TranR*, based on the approach introduced in Sect. 2.3.2. The data for calculating *TranR* are collected from the China Emission Accounts and Datasets (CEADs) and the WIND database. Figure 4a plots the level of transition risks of all banks in the sample from 2010 to 2019. The general trend of the overall level of transition risk is decreasing during the sample period, which can be explained by China's great achievement in reducing carbon intensity during this decade (Lee and Wang 2022). The introduction of a general guidance to establish a green financial system in 2015 has especially contributed to the reduction in transition risk in these banks (Ji and Zhang 2019). Although there are large variations across individual banks, the average level of transition risk stabilizes in the last four years of observation. Figure 4b compares the level of transition risk between city and rural commercial banks in each of the sample years. Both groups show decreasing trends in their levels of transition risk. The average value of transition risk for rural commercial banks is generally higher than that for city commercial banks, though larger variations are observed in city commercial banks. The observed differences in the level of transition risk between these two groups of banks are worth further investigation.

Both *PhyR* and *TranR* are log-transformed. Zhang et al. (2024) argue that physical risk and transition risk may be related as both risks capture the impacts of climate change. The authors therefore calculate the correlation between these two types of risks. The correlation shows no obvious time variations over the entire sample period and the average value of -0.1104 suggests a clear difference between these two types of climate risks. The negative magnitude of the correlation coefficient indicates a negative correlation between these two types of climate risks, albeit a weak one. A plausible explanation is that climate transition risk and climate physical risk arise from different sources, while governments and businesses may prioritize different aspects of climate change risk based on their policy goals and economic strategies. A strong emphasis on transitioning to a low-carbon economy might lead to proactive policies that reduce climate transition risk but may not necessarily reduce vulnerability to physical risks. Conversely, regions or sectors focusing on adapting to physical risks might not be at the forefront of sustainable transition efforts.

For the control variables, Zhang et al. (2024) first account for the potential influences of bank-specific characteristics, including banks' return on assets, loan deposit ratio, loan provision rate, debt asset ratio, and log-transformed total assets. Return on Assets assesses a bank's profitability by measuring its net income in relation to its total assets and reflects the overall financial performance of banks, which can be a key factor in understanding how climate risks may impact financial institutions.

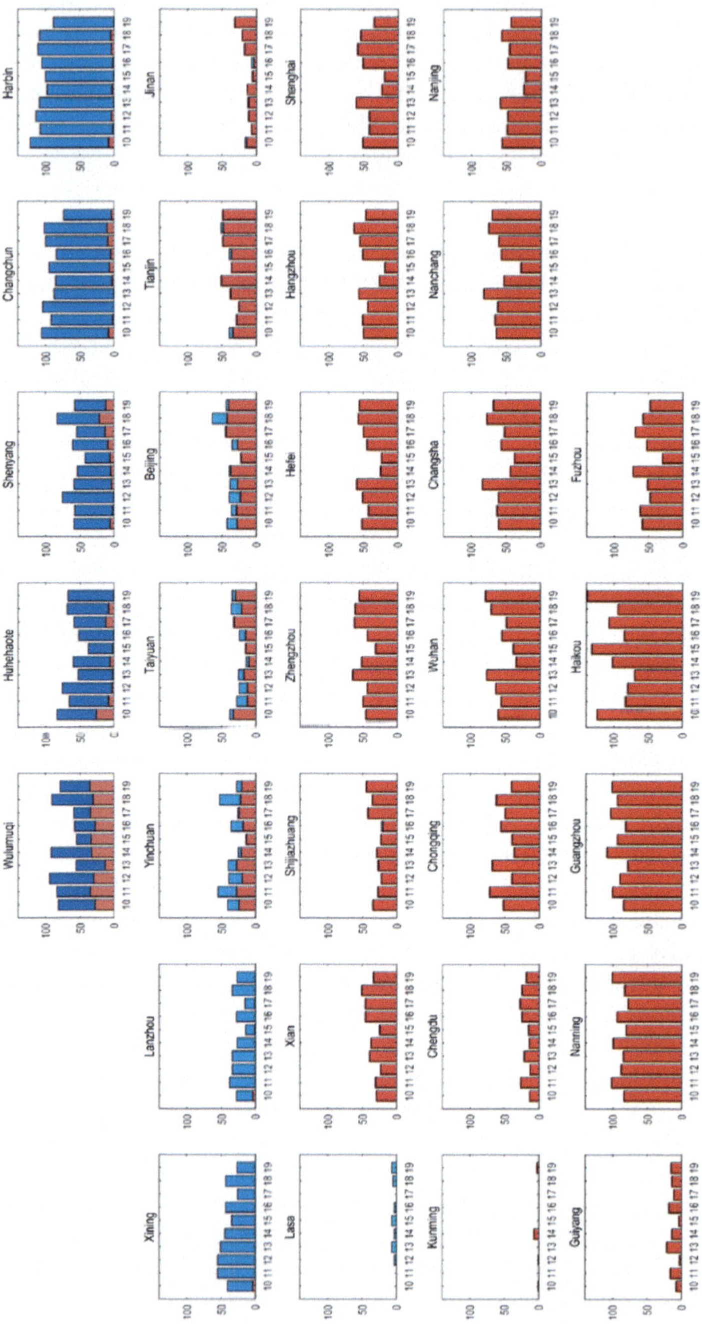

Fig. 3 Extreme weather days in China's capital cities: 2010–2019 (Zhang et al. 2024). *Note* In this figure, blue bars represent extremely cold days and red extremely hot days

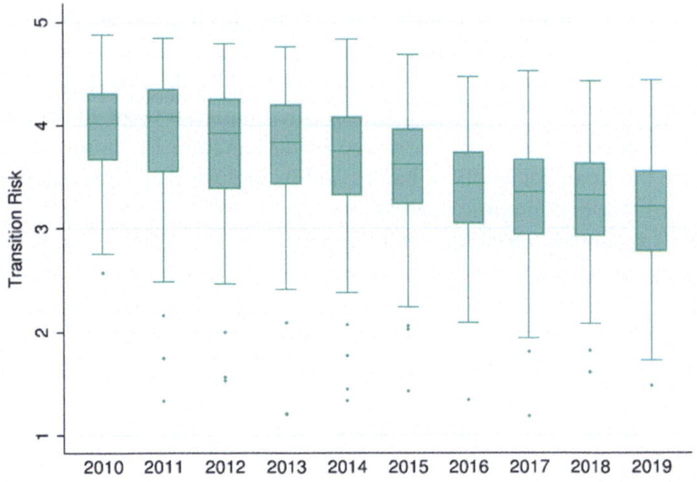

(a) All banks

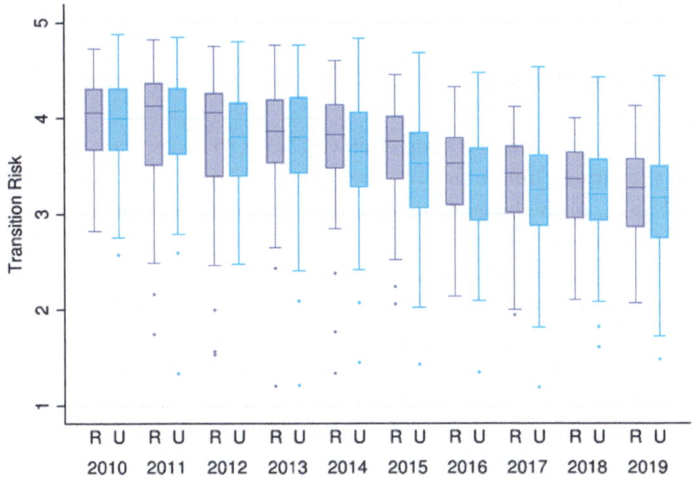

(b) City versus rural commercial banks

Fig. 4 Transition risks for Chinese regional commercial banks (Zhang et al. 2024). *Note* In this figure, R and U refer to rural and urban banks, respectively. The unit in the graph is the logarithm of the transition risk measure *TranR*, calculated as the a bank's sum of loans to each sector multiplied by the carbon intensity of the corresponding sector, scaled by the total assets of the bank

The loan deposit ratio is the proportion of a bank's assets that are tied up in loans compared to its deposits, indicating a bank's lending practices and liquidity. The loan provision rate is the percentage of a bank's loans that are set aside as provisions for potential losses. This variable is critical for understanding how banks prepare for and manage credit risks. The debt asset ratio measures the proportion of a bank's assets that are financed by debt and provides insights into a bank's leverage and financial structure. Taking the natural logarithm of total assets is a common practice in financial analysis to account for the impact of bank scale. For regional economic development, the authors include log-transformed regional GDP, to account for the economic conditions in the regions where banks operate. Economic development can influence the financial health of banks, and its inclusion ensures that the analysis considers the broader economic context.

The data of control variables are obtained from the WIND database and are winsorized at the 1 and 99% levels to mitigate the impact of extreme values or outliers in the datasets. When variables are in natural logarithm form, 1 is added before taking the log to handle cases where the variable of interest contains zero values, preventing issues with undefined logarithms.

4 Empirical Results

4.1 Baseline Results

4.1.1 Full Sample Results

The main research question of Zhang et al. (2024) is to investigate the influences of physical and transition climate risks on loan quality and stability of China's regional commercial banks. In the baseline model, the dependent variable is the NPL of the banks in the sample, and the key independent variable is either physical risks *PhyR* or transition risks *TranR* introduced in the former section. In the baseline model, both time fixed effect and individual fixed effect are controlled for. Bank-specific variables and macroeconomic variables are included as controls.

For each type of climate risks, Zhang et al. (2024) conduct three sets of regressions: unconditional regressions with no control variables, regressions conditional on bank-specific characteristics, and regressions conditional on both bank and regional economic characteristics. For the role of physical climate risks, the authors find that the coefficients are positive and significant in all three regression models, ranging from 0.14 to 0.161 in magnitude. These results suggest that higher levels of NPLs are associated with elevated physical climate risks. When all the control variables are included, an increase of one unit in physical climate risk leads to a 0.161% rise in banks' NPLs. Zhang et al. (2024) also point out that based on the difference between the maximum and minimum of *PhyR*, the difference in NPLs between the corresponding banks can reach 0.746%, which translates to a roughly 36% increase relative to the mean NPL level (2.037%). This implies that the impact of physical climate risks on banks' loan quality is not only statistically but also economically significant. The coefficients for transition risk variables are also significant across all model specifications, indicating that climate transition risks can lead to higher

NPL levels in these banks. Similar to the interpretation for physical climate risks, the magnitude is also economically significant.

For control variables, the regression results in Zhang et al. (2024) are generally consistent with economic intuitions. Most are comparable with evidence in the existing literature (for example, Li and Pan (2022)). Banks with better financial performance (ROA) are associated with lower levels of NPLs (Khan et al. 2020), while higher loan deposit ratios (LDR) and loan provision rates (LPVR) tend to be associated with higher NPLs. Similar to Umar and Sun (2018), the results for capital structure and bank size are inconsistent between models of physical risks and those of transition risks, which may be attributed to sample differences, as almost 50% of the observations are dropped in the transition risk models. The coefficient on regional GDP is significant in models involving physical climate risks. This is in line with the evidence in Umar and Sun (2018) and economic intuition, as banks operating in more economically developed regions tend to have fewer poor-quality loans.

Zhang et al. (2024) not only investigate the potential impact of physical climate risks as a whole on bank loan quality and stability, they go further to examine whether extremely high and low temperatures have varying impacts on NPLs. They use the variables High and Low to replace the former variable *PhyR* to separately test the effects of extremely hot and cold weather conditions on the level of bank NPLs, still by three model specifications including no controls, only bank-specific controls, or all control variables.

Findings based on such a comparison further enrich the literature on the links between climate risks and financial stability. Specifically, Zhang et al. (2024) find that only the physical climate risk measured by the count of extremely hot days holds significance for banks' loan quality in all three models, while the coefficients for extreme cold days are not significant. This can be interpreted as the heightened levels of these banks' NPLs resulting from physical climate risks predominantly stem from extremely hot weather. While both types of extreme weather can cause severe damage in production or human health, their findings suggest that in the context of financial stability in the banking sector, extreme heat is more detrimental. This is not entirely surprising. As known to many, extreme hot weather has emerged as a major global climate risk concern (Eckstein et al. 2021), which can lead to drought and other climate hazards, making it a more severe threat than extremely cold weather conditions.

4.1.2 Comparing City and Rural Commercial Banks

The distinction between city commercial banks and rural commercial banks in China has its roots in the historical evolution of the country's banking system. The original forms of these banks, namely the former city credit unions and rural credit unions, were established with different objectives and purposes. Understanding this historical context is essential for comprehending the unique challenges and focuses of each type of bank, especially in the context of climate risks. The precursor to city commercial banks in China, the city credit unions, were initially designed to cater to the financial needs of urban areas, focusing on the burgeoning urban economy and the diverse financial requirements of urban residents and businesses. City commercial banks typically operate in metropolitan or urban settings, serving a diverse clientele that includes large enterprises, small and medium-sized businesses, and urban residents. Their financial services are geared towards the dynamics of urban economic activities. On the other hand, rural commercial banks evolved from the restructuring of the former rural credit unions. They were established to address the financial needs of the agricultural sector, small and medium enterprises (SMEs), and residents in rural areas. Rural commercial banks play a crucial role in supporting the rural economy, which is often characterized by agriculture-dependent livelihoods. Their services are tailored to meet the specific challenges and opportunities present in rural communities.

Given the historical purposes and objectives of these two groups of banks, there are inherent differences in their susceptibility to climate risks, particularly physical risks associated with climate change. The agricultural sector, being a significant focus of rural commercial banks, is naturally more vulnerable to the impacts of extreme weather conditions, such as droughts, floods, and changes in temperature patterns. The livelihoods of rural communities often depend heavily on agriculture, making them more exposed to the immediate consequences of climate-related events. Issues such as crop failures, livestock losses, and disruptions in supply chains can have a direct impact on the financial health of rural commercial banks.

Zhang et al. (2024) therefore conjecture that these two groups of banks had different origins and tend to have had varied business purposes and borrower profiles, plausibly leading to notable variations in climate risk exposure of their loan portfolios. The authors proceed to investigate whether the impacts of both physical and transitional climate risks on these banks' loan quality would vary between city and rural commercial banks. Zhang et al. (2024) separately analyze the impacts of climate risks for each group of banks. The dependent variable remains to be NPLs of each subsample of banks, while the key explanatory variables in each mode are *PhyR*, High, Low, *TranR*, respectively. All control variables and fixed effects are included in each mode.

Comparing the results of the two bank groups, Zhang et al. (2024) indeed find that only rural commercial banks exhibit significant responses to climate risks in all cases, except for extremely cold days. In comparison, bank loan quality of urban commercial banks is not significantly affected by any type of climate risks discussed in their analysis. Generally, these results suggest that rural commercial banks are more susceptible to encountering difficulties when confronted with climate risks. Zhang et al. (2024) suggest that the stronger impact of physical climate risks on rural banks' loan quality is potentially caused by their direct impact on agricultural activities or production. These findings emphasize the need for tailored risk management strategies that consider the distinct vulnerabilities and strengths of each type of bank in the face of a changing climate. On the other hand, we should be cautious when trying to interpret the insignificant results for urban commercial banks in terms of climate transition risks, considering the smaller number of observations for this group.

4.2 *Robustness Checks*

The results of the baseline regressions in Zhang et al. (2024) indicate that both physical and transition climate risks exert significant and adverse impacts on the loan quality of Chinese regional commercial banks, especially extremely hot weather conditions. By comparing the rural and urban commercial banks, the former group is more susceptible to both types of climate risks. These results offer crucial insights for Chinese regulators, emphasizing the significance of climate risk in maintaining the stability of the financial system. To check the robustness and address potential technical concerns, Zhang et al. (2024) conduct a series of additional tests. The results are reported in this section.

4.2.1 Changing Thresholds for Extreme Weather Conditions

Given the ambiguity surrounding the definition of extreme temperatures, Zhang et al. (2024) reset the thresholds of extreme hot and cold days when constructing the measures of physical climate risks. This adjustment aims to establish more stringent criteria for extreme temperature events, reflecting harsher weather conditions that could affect the financial sector. The revised thresholds implemented by Zhang et al. (2024) involve increasing the upper threshold for extreme heat from the former 32 to 37°C. This new upper threshold aligns with the code orange extreme heat warning adopted in China, signalling conditions under which outdoor activities should be suspended. Simultaneously, the lower threshold for extreme cold is decreased from −15 to −20°C. These adjustments are made to better capture the severity of weather events and their potential impacts on regional commercial banks.

Despite the stricter thresholds, the results remain consistent with the baseline model. The magnitudes of the coefficients of key explanatory variables are smaller than those obtained in the baseline results. However, the major conclusions drawn from the study persist, indicating that physical climate risks, especially in the context of extreme heat, contribute to increased non-performing loans (NPLs) in regional commercial banks in China. It is interesting to note that, after adopting stricter temperature thresholds, the study reveals marginally significant negative impacts of extreme cold days on the loan quality of these banks. This implies that extreme cold days, if severe enough, are not entirely harmless but can also have adverse effects on banks' loan quality.

4.2.2 Dynamic Analysis with Lagged NPLs

Recognizing the importance of considering the persistence of loan quality in banks and potential lagged effects of non-performing loans (NPLs), Zhang et al. (2024) introduce autoregressive terms into the regressions, thereby transforming the panel analysis into a dynamic form. This dynamic modelling approach enables the researchers to account for the temporal dynamics and potential time lags associated with the impact of NPLs on loan quality.

To implement this dynamic panel model, Zhang et al. (2024) draw on the technique proposed by Arellano and Bond (1991) and Blundell and Bond (1998), which involves both difference-GMM (Generalized Method of Moments) and System-GMM estimations. Difference-GMM focuses on first-differenced equations, while System-GMM incorporates both differenced and level equations, providing a comprehensive approach to modelling the dynamic relationships within the panel data. The use of these econometric methods allows the researchers to capture the time-series dimension of the data and examine how past values of NPLs affect current loan quality in regional commercial banks in China. The autoregressive terms, represented by lagged NPLs, play a crucial role in this dynamic panel model. The results show that these lagged NPLs are significant in all models, emphasizing the necessity of controlling for the temporal dynamics and lagged effects of non-performing loans. This finding underscores the importance of understanding how the history of NPLs can influence the current state of loan quality in the banking sector.

The robustness of the main findings is further confirmed through the results of the dynamic panel model. In particular, all results, except for the outcomes of the System-GMM estimation on physical climate risks, align with the baseline regression results. This consistency strengthens the reliability of the study's main conclusions. It therefore suggests that the observed impact of physical climate risks, especially in the context of extreme temperatures, on non-performing loans in regional commercial banks remains robust even when accounting for the dynamic nature of the relationships over time.

4.2.3 Incorporating Lagged Variables

Zhang et al. (2024) incorporate one-period lagged terms for all control variables and lagged terms for climate risk variables into their regressions. This adjustment is motivated by the understanding that the impact of climate-related factors on banks' loan quality may not be immediate and could take time to materialize. By introducing lagged terms, the researchers aim to address potential delays in the manifestation of loan deterioration due to climate uncertainties, acknowledging that the damage from the climate side may have a time lag before becoming evident. Meanwhile, in the context of China's banking practices, Zhang et al. (2024) note the common classification of banks' non-performing loans (NPLs) into three categories: overdue loans, idle loans, and bad loans. Overdue loans specifically refer to those that are overdue within a 90-day period. This classification implies that there is a time delay before troubled loans are eventually classified as NPLs. The incorporation of lagged terms in the analysis aligns with this understanding and allows the researchers to account for the temporal aspect of loan classification.

The incorporation of one-period lagged terms for control variables and climate risk variables is a strategic move to account for the dynamic nature of the relationships under investigation. By doing so, the study recognizes the complexity of the processes involved in assessing loan quality and aims to better capture the temporal nuances associated with climate-related impacts on regional commercial banks in China. The key findings after including the lagged terms of control variables and climate risk variables remain consistent with the baseline regression findings. This consistency provides strong support for the robustness of the main results, even after considering potential delays in the manifestation of climate-related impacts on loan quality.

4.2.4 Excluding Municipalities from the Sample

In the original sample, Zhang et al. (2024) include four municipalities, which are provincial-level cities: Beijing, Tianjin, Shanghai, and Chongqing. The presence of these municipalities in the sample introduces a potential influence on the outcomes, given their distinct characteristics and possibly different exposure to climate risks compared to pure prefectural cities. To address this concern and test the robustness of their findings, the researchers conduct an additional analysis by excluding these municipalities from the sample. After excluding Beijing, Tianjin, Shanghai, and Chongqing, the new sample consists of 581 banks, and the total number of observations becomes 3,397. This adjustment allows the researchers to specifically assess the impact of physical and transition climate risks on non-performing loans (NPLs) in a sample that comprises only prefectural cities, providing a more focused analysis on regions that might be more comparable in terms of economic and environmental characteristics.

The results of this additional robustness check reveal that the difference between the outcomes based on the new sample and the original full sample is almost negligible. Despite excluding the four municipalities, both physical and transition risks continue to contribute to elevated NPLs in regional commercial banks. This consistency in the findings supports the robustness of the main conclusions drawn from the study even after excluding the provincial-level cities. The fact that the impact of climate risks on NPLs persists in the absence of these major municipalities suggests that the observed relationships are not heavily driven by the unique characteristics of Beijing, Tianjin, Shanghai, and Chongqing. The researchers' decision to perform this sensitivity analysis enhances the credibility of their main conclusions and reinforces the notion that the influence of climate risks on banks' loan quality is a broader phenomenon applicable to a diverse set of regions, not limited to the specific circumstances of major metropolitan areas.

5 The Green Finance Reform: A Quasi-Natural Experiment

Transition climate risk arises from societal efforts to address climate change, and related policies can impact firms by either increasing costs (such as emissions trading) or providing financial benefits to support low-carbon transition (such as green finance reform, Liu and Wang (2023)). Motivated by this rationale, Zhang et al. (2024) further investigate the effects of policy shocks associated with the low-carbon transition. The authors use a green finance reform policy in China as a quasi-natural experiment to explore the role of transition risk and its potential causality with the NPLs in China's regional commercial banks.

5.1 *Formulation of Hypotheses*

In 2017, a notable policy initiative took shape in China with the State Council's approval of green finance pilot zones in eight cities spanning five provinces: Zhejiang, Jiangxi, Guangdong, Guizhou, and Xinjiang. This strategic move by the Chinese government aimed to foster the development of green finance by designating specific zones for piloting innovative approaches and products. The overarching objectives of establishing these green finance pilot zones included supporting the creation of green financial products, promoting the growth of green institutions, and constructing a financial services system tailored for the needs of green industrial upgrading (Yan et al. 2022). This policy reform is considered a positive step in addressing environmental concerns and promoting sustainable financial practices. By focusing on these designated pilot zones, the Chinese government aimed to facilitate the integration of green finance into mainstream financial activities, aligning economic growth with environmental sustainability goals. The establishment of these zones signifies a commitment to exploring and refining financial mechanisms that can contribute to a more sustainable and environmentally friendly economic landscape.

Against this backdrop, Zhang et al. (2024) formulate a testable hypothesis related to the impact of this policy on banks' exposure to transition risks and, consequently, their levels of non-performing loans (NPLs). The first hypothesis posits that banks operating within these green finance pilot zones, compared to those in non-reform cities, would experience lower exposure to transition risks. The rationale behind this expectation is that the policy measures introduced in these zones are designed to mitigate uncertainty and create a supportive environment for the development of green finance.

In addition to examining the impact of green finance pilot zones on transition risks, Zhang et al. (2024) formulate a second hypothesis that focuses on the potential adjustments in the loan portfolios of banks within these designated zones. This hypothesis is rooted in the expectation that, in response to the policy change, banks operating in green finance pilot zones would strategically modify their lending practices. The specific adjustment hypothesized is a lower share of high-carbon loans within their portfolios following the implementation of the green finance policy, compared to a control group. The rationale behind this hypothesis is tied to the recognition that high-carbon loans typically entail greater transition risks for banks. These loans are associated with industries or projects that are more vulnerable to shifts in environmental regulations, market preferences, and global efforts to address climate change. As a result, they may imply higher potential losses for banks due to the increased uncertainty and risks associated with the transition to a more sustainable and low-carbon economy. This hypothesis suggests that the implementation of the green finance policy would incentivize banks within the pilot zones to align their lending practices with environmental sustainability goals. By reducing the share of high-carbon loans, these banks may be proactively managing their exposure to transition risks and positioning themselves in line with the broader objectives of the green finance initiative.

5.2 *Effects of the Green Finance Polity*

Zhang et al. (2024) test both hypotheses in a Difference-in-Differences (DID) setup, using both basic DID regressions and regressions after propensity score matching (PSM). In their DID framework, banks in the designated green finance pilot zones constitute the treatment group, while those in non-pilot zones serve as the control group. The dependent variable is specified differently for each hypothesis: either the Non-Performing Loans (NPLs) or the share of high-carbon loans scaled by total assets for a given bank, corresponding to the first and second hypotheses, respectively.

To capture the temporal dynamics introduced by the policy, the researchers include a dummy variable labeled "Pilot" in the regression analysis. This variable takes a value of one after the policy is implemented in 2017 and zero otherwise. Another dummy variable, "Treat," is introduced to indicate whether a bank is located in a pilot zone. The critical element of the DID setup involves the inclusion of the interaction term between "Pilot" and "Treat" as the key parameter of interest. This interaction term forms the basis for assessing the differential impact of the policy between treatment and control groups over time.

Before testing the hypotheses, Zhang et al. (2024) provide a visual representation of NPLs and the share of high-carbon loans for both the control and treatment groups. Figure 5a and b present graphical insights into the trends within these variables. The electricity, heating, gas, and water supply (EHGW) sector is considered the high-carbon sector, given its much higher carbon intensity than others.

The results from the DID analysis reveal no significant differences in NPLs between the treatment and control groups before the establishment of the pilot zones. However, a distinct gap emerges from 2017 onward, following the implementation of the green finance policy. Banks in the treatment group consistently exhibit lower NPLs on average compared to those in the control group. This observed gap in

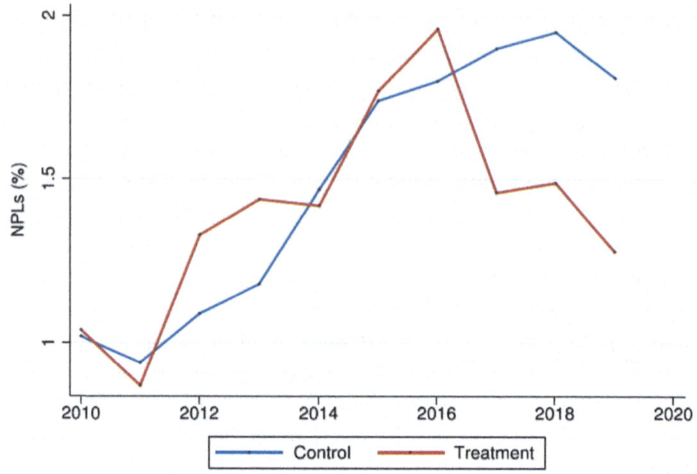

(a) Non-performing loans

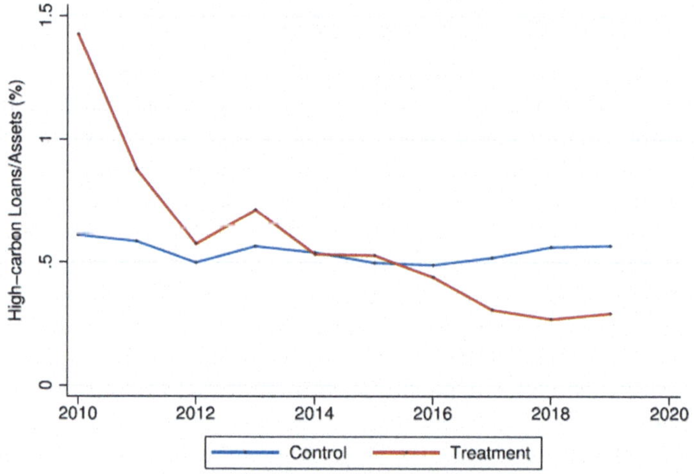

(b) High carbon loans

Fig. 5 Differences in NPLs and high carbon loans between banks in non-pilot and pilot zones (Zhang et al. 2024)

NPLs is consistent with the first hypothesis posited by Zhang et al. (2024). The findings validate their proposition that the establishment of green finance pilot zones contributes to an improvement in the loan quality of banks located within these zones. The temporal shift in NPLs indicates a positive and sustained impact of the policy on the financial health of banks operating in alignment with green finance initiatives.

Similarly, the DID analysis reveals a clear gap in high-carbon loan shares between the treatment and control groups after the policy implementation. Banks in the treatment group exhibit a lower share of high-carbon loans, aligning with the expectations outlined in the second hypothesis. This result signifies a strategic shift in the loan portfolios of banks within the green finance pilot zones towards greener sectors with lower carbon intensity.

To further validate the robustness of their findings, Zhang et al. (2024) conduct parallel trend tests. These tests assess the parallel trends assumption crucial for the validity of the DID analysis. The results, as depicted in Fig. 6, support the conclusions drawn from the DID analysis. The parallel trend tests provide additional evidence that the observed changes in NPLs and high-carbon loan shares are attributable to the establishment of green finance pilot zones and not driven by pre-existing trends or external factors.

By focusing on the quasi-natural experiment provided by the establishment of green finance pilot zones, the findings derived from Zhang et al. (2024) provide valuable insights with direct policy implications for regulators and policymakers. The evidence suggests that the implementation of this policy is significantly beneficial in reducing transition risks for banks and concurrently improving their loan quality, contributing to an overall enhancement of financial stability. The primary objective of the green finance policy is to encourage banks, particularly those in the designated green pilot zones, to prioritize low-carbon and environmentally sustainable projects when granting loans. The research findings underscore the effectiveness of this policy measure in achieving its intended goals. The success of the green finance policy in incentivizing banks to support low-carbon projects emphasizes the importance of aligning financial sector practices with broader environmental and sustainability objectives.

6 The Role of Bank Competition

While the above analysis indicates that the implementation of green finance policies can reduce transition risk and enhance the loan quality of regional banks, another potential channel to alleviate climate risk shocks is through the development of regional financial markets. There is a growing literature on the role of financial market development in mitigating the adverse impacts of climate risks. For example, Zhang and Managi (2020) study the relationship between financial development and natural disasters of the pacific small island states, and find that financial development and governments' risk management power contribute to alleviating the effects of climate shocks. Chen et al. (2022) find significantly adverse impacts of climate physical and transition risks on the foreign direct investment inflows of 108 developing counties, but improved national governance can effectively reduce such negative impacts. Fu et al. (2014) and Fiordelisi and Mare (2014) suggest that banking competition can contribute to financial stability, based on observations in the Asian

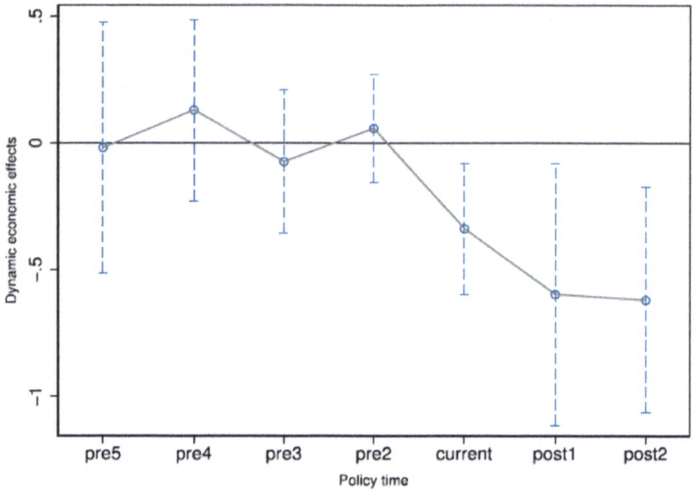

(a) Non-performing loans

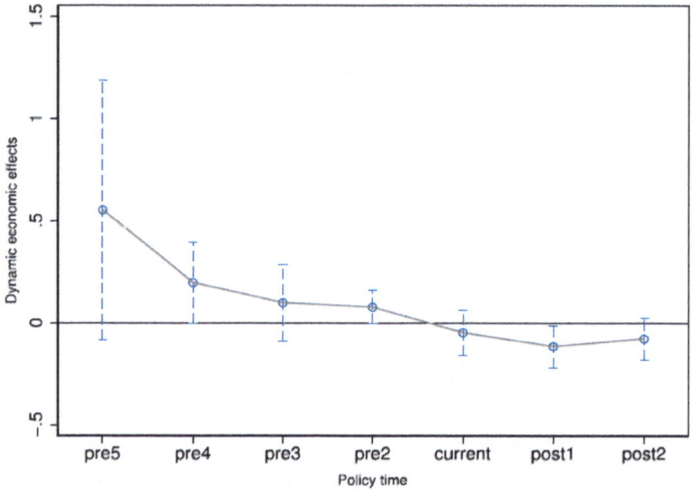

(b) High carbon loans

Fig. 6 Parallel trend tests of the green finance policy (Zhang et al. 2024)

Pacific and European markets, respectively. The former study shows that competition can lower banks' risk-taking and therefore enhance stability, while the latter documents reduced instability in the banking sector as a result of competition among European cooperative banks.

In the context of China, there has been ongoing reforms in the banking sector aiming to establish a market-oriented system and enhance competition, thereby improving efficiency and overall performance. Existing evidence shows that market reforms in China can lead to increased competition and efficiency in the banking sector, resulting in improved bank performance (Fu and Heffernan 2009). The historical landscape of China's banking sector has witnessed a significant transformation, particularly in terms of market concentration and the emergence of diverse banking entities. Traditionally, the sector was characterized by high concentration, primarily dominated by the big five state-owned banks. These major players, known as the big five, held a substantial share of the market and played a central role in China's financial system.

However, over time, there has been a notable shift in the competitive dynamics of the banking sector. The emergence of joint-stock banks and regional commercial banks has introduced increased competition and diversity into the financial landscape (Gao et al. 2019). This shift has been instrumental in breaking down the highly monopolistic structure that characterized the sector in the past. According to data released by the CBIRC, as of the end of June 2022, there were a total of 4,599 bank-type financial institutions in China. Notably, regional commercial banks accounted for a significant share of 85.8%, comprising 3,946 institutions. This category includes 125 city commercial banks, 1,600 rural commercial banks, and 2,221 other rural financial institutions. In terms of total assets across all commercial banks, regional commercial banks, when combined (city and rural commercial banks), held a substantial share of 26.4%. This indicates the growing influence and market presence of regional commercial banks in China's financial landscape. Although the big five state-owned commercial banks still command a significant share, representing 41.9% of total assets, the dynamics have evolved, and the previously highly monopolistic situation has undergone substantial changes.

The diversification and increased prominence of regional commercial banks highlight a more competitive and dynamic banking environment in China. While the big five continue to play a foundational role, the growing role of regional commercial banks reflects a trend toward greater diversity and competition within the sector. Motivated by the understanding that the competitive dynamics within the banking sector may play a crucial role in shaping how banks respond and adapt to environmental challenges, Zhang et al. (2024) extend their investigation to explore the influence of bank competition on the ability of regional commercial banks to address climate risks.

To measure the level of banking competition at the city level, the researchers employ two widely recognized metrics: the Herfindahl–Hirschman Index (HHI) and the concentration ratio of the five largest state-owned banks (CR5). These measures are constructed using branch information provided by the China Banking Regulatory Commission for each city. The adoption of these measures follows the existing literature on bank competition (Chong et al. 2013). The Herfindahl–Hirschman Index (HHI) is a standard measure of market concentration. In the context of this study, higher HHI values indicate less competition in a city's banking sector, reflecting a more concentrated market. The concentration ratio of the CR5 provides an additional perspective on market concentration, with higher values implying a lower degree of competition among the largest state-owned banks in a city.

Given the argument that higher competition may enhance banks' efficiency and risk management, Zhang et al. (2024) test the hypothesis if banks in cities with higher concentration (equivalent to lower competition) exhibit greater exposure to climate risk, or vice versa. The authors incorporate interaction terms between climate risks and competition measures in the baseline regressions to test this hypothesis. The regression results present mixed evidence regarding the impact of physical and transition risks.

In models investigating the effects of physical climate risks, the findings presented by Zhang et al. (2024) reveal significant and positive coefficients for the interaction terms involving climate risk and regional concentration in the banking sector. This suggests that higher regional concentration, indicative of less competition, amplifies the adverse impact of physical climate risks on loan quality, as evidenced by an increase in NPLs. In contrast, lower concentration or higher levels of bank competition appear to assist regional banks in better navigating and mitigating the effects of physical climate risks. The plausible explanation for this phenomenon is rooted in the idea that banks operating in a highly competitive business environment may find it imperative to enhance their risk management practices to not only survive but also thrive amid intensified competition.

However, the models examining the effects of transition risks do not present a similar mitigating effect of competition on such risks. This absence of a mitigating mechanism arising from competition can be attributed to the complex nature of uncertainties caused by transition risks. Transition risks, related to the shift towards a more sustainable and low-carbon economy, introduce multifaceted challenges that may not be as readily addressed through increased competition alone. Moreover, the recent introduction of transition policies applies only to a subset of banks rather than the entire banking sector, adding an additional layer of complexity to the evaluation of the impact of competition on mitigating transition risks. The intricate relationship between competition and risk becomes even more complicated with the implementation of green finance policies. The traditional standard mechanisms that might explain the relationship between competition and risk may not fully capture the nuanced dynamics introduced by policies aimed at fostering sustainable finance. The shift towards green finance policies implies a fundamental restructuring of priorities and risk assessments within the banking sector, making the relationship between competition and risk multifaceted and context-dependent.

In summary, these findings shed light on the nuanced interactions between competition, climate risks, and the banking sector. While competition appears to have a mitigating effect on the adverse impact of physical climate risks on loan quality, the same does not hold true for transition risks. The evolving landscape of green finance policies further complicates this relationship, emphasizing the need for a more sophisticated understanding of how competition and policy interventions intersect in shaping risk dynamics within the banking sector.

7 Conclusions

As climate change continues to unfold at an accelerated pace, the challenges it presents cut across geographical, political, and economic boundaries. Mitigating and adapting to the impacts of climate change requires collaborative efforts, innovative solutions, and a shared commitment to building a more resilient and sustainable future. The recognition of climate change as a rapidly intensifying global phenomenon serves as a clarion call for renewed and accelerated action on the part of governments, businesses, and individuals alike. Only through united and resolute efforts can the world hope to navigate the complexities of climate change and safeguard the well-being of current and future generations.

This chapter reviews and discusses the research and findings in Zhang et al. (2024), which seeks to explore the impact of climate risks on the financial stability of Chinese banks, responding to the growing body of literature addressing the socio-economic consequences of climate change. Despite climate risks not yet being formally incorporated into the policy framework of Chinese authorities, it has become a subject of increasing interest to financial regulators and central banks. Given China's vast geographical expanse and exposure to diverse climate challenges, coupled with its commitment to carbon neutrality by 2060 and introduction of a series transition policies, Zhang et al. (2024) investigate how banks in the country respond to climate-related shocks. The aim is to provide valuable insights for regulators in formulating effective measures to manage climate risks and maintain financial stability.

The study of Zhang et al. (2024) employs two measures to assess climate risk: physical and transition climate risks. Physical climate challenges are gauged using a city's extreme temperature each year, while a bank-specific carbon-based measure serves as a proxy for transition risk. Drawing from a sample of regional commercial banks in China, the study establishes that both physical and transition climate risks significantly impact financial stability by elevating levels of NPLs. Specifically, climate risk adversely affects financial stability by diminishing the loan quality of banks, with rural commercial banks being more susceptible. Given their relatively smaller size, the higher levels of troubled loans in these banks can inflict more significant damage, warranting increased attention from regulators. The robustness of these findings is confirmed through various tests.

Additionally, Zhang et al. (2024) delve into how transition policies may influence the loan quality of regional commercial banks, providing causal evidence that transition risk is a pertinent factor for financial stability. Using the establishment of green finance pilot zones by the Chinese government in 2017 as a quasi-natural experiment to represent lower transition risks, the authors examine how this policy impacts banks' loan quality and behavior. The analysis reveals that the policy, indicative of lower transition risks, can reduce NPLs, potentially due to adjustments in loan portfolios by banks operating in the pilot zones. These findings suggest the significant and positive role regulators can play in reducing climate uncertainty and enhancing financial stability, through adjusting banks' incentives and operations.

Furthermore, Zhang et al. (2024) investigates the role of regional bank competition in mitigating the adverse stability shocks of climate risks. In line with the existing literature, it finds that higher levels of regional bank competition can reduce banks' exposure to climate risks, specifically in the context of physical risks. The underlying mechanisms are grounded in the understanding that competition enhances efficiency, compels better risk management practices, and ultimately improves bank performance.

However, caution is advised by the authors in interpreting these results, acknowledging certain limitations of this study. The complexity of climate risk measurements, despite the efforts of Zhang et al. (2024) to justify physical and transition risks, leaves room for additional climate challenges which are not fully captured in the study. Additionally, the evolving role of the Chinese banking sector in the country's green transition, following dual carbon targets, introduces new features not covered by the data. Future research with updated data is essential to address these aspects.

In conclusion, Zhang et al. (2024) provide crucial empirical evidence for financial regulators and bank managers, emphasizing the significance of integrating climate risk considerations into bank operations, particularly in the lending process. Amidst global efforts to combat climate change, uncertainties associated with both physical and transitional aspects can exert substantial impacts on the financial sector, potentially jeopardizing the collective efforts to address climate change. Recognizing the pivotal role of banks as significant financial intermediaries, it becomes imperative for financial regulators and practitioners to acknowledge the relevance of climate risk and incorporate it into their strategies for the sake of maintaining financial stability.

References

Arellano M, Bond S. 1991. Some tests of specification for panel data: Monte Carlo evidence and an application to employment equations. Rev. Econ. Stud. 58 (2), 277–297.

Battiston S, Mandel A, Monasterolo I, Schütze F, Visentin G. 2017. A climate stress-test of the financial system. Nat. Clim. Change 7 (4), 283–288.

Battiston S, Dafermos Y, Monasterolo I. 2021. Climate risks and financial stability. J. Financ. Stab. 54, 100867.

Bauer M D, Huber D, Rudebusch G D, Wilms O. 2023. Where is the carbon premium? Global performance of green and brown stocks. J. Clim. Finance, 100006.

Blundell R, Bond S. 1998. Initial conditions and moment restrictions in dynamic panel data models. J. Econom. 87 (1), 115–143.

Bolton P, Després, M, da Silva L A P, Samama F, Svartzman R. 2020. The Green Swan. BIS Books.

Bolton P, Kacperczyk M. 2021. Do investors care about carbon risk? J. Financ. Econ. 142 (2), 517–549.

Bouri E, Iqbal N, Klein T. 2022. Climate policy uncertainty and the price dynamics of green and brown energy stocks. Finance Res. Lett. 47, 102740.

Breitenstein M, Nguyen D K, Walther T. 2021. Environmental hazards and risk management in the financial sector: a systematic literature review. J. Econ. Surv. 35(2), 512–538.

Caldecott B, Harnett E, Cojoianu T, Kok I, Pfeiffer A. 2016. Stranded Assets: A Climate Risk Challenge. Inter-American Development Bank, Washington DC.

Campiglio E, Dafermos Y, Monnin P, Ryan-Collins J, Schotten G, Tanaka M. 2018. Climate change challenges for central banks and financial regulators. Nat. Clim. Change 8 (6), 462–468.
Chen Y, Zhang D, Wu F, Ji Q. 2022. Climate risks and foreign direct investment in developing countries: the role of national governance. Sustain. Sci. 17 (5), 1723–1740.
Chen J, Liu X, Ou F, Lu M, Wang P. 2023a. Green lending and stock price crash risk: evidence from the green credit reform in China. J. Int. Money Financ. 130, 102770.
Chen Y, Guo K, Ji Q, Zhang D. 2023b. "Not all climate risks are alike": heterogeneous responses of financial firms to natural disasters in China. Finance Res. Lett. 52, 103538.
Chenet H, Ryan-Collins J, Van Lerven F. 2021. Finance, climate-change and radical uncertainty: towards a precautionary approach to financial policy. Ecol. Econ. 183, 106957.
Chong T T L, Lu L, Ongena S. 2013. Does banking competition alleviate or worsen credit constraints faced by small- and medium-sized enterprises? Evidence from China. J. Bank. Finance 37 (9), 3412–3424.
Dafermos Y, Nikolaidi M, Galanis G. 2018. Climate change, financial stability and monetary policy. Ecol. Econ. 152, 219–234.
Dai Z, Zhang X. 2023. Climate policy uncertainty and risks taken by the bank: evidence from China. Int. Rev. Financ. Anal. 87, 102579.
Eckstein D, Künzel V, Schäfer L. 2021. The Global Climate Risk Index 2021. Germanwatch, Bonn.
Fiordelisi F, Mare D S. 2014. Competition and financial stability in European cooperative banks. J. Int. Money Financ. 45, 1–16.
Fu X M, Heffernan S. 2009. The effects of reform on China's bank structure and performance. J. Bank. Finance 33 (1), 39–52.
Fu X M, Lin Y R, Molyneux P. 2014. Bank competition and financial stability in Asia Pacific. J. Bank. Finance 38, 64–77.
Gao H, Ru H, Townsend R, Yang X. 2019. Rise of bank competition: Evidence from banking deregulation in China. Technical report. National Bureau of Economic Research.
Gavriilidis K. 2021. Measuring climate policy uncertainty. Available at SSRN 3847388.
Griffin P, Lont D, Lubberink M. 2019. Extreme high surface temperature events and equity-related physical climate risk. Weather Clim. Extrem. 26, 100220.
Guesmi K, Makrychoriti P, Spyrou S. 2023. The relationship between climate risk, climate policy uncertainty, and CO2 emissions: empirical evidence from the US. J. Econ. Behav. Organ. 212, 610–628.
Guo J, Long S, Luo W. 2022. Nonlinear effects of climate policy uncertainty and financial speculation on the global prices of oil and gas. Int. Rev. Financ. Anal. 83, 102286.
Hong H, Li F W, Xu J. 2019. Climate risks and market efficiency. J. Econom. 208 (1), 265–281.
Hong H, Karolyi G A, Scheinkman J A. 2020. Climate finance. Rev. Financ. Stud. 33 (3), 1011–1023.
Huang H H, Kerstein J, Wang C, Wu F. 2022a. Firm climate risk, risk management, and bank loan financing. Strateg. Manag. J. 43 (13), 2849–2880.
Huang H, Mbanyele W, Wang F, Song M, Wang Y. 2022b. Climbing the quality ladder of green innovation: does green finance matter? Technol. Forecast. Soc. Change 184, 122007.
Javadi, S., Masum, A.-A., 2021. The impact of climate change on the cost of bank loans. J. Corp. Finance 69, 102019.
Ji Q, Zhang D. 2019. How much does financial development contribute to renewable energy growth and upgrading of energy structure in China? Energy Policy 128, 114–124.
Jung S.H, Feng T. 2020. Government subsidies for green technology development under uncertainty. Eur. J. Oper. Res. 286 (2), 726–739.
Khan M.A, Siddique A, Sarwar Z. 2020. Determinants of non-performing loans in the banking sector in developing state. Asian J. Account. Res. 5 (1), 135–145.
Klomp J. 2014. Financial fragility and natural disasters: an empirical analysis. J. Financ. Stab. 13, 180–192.
Krueger P, Sautner Z, Starks L T. 2020. The importance of climate risks for institutional investors. Rev. Financ. Stud. 33 (3), 1067–1111.

Lee S O, Mark N C, Nauerz J, Rawls J, Wei Z. 2022. Global temperature shocks and real exchange rates. J. Clim. Finance 100004.
Lee C-C, Wang F. 2022. How does digital inclusive finance affect carbon intensity? Econ. Anal. Policy 75, 174–190.
Lemoine D. 2021. The climate risk premium: how uncertainty affects the social cost of carbon. J. Assoc. Environ. Resour. Econ. 8 (1), 27–57.
Li S, Pan Z. 2022. Climate transition risk and bank performance: evidence from China. J. Environ. Manag. 323, 116275.
Liu S, Wang Y. 2023. Green innovation effect of pilot zones for green finance reform: evidence of quasi natural experiment. Technol. Forecast. Soc. Change 186, 122079.
Long S, Lucey B, Kumar S, Zhang D, Zhang Z. 2022. Climate finance: what we know and what we should know? J. Clim. Finance 1, 100005.
Löschel A, Lutz B J, Managi S. 2019. The impacts of the EU ETS on efficiency and economic performance–an empirical analyses for German manufacturing firms. Resour. Energy Econ. 56, 71–95.
Lynas M, Houlton B Z, Perry S. 2021. Greater than 99% consensus on human caused climate change in the peer-reviewed scientific literature. Environ. Res. Lett. 16(11), 114005.
Monasterolo I. 2020. Climate change and the financial system. Annu. Rev. Resour. Econ. 12, 299–320.
Nguyen Q, Diaz-Rainey I, Kuruppuarachchi D, McCarten M, Tan E K. 2023. Climate transition risk in us loan portfolios: are all banks the same? Int. Rev. Financ. Anal. 85, 102401.
Park S K. 2021. Legal strategy disrupted: managing climate change and regulatory transformation. Am. Bus. Law J. 58 (4), 711–749.
Ramelli S, Ossola E, Rancan M. 2021. Stock price effects of climate activism: evidence from the first global climate strike. J. Corp. Finance 69, 102018.
Reinders H J, Schoenmaker D, van Dijk M. 2023. A finance approach to climate stress testing. J. Int. Money Financ. 131, 102797.
Ren X, Qin J, Dong K. 2022. How does climate policy uncertainty affect excessive corporate debt? The case of China. J. Environ. Assess. Policy Manag. 24 (02), 2250025.
Rosvold E L, Buhaug H. 2021. Gdis, a global dataset of geocoded disaster locations. Sci. Data 8 (1), 61.
Semieniuk G, Campiglio E, Mercure J F, Volz U, Edwards N R. 2021. Low-carbon transition risks for finance. Wiley Interdiscip. Rev.: Clim. Change 12 (1), e678.
Umar M, Sun G. 2018. Determinants of non-performing loans in Chinese banks. J. Asia Bus. Stud. 12 (3), 273–289.
Xu X, Huang S, Lucey B M, An H. 2023. The impacts of climate policy uncertainty on stock markets: comparison between China and the US. Int. Rev. Financ. Anal. 88, 102671.
Yan C, Mao Z, Ho K-C. 2022. Effect of green financial reform and innovation pilot zones on corporate investment efficiency. Energy Econ. 113, 106185.
Zhang D, Managi S. 2020. Financial development, natural disasters, and economics of the Pacific small island states. Econ. Anal. Policy 66, 168–181.
Zhang D, Cai J, Dickinson D G, Kutan A M. 2016. Non-performing loans, moral hazard and regulation of the Chinese commercial banking system. J. Bank. Finance 63, 48–60.
Zhang D, Cai J, Liu J, Kutan A M. 2018. Real estate investments and financial stability: evidence from regional commercial banks in China. Eur. J. Finance 24(16), 1388–1408.
Zhang D, Hu M, Ji Q. 2020. Financial markets under the global pandemic of Covid-19. Finance Res. Lett. 36, 101528.
Zhang X, Zhang S, Lu L. 2022. The banking instability and climate change: evidence from Chinda. Energy Econ. 106, 105787.
Zhang D, Wu Y, Ji Q, Guo K, Lucey B. 2024. Climate impacts on the loan quality of Chinese regional commercial banks. Journal of International Money and Finance, 140, 102975.
Zhenmin L, Espinosa P. 2019. Tackling climate change to accelerate sustainable development. Nat. Clim. Change 9 (7), 494–496.

Zscheischler J, Westra S, Van Den Hurk B J, Seneviratne S I, Ward P J, Pitman A, AghaKouchak A, Bresch D N, Leonard M, Wahl T. 2018. Future climate risk from compound events. Nat. Clim. Change 8 (6), 469–477.

ESG and Corporate Climate Actions

Lei Lei and Dayong Zhang

Abstract The rise and development of environmental, social and governance (ESG) globally has become a compelling trend in the twenty-first century. ESG represents the three key dimensions of environmental, social and corporate governance, and they have become an important topic of concern for investors and corporations. This chapter first introduces the concept and connotation of ESG, reviews its developmental history and relevant theoretical foundations, and describes the basic connection between ESG and climate change. Second, this chapter reviews current discourse in the literature on ESG and corporate behaviour, particularly studies related to climate change, in terms of both corporate ESG performance and related information disclosure. Finally, this chapter briefly describes possible directions for future research based on the existing research base. This chapter will help provide an in-depth understanding of ESG-related concepts, a comprehensive understanding of ESG's historical evolution and current development, and an understanding of current corporate behaviour related to ESG and climate change.

Keywords ESG · Corporate climate actions · Corporate governance

1 ESG Concepts and Connotations

This section focusses on the basic concepts and connotations associated with ESG and introduces the history of ESG's development further, along with relevant theoretical foundations. We also elaborate on the connection between ESG and climate change.

L. Lei (✉)
School of Accounting, Southwestern University of Finance and Economics, 555 Liutai Avenue, Chengdu 611130, China
e-mail: lei_lei@swufe.edu.cn

D. Zhang
Research Institute of Economics and Management, Southwestern University of Finance and Economics, Chengdu 611130, China

F. Wu et al. (eds.), *Climate Finance*, Climate Change and Energy Transition,
https://doi.org/10.1007/978-981-97-3308-8_6

1.1 ESG Definition

ESG is an acronym for *environmental, social* and *governance* and is an investment philosophy and corporate evaluation standard that focusses on companies' nonfinancial performance in terms of environmental protection, social responsibility and corporate governance. The ESG system comprises three key components: ESG disclosure; ESG evaluation and ESG investment.

ESG disclosure is the process by which a business enterprise or asset management organisation transparently discloses its ESG information to investors (i.e., shareholders), stakeholders and the public. MSCI, the leading international ESG evaluator, defines ESG evaluation as a measure of a company's resilience to long-term, material ESG risks in the industry. ESG investment, according to the United Nations' Principles for Responsible Investment (UNPRI), is a process that involves integrating ESG information into a company's investment strategy. More specifically, it entails integrating environmental, social and corporate governance factors into investment decisions and active ownership. Environmental factors include issues such as climate change, resource depletion, waste, pollution and deforestation. Social factors include issues such as human rights, modern slavery, child labour, working conditions and employee relations. Corporate governance includes issues such as bribery and corruption, executive compensation, board diversity and structure, political lobbying and contributions, and tax strategies.

ESG has multiple meanings. First, ESG is a value concept that advocates for synergistic and sustainable development of the environment, society and economy through investment. It also advocates for improvements in corporate governance, including the introduction of public interests, such as environmental protection and social development, into companies' value systems to realise the overall enhancement of social value in companies' business activities. Second, ESG provides an investment evaluation system that comprises financial and nonfinancial dimensions, as well as a measurable and comparable evaluation method. Finally, ESG is an investment strategy that emphasises how inputs such as CSR can help improve financial performance and reduce business risks, as investors have shifted from focussing only on traditional financial indicators to also measuring enterprises' social benefits comprehensively.

1.2 ESG Development

ESG-related ideas have a long history, dating back as far as the practice of responsible investing in connection with religious practices in B.C. Initially, certain investors screened for sinful stocks—such as alcohol, tobacco and gambling—in the name of religious beliefs, but today, investors and corporations focus on risks related to ESG from a broader perspective. From its religious origins to its modern form, ESG ideas have gone through three major stages of development, as described below.

1.2.1 Ethical Investing (Prior to the 1960s)

ESG-related concepts first originated as ethical investing in connection with religious investment philosophies and activities, in which religious groups refused to invest in industries with perspectives that were contrary to their doctrinal beliefs. Morality always has been a fundamental consideration in ethical investment decisions, but the application of the principle has varied. Some religious groups view ethical investments as investment guidelines, while others make ethical investments because of legal requirements. Ethical investment philosophies also vary by religious group, resulting in many different interpretations of the topic.

In biblical times, Jewish law mandated ethical investment. In the first five books of the Bible, written by Moses between 1500 and 1300 B.C.E., the Jewish concept of *Tzedek* (meaning 'justice' and 'equality') appears, a concept that speaks to the need for justice and fairness in all aspects of life and is intended to redress human-caused imbalances, including economic activity. Investment makes people property owners, and people have a responsibility to use ownership to prevent direct and potential harm.

In the United States, responsible investing originated in the early eighteenth century. In 1703, the Methodist denomination of Protestant Christianity was founded in the U.S. The Methodists spread their religious teachings through capital market investment activities by boycotting the slave trade, smuggling and conspicuous consumption, as well as refusing to invest in companies that manufactured alcohol or tobacco products and supported gambling. Subsequently, other religious groups followed the Methodists' lead. The Quakers prohibited investments related to the slave trade and war. Members of this denomination also have since established two financial institutions famous in modern history: Barclays Bank and Lloyds Bank.

Early responsible investment practices were popular only with religious organisations, mainly in the form of resistance to sinful industries, and despite their popularity and long history, they did not make a notable impact on capital markets and corporate activity. This phenomenon did not change until the 1920s, when the corporate social responsibility (CSR) concept evolved. Some scholars did not explicitly define CSR outright, but they argued that businesses' responsibility goes beyond making profits. Oliver Sheldon, in his book *The Philosophy of Management*, suggested that the responsibility of business is to pursue its own profits while improving the community's interests. Since then, despite more than 20 years of debate, the CSR concept had not changed significantly. It was not until 1953 that Howard Bowen gave a more rigorous definition of CSR in his book *Social Responsibility of the Businessmen*, in which he defined CSR as the policies, programmes and actions that businesses take to satisfy societal goals and values. The author argued that large corporations can influence citizens' lives in various ways and should fulfil greater social responsibilities.

1.2.2 Corporate Social Responsibility (1960s to Early 2000s)

Starting in the 1960s, CSR gradually moved from religious organisations to the public realm, and the responsible investing concept began to encompass social issues such as war, civil rights, labour and the environment.

By the late 1960s, the popularisation and development of CSR was driven directly by public discontent with the Vietnam War in the U.S. For example, Vietnam War protesters boycotted companies that supplied weapons for the war effort and demanded that university endowments no longer invest in defence contractors. In 1968, the Medical Human Rights Commission acquired shares in Dow Chemical and filed a proxy statement recommending that Dow's bylaws be changed to prohibit the sale of napalm to any buyer unwilling to provide assurances that the substance would not be used on human beings, a statement that prompted Dow to cease production of napalm quietly a year later. Against the backdrop of rapidly rising demand for responsible investment, the Pax World Fund, the first socially responsible mutual fund in the United States, was established in 1971 to discourage investment in companies that profited from the Vietnam War.

Simultaneously, the public and international organisations began to pay attention to environmental protection issues, and CSR's connotation gradually was extended to environmental protection and climate change concepts. In 1962, the environment-themed book *Silent Spring* was published, depicting an environmental pollution disaster and triggering public concerns and reflection on environmental issues. In 1972, the United Nations Conference on the Human Environment (UNCEN) adopted the world's first programmatic document to protect the environment, 'Declaration on the Human Environment'. In the 1980s, several major environmental disasters occurred worldwide, including the 1984 toxic gas leak from a pesticide plant in India, the 1986 accident at the Chernobyl nuclear power plant in Ukraine and the massive 1989 oil spill from an Exxon Valdez tanker in the Gulf of Alaska, which triggered concerns about the environment and climate change, and helped develop responsible investment in the environmental field. In 1990, the Domini 400 Social Index, now known as the MSCI KLD 400 Social Index—the first market capitalisation-weighted index to track responsible investing—was launched. In 1992, the United Nations Conference on Environment and Development (UNCED) adopted Agenda 21, which advocates for environmental protection while promoting development. In 1997, the Global Reporting Initiative (GRI) was established to improve business organisations' sustainability reporting, and the Standards for the Preparation of Sustainability Reports (STRS), issued by the GRI, became one of the most universally accepted reporting systems in the world today.

The academic definition of CSR also evolved during this period. In the 1960s, the CSR concept remained largely ethically oriented. Some scholars suggested that CSR entails fulfilment of public expectations and enhancement of socioeconomic well-being, in addition to personal and corporate interests. In the 1970s, the CSR concept was differentiated and diversified. Economists provided a new perspective that socially responsible businesses should consider multiple interests that include their employees, suppliers, distributors, the local community and the country as a whole, not merely focus on making profits for shareholders. The U.S. Committee for Economic Development, in its report 'Social Responsibilities of Business Corporations', suggests that CSR comprises three circles: The inner circle represents the basic responsibilities of business, such as promoting economic growth, creating jobs and providing products for economic functions. The middle circle represents awareness and action on evolving social values and priorities outside of economic functions, such as environmental protection, customers' right to know and employees' right to fairness. The outer circle represents businesses' responsibility to improve the social environment, such as combating poverty and preventing urban decay. Furthermore, new CSR concepts, such as enlightened self-interest and good neighbour, emerged during this period.

In the 1980s, the CSR concept entered a mature stage. The most representative was Edward Freeman's pioneering work on stakeholder theory, *Strategic Management: A Stakeholder Approach*, published in 1984, which points out that a company's success depends on its ability to manage its stakeholders and defined a stakeholder as any group or individual that can influence or be influenced by achievement of an organisation's objectives. Freeman's stakeholder theory is viewed as a rejection of Friedman's shareholder centrism, which asserts that firms should be accountable only to shareholders and that their only responsibility is to earn profits for them, while the former views firms as a collection of different stakeholders' interests and argues that firms' responsibility should be to maximise stakeholders' interests rather than shareholders' interests. The introduction of stakeholder theory has led to the evolution of CSR from concept to theory.

Between the 1990s and the beginning of the twenty-first century, the CSR concept began to take on a managerial orientation. During this period, in addition to the famous pyramid theory of CSR (economic, legal, ethical and philanthropic responsibilities from the bottom to the top) and the triple bottom-line theory (economic, environmental and social), more scholars called for CSR to be included in enterprises' overall strategic management framework.

1.2.3 Modern ESG Concepts (Early 2000s to the Present)

After the beginning of the twenty-first century, the CSR concept gradually evolved in the direction of sustainable development and corporate citizenship. During this period, the CSR concept increasingly was influenced by the standard-setting of international organisations, placing greater emphasis on CSR's role in sustainable development and eventually converging into the increasingly mainstream ESG or sustainability reporting category.

The modern ESG concept has evolved under the impetus of the UN and other international organisations, and ESG investing has continued to grow globally. In 2000, UN Secretary-General Kofi Annan launched the Global Compact, an initiative to encourage integration of environmental, social and corporate governance into capital markets, which coined ESG investing. In 2004, the UN Global Compact, together with 20 financial institutions, released the landmark *Who Cares Wins* report, which invited participants from different financial sectors to make a series of recommendations on how to incorporate ESG considerations into financial market research, analysis and investment. Data from the report indicate that companies that perform better in the ESG domain also perform better in terms of increasing shareholder value and corporate profits, improving corporate reputation and promoting social sustainability. Therefore, ESG is an important factor in influencing shareholders' long-term interests. The report marks ESG as an important criterion for examining assets' nonfinancial factors. In 2006, former UN Secretary-General Annan launched the UN's Principles for Responsible Investment (UNPRI) to promote incorporation of ESG indicators into major asset managers' investment decisions, and to help UNPRI signatories enhance their sustainable investment capabilities, avoid risks and optimise their investment performance in practice. Since then, with UNPRI's support, ESG investment has grown rapidly worldwide.

Since it was created, ESG has inherited some aspects of CSR, and without CSR's century-long evolution, there would be no ESG today. The ESG concept can be viewed as an advancement of CSR that gradually formed due to changes in external factors at a certain stage in CSR's development. The external factors that prompted CSR to evolve into ESG mainly came from three aspects: the UN's active promotion of environmental protection and sustainable development; strong demand for ESG information in the capital market and international organisations' unremitting attempts to formulate ESG standards.

Concerned about economic, social and environmental development's inadequacy and incoherence, the UN has been promoting economic and social development, and solving environmental issues since the 1970s. In 1972, the first United Nations Conference on the Human Environment (UNCHE) was held in Stockholm, Sweden, and in 1973, the United Nations Environment Programme (UNEP) was created. In December 1983, the UN established the World Commission on Environment and Development (WCED), chaired by Mrs. Brundtland, who also served as the Norway's prime minister for three terms (1981, 1986–89, and 1990–96). After more than three years of unremitting efforts, the WCED submitted a study, *Our Common Future,* to the UN in 1987, formally introducing and defining the sustainable development concept. *Our Common Future* defined sustainable development as development that meets present needs without jeopardising future generations' ability to meet their own needs. In June 1992, the United Nations Conference on Environment and Development (UNCED) was held in Rio de Janeiro, Brazil, where the Rio Declaration on Environment and Development (also known as the Earth Charter) was adopted, with more than 150 countries signing the Convention on Biological Diversity (CBD), the Framework Convention on Climate Change (FCCC) and other important documents. In 2000, the United Nations Global Compact, the world's largest sustainable development organisation, was established. In 2004, the UN released the study *Who Cares Wins*, which proposed the ESG concept for the first time. In 2006, the UN released its Principles for Responsible Investment. In September 2015, 193 member states adopted the United Nations 2030 Agenda for Sustainable Development at the United Nations Summit on Sustainable Development in New York City, setting 17 Sustainable Development Goals (SDGs). Years of unremitting UN efforts have made nations worldwide and the public increasingly aware that ESG is an important foundational and institutional arrangement for ensuring sustainable development, while promoting the evolution of CSR, with its strong ethical and philanthropic overtones, into ESG, which focusses on economically, socially and environmentally sustainable development.

Since the signing of the Paris Agreement, the economic and social transformation towards low-carbon and green development has become a consensus. In this context, the capital market has formed a strong demand for sustainable development, particularly ESG information, as CSR reports with voluntary disclosure no longer can meet the capital market's needs, objectively leading to a shift from CSR to ESG.

CSR's evolution into ESG cannot be separated from international organisations' active participation in the development of ESG standards. The GRI—created in 1997 and based in Amsterdam, the Netherlands—proposed a four-module guideline system (Generic Guidelines Module, Economic Issues Module, Environmental Issues Module and Social Issues Module), which has become one of the most widely used frameworks for ESG reporting in the corporate world to date. In 2007, the Climate Disclosure Standards Board (CDSB), based in London, was established and proposed a framework for climate change disclosure based on seven principles and 12 elements. In 2011, the Sustainability Accounting Standards Board (SASB), based in San Francisco, was established and issued Sustainability Accounting Standards (SASs) covering 77 industries in 11 economic sectors. In 2015, following a request at the G20 Finance Ministers and Central Bank Governors' Meeting, the Financial Stability Board (FSB) established the Task Force on Climate-related Financial Disclosure (TCFD), which proposed the TCFD framework comprising four core elements (governance, strategy, risk management, and metrics and targets) and 11 disclosure requirements and became the most widely utilised standard for climate-related information disclosure. The reporting standards that GRI, CDSB, SASB and TCFD issued have become an important technical force driving the development of ESG reporting, accelerating CSR's evolution into ESG and cultivating ESG from concept to sustainability reporting.

However, GRI, CDSB, SASB and TCFD standards are different and not authoritative enough, which not only increases the cost of compilation of ESG-related disclosure reports for enterprises and financial institutions, but also increases the cost of analysis for users. For this reason, international organisations—such as the G20, International Organisation of Securities Commissions (IOSCO), International Federation of Accountants (IFAC) et al.—have declared a need to change this system in which several different ESG or sustainability reporting standards exist and called for the establishment of more authoritative and consistent international standards as soon as possible. Following the European Commission's mandate to the European Financial Reporting Advisory Group (EFRAG) in April 2021 to develop a European Sustainability Reporting Standard (ESRS), the International Financial Reporting Standards Foundation (IFRS) announced, at the 26th United Nations Climate Change Conference in Glasgow in November 2021, the creation of the International Sustainability Standards Board (ISSB), which will be responsible for developing the IFRS Sustainability Disclosure Standards (ISDS). In 2022, the Council of the European

Union formally approved the Corporate Sustainability Reporting Directive (CSRD), laying a solid legal foundation for the development and implementation of the ESRS. Simultaneously, the U.S. Securities and Exchange Commission (SEC) issued a new regulation on climate disclosure.

On June 26, 2023, the ISSB officially issued the IFRS S1 General Requirements for Disclosure of Sustainability-related Financial Information (IFRS S1) and Climate-related Disclosures (IFRS S2). The release of these two standards marked the beginning of a new era of sustainable information disclosure, which is an important infrastructure for achieving green and low-carbon transformation and social equity and justice, and is of great significance for promoting sustainable development of the economy, society and the environment. The European Commission (EC) also published the first batch of 12 ESRSs on July 31, 2023, including two cross-cutting guidelines and 10 guidelines on ESG topics. This is a milestone in the development of sustainable development reporting standards following the ISSB's release of IFRS S1 and S2.

1.3 ESG's Theoretical Foundation

As a new concept and method, ESG requires both applied research at the technical level and theoretical construction at the academic level to ensure its sustainable development. In this subsection, we introduce several theories that form the basis of ESG concepts.

1.3.1 The Theory of Economic Externalities

Externalities, also known as external and spillover effects, are important research objects in economics, providing a theoretical basis for the government to regulate enterprises' business activities and information disclosure (including the disclosure of financial and ESG reports) outside of the market mechanism. The theory of economic externalities has a long history and has been used widely in the environmental aspect of ESG.

Adam Smith, who originated market economy theory, believed that a free economic system encourages and allows individuals to pursue their own interests. However, the market mechanism is not perfect. The best example is that economic externalities lead to market failures in which market prices fail to reflect marginal social costs and benefits of production. Economic externalities indicate that it is difficult to achieve optimal allocation of resources and maximisation of social benefits by relying solely on the market mechanism.

In 1890, Alfred Marshall first proposed the external economies concept in his *Principles of Economics*, pointing out that we can divide the economies derived from the production scale of any product into two types: economies that depend on the industry's general development and economies that depend on organisational resources and management efficiency. The former can be described as external economies, while the latter can be described as internal economies. Although the author proposed the external economies concept, he did not explicitly propose the externalities concept. However, the economic community generally regards external economies as the prototype and source of externalities.

In 1920, Arthur Pigou published *The Economics of Welfare*, introducing the economic externalities concept based on Marshall's external economies. This shifted the focus of externality research from the impact of external factors on enterprises to the impact of enterprises or residents on other enterprises or residents, marking the official birth of the theory of economic externalities. Pigou believed that as long as the marginal private net output value and marginal social net output value conflicted, economic externalities would exist. Using the terminology of marginal cost and marginal revenue, when marginal private (including individuals and enterprises) costs are less than marginal social costs, there will be negative externalities, i.e., other social entities bear costs that should be borne by private individuals. When marginal private benefits are less than marginal social benefits, there will be positive externalities, i.e., other social entities receive benefits that private individuals should enjoy exclusively. Therefore, Pigou proposed taxing enterprises with marginal private costs that are less than marginal social costs and providing subsidies to enterprises with marginal private benefits that are less than marginal social benefits. Through this form of taxation and subsidies, internalisation of external effects can be achieved, and resource allocation can be optimised as much as possible to achieve Pareto optimality. This policy proposal later became known as the Pigouvian Tax. The imposition of emission fees, the introduction of environmental taxes and subsidies for zero-emission vehicles all can be viewed as being forms of the Pigouvian Tax and can find theoretical support in Pigou's economic externalities work.

However, Ronald Coase pointed out the Pigouvian Tax's drawbacks and proposed an idea that later became the Coase Theorem, which posited that economic externalities are not an inevitable result of market mechanisms, but rather are due to unclear property rights. As long as property rights are clear, economic externalities can be resolved by contracting or through voluntary negotiation between the parties involved. Coase believes that the Pigouvian Tax may not be the optimal policy solution for addressing economic externalities. In situations in which transaction costs are zero and property rights can be defined clearly, the parties involved can achieve optimal resource allocation through voluntary negotiation, and the Pigouvian Tax is unnecessary. In situations in which transaction costs are not zero, resolving externalities issues requires resorting to administrative intervention based on cost–benefit analyses. At this point, the Pigouvian Tax may be an efficient institutional arrangement, but it also may be an inefficient or ineffective institutional arrangement. If the administrative intervention used incurs a cost lower than its benefits, the Pigouvian Tax can be an efficient institutional arrangement for addressing economic externalities. Conversely, the Pigouvian Tax also can be an inefficient or even ineffective institutional arrangement.

The most direct implication of economic externality theory for ESG is that ecological environmental resources, as a public good with unclear property rights, cannot be fully resolved by the market mechanism. Instead, government intervention and regulation are required. Such intervention and regulation can manifest in a purely administrative way, such as imposing resource taxes, charging fees for pollution discharges and emissions or assigning emission quotas, or in a quasi-market way, such as establishing carbon emission trading markets. No matter what kind of interventions and regulations are employed, they all require enterprises to disclose environmental information. ESG reporting is an important policy option to encourage enterprises to disclose environmental information. An ESG report not only can provide a decision-making basis for administrative intervention and regulation, but also significantly reduces transaction costs of administrative intervention and regulation.

Second, ESG reports should disclose not only negative externalities derived from corporate business activities, but also positive externalities generated by corporate business activities. Both should not be neglected, or else resource optimisation allocation could become a pipe dream. From an economics perspective, while implementing punitive policies to correct enterprises' environmental externalities may be effective, the supervisory costs are often very high. However, implementing incentive policies for positive externalities can guide enterprises effectively towards low-carbon development and green transformation, usually with minimal supervisory costs.

Finally, the externality space's scope in environmental aspects must be defined clearly for ESG reports to disclose information on greenhouse gas (GHG) emissions comprehensively and accurately. More specifically, ESG reporting standards should clarify whether they are disclosing only direct GHG emissions generated by the company's own business activities, or whether to expand the disclosure scope to the entire supply chain, covering both direct and indirect GHG emissions generated by enterprise activities. Limiting GHG emissions to the enterprise scope is easier to operate, has lower disclosure costs and is easy to verify, but it may underestimate the amount of GHG emissions associated with enterprise activities. Conversely, expanding GHG emissions to the entire supply chain can reflect GHG emissions associated with enterprise activities more accurately, but it is hard to accomplish, has higher disclosure costs and is difficult to verify.

1.3.2 Stakeholder Theory

With the development of productivity and companies' increasingly complex management activities, owners gradually become overwhelmed and begin to seek professional managers with the capabilities to manage companies. This has led to professional managers running companies, with the companies gradually presenting a separation between ownership and management, leading to the emergence of principal-agent relationships. Michael Jensen and William Meckling have examined the conflicts of interest between management and owners based on principal-agent relationships and formally have proposed principal-agent theory. Compared with owners, management has more internal information on a company's operational management process. To pursue their own interests, they may make decisions that weaken owners' interests and even jeopardise companies' survival and development. This is the first type of principal-agent problem between principals (owners) and agents (management). More specifically, if the company is viewed as a linkage of contractual relationships, it should not focus too much on whether it should bear social responsibilities; otherwise, it will lead to serious misdirection. The company is only a legal fiction, so through complex procedures, it promotes individuals with conflicting goals to achieve a balance within the framework of contractual relationships. Therefore, in the separation of ownership and management rights, as residual claimants of company profits and property, shareholders hire managers as agents to manage the company's operation and management. Management's responsibility, playing the role of agent, is to maximise shareholder value.

Since the 1980s, labour-capital relations in Western developed countries have become increasingly tense. Granting large stock options to corporate management in the name of maximising shareholder value has widened the wealth gap further, and pursuing corporate interests while disregarding environmental protection has led to sharp public criticism, prompting a fundamental rethinking of shareholder supremacy (shareholder value maximisation) and eventually leading to the rise of stakeholder theory. It can be said that stakeholder theory emerged out of the debate about shareholder supremacy. Stakeholder theory believes that shareholder supremacy values are too narrow and emphasises the concept that capital employs labour. Shareholder supremacy thinking fundamentally denies other stakeholders' important contributions, particularly human capital, and ignores enterprise value creation beyond shareholders. Stakeholder doctrine argues that from ethical, moral and sustainable development perspectives, corporate management should be responsible not only to shareholders for creating value, but also to other stakeholders.

Edward Freeman systematically presented stakeholder theory in 1984, defining stakeholders as any group or individual who can influence or be influenced by the achievement and process of an organisation's goals. Specifically, three stakeholder categories exist: ownership stakeholders (e.g., shareholders, including directors and managers, who hold shares); economic dependence stakeholders (e.g., employees, creditors, suppliers, consumers, competitors, communities, etc.) and social stakeholders (e.g., governments, media, special interest groups, etc.). In 2010, Freeman et al. (2010) divided stakeholders into two categories: primary stakeholders (e.g., capital investors, suppliers, consumers, employees and communities) and secondary stakeholders (e.g., governments, competitors, media, special interest groups and consumer protection groups). Stakeholder theory posits that an enterprise comprises various stakeholders' interests, and that the enterprise's managers should consider both shareholders and other stakeholders' interests, i.e., they should be responsible not only to the main capital providers (shareholders), but also to other stakeholders. Responsibility to other stakeholders beyond shareholders should be incorporated into corporate management's overall fiduciary responsibilities, thereby creating the broader CSR concept. Fulfilling social responsibilities is enterprises' moral responsibility, but enterprises also inherently need to attract and maintain strategic resources. Without other stakeholders' input and consumers' full support, enterprises cannot sustainably create value for shareholders.

Stakeholder theory carries significant implications for ESG. First, it lays a solid theoretical foundation for the popularisation and development of the ESG concept, prompting enterprises to pay more attention to ESG issues, provide an effective social atmosphere for development of ESG reports and help enterprises balance corporate and social benefits. Second, stakeholder theory's increasing popularity urges corporate management to take an unprecedented approach to balancing shareholders and other stakeholders' needs, which may lead to changes in corporate governance structures. In the future, more members of corporate boards will be non-shareholder stakeholders, such as employee representatives, environmentalists and consumer advocates. Finally, the rise of stakeholder theory forces companies to provide ESG reports that focus on stakeholders, in addition to financial reports, to meet the information needs of stakeholders who are evaluating whether the company effectively fulfils its social responsibilities.

1.3.3 Sustainable Development Theory

The sustainable development concept originated from environmental issues, and its origins can be traced back to the Stockholm World Environmental Conference in 1972. In 1980, the International Union for Conservation of Nature and Natural Resources (IUCN) published the *World Conservation Strategy*, which explicitly mentioned the term 'sustainable development'. However, the UN officially put forth the true sense of sustainable development theory. To address increasingly severe environmental and economic issues and find solutions, the UN established the World Commission on Environment and Development (WCED) in December 1983. After more than three years of unremitting efforts and the support of countries worldwide, WCED submitted its *Our Common Future* report to the UN in March 1987, where it was debated before the 42nd UN General Assembly adopted it in April 1987. *Our Common Future* officially was published in April 1987 and elicited a warm response worldwide, marking the official birth of sustainable development theory. The report comprised three parts—common concerns, common challenges and common efforts—and incorporated the sustainable development concept throughout.

In the report's second chapter, WCED defined sustainable development as development that meets the present generation's needs without compromising future generations' ability to meet their own needs. WCED's specific elaboration of the sustainable development concept includes 10 aspects: (1) meeting human needs and pursuing a better life is the main goal of development, and sustainable development requires meeting basic human needs and providing opportunities for people to pursue a better life; (2) sustainable development advocates for a value system that controls consumption levels within the ecological environment's tolerable range; (3) economic growth must comply with sustainable development's basic principles and not exploit others, as sustainable development requires improving production potential and ensuring fair opportunities to meet human needs; (4) sustainable development requires that population development be in harmony with the changing ecological environment's production potential; (5) sustainable development demands curbing excessive exploitation of resources that endangers future generations' ability to meet their basic needs; (6) sustainable development requires that humans not harm the natural systems that support life on Earth, including the atmosphere, water, soil and biology; (7) sustainable development requires that countries worldwide ensure fair access to limited resources and alleviate resource pressures through technological means; (8) sustainable development requires rational use of renewable resources, prevention of excessive development and utilisation, and control of non-renewable resource extraction rates to avoid endangering future generations' development; (9) sustainable development requires protecting plants and animals, and preventing species diversity reduction that affects future generations' choices; and (10) sustainable development requires minimising human activities' negative impact on air, water and natural elements to maintain the ecosystem's integrity.

WCED's principles have been recognised widely by the UN, World Bank, European Union, other international organisations and most UN member countries, and has become an important cornerstone of sustainable development theory. Thanks to WCED and other international organisations' research achievements, the UN held a Sustainable Development Summit in New York in September 2015, during which 193 member states adopted the *Transforming Our World: The 2030 Agenda for Sustainable Development*, which proposed 17 sustainable development goals (SDGs) aimed at guiding member states to address environmental, social and economic issues from 2015 to 2030.[1]

A review of ESG initiatives and proposals that several international organisations put forth reveals that most ESG reporting frameworks aim to provide information that helps stakeholders assess the risks and opportunities associated with a company's sustainable development. Therefore, sustainable development theory's far-reaching influence on ESG is evident. Furthermore, many ESG reporting frameworks draw on the essence of sustainable development theory in their indicator system design, particularly in terms of social and environmental sustainability. For example, the GRI's four-module criterion system includes economic, environmental and social modules that share the same design concept as the social, economic and environmental trilemma of sustainable development. The SASB's five-dimension reporting framework comprises three dimensions—environmental protection, social capital and human capital—with 17 indicators that contain ideas on social and environmentally sustainable development. The TCFD's four-element climate disclosure framework and the CDSB's environmental and climate change disclosure framework focus on environmentally sustainable development without mentioning economic and social sustainable development, but their propositions and disclosure matters in the area of the environment are highly consistent with sustainable development

[1] The 17 SDGs include: (1) no poverty; (2) zero hunger; (3) good health and well-being; (4) quality education; (5) gender equality; (6) clean water and sanitation; (7) affordable and clean energy; (8) decent work and economic growth; (9) industry, innovation and infrastructure; (10) reduced inequalities; (11) sustainable cities and communities; (12) responsible consumption and production; (13) climate action; (14) life below water; (15) life on land; (16) peace, justice and strong institutions; and (17) partnerships for goals.

theory. Moreover, sustainable development theory generally does not address specific corporate governance issues directly. However, its policy recommendations usually require governments or other organisations to prioritise institutional changes and innovations to ensure that the governing body adopts appropriate procedures and methods to address sustainable development issues in social, economic and environmental areas. In this sense, the 'G' in ESG reporting can be viewed as a mechanism for implementing sustainable development theory policy recommendations.

1.4 ESG and Climate Change

The 'S' and 'G' aspects of ESG entail more flexible issues with distinct social attributes, making it difficult for countries worldwide to reach a consensus. However, the 'E' in ESG entails more rigid issues, with stronger technical than social attributes. Under international treaties such as the UN Framework Convention on Climate Change and the Paris Agreement, countries worldwide are more likely to reach a consensus on the 'E' aspect. The 'E' in ESG encompasses a wide range of topics (e.g., climate change, air pollution, water and marine resources, biodiversity and ecosystems, resource utilisation and the circular economy), among which reducing GHG emissions to mitigate climate change is the most pressing sustainable development issue and a top concern of the international community.

GHGs generate environmental effects that lead to climate change, resulting in biodiversity loss and ecosystem degradation, and posing a serious threat to the sustainable development of the economy and society. To curb climate change problems from GHGs, the 21st UN Climate Change Conference held in Paris in December 2015 adopted the Paris Agreement. In April 2016, 190 countries and the European Union Commission signed the agreement, which established a goal of controlling temperature rise in the twenty-first century to within 1.5 °C above the average temperature before the Industrial Revolution. Signatories are obliged to conserve energy, reduce emissions and make independent contributions to achieving the temperature control target. The Intergovernmental Panel on Climate Change (IPCC) released its *Special Report on Global Warming of 1.5 °C* in 2018, stating that if global temperature rise is not controlled within 1.5 °C above the pre-industrial level, and the goal of achieving net-zero emissions by 2050 is not met, humanity will miss the best opportunity to avoid catastrophic climate breakdown. In its *Sixth Assessment Report* released in 2021, the IPCC confirmed further that climate change is affecting every region on Earth and increasingly is manifesting through extreme weather, severe droughts and forest fires.

Climate change has garnered significant attention from the international community, making it a key focus of ESG and sustainable development. On one hand, climate change is an important aspect of ESG, and its impact on ESG is manifested in multiple ways. First, climate change directly impacts the environment, eliciting extreme weather events, sea level rise, etc., that can affect enterprises' operations and finances.

Second, climate change impacts society through population migration, intensification of social inequalities, etc., which can affect enterprises' workforce, customer base and social reputation. Finally, climate change impacts enterprises' governance structures—such as policy development, compliance requirements, etc.—which can affect enterprises' strategic planning and business operations. However, ESG factors also impact climate change. First, a company's ESG performance affects its GHG emissions and energy consumption. Second, a company's ESG performance affects its ability and determination to address climate change. Finally, a company's ESG performance affects its status and influence in the supply chain, thereby affecting its contribution to climate change.

2 Corporate Performance on ESG and Climate Change

In this section, we review the current literature on the relationship between a series of corporate behaviours, including ESG performance. Specifically, we first review the influencing factors associated with a company's ESG performance identified in the current literature, including market characteristics, board and management characteristics, ownership structure, etc. Second, we briefly summarise the economic consequences of a company's ESG performance, including the risks that the company faces and its value.

2.1 Influencing Factors

In this subsection, we discuss the factors that make significant impacts on corporate ESG performance. The factors are introduced following an order from a macro level to a micro level. We observe that country and market characteristics, industry characteristics, board and management structures, and ownership structures can play important roles in influencing corporate ESG performance.

2.1.1 Market Characteristics

Corporate ESG performance is influenced by the country in which it operates, mainly due to each country or region's political, economic and cultural factors' impact on the company's operations and decision-making. In terms of policy environment, different countries and regions have different policy environments, such as environmental protection regulations, labour regulations, corporate governance regulations, etc. These policies directly affect corporate ESG performance. Other factors that affect ESG performance include (1) level of economic development—countries and regions with high levels of economic development typically have more comprehensive legal systems, regulatory frameworks and market mechanisms; (2)

societal culture, in which differences exist in the degree of emphasis and cognition on environmental protection, labour rights, corporate governance, etc., in different countries and regions; and (3) industry and market competition conditions, which vary in different countries and regions. To sum up, when discussing a company's ESG performance, the influence of the country in which it operates must be fully considered, and corresponding strategies and measures need to be formulated.

Cai et al. (2016) examined the reasons for differences in corporate social performance (CSP) ratings among companies in different countries. The authors analysed CSP ratings on more than 2,600 companies across 36 countries and found that company characteristics explained little variation in CSP ratings. Instead, national factors—such as the nation's culture, institutions and stage of economic development—were cited as important reasons for differences. The authors also found that countries with high per capita income, strong civil liberties and political rights, and a culture of harmony and autonomy tend to have particularly high CSP ratings. They also observed that compared with nonmultinational companies and pure domestic companies, home-country factors explained a small portion of the overall change in CSP for multinational and cross-listed companies. Liang and Renneboog (2017) examined the relationship between CSR ratings and legal origins of countries in which they are based, and they found that a company's CSR rating is related closely to the legal origin of the country in which it operates. They suggested that legal origin is a better predictor of CSR ratings than factors such as 'doing well by doing good' or company and country characteristics. Their results also indicate that compared with common law firms, civil law firms respond strongly to CSR's impact on companies. This paper suggests that CSR is a balance between shareholder concerns and other stakeholders' concerns.

Besides country-specific characteristics, Boubakri et al. (2016) found that cross-listing positively impacts CSR performance, particularly for companies from countries with weaker institutions and more foreign liabilities. The research results suggest that cross-listing can improve CSR practices and enhance corporate valuation. Jha and Cox (2015) found that corporate headquarters' location is another important factor that affects corporate ESG performance. They argued that companies' motivation to take social responsibility may stem from an altruistic tendency fostered by the social capital of the region where a company's corporate headquarters are located. By examining the relationship between social capital and CSR, they found that companies in regions with high social capital exhibit higher social responsibility. Industry and market conditions within a country are also an important factor that could affect corporate ESG performance. For example, Borghesi et al. (2014) found better ESG performance among firms in the consumer goods and computer hardware industries and worse ESG performance among firms in the petroleum and natural gas industries.

As for corporate performance on climate change, Lee and Luo (2021) found strong evidence that the local community is an important factor that forces local firms to take action on environmental issues, thereby resulting in lower levels of toxic emissions. Dai et al. (2021a) found strong evidence that when firms face more and more intense regulations on carbon emissions, these firms outsource part of their own emissions to their suppliers in other countries that have more-lenient emission-reduction policies, instead of taking significant actions to reduce emissions. Thus, with these actions, global emissions levels essentially remain the same, rather than decrease.

2.1.2 Board and Management Characteristics

Corporate ESG performance is influenced by a company's board of directors and management team, who play crucial roles in strategic planning, decision-making and execution. First, the board and management team are responsible for developing the company's strategic plan, including ESG-related goals and initiatives. They need to consider market demand, industry competition, policy regulations and other factors comprehensively to formulate ESG strategies that are in line with the company's actual situation and long-term development goals. In the decision-making process, the board and management team need to evaluate ESG factors' potential risks and opportunities for the company and make decisions in line with the company's interests. For example, in making investment decisions, they need to evaluate investment projects' environmental and social impacts, and consider how to reduce potential risks by improving ESG performance. Moreover, they ultimately are responsible for achieving the company's ESG goals and need to ensure that the company has the ability and resources to achieve these goals, including personnel training, technological investment, resource allocation, etc. Simultaneously, they also need to supervise various departments within the company to comply with ESG-related regulations, standards and best practices during the execution process. Finally, they also need to establish a sound ESG risk assessment and management mechanism to identify, evaluate and manage ESG risks that the company faces during its business processes. This helps the company take timely measures to reduce potential risks and improve its robustness and sustainability. To sum up, the board and management team play a critical role in the company's strategic planning, decision-making and execution, as their attitudes and actions directly affect the company's ESG performance. Therefore, strengthening the board and management team's emphasis on ESG and governance capabilities related to ESG is key to promoting the company's ESG performance.

A company's chief executive officer (CEO) is one of the most important roles within a corporate management team; thus, a CEO's characteristics exert significant influence on corporate ESG performance. Borghesi et al. (2014) found that a CEO's age is a key factor, i.e., younger CEOs tend to invest more in improving corporate ESG performance. One potential reason for this behaviour is concerns over reputation, as the authors found that the level of media scrutiny surrounding the firm and its CEO is related positively to the firm's ESG performance. McCarthy et al. (2017) examined the relationship between CSR and CEO confidence and found that more confident CEOs tend to underestimate company risks and, therefore, engage in less hedging. Therefore, CEO confidence is correlated negatively with CSR level. This effect is stronger at the institutional level of CSR (e.g., in the community and labour diversity) than at the technological level (e.g., company governance and product quality). The study also ruled out other explanations, including narcissism, and found that the negative relationship between CEO confidence and CSR remains even after controlling for CEO characteristics and other factors. Ferrell et al. (2016) also found that excessive CEO compensation measures are correlated negatively with ESG scores and concluded that a negative correlation exists between excessive CEO compensation and ESG scores. High compensation unrelated to performance leads to less investment in ESG activities, which supports the view of good governance. To support their hypothesis further, the authors demonstrated that a company's performance-based compensation sensitivity is correlated positively with its ESG score.

Geographic and political factors also matter when considering the relationship between management decision-making and corporate ESG performance. For example, Landier et al. (2009) examined geographic diversification's impact on corporate decision-making and found that companies with geographic diversification had lower employee friendliness, and that departments closer to the companies' headquarters were less likely to face layoffs. The authors suggest that informational and social factors played a role in these findings. In industries in which information is difficult to transmit over long distances, companies are more likely to protect employees in nearby locations. Furthermore, the stock market responded positively to state-based departments' divestures. Di Giuli and Kostovetsky (2014) examined the relationship between a political stance and CSR ratings based on the US sample. The authors found that companies whose founders, CEOs and directors are Democrats, as well as companies headquartered in states with Democratic leanings, scored higher on CSR ratings than companies with Republican founders and leaders. Democratic-leaning companies spend more on CSR than Republican-leaning companies, but no evidence has been found to indicate that these expenditures result in increased sales.

In terms of corporate performance on climate change, Benjaafar et al. (2012) discussed the integration of carbon emissions into operational decisions in supply chain management. The authors explained how to modify traditional models to support decision-making that considers both cost and carbon footprint simultaneously. They examined carbon-reduction requirements' impact on operational adjustments and investigated the benefits of cooperation between enterprises within the same supply chain. The research emphasised business decisions' importance in assessing regulatory policies and investments' impact on carbon efficiency technologies.

2.1.3 Ownership Characteristics

Corporate ESG performance is influenced by ownership structure, which can affect strategic decisions, governance structure and business behaviour. First, different ownership structures may lead to varying strategic decisions. For example, companies with decentralised ownership may focus more on short-term interests and financial performance, while companies with centralised ownership may focus more on long-term strategies and sustainable development. A company's ownership structure can affect its ESG performance by influencing incentives for and constraints on managers. Second, a company's ownership structure also can affect its governance structure, which affects its ESG performance. For example, family-owned or individually owned companies may lack effective oversight mechanisms and transparency, resulting in insufficient attention paid to resolving ESG issues. However, institutional investors or publicly held companies may be more focussed on ESG performance because it affects the company's reputation and market value. Third, a company's ownership structure also can affect its business behaviour, including considerations related to the environment, society and governance. For example, a company's owner may make a direct impact on the company's business behaviour, such as the emphasis and investment level placed on environmental protection, social responsibility and corporate governance. Fourth, different ownership structures may lead to varying risks and returns. For example, companies with centralised ownership may face greater operational risks, but also may receive higher returns. However, companies with decentralised ownership may face lower operational risks, but also may receive lower returns. This difference in risk and return may affect a company's ESG performance. Thus, a company's ownership structure can affect its ESG performance by influencing its strategic decisions, governance structure and business practices. Therefore, companies need to consider ownership structure's impact fully when improving their ESG performance, and develop corresponding strategies and measures.

As important participants in the capital market, institutional investors can make a significant impact on a company's governance structure and decision-making, thereby influencing its ESG performance. First, institutional investors typically possess large asset sizes and voting rights, allowing them to influence a company's governance structure and decision-making. They can express their opinions and demands by voting at shareholder meetings or communicating with the company's management, thereby influencing the company's ESG performance. Dyck et al. (2019) found that higher institutional holdings are associated with better corporate ESG performance, implying that institutional investors care about corporate ESG issues.

Second, institutional investors typically focus on long-term value and sustainable development, placing greater emphasis on a company's ESG performance. They incorporate ESG factors into investment decisions by selecting companies with effective ESG performance for investment to achieve their investment goals and values, and this phenomenon can be even stronger for institutional investors with a longer investment horizon. Dimson et al. (2015) analysed a proprietary database that records ESG engagements with US-listed companies from 1999 to 2009 and found that engagement that institutional investors initiated is more likely to succeed if the engaged firm cares about its reputation, and that collaboration among institutional activists can improve this engagement's success rate.

Overall, as an important force in the capital market, institutional investors can influence a company's ESG performance through various means. They can participate in corporate governance, incorporate ESG factors into investment decisions, take joint actions with other investors and influence market public opinion to exert their influence. Therefore, when improving ESG performance, companies need to consider institutional investors' role and influence fully, and actively communicate and collaborate with them.

Family ownership also can exert an important influence on corporate ESG performance. More specifically, family ownership can affect a company's governance structure, thereby influencing its ESG performance. Family owners typically have representative seats on the company's board of directors and can influence decision-making and supervisory mechanisms. Family owners also may pay more attention to the company's social responsibility and sustainable development; thus, they may focus more on ESG factors in the governance structure. Furthermore, family ownership can affect a company's operating behaviour, thereby influencing its ESG performance. Family owners typically pay more attention to the company's cultural and values legacy, so they may focus more on ESG factors such as environmental protection, social responsibility, etc., in the operation process. Furthermore, family owners may pay more attention to the company's long-term development and stable returns, so they may focus more on improving governance mechanisms, such as risk management, internal controls, etc. Abeysekera and Fernando (2020) examined differences in attitudes towards ESG between family and nonfamily firms, and found that firms with stronger family ownership were more responsible to shareholders when making ESG-related decisions. Therefore, when improving ESG performance, companies need to consider family ownership's impact fully and formulate corresponding strategies and measures.

State ownership's impact on corporate ESG performance is also a relevant factor, mainly because state ownership can influence a company's governance structure, business practices and strategic decision-making, thereby affecting its ESG performance. As for governance structure, under state ownership, the state typically has representative seats on the company's board of directors and can influence decision-making and supervisory mechanisms. State owners typically place more emphasis on CSR and sustainable development, so they may pay more attention to ESG factors in the governance structure. As for business practices, state owners typically place more emphasis on long-term development and stable returns, so they may pay more attention to improving the company's governance mechanisms, such as risk management, internal controls, etc. Furthermore, state owners also may promote ESG performance by formulating relevant policies and regulations. As for strategic decision-making, state owners typically place more emphasis on social benefits and public interests, so they may pay more attention to ESG factors in making strategic decisions. For example, state owners may incorporate environmental protection, social responsibility and other ESG factors into the company's strategic planning and promote active social responsibility fulfilment. Consistent with these ideas, Hsu et al. (2021) found that state-owned companies pay more attention to corporate ESG performance, and that the positive effect is even stronger for firms from countries without strict ESG-related regulations. This finding indicates that state ownership plays an important role in dealing with corporate ESG issues.

Specifically for climate change-related behaviour, institutional investors nowadays believe that climate risks make material impacts on their portfolio firms, and they take impactful actions to improve their climate risk management and engagement. Azar et al. (2021) found that the 'Big Three' (i.e., BlackRock, Vanguard and State Street Global Advisors) institutions are engaged actively in dealing with climate change issues and found that a higher percentage of shares held by the Big Three is associated with a lower level of corporate carbon emissions. Flammer et al. (2021) found that environmental shareholder activism increases voluntary corporate disclosure of climate change risks, particularly when initiated by institutional investors, especially long-term ones.

2.2 *Economic Consequences*

In this subsection, we change course and discuss corporate ESG performance's economic consequences. We review the current literature concerning what risks firms face from ESG measures and how ESG factors impact firms' performance and valuation.

2.2.1 Firm Risks

Corporate ESG performance influences firm risks, mainly because ESG factors are related closely to the enterprise's operational and financial status. Various types of firm risks include systematic and regulatory risks. As for systematic risks, Albuquerque et al. (2019) built a theoretical model that includes a corporate ESG factor in the firm decision-making process and discussed how the corporate ESG factor would impact a firm's operations and competitive status. The authors found that better corporate ESG performance could help firms decrease systematic risk, an effect more obvious for firms with high product differentiation. Moreover, compared with natural arbitrage-seeking mutual funds or hedge funds, institutions constrained by social norms, such as pension plans, hold fewer sin stocks, which have higher expected returns than other comparable stocks, consistent with their being ignored by investors who are constrained by norms and face greater litigation risks exacerbated by social norms. Furthermore, engagement on ESG issues can benefit shareholders by reducing a company's downside risk, measured using lower partial moments and value at risk. Furthermore, the measured risk effect differs between engagement success and engagement topics. When dealing with environmental issues (primarily climate change), engagement appears to be most effective at reducing downside risk.

As for the question of how climate change affects firm risks, a key challenge in assessing these impacts is that it is difficult to measure how climate change affects individual companies, as the impact is multifaceted and comes from multiple sources. Sautner et al. (2023) developed a method to determine the level of concern about climate change among participants in earnings conference calls. The method uses a machine learning keyword discovery algorithm and captures firm risks tied to climate change-related opportunities, physical impacts and regulatory shocks. Furthermore, in the face of increasingly severe climate change challenges, do capital markets and their participants, including firms, have sufficient awareness of and take corresponding measures to address these challenges? To address this question, Stroebel and Wurgler (2021) conducted an anonymous global survey of financial economists, financial practitioners and economists from regulatory agencies and central banks. The survey results indicate that the respondents believe regulatory risks are the greatest climate-related risks that investors and companies will face in the next five years, while physical risks are the greatest risks in the next 30 years. Another survey has been conducted to learn how institutional investors perceive climate risks, whether systematic cross-sectional changes in their views on climate risks exist, as well as their strategies for managing these risks. The results indicate that institutional investors recognise that risks resulting from climate change, particularly regulatory risks, have become increasingly apparent and have made a financial impact on their portfolio companies that cannot be ignored. As for firm risks' real impact, climate policy uncertainty already is priced into the options market. As for companies with carbon-intensive business models, the cost of protecting against downside-tail risks is higher, and the cost of hedging against downside-tail risks sometimes can be amplified when public attention paid to climate change surges.

2.2.2 Firm Performance and Valuation

The impact of a company's ESG performance on its value mainly is tied to how ESG factors reflect the company's comprehensive strength, social responsibility, risk management capabilities and financial performance. First, ESG factors are important indicators of a company's comprehensive strength. Effective ESG performance indicates a high level of quality in these areas, thereby enhancing the company's overall strength and competitiveness. Second, ESG factors are an important manifestation of a company's social responsibility. ESG performance reflects the company's contributions to and impacts on society, the environment and the economy. Effective ESG performance means that the company actively fulfils its social responsibility; pays attention to employee welfare, environmental protection and public welfare undertakings; and wins social recognition and trust. Furthermore, ESG factors also can affect a company's risk management capabilities. If a company has deficiencies in ESG aspects, it may result in increased costs and risks, thereby affecting the company's profitability and long-term development. Effective ESG performance can enhance a company's brand image and market value, attract more investors and consumers, and increase the company's financial performance. Albuquerque et al.'s (2019) theoretical discussion supported these ideas, as the authors demonstrated that better corporate ESG performance could increase firm value.

However, a huge debate has been brewing in empirical discussions about the relationship between corporate ESG performance and firm value. As for the positive effect, Ferrell et al. (2016) found that a positive correlation exists between CSR and value, and that CSR weakens the negative correlation between management entrenchment and value. Servaes and Tamayo (2013) found that a significant positive correlation exists between CSR and corporate value among companies with higher consumer awareness, implying that CSR activities can add value to companies only under certain conditions. Lins et al. (2017) found that during the 2008–2009 Global Financial Crisis, high CSR companies had higher stock returns than low CSR companies. Edmans (2011) found a similar positive impact on stock returns when measuring corporate ESG performance based on employee satisfaction. Flammer (2015) examined the impact of shareholders' CSR proposals on corporate financial performance and found that adoption of closely linked CSR proposals elicits positive announcement returns and better accounting performance, indicating that these proposals have value-enhancing effects.

As for negative or no effect, Di Giuli and Kostovetsky (2014) examined the relationship between changes in a company's three-year ESG score and its concurrent revenue growth and did not find a significant relationship. They also found a significant negative correlation between changes in a company's ESG performance and changes in return on assets (ROA) or stock returns over the same three-year period. They interpreted these results cautiously, suggesting that 'any benefits to stakeholders from social responsibility come at the direct expense of firm value'. They also concluded that when companies expand their ESG policies, the subsequent result is poor stock performance and long-term ROA deterioration. Masulis and Reza (2015) investigated the relationship between corporate philanthropy and firm value afterward and found that when corporate giving increases, the capital market and shareholders will decrease their valuations of the firm.

Many studies also have examined ESG's effects on corporate cost of capital. Theoretically, Pástor et al. (2021) posited that investors' preferences for green and brown stocks explicitly exist in their utility functions. Using their general equilibrium model, the authors analysed this preference's financial and real impacts and found that green companies have lower cost of capital. Similarly, Pedersen et al. (2021) explicitly assumed that investors have ESG preferences and demonstrated that the cost of capital for green stocks depends on uninformed investors' wealth. Baker et al. (2022) suggested that green companies must meet special conditions to obtain lower funding costs, or else some investors may seek to hedge high-pollution states, which would increase brown companies' hedging interest and reduce their funding costs. Empirically, Hong and Kacperczyk (2009) focussed on the equity market and found that better ESG performance could help firms reduce the cost of equity capital. Nevertheless, Flammer (2021) tested the relationship between corporate ESG performance and the cost of capital in the bond market, but did not find evidence that better ESG performance leads to lower capital costs.

As for consequences to the company from climate change-related performance, Chava (2014) analysed the impact of a company's environmental performance on its equity and debt capital costs. The author found that investors expect much higher returns on stocks screened out by environmental criteria, such as climate change issues. Lending institutions also charge significantly higher interest rates on bank loans issued to companies with these environmental issues. Furthermore, compared with companies without environmental issues, those with environmental issues have fewer participating banks in their syndicated loans. Furthermore, direct evidence has been found on the relationship between corporate climate change-related performance and firm valuation, indicating that on average, for every 1,000 tons of carbon emissions a company produces, its value decreases by $212,000.

3 Corporate Disclosure on ESG and Climate Change

In this section, we review the current literature on the relationship between a series of corporate behaviours and their ESG disclosure choices. This section's structure is similar to the previous one. First, we review the influencing factors of corporate ESG disclosure choices identified in the current literature, including market characteristics, board and management characteristics, ownership structure, etc. Second, we briefly summarise the economic consequences caused by corporate ESG disclosure choices, including market reactions and firm valuation.

3.1 Influencing Factors

In this subsection, we discuss the factors that impose significant impacts on corporate ESG disclosure. We start with market characteristics, including country and industry details. We then introduce board and management characteristics that could change corporate disclosure choices. Finally, we introduce the role played by ownership structure.

3.1.1 Market Characteristics

Companies' ESG information disclosure is influenced by the countries in which they operate, mainly due to differences in political, economic, cultural and social backgrounds among different nations and regions. These factors can affect how much importance companies place on ESG information disclosure, what content they disclose and in what manner.

First, different countries and regions have varying requirements and regulations for ESG information disclosure. Some require that companies disclose ESG information, while others have no clear laws or regulations. This may result in differences and inconsistencies in how companies disclose ESG information. Indeed, when we examined mandatory ESG disclosure policies worldwide, huge differences in disclosure requirements were found. Most countries do not have mandatory regulations, and for those that do, the form is not unified (either comply or explain). As for countries that do not have mandatory disclosure requirements, firms can choose to disclose ESG information voluntarily. However, this leads to another debate: When a firm chooses to disclose ESG information, is it more about marketing the company as 'green' and less about effective ESG performance (a practice known as 'greenwashing')?

Second, cultural and social background also can affect companies' attitudes and behaviours towards ESG information. Some countries and regions prioritise environmental protection, social responsibility and corporate governance, so companies in these regions perform well in these areas and are more willing to disclose ESG information. For example, Innes and Sam (2008) examined the determinants and impacts of corporate participation in the *33/50 Programme*, a voluntary emission-reduction programme that government regulatory agencies initiated. The authors found evidence that supported a law enforcement theory that predicts participation in the programme will be rewarded with relaxed regulatory scrutiny, which will incentivise corporate participation and elicit rewards from regulatory agencies for reduced pollution. This paper also found that companies operating in states with high levels of support from environmentalists are more likely to participate in the programme.

Furthermore, different industries and markets have varying ESG information disclosure policies. Some prioritise sustainable development and social responsibility, in which companies need to disclose more ESG information to attract investors and customers. Other industries and markets may prioritise financial performance and profit levels, in which companies may disclose less ESG information. For example, Gamerschlag et al. (2011) found that firms in 'polluting' industries, such as energy and consumer products, are more likely to disclose more information on environmental issues. Similarly, firms in the 'sin' industry tend to disclose more ESG information as they try to decrease litigation risks generated from ESG-related controversies.

As for corporate disclosure on climate change, particularly carbon emissions, Alrazi et al. (2016) used a comprehensive disclosure index to measure the quality of carbon emissions disclosure and overall environmental disclosure among 205 power-generation companies in 35 countries. The study demonstrated that companies in countries with a high commitment to the environment and a carbon emissions trading system are more likely to disclose comprehensive environmental information. In terms of informal institutional aspects, Luo and Tang (2016) found that cultural dimensions—such as power distance, uncertainty avoidance, individualism and long-term orientation—are significantly related to companies' tendency to disclose carbon information.

The market's operation mechanism also can affect corporate carbon disclosure significantly. In terms of market competition, Ott et al. (2017) conducted an empirical analysis of relevant company data from 60 countries or regions and found that market competition pressure may affect voluntary disclosure of carbon emissions activities. When the substitutability of a company's industry is strong or market size is large, the company will face greater market competition pressure and is less willing to provide additional information to competitors. Therefore, these companies are less likely to respond to the CDP questionnaire survey. In terms of factor markets, Rankin et al. (2011) found that in carbon-intensive industries, firms tend to disclose more carbon information than those in other industries, as they face higher regulatory pressure.

Furthermore, some studies focus on external stakeholders, such as nongovernmental organisations. For example, Liesen et al. (2015) conducted an empirical test on EU companies that voluntarily disclosed GHG emissions between 2005 and 2009, and found that external stakeholders, such as nongovernmental organisations and the public, also are influencing corporate carbon emissions disclosure factors. Thus, companies are more willing to make GHG disclosures to alleviate pressure from external stakeholders. However, the study also pointed out that external stakeholders only affect the existence of corporate GHG disclosure, while GHG reports' completeness requires mandatory disclosure regulations.

3.1.2 Board and Management Characteristics

Companies' disclosure of ESG information is influenced by the characteristics of their board of directors and management, mainly because the board and management play an important role in corporate decision-making and operations. Their cognition, attitude and actions towards ESG issues will affect corporate ESG disclosure directly or indirectly.

First, the board of directors is the company's highest decision-making body, responsible for formulating corporate development strategies, making major decisions and supervising corporate operations and management. Shareholders usually elect board members to represent their interests. If board members lack awareness and understanding of ESG issues or attach less importance to them, they may tend to allocate more resources to traditional financial indicators and pay relatively less attention to ESG information disclosures. Consistent with this logic, Teoh et al. (2022) employed machine-learning techniques to measure board members' trustworthiness and found that managers tend to invest more human capital and effort in ESG activities when they perceive the board to have opinions on ESG that are consistent with their views. Moreover, a higher level of board diversity also could lead to better ESG practices, such as more equitable pay and inclusive corporate culture.

Second, managers are the core of corporate daily operational management, responsible for formulating and implementing various policies and plans. Their attitude towards ESG issues affect enterprises' ESG information disclosures directly. If management has a positive attitude towards ESG issues and is willing to bear corresponding responsibilities and risks, they may pay more attention to the collection, collation and disclosure of ESG information to convey the company's sustainable development capabilities and social responsibility to the market. Various managerial factors have been identified that could shape managerial attitudes towards ESG. For example, Lewis et al. (2014) found that managers' education background and the training they receive are related to firms' ESG reporting. Other potential factors include managers' personal views on ESG, their ethnic background, prior expertise with ESG and family background.

As for corporate disclosures on carbon emissions, Liao et al. (2015) found that a significant positive correlation exists between the proportion of female directors on the board and carbon information disclosure quality. The authors also further found that hiring more independent directors or establishing an environmental committee on the board will increase the company's ecological transparency tendencies, thereby improving its carbon information disclosure quality. Bui et al. (2020) found that increasing frequency of reporting to the board and expanding the time window for carbon reporting can improve carbon information disclosure significantly. Furthermore, regarding management ownership's impact, Tauringana and Chithambo (2015) examined GHG disclosures by 215 companies in the FTSE 350 index of the London Stock Exchange between 2008 and 2011 and found that director ownership is correlated negatively with the company's willingness to disclose carbon information because return on environmental investment entails a high degree of uncertainty, and directors with greater ownership are less willing to engage in energy conservation and emission-reduction activities, including carbon disclosure.

3.1.3 Ownership Characteristics

Ownership characteristics influence corporate ESG disclosure, mainly because companies with different ownership characteristics have differences in governance structure, management philosophy, strategic decision-making and other factors that may affect the degree of emphasis on ESG information, disclosure content and disclosure methods. First, institutional investors demand ESG information disclosure more stridently, and they are increasingly paying attention to corporate ESG performance in their investment decisions. They believe that ESG information is an important gauge for evaluating companies' long-term value and risks. McCahery et al. (2022) surveyed institutional investors to understand why they consider ESG factors in their investment management and found that limited partners (LPs) are motivated by effects on financial performance, whereas general partners (GPs) care more about ESG factors in response to clients' sustainability demands.

Second, institutional investors can guide the market's attention towards corporate ESG performance. Institutional investors, as important market participants, can influence the overall market trend by paying attention to and demanding corporate ESG disclosure. If more and more institutional investors begin to value corporate ESG performance, the market's demand for corporate ESG information disclosure will continue to increase. For example, Pawliczek et al. (2021) examined the impact of BlackRock's annual 'Dear CEO' letter on the portfolio companies' behaviour and found that portfolio companies' information disclosure after receiving the letter reflects themes discussed in the letter, including ESG related content.

Third, institutional investors can provide professional knowledge and resource support because they usually have rich professional knowledge and experience and, thus, can provide professional advice and suggestions on corporate ESG disclosure. For example, Siew et al. (2016) found a significant negative correlation between corporate ESG disclosure and the bid-ask spread, indicating that institutional investors' presence reduces market information asymmetry.

Ownership concentration is another important factor that influences corporate ESG disclosure, mainly because ownership concentration can lead to large shareholders' interests being prioritised at the expense of small shareholders and stakeholders' interests, thereby reducing ESG disclosure quality and transparency. Consistent with this argument, Höllerer (2013) found that dispersed private-sector ownership is related positively to the likelihood that a firm makes ESG disclosures. Thus, firms with more concentrated ownership are less likely to disclose ESG information.

As for corporate disclosure on climate change, Cohen et al. (2023) examined the relationship between institutional investors' demand for climate-related information, companies' decision to disclose this information and their carbon emissions. The results indicate a positive relationship between institutional ownership in CDP-signing countries and the likelihood of disclosing climate information, and that this disclosure subsequently is related to lower carbon emissions. Ceccarelli et al. (2023) focussed on the mutual fund industry and found that mutual funds disclose carbon information and get a 'low carbon' label to attract fund flows from institutional investors.

3.2 *Economic Consequences*

In this section, we review the literature on corporate ESG disclosure's economic consequences, including climate-related disclosures. More specifically, we first discuss the question of whether and how the capital market reacts to corporate ESG disclosure. We then further examine corporate ESG disclosure's effect on firm performance and valuation.

3.2.1 Capital Market Reaction

First, in the equity market, corporate ESG disclosure can help equity investors better understand companies' business conditions, strategic direction and social responsibility. This information can help investors assess companies' value and risks more comprehensively, and make more-informed investment decisions. For example, Flammer (2013) found that stock prices are related positively to good ESG news and negatively to bad news. The author demonstrated further that the relationship between stock prices and ESG news is asymmetrical, as investors react more to bad news. Christensen et al. (2017) demonstrated further that the corporate ESG disclosure medium also matters. The authors found that the market reacts strongly to ESG information disclosed through corporate financial statements, even though the same piece of information already has been disclosed in other places, such as government websites.

Corporate ESG disclosure also can help equity investors better understand enterprises' business philosophy, governance structure and risk management, thereby enhancing their investment confidence. This helps increase investors' loyalty and participation, bringing more financial and other resources to companies, particularly during market crises. Consistent with this idea, during the COVID-19 pandemic, firms with better ESG profiles experienced higher stock returns and suffered less from volatility. Ding et al. (2021) found that firms suffered fewer financial losses and had stronger immunity from financial downturns during the COVID-19 pandemic when they disclosed more ESG-related information, such as their ESG activities.

Furthermore, corporate ESG disclosure affects equity investors' investment strategy and, thus, these firms' capital costs. As for equity investors concerned about social responsibility, ESG information disclosure directly affects their investment strategies. If companies actively can disclose ESG information and demonstrate effective social responsibility performance, these investors may be more inclined towards investing in the company to support its sustainable development and social responsibility efforts. Therefore, the cost of capital for this type of firm will be lower. For example, Plumlee et al. (2015) examined the relationship between voluntary environmental information disclosure quality and corporate value, and found that the former is associated negatively with equity costs.

Second, in the debt market, corporate ESG disclosure significantly impacts corporate lenders and bondholders, helping them assess the company's credit risk, solvency and sustainability efforts. Therefore, companies should strengthen their ESG information disclosure quality and transparency to meet lenders and bondholders' needs and expectations. Christensen et al. (2021) argued that a CSR reporting mandate 'likely would reduce the search and information processing costs for bond investors and should make it easier to compare firms, particularly if investors have preferences for certain CSR topics'.

Third, financial intermediaries, such as financial analysts and the media, also are concerned about corporate ESG disclosure. As for financial analysts, corporate ESG disclosure provides more information to help them assess companies' value and risks, then helps them make more accurate forecasts and recommendations. Dhaliwal et al. (2012) demonstrated that financial analysts make fewer forecast errors when assessing firms that make ESG disclosures. Similarly, financial analysts can evaluate a firm's fundamental risks more accurately if the firm discloses more specific information, including ESG-related content. Ioannou and Serafeim (2015) found that firms' ESG practices, including disclosures, affect financial analysts' views on stock recommendations. As for the media, they often focus on a company's ESG performance and can help firms enhance their visibility and reputation. Cahan et al. (2015) demonstrated that the media tend to report more information on companies with better ESG reputations, but media coverage also could reinforce bad ESG news at a company, thereby eliciting a negative effect.

As for climate-related disclosure, previous literature found that capital markets in different institutional settings respond differently to carbon emissions information disclosure. Ziegler et al. (2011) found that in European and American markets, companies with higher climate change disclosure levels demonstrated better stock performance. Bolton and Kacperczyk (2021) demonstrated that firms which disclose their carbon emissions generate larger stock returns. Furthermore, Schiemann and Sakhe (2019) found that carbon information disclosure can reduce bid-ask spreads.

3.2.2 Firm Performance

Corporate ESG disclosure could impose significant influences on corporate investment, financing and business activities. First, corporate ESG disclosure can help companies understand investment projects' ESG performance, thereby better evaluating their operational risks and potential returns. This information can help companies make more comprehensive and accurate judgements, including investment decisions, while avoiding potential losses due to ESG issues. For example, Allman and Won (2022) demonstrated that corporate ESG disclosure could help firms improve their investment efficiency, particularly firms constrained financially or that have more entrenched managers. Fiechter et al. (2022) investigated mandatory ESG disclosure requirements' real effects and found that affected firms have higher ESG investments, elicit better returns and receive higher valuations after ESG disclosures.

Second, investors are more likely to focus on companies with more ESG disclosures when looking for prospects, as they are more likely to have sustainable business capabilities and effective social responsibility performance. These companies usually can obtain funding at lower costs and gain a better reputation and more trust in the market. Consistent with this idea, Christensen et al. (2017) argued that when firms provide more information on their ESG activities, equity and debt investors can better recognise managers' behaviour and reduce information asymmetry issues between corporate insiders and outsiders.

Third, corporate ESG disclosure directly impacts the company's business activities. If a company fails to fulfil its social responsibilities, its relationships with suppliers, customers and employees may be affected, which then affects its operating efficiency. For example, Dai et al. (2021b) found that corporate customers impose significant effects on their suppliers and make them disclose more ESG-related information, as well as take more impactful actions. Dyck et al. (2008) also argued that stakeholders could exert their influence on corporate behaviour, including ESG practices, through means such as public shaming.

Furthermore, a company's ESG performance is related directly to its brand image and reputation. If a company actively can disclose ESG information and demonstrate effective performance, this will help enhance its brand image and market recognition, thereby improving its market competitiveness. This also means that when a firm discloses undesirable ESG behaviour, its industry peers will avoid disclosing similar actions, implying that firms care about potential reputational damage caused by undesirable ESG practices. Chen et al. (2018) also found that industrial wastewater and SO_2 emissions are lower in cities that have mandatory ESG disclosure requirements imposed on local firms.

Much evidence also exists on practices that specifically focus on climate change disclosure worldwide. In the US, the government mandated GHG emissions disclosure for thousands of manufacturing facilities in 2010. Tomar (2023) examined how this change in the disclosure environment influences corporate behaviour and found that the affected facilities reduced carbon emissions by 7.9% afterwards. Similarly, Downar et al. (2021) found that affected listed firms in the UK reduced carbon emissions by 8% after mandatory disclosure requirements were adopted in 2013.

4 Conclusions and Future Research

This chapter introduces the basic concepts of ESG and climate change, and reviews the current literature related to corporate behaviour on ESG and climate change. Clearly, the academic community has generated diverse literature on ESG and climate change, making contributions to promoting sustainable development. However, current corporate ESG reports' information quality generally is not high, and the quality of empirical research based on these reports inevitably is affected. Furthermore, current empirical ESG research focusses on discussing influencing factors, economic consequences and market reactions. Although this research has found a correlation between ESG information, corporate characteristics, firm value and stock price response to varying degrees, few studies have demonstrated causal relationships between them. Scholarly research on ESG-related topics remains in the exploratory stage, and extant research that treats ESG as an integrated concept remains lacking.

With the gradual introduction of ESG reporting standards and certification mechanisms, ESG information quality will improve greatly, and the corporate value creation concept will undergo a significant transformation. This provides a rare opportunity to improve ESG research quality, and academic research around ESG will become more diverse and colourful, with the following trends.

Policy research on ESG reporting standards will elicit participation in academia. More specifically, sustainability reporting standards, or disclosure guidelines, are important foundational elements and institutional arrangements for ESG reporting. With the introduction and implementation of ESG reporting standards, more and more companies will disclose ESG information. Academia's involvement in policy research helps standard-setting bodies better understand these standards' cost-effectiveness and economic consequences, thereby improving the relevance and applicability of ESG or sustainable development information disclosure.

The ESG research field will expand further. More specifically, this field increasingly will indicate an interdisciplinary integration trend. In addition to ESG factors' impact on companies, corporate ESG practices may be affected by macroeconomic policies, legal systems, social culture, population, international trade, technological innovation and other factors, all of which can affect firms' value, financial health and capital market performance.

ESG research based on big data and artificial intelligence (AI) will be applied more widely. With the continuous development of big data and AI technology, more and more scholars will apply these technologies to analyse and study ESG data. By mining and analysing massive amounts of data, we can study ESG factors' impact on companies in a more in-depth way, providing more accurate decision support for corporate management.

Cross-border comparative research and international cooperation will become more frequent as well. As globalisation proliferates further, more and more multinational companies are beginning to promote and apply ESG practices globally. Therefore, cross-border comparative research and international cooperation will become more frequent and important. By comparing ESG practices in different countries and regions, we can better understand different cultures and systems' impact on firms and promote international cooperation and exchange.

Regulation of ESG practices will become stricter, but the question remains about how to regulate these practices. Academia can provide more advice to regulators based on policy evaluations. As ESG practices' popularity and depth increase, regulators will impose stricter regulations on ESG practices. Simultaneously, investors and stakeholders increasingly are concerned about corporate ESG performance, which will prompt companies to pay more attention to compliance and transparency in ESG practices.

References

Abeysekera, A. P., & Fernando, C. S. (2020). Corporate social responsibility versus corporate shareholder responsibility: A family firm perspective. *Journal of Corporate Finance, 61*, 101370.

Albuquerque, R., Koskinen, Y., & Zhang, C. (2019). Corporate social responsibility and firm risk: Theory and empirical evidence. *Management Science, 65*(10), 4451–4469.

Allman, E., & Won, J. (2022). The effect of ESG disclosure on corporate investment efficiency. In *Proceedings of Paris December 2021 Finance Meeting EUROFIDAI-ESSEC*.

Alrazi, B., De Villiers, C., & Van Staden, C. J. (2016). The environmental disclosures of the electricity generation industry: a global perspective. *Accounting and Business Research, 46*(6), 665–701.

Azar, J., Duro, M., Kadach, I., & Ormazabal, G. (2021). The big three and corporate carbon emissions around the world. *Journal of Financial Economics, 142*(2), 674-696.

Baker, S. D., Hollifield, B., & Osambela, E. (2022). Asset prices and portfolios with externalities. *Review of Finance, 26*(6), 1433–1468.

Benjaafar, S., Li, Y., & Daskin, M. (2012). Carbon footprint and the management of supply chains: Insights from simple models. *IEEE Transactions on Automation Science and Engineering, 10*(1), 99–116.

Bolton, P., & Kacperczyk, M. (2021). Do investors care about carbon risk?. *Journal of Financial Economics, 142*(2), 517–549.

Borghesi, R., Houston, J. F., & Naranjo, A. (2014). Corporate socially responsible investments: CEO altruism, reputation, and shareholder interests. *Journal of Corporate Finance, 26*, 164–181.

Boubakri, N., El Ghoul, S., Wang, H., Guedhami, O., & Kwok, C. C. (2016). Cross-listing and corporate social responsibility. *Journal of Corporate Finance*, 41, 123–138.

Bui, B., Houqe, M. N., & Zaman, M. (2020). Climate governance effects on carbon disclosure and performance. *The British Accounting Review, 52*(2), 100880.

Cahan, S. F., Chen, C., Chen, L., & Nguyen, N. H. (2015). Corporate social responsibility and media coverage. *Journal of Banking & Finance, 59*, 409–422.

Cai, Y., Pan, C. H., & Statman, M. (2016). Why do countries matter so much in corporate social performance?. *Journal of Corporate Finance*, 41, 591–609.

Ceccarelli, M., Ramelli, S., & Wagner, A. F. (2023). Low carbon mutual funds. *Review of Finance,* Forthcoming.

Chava, S. (2014). Environmental externalities and cost of capital. *Management Science, 60*(9), 2223–2247.

Chen, Y. C., Hung, M., & Wang, Y. (2018). The effect of mandatory CSR disclosure on firm profitability and social externalities: Evidence from China. *Journal of Accounting and Economics, 65*(1), 169–190.

Christensen, H. B., Floyd, E., Liu, L. Y., & Maffett, M. (2017). The real effects of mandated information on social responsibility in financial reports: Evidence from mine-safety records. Journal of Accounting and Economics, 64(2-3), 284–304.

Christensen, H. B., Hail, L., & Leuz, C. (2021). Mandatory CSR and sustainability reporting: Economic analysis and literature review. *Review of Accounting Studies*, *26*(3), 1176–1248.

Cohen, S., Kadach, I., & Ormazabal, G. (2023). Institutional investors, climate disclosure, and carbon emissions. *Journal of Accounting and Economics*, *76*(2–3), 101640.

Dai, R., Duan, R., Liang, H., & Ng, L. (2021a). Outsourcing climate change. *European Corporate Governance Institute–Finance Working Paper*, (723).

Dai et al. 2021b Dai, R., Liang, H., & Ng, L. (2021). Socially responsible corporate customers. *Journal of Financial Economics*, *142*(2), 598–626.

Dhaliwal, D. S., Radhakrishnan, S., Tsang, A., & Yang, Y. G. (2012). Nonfinancial disclosure and analyst forecast accuracy: International evidence on corporate social responsibility disclosure. *The Accounting Review*, *87*(3), 723–759.

Di Giuli, A., & Kostovetsky, L. (2014). Are red or blue companies more likely to go green? Politics and corporate social responsibility. *Journal of Financial Economics*, *111*(1), 158–180.

Dimson, E., Karakaş, O., & Li, X. (2015). Active ownership. *The Review of Financial Studies*, *28*(12), 3225–3268.

Ding, W., Levine, R., Lin, C., & Xie, W. (2021). Corporate immunity to the COVID-19 pandemic. *Journal of Financial Economics*, *141*(2), 802–830.

Downar, B., Ernstberger, J., Reichelstein, S., Schwenen, S., & Zaklan, A. (2021). The impact of carbon disclosure mandates on emissions and financial operating performance. *Review of Accounting Studies*, *26*, 1137–1175.

Dyck, A., Volchkova, N., & Zingales, L. (2008). The corporate governance role of the media: Evidence from Russia. *The Journal of Finance*, *63*(3), 1093–1135.

Dyck, A., Lins, K. V., Roth, L., & Wagner, H. F. (2019). Do institutional investors drive corporate social responsibility? International evidence. *Journal of Financial Economics*, *131*(3), 693–714.

Edmans, A. (2011). Does the stock market fully value intangibles? Employee satisfaction and equity prices. *Journal of Financial Economics*, *101*(3), 621–640.

Ferrell, A., Liang, H., & Renneboog, L. (2016). Socially responsible firms. *Journal of Financial Economics*, *122*(3), 585–606.

Fiechter, P., Hitz, J. M., & Lehmann, N. (2022). Real effects of a widespread CSR reporting mandate: Evidence from the European Union's CSR Directive. *Journal of Accounting Research*, *60*(4), 1499–1549.

Flammer, C. (2013). Corporate social responsibility and shareholder reaction: The environmental awareness of investors. *Academy of Management Journal*, *56*(3), 758–781.

Flammer, C. (2021). Corporate green bonds. *Journal of Financial Economics*, *142*(2), 499–516.

Flammer, C., Toffel, M. W., & Viswanathan, K. (2021). Shareholder activism and firms' voluntary disclosure of climate change risks. *Strategic Management Journal*, *42*(10), 1850–1879.

Flammer, C. (2015). Does corporate social responsibility lead to superior financial performance? A regression discontinuity approach. *Management Science*, *61*(11), 2549–2568.

Freeman, R. E., Harrison, J. S., Wicks, A. C., Parmar, B. L., & De Colle, S. (2010). Stakeholder Theory: The State of the Art. Cambridge: Cambridge University Press.

Gamerschlag, R., Möller, K., & Verbeeten, F. (2011). Determinants of voluntary CSR disclosure: empirical evidence from Germany. *Review of Managerial Science*, *5*, 233–262.

Höllerer, M. A. (2013). From taken-for-granted to explicit commitment: The rise of CSR in a corporatist country. *Journal of Management Studies*, *50*(4), 573–606.

Hong, H., & Kacperczyk, M. (2009). The price of sin: The effects of social norms on markets. *Journal of Financial Economics*, *93*(1), 15–36.

Hsu, P. H., Liang, H., & Matos, P. (2021). Leviathan Inc. and corporate environmental engagement. *Management Science*.

Innes, R., & Sam, A. G. (2008). Voluntary pollution reductions and the enforcement of environmental law: An empirical study of the 33/50 program. *The Journal of Law and Economics, 51*(2), 271–296.
Ioannou, I., & Serafeim, G. (2015). The impact of corporate social responsibility on investment recommendations: Analysts' perceptions and shifting institutional logics. *Strategic Management Journal, 36*(7), 1053–1081.
Jha, A., & Cox, J. (2015). Corporate social responsibility and social capital. *Journal of Banking & Finance, 60*, 252–270.
Landier, A., Nair, V. B., & Wulf, J. (2009). Trade-offs in staying close: Corporate decision making and geographic dispersion. *The Review of Financial Studies, 22*(3), 1119–1148.
Lee, N., & Luo, J. (2021). Are native plants green? Assessing environmental performances of locally-owned facilities. *SSRN*, 3830153.
Lewis, B. W., Walls, J. L., & Dowell, G. W. (2014). Difference in degrees: CEO characteristics and firm environmental disclosure. *Strategic Management Journal, 35*(5), 712–722.
Liang, H., & Renneboog, L. (2017). On the foundations of corporate social responsibility. *The Journal of Finance, 72*(2), 853–910.
Liao, L., Luo, L., & Tang, Q. (2015). Gender diversity, board independence, environmental committee and greenhouse gas disclosure. *The British Accounting Review, 47*(4), 409–424.
Liesen, A., Hoepner, A. G., Patten, D. M., & Figge, F. (2015). Does stakeholder pressure influence corporate GHG emissions reporting? Empirical evidence from Europe. Accounting, Auditing & Accountability Journal, 28(7), 1047–1074.
Lins, K. V., Servaes, H., & Tamayo, A. (2017). Social capital, trust, and firm performance: The value of corporate social responsibility during the financial crisis. *The Journal of Finance, 72*(4), 1785–1824.
Luo, L. L., & Tang, Q. (2016). Does national culture influence corporate carbon disclosure propensity?. *Journal of International Accounting Research, 15*(1), 17–47.
Masulis, R. W., & Reza, S. W. (2015). Agency problems of corporate philanthropy. *The Review of Financial Studies, 28*(2), 592–636.
McCahery, J. A., Pudschedl, P. C., & Steindl, M. (2022). Institutional Investors, Alternative Asset Managers, and ESG Preferences. *European Business Organization Law Review, 23*(4), 821–868.
McCarthy, S., Oliver, B., & Song, S. (2017). Corporate social responsibility and CEO confidence. *Journal of Banking & Finance, 75*, 280–291.
Ott, C., Schiemann, F., & Günther, T. (2017). Disentangling the determinants of the response and the publication decisions: The case of the carbon disclosure project. *Journal of Accounting and Public Policy, 36*(1), 14–33.
Pástor, Ľ., Stambaugh, R. F., & Taylor, L. A. (2021). Sustainable investing in equilibrium. *Journal of Financial Economics, 142*(2), 550–571.
Pawliczek, A., Skinner, A. N., & Wellman, L. A. (2021). A new take on voice: the influence of BlackRock's 'Dear CEO' letters. *Review of Accounting Studies, 26*(3), 1088–1136.
Pedersen, L. H., Fitzgibbons, S., & Pomorski, L. (2021). Responsible investing: The ESG-efficient frontier. *Journal of Financial Economics, 142*(2), 572–597.
Plumlee, M., Brown, D., Hayes, R. M., & Marshall, R. S. (2015). Voluntary environmental disclosure quality and firm value: Further evidence. *Journal of Accounting and Public Policy, 34*(4), 336–361.
Rankin, M., Windsor, C., & Wahyuni, D. (2011). An investigation of voluntary corporate greenhouse gas emissions reporting in a market governance system: Australian evidence. Accounting, Auditing & Accountability Journal, 24(8), 1037–1070.
Sautner, Z., Van Lent, L., Vilkov, G., & Zhang, R. (2023). Firm-level climate change exposure. *The Journal of Finance, 78*(3), 1449–1498.
Schiemann, F., & Sakhel, A. (2019). Carbon disclosure, contextual factors, and information asymmetry: The case of physical risk reporting. *European Accounting Review, 28*(4), 791–818.
Servaes, H., & Tamayo, A. (2013). The impact of corporate social responsibility on firm value: The role of customer awareness. *Management Science, 59*(5), 1045–1061.

Siew, R. Y., Balatbat, M. C., & Carmichael, D. G. (2016). The impact of ESG disclosures and institutional ownership on market information asymmetry. *Asia-Pacific Journal of* Accounting & Economics, 23(4), 432–448.

Stroebel, J., & Wurgler, J. (2021). What do you think about climate finance?. *Journal of Financial Economics, 142*(2), 487–498.

Tauringana, V., & Chithambo, L. (2015). The effect of DEFRA guidance on greenhouse gas disclosure. *The British Accounting Review, 47*(4), 425–444.

Teoh, S. H., Yan, J., & Yoon, A. (2022). ESG and shareholder value: The role of board facial impressions and perceived trustworthiness. Available at SSRN 4273360.

Tomar, S. (2023). Greenhouse gas disclosure and emissions benchmarking. *Journal of Accounting Research, 61*(2), 451–492.

Ziegler, A., Busch, T., & Hoffmann, V. H. (2011). Disclosed corporate responses to climate change and stock performance: An international empirical analysis. *Energy Economics, 33*(6), 1283–1294.

Governance and Climate Finance in the Developing World

Byeong-Hak Choe and Tilsa Ore-Monago

Abstract We investigate the relationship between governance and climate finance, particularly in the energy transition context in developing countries. Our aim is to examine how governance qualities in developing countries impact financial contributions from contributor countries intending to fund mitigation projects in the energy sector. We have compiled a dataset of yearly climate finance contributions at the project level spanning from 2011 to 2019. Our analysis, which utilizes random forests and Least Absolute Shrinkage and Selection Operator (LASSO) estimations, reveals that climate finance contributions, particularly those for energy-related projects, are significantly linked to good governance, including a robust legal system, the rule of law, and accountability. Ultimately, this study provides valuable insights into the dynamics between governance and climate finance in developing countries and informs policy decisions to support effective climate action in the energy sector.

1 Introduction

Climate change has a global impact and requires being tackled globally. To feasibly reach the goal of net-zero by 2050, international climate finance must increase by a factor of six by 2030 (CPI 2021). Considering the existing income disparities in the world, climate finance flows from developed to developing economies are crucial.

However, this effort requires that finance is effectively used to secure decarbonization and a just transition. On the other hand, since mitigation projects tend to target the energy sector, which is characterized by significant sunk costs and high long-term rents, energy-related projects within countries with poor governance can be subject to increasing asymmetric information problems. This may include moral hazard from contract parties by renegotiations (Choe 2020) or increased corruption.

B.-H. Choe (✉)
School of Business, State University of New York at Geneseo, New York, USA
e-mail: bchoe@geneseo.edu

T. Ore-Monago
Baker Institute for Public Policy, Rice University, Houston, USA
e-mail: tilsa@rice.edu

F. Wu et al. (eds.), *Climate Finance*, Climate Change and Energy Transition,
https://doi.org/10.1007/978-981-97-3308-8_7

Governance factors are relevant for climate finance effectiveness, given the existing strong correlation between climate change vulnerability and perceived corruption at the country level. Moreover, Nest et al. (2023) identify other risk factors such as inadequate monitoring, multiplicity of actors, and unclear and evolving rules in renewable energy projects, which increases developing countries' vulnerability to corruption. Thus, it is crucial to assess the impact of climate finance in the developing world since developing countries are the most vulnerable to climate change and weak institutions with poor governance. Low-quality governance can be a significant barrier to emissions reduction in these countries. For that reason, we conduct a study to characterize climate finance, particularly for the financial flows from developed to developing countries, to identify potential hindrances to the effectiveness of climate finance allocation.

Under our analysis, accounting for a wide range of governance dimensions can help to improve funding allocation mechanisms. Thus, our study contributes to the literature by including such a dimension, which has not yet been fully studied (Nest et al. 2020; Kouwenberg and Zhen 2023). For our empirical analysis, we construct a dataset from various sources (UNFCCC Climate Finance Data Portal 2023; Global Environment Facility 2023; IMF 2023); with country governance indicators from the PRS Group (2023) and the World Bank (2023a). We use machine learning methods on the dataset for climate finance funds during the period 2011–2019 at the project level to evaluate how developing countries' governance qualities impact developed countries' financial contributions.

Thus, we study the determinants of funding contributions for climate change projects, particularly for energy-related ones. We find that governance, energy, and environmental factors in developing countries determine the size of funding contributions for their climate finance projects, particularly energy-related projects.

A higher quality of governance allows for greater economic stability and predictability, which favors investment flows. Developing countries need to work more to improve their governance, but bigger efforts need to be made considering the rapid climate change. This includes urgently improving climate finance access by simplifying and standardizing administrative processes and providing capacity-building support and ensuring higher participation of local stakeholders in the decision-making for climate change projects. It is also crucial to have more clarity between climate finance and development aid. They should not be treated as the same, as the incentives for those two funding aids are not equivalent.

Section 2 discusses climate change and the global sustainability goals. Section 3 discusses various topics in climate finance, such as types of instruments, its differences from development aid, and the different incentives in each case. Section 4 presents a brief analysis of clean energy markets and their relationship with climate finance. Section 5 presents the factors of climate finance. Section 6 presents and discusses the empirical analysis. Lastly, Sect. 7 concludes the study.

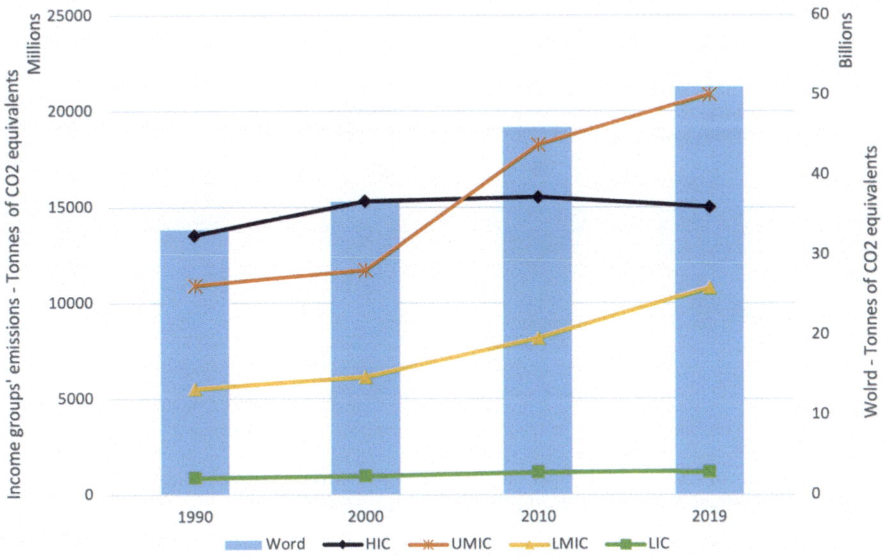

Fig. 1 Evolution of total GHG emissions by income group, tonnes of CO_2e (1990–2019). *Notes* HIC = High-income countries, UMIC = Upper-middle income countries, LMIC = Lower-middle income countries, and LIC = Low-income countries. *Source* Our World in Data based on the Global Carbon Project 2022

2 Climate Change and Sustainability Goals

Climate change is manifesting more often via extended heat waves or unexpected cold seasons in conventionally warm areas, which is affecting humanity and the ecosystem in several ways. Compared to developed countries, developing countries have faced and are projected to continue experiencing more severe adverse effects of climate change, such as water stress, reduced food security, forced climate migration, and increased morbidity. This happens despite the fact that developing countries contribute the least to climate change (IPCC 2023). According to the IPCC (IPCC 2023), global surface temperatures for the period 2011–2020 were 1.1°C higher than the levels recorded in the mid-nineteenth century. Greenhouse gas (GHG) emissions, most of which are CO_2 emissions,[1] have been consistently increasing decade by decade. Between 2000 and 2010, global GHG emissions increased by 25.4%, followed by an 11% rise from 2010 to 2019. These surges are primarily attributed to upper-middle income countries, including China (see Fig. 1). Notably, low-income countries have substantially slowed down their emission rates: these countries saw a 4% increase from 2010 to 2019, a marked reduction from the 21% growth recorded between 2000 and 2010.

[1] According to the World Resource Institute, CO_2 emissions in 2019 represented around 75% of GHG emissions (see https://www.wri.org/insights/4-charts-explain-greenhouse-gas-emissions-countries-and-sectors).

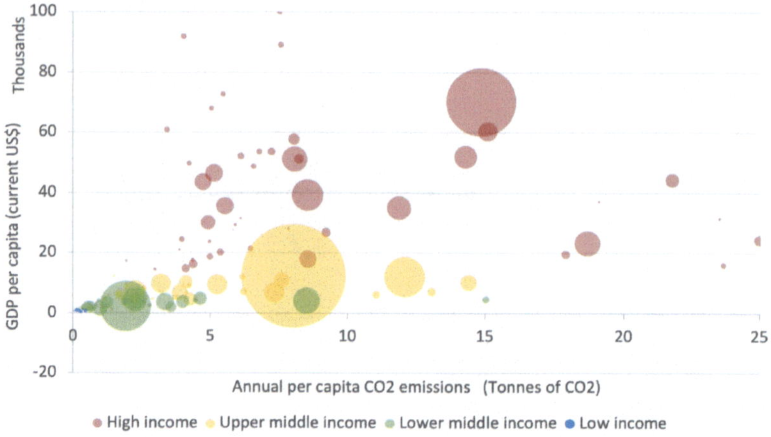

Fig. 2 Emissions of CO_2 and GDP per capita (2021), *Notes* Bubble size indicates the country's annual CO_2 emissions. *Source* Our World in Data, World Bank dataset

GHG emissions are primarily driven by extensive global energy use, and energy consumption, and consequently CO_2 emissions, are strongly associated with industrialization and economic growth. This explains why historically, high-income countries have been, and continue to be, among the largest emitters (see Fig. 2). In the past decade, major emerging economies, such as China, have exceeded the proportion of emissions contributed by high-income countries to global GHG emissions.

As of 2019, global GHG emissions reached 51 million tonnes. The four leading sectors, accounting for 57% of these high emissions, are electricity and heat, transport, manufacturing and construction, and agriculture (see Fig. 3). While this ranking holds true for high-income countries, it shifts for low-and lower-middle-income countries, where agriculture accounts for a more significant portion of emissions. Electricity and transportation are still important for lower-middle-income countries (see Fig. 4).

Reducing global GHG emissions is challenging, as it involves addressing significant disparities. As emissions levels are positively associated with economic growth, it is reasonable to anticipate an increase in emissions from lower-income countries, which currently emit the least, as their economies continue to grow. Additionally, it is also projected that high-income countries will see minimal reductions in emissions, because they prefer maintaining their high standards of living (Tirole 2017).

Tackling climate change requires global climate policy solutions, and there are two main types of policies to address its negative consequences: (i) mitigation policies aimed at reducing emissions and decarbonizing economies, and (ii) adaptation policies aimed at adjusting socioeconomic systems and enhancing resilience to current and future climate change impacts.

Mitigation actions can be considered a public good, as they benefit everyone in the global society. This, however, also leads to a situation where individuals might wait for others to reduce their emissions, thus reaping the benefits of mitigation

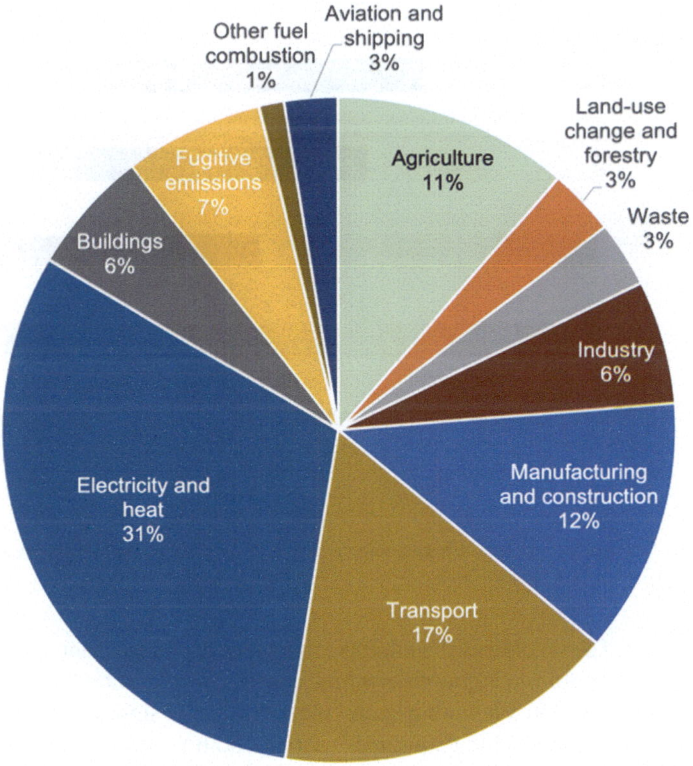

Fig. 3 Greenhouse gas emissions by sector, 2019. *Source* Our World in Data based on the Global Carbon Project 2022

without incurring the costs. This scenario is referred to as the free-rider problem in economics. Climate policy—aimed at combating climate change—is often linked to a typical 'tragedy of the commons' situation: although reducing emissions is universally beneficial, particularly for future generations, individual incentives to undertake such actions are minimal due to the free-riding issue (Bracking and Benjamin 2021). A key aspect of reducing emissions is the need for collective action, as isolated efforts are insufficient to prevent the greater adverse impacts of emissions. The Kyoto Protocol, established in 1997, where signatory parties (developed countries) agreed to reduce their emissions by 2012 and implemented a tradable emissions permit system, did not work as incentives to adhere to the agreement were undermined by the free-rider problem (Tirole 2017).

Conversely, adaptation actions, focused on equipping vulnerable populations–predominantly in developing countries–to deal with the adverse effects of climate change, are not aligned well with the definition of a public good. While adaptation actions are crucial to prevent suffering in populations that are the least responsible for emission issues, these measures are often localized, benefiting countries that

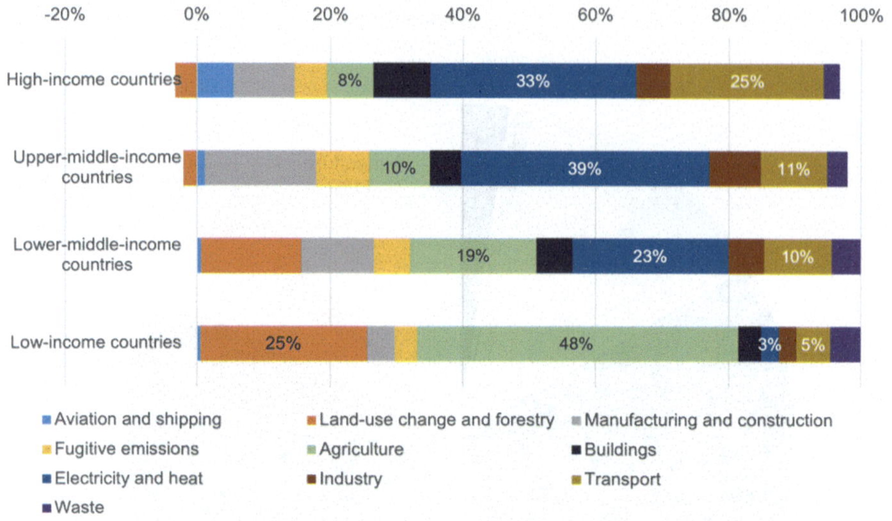

Fig. 4 Share of per capita greenhouse gas emissions by sector, 2019. *Source* Our world in data based on the global carbon project 2022

implement them. The incentives to undertake these efforts are substantial for affected countries. However, for other countries which are less impacted by these issues, the incentive to participate in alleviating such vulnerabilities is significantly lower.

The implementation of climate policies requires both political will and financial access. Regarding political will, two key events happened in 2000 and 2015. In 2000, the United Nations named climate change its seventh Millennium Development Goal and in 2015 as one of its 17 Sustainable Development Goals. The 13th goal explicitly calls upon us to "take urgent action to combat climate change and its impacts," while related references are implicit within other goals such as those that aimed at affordable and clean energy (goal 7), access to clean water and sanitation (goal 6), and sustainable cities and communities (goal 11).[2] In December 2015, the Paris Agreement set the ambitious target of limiting the global temperature increase to 1.5 °C or, at most, 2 °C by 2050. Currently, 194 parties (193 countries and the European Union) are signatories to the Paris Agreement. Under the Paris Agreement, parties have committed to submitting their Nationally Determined Contributions (NDCs), which outline plans for reducing GHG emissions and actions to adapt to the impacts of climate change.

Regarding finance access, the Paris Agreement notably enhanced climate finance through the commitment (although voluntary) of developed countries to providing financial support. The agreement also includes assistance for capacity-building related to climate issues in developing countries, along with support for enhancing technology development and transfer to mitigate and adapt to climate change. Furthermore, an Enhanced Transparency Framework (ETF) was established,

[2] See United Nations website https://sdgs.un.org/.

mandating all countries from 2024 onwards, to report their actions and progress on climate-related mitigation and adaptation efforts, as well as the support they have either given or received in pursuit of the climate goals.[3]

3 Climate Finance

Climate finance refers to funds mobilized for climate change mitigation and adaptation activities around the world. This includes financial flows from developed countries to less developed countries, as stipulated in the Paris Agreement.[4] In the Paris Agreement of 2015, developed countries committed to jointly mobilize USD 100 billion per year in climate finance by 2020, and to continue this level of annual spending through 2025. The sources of this funding are diverse, ranging from public and private to bilateral and multilateral channels, including the United Nations Green Climate Fund. These funds are intended to assist developing countries in their efforts to mitigate and adapt to climate change.

According to UNFCCC figures in 2022 (UNFCCC 2022), global climate finance reached an annual average of USD 803 billion between 2019 and 2020, 12% higher than in the 2017–2018 period. Likewise, the least developed countries (LCDs) received roughly 20% of the total global climate finance. Overall, developing countries received around USD 66 billion in private climate finance between 2016 and 2020 (mobilized via bilateral and multilateral channels). Around 86% of these climate funds were given for mitigation projects, and 53% of those mitigation projects were energy-related (mostly for renewable energy).

The pronounced focus on financing energy projects, especially those involving renewable and clean energy, is linked to the significant impact of the energy sector on global carbon emissions. There is a collective sense of urgency and higher incentives to decarbonize this sector, where the costs of implementation have decreased substantially over time due to technological advancements (IEA, 2023). Similarly, the transportation sector is anticipated to be the next target for climate finance initiatives.

Although climate finance is on the rise, the current flow remains substantially inadequate for achieving the net-zero goals: the current funding may need to increase by at least five times to reach an annual climate investment of USD 4.35 to 5 trillion by 2030 (CPI 2021; Kouwenberg and Zhen 2023). The concern deepens when considering that the annual climate-related financing for 2019–2020 (USD 803 billion per year) still falls below the global investment in fossil fuels during the same period (USD 892 billion). Furthermore, annual fossil fuel subsidies amount to more than

[3] Based on information available on the UNFCCC website. For more, see https://unfccc.int/process-and-meetings/the-paris-agreement.

[4] A more precise definition is given in UNFCCC (2022): "Climate finance aims at reducing emissions, and enhancing sinks of greenhouse gases and aims at reducing the vulnerability of, and maintaining and increasing the resilience of, human and ecological systems to negative climate change impacts".

half of the climate finance flows, at USD 450 billion (UNFCCC 2022). This substantial gap between current and necessary investment levels can be partially attributed to the free-rider problem. It is, therefore, crucial to understand the workings of climate finance and its incentive mechanisms.

3.1 Types of Financing

Funds can be provided by the public sector, private sector, or a combination of both. Funds can come from direct national and sub-national governments, private financial institutions, philanthropic foundations, and multilateral institutions. Funds can also come from intermediaries such as development financial institutions (DFI)–development banks–comprising national, non-profit organizations, and multilateral and bilateral funds, to promote and finance economic development projects on a non-commercial basis.

DFIs play an essential role in climate finance since they enable the financing of public and private sector investments in climate change projects that would otherwise not be developed due to high financial risk. There are also climate-specific funding mechanisms, such as UNFCCC funds, non-UNFCCC funds, and national climate funds. These include the Global Environment Facility (GEF), the Green Climate Fund (GCF), the Adaptation Fund (AF), and the Climate Investment Funds (CIF). In addition, there are issuers of green bonds and green, social, and sustainability bonds (GSS). From these, the GEF, the World Bank's CIF, and the GCF jointly constitute the main pillars of public finance via multilateral channels (Bracking and Benjamin 2021).

Regarding the type of financial instrument, climate finance is similar to financial assistance for economic development in that a fund is given through grants, debt, loans (including concessional or soft loans), equity, and guarantees. Below, we provide a brief definition of each instrument.

- Grants are given free of interest and with no repayment obligation.
- Loans are subject to an interest rate and a repayment schedule; when the interest rate is significantly lower than that of a commercial loan, the instrument is known as a concessional loan.
- Equity finance refers to early-stage investment or capital provided for developing a project in exchange for a portion of ownership.
- Guarantees cover borrower's obligations in the case of default, reducing the risk faced by the lender.

The incentives for lender and recipient countries in the realm of climate finance differ according to the type of financial instrument used. Loans, for instance, offer robust incentives for borrowers to implement climate change projects effectively due to the repayment obligation and the interest rate attached to the loan; these incentives may intensify with repeated interactions between the donor and recipient countries. In contrast, equity finance creates stronger incentives for lender countries to enhance monitoring and project evaluation. Guarantees play a crucial role in reducing investment risk, which can encourage more significant investment volumes. Additionally, guarantees may be more readily available to borrower parties who are more credible and stable for ongoing interactions.

The optimal use of climate finance instruments can improve climate finance allocation and accelerate climate action. Achieving net-zero goals requires widespread climate action, which requires abundant and accessible climate finance.

3.2 Climate Finance Access

Accessing climate finance has been particularly challenging for LDCs and Small Island Developing States (SIDS). These challenges stem from the diverse requirements attached to various sources of climate finance, as summarized by the UNFCCC (2022) (p. 124). We have slightly modified this summary to encompass two main factors:

- The project adequacy and predictability conditions involve the level of funding available relative to needs (mitigation-adaptation balance), the nature of the funding available relative to needs (financial instrument and time horizon), and the nature of macroeconomic conditions and impact on capital access. Likewise, this should include an enabling environment such as policies and regulations governing sectoral transitions.
- The technical and administrative skill set involves the capacity and capability to identify and articulate financial needs and priorities, to prepare projects, and the procedural capability to deal with eligibility criteria, as well as accreditation and financial approval processes, that is, capacity building, which was also highlighted as necessary during the IMF 2023 Spring Meetings.

Argueta et al. (2021) analyze the accessibility of climate finance for LDCs and SIDS. According to them, multilateral climate funds have been less accessible to developing countries than other sources, such as private and bilateral sources, DFIs, and multilateral development banks (MDBs).

Barriers to accessing climate finance relate to strong requirements that countries may not be able to satisfy. For example, Argueta et al. (2021) find that the requirement of historical climate data (for the last 30 years) to support the climate change-related rationale of projects has hindered recipient countries' access to climate finance. This is because low-income countries often lack such data or the means to obtain it. Argueta et al. (2021) also find that the criteria concerning the r characteristics of recipient countries, such as their income level, tend to force them to obtain required levels of co-finance or private sector investment. This is particularly pertinent for countries with high debt and limited fiscal resources, especially in the aftermath of the COVID-19 pandemic, which may make them ineligible for non-concessional loans.

Another obstacle in climate finance is the lack of standardization and simplification of requirements, criteria and/or processes to access climate finance across financial sources, and multilateral and bilateral sources. Processing costs may increase when the capacity-building and administrative skills of recipient countries are low. There is also a lack of clarity between development finance and climate finance for adaptation actions. This adds confusion and inefficiencies to the process and to funds allocation. This lack of clarity stands out as an obstacle for multilateral climate finance because coordination problems may arise between the multilateral MDB's CIF, and the GCF administered by the UNFCCC.[5] Moreover, this lack of clarity can be detrimental at the domestic level, where coordination failures between assigned agencies with overlapping functions may prevent or slow project developments (Skovgaard, 2023).

Lastly, an aspect highlighted by Argueta et al. (2021) is that bilateral channels tend to be less transparent and more discretionary. Since most climate finance flows are given by bilateral channels, recipient countries perceive that finance would often be linked to contributors' interests and policy goals, such as geopolitical ties and proximity. This is consistent with the finding of Burnside and Dollar (2000) regarding development aid.

In sum, the economic conditions of recipient countries that support project predictability and the presence of adequate regulatory environments are crucial for enabling project development. These conditions are related to a country's institutional capacity and maturity to comply more effectively with climate finance requirements and accreditation standards. These factors are closely related to a country's governance. Additionally, repeated interactions between donor and recipient countries can create a learning process regarding procedural matters. This also highlights governance as either an enabler or a barrier to further climate finance. Nest et al. (2020), for example, underline corruption as a crucial governance issue that may undermine climate-related achievements. They note that countries receiving about 40% of climate-related official development assistance (ODA) are among those most at risk of corruption. These issues are further discussed in Sect. 5.

3.3 Stylized Facts About Climate Finance

Based on the UNFCCC (2022) and CPI (2021), some important facts for the period 2019–2020 can be highlighted:

[5] According to Skovgaard et al. (2023), under CIF, climate finance is seen as development finance, where MDBs develop projects and, the decisions are shaped by the "contributors" criteria, while under GCF, climate finance is seen as different from development aid, so its mechanisms are intended to be different, funds are provided by "contributors" and recipient country with other stakeholder will take active part on the decision-making of the project development. CIF also tends to provide moderately concessional lending and few grants, whereas GCF tends to provide more concessional loans and grants.

Global climate finance flows

- Public sector finance, through mostly DFIs, accounted for more than half (51%) of climate finance during the period 2019–2020. Roughly 37% of total public finance was given by national DFIs, and around 20% of it came from multilateral DFIs.
- The private sector—comprised mainly of corporations, commercial financial institutions, and households and individuals—contributed 49% of the annual climate finance.[6] Corporations contributed 40% of the total private finance, but commercial banks accounted for 39% of the private finance, showing a significant increase from the previous period as more commercial banks have been financing clean energy projects.
- Global climate finance grew 12% in the period 2017–2018 driven mainly by investments in the energy efficiency of buildings, sustainable transport and adaptation finance.
- Global climate finance was given through loans (debt), representing 61% of the total, followed by equity investments (33%), according to CPI (2021). Only 6% was raised as grants, of which 55% correspond to international flows.
- Around 90% of the global climate finance went to mitigation projects.
- Geographically, global climate finance is concentrated in East Asia and the Pacific (43%), Western Europe (20%), and the United States and Canada (20%).

To achieve the net-zero goals, a substantial expansion of global climate finance is essential, including a broadening of private finance involvement. According to the IEA and IFC (2023), private finance is currently highly concentrated on projects in the developed world, while emerging and developing countries are often overlooked. Addressing this imbalance necessitates the development of carbon markets and the establishment of standards and certifications for environmental, sustainable, and governance (ESG) practices to mobilize capital for climate change projects.

Flows from developed to developing countries

- The commitment made under the Paris Agreement to jointly mobilize USD 100 billion per year in climate finance by 2020 was not fully met.
- Most climate finance flows from developed to developing countries (79%) were provided by bilateral, regional, and other channels. The rest (21%) was given by multilateral DFIs and multilateral climate funds.
- According to the UNFCCC (2022), there is no clear estimate of private climate finance to developing countries. However, the total private climate finance mobilized by multilateral funds to developing countries may have amounted to USD 66.8 billion, 86% of which was provided for mitigation projects. Half of the 86% specifically went to funding the energy sector. Private climate finance for adaptation targeted projects for industry, mining, and construction projects.

[6] Households contributions would come basically from their spending on electric vehicles, estimated to be around USD 25 billion per year in the period 2019/2020.

Table 1 Public climate finance flows to developing countries by channel, area of support and type of instrument (2019/2020)

	Annual average (USD billion)	Area of support				Financial instrument		
		Mitigation (%)	Adaptation (%)	Cross-cutting (%)	REDD +	Grants (%)	Loans (%)	Other (%)
Bilateral climate finance	31.6	57	28	15	–	49	49	1.5
Multilateral climate funds	3.1	37	19	35	9%	62	34	4
MDB climate finance	38.3	62	36	2	–	8	78	13

Source Taken from UNFCCC (2022) (p. 106)

- A large share of climate finance flows was directed at mitigation projects. 57% of funds from bilateral channels were for mitigation activities, and only 28% were for adaptation projects.
- Climate finance flows were channelled by multilateral means. Likewise, more than 90% of multilateral finance was given to adaptation, cross-cutting, and other general projects.
- Public finance for mitigation projects was mostly given by loans, while public finance for adaptation projects was predominantly given by grants (UNFCCC 2022).
- In geographic terms, most of the climate finance for developing countries was provided to Asia (36%), followed by Africa (27%) and then Latin America (16%).
- Out of the USD 13.6 billion committed for climate-related projects from the GCF, only USD 5.1 billion (37.5%) was disbursed.

In Table 1, the distribution of public climate finance provided by bilateral and multilateral channels is presented by area of support and type of financial instrument. It is noticeable that climate finance given by MDBs is funding mitigation projects via loans.

3.4 Climate Finance, Foreign Aid and Incentives

Traditionally, financing for economic development projects to enhance the economic development and social welfare of recipient countries has been provided to developing countries under foreign aid that has been defined as official development assistance (ODA) by the Organization for Economic Co-operation and Development (OECD)'s Development Assistant Committee. In this case, contributor countries are essentially OECD country members, and ODA recipients are developing countries including upper-middle-income countries.[7]

Climate finance has been widely allocated to the developing world through ODA means, likely due to the experience accumulated in aid resource allocation by the ODA system. Likewise, climate finance to developing countries and ODA are both mostly given through bilateral channels. Approximately 89% of the climate finance flows from developed to developing countries was given through bilateral, regional, and other channels in the period 2019–2020 (UNFCCC 2022). In the case of foreign aid, in 2020, 71.4% of the total aid under ODA (USD 162.27 billion) was also given through bilateral channels, while 28.6% was given through multilateral channels.[8]

While development aid and climate finance may share certain similarities in their provision methods, it is important to note some key distinctions regarding the nature of climate finance in contrast to foreign development aid:

i Climate finance entails all financial flows used for climate-related projects everywhere. Aid is basically restrained to funds provided to help less developed countries.
ii Climate finance has the global objective of fighting and adapting to climate change, which constitutes a public good, meaning that any improvement is shared by everyone. As the project advances, foreign aid has fewer incentives which are not easily shared. Browne (Browne 2022) argues that climate finance should be seen as restitution rather than aid since the countries most affected by climate change tend to be poorer and are indeed those with the least emissions.
iii The sense of urgency might be stronger for climate finance than in traditional foreign aid, due to the net-zero goals, to which most countries have committed.

Given that climate finance mostly uses an ODA-like system to allocate funds, it is important to review how the ODA mechanisms work to improve efficiency in climate finance.

Despite expectations, foreign aid has not been very successful in bridging the investment gap in poor countries or increasing growth rates. Empirical evidence suggests that aid increases consumption rather than investment (Easterly 2007). This is likely due to political variables in recipient countries. Politicians in these countries are presumably inclined to use aid to maximize the welfare of elites rather than the welfare of society (Boone 1996). Thus, aid might enrich corrupt elites and incentivize corruption and violence (Fisman and Miguel 2008). These findings have important implications for foreign aid and climate finance. For the effective allocation of these resources to reach their goals, it is important to address the political factors that can lead to their misuse.

---

[7] The list of recipient countries is updated every three years based on per capita income. See the OECD website for more information: https://www.oecd.org/dac/financing-sustainable-development/development-finance-standards/official-development-assistance.htm.

[8] By 2022, that share changed to 74.6% and 25.4%, respectively (of a total of USD 204 billion). For more information see https://stats.oecd.org/Index.aspx?QueryId=65072.

Several empirical studies have found that aid has not necessarily been directed toward countries in greater need, due to strategic or political interests that influence contributors' incentive to allocate aid (Burnside and Dollar 2000; Boone 1996; Alesina and Dollar 2000; Kuzienko and Werker 2006). In particular, Burnside and Dollar (2000) find, in a sample of 56 countries, that strategic factors are strong determinants of aid allocation in the specific case of bilateral aid. They also find that, unlike aid, private flows–namely, foreign direct investment–are highly responsive to economic incentives (economic conditions, such as openness and property rights protection).

It is worth mentioning that while the aid provided by ODA was traditionally given through grants, grants now account for a small share of overall ODA finance. Instead, debt-financing is currently prevalent (Bracking and Benjamin 2021). International public climate finance relies mostly on loans, whereas debt-financing constitutes roughly 64% of the joint total provided by bilateral and multilateral development banks and multilateral climate funds. Interestingly, adaptation climate finance is largely provided by grants and mitigation finance by loans (UNFCCC 2022). Adaptation climate finance might be similar to aid. In fact, Argueta et al. (2021) find that, for financing purposes, there is a lack of distinction regarding what constitutes a climate adaptation project versus aid.

Aid is often driven by both contributors 'own interests and recipients' needs. Its effectiveness often hinges on the commitment of recipient governments to utilizing aid efficiently. In the context of climate finance, contributors' interest might be heightened by the Paris Agreement commitments and the expected impact of climate projects. This is especially true for mitigation projects, which have shareable and non-excludable benefits if successful (Choe 2020). This also explains why bilateral climate finance is mostly directed to mitigation actions and why adaptation projects are left behind.

In aid and climate finance, there exist important principal-agent problems that require analysis to align objectives and offer the right incentives. Contrary to the belief that multilateral finance can be more effective and efficient –and able to make conditional aid less political–, most aid and climate finance are given bilaterally. In the context of aid, Milner (2006) investigates the asymmetric information problem in the first stage–from the public to the contributor's government–to explain the trend of delegating aid provision to multilateral agencies. According to the author, evidence shows that the multilateral scheme might be used by contributors as a signal of the right use of money paid by the public (taxpayers), especially when public opinion about aid is negative. Thus, when people are not informed about aid effectiveness, governments are biased towards the use of a bilateral schemes, which allows them to exert more control.

Although a bilateral scheme reduces the principal-agent problem by avoiding the inclusion of an extra agent (multilateral agency), it is often driven by the donor's/contributor's strategic and political interests.[9] In the context of climate finance, to accelerate the energy transition and guarantee energy security, it is plausible that

[9] This would partially explain why aid does not show a positive effect on growth and development.

bilateral climate finance could be influenced by the strategic presence of critical extractive resources, such as minerals, in recipient countries.

From a theoretical perspective, one solution to the principal-agent problem between donors/contributors and recipients is the implementation of conditional projects (as opposed to direct financial transfers). This approach can help to align the interests of both donors/contributors and recipients (Jain 2007). Another solution involves enhancing the monitoring of financed projects. In this context, a bottom-up approach, such as community engagement and reporting, can be beneficial. Expanding the involvement of stakeholders, including local and indigenous communities, is recognized as crucial for effective finance delivery. Consequently, there is a growing emphasis on the 'country ownership' concept in climate finance and project development. This approach is evident in financial mechanisms under the UNFCCC, such as the GCF (UNFCCC 2022; Argueta et al. 2021; Browne 2022).

Like aid, climate finance often results in increased government revenues. As governments' objective function might differ from social welfare, under no monitoring or supervision, a risk of rent-seeking behavior (private consumption of rent-seekers) of those in power could negatively impact the project's outcomes. Consequently, it is advisable that more funds be allocated to less corrupt countries. Nonetheless, if fund allocation is discretionary, contributors do not systematically allocate finance or aid to less corrupt countries. Thus, political equilibrium is crucial for the positive impact of project finance and/or aid. Democracies have been shown to diminish the counter-effect of corruption (or perverse incentives) on these funds in recipient countries (Svensson 2000; Economides et al. 2008).

Corruption is perhaps the main reason for foreign aid's failure, a characteristic that is not only present in recipients' governments, but also within contributors' aid agencies.[10] Although corruption is difficult to combat and it may not be possible to eliminate it, it is possible to limit its scope:

- One approach is to favor debt financing over grants. Quazi (2006) argues that loans are typically used for investment projects, while grants are often diverted to public consumption or unproductive initiatives. Grants are at higher risk of being stolen by corrupt governments compared to loans, which require credit assessments and repayment. Consequently, loans can motivate lenders to closely monitor the outcomes of their funded projects and reduce the perverse incentives for misappropriation.
- Another strategy involves enhancing enforcement and conducting post-evaluations of financed projects or the use of aid. Fisman and Miguel (2008) argue that increased enforcement significantly reduces corruption. This is particularly important in climate finance given the lack of evaluation of funds usage (Bracking and Benjamin 2021).

[10] Studies on the membership structure of the Security Council (SC) of the United Nations (UN) have shown evidence of bribery among rotating members of the SC, influencing the amount of aid allocated by the US through the UN (Kuzienko and Werker 2006).

Governance factors, including corruption, the rule of law (or protection of private property), political stability and accountability, can impact the allocation of climate finance. This is particularly relevant when projects are financed through loans, as these factors are associated with the level of risk involved. The significance of governance factors becomes even more pronounced in the context of energy-related projects, which are capital-intensive and require substantial investment.

4 Energy-Related Projects

Climate finance for energy-related projects accounts for a significant share of total mitigation finance contributions. Indeed, for the period 2019–2020, projects related to renewable energy generation accounted for the largest sector of global climate finance (UNFCCC 2022). Over the past few decades, this trend has coincided with a significant reduction in the costs of non-conventional renewable energy sources, such as wind and solar power, which made these technologies both accessible and cost-competitive in the electricity generation market (IRENA 2022).

The 2015 Paris Agreement stimulated climate finance commitments, and although actual disbursements were minimal, energy projects could receive funding. As shown in Fig. 5, while climate finance commitments increased almost exponentially for non-energy projects after 2015, disbursed funds were significantly reduced. Among the provided funds, energy projects received relatively larger amounts than non-energy projects, particularly through mitigation finance.

Renewable energy sources like solar and wind are being adopted in various countries, but their deployment in emerging economies encounters significant barriers. The limited implementation of clean energy projects in these regions can be attributed to the nature of the investment: solar and wind projects require high initial costs but have low ongoing operating expenses, leading to substantial upfront capital requirements for investors. These risks are exacerbated by economic instability and uncertainty in the country. Investment risk can be relatively small in a country with robust institutions, ensuring demand security (e.g., through power purchase agreements) and reducing the likelihood of renegotiation (Choe 2020), or even the risk of expropriation.

Figure 6 shows how the total contribution during the period 2011–2020 varies by grant status and whether the project is related to energy. For the energy projects, most of the contribution comes from non-grants (loans), while it is the opposite for the non-energy projects.

The World Bank (2023b) identifies two barriers for low- and middle-income countries to mobilize the required finance: (i) limited affordability or limited fiscal flexibility of governments to incur in clean energy public investment, and (ii) limited access to private capital and the high capital costs, which are associated with weak or underdeveloped financial markets (usually not aligned to international financial market standards), poor or weak policy and regulatory frameworks, and lack of adequate institutional capacity.

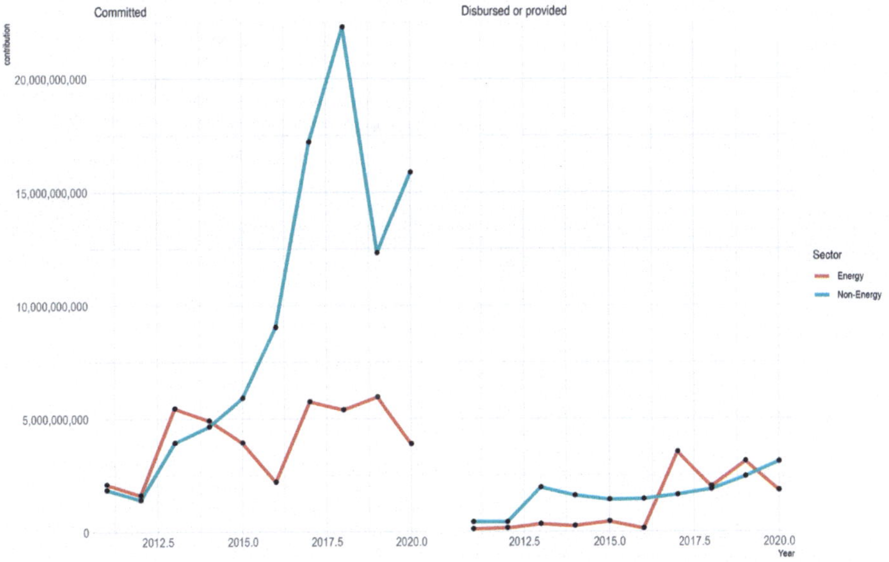

Fig. 5 Climate finance contributions to projects by sector and by status. *Source* UNFCCC Climate Finance Data Portal, (2023)

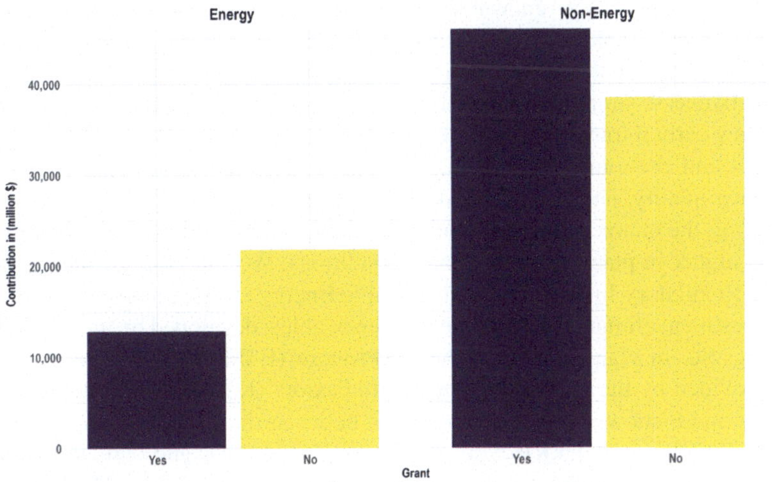

Fig. 6 Climate finance contributions to projects by sector and by grant (Yes is grant; No otherwise). *Source* UNFCCC Climate Finance Data Portal, 2023

A key factor that impedes many low- and middle-income countries is the prevalence of fossil fuel subsidies, which is a cause of fossil fuel dependency. Governments are under societal pressure to keep subsidies on transport and cooking fuels, which are essential for the population at large. However, they also lack the fiscal resources

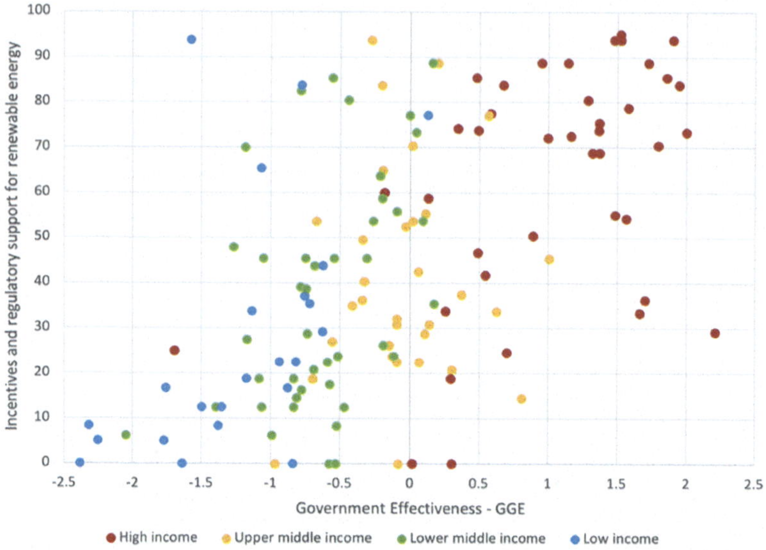

Fig. 7 Incentives and regulatory support indicator versus government effectiveness, 2019. *Source* RISE 2019 and World Governance Indicators

to promote and invest in renewable energy projects, which require high up-front costs (The World Bank 2023b). To speed the energy transition, and expand mitigation projects, Nest et al. (2020) proposes climate finance to be optimized for impact and effectiveness, strengthening anti-corruption efforts, particularly on renewable energy, low carbon transport, and energy efficiency projects.

Market and economic conditions, the regulatory framework, capacity building, governance quality, and political risk can be crucial for clean energy investment. Considering the characteristics of the investment, clean energy project investments could be higher in places with favorable conditions. We can observe such a pattern from the Regulatory Indicators for Sustainable Energy (RISE), a proxy for progress in the investment climate for investment in renewables, developed by the World Bank and Energy Sector Management Assistance Program (ESMAP), and governance indicators provided by the World Governance Indicators (Kaufmann and Kraay 2023). Figures 7 and 8 show a positive association between the government effectiveness indicator (GGE)[11] and the RISE sub-indicator of incentives and regulatory support for renewable energy, and the same indicator with the overall renewable energy pillar indicator. The positive association is preserved across income level groups, such that a lower GGE is observed for lower-income countries that also have a lower renewable energy investment climate.

[11] The higher, the better.

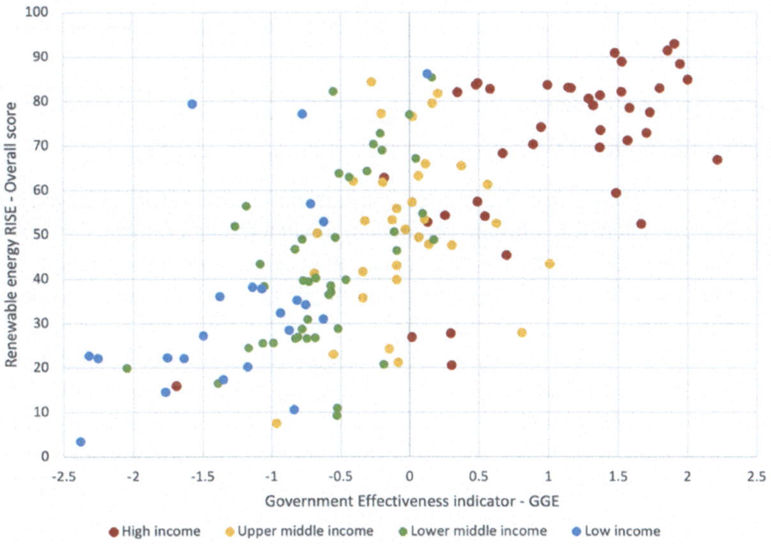

Fig. 8 Renewable energy indicator versus government effectiveness, 2019. *Source* RISE 2019 and World Governance Indicators

5 Factors Influencing Climate Finance Allocation

Following our analysis and based on the theory and literature, we identify the following factors that may influence climate finance in developing countries.

- **Global climate change factors**: a distinctive characteristic of climate finance is the sense of urgency motivated by increasing global GHG emissions or rising temperatures. Thus, indicators of worsening climate conditions may increase climate finance mobilization.
- **Project level factors**
  - **Type of support**: Considering the objectives of climate finance, and the non-excludability of emissions reductions, mitigation projects may receive more support than adaptation projects.
  - **Sector of the project**: In the same line, due to the role of the sector in emissions, energy-related projects, and transport-related projects are expected to be more likely to receive funding.
  - **Type of finance instrument**: From the literature and our analysis, since climate finance is provided mostly by debt-financing (loans), project finance could be highly responsive to economic conditions such as economic openness, economic risks, and property rights protection.
  - **Status of funds**: Since climate finance commitments are not binding by design, contributor countries often pledge large amounts without providing the full extent of the committed funding for the projects.

If commitments were binding, we would see a smaller gap between committed and disbursed projects.

- **Recipient country factors**:
  - **Economic factors**: We summarize the economic factors below:
    - Size of the economy: Income level is part of the criteria for accessing climate finance. Therefore climate projects in lower-income countries are expected to receive climate finance. Also, despite the income classification, income stability and a balanced budget that indicates fiscal discipline can encourage higher project investments. The size of the population is another factor to consider since the impact of projects can be greater in larger populations. In the case of energy-related projects, since a larger population has a greater need for energy consumption, the demand for clean energy projects is expected to increase. Indeed, a study on the determinants of firms' green investments finds a positive effect of gross domestic product (GDP) and population size on green investment levels (Barabanov, 2021).
    - Economic risk factors, including macroeconomic factors, that bring economic stability and predictability can incentivize private investment as economic stability lowers the investment risk. This is more relevant for debt financing projects. Moreover, governments with a stable budget or fiscal balances are associated with fiscal discipline, lower default risk, and greater reliability. Thus, we expect lower climate finance for countries with budget imbalances. Conversely, the economic openness (or openness to trade) of recipient countries signals stronger interest in aligning with international standards, thereby increasing reliability and the attractiveness for climate investment or finance.
    - Strong financial markets can help to mobilize funds more easily through new financial instruments (e.g., blended finance or corporate financial instruments). Therefore, countries with better financial markets may be more likely to receive climate finance.
  - **Socioeconomic factors**: Countries with impoverished populations vulnerable to climate change disasters are likely to receive more climate finance, at least in terms of funds for adaptation. Likewise, high unemployment levels and low consumer confidence usually lead to social and economic instability, which can adversely affect project investments.
  - **Energy environmental factors**:
    - Countries with higher GHG emissions and/or higher levels of energy intensity (i.e. low energy efficiency) may receive more funds to help them reduce emissions. Additionally, countries with higher rates of nature depletion are expected to be more likely to receive funding due to the urgency and significance of addressing such challenges.

- Countries may have higher incentives to promote renewable energy projects (such as solar photovoltaic projects) when they have a large population with low access to electricity, aiming to increase electricity access.
- The role of renewable/clean energy in their energy matrix for climate finance is expected to be positive. Having relatively clean energy matrices may show a stronger commitment to cleaner energy technology and, therefore, may be more likely to foster the adoption of clean energy. However, it is also plausible that higher penetration of renewable energy in one period reduces the likelihood of receiving finance for renewable energy projects in the following period.
- From the openness to trade perspective, higher trade flows of low-carbon energy products may show the greater readiness of countries to foster clean energy projects. Therefore, higher funding is expected in this case.
- Lastly, the strategic existence of essential extractive resources, like minerals, in recipient countries could impact the size of bilateral climate finance. This approach is often aimed at securing future access to these resources to support the contributors' energy transition needs.

– **Governance factors**: Investment decisions are inherently long-term, emphasizing the importance of stable and predictable policies and regulations free from political bias. For example, countries with transparent rules, robust protection of property rights, and an efficient legal system create a conducive environment for investment and private sector growth. Effective governance is characterized by strong, stable institutions, high capacity-building, and minimal bureaucracy, enabling governments to facilitate market interactions by reducing transaction and contract costs. Conversely, perceived corruption, often thriving in environments lacking transparency and accountability, weak rule of law, or inadequate protection of private property, and political instability, can negatively impact climate finance allocation. These factors heighten project risks, particularly for projects financed through loans. Consequently, it is reasonable to expect that projects in more corrupt countries may receive less funding, especially in the form of loans.

In the following Sect. 6, utilizing data from the years 2011–2019, we conduct tests on whether the anticipated associations between climate finance and these factors are observed in real-world scenarios.

6 Empirical Analysis

6.1 Data

For our empirical analysis, we construct a dataset on global climate finance, governance, various indicators for energy, the environment, and the economy, and various indicators for financial and economic risks from various sources including the UNFCCC Climate Finance Data Portal (2023), IMF (2023), the World Bank (2023b), Global Environment Facility (2023), Food and Agriculture Organization (2023), Kaufmann and Kraay (2023), the PRS Group (2023), and Climate Watch (2023).[12] We restrict our analysis to the period 2011–2019 and exclude year 2020 from our analysis to avoid distortions in the climate finance trends due to the COVID-19 pandemic.

The dataset consists of various determinants for funding contributions for a climate change project, denoted as $Contribution_{p,s,r,n,c,y}$ and given in USD. Subscripts p, s, r, n, c, and y on the variables in this section represent observation units for a climate change project (p) in a sector (s) in a recipient country (r) on a continent (n) contributed by a contributor country/organization (c) in year (y).[13]

Table 2 provides a summary statistics for $Contribution_{p,s,r,n,c,y}$ by $Energy_s$, a dummy variable for the energy sector.[14]

$\mathbf{Governance}_{r,y-2}$ is the vector of two-year lagged governance-related indicators, which encompasses several aspects of governance, including (1) control of corruption, (2) voice and accountability, (3) regulatory quality, (4) government effectiveness, (5) rule of law, and (6) political stability and absence of terrorism/violence.[15] The indicators for these six categories, provided by Kaufmann and Kraay (2023) (WGI), are described in Table 9; the WGI indicators vary within the [−2.5, 2.5]

[12] Another data source that we initially considered is the regulatory indicators for sustainable energy (RISE) created by the Energy Sector Management Assistance Program (ESMAP) from the World Bank. RISE indicators are constructed to assess energy policy and regulatory framework that support investment in clean energy and access to it. RISE depends on four pillars: access to electricity, access to clean cooking, energy efficiency, and renewable energy. For our study, we did not get access to such dataset, so instead, we used available energy sector indicators that may capture some of RISE's information.

[13] Note that one climate change project can involve multiple sectors (i.e., (1) the agricultural sector and (2) the water sector), except for the energy sector. For climate change projects involving multiple sectors, we assume that the funding contribution is equally allocated across all the involved sectors. The number of such climate change projects is 2,174, while the number of all the projects is 16,804. In particular, for the energy sector, we use observations with climate change projects that involve solely the energy sector. Additionally, we also assume that if the project encompasses multiple countries, the funding contribution for such project is equally allocated. The number of the projects that were in multiple countries is 1,535.

[14] Out of 52,833 observations, 738 exhibit a negative $Contribution_{p,s,r,n,c,y}$. The empirical analysis presented in this section is anticipated to remain robust, even when incorporating these observations with negative contributions.

[15] We consider the two-year lagged governance variables because one country's governance quality tends to evolve slowly.

Table 2 Summary statistics for contribution$_{p,s,r,n,c,y}$

Variable	$Energy_s$	Mean	Std.Dev	Min	Q1	Median	Q2	Max
$Contribution_{p,s,r,n,c,y}$	Yes	5,723,235.24	23,554,437.7	−38,382,142	42,779.5	410,000	2,100,000	551,380,000
	No	1,807,144.37	10,410,810.8	−33,924,246	16,832	102,631.12	530,000	398,300,584

Table 3 Summary statistics for **Governance**$_{r,y-2}$

Variable	*Energy*$_s$	Mean	Std.Dev	Min	Q1	Median	Q2	Max
Contract_ viability $_{r,y-2}$	Yes	2.5617	0.2989	0.5	2.4203	2.5	2.6667	4
	No	2.5291	0.3241	0.5	2.4203	2.5	2.6205	4
Control_of_ corruption $_{r,y-2}$	Yes	−0.544	0.334	−1.7698	−0.7088	−0.5598	−0.4375	1.6366
	No	−0.5799	0.3367	−1.7698	−0.7088	−0.5598	−0.4535	2.0705
Ethnic_ tensions $_{r,y-2}$	Yes	3.4198	0.7794	1	3.022	3.3292	4	6
	No	3.4462	0.8149	1	3	3.3473	4.0147	6
Government_ cohesion $_{r,y-2}$	Yes	2.7681	0.3069	1.875	2.5938	2.7378	2.9142	4
	No	2.7461	0.2994	1.7083	2.5417	2.7378	2.9142	4
Law_and _ order $_{r,y-2}$	Yes	3.0872	0.6498	0.5	2.5	3.0285	3.5	5
	No	2.9666	0.7134	0.5	2.4167	3.012	3.375	6
Legislative_ strength $_{r,y-2}$	Yes	2.3991	0.3268	1.5	2.2311	2.344	2.4583	4
	No	2.3686	0.2997	1.5	2.2256	2.3333	2.44	4
Rule of_law $_{r,y-2}$	Yes	0.0769	0.937	−4.80	−0.520	−0.130	0.504	7.67
	No	−0.0115	1.01	−5.17	−0.485	−0.130	0.414	9.60
Popular_ support $_{r,y-2}$	Yes	2.085	0.2651	0	2	2.0579	2.1595	3.6667
	No	2.065	0.2641	0	2	2.0564	2.1355	3.6667
Voice_and_ accountability $_{r,y-2}$	Yes	−0.3495	0.4723	−2.2592	−0.5749	−0.3825	−0.0463	1.2134
	No	−0.3727	0.4795	−2.2592	−0.5858	−0.3325	−0.0408	1.3875

range such that higher values mean better governance. The vector **Governance** $_{r,y-2}$ also includes additional indicators for more details in each category of the WGI provided by the PRS Group (2023), and described in Table 10. The PRS indicators vary in range, but for all of them, higher values indicate better situations. Table 3 provides summary statistics for the selected variables in vector **Governance** $_{r,y-2}$.

EnergyEnvironment $_{r,c,y-1}$ is the vector of one-year lagged environment-and energy-related indicators for the recipient country r. The vector **EnergyEnvironment** $_{r,c,y-1}$ includes (1) energy intensity, (2) exports and imports of low carbon technology products between the recipient and the contributor countries,[16] (3) greenhouse gas emissions from various sectors, (4) access to electricity in urban and rural areas, (5) fuel imports and exports, (6) depletion of energy and natural resources, (7) rents from natural resources, and (8) access to basic drinking water. The details on these variables are provided in Table 11 in the Appendix. Table 4 provides summary statistics for the selected variables in vector **EnergyEnvironment** $_{r,c,y-1}$.

[16] Products based on low-carbon technology generate fewer greenhouse gas emissions than traditional energy solutions, serving a critical function in transitioning to a low-carbon economy. Examples of such low-carbon technologies encompass mechanisms such as wind turbines, solar panels, biomass systems, and carbon capture equipment (IMF 2023).

Table 4 Summary statistics for **EnergyEnvironment** $_{r,c,y-1}$

Variable	*Energys*	Mean	Std.Dev	Min	Q1	Median	Q2	Max
Access_to_electricity_urban $_{r,y-1}$	Yes	89.2881	13.9612	7.2	76.6907	97.3018	99.6732	100
	No	88.2863	15.429	7.2	75.3419	97.2573	99.0926	100
Electricity_capacity_renewable_excluding_hydro $_{r,y-1}$	Yes	7.3442	5.7644	0	2.8122	6.6415	10.614	63.2237
	No	8.015	6.5885	0	3.3301	7.508	10.7074	63.2237
Exports_of_low_carbon_tech_products $_{r,y-1}$	Yes	74.25	321.1643	0	0.9737	1.6765	2.364	1572.3721
	No	54.2598	274.4348	0	0.917	1.6147	2.2001	1572.3721
GHG_emissions_LUCF $_{r,y-1}$	Yes	35.2789	120.5791	−707.6	−0.6823	37.1175	55.5414	1147.43
	No	48.7781	117.7534	−707.6	0.0907	39.0036	57.54	1147.43
GHG_emissions_manufacturing_construction $_{r,y-1}$	Yes	88.8133	320.6468	0	2.5687	8.6653	31.32	3111.27
	No	56.1213	202.722	0	2.3496	5.78	18.8135	3111.27
GHG_emissions_other_fuel_combustion $_{r,y-1}$	Yes	8.1768	23.1904	0	0.4674	1.2285	5.43	208.9
	No	5.6401	15.0632	0	0.42	1.09	4.0806	208.9
Fuel_exports $_{r,y-1}$	Yes	11.9092	12.0131	0	7.2097	9.9273	13.878	99.9865
	No	11.754	11.5476	0	5.522	9.9273	15.4025	99.9865
Natural_resources_rents $_{r,y-1}$	Yes	5.1691	4.2225	0	2.2553	3.8902	7.4886	56.3427
	No	5.3757	4.5415	0	2.4374	3.9687	7.6629	79.4309

EconomicRisks $_{r,y-1}$ is the vector of one-year lagged economy—related risk indicators for the recipient country *r*. The vector **EconomicRisks** $_{r,y-1}$ includes risks associated with (1) budget balance, (2) debt service, (3) exchange rate stability, (4) foreign debt, (5) inflation, (6) international liquidity, (7) current account, (8) GDP growth, and (9) GDP per capita. The details of these variables are provided in Table 13 in the Appendix. Table 5 provides summary statistics for the selected variables in vector **EconomicRisks** $_{r,y-1}$.

SocioeconomicFactors $_{r,y-1}$ is the vector of one-year lagged socioeconomic indicators for the recipient country *r*. The vector **SocioeconomicFactors** $_{r,y-1}$ includes (1) GDP per capita based on purchasing power parity (GDP PPP), (2) the size of the population, (3) unemployment, (4) consumer confidence, and (5) poverty. The details of these variables are provided in Table 12 in the Appendix.

Table 5 Summary statistics for **EconomicRisks** $_{r,y-1}$

Variable	*Energy* $_s$	Mean	Std.Dev	Min	Q1	Median	Q2	Max
Risk_for_budget balance $_{r,y-1}$	Yes	5.636	0.8243	1	5.2251	5.6736	6.1039	10
	No	5.6728	0.8702	0	5.2276	5.6736	6.25	10
Risk_for_current_account_as_percentage_of_XGS $_{r,y-1}$	Yes	10.4698	1.5968	0	9.1712	10.9167	11.5	15
	No	10.4015	1.6914	0	9.3333	10.875	11.439	15
Risk_for_debt_service $_{r,y-1}$	Yes	9.4513	0.5888	0	9.25	9.5534	9.7918	10
	No	9.4607	0.6349	0	9.25	9.5496	9.8039	10
Risk_for_international_liquidity $_{r,y-1}$	Yes	2.5993	0.9963	0	1.947	2.5833	3.2959	5
	No	2.6148	1.0765	0	1.947	2.7266	3.3362	5
Risk_for_per capita_GDP $_{r,y-1}$	Yes	0.7711	0.7155	0	0.1359	0.6336	1.3288	5
	No	0.7447	0.702	0	0.1216	0.5984	1.3383	5

$\mathbf{X}_p$ is the vector of project characteristics. The vector $\mathbf{X}_p$ includes (1) whether the funding contribution is a grant; (2) whether the funding for the project p is only committed or is disbursed/provided; (3) whether the funding contributor for the project p is a single country or a multilateral fund/organization such as the Special Climate Change Fund and the Global Environmental Facility; (4) whether the project p is adaptation, mitigation, or cross-cutting; and (5) whether the project is aimed at lowering carbon emissions through sustainable forest management and the preservation and increase of forest carbon stocks (known as REDD+).

6.2 Empirical Model

In this subsection, we use the panel dataset described in the previous subsection to estimate the climate funding decisions regarding climate change projects in recipient countries, particularly for projects in the energy sector, provided in Eq. (1).

$$
\begin{aligned}
Contribution_{p,s,r,n,c,y} = \; & \big(\boldsymbol{\beta}_{\mathbf{G}}\ \mathbf{Governance}_{r,y-2} + \\
& \boldsymbol{\beta}_{\mathbf{E}}\ \mathbf{Energy\ Environment}_{r,c,y-1} + \\
& \boldsymbol{\beta}_{\mathbf{E}}\ \mathbf{EconomicRisks}_{r,c,y-1} + \\
& \boldsymbol{\beta}_{\mathbf{R}}\ \mathbf{SocioecomicFactors}_{r,y-1}\big) \times Energy_s + \\
& \gamma \mathbf{X}_p + \alpha + \mu_s + \psi_r + \kappa_n + \chi_c + \phi_{c,r} + \eta_y + \epsilon_{p,s,r,n,c,y}
\end{aligned} \tag{1}
$$

Equation (1) can be estimated by applying ordinary least squares (OLS) models with pooled cross-sections in the dataset. However, several unobserved factors might potentially affect the funding decisions. Even after controlling for the effects of governance, environmental, energy, and economic factors, and economic and political risks, funding decisions can be made for other reasons that we are not directly observing. For example, we do not directly observe private information about the relationship between the contributor and the recipient countries that can influence the funding decisions. Therefore, we should consider controlling for a contributor-recipient-specific unobserved effect.

Fixed-effects (FE) estimators are often considered to control individual-specific unobserved effects. Some country-level or sector-level unobserved factors, such as private information about the two countries' relationships relating to funding contracts, can be correlated to variables considered and might not be randomly distributed.

Equation (1) assumes that the relationship between $Contribution_{p,s,r,n,c,y}$ and each of the variables in the vectors, $\mathbf{Governance}_{r,y-2}$, $\mathbf{EnergyEnvironment}_{r,c,y-1}$, $\mathbf{SocioeconomicFactors}_{r,y-1}$, and $\mathbf{EconomicRisks}_{r,y-1}$ varies according to whether the project p is related to energy. Considering the special characteristics of the energy sector, this assumption is valid. However, this assumption about the interaction leads to 2,714 independent variables in the model. Accordingly, the simple linear FE estimator will suffer from the consequences of multicollinearity.

To robustly perform variable selection, we estimate the bootstrapped cross-validation (CV) Least Absolute Shrinkage and Selection Operator (LASSO) regression model, quantifying the uncertainty regarding variable selection. We also estimate the bootstrapped random forests model to determine variable importance, indicating which variables are more important than others. This combination is beneficial because the random forest may capture complex interactions and non-linear relationships between $Contribution_{p,s,r,n,c,y}$ and each of the variables in the vectors $\mathbf{Governance}_{r,y-2}$, $\mathbf{EnergyEnvironment}_{r,c,y-1}$, $\mathbf{SocioeconomicFactors}_{r,y-1}$, and $\mathbf{EconomicRisks}_{r,y-1}$ that LASSO can miss.

Furthermore, LASSO can help to control for overfitting and provide a more parsimonious model, especially when the model has high-dimensional controls. The bootstrapped CV LASSO selects only a small subset of variables ranging from 4 to 36 out of 2,714, excluding the fixed effect dummies.[17] Additionally, we estimate the bootstrapped Random Forests model to determine variable importance, indicating which independent variables might be more important than others.

6.3 *Results*

Figure 9 shows the 20 most important variables excluding variable $Grant_p$ and the fixed-effect dummies, selected by the metric of variable importance in the Random

[17] The number of independent variables selected by the LASSO depends on the size of the penalty parameters, lambdas. For the penalty parameters lambdas, the minimum mean CV error and the CV error that is within one standard error of the CV error.

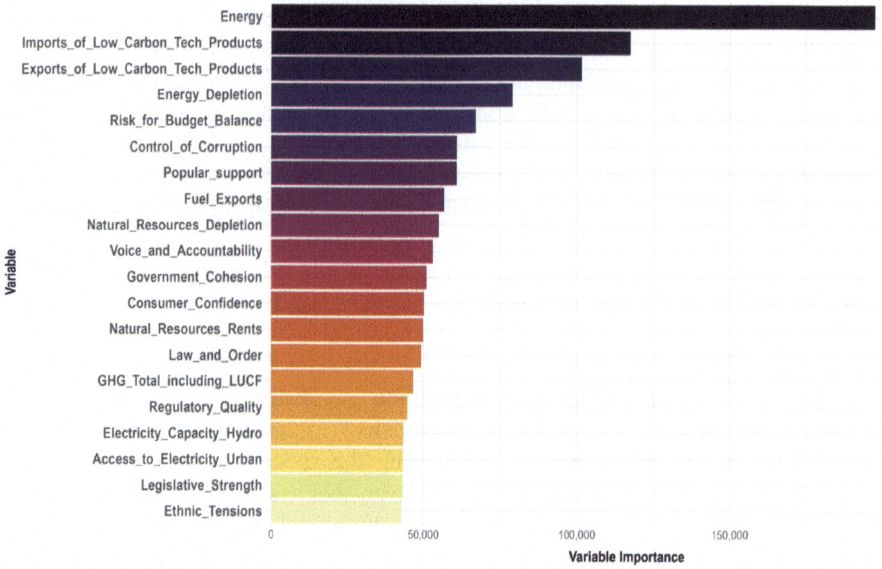

Fig. 9 Top 20 most important variables from the random forests estimation

Forests estimation.[18] Variable importance from the random forest estimation provides insights into how strongly these variables in the vectors–**Governance** $_{r,y-2}$, **EnergyEnvironment** $_{r,c,y-1}$, **SocioeconomicFactors** $_{r,y-1}$, and **EconomicRisks** $_{r,y-1}$–are likely to be associated with the funding contribution, $Contribution_{p,s,r,n,c,y}$. This is because changes in a variable with higher importance tend to result in significant changes in the outcome variable.

Table 6 presents the estimated beta coefficients for the selected variables in **Governance** $_{r,y-2}$ in Eq. (1) from the bootstrapped CV LASSO. LASSO selects those governance-related variables that interact with $Energy_s$. Columns (1)–(6) contain the estimates depending on what FEs are controlled. Table 14 in the Appendix provides the OLS counterpart.

Overall, the estimated coefficients on variable $Energy_s$ in Table 6 are all with relatively small bootstrap standard errors, implying reliable estimates. The estimated coefficients on variables $Legislative\ Strength_{r,y-1} \times Energy_s$, $Popular\ support_{r,y-1} \times Energy_s$, and $Voice\ and\ Accountability_{r,y-1} \times Energy_s$ are all positive with relatively small standard errors. Variable $Rule\ of Law_{r,y-1} \times Energy_s$ is selected only when all FEs are controlled.

[18] Figure 9 omits the variable $Grant_p$, which is selected to be the most important variable in the random forest estimation. The variable importance of $Grant_p$ is 10.18 times greater than the variable $Energy_s$. This ranking is determined by the relative contribution each variable makes to the predictive power of the model. When the values of these variables change, the model's predictions are most affected. Hence, they appear higher in a variable importance ranking.

Table 6 Bootstrapped CV LASSO estimates for **Governance** $_{r,y-2}$

Interaction w/*energy* LASSO	(1)	(2)	(3)	(4)	(5)	(6)
Contract _viability						
Contract _viability:Energy	−438,134.76 (9618.37)	−453,127.89 (8255.11)	−454,461.12 (8389.78)	−434,525.2 (4304.1)	−492,357.5 (0)	
Control _of _corruption	11,762.31 (1186.23)	19,399.11 (168.32)	16,992.94 (74.73)			
Control _of _corruption:Energy	582,911.1 (6297.5)	592,918.8 (4599.4)	593,335.75 (4641.52)	592,595.79 (1239.07)	361,260.5 (0)	
Ethnic_tensions						
Ethnic_tensions:Energy					−4772.47 (0)	−302,109.7 (125,966.2)
Law_and_order						
Law_and _order:Energy	203,360.5 (8403.2)	196,393.22 (7780.82)	199,595.08 (8104.24)	137,202.16 (7648.42)	168,677.5 (0)	
Legislative_strength						
Legislative_strength:Energy	490,787.77 (3537.34)	390,372.72 (3078.77)	392,227.09 (3266.08)	436,696.87 (3216.28)	594,191.5 (0)	748,536.5 (295,523.1)
Popular_support	206,317.4 (1579.97)	180,663.21 (1297.89)	182,251.47 (1458.32)	163,337.1 (1087.1)	166,903.8 (0)	
Popular_support:Energy	451,151.04 (5883.64)	470,173.77 (4346.29)	469,465.62 (4274.76)	448,819.99 (2518.11)	505,163.4 (0)	95,208.68 (53,034.54)
Rule_of_law	54,696.1 (951.18)	3290.11 (1560.13)	3411.88 (1547.83)			
Rule_of_law:Energy						194,095.82 (72,990.15)

(continued)

Table 6 (continued)

Interaction w/*energy* LASSO	(1)	(2)	(3)	(4)	(5)	(6)
Voice_and accountability	18,567.26 (623.38)					
Voice_and accountability:Energy	830,354.3 (13,548.4)	793,857.6 (10,806.6)	791,048 (10,522.8)	751,479.7 (10,651.04)	939,435.3 (0)	692,649.8 (303,641.1)
Year FE	No	Yes	Yes	Yes	Yes	Yes
Continent FE	No	No	Yes	Yes	Yes	Yes
Recipient FE	No	No	No	Yes	Yes	Yes
Contributor FE	No	No	No	No	Yes	Yes
Contributor-recipient FE	No	No	No	No	No	Yes

Estimates are the mean values of bootstrap estimates
Bootstrapped standard errors are in parentheses

Table 7 presents the estimated beta coefficients for the selected variables in **EnergyEnvironment** $_{r,c,y-1}$ in Eq. (1) from the bootstrapped CV LASSO. Columns (1)-(6) contain the estimates depending on which FEs are controlled. Table 15 in the Appendix provides the counterpart from the OLS.

Overall, the estimated coefficients on variable $Energy_d$ in Table 7 are all with small bootstrap standard errors, implying that they are reliable estimates. The estimated coefficients on variables $Access\ to\ Electricity\ Urban_{r,y-1} \times Energy_s$ and $Exports\ of\ Low\ Carbon\ Tech\ Products_{r,y-1} \times Energy_s$ are negative and positive, respectively, with relatively small standard errors. Variable $Fuel\ Exports_{r,y-1} \times Energy_s$ is selected only when all FEs are controlled. Most GHG emissions variables inter-acting with $Energy_s$ are not selected when controlling the contributor FE and contributor-recipient FE.

Table 8 presents estimated beta coefficients for the selected variables in **EconomicRisks** $_{r,y-1}$ as well as $Population_{r,y-1}$ in Eq. (1) from the bootstrapped CV LASSO. Columns (1)–(6) contain the estimates depending on which FEs are controlled. The estimated coefficients on variables $Risk\ for\ Budget\ Balance_{r,y-1} \times Energy_s$ are negative with relatively small standard errors. Table 16 in the Appendix provides the OLS counterpart.

6.4 Discussion

Based on the Random Forest and LASSO estimations, our analysis shows that governance factors indeed play a crucial role in climate finance allocation. Additionally, we find that energy, environmental, and socioeconomic factors are associated with funding contributions for energy projects in developing countries. Below we discuss some of the main findings.

As expected, a strong legal system, paired with clear rules, reliable enforcement, and solid social accountability are not only found to be important factors for climate finance, but also particularly relevant for energy-related projects. Yet stronger popular support for the government in place, and higher control of corruption levels are associated with more political stability and reliability, therefore, they bring favorable conditions for higher climate finance contributions, with special emphasis in the energy sector, which involves mostly renewable energy projects. Good governance reduces uncertainty and investment risks, making project investment relatively more attractive.

- Legislative strength: The estimated coefficients for variable Legislative Strengthr, y−1 × Energys implies that all else being equal, an increase in Legislative Strengthr,y−1 score by one standard deviation (0.33) is associated with an increase in $Contribution_{p,s,r,n,c,y}$ for the energy-related climate change project of $748,536.
- Popular support: The estimated coefficients for variable $Popular\ Support_{r,y-1} \times Energy_s$ implies that all else being equal, an increase in $Popular\ support_{r,y-1}$ of

Table 7 Bootstrapped CV LASSO estimates for **EnergyEnvironment** $_{r,c,y-1}$

Interaction w/*energy* LASSO	(1)	(2)	(3)	(4)	(5)	(6)
Access to electricity urban	−141,992.37 (4993.34)	−168,463.15 (2696.49)	−166,600.47 (2508.34)			
Access_to_electricity_urban:Energy	−1,896,060.7 (13,933.1)	−1,862,315.6 (10,753.6)	−1,860,602.9 (10,580.6)	−1,812,734 (7140.4)	−1,593,928 (0)	−1,089,217 (432,877)
Electricity_capacity_renewables_excluding_hydro						
Electricity _capacity_renewables_excluding _hydro:Energy	−49,413.63 (4991.28)			−95,519.25 (1842.21)	−212,452.4 (0)	
Exports _of_low_carbon_tech_products	−792.7 (15.37)	−472.08 (10.51)	−473.42 (10.65)	−650.79 (8.56)	−723.14 (0)	−529.42 (244.25)
Exports_of_low _carbon_tech_products:Energy	690.46 (9.76)	713.85 (8.34)	713.96 (8.36)	788.2 (5.22)	1162.02 (0)	836.18 (355.12)
GHG_land_use_change_and_forestry						
GHG_land_use_change_and_forestry:Energy	31,681.08 (3200.11)	40,874.47 (4128.73)	42,928.9 (4336.25)	1045.06 (105.56)		
GHG_manufacturing_construction						
GHG_manufacturing_construction:Energy	−96,053.59 (9702.38)	−74,702.88 (7545.75)	−75,330.37 (7609.13)	−41,299.64 (4171.68)		
GHG_other_fuel_combustion						
GHG_other_fuel_combustion:Energy				−75,002.37 (7576)	−18,410.82 (0)	
Fuel_exports						
Fuel exports:Energy						−104,045.64 (73,300.47)

(continued)

Table 7 (continued)

Interaction w/*energy* LASSO	(1)	(2)	(3)	(4)	(5)	(6)
Natural_resources_rents	283,561.64 (890.57)	188,055.44 (957.58)	188,586.97 (1011.27)	51,879.36 (202.31)	22,940.64 (0)	40,072.62 (20,184.63)
Natural_resources_rents:Energy	195,693.32 (637.21)	256,816.45 (94.46)	255,788.13 (198.33)	258,552.2 (86.04)	82,848.16 (0)	
Year FE	No	Yes	Yes	Yes	Yes	Yes
Continent FE	No	No	Yes	Yes	Yes	Yes
Recipient FE	No	No	No	Yes	Yes	Yes
Contributor FE	No	No	No	No	Yes	Yes
Contributor-recipient FE	No	No	No	No	No	Yes

Estimates are the mean values of bootstrap estimates
Bootstrapped standard errors are in parentheses

Table 8 Bootstrapped CV LASSO estimates for **EconomicRisks** $_{r,y-1}$ and population$_{r,y-1}$

Interaction w/*energy* LASSO	(1)	(2)	(3)	(4)	(5)	(6)
Population	−8.14 (0.82)					
Population:energy	3026.76 (32.46)	3141.89 (25.97)	3135.34 (25.31)	3134.85 (22.35)	2969.48 (0)	1724.26 (662.65)
Risk_for_budget_balance					60,126.16 (0)	
Risk_for_budget_balance:Energy	−776,515.25 (10,027.54)	−762,734.14 (8137.59)	−759,797.6 (7840.97)	−766,949.11 (4859.94)	−602,339.6 (0)	−450,639.5 (187,599.1)
Risk_for_current_account_as_percentage_of_XGS						
Risk_for_current_account_as_percentage_of_XGS:Energy	637,407.43 (21,392.72)	625,703 (17,508.2)	625,932.76 (17,531.41)	675,757.97 (14,032.28)	667,225.8 (0)	196,206.6 (125,966.2)
Risk_for_current_account_as_percentage_of_XGS						
Risk_for_current_account_as_percentage_of_XGS:Energy	637,407.43 (21,392.72)	625,703 (17,508.2)	625,932.76 (17,531.41)	675,757.97 (14,032.28)	667,225.8 (0)	196,206.6 (144,567.2)
Risk_for_debt_service	9237.52 (933.08)	49,604.49 (1531.41)	49,588.22 (1529.76)	89,409.12 (1438.46)	133,336.9 (0)	
Risk_for_debt_service:Energy						−38,817.7 (29,100.71)
Risk_for_international_liquidity						
Risk_for_international_liquidity:Energy	709,195.55 (21,401.54)	658,733.02 (16,488.77)	655,567.6 (16,169.03)	765,431.92 (17,309.82)	526,185.4 (0)	92,210.33 (68,710.91)
Risk_for_per_capita_GDP						

(continued)

Table 8 (continued)

Interaction w/*energy* LASSO	(1)	(2)	(3)	(4)	(5)	(6)
Risk_for_per_capita_GDP:Energy	−367,619.08 (21,463.25)	−320,923.9 (16,603.4)	−320,044.34 (16,514.56)	−376,630.4 (16,141.01)	−319,745.6 (0)	−17,535.13 (14,091.55)
Year FE	No	Yes	Yes	Yes	Yes	Yes
Continent FE	No	No	Yes	Yes	Yes	Yes
Recipient FE	No	No	No	Yes	Yes	Yes
Contributor FE	No	No	No	No	Yes	Yes
Contributor-recipient FE	No	No	No	No	No	Yes

Estimates are the mean values of bootstrap estimates
Bootstrapped standard errors are in parentheses

one standard deviation (0.27) is associated with an increase in $Contribution_{p,s,r,n,c,y}$ for the energy-related climate change project of $95,209.

- Rule of law: The estimated coefficients for variable $Rule\ of\ Law_{r,y-1} \times Energy_s$ implies that all else being equal, an increase in $Rule\ of\ Law_{r,y-1}$ of one standard deviation (1.00) is associated with an increase in $Contribution_{p,s,r,n,c,y}$ for the energy-related climate change project of $194,095.
- Voice and accountability: The estimated coefficients for variable $Voice\ and\_Accountability_{r,y-1} \times Energy_s$ implies that all else being equal, an increase in $Voice\ and\ Accountability_{r,y-1}$ of one standard deviation (0.47) is associated with an increase in $Contribution_{p,s,r,n,c,y}$ for the energy-related climate change project of $692,650.

Regarding the energy and environment factors, as expected, we find that greater access to electricity leads to lower contribution, particularly in energy. Note that a significant portion of the climate finance projects are mitigation projects that consist mostly of energy projects. For low-income countries, higher electricity service coverage would allow them to focus on solving problems in other sectors or perhaps on adaptation projects.

The GHG emissions of recipient countries were expected to influence climate finance contributions. According to our results, the effect may not be evident with the emitter sector whenever the attention is focused on energy-related projects. For example, if there is no unobserved heterogeneity between the contributor and the recipient countries (i.e., a strategic relationship between these countries), higher emissions from land use change and forestry are associated with higher contributions for energy projects. In addition, energy projects may be funded as a quick way to mitigate country emissions given the difficulty that lower-income countries have in reducing emissions from land use. Furthermore, as higher emissions from manufacturing and construction tend to diminish contributions to energy projects, we may expect that climate finance would flow towards mitigation actions for manufacturing and construction. However, these expected effects do not seem significant if there exists a contributor-recipient relationship associated with variables considered in the model, such as the bilateral trade pattern in low carbon technology products.

Additionally, our data suggest that countries with higher natural resource rents receive more climate change contributions, and this pattern is maintained when we account for fixed effects on contributor countries, but it loses significance when contributor-recipient FE are used.

Contributions for energy projects seem to decrease with the recipient country's installed capacity of renewable energy, but the effect disappears when we control for contributor-recipient FE. Likewise, trade flows of low carbon technological products, specifically export flows, are positively associated with increasing contributions for energy-related projects.

- Access to electricity in urban areas: The estimated coefficients for variable

  $Access\ to\ Electricity\ Urban_{r,y-1} \times Energy_s$ implies that all else being equal, an increase in $Access\ to\ Electricity\ Urban_{r,y-1}$ of one standard deviation is associated with a decrease in $Contribution_{p,s,r,n,c,y}$ for the energy-related climate change project of $1,089,217.[19] Countries with low access to electricity, particularly in urban areas, have a strong incentive to invest in energy infrastructure such as electricity grids.
- Exports of low carbon technology products: The estimated coefficients for variable

  $Exports\ of\ Low\ Carbon\ Technology\ Products_{r,y-1} \times Energy_s$ imply that all else being equal, an increase in $Exports\ of\ Low\ Carbon\ Technology\ Products_{r,y-1}$ of one standard de- viation (353.44) is associated with an increase in $Contribution_{p,s,r,n,c,y}$ for the energy-related climate change project of $836.18. This result is intuitive in the sense that contributor countries have strong incentive to invest in countries producing a large number of low carbon technology products to promote the transition to a low carbon economy around the globe.

Besides the previous results, we find a few counter-intuitive results regarding the governance indicator–ethnic tensions–and the macroeconomic factor risk of budget balance. We discuss each of these results below.

- Ethnic tensions: The estimated coefficients for variable

  $Ethnic\ Tensions_{r,y-1} \times Energy_s$ imply that all else being equal, an increase in $Ethnic\ Tensions_{r,y-1}$, meaning a reduction in ethnic tensions, of one standard deviation (0.78) is associated with a decrease in $Contribution_{p,s,r,n,c,y}$ for the energy-related climate change project of $302,110.

  This result may seem counter-intuitive, as it suggests that countries with fewer ethnic tensions are the ones that need to address climate change issues. One possible explanation for this result is that some countries with low ethnic tensions might be dependent upon fossil fuel rents. These countries have less incentive to switch from fossil fuel to renewable energy sources. Figure 10 illustrates the correlation between ethnic tensions and fossil fuel consumption, demonstrating a positive association between the two, irrespective of the types of projects involved.
- Risk for budget balance: The estimated coefficients for variable

  $Risk\ for\ Budget\ Balance_{r,y-1} \times Energy_s$ imply that all else being equal, an increase in $Risk\ for\ Budget\ Balance_{r,y-1}$ score, meaning less risk for budget balance, of one standard deviation (0.82) is associated with a decrease in $Contribution_{p,s,r,n,c,y}$ for the energy-related climate change project of $450,640. This result is also counter-intuitive in that a contributor country might be more likely to invest in countries with low risks for government budget balance. One possible explanation for this result is that some countries with low risks for budget balance might be dependent upon fossil fuel rents. These countries have less incentive to switch from fossil fuel to renewable energy sources (Fig. 11).

[19] In the estimation, we standardize the numeric type of the independent variables.

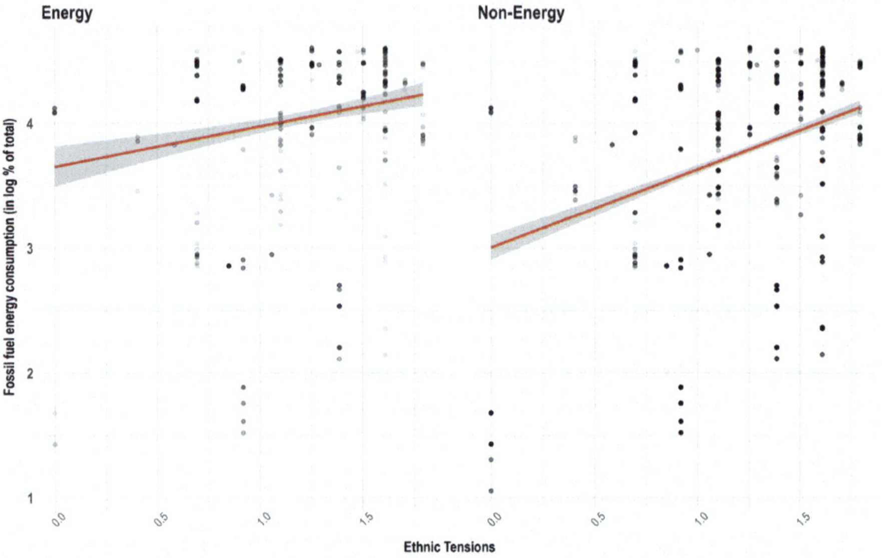

Fig. 10 Ethnic tensions and fossil fuel consumption

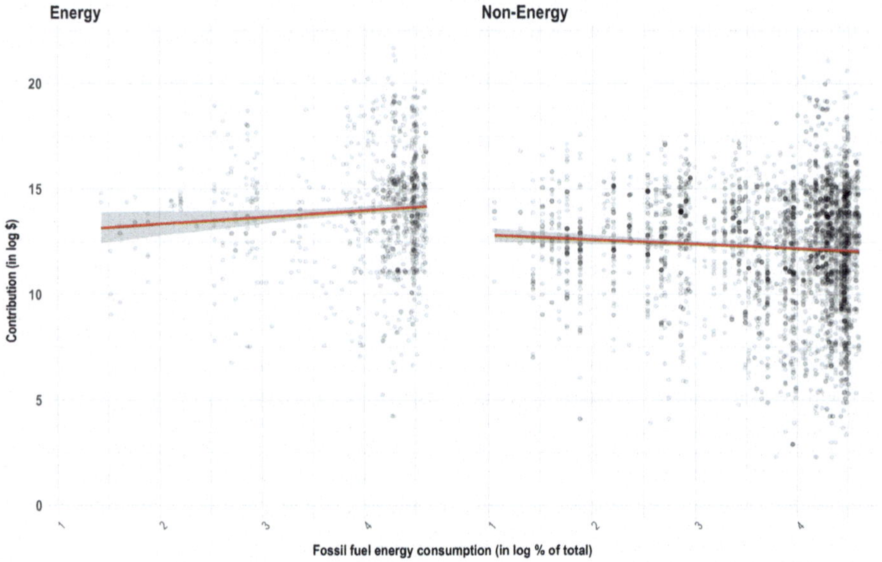

Fig. 11 Budget balance risk and fossil fuel consumption

7 Conclusion

We study the determinants of funding contributions for climate change projects, particularly for energy-related ones. We find that various factors in governance, economy, energy, and the environment in developing countries determine the size of funding contributions for the energy projects in their countries.

The results of our study imply that governance quality can shape the feasibility of energy projects in the developing world. Although governments are capable of implementing energy policies, a low quality of governance can slow down the financing of energy projects in developing countries. The results of our study also confirm that it is important for recipient countries to understand the microeconomic mechanism of financing energy projects through various factors in energy markets, macroeconomic conditions, and the environment in their local setting.

The results have policy implications for both contributors' and recipients' climate change projects and funding decisions. First, recipient countries with improved governance quality can raise higher climate funds for energy projects. In particular, a strong legal system, rule of law, and accountability arise as the most influential governance factors. For example, recipient countries can take steps to enhance these factors to implement energy projects that tend to require an enormous amount of funding from contributors. This would help to convince contributors to invest in their energy projects.

We leave several important questions that are worth investigating in future research. First, we do not consider the effectiveness of climate finance on mitigating GHG emissions in the energy sector through a cost–benefit analysis. Although there would be a positive association between the size of funding contributions and the amount of GHG emissions reduction, it is empirically challenging to evaluate the welfare implications of climate finance. This task may require more detailed data concerning how much of an emission reduction a specific energy project realizes. A post-evaluation of the energy project should facilitate this task. Second, we do not model the strategic interaction between the contributor and the recipient. For example, contributors can use contribution as a strategic instrument to influence other activities involving both parties. This type of strategic behaviors regarding climate finance may play an important role in transitioning to a low-carbon economy in the developing world.

Appendix

A. Variable Description

Variable descriptions in this section are from the original sources (Tables 9, 10, 11, 12 and 13).

B. OLS estimates

(See Tables 14, 15 and 16).

C. Difference in Results between the Random Forests, LASSO, and OLS

Table 9 The World Bank's Governance Indicators

Variable	Description
Control of corruption	The extent to which public power is exercised for private gain, including both petty and grand forms of corruption, as well as"capture" of the state by elites and private interests
Voice and accountability	Perceptions of the extent to which a country's citizens are able to participate in selecting their government, as well as freedom of expression, freedom of association, and a free media
Regulatory quality	Perceptions of the government's ability to formulate and implement sound policies and regulations that permit and promote private sector development
Government effectiveness	Perceptions of the quality of public services, the quality of the civil service and the degree of its independence from political pressure, the quality of policy formulation and implementation, and the credibility of the government's commitment to such policies
Rule of law	The extent to which agents have confidence in and abide by the rules of society, particularly the quality of contract enforcement, property rights, the police, and the courts, as well as the likelihood of crime and violence
Political stability and absence of terrorism/ violence	Perceptions of the likelihood of political instability and/or politically motivated violence, including terrorism

Table 10 The PRS group's governance indicators

Variable	Description
Government cohesion	The extent to which the executive/cabinet is coalesced aroundthe government's general policy goals
Legislative strength	Whether the government can realize its policy program through the legislative arm of government
Repatriation	The extent to which profits can be transferred out of the host country (impediments include exchange controls, excessive bureaucracy, a poor banking system, etc.)
Popular support	The level of support for the government and/or its leader, based on credible opinion polls
Civil war	The actual or potential risk of civil war (where a rebel force, which holds territory, is in armed conflict with the security forces of the government, and where both forces are citizens of the state in which the conflict occurs)
Terrorism	The actual or potential risk of terrorism (where forces opposed to the government carry out violent acts against civilian or state targets to achieve a political goal). The fundamental difference between a terrorist campaign and a civil war is that the former do not hold and administer territory within a nation state
Civil disorder	The potential risk to governance or investment from mass protest, such as anti-government demonstrations, or strikes
War	Actual or potential armed conflict with another nation borne out of the desire of either combatant state to subjugate the governance of people and/or acquire territory of the other, primarily through the use of its own armed forces
Cross-border conflict	Actual or potential conflict with another nation state that does not affect the whole nation and which can range in severity from cross-border armed conflict and incursion to territorial claims subject to civil mediation or litigation
Foreign pressures	Actual or potential risk posed by pressures brought to bear on the government by one or more foreign states to force a change of policy. Such pressures can range from diplomatic pressures, through suspension of aid and/or credits, to outright sanctions
Military in politics	A measure of the military's involvement in politics. Since the military is not elected, involvement, even at a peripheral level, diminishes democratic accountability. Military involvement might stem from an external or internal threat, be symptomatic of underlying difficulties, or be a full-scale military takeover. Over the long term, a system of military government will almost certainly diminish effective governmental functioning, become corrupt, and create an uneasy environment for foreign businesses
Religious tensions	A measure of religious tensions arising from the domination of society and/or governance by a single religious group–or a desire to dominate–in a way that replaces civil law with religious law, excludes other religions from the political/social processes, suppresses religious freedom or expressions of religious identity. The risks involved range from inexperienced people imposing inappropriate policies to civil dissent or civil war

(continued)

Table 10 (continued)

Variable	Description
Law and order	Two measures comprising one risk component. Each sub-component equals half of the total. The "law" sub-component assesses the strength and impartiality of the legal system, and the"order" sub-component assesses popular observance of the law
Ethnic tensions	A measure of the degree of tension attributable to racial, national, or language divisions. Lower ratings (higher risk) are given to countries where tensions are high because opposing groups are intolerant and unwilling to compromise
Democratic accountability	A measure of, not just whether there are free and fair elections, but also how responsive the government is to its people. The less responsive it is, the more likely it will fall. Even democratically elected governments can delude themselves into thinking they know what is best for the people, regardless of clear indications to the contrary from the people
Contract viability	The risk of unilateral contract modification or cancellation and, at worst, outright expropriation of foreign owned assets
Bureaucracy quality	that tends to minimize revisions of policy when governments change. In low-risk countries, the bureaucracy is somewhat autonomous from political pressure

Notice that some variables that appear as the top 20 most important variables in the random forests estimation (see in Fig. 9) do not appear in the LASSO estimates in Tables 6, 7, and 8. First, some interactions the Random Forest model takes into account are not necessarily the interaction with $Energy_s$. Therefore, the Random Forest estimation might miss the relationships with $Energy_s$ presented in Tables of the LASSO estimates. Second, the Random Forest captures the non-linear relationship between funding contributions and an independent variable, while LASSO assumes a linear relationship between them. Therefore, the linearity assumption in the LASSO model we estimate may not capture the non-linear relationship with contributions.

Table 11 The World Bank, the IMF, and the FAO's data on energy and the environment

Variable	Description
Energy intensity level of primary energy (MJ/$2017 PPP GDP)	Energy intensity level of primary energy is the ratio between energy supply and gross domestic product (GDP) measured at purchasing power parity (PPP). Energy intensity is an indication of how much energy is used to produce one unit of economic output. A lower ratio indicates that less energy is used to produce one unit of output
Exports and imports of low carbon technology products	Low-carbon technologies include mechanics like wind turbines, solar panels, biomass systems and carbon capture equipment
Greenhouse gas emissions from various sectors	Greenhouse gas emissions from each of various sectors, including (a) energy, (b) electricity and heat, (c) transportation, (d) manufacturing and construction, (e) agriculture, (f) fugitive emissions, (g) industrial process, (h) building, waste, (i) land use change and forestry, (j) bunker fuels, and (k) other fuel combustion
Access to electricity in urban and rural areas	Access to electricity is the percentage of the population with access to electricity. Electrification data are collected from industry, national surveys and international sources
Fuel imports and exports	Fuels comprise the commodities in mineral fuels, lubricants and related materials
Energy depletion	Energy depletion is the ratio of the value of the stock of energy resources to the remaining reserve lifetime (capped at 25 years). It covers coal, crude oil, and natural gas
Natural resources depletion	Natural resource depletion is the sum of net forest depletion, energy depletion, and mineral depletion. Net forest depletion is unit resource rents times the excess of roundwood harvest over natural growth. Energy depletion is the ratio of the value of the stock of energy resources to the remaining reserve lifetime (capped at 25 years). It covers coal, crude oil, and natural gas. Mineral depletion is the ratio of the value of the stock of mineral resources to the remaining reserve lifetime (capped at 25 years). It covers tin, gold, lead, zinc, iron, copper, nickel, silver, bauxite, and phosphate
Natural resources rents	Total natural resources rents are the sum of oil rents, natural gas rents, coal rents (hard and soft), mineral rents, and forest rents
Access to basic drinking water	Percentage of the population using at least basic drinking water services

Also, notice that the OLS estimates, provided in the previous section of the Appendix, tend to be much larger than the LASSO estimates. This could be due to severe multicollinearity that OLS cannot handle well without carefully selecting a small set of relevant variables to explain the variation in contributions. Secondly, the OLS estimation is susceptible to overfitting to data, resulting in a significant bias in the estimates.

Table 12 The World Bank, IMF, and PRS group's finance and economic indicators

Variable	Description
GDP PPP	GDP, PPP (constant 2017 international $)
Population	Population, total
Unemployment	The official rate as defined by credible sources (e.g. IMF, World Bank, CIA Factbook); significant levels of underemployment or employment in the informal economy in emerging markets can affect the rating
Consumer confidence	The level of consumer confidence vis-à-vis credible surveys, where available, or approximations based on employment trends, economic growth and investment, etc
Poverty	The level of poverty vis-à-vis credible sources (e.g., IMF, World Bank, CIA Factbook)

Table 13 The PRS group's data on financial and economic risks

Variable	Description
Risk for budget balance	Ranging from high % of 4.0+ with risk points at 10.0, to a low of −30.0 with 0.0 points. The higher the points, the lower the risk
Risk for debt service	Ranging from high % of >85.0 with risk points at 0.0, to a low of 0.0 with 10.0 points. The higher the points, the lower the risk
Risk for exchange rate stability	Ranging from high % change of either 0.0−9.9 appreciation or depreciation of 0.1–4.9 with risk points at 10.0, to a midpoint of either appreciation at 50.0 + or depreciation of 30.0−34.9 with risk points at 5.0 to a low depreciation of 100.0+ with 0.0 points. The higher the points, the lower the risk
Risk for foreign debt	Ranging from high % of >200.0 with risk points at 0.0, to a low of 0.0 with 10.0 points. The higher the points, the lower the risk
Risk for GDP growth	Risk points determined by expressing this number as a percentage of the average of the estimated total GDP of all countries covered by ICRG, then assigning risk points, ranging from high % of 6+ with risk at 10.0, to a low of <0.4 with 5.0 points. The higher the points, the lower the risk
Risk for inflation	Ranging from high % of 130+ with risk points at 0.0, to a low of 0.0 with 10.0 points. The higher the points, the lower the risk
Risk for international liquidity	Ranging from high % of 15.0+ with risk points at 5.0, to a low of 0.0 with 0.0 points. The higher the points, the lower the risk
Risk for per capita GDP	Risk points determined by expressing this number as a percentage of the average of the estimated total GDP of all countries covered by ICRG, then assigning risk points ranging from high % of 250+ with risk at 5.0 points, to a low of <10 with 0.0 points. The higher the points, the lower the risk

Table 14 OLS estimates for G **Governance** $_{r,y-1}$

Interaction w/*energy* OLS	(1)	(2)	(3)	(4)	(5)	(6)
Contract_viability	−35,102.44 (96,479.68)	−82,051.92 (99,925.25)	−59,691 (101,690.12)	−49,872.22 (134,531.58)	−161,234.72 (132,196.94)	62,689.8 (141,615.06)
Contract_viability:Energy	−48,778.7 (327,536.69)	−8054.12 (327,488.65)	−22,534.88 (327,855.28)	91,834.12 (332,017.15)	−88,589.81 (326,304.81)	1,374,662.29 (340,527.45)
Control_of_corruption	−45,523.44 (125,259.6)	17,670.31 (128,661.89)	3618.45 (134,006.32)	-984,320.62 (292,054.64)	−606,891.14 (287,424.23)	−779,235.99 (303,315.91)
Control_of_corruption:Energy	479,154.07 (411,389.93)	513,425.09 (411,305.51)	498,711.38 (411,484.62)	391,876.36 (417,810.74)	773,348.42 (410,948.04)	243,580.98 (437,654.71)
Ethnic_tensions	206,021.61 (115,799.65)	202,169.84 (116,466.67)	−15,705.88 (145,014.28)	−808,831.39 (714,856.11)	−1,104,970.56 (702,469.79)	−115,578.37 (745,572.71)
Ethnic_tensions:Energy	−1,234,956.42 (388,363.79)	−1,275,947.58 (388,254.02)	−1,275,491.32 (388,722.38)	−1,286,763.04 (398,317.75)	−1,400,135.99 (391,839.47)	−2,747,802.17 (454,271.02)
Government_cohesion	46,656.12 (99,310.47)	20,303.71 (102,480.49)	32,763.52 (103,463.02)	42,575.17 (128,384.98)	210,427.19 (126,233.27)	−1083.13 (133,310.94)
Government_cohesion:Energy	−499,014.13 (333,226.46)	−524,610.17 (333,306.85)	−547,698.44 (333,515.83)	−554,050.43 (336,604.53)	−683,915.17 (330,847.52)	−1,425,522.27 (341,485.07)
Law_and_order	−87,986.97 (151,385.29)	−12,293.26 (153,395.57)	−118,789.2 (169,045.97)	−27,259.69 (472,105.08)	−146,405.4 (463,576.71)	184,655.72 (489,899.19)
Law_and_order:Energy	1,514,255.76 (574,460.63)	1,529,389.41 (574,774.93)	1,509,746.21 (574,929.48)	1,459,576.22 (587,267.61)	1,304,585.39 (576,529.8)	247,026.39 (604,316.99)
Legislative_strength	113,612.17 (92,599.9)	−23,609.04 (95,998.25)	6007.27 (97,148.42)	85,920.25 (128,633.86)	160,511.8 (126,359.79)	26,191.23 (131,415.72)
Legislative_strength:Energy	1,629,518.81 (314,903.18)	1,662,857.44 (315,068.97)	1,693,758.97 (315,219.24)	1,724,196.63 (317,902.4)	2,042,727.48 (312,519.83)	2,669,907.02 (324,019.97)

(continued)

Table 14 (continued)

Interaction w/*energy* OLS	(1)	(2)	(3)	(4)	(5)	(6)
Popular_support	251,528.29 (81,789.17)	213,664.75 (83,125.66)	190,019.12 (85,488.5)	191,864.61 (100,819.11)	177,786.07 (99,103.04)	165,328.4 (103,092.75)
Popular_support:Energy	802,538.63 (283,734.88)	767,748.12 (283,633.23)	749,707.27 (283,733.01)	604,093.82 (285,995.79)	598,228.54 (281,108.21)	901,968.48 (287,371.65)
Voice_and_accountability	155,129.96 (203,510.27)	15,153.98 (205,908.51)	−89,597.76 (219,211.83)	81,414 (548,979.75)	96,962.84 (540,497.55)	1,269,316.8 (570,652.94)
Voice_and_accountability:Energy	4,773,541.1 (635,624.08)	4,781,733.85 (635,540.4)	4,753,682.19 (637,008.97)	4,953,584.12 (645,183.87)	4,412,652.84 (635,190.4)	4,408,768.24 (706,227.64)
Year FE	No	Yes	Yes	Yes	Yes	Yes
Continent FE	No	No	Yes	Yes	Yes	Yes
Recipient FE	No	No	No	Yes	Yes	Yes
Contributor FE	No	No	No	No	Yes	Yes
Contributor-recipient FE	No	No	No	No	No	Yes
N	52,833	52,833	52,833	52,833	52,833	52,833
R^2	0.3304	0.3317	0.3318	0.3347	0.3623	0.4524

Standard errors are in parentheses

Table 15 OLS estimates for **EnergyEnvironment** $_{r,c,y-1}$

Interaction w/*energy* *OLS*	(1)	(2)	(3)	(4)	(5)	(6)
Access_to_electricity_urban	−644,341.24 (290,567.81)	−725,645.11 (291,859.88)	−697,680.45 (294,638.67)	−370,698.61 (703,966.36)	−379,166.53 (692,093)	−207,322.81 (719,031.83)
Access_to_electricity_urban:Energy	−1,981,297.48 (1,062,146.44)	−1,912,224.91 (1,061,883.36)	−1,894,638.86 (1,062,674.6)	−1,937,119.02 (1,074,903.57)	−1,844,271.54 (1,056,791.85)	−1,433,774.38 (1,079,551.91)
Electricity_capacity_renewables_excluding_hydro	−248,444.54 (138,560.02)	−126,773.13 (143,306.97)	−220,569.16 (152,898.5)	−658,564.21 (505,564.57)	−1,628,067.91 (497,991.09)	67,043.84 (531,343.97)
Electricity_capacity_renewables_excluding_hydro:Energy	1,817,982.64 (518,175.64)	1,902,815.71 (518,245.8)	1,858,905.29 (518,701.36)	1,825,503.07 (525,486.75)	1,818,478.87 (515,951.89)	2,305,746.31 (528,887.87)
Exports_of_low_carbon_tech_products	−1595.64 (209.09)	−1372.11 (228.02)	−1333.5 (229.09)	−1596.18 (263.71)	−1724.54 (259.58)	−1481.51 (259.57)
Exports_of_low_carbon_tech_products:Energy	1060.3 (587.54)	1065.42 (587.16)	1069.1 (587.22)	1297.33 (589.11)	1939.45 (578.87)	2376.22 (559.3)
Fuel_exports	−172,068.97 (140,659.23)	33,409.11 (150,475.47)	54,149.24 (155,088.47)	383,566.32 (261,259.38)	303,367.7 (256,874.61)	168,872.2 (272,247.76)
Fuel_exports:Energy	−1,601,683.69 (492,975.26)	−1,637,212 (492,968.2)	−1,564,494.81 (493,541.94)	−1,347,742.9 (499,609.32)	−1,131,320.58 (492,089.51)	−2,302,302.1 (517,144.81)
GHG_land_use_change_and_forestry	−2,229,840,561.24 (1,442,644,079.03)	−1,968,551,994.6 (1,467,883,931.34)	−1,762,430,362.97 (1,472,251,233.15)	−835,064,119.84 (1,626,588,971.17)	−99,823,965.73 (1,595,737,015.7)	988,735,214.31 (1,602,042,806.25)
GHG_land_use_change_and_forestry:Energy	23,461,225,510.89 (4,688,185,746.81)	24,323,245,897.18 (4,686,344,217.25)	24,107,110,179.74 (4,688,456,122.92)	25,115,876,331.41 (4,711,781,513.52)	24,256,446,263.72 (4,624,789,889.01)	26,917,206,673.57 (4,558,116,958.94)

(continued)

Table 15 (continued)

Interaction w/*energy* *OLS*	(1)	(2)	(3)	(4)	(5)	(6)
GHG_manufacturing_ construction	−1,114,540,688.14 (1,321,641,964.2)	−1,111,285,226.51 (1,327,845,336.29)	−1,938,991,711.08 (1,364,717,140.38)	−3,289,002,880.77 (1,538,044,041.34)	−4,707,185,168.24 (1,511,561,291.59)	−1,122,090,012.38 (1,512,558,120.91)
GHG_manufacturing_ construction:Energy	19,625,567,733.44 (4,408,036,720.72)	19,602,547,989.49 (4,405,196,878.53)	19,762,885,244.29 (4,407,385,034.7)	20,161,585,314.12 (4,433,424,375.14)	21,134,734,972.19 (4,347,849,691.35)	24,874,229,513.71 (4,342,228,475.54)
GHG_other_fuel_ combustion	−110,282,228.54 (130,078,823.29)	−110,506,085.86 (130,683,625.82)	−192,135,986.01 (134,326,209.01)	−324,500,656.37 (151,492,609.9)	−462,191,475.38 (148,882,329.34)	−110,763,239.25 (148,999,740.23)
GHG_other_fuel_ combustion:Energy	1,941,995,248.31 (433,890,301.35)	1,939,698,308.08 (433,609,754.31)	1,955,230,889.85 (433,823,586.35)	1,994,689,426.61 (436,397,651.35)	2,089,418,831.39 (427,974,050.21)	2,465,225,217.2 (427,487,743.68)
Natural_resources_ rents	508,720.3 (232,540.36)	329,321.47 (240,509.12)	200,504.16 (255,732.9)	461,866.92 (540,062.14)	1,020,486.53 (530,565.61)	−92,789.82 (570,812.05)
Natural_resources_ rents:Energy	20,212.24 (745,212.53)	138,234.81 (745,502.52)	183,247.73 (745,739.78)	302,587.22 (758,601.42)	−276,222 (747,073.6)	2,418,235.61 (813,733.51)
Year FE	No	Yes	Yes	Yes	Yes	Yes
Continent FE	No	No	Yes	Yes	Yes	Yes
Recipient FE	No	No	No	Yes	Yes	Yes
Contributor FE	No	No	No	No	Yes	Yes
Contributor−recipient FE	No	No	No	No	No	Yes
N	52,833	52,833	52,833	52,833	52,833	52,833
R^2	0.3304	0.3317	0.3318	0.3347	0.3623	0.4524

Standard errors are in parentheses

Table 16 OLS estimates for population$_{r,y-1}$ and **EconomicRisks** $_{r,y-1}$

Interaction w/*energy* OLS	(1)	(2)	(3)	(4)	(5)	(6)
Population	−1002.29 (342.97)	−815.26 (344.64)	-883.36 (357.61)	1229.2 (759.32)	1090 (747.18)	520.79 (798.85)
Population:Energy	2820.72 (1039.36)	2884.38 (1039.05)	2836.36 (1039.6)	2551.15 (1056.33)	2609.44 (1045.44)	3521 (1122.29)
Risk_for_budget_balance	219,002.74 (86,866.65)	194,386.93 (87,860.23)	178,751.95 (93,442.58)	40,203.1 (128,097.99)	119,188.55 (125,987.85)	−4204.44 (133,029.85)
Risk_for_budget_balance:Energy	−747,393.07 (274,830.64)	−758,167.28 (275,367.2)	−742,916.72 (275,765.62)	−654,427.8 (278,716.43)	−535,852.94 (273,842.22)	−934,907.6 (287,063.34)
Risk_for_current_account_as_percentage_of_ XGS	86,217.12 (244,200.13)	87,458.56 (253,496.33)	124,967.24 (256,531.45)	790,591.94 (353,780.9)	526,580.97 (347,081.23)	280,986.72 (365,380.04)
Risk_for_current_account_as_percentage_of_ XGS:Energy	3,824,568.95 (773,588.07)	3,836,304.45 (773,088.46)	3,819,485.18 (773,172.77)	3,736,987.49 (780,447.29)	3,569,242.2 (766,556.81)	2,174,571.95 (812,554.55)
Risk_for_debt_service	259,323.41 (78,052.09)	279,199.61 (83,301.98)	208,850.35 (87,300.18)	379,298.37 (113,541.61)	483,069.7 (111,862.39)	257,667.52 (119,186.41)
Risk_for_debt_service:Energy	−784,309.37 (249,117.9)	−761,134.93 (249,328.5)	−732,988.87 (249,620.49)	−796,031.92 (252,100.44)	−863,956.42 (247,677.41)	−698,166.01 (257,364.43)
Risk_for_international_liquidity	−81,010.54 (115,999.14)	−80,480.87 (118,599.61)	−97,057.72 (130,869.49)	−313,732.17 (245,692.72)	−566,542.33 (241,447.9)	−422,963.21 (251,500.12)
Risk_for_international_liquidity:Energy	2,661,305.31 (348,905.31)	2,657,752.04 (348,852.54)	2,622,738.98 (349,288.39)	2,742,981.93 (354,497.57)	2,511,399.39 (348,684.54)	2,897,227.66 (376,753.91)
Risk_for_per_capita_GDP	186,870.32 (191,126.29)	322,347.38 (193,956.45)	32,921.1 (233,506.24)	−1,280,333.04 (475,773.7)	−1,433,143.01 (467,257.67)	−689,698.18 (488,117.88)
Risk_for_per_capita_GDP:Energy	−2,295,888.04 (593,728.47)	−2,386,470.64 (593,632.12)	−2,348,249.6 (595,582.59)	−2,371,198.25 (609,863.61)	−2,253,457.53 (598,652.4)	−1,453,580.67 (665,440.95)
Year FE	No	Yes	Yes	Yes	Yes	Yes

(continued)

Table 16 (continued)

Interaction w/*energy* OLS	(1)	(2)	(3)	(4)	(5)	(6)
Continent FE	No	No	Yes	Yes	Yes	Yes
Recipient FE	No	No	No	Yes	Yes	Yes
Contributor FE	No	No	No	No	Yes	Yes
Contributor-recipient FE	No	No	No	No	No	Yes
N	52,833	52,833	52,833	52,833	52,833	52,833
R^2	0.3304	0.3317	0.3318	0.3347	0.3623	0.4524

Standard errors are in parentheses

References

Alesina, A., & Dollar, D. (2000). Who gives foreign aid to whom and why? Journal of Economic Growth, 5(1), 33–63.

Argueta, B., Chhetri, R., Eckstein, D., & Kohler, M. (2021). Access to climate finance for the most vulnerable. Climate Finance Advisory Service (CFAS). eprint: https://cfas.info/sites/default/files/anhang/CFASPolicyBriefAccesstoclimate%20finance0.pdf

Barabanov, S., Basnet, A., Walker, T., Yuan, W., & Wendt, S. (2021). Firm-and country-level de-terminants of green investments: An empirical analysis. Managerial Finance, 47(11), 1672–1692.

Boone, P. (1996). Politics and the effectiveness of foreign aid. European Economic Review, 40, 289– 329.

Bracking, S., & Benjamin, L. (2021). Climate finance governance: Fit for purpose? WIREs Climate Change.

Browne, K. (2022). Rethinking governance in international climate finance: Structural and alternative approach. WIREs Climate Change.

Burnside, C., & Dollar, D. (2000). Aid, policies, and growth. The American Economic Review, 90(4), 847–868.

Choe, B.-H. (2020). Climate finance under conflicts and renegotiations: A dynamic contract approach. Unpublished manuscript.

CPI. (2021). Global landscape of climate finance 2021. Climate Policy Initiative (CPI). eprint: https://www.climatepolicyinitiative.org/publication/global-landscape-of-climate-finance-2021/

Easterly, W. (2007). The elusive quest for growth: Economists' adventures and misadventures in the tropics. The MIT Press.

Economides, G., Kaluvitis, S., & Philippopoulos, A. (2008). Does foreign aid distort incentives and hurt growth? theory and evidence from 75-aid recipient countries. Public Choice, 134, 463–488.

Fisman, R., & Miguel, E. (2008). Economic gangsters. Princeton University Press.

Food and Agriculture Organization. (2023). Database. Global Environment Facility. Retrieved July 23, 2023, from https://www.fao.org/faostat/en/#data

Global Environment Facility. (2023). Project database. Global Environment Facility. Retrieved July 23, 2023, from https://www.thegef.org/projects-operations/database

IEA, & IFC. (2023). Scaling up private finance for clean energy in emerging and developing economies. International Energy Agency and International Finance Corporation.

IMF. (2023). Climate change indicators dashboard. IMF. Retrieved July 24, 2023, from https://climatedata.imf.org

IPCC. (2023). Climate change 2023: Synthesis report - summary for policymakers. Intergovernmental Panel on Climate Change (IPCC).

IRENA. (2022). Renewable power generation costs in 2021. International Renewable Energy Agency IRENA. Retrieved from https://www.irena.org/publications/2022/Jul/Renewable-Power-Generation-Costs-in-2021

Jain, S. (2007). Project assistance versus budget support: An incentive-theoretic analysis of aid conditionally. Review of World Economics, 143(3), 694–719.

Kaufmann, D., & Kraay, A. (2023). Worldwide governance indicators (wgi) project. World Bank Retrieved April 28, 2023, from https://info.worldbank.org/governance/wgi

Kouwenberg, C., R. ; Zhen. (2023). A review of the global climate finance literature. Sustainability, 15(1255).

Kuzienko, I., & Werker, E. (2006). How much is a seat o the security council worth? foreign aid and bribery at the United Nations. Journal of Political Economy, 114(5), 905–930.

Milner, H. (2006). Why multilateralism? foreign aid and domestic principal-agent problems. Delegation and agency in international organizations, 107–139.

Nest, M., Mullard, S., & Wathne, C. (2020). Corruption and climate finance: Implications for climate change interventions. Chr. Michelsen Institute - CMI, U4 Anti-corruption Resource Center, U4 Brief 2020:14. eprint: https://www.u4.no/publications/corruption-and-climate-finance.pdf

Quazi, R. (2006). Effects of foreign aid on GDP growth and fiscal behavior: An econometric case study of bangladesh. The Journal of Developing Areas, 38(2), 95–117.

Skovgaard, J., Adams, K., Dupuy, K., Dzebo, A., Funder, M., Fejerskov, A., Shawoo, Z. (2023). Multilateral climate finance coordination: Politics and depoliticization in practice. Global Environmental Politics, 23(2), 125−147.

Svensson, J. (2000). Foreign aid and rent-seeking. Journal of International Economics, 51, 437–461.

The PRS Group. (2023). The international country risk guide (icrg). The PRS Group. Retrieved July 24, 2023, from https://www.prsgroup.com/explore-our-products/icrg/

The World Bank. (2023a). Databank. The World Bank. Retrieved July 24, 2023, from https://databank.worldbank.org

The World Bank. (2023b). Scaling up to phase down: Financing energy transitions in the power sector. The World Bank.

Tirole, J. (2017). Economics for the common good. Princeton University Press.

UNFCCC. (2022). Fifth biennial assessment and overview of climate finance flows. United Nations Framework Convention on Climate Change, UNFCCC Standing Committee on Finance. eprint: https://unfccc.int/news/four-new-reports-set-scene-for-discussions-on-climate-finance-at-cop27

UNFCCC Climate Finance Data Portal. (2023). Biennial reports data interface (br-di). United Na-tions Climate Change. Retrieved April 28, 2023, from https://unfccc.int/climatefinance

Climate Watch. (2023). Data explorer. Climate Watch. Retrieved April 28, 2023, from https://www.climatewatchdata.org

Climate Finance and Investment in Africa: A Case Study of Ghana

Solomon Nborkan Nakouwo and Dayong Zhang

Abstract This chapter discusses the critical issues surrounding climate finance and investment in Africa, with a specific focus on Ghana. It is evident that climate change poses a significant threat to the development and survival of the African continent. Particularly noteworthy are the escalating temperatures, unpredictable rainfall patterns, and rising sea levels, which have profound implications for African nations. While the Ghanian government has taken steps to create a favourable climate finance environment through various policies and institutions, obstacles continue to persist, including inadequate financial resources, weak institutional frameworks, and a lack of coordination, all of which hinder Ghana's ability to attract climate finance. This chapter stresses the need for a coordinating mechanism involving government agencies, the private sector, civil society, and local communities. Additionally, social and environmental safeguards must be integrated into climate finance, which would promote sustainable development, poverty reduction, and gender equality.

Keywords Climate finance · Green transition · Green investment · Case study

1 Introduction

One of the major present-day issues across the world that has significant environmental, social, and economic repercussions is climate change. The impacts of climate change are mostly felt by developing countries, like those found in Africa. It is challenging for developing nations to adapt to changing climatic conditions and to devise effective strategies for mitigating the devastating effects of the climate change events. Due to African countries' climate-sensitive sectors, including agriculture, forestry, and fisheries, it is necessary to have sufficient financing available for climate resilience and sustainable development in Africa. There is thus a need to understand the climate finance and investments that are currently being channelled

S. N. Nakouwo · D. Zhang (✉)
Research Institute of Economics and Management, Southwestern University of Finance and Economics, 555 Liutai Avenue, Chengdu 611130, China
e-mail: dzhang@swufe.edu.cn

F. Wu et al. (eds.), *Climate Finance*, Climate Change and Energy Transition,
https://doi.org/10.1007/978-981-97-3308-8_8

to Africa from developed economies, their limitations, and how they are being used to fund climate actions in African countries.

In the past few decades, governments and non-governmental organisations have dedicated resources to mitigation and adaptation measures at various levels and across a number of regions in Africa. This type of financing is critical for driving economies along low-carbon and climate-resilient trajectories. For example, the World Bank and the African Development Bank (AfDB) group channel funds for climate-related projects across the continent, with the latter doing so through the Africa Climate Change Fund (ACCF) and Climate Investment Funds (CIF). In addition, the United Nations Development Programme (UNDP) and the United Nations Framework Convention on Climate Change (UNFCCC) play pivotal roles in climate change policy formulation and enforcement in Africa (Leal Filho et al. 2018).

1.1 Overview of Climate Change in Africa: Contributions and Impacts

1.1.1 Africa's Contribution to Global Warming

The primary driver of climate change is the generation of greenhouse gases (GHGs) by humans. Only 10 nations are responsible for around 60% of global warming gases, with the 100 nations with the lowest emissions contributing less than 3% (Climate Watch 2023). Total historical GHG emissions, including land-use change and forestry (LUCF) in million tonnes of carbon dioxide ($MtCO_2e$) over three decades from 1991 to 2020, show that all African countries together contribute about 10% of the total global GHG emissions (see Table 1). It is important to note that the LUCF industry has the potential to both absorb and release carbon dioxide. While trees and other plants remove carbon dioxide from the air, cutting them down, subjecting them to combustion, or converting their spaces to other land uses results in further emissions. The outcome of this sector's carbon sequestration and emissions within a country's borders determines whether the net emissions are positive or negative.

1.1.2 Impacts of Climate Change in Africa

The last century has witnessed rising average temperatures in most parts of Africa. For example, in 2020, nine of the ten countries most affected by climate change were African (Reuters 2023; UNDP Climate Promise 2023). As observed in projections provided by the Intergovernmental Panel on Climate Change (IPCC), the rate of surface temperature increase has generally been more rapid in Africa than the global average, with human-induced climate change being the dominant driver (Intergovernmental Panel on Climate Change (IPCC) 2023). Heatwaves have negative impacts on human health, agriculture, and the natural environment, given the already rising

Table 1 Total historical GHG emissions in million tonnes of CO_2 ($MtCO_2e$) over three decades (1991–2020): Africa's contribution

Year	World total	% Change world (%)	Africa total	% Change Africa (%)	Share of Africa (%)
1991	32,835.51	0.53	3166.06	2.69	9.64
1992	32,736.21	−0.30	3188.44	0.71	9.74
1993	32,884.18	0.45	3243.80	1.74	9.86
1994	33,162.74	0.85	3353.56	3.38	10.11
1995	33,960.87	2.41	3440.12	2.58	10.13
1996	34,351.00	1.15	3485.30	1.31	10.15
1997	35,715.00	3.97	3534.68	1.42	9.90
1998	35,261.24	−1.27	3621.89	2.47	10.27
1999	35,264.63	0.01	3623.58	0.05	10.28
2000	35,994.91	2.07	3647.66	0.66	10.13
2001	36,066.81	0.20	3735.75	2.41	10.36
2002	37,012.72	2.62	3803.80	1.82	10.28
2003	38,009.25	2.69	3972.00	4.42	10.45
2004	39,849.51	4.84	4064.72	2.33	10.20
2005	40,784.41	2.35	4215.58	3.71	10.34
2006	42,278.18	3.66	4245.41	0.71	10.04
2007	43,061.38	1.85	4337.20	2.16	10.07
2008	43,316.76	0.59	4458.57	2.80	10.29
2009	43,270.13	−0.11	4431.50	−0.61	10.24
2010	45,080.62	4.18	4588.90	3.55	10.18
2011	45,256.47	0.39	4740.24	3.30	10.47
2012	45,800.17	1.20	4937.01	4.15	10.78
2013	46,443.60	1.40	4949.90	0.26	10.66
2014	47,106.48	1.43	5004.53	1.10	10.62
2015	47,059.77	−0.10	5044.13	0.79	10.72
2016	47,691.83	1.34	5141.98	1.94	10.78
2017	48,390.92	1.47	5237.31	1.85	10.82
2018	49,585.91	2.47	5285.63	0.92	10.66
2019	49,880.60	0.59	5331.61	0.87	10.69
2020	47,513.15	4.75	5162.13	3.18	10.86

Data Source Climate Watch (2023)

temperatures. The continent of Africa is heavily dependent on rainfed agriculture and is therefore more prone to changing rain patterns. Agriculture is among the most important economic sectors in many African counties, with significant contributions to employment and GDP. Changing rainfall patterns, increasing temperatures, droughts, and flooding have continued to affect agricultural production, leading to food insecurity across Africa. Furthermore, variable, infrequent, yet hot and dry weather that causes evaporation results in reduced water availability and quality in terms of agriculture, production, and human consumption (United Nations Development Programme (UNDP) 2016). This is probably one of the most important challenges for Africa, since water depletion has a direct impact on economic development and human well-being. The severe conditions of droughts and heavy downpours of rain in recent years have caused significant damage to crops and affected food security, which will likely degenerate into further acute poverty if nothing is done quickly.

Water availability and quality are affected by climate change, thereby increasing Africa's vulnerability to water scarcity. Water stress increases due to changes in rainfall patterns, in addition to a high rate of population growth with increasing demand for water in areas where the natural water supply is insufficient. Subsequently, water deficits impact the output of agriculture, leading to food shortages. In Africa, the adverse effects of climate change exacerbate general health-related problems, such as low healthcare accessibility in poor communities and increased populations, such as refugees. The increased occurrence and severity of heat waves, in turn, cause heat-related illnesses and death. Malaria and dengue fever are some of the most common vector-borne diseases in the tropical and subtropical climates in Africa, which spread because of high temperatures.

The African continent has an extensive coastline stretching thousands of kilometres, with many populations living on these coastal bases. The sea-level rise poses a danger to these communities, ports, and their coastal ecological systems. For instance, IPCC predicts that, a one-metre increase in sea level, will cause the displacement of 8 million people in Egypt alone, assuming no protection and existing population levels (Intergovernmental Panel on Climate Change (IPCC) Reports 1997). This would result in the exacerbation of already-existing social and economic disparities. Furthermore, Africa has a wide range of diverse ecosystems with numerous indigenous species that are essential for environmental sustainability. However, such biodiversity is greatly threatened by climate change, which includes disturbances in ecosystems and extinction of species due to warming. Decreases in biodiversity have detrimental effects on agriculture, tourism, and human health.

Very often, conflicts in Africa arise over scanty resources, such as water and arable land, which are now quite prevalent due to climate change. These conflicts often result in internal displacements and migration, which could culminate in humanitarian crises and further complications in the already complex socio-political dynamics of the region. As people move from place to place, host nations face challenges in providing health care, education, and social protection for vulnerable persons due to high migrant flows triggered by climate change (International Organization for Migration (IOM) 2020).

For Africa to meet the climate change goals outlined by the nationally determined contributions (NDCs) of committed countries, sufficient finance is crucial. The estimated funding required for African countries' NDCs from 2020 to 2030 was estimated at USD 2.8 trillion, representing more than 93% of Africa's GDP (UNDP Climate Promise 2023). In response to the demand for climate funding by African countries, the ACCF was created in 2014 by the AfDB. With a trust fund size of USD 25.71 million, the ACCF has approved 26 grant projects that have provided support for more than 26 African countries in several climate change projects. Similarly, the UNFCCC and many other partners have launched intergovernmental international organisations to help speed up actions and support adaptation measures with a focus on the most vulnerable countries (Leal Filho et al. 2018). However, there is still a huge financing gap, even though many domestic public resources are committed to such causes. To help bridge this financing gap, in 2009, developed countries at the 15th Conference of Parties (COP15) of the UNFCCC in Copenhagen committed to a collective goal of mobilising USD 100 billion per year by 2020 for climate action in developing countries (OECD Climate Change 2023). The Organisation for Economic Co-operation and Development (OECD) reported that developed countries had mobilised USD 83.3 billion in 2020 and provided USD 89.6 billion (about USD10 billion short) in 2021 (OECD Climate Change 2023). Despite a steady increased in the yearly funds mobilized relative to previous years, the data indicates that the USD100 billion goal is still yet to be met.

Looking at the unique, yet profound and multifaceted vulnerability of Africa to the effects associated with climate change, it is evident that large amounts of continued monetary support are needed to establish a climate-resilient regime in Africa. Evidence shows that the African continent requires robust strategies, policies, and funds to tackle these climatic change challenges. Therefore, more international cooperation and boosted climate finance are needed to assist African countries in their efforts to promote climate change adaptation and mitigation actions.

1.2 Regional Variations in Climate Change Effects

The African continent is not homogeneous in terms of climate change. Africa is characterised by diverse topographical, climatic, and socioeconomic settings that create significant variation in its impacts and effects. Africa's climate is dominated by desert conditions along vast stretches of its northern and southern fringes. The central portion of the continent is wetter, with tropical rainforests, grasslands, and semi-arid climates (see Fig. 1) (Britannica 2023).

The heterogeneity of climatic conditions across various African regions results in regional variabilities of climate change impacts. For instance, there have been increased dry spells in some areas, while others experience pluvial flooding and noticeable reductions in mean precipitation (United Nations Framework Convention on Climate Change (UNFCCC) 2020). These differences call for regional contextualised climate finance and investment solutions. For example, water scarcity has

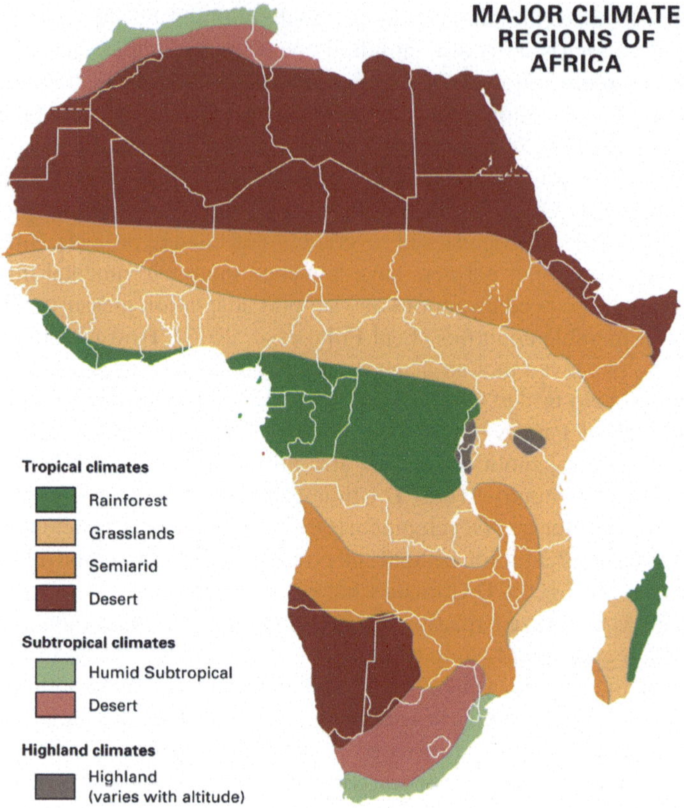

Fig. 1 African climate—regional variations. *Source* Britannica (2023)

become more prevalent in Northern Africa, whereas altered rainfall patterns continue to affect food security in sub-Saharan Africa. Specifically, crop yields in sub-Saharan Africa have decreased as a result of climate change, thereby lowering agricultural productivity. Changing weather patterns create a broad range of security risks, including climate-induced migration, which is common in the Horn of Africa. The coastal regions around the south Indian Ocean and other areas neighbouring the continent are at risk of rising sea levels. In early 2022, four consecutive tropical cyclones developed in the southern Indian Ocean, crossed over Africa, and made landfall in Madagascar and other parts of East Africa (EUMETSAT 2023). While oceans absorb approximately 90% of anthropogenic warming, it has been noted that the Indian Ocean is warming at a faster rate (Roxy et al. 2020). This has probably raised the occurrence of tropical cyclones in East and Southern Africa, as 2018 and 2019 contained the strongest tropical cyclones on record that affected Mozambique and Somalia. Today, cyclones affect not only coastal areas but also inland countries, such as Zimbabwe and Malawi.

Temperatures in major cities in East Africa have also increased above the global average warming since pre-industrial times. Since 1860, Addis Ababa (Ethiopia) has experienced warming of 2.2 °C, with 2.09 °C of warming being reported in Khartoum (Sudan), 1.9 °C in Dar es Salaam (Tanzania), 1.9 °C in Mogadishu (Somalia), and 1.9 °C of warming being recorded in Nairobi (Kenya) (ICPAC 2021). On the whole, East Africa has encountered varying climatic challenges. Weber et al. (2018) has posited that even if the increase in global temperatures is limited to well below 2 °C, in accordance with the ambitious target of the Paris Agreement, some regions might still be substantially affected by climate change, especially in continents like Africa, where the socio-economic conditions are strongly linked to climatic conditions.

While coastal areas are facing increased flooding as a result of rising sea levels, regions such as the Ethiopian Highlands suffer from more frequent droughts. The changing climate patterns have also impacted the Great Lakes and the economies that depend on agriculture. Rising ocean levels continue to threaten dozens of Africa's rapidly expanding coastal metropolises, resulting in shrinking land areas, coastal flooding, and more powerful storm surges, thus calling for better mitigation efforts (The Africa Center for Strategic Studies 2022).

In the case of Southern Africa, countries are experiencing an increased incidence and severity of droughts and heatwaves, which mainly affect the availability of water for domestic use, as well as for agriculture. Mozambique and Madagascar, among other countries, are also experiencing intensive cyclones, which cause severe socioeconomic disruptions.

With increased temperature and altered rainfall patterns, the Sahel is vulnerable to desertification and food insecurity. Such changes are also increasing temperatures and reducing rainfall over the North Africa region, which is predominantly a desert, thus worsening the already-existing water shortage problem in the region. Increased temperature and rainfall pattern changes in the Nile Basin have led to water stress and decreased agricultural productivity. In Central Africa, a variation in rainfall patterns is being noted in the Congo Basin and its large rainforests (Barimalala et al. 2023). The area is relatively less arid than other regions; however, more variable rainfall affects useful river flows, hydroelectric power generation, and biodiversity.

West Africa consists of a combination of both coastal and inland countries, which are also experiencing changing rainfall patterns, resulting in wider droughts and floods. Such variability has great effects on the important economic sector of agriculture and contributes to desertification, especially in the Sahel region. However, the southern parts of West Africa are affected by the type of climate change that contributes to soil erosion and flooding, while the northern areas continue to record some of their highest annual temperatures (UN Climate Change News 2020).

Each region in Africa requires targeted climate finance and investment solutions due to its distinct climate challenges. Consequently, the challenge for Africa is to understand these regional variations so that it can come up with effective climate finance and investment strategies that are tailor-made to appropriately address these specific problems.

1.3 Climate Action and Plans Across Africa

It is interesting to note that Africa has contributed the least towards the global emissions of GHG relative to other continents, and yet the continent remains one of the most affected by climate change. This paradox exists because the impacts of GHGs are borderless; in other words, it is impossible to completely contain the emitted gases within the geographical areas in which they are generated. There is, therefore, the need for global joint climate actions and coordinated strategic plans in the fight against global warming and its detrimental impacts. In this regard, the governments of African nations have recognised this need and shown strong commitments to dealing with climate change, especially in the African Union's Agenda 2063 (Cross 2017) and African Renewable Energy Initiatives. Key African climate change policies, initiatives, and agreements include the New Partnership for Africa's Development Climate Change Fund (NEPAD Climate Change Fund). In addition, African states are beginning to appreciate the need for collective regional efforts to combat climate change. A clear example is the continent's Agenda 2063, a strategic agenda that stresses climate-resilient economies and sustainable natural resource management. The transformation framework of Agenda 2063 recognizes the diversity of the continent. Each country being inspired by the same set of goals and targets will develop policies and strategies adapted to its circumstances while learning from the diverse, unique and shared experiences of various countries and regions as a basis of forging an African approach to transformation (African Union (AU) 2015). The Paris Agreement also inspired African states to develop their NDCs. Each country's strategies are described in the NDCs, which display the targeted climate actions and goals (United Nation (UN) 2017). The variations across the NDCs are particularly significant when assessing how different conditions relate to the environmental, economic, and social factors that apply across African states and sub-regions. For instance, in Kenya and Ethiopia, priority is given to renewable energy projects, while Nigeria focuses on reforestations and afforested initiatives.

Being a continent that is highly vulnerable to climate change—with drought, floods, and even desertification being some of the main effects—adaptation measures are predominant in many countries on the African continent. These include growing climate-resilient agriculture, increased water saving, and investment in worn-out infrastructure. African governments are also increasingly recognising the importance of local knowledge and participation in their climate action plans. Local community involvement could guarantee that climate action plans are in line with the systems and cultures of the direct beneficiaries, thereby increasing their success rate over time.

In many cases, climate actions in Africa have been deeply shaped by financial inputs. A number of crucial resources have been contributed by international partnerships and instruments in the form of bilateral and multilateral cooperation. Substantial efforts have been channelled toward the development of NDCs, such as climate-smart agriculture practices and renewable energy programmes. Despite the progress achieved, resource and technology limitations are still significant obstacles. However, these limitations may be potential sources of opportunity for regional integration, broader international cooperation, technology transfers, and the overall creation of a sustainable economy.

1.3.1 Overview of Key Initiatives and Plans

The intensity of the impacts of climate change in Africa calls for a collective and well-coordinated approach, as it presents an unprecedented challenge. Africa's unique vulnerabilities and opportunities in the face of climate change have attracted several key initiatives and strategic plans, both continentally and globally, in recent years. These initiatives aim to tap into renewable energy potential and fight desertification. They have been critical milestones along Africa's sustainability journey and improved resilience to climate change. Although they have encountered some challenges, if they continue to be implemented, their impacts could be felt across the continent in terms of environmental benefits, economic gains, and social implications. Some of these major initiatives are outlined below.

Africa Renewable Energy Initiative (AREI)

The Africa Renewable Energy Initiative (AREI) is an ambitious effort launched in 2015 by the African Union (AU), together with the African Group of Negotiators, Least Developed Countries Group, United Nations, and International Renewable Energy Agency (IRENA), among other partners (Engel 2023). This initiative was designed to help unlock the huge renewable energy potential in Africa and scale up access to clean, reliable, and affordable electricity in African countries. AREI's leading objective is to reach a minimum of 10 gigawatts (GW) of additional new renewable energy generation capability by 2020 and at least 300 GW by 2030. It also seeks to provide technical assistance and capacity-building support to relevant national and regional stakeholders (United Nations 2015). AREI aims to provide sustainable and affordable energy for all, especially in underserved rural areas. The initiative is part of a wider sustainable development project with a variety of climate change objectives, and it is expected to significantly help the region achieve its Paris Agreement goals. The AREI encourages collaboration between various African regions to tap into the potential of different kinds of renewable energy, such as solar, wind, hydro, and geothermal sources. These proposed initiatives include technology transfer, innovation, and local capacity building in renewable energy technologies. Public and private financing are combined to fund AREI. The major international donors in support of the objectives of AREI are Germany, France, and the European Union (AREI 2019). The organisation provides a conducive policy environment in African countries for investment attraction and renewable energy technology deployment. However, there is still the major challenge of setting up the required infrastructure for renewable energy, especially in remote regions. Therefore, it is essential to ensure consistent and adequate funding. AREI has also created employment opportunities and innovation projects along technological lines, while further promoting the diversification of the economy.

Great Green Wall Initiative

The Great Green Wall Initiative is a continent-wide project designed to combat desertification and land degradation in the Sahara and Sahel, the most vulnerable zones of Economic Community of West African States (ECOWAS) with respect to climate change. The AU initiated this project in 2007 with the aim of creating a mosaic of green productive landscapes across North Africa, the Sahel, and the Horn. The primary objective was to stop the spread of the Sahara Desert by planting a long wall of trees across the African continent, starting from Senegal in the West to Djibouti in the East. Its ambition is to restore 100 million hectares of currently degraded land, sequester 250 million tonnes of carbon, and create 10 million green jobs by 2030 (United Nations Convention to Combat Desertification (UNCCD) 2007). Thousands of villages throughout Africa are expected to be reborn as a result of this massive undertaking, which is taking place in 22 different nations. With the Pan-African Agency of the Great Green serving as the guiding light, this organisation has united African nations with their foreign counterparts. This groundbreaking effort has received over USD 8 billion in funding. The initiative is also focused on maintaining biodiversity, improving natural habitats, and developing more climate-change-resilient ecosystems. By mainly engaging in sustainable land and water management practices, it aims to enhance living conditions for the affected communities, primarily in rural areas. Generally, the initiative is a grassroots operation that involves tree planting and sustainable land management practices in the local communities. This approach to land management combines reforestation with the sustainable practice of agriculture. Some of the project's international partners include the United Nations, the World Bank, and the European Union, among others. Nevertheless, there are logistical challenges to its execution due to the sheer scale of the project. The project also emerged at a time when there were increasingly erratic weather patterns due to climate change. Regardless, the initiative is still aimed at promoting rural development, poverty alleviation, and community empowerment.

African Union's Agenda 2063

Agenda 2063 is the AU's strategic framework for the socioeconomic transformation of the African continent over 50 years from 2013 to 2063. This is Africa's blueprint and master plan for transforming Africa into the global powerhouse of the future (Union 2013). It presents a compelling vision for an integrated, high-performance African economy capable of sustainable growth and development. A crucial element in realising their vision is mitigating climate change and supporting the transformation of the economies. Accordingly, emphasis must be placed on sustainable and inclusive people-centred economic growth. The initiative is devoted to the formulation and implantation of climate-resilient and low-carbon development strategies to reduce environmental impacts. By 2063, Africa is expected to have undergone a total change in its economies anchored on diversification and industrialisation. Its agenda is aligned with its long-term vision of national development plans, as its focus remains on regional cooperation to promote economic growth. Agenda 2063 also seeks to instil the use of green technologies and practices within different sectors. It anticipates enhancing partnerships internally among African states and with international partners for the purposes of technology transfer, capacity building, and financing. However, developing strong policy and institutional frameworks for implementation is not easy. Accordingly, the AU is currently attempting to generate sufficient resources for the continuous financing of Agenda 2063 projects and initiatives. As a broader initiative, the agenda also seeks to attend to exploitation, innovation, sustainable industrialisation, and intra-African trade.

Africa Climate Change Fund (ACCF)

The AfDB established the ACCF in April 2014 with an initial contribution of € 4.725 million from the Government of Germany, with the aim of supporting African countries in transitioning to sustainable, low-carbon growth and building climate resilience. The ACCF was converted to a multi-donor trust fund in 2017, with contributions from the governments of Flanders, Belgium, and Italy. Global Affairs Canada and the Government of Quebec joined the fund in 2020 and the Global Center on Adaptation in 2022. The current trust size is USD 25.71 million (African Development Bank (AfDB) 2023). The role of the ACCF in funding climate change projects and strategies throughout Africa cannot be overstated. It sets out to build resilience by assisting countries in embracing strategies that will help them adapt to climate change effects, achieve low-carbon development through transitioning into low-carbon-based economies, and enhance capacity building and technical assistance for improved climate governance, as well as policy implementation among African countries. The ACCF is also involved in the provision of grants for projects that deal with climate adaptation and mitigation, thereby supporting the development and implementation of good climate policies, as well as promoting the dissemination of best practices learned from efforts in adapting to and mitigating climatic changes. Since its establishment in 2014, 26 of the awarded projects amounting to USD 15.89 million have been authorised by the ACCF Governing Committees (African Development Bank (AfDB) 2023). One of the main challenges facing the ACCF is the assurance that resources are assigned and allocated efficiently and equitably among various projects or countries. Additional challenges include evaluating the sustainability and overall effect of funded projects over long periods, as well as involving different stakeholders, such as government NGOs and local communities, to guarantee relevance. The ACCF is an integral effort in climate action towards bridging financial gaps and ensuring the development of efficient solutions to counter global warming in Africa.

Nationally Determined Contributions (NDCs)

The Paris Agreement requires that all parties establish self-defined NDCs and be committed to the actual goals of climate change mitigation and adaptation. African countries have presented their NDCs by pointing out the specifics of each country and indicating that they are participating in global efforts to reduce the impact of global warming. At present, 53 African counties have actively filed their NDCs in accordance with Article 4, paragraph 12 of the Paris Agreement. NDCs usually have targets for minimising greenhouse gas (GHG) emissions, most often with specific commitments to renewable energy transition and increased energy efficiency, as well as improved carbon sinks. They also articulate strategies for mitigating the effects of climate change and addressing vulnerabilities in sectors such as agriculture, water resources, and health (Onuoha et al. 2023). The NDCs are anchored in national development objectives to ensure that climate actions support the goals of economic and social development. African countries are incorporating NDCs into national policies as an implementation strategy, making climate action a core feature of development planning. Ensuring international and domestic finance for conducting NDC commitment, including expenditures for green technology and infrastructure, is paramount. African countries are also interested in developing national capacities for NDC implementation, monitoring, and updating, as well as reporting on progress. As at the end of 2022, a total of 47 African countries submitted their updated NDCs. These new NDCs have higher levels of ambition and quality and are more inclusive. Emission reduction targets in African NDCs have been increased by 6.9% on average over a wider scope of gases and sectors. The new NDCs display more detailed implementation, financing, and Monitoring, Reporting and Verification (MRV) plans, with more than 80% of updated NDCs provide cost estimates for their implementation, which will make it easier to develop investment plans, and total estimates amount to USD 1.2 trillion leading up to 2030 (The Africa NDC Hub 2022). Despite the enthusiasm, African countries are particularly constrained by generating the necessary funds and technical capacity needed to fully implement their NDCs. They have also faced challenges in providing forthright data systems for monitoring purposes to take stock of what has been done and make necessary adjustments. Nevertheless, the NDCs still have the potential to promote sustainable development, enhance energy access, and develop more green jobs.

1.3.2 Role of International Agreements in Promoting Climate Actions in Africa

International agreements play a crucial role in climate finance and investment strategies in Africa. They act as a basis for cooperation, direction, and resourcing. Policies at the local level are also influenced by international agreements, and such an effect makes countries more inclined to adopt climate change domestication. The key agreements in this regard are the Paris Agreement, the Glasgow Climate Pact, and UN Sustainable Development Goals (SDGs).

Paris Agreement

The Paris Agreement is a global convention adopted in 2015 at the twenty-first session of the Conference of the Parties (COP21) to the UNFCCC. This initiative gives all countries one common point of reference in addressing climate change and adaptation, which is supported by increased financing for developing countries. Under the Paris Agreement, African countries have developed their NDCs, which provide the targets and their commitments to mitigating greenhouse gas emissions and adapting to climate change impacts. In particular, this agreement allows for financial support to be provided to African countries to develop renewable power sources, forestry, and sustainable agriculture. Moreover, technological and capacity-building support in Africa is accommodated by the Paris Agreement. From this point of view, the Paris Agreement enables the adaptation of green technologies and relevant building capacities for many African nations that are moving towards sustainability.

Glasgow Climate Pact

The Glasgow Climate Pact, which was ratified at the 26th session of the Conference of the Parties (COP26) to the UNFCCC in Glasgow (2021), builds upon the Paris Agreement's commitments to underline the growing demand for such action and support. The pact reaffirms the commitment of developed countries to raise US 100 billion per annum for climate action in developing states, which is particularly important with regard to Africa's climate finance. It acknowledges the special climate change risks facing African states and their need for adequate resources to tackle them. The agreement emphasises the need to build resilience and develop climate adaptation measures in Africa, calling on all nations to phase down unabated coal power and inefficient subsidies for fossil fuels.

Sustainable Development Goals (SDGs)

The 2030 Agenda for Sustainable Development is a central blueprint for achieving a better and more sustainable future for all. In particular, SDG 13 targets climate change. The framework allows African countries to embed climate change in their national policies, strategies, and planning with SDG 13 as a guiding principle. This is immensely important for African countries, because SDGs have adopted an 'agenda' approach by linking climate actions to other meaningful goals, such as poverty alleviation, health, education, and economic development. Generally, the SDGs provide a framework for monitoring and reporting climate action and promoting transparency and accountability in the context of climate projects.

Collectively, these international agreements provide African countries with a roadmap for sustainable development and climate resilience. This implies that for Africa's case of climate change to be addressed, there is a need for global partnerships, adequate funding, technology transfer, and capacity building.

1.4 Demand for Climate Finance in Africa

Investment in climate change in Africa has become a necessity to target the continent's specific vulnerabilities with respect to the attainment of the SDGs. In Africa, climate finance has been geared towards adaptation and mitigation measures. Adaptation aims at the development of resilience in communities, infrastructure, and economies for climate change impacts. Such projects include enhanced water management, climate-resilient agriculture, and the reinforcement of improved coastal defenses. Mitigation, however, seeks to lower greenhouse gas emissions through initiatives of developing clean or renewable energy, conserving forests, and sustainable transport systems, among others.

Climate phenomena such as droughts, floods, and rising sea levels are often experienced in Africa, a continent with diverse ecosystems and economies that rely heavily on agriculture and natural resources. According to estimates from the Climate Policy Initiative, the continent requires USD 277 billion every year to work in accordance with the NDCs so as to meet 2030 climate goals. However, at the moment, annual climate finance flows in Africa are only around USD 30 billion. This leaves Africa with a huge financing gap, as the demand continues to increase year after year. According to the African Economic Outlook 2022 report by the AfDB, the continent has an estimated climate finance gap of up to USD 1.2 trillion annually from 2020 to 2030 (African Development Bank (AfDB) 2022). With this escalating demand for climate financing in Africa, the AfDB has moved to triple its climate financing commitment as a means of promoting a resilient Africa. In addition, the Global Center on Adaptation and others including Denmark, France, the Netherlands, Norway, and the United Kingdom have pledged to provide substantial financial support for Africa's climate projects by prioritizing Africa in their adaptation finance scaling efforts, including through support to the Africa Adaptation Acceleration Program (AAAP), and called on other developed nations to take similar steps to close the adaptation finance gap affecting African nations on the climate frontlines (Global Center on Adaptation 2023).

To address climate change, 29 donor nations provided climate-targeted official development assistance (ODA) to African nations between 2018 and 2020, which amounted to USD 27.8 billion (Development Initiatives 2022). Within this period, 73.7% of all ODA pertaining to climate change in Africa came from the top five donors (see Fig. 2). Funded adaptation initiatives mirrored the priorities in the nation's adaptation plans and NDCs, as the allocation of funds by purpose (adaptation or mitigation) varies from country to country. To be effective over the long term, adaptation funding needs a solid framework for implementation. More general vulnerabilities,

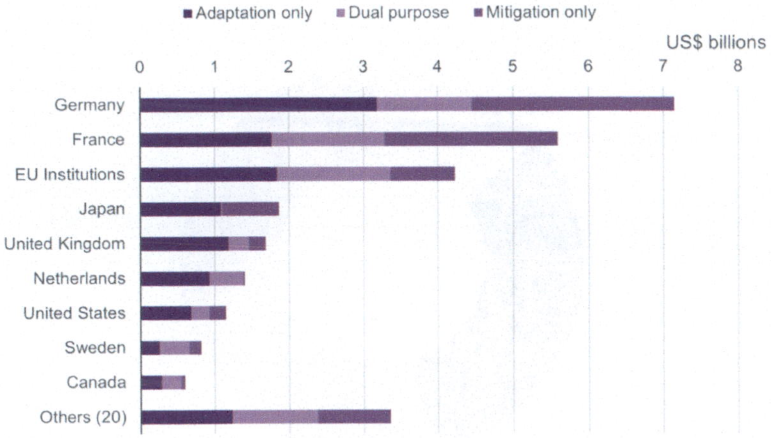

Fig. 2 Major donors of climate-related ODA to Africa, 2018–2020. *Source* Development Initiatives (2022)

such as those associated with instability and conflict in some African countries, may also be reflected in this mix of finances.

Multilateral climate funds, such as the Green Climate Fund (GCF), are also major sources of climate financing, aside from bilateral funding sources. In total, Africa has received 46% of adaptation finance disbursed by multilateral funds globally, which has amounted to USD 2.95 billion. Out of this distributed multinational climate fund, only 14% was allocated to fragile and conflict-affected states (FCAS) in Africa, while 32% was channelled to other more stable African countries (see Fig. 3). Oftentimes, the FCAS in Africa are the most susceptible to the effects of climate change. These nations have a weak ability to deal with climatic shocks, as well as broader and interconnected social, economic, and political unrest. In contexts of heightened vulnerability, where risk management capabilities are inadequate, and climate shocks have the potential to trigger broader, longer-lasting crises, adaptation funding—particularly for projects involving cross-border approaches—becomes even more crucial.

Grants accounted for 65% of the climate finance committed to Africa (Fig. 4). On the one hand, multilateral climate funds provide grants to African countries, which constitute the majority of the climate funding provided to these countries. On the other hand, 33% is provided in the form of concessional loans (see Fig. 4). It is possible for climate-vulnerable countries that are experiencing significant levels of debt distress to suffer negative consequences from allocation in the form of loans. As a result of debt distress, a nation may become more susceptible to the effects of climate change. In extreme circumstances, when debt hardship becomes rampant, such conditions can add to unmanageable debt loads and worsen the country's situation, leading to an economic crisis. To prevent climate-vulnerable nations from becoming entangled in crisis cycles, it is of the utmost importance that climate change finance come mostly in the form of grants.

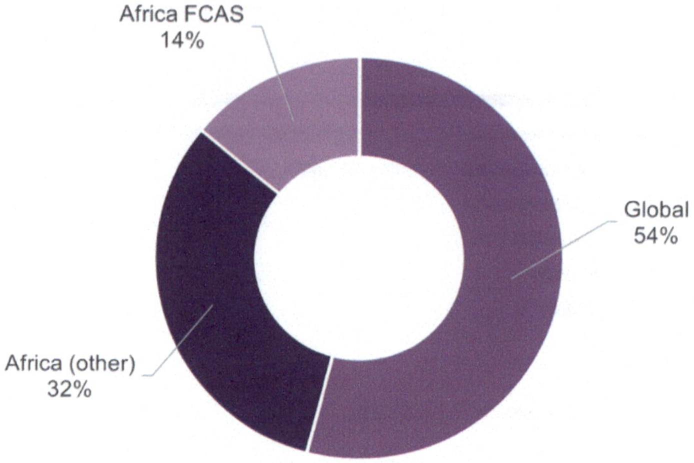

Fig. 3 Share of multilateral climate funds. *Source* Development Initiatives (2022)

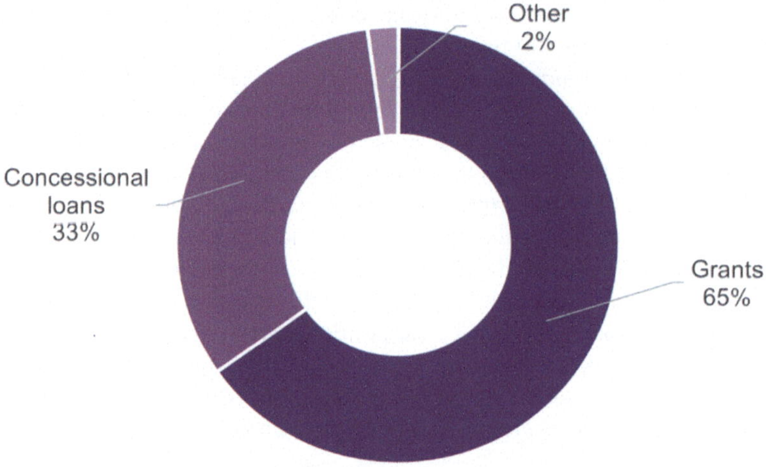

Fig. 4 Types of climate funding for Africa. *Source* Development Initiatives (2022)

In a related vein, ODA for climate change mitigation, adaptation, and dual objectives increased between 2018 and 2020. Nevertheless, the yearly pledge of USD 100 billion was still unmet, and the amounts allocated differed substantially among nations. From 2018 to 2020, Africa received a cumulative total of USD 27.8 billion in climate-related ODA, which was largely channelled to countries south of the Sahara (Development Initiatives 2022). Out of this, USD 22.4 billion was allocated to country-specific projects, and USD 5.5 billion was committed to projects at the regional level (see Fig. 5).

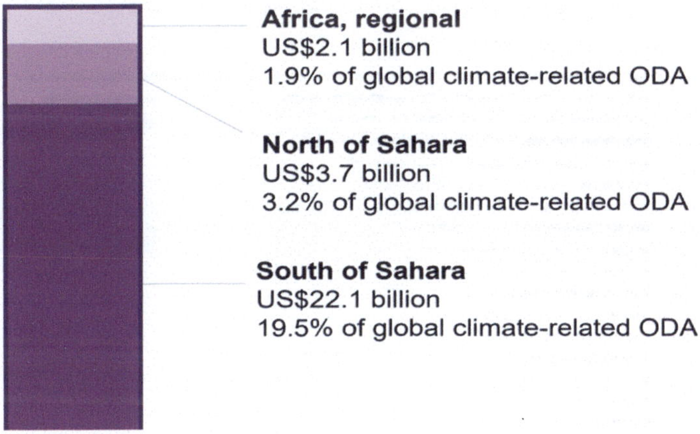

Fig. 5 Climate-related ODA to Africa Between 2018 and 2020. *Source* Development Initiatives (2022)

Generally, it can be concluded that ODA to Africa related to climate change is unevenly allocated. Between 2018 and 2020, 27.3% of all climate-related aid went to only three countries in Africa (Kenya, Ethiopia, and Morocco) (Fig. 5). Despite the fact that the continent received over 25% of all climate-centred ODA within this three-year period, the uneven distribution of these climate funding aids left the majority of the African countries with meagre amounts, thereby causing them to struggle with their adaptation actions (Fig. 6).

Whereas climate finance is in high demand in Africa, problems such as capital inadequacy, technology gaps, capacity-building weaknesses, policy incompetence, and political instabilities continue to worsen the situation in many countries on the continent. Nevertheless, many African governments have a strong desire for technology transfers and requisite capacities to drive sustainable climate solutions to boost economic development. Owing to this enthusiasm, it is worth pointing out that for climate projects to be successful and drive growth in Africa, expertise and capacity at the local level with respect to planning, implementation, and management must be developed. Furthermore, enabling policies and governance structures are necessary to facilitate the flow of climate finance and its efficient deployment.

Overall, the high demand for climate finance in Africa shows the commitment of the continent towards the fight against the damaging effects of climate change. In fact, a significant amount of progress has been made in the process of resource mobilisation. That being said, there is still a substantial climate financing gap that needs to be filled to satisfy all of the continent's demands and successfully reach climate change targets. Supporting Africa in the fight is not only important for African countries in terms of ensuring their self-sustainability and prosperity, but it is also a critical measure to curb global warming.

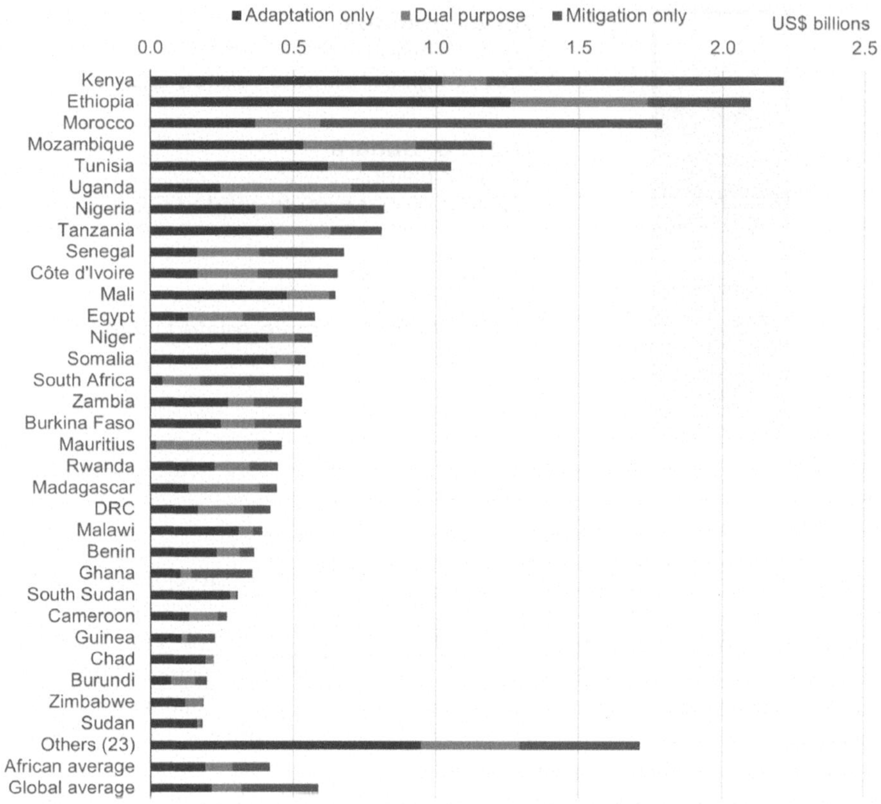

Fig. 6 Climate-related ODA volumes to countries in Africa, 2018–2020. *Source* Development Initiatives (2022)

1.4.1 Importance of Financial Support in Combating Climate Change

Investments in renewable energy, climate-smart agriculture, and infrastructure resilient to climate change are essential for the development of the African continent. The finance gap and the peculiar problems affecting Africa show that the continent needs sufficient climate funding support. More specifically, financial support in the fight against climate change is important for a number of reasons in Africa, which will be outlined below.

Adaptation Measures

There are many reasons why Africa needs to adapt to climate change, and hence, the requirement for financial assistance becomes inevitable. Indeed, Africa remains the most vulnerable to the impacts of climate change for a number of reasons, including poverty, poor infrastructure, and weak technology. Thus, adaptive strategies must be financially supported to ensure the continent's sustainable growth. Generally, the economic growth of Africa is related to climate-sensitive sectors, including farming and environmental administration. The majority of the population depends on rainfed agricultural activities as a means of survival, thereby exposing them to climate-related hazards. Financial support helps farmers embrace climate-based agriculture practices, including efficient irrigation systems, drought resilient crop varieties, and sustainable land management technologies. These practices can be used as a means of increasing production, exercising resilience against climatic effects, and ensuring food safety during climatic change.

Most African infrastructure is poor at adapting to climate change. In so many parts of the continent, where there are insufficient road networks and drainage systems, floods caused by excess rainfall can cause greater losses (Boko et al. 2007). In other instances, heavy rains may cause floods, which destroy public utilities, like road networks and water supplies, leading to difficulties in transport and communications, among other challenges in accessing important services. Climate-resistant infrastructure costs a lot of money, and it is therefore imperative that such investments are backed by financial support.

Moreover, Africa does not have the appropriate technology required for effective adaptation to climate change. The availability of climate data, early warning systems, and advanced technologies in Africa is restricted, making it hard for the continent to prepare and respond to such threats. Financing can promote technology transfer, capacity building, and information exchange by helping Africa create functional adaptation approaches. In addition, this support could enhance creativity and nurture the development of localised answers aimed at addressing distinctively African problems.

Finally, tackling climate change adaptation in Africa is both an environmental necessity and a moral responsibility. African nations are always the minor contributors to global warming gases but bear most of the consequences. A changing climate worsens inequity situations and impedes the attainment of sustainable development aims. African countries require financial support from the developed world in fulfilment of the principle of equity, which will consequently usher in a fairer and lasting tomorrow.

Therefore, in light of the above considerations, climate change adaptation has become crucial for Africa, considering that it is especially vulnerable to climate change, dependent on climate-sensitive sectors, and has poor infrastructure and an inadequate technology base, yet still bears the moral responsibility to enact climate justice. Effective adaptation measures, resilience building, and sustainable development require significant financial support. Investing in Africa's adaptation efforts would thus benefit the continent while also contributing towards global efforts to mitigate climate change for an equal world.

Mitigation Actions

Mitigating the impact of climate change includes the actions taken to cut down emissions and maintain a steady state within the earth's climate system. Africa is a sensitive area that is particularly vulnerable to climate change because it relies mainly on agriculture, with very little capacity to be adaptive, and many poor people. As such, Africa should receive adequate financing if it aspires to effectively control climate change in an effective manner. To build resilience in Africa, measures such as building early warning centres, flood defenses, and resilient agriculture practices are of necessity. However, without substantial financial inputs, the mentioned measures cannot be implemented by the African states due to a lack of capacity, thus making their people and economies especially vulnerable to climate change effects.

The continent of Africa is rich in renewable energy sources, such as solar, wind, and hydropower. However, due to the significant capital costs involved in setting up renewable energy facilities, deployment proves elusive. African states can also be assisted in going green through the financing of renewable energy projects, capacity building, and technology transfer. Such moves will help reduce carbon emissions and improve energy access while reducing dependency on petroleum. Also, as agricultural activity remains the major source of employment in many African countries and constitutes an important contribution towards food security, provisions of financial support to African famers could facilitate their undertaking of some climate-smart agriculture practices, such as conservation agriculture, agroforestry, and efficient irrigation technology. Such activities may improve productivity, lower emission levels, and mitigate climate change impacts.

Forests with enormous potential for carbon sequestration exist in large proportions in Africa, and they remain critical for sustaining biodiversity. Financial support is required to assist African nations in curbing deforestation and forest degradation, which are major causes of GHG emissions. Reforestation in such lands could further assist in restoring degraded lands to improve carbon sink capacity. Reforestation has been found to be useful in environmental conservation as it reduces global warming, protects the local flora and fauna, and creates jobs, thus supporting the livelihood of people (Climate Impact Partners 2023).

Additionally, African countries may not have adequate skills, information, or technology to mitigate climate change. The provision of financial support in African states will promote activities such as training and technology exchange, as well as aid in developing climate change counteract measures. Accordingly, developed countries are making commitments to provide financial assistance to African countries in their endeavours to cope with the mitigation and adaptation of climate change actions. For instance, at the 28th Conference of Parties (COP28) of the UNFCCC, Parties within COP have pledged USD 700 million in funding to help lower-income countries recover from the effects of climate change. While this is a huge milestone for climate justice, the funding still falls extremely short of what climate-vulnerable populations will need to rebuild their homes, livelihoods and communities when climatic disasters inevitably strike (Afghanaid 2023).

In sum, it is imperative that African countries receive adequate financial support as they battle climate change. Building resilience, transitioning into renewable energy, adopting sustainable agricultural practices, conserving forests, and enhancing capacity and technology transfer are crucial. The international community can help Africa cope with the effects of climate change so as to reduce vulnerabilities towards sustainable development through financial assistance.

Enabling Technology Transfer and Capacity Building

Financial support for Africa's efforts to overcome climate change is essential, as it allows for technology transfer and the strengthening of capacity. Technology requirements for the successful adaptation of mitigation measures in many African countries do not exist. These include access to sophisticated renewable energy technology, climatic monitoring systems, and climatic modelling mechanisms. Financial assistance plays an enormous role in closing this gap, as it may be used to facilitate technology transfers, finance research and development (R&D), and enable initiatives.

The African continent has aimed to realise the SDGs with regard to climate change, the alleviation of poverty, and sustainable economic growth. These goals, however, come with a huge financial need. Integrating climate change considerations into African countries' development plans and policies could be financially supported, which would assist their efforts in meeting the SDGs. The commitment that Africa has undertaken in the international climate treaties includes reducing carbon footprints and boosting its adaptability to global change. Nevertheless, implementing these commitments requires a lot of money. Funding would help Africa meet its pledge to climate change through financing renewable energy, energy conservation, and adaptation to environmental changes. Technology transfer that entails sharing green technologies and knowledge-based resources with less-developed states is also vital. These technologies may be facilitated through financial assistance in acquiring the technologies, training in how to use them, and further developmental capacities.

Africa faces a huge financial deficit when it comes to fighting the effects of global warming. These countries can rarely afford the high costs incurred by climate change mitigation and adaptation. The financial gap could be bridged through the provision of grants, concessional loans, and technical advice to African countries, so that they may invest in climate-friendly technologies and build capacity for tackling different climate change challenges.

Ultimately, technology transfer and capacity building are key determinants of Africa's ability to tackle climate change effectively. The provision of finance acts as a major tool capable of addressing the technological and financial gaps in Africa. Funding for technology transfer, R&D, and climate change-related capacity-building measures will enable African countries to reinforce their climate change resilience and meet the SDGs and international climate commitments while bridging climate financing gaps. In effect, climate finance is an essential component of the climate change war in Africa. Financial support not only helps nations to make the required changes, but also minimises impacts in the future, thereby building a sustainable and resilient future.

1.4.2 Challenges in Securing Adequate Climate Finance in Africa

Africa faces challenges in attracting climate finance despite the continent's huge demand for climate finance and investment. As a result, implementing climate action plans becomes difficult due to a lack of funds. Securing sufficient climate finance is one of the pivotal phases in Africa's pursuit of dealing with climate change and promoting green growth. However, the continent has many challenges that impede the proper mobilisation and utilisation of climate finance.

Limited Access to International Climate Finance Mechanisms

Indeed, one of the biggest challenges Africa faces in its efforts towards securing sufficient financial aid and investments to combat the effects of climate change is the limited access to international climate finance mechanisms. Most African states are deficient in critical institutional capabilities, technical competence, and sufficient finances to facilitate effective engagement with international climate change capital resources. This inhibits them from formulating strong project proposals that fulfil strict eligibility requirements across a range of applications that are not easy to follow. In addition, African countries generally have limited information and knowledge on existing climate funds. These mechanisms could remain inaccessible if people are uninformed about the available range of funding sources, eligibility for funding, and how to apply for such assistance. The lack of knowledge of climate options hinders many from accessing any such avenue.

Moreover, Africa lacks favourable investment conditions to attract substantial amounts of climate-related investment. Challenges faced in the creation of conducive environments for investments in climate finance in Africa include political instability, poor governance, corruption, and other regulatory constraints. These factors repel potential investors and hinder African countries' efforts to attract private sector investment, which could be used to tackle climate change effects. Similarly, many international climate finance systems are primarily providing loans, and grant or concession financing is not significantly attracted by the African continent. African nations, most of which are already overburdened by debt, may be hesitant to commit to new loans. For example, the runaway debt burden in Africa has led to many countries defaulting or at the brink of defaulting on their external debt in a desperate move to restore macroeconomic sustainability. As at 2023, 23 low-income African countries are at high risk, or already in debt distress according to the IMF and World Bank. 4 African sovereigns namely Zambia, Mali, Ghana, and Mozambique have defaulted or stopped debt servicing and are turning to the IMF for support (African

Forum and Network on Debt and Development (AFRODAD) 2023). This makes difficult for these countries to contract additional loan facilities to finance climate change actions.

Limited Domestic Financial Mechanisms and Institutional Capacity

Limited domestic financial mechanisms and institutional capacity is one of the major challenges Africa faces in gaining access to sufficient climate funds and investments to combat the effects of climate change. The underlying causes of these challenges include poor financial management, fragile institutions, and a lack of appropriate technologies. Many African countries have poor financial systems that suffer from limited access to capital markets, weak banking industries, and deficient financial infrastructure. This hinders them from realising the optimal usage of climate finance within their respective countries. In contrast, an effective financial system would promote further public investment, innovative financial product development, and good management of climate change funds, among other features.

Poor governance, corruption, and limited transparency are great obstacles to safeguarding climate change financing. These problems create doubt among investors and discourage international funding for climate change mitigation programmes. The limited accountability mechanisms and the inadequate regulatory framework make the challenge even harder to address by simply enhancing climate-fund management. Weak institutions and ineffective policies to attract external climate funds, coupled with limited domestic resource mobilisation negatively impacts climate change intervention and undermining mitigation efforts to reduce emissions (World Bank Group 2023). There has become a struggle to secure adequate climate finance due to increased competition among nations that depend on external resources. In terms of domestic sources, weak tax systems, low fiscal space, and other competing demands usually obstruct the process of domestic resource mobilisation.

The technical knowledge gap in climate financing and inadequate risk management capacities are also considerable barriers to accessing adequate climate financing by Africa. There are new emerging risks associated with climate change; hence, countries need to have established risk management systems. Unfortunately, African countries do not have the means or expertise to properly assess climate-related risks. This adds to the perceived risks of making investments in climate-related initiatives, thus scaring off would-be investors and financers. These issues call for a broad-based response that incorporates capacity enhancement in fiscal areas of the state, which would improve national governance mechanisms, boost domestic revenue mobilisation initiatives, and strengthen internal risk management processes.

Policy and Regulatory Barriers and Political Instability

The process of securing the required climate finance and investment is often hampered by existing policy, regulatory barriers, and political instability in Africa. The continent's inability to address these challenges undermines its response to climate change and adaptation. Some African nations have ill-defined, sporadic, and contradictory policies regarding climate change. These inconsistencies create uncertainties among investors, which make it hard for them to secure climate finances. Moreover, a lack of broad policies and legislative regimes impedes the launching of climate-friendly projects on a large scale, as well as hinders the expansion of renewable energy and environmentally friendly practices. The lack of adequate institutional capacities in African countries makes it hard for them to create and implement the best climate change policies. These limited capacities include a lack of technical competencies, insufficient supervision and evaluation mechanisms, and a general absence of effective inter-agency coordination. Credibility becomes affected due to limited capacity, which affects investment and climate financing in Africa because such projects must be carried out in trusted working institutions.

The African region is marred by a lot of political instability, coupled with widespread corruption that hinders investor confidence. These factors act as dissuasive features for domestic and external investors, and thus they may withhold investment in climate-change-related ventures. Corruption undermines confidence, raises the costs of projects, and directs funds away from climate change programmes. Unwarranted political instabilities, such as the fluctuation of governments or policy reversals, cause uncertainties that drive away investors who may otherwise commit to long-term measures for coping with climate change effects. Political instability, poor governance, and infrastructural challenges have contributed to a negative perception of Africa as a high-risk investment destination. Such conditions make potential investors believe that there are higher costs involved in investing in climate change-related projects, thus decreasing the attractiveness of such initiatives. The perception of high investment costs and the potential uncertainty of returns further hinder engagement of the private sector and limit access to financing.

Consequently, the existing policy and regulatory barriers, along with political instability, make it difficult for Africa to acquire sufficient climatic finances and investments. These issues must be addressed in an integrated manner by working with different stakeholders comprising fortified policy frameworks and institutions that combat corruption, a simple banking system, and improved data collection and sharing. Addressing these barriers adequately will make it possible for Africa to develop effective measures for counteracting the consequences of climate change and building a sustainable future.

Low Private Sector Engagement

Low engagement in the private sector is among the main challenges that hamper Africa from receiving sufficient climate financing and the required investments to combat climate effects. The continental struggle regarding how best to handle climate issues becomes difficult due to poor private sector participation, as well as the absence of appropriate technologies and resources. Notably, many developing nations, especially in Africa, usually have insufficient budget allocations towards climate change mitigation and adaptation efforts. Private sector involvement is necessary, as the public sector alone is unable to offer sufficient funding. Nevertheless, the private sector is more often cautious about its investments in climate-related projects because of the perceived uncertainties, risks, and lower returns.

African states have a poor investment climate, and this can be attributed to a lack of proper legal frameworks, poor road networks, and widespread corruption. These factors lead many in the private sector to consider climate change projects as unattractive investment avenues. Stable and transparent policies, regulations, and institutions in which investors' funds may be secured and earn returns are needed by investors. Investment risks associated with climate change projects derive from uncertainties in policy changes, markets, and the future of payoffs, which also make private investors tread cautiously in the African market. In addition, African countries suffer from political instability and weak governance and are especially vulnerable to climatic impacts, thus making potential investors perceive an elevated level of risk. The perception of this risk discourages the private sector from indulging in climate finance and investment.

Regrettably, the private sector in Africa is seldom aware and has little or no knowledge of the advantages of climate-related investments. The identification of the available investment options is hindered by poor information on the nature and hazards of climate change. Also, there is a lack of techno-capability in the private domain for designing low-carbon options. As such, Small and Medium Enterprises (SMEs) in Africa encounter various challenges when seeking financing for climate-based investments. Financial institutions are normally ignorant about issues concerning climate change and thus have less supply of appropriate financial instruments. Low levels of collateral, low-quality credit history, and poor financial literacy among SMEs further inhibit their access to climate finance.

Hence, providing sufficient resources to combat the effects of climate change on Africa requires tackling low private-sector engagement in climate finance and investment. By promoting conduciveness investment climate for private investors, generating awareness among potential investors on the benefits of investing in climate related projects, and mitigating the risks of investments and innovations in finance, Africa will attract sufficient funding and expertise to address the threats posed by climate change.

2 Current Climate Change Situation in Ghana

Ghana, like many other African countries, has been facing significant impacts of climate change over the years. Ghana is highly vulnerable to global climate change because its economy is predominantly supported by climatic-sensitive sectors, such as agriculture, forestry, and fishing. Ghana has made several efforts to improve its climate finance outlook amid these challenges. Specifically, the Ghana government has explored various means to attract climate finance in partnership with international and domestic donors and investors. An example is the nation's involvement in global actions such as the GCF, which actively supports climate activities. The critical factor that secures climate finance from the GCF is innovativeness, and funded programmes include the Ghana Shea Landscape Emission Reductions Project and the Program on Affirmative Finance Action for Women in Africa (AFAWA). Ghana has also come to appreciate the necessity of public–private partnerships (PPPs) in driving climate finance. This approach has allowed the nation to combine public funds with a partner's private investment in climate-resilient and low-carbon projects. Notably, the expansion of climate finance crucially revolves around the private sector, which is critical for scaling up climate finance and ensuring sustainable economic growth.

Several institutions are responsible for addressing climate change in Ghana. These include the Ministry of Environment, Science, Technology, and Innovation (MESTI), the Environmental Protection Agency (EPA), the Ministry of Finance (MoF), the National Development Planning Commission (NDPC), and the Ministry of Energy (MoE). MESTI is Ghana's lead agency for climate change coordination and implementation (MESTI 2021). MESTI's portfolio is very broad, and climate change is only a small part of what falls into the ministry's purview. MESTI receives technical support from the EPA, which also serves as the focal point of contact for the UNFCCC and coordinates Ghana's participation in international processes. Several ministries, departments, and agencies (MDA) have established climate change focal units. For example, the National Resources, Environment and Climate Change (NREC) Unit at the MoF oversees and coordinates climate finance in Ghana. The Climate Change Unit at the Forestry Commission serves as the national Reducing Emissions from Deforestation and Forest Degradation (REDD+) Secretariat, while at the Energy Commission, the Renewable Energy, Energy Efficiency, and Climate Change Divisions oversee climate change issues in the energy sector (United States Department of Agriculture (USDA) 2023).

Ghana must overcome various hurdles to fully realise the benefits of climate finance. These include minimal access capabilities to international climate funds, challenges in coordinating all the relevant stakeholders, and more specific policy frameworks that limit the attraction and use of climate finance. However, these challenges are also windows of opportunity for growth and improvement. In particular, the building of institutional capacities, the creation of enabling policies, and the promotion of PPPs would further enhance the climate finance landscape in Ghana.

As the need for innovative financial instruments, improved governance arrangements, and wider stakeholder involvement in navigating climate finance in Ghana becomes apparent among stakeholders, new pathways are emerging. This suggests that the country is incorporating climate concerns into its development agenda by seeking sustainable development and resilience to climatic conditions.

2.1 General Information About Ghana

Located in West Africa, Ghana is bordered on the west by Côte d'Ivoire, Burkina Faso to the north, Togo to the east, and the Gulf of Guinea to its south. It has an area of about 238,533 km^2. With two (rainy and dry) seasons in both the south and north regions, Ghana's climate ranges from tropical in the south to almost arid in the north. The country has a varied topography, which includes coastal savannahs to the south, tropical rainforests westward, and semi-arid regions in its north. Such a variable climate affects the agricultural sector, which is crucial in terms of crop yields and food security.

With a population of about 31.73 million, the country has rich cultural diversity encompassing different ethnic, linguistic, and religious groups. English, the country's official language, enables Ghana to act as a regional centre for trade and foreign relations. The largest city is the capital Accra, which serves as the economic and administrative hub of the country. Economically, the country is one of Africa's strongest economies, with a broad endowment of natural resources, including oil, gold, and cocoa. Nevertheless, it experiences problems such as unequal incomes and dependence on primary commodities. Agriculture continues to be a major sector in terms of the employing the largest section of the workforce and its significant contribution to the national GDP. At the same time, urbanisation and industrialisation continue on an upward trend, with services and manufacturing sectors increasing in their economic impact in recent years (Statista 2023).

Ghana is also politically acclaimed for its stability of democratic governments. In 1992, it became a democratic nation and has since maintained a strong example of peaceful elections conducted at regular intervals in the region. Nevertheless, deforestation, water pollution, and inadequate waste management continue to negatively affect the developmental strides in Ghana. To make matters worse, climate change has led to other problems, as it has had an adverse effect on agriculture, health, and economic growth in this region. Solving these problems is critical for the long-term development of Ghana and constitutes an important facet of the climate finance and investment terrain.

With the current state of affairs in this dynamic economy, the challenges of climate change are increasingly intensified in Ghana and largely affect its rural communities that predominantly depend on agriculture. How a country responds to climate change in terms of finance and investment is important for the course of its sustainable development. In the African context, Ghana leads by example when it comes to seeking international climate finance and engaging with sustainable projects and PPPs.

2.2 Economic Development and Environmental Impact

In recent years, Ghana has been celebrated for its political stability and its economic advancement in the West Africa region. Ghana's transition to middle-income status has resulted from this growth, with a major boost in oil production and other sectors, such as agriculture based on cocoa exports, gold mining, and energy coming mainly from fossil fuel sources. The resultant growth has helped improve infrastructure, healthcare, and education. However, this advancement has come along with problems, such as income gaps and regional imbalances, that jeopardise the country's long-term growth trajectory, in addition to eminent environmental challenges. One such case is the practice of traditional farming systems (e.g., slashing and burning bushes) and logging activities that lead to a high risk of deforestation, which have adversely affected biodiversity and further contributed to climate change. In the same vein, mining activities, especially the gold mining process, have led to land degradation and water pollution and have also posed dangers to human health. Moreover, overreliance on the traditional farming methods of burning contributes significantly to GHG emissions, which in turn negatively affects agricultural productivity.

Increased temperatures, erratic rainfall, and sea level rises are largely human-induced through economic activities. These changes threaten food security and livelihoods, especially for rural-based communities. In Ghana, the agricultural sector has become both the victim and contributor of these environmental challenges. Many agricultural practices come with negative side effects on the climate, including GHG emissions, deforestation, soil degradation, and depletion of water resources. At the same time, agriculture is adversely affected by climate change.

Mineral mining, especially gold mining, is a leading economic activity that has greatly affected the environment. These effects include deforestation, water pollution, and soil contamination. The sector's environmental footprint has necessitated a call for sustainable mining practices and sound ecological regulations. Fossil fuels and conventional biomass are largely used in Ghana's energy sector, with the resultant production of GHG. Therefore, Ghana has to make efforts towards the transition to renewable energy sources to further reduce its carbon footprint. In Ghana, rapid urbanisation has placed the environment under pressure in cities, a phenomenon triggered by air and water pollution, poor waste management, and environmental degradation. Thus, sustainable urban planning is also required, and further investment in green infrastructure is urgently needed.

Ghana has been successful in incorporating environmental factors into the planning of its economy. Specifically, the government of Ghana has put in place different policies and regulations that are concerned with enhancing sustainable development and protecting the environment. This entails promoting the use of renewable energy, adopting better agricultural practices, and encouraging sustainable mining practices. Climate finance has a role to play in supporting Ghana's transition to a sustainable development pathway. Investment in renewable energy, sustainable agriculture, and environmental conservation is critical for balancing economic growth with environmental protection. In this context, international funding, including that from the GCF and local initiatives, is key.

Overall, Ghana has experienced a variety of environmental concerns that call for immediate action as part of its economic development toward enhancing its socioeconomic status. Climate finance and investment are, consequently, important aspects of development in the country to ensure that Ghana's economy will rest on sustainable green growth.

2.2.1 Key Industries and Their Environmental Footprints

Ghana is endowed with certain essential industries, such as agriculture and mining, that account for a large portion of its economy but also have significant environmental footprints, thereby calling for more sustainable practices. Other leading industries include energy, manufacturing, and the tourist sector.

The agriculture sector is not only a major employer in the Ghanaian economy; it is also a major contributor to environmental challenges in the country. Slash and burn agriculture, as well as the misuse of fertilisers, lead to phenomena such as deforestation, soil depletion, and water pollution. At the same time, agricultural production is adversely influenced by issues related to global warming, such as unusual rainfall patterns and increasing warmth. In 2020, the agriculture sector of Ghana contributed 11.8 million tonnes of CO_2 equivalent ($MtCO_2e$) GHG emissions, which represented 30.27% of its total emissions excluding land-use change and forestry (39.1 $MtCO_2e$), and 82.06% including LUCF (14.41 $MtCO_2e$), as illustrated by Fig. 7 (Climate Watch 2021). Burning (savanna), enteric fermentation, and manure left on pastures are the major drivers of the agriculture sector's GHG emissions. This is an indication that the traditional farming method (slash and burn) predominantly practiced in Ghana is a cause of concern. The good news is that, though still high, the contributions of burning (Savanna) to total GHG emissions have exhibited a downward trend in recent years (Climate Watch 2021). In effect, GHG emissions from agriculture consist mainly of non-CO_2 gases produced by crop and livestock production and management activities.

Ghana depends on the energy sector, which relies on fossil fuels as well as renewables. For instance, in Ghana, carbon emissions still arise from the power production and transport sectors, where fossil fuel is still used despite the opportunities to invest in the renewable energy sector. Efforts to increase renewable energy sources are crucial to lowering the country's carbon footprint. In 2020, the energy sector was the highest contributor to the total GHG emissions, with a share of 21.94 $MtCO_2e$ GHG emissions, representing 56.16% of the total emissions, including those associated with LUCF. In terms of the energy sub-sector emissions level, based on energy usage, motor gasoline, liquefied petroleum gas (LPG), and gas-diesel oil are the leading drivers of GHG emissions coming from the energy sector in Ghana. Figure 8 illustrates the energy sub-sectors' contributions to total GHG emissions in Ghana.

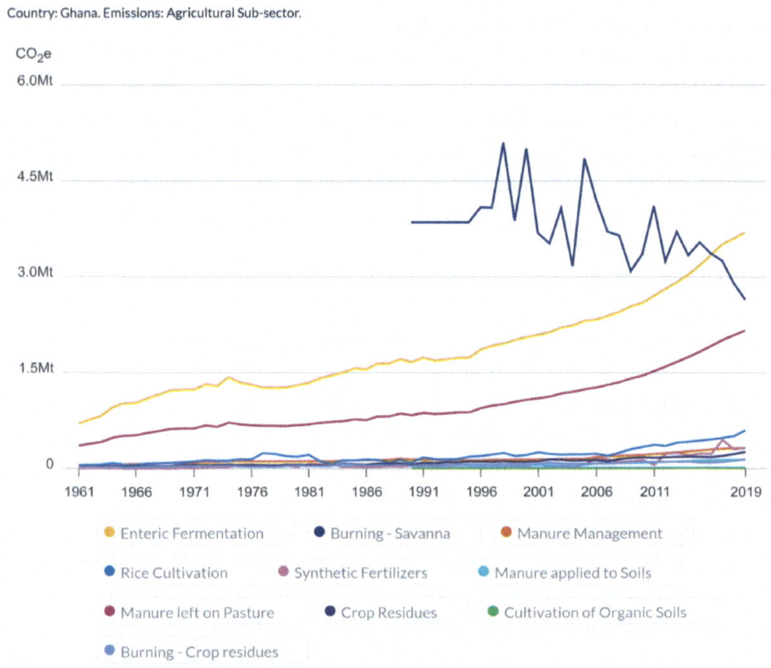

Fig. 7 Agriculture sub-sectors' contributions to total GHG emissions in Ghana (in $MtCO_2e$). *Source* Climate Watch (2021)

Ghana's rich cultural heritage and natural attractions make tourism a vital industry in the country. The environmental impacts of tourism include transportation carbon emissions, waste generation, and the use of natural resources. Nonetheless, these impacts can be mitigated through the promotion of eco-tourism and sustainable practices.

2.3 *Energy, Emissions, and Climate Action Plans*

Ghana's energy production industry is one of the key sectors in the economy, with a blend of hydropower and crude and alternative energy. Ghana, however, continues to stagnate in achieving sustainable and environmentally friendly energy production, despite its strides in this direction. This has resulted in high GHG levels resulting from the use of fuel. Large sections of Ghana's population rely on biomass, such as wood or charcoal, for cooking and heating purposes. Dependence on biomass is responsible for deforestation, carbon intensity, and related environmental and health problems. In fact, one of the major sources of energy is the Akosombo Dam, as Ghana has historically depended on hydroelectric power. Though hydroelectricity provides a cleaner substitute for fossil fuels, fluctuating water levels partly related to

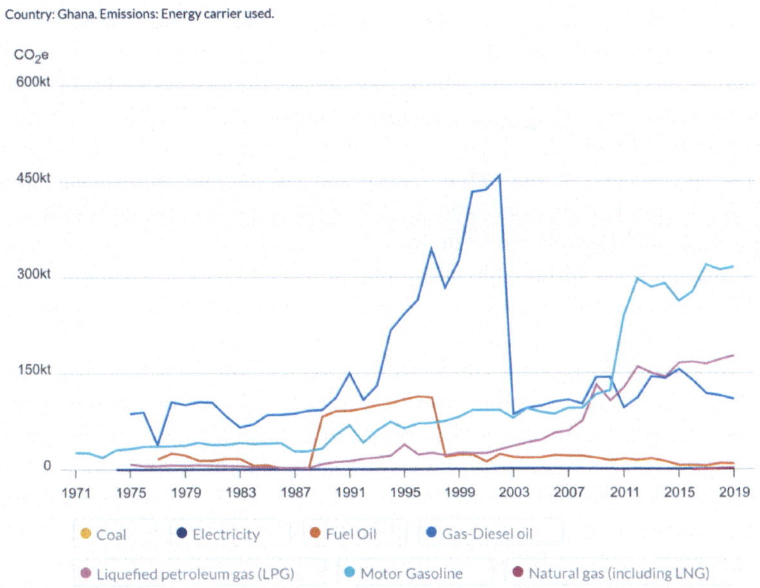

Fig. 8 Energy sub-sectors' contributions to total GHG emissions in Ghana (in $MtCO_2e$). *Source* Climate Watch (2021)

climate change have cast doubt on its continued reliability. In recent years, there have been discoveries of oil and natural gas in Ghana (International Trade Administration 2023), and this has shifted energy reliance towards these resources. While their use as supplementary tools in addressing consumer demand contributes to economic growth, it has also caused increased carbon emissions and further environmental problems.

Generally, emissions in Ghana have been rising with industrialisation and urbanisation, although they are relatively low on a global scale. These emissions are mainly contributed by the energy sector through electricity generation and transportation. Such increases emphasise the urgency of climate action plans and the transition to cleaner energy solutions. Ghana is committed to international climate agreements and has also launched the National Climate Change Policy, which provides strategic direction for coordinating issues of climate change in the country. Some of the country's pledges in the Paris Agreement were to cut emissions and increase renewable energy adoption (Climate and Clean Air Coalition (CCAC) 2023). Ghana's NDCs highlight specific emission reductions that aim at developing a low-carbon-based economy. Ghana has also been promoting the use of renewable energies, such as solar and wind energy, in preparation for oil exhaustion. In addition to reducing emissions, these initiatives would further bolster energy security and catalyse economic development.

According to Climate Watch (2021), Ghana was the world's 138th largest emitter in 2020, with a total share of 0.03% (see Table 2). Thus, GHG emissions from Ghana are relatively small in the grand scheme of things. Compared to more industrialised nations, as a developing country, Ghana has a smaller industry and lower levels of energy consumption. Agriculture, deforestation, and waste management are the main sources of GHG emissions. Many Ghanaians still rely on traditional biomass for their cooking and heating needs, making far lower levels of GHGs than would be the case with fossil fuels. At the same time, efforts are underway to reduce emissions through such projects as renewable energy and sustainable land management. In comparison with other larger economies, Ghana's overall contributions still remain rather insignificant. However, despite its low level of emissions by global standards, Ghana's insistence on sustainable development and emission reductions makes it a model for other countries seeking to lower their carbon footprints. In other words, Ghana's move towards a sustainable energy future is important not just for controlling emissions, but also for providing an example of climate action in Africa. The country's effort to blend economic growth with environmental sustainability, through innovative energy solutions and well-crafted climate action plans, will hopefully help it meet its carbon-target objectives in the international fight against global warming.

Overall, Ghana's energy sector plays a crucial role in its economic development, with a diverse mix of energy sources contributing to its energy matrix. The country's energy consumption primarily relies on a combination of traditional biomass, hydroelectric power, and fossil fuels, including oil and natural gas. In Ghana, total GHG emissions, including LUCF, came to 14.41 $MtCO_2e$ in 2020 (see Fig. 9). The energy sector was the leading contributor to this total emissions level. This is not unexpected, given that certain energy activities, such as the generation of electricity, its transportation, and its use by industry, are well known to be responsible for discharging large quantities of GHGs, primarily carbon dioxide, into the air.

Agriculture was the second-largest source of GHG emissions in Ghana. Agriculture plays an important role in Ghana's economy, but it is not without its own contributions to GHGs—in particular through activities such as the raising of livestock and rice cultivation in paddies. There are also emissions associated with the use of synthetic fertilisers. Reducing emissions in this sector could involve more sustainable farming methods, such as organic production and improved ways of raising livestock.

In terms of greenhouse gas emissions, the waste sector ranks third. Inconsiderate waste disposal, such as throwing organic refuse into landfills, leads to the emission of methane gas, a potent greenhouse agent. Waste management, including recycling, composting, and the capture of methane from landfills, can reduce emissions in this sector.

Remarkably, since 2016, Ghana has made great strides in reducing emissions from the LUCF sector. Figure 9 shows negative emissions from the LUCF sector since 2016, which means that the amount of carbon dioxide reabsorbed through tree planting and forest preservation efforts is greater than the amount released from deforestation. This is something to be commended and points towards the significance of sustainable land management in addressing climate change.

Table 2 Historical total GHG emissions ($MtCO_2e$) over three decades (1991–2020): Ghana's contribution

Year	World total	% Change world (%)	Ghana total	% Change Ghana (%)	Share of Ghana (%)
1991	32,835.51	0.53	21.61	0.23	0.07
1992	32,736.21	−0.30	22.02	1.90	0.07
1993	32,884.18	0.45	22.17	0.68	0.07
1994	33,162.74	0.85	22.45	1.26	0.07
1995	33,960.87	2.41	22.82	1.65	0.07
1996	34,351.00	1.15	23.73	3.99	0.07
1997	35,715.00	3.97	24.96	5.18	0.07
1998	35,261.24	−1.27	28.58	14.50	0.08
1999	35,264.63	0.01	27.25	−4.65	0.08
2000	35,994.91	2.07	27.57	1.17	0.08
2001	36,066.81	0.20	62.01	124.92	0.17
2002	37,012.72	2.62	63.27	2.03	0.17
2003	38,009.25	2.69	63.77	0.79	0.17
2004	39,849.51	4.84	62.62	−1.80	0.16
2005	40,784.41	2.35	64.91	3.66	0.16
2006	42,278.18	3.66	66.13	1.88	0.16
2007	43,061.38	1.85	66.38	0.38	0.15
2008	43,316.76	0.59	66.15	−0.35	0.15
2009	43,270.13	−0.11	67.31	1.75	0.16
2010	45,080.62	4.18	68.97	2.47	0.15
2011	45,256.47	0.39	54.50	−20.98	0.12
2012	45,800.17	1.20	56.32	3.34	0.12
2013	46,443.60	1.40	58.40	3.69	0.13
2014	47,106.48	1.43	57.94	−0.79	0.12
2015	47,059.77	−0.10	59.65	2.95	0.13
2016	47,691.83	1.34	5.82	−90.24	0.01
2017	48,390.92	1.47	7.58	30.24	0.02
2018	49,585.91	2.47	9.22	21.64	0.02
2019	49,880.60	0.59	11.22	21.69	0.02
2020	47,513.15	−4.75	14.41	28.43	0.03

Data Source Climate Watch (2023)

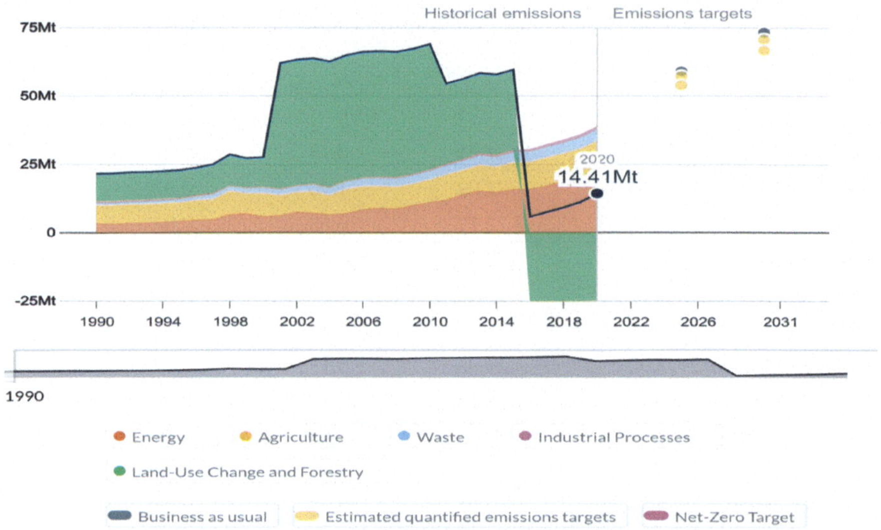

Fig. 9 GHG emissions and emissions targets in Ghana (in $MtCO_2e$). *Source* Climate Watch (2021)

Finally, Ghana's sectoral contributions to GHG emissions are mainly made by the energy sector; agriculture and waste followed. The reduction of emissions should include switching to cleaner sources of energy and developing sustainable forms of agriculture and waste disposal systems. It is also important that LUCF activities continue along the investment stage.

Table 3 and Fig. 10 present the total historical GHG emissions in Ghana over three decades (i.e., from 1990 to 2020). The data show the proportions of major gases grouped into methane (CH_4), carbon dioxide (CO_2), fluorinated gases (F-gas), and nitrous oxide (N_2O) over these years. By looking into the growth trends in each category of GHG emissions, one can gain a better understanding of Ghana's environmental impact over time. Ghana's total GHG emissions varied widely from 1990 to 2020. Its emissions began at 21.56 $MtCO_2e$ in 1990 and grew gradually to a total of 68.97 $MtCO_2$, but in 2011, there was a large fall, where emissions dropped by 20.98% to reach just 54.5 $MtCO_2e$ (Table 3). This decrease was due to a number of factors, such as shifts in industrial activity and the adoption of climate change mitigation policies (Sova et al. 2014). Also, CO_2 is a major source of GHG emissions in Ghana, which is produced by the burning of fossil fuels and forest destruction. In recent years, carbon dioxide emissions had steadily fallen beginning from 2016 and to reached a reduction of −19.68% in 2020. The decrease can be attributed to the country's efforts to switch over to cleaner energy sources and sustainable practices (Sova et al. 2014).

There was a similar pattern for the main source of methane emissions, which come mainly from agricultural activities, as well as waste management and energy production. From 1990 to the end of 2020, Ghana's methane emissions steadily increased. In particular, they rose by a hefty 5.63% in 1996, a larger percentage than ever seen

Table 3 Historical total GHG emissions ($MtCO_2e$) over three decades (1991–2020): proportions of major gases in Ghana

Year	GHG total	%Δ GHG total (%)	CH_4	%ΔCH_4 (%)	CO_2	%ΔCO_2 (%)	F-gas	%ΔF-gas (%)	N_2O	%ΔN_2O (%)
1991	21.61	0.23	5.32	4.31	12.11	−2.10	0.59	1.72	3.58	1.99
1992	22.02	1.90	5.29	−0.56	12.51	3.30	0.66	11.86	3.56	−0.56
1993	22.17	0.68	5.36	1.32	12.55	0.32	0.66	0.00	3.59	0.84
1994	22.45	1.26	5.54	3.36	12.77	1.75	0.54	−18.18	3.60	0.28
1995	22.82	1.65	5.68	2.53	13.04	2.11	0.47	−12.96	3.62	0.56
1996	23.73	3.99	6.00	5.63	13.34	2.30	0.50	6.38	3.88	7.18
1997	24.96	5.18	6.86	14.33	13.46	0.90	0.60	20.00	4.05	4.38
1998	28.58	14.50	8.15	18.80	15.30	13.67	0.27	−55.00	4.86	20.00
1999	27.25	−4.65	7.16	−12.15	15.68	2.48	0.30	11.11	4.11	−15.43
2000	27.57	1.17	7.78	8.66	14.81	−5.55	0.27	−10.00	4.71	14.60
2001	62.01	124.92	6.58	−15.42	51.28	246.25	0.28	3.70	3.88	−17.62
2002	63.27	2.03	6.66	1.22	52.50	2.38	0.29	3.57	3.81	−1.80
2003	63.77	0.79	7.12	6.91	52.22	−0.53	0.28	−3.45	4.16	9.19
2004	62.62	−1.80	6.90	−3.09	51.76	−0.88	0.27	−3.57	3.69	−11.30
2005	64.91	3.66	7.83	13.48	52.16	0.77	0.27	0.00	4.65	26.02
2006	66.13	1.88	7.65	−2.30	53.63	2.82	0.31	14.81	4.54	−2.37
2007	66.38	0.38	7.49	−2.09	54.25	1.16	0.35	12.90	4.29	−5.51
2008	66.15	−0.35	7.65	2.14	53.80	−0.83	0.40	14.29	4.30	0.23
2009	67.31	1.75	7.58	−0.92	55.15	2.51	0.44	10.00	4.14	−3.72
2010	68.97	2.47	7.89	4.09	56.21	1.92	0.49	11.36	4.39	6.04
2011	54.50	−20.98	8.94	13.31	40.19	−28.50	0.58	18.37	4.80	9.34

(continued)

Table 3 (continued)

Year	GHG total	%Δ GHG total (%)	CH_4	%ΔCH_4 (%)	CO_2	%ΔCO_2 (%)	F-gas	%ΔF-gas (%)	N_2O	%ΔN_2O (%)
2012	56.32	3.34	8.70	−2.68	42.26	5.15	0.67	15.52	4.69	−2.29
2013	58.40	3.69	9.31	7.01	43.28	2.41	0.76	13.43	5.05	7.68
2014	57.94	−0.79	9.42	1.18	42.75	−1.22	0.84	10.53	4.92	−2.57
2015	59.65	2.95	9.83	4.35	43.70	2.22	0.93	10.71	5.18	5.28
2016	5.82	−90.24	9.94	1.12	−10.41	−123.82	1.04	11.83	5.25	1.35
2017	7.58	30.24	10.72	7.85	−9.82	−5.67	1.14	9.62	5.54	5.52
2018	9.22	21.64	10.76	0.37	−8.17	−16.80	1.24	8.77	5.39	−2.71
2019	11.22	21.69	11.24	4.46	−6.91	−15.42	1.35	8.87	5.54	2.78
2020	14.41	28.43	11.99	6.67	−5.55	−19.68	1.45	7.41	6.52	17.69

Data Source Climate Watch (2023)

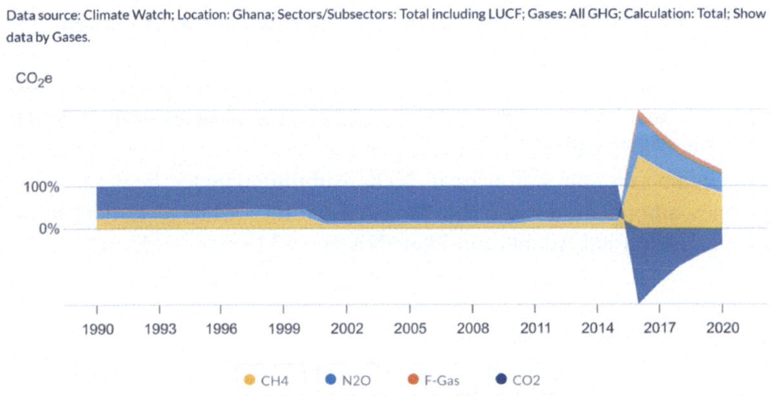

Fig. 10 Ghana's Historical Emissions by Gases (in $MtCO_2e$). *Data Source* Climate Watch (2021)

before. However, after 2006, methane emissions remained stable, with slight variations. This would indicate that Ghana has been effective in controlling and reducing methane emissions, possibly through improved waste disposal management, or by adopting more environmentally friendly agricultural methods.

Hydrofluorocarbons (HFCs) and perfluorocarbons (PFCs), commonly called fluorinated gases or F-gas, are mainly used in industrial applications, including refrigeration, air conditioning systems, and electronics manufacturing. According to the statistics, F-gas emissions in Ghana varied greatly. In 1998, they dropped by as much as −55.00%. However, emissions of F-gas increased after that time. This shows the need for stricter legislation and alternative technologies to lower gas levels.

Nitrous oxide emissions, produced mainly from agricultural and industrial activities, also exhibited a relatively stable trend, with small fluctuations over the 30 years. Since nitrous oxide emissions remained consistent in these sectors, the data indicate that Ghana has opted for effective management practices.

Generally speaking, the GHG emission analysis of Ghana presents both positive and negative aspects. Slightly reduced emissions of carbon dioxide and methane are mainly a reflection that the country is moving towards cleaner energy sources and improved waste handling theory. Furthermore, stable nitrous oxide emissions require constant monitoring and adjustment of agricultural and industrial techniques.

Ghana has exhibited active involvement in international projects, such as the Paris Agreement, and committed to long-term goals of developing sustainable energy sources, promoting climate change policy, and planning periodically updated national plans for adaptation at the local/regional and individual-citizen levels. As a contributor to global climate goals and for the benefit of its own citizens, Ghana will have to actively pursue further GHG emission reductions through more sustainable development.

2.3.1 National Policies and Strategies for Climate Action in Ghana

Ghana needs to pay attention to its active climate change initiatives and foster low-carbon growth development. National climate change policies and strategies have been formulated to enable Ghana to respond to the challenges of climate change. Central to Ghana's climate action are its NDCs submitted under the Paris Agreement. The key ones among the lot are the National Climate Change Policy, Renewable Energy Policy, National Adaptation Plan (NAP), and Forest and Land Use Policy.

National Climate Change Policy

Ghana's National Climate Change Policy is an expansive framework that sets out the country's strategy and approach to climate change. The policy was formulated in 2013 and revised in 2019 to match international commitments, such as the Paris Agreement (Ministry of Environment Science, Technology and Innovation 2013). In terms of mitigation, a low-carbon and green development model is the policy's goal. In key sectors, such as energy, transport, agriculture, and waste management, it establishes concrete targets for cutting emissions. These goals are aimed at the use of renewable energy and other means to increase efficiency, as well as a sustainable land-use policy. For the purposes of adaptation, the policy acknowledges that building resilience and adapting to climate change are necessary. The National Climate Change Policy aimed at strengthening resilience in vulnerable areas, such as agriculture, water resources, and coastal regions (Ministry of Environment Science, Technology and Innovation 2013). It also promotes the incorporation of climate change into development planning and decision-making.

The policy gives priority to technology transfer and capacity building in climate change mitigation and adaptation. It fosters the development and application of climate-friendly technologies, as well as cooperation between partners from around the world. Adequate financial resources to put climate change actions into practice are acknowledged by the policy. It requires domestic and international sources of funding to be provided, including investment from the public or private sectors at home, climate financing mechanisms abroad, and cooperation at an international level. The policy emphasises the need for effective coordination and governance structures to ensure that climate change actions are properly completed. Specifically, it urges the creation of a National Climate Change Secretariat to monitor policy implementation, coordinate interdepartmental efforts, and liaise with stakeholders.

Ghana's National Climate Change Policy serves as a reference point to guide climate action at the national, regional, and local levels. Its aim is to inject climate change considerations into the development planning process and foster sustainable and resilient paths of development. The policy is in line with the overriding objectives of Ghanaian development, which consist of poverty alleviation and sustainable economic growth, with the ultimate goal of achieving inclusive growth by creating opportunities for all.

Renewable Energy Policy

Ghana's Renewable Energy Policy is an important part of the country's national climate action strategy. Its purpose is to promote the development and use of sources of renewable energy to reduce greenhouse gas emissions, expand access to energy, and enhance the security of supplies. The policy stipulates several goals and targets to be reached by 2030. The listed objectives include raising the share of renewable energy in the country's overall mix to at least 10%, stimulating use by remote areas and off-grid communities, and attracting private sector investment into building new projects (Ministry of Energy 2021).

In pursuit of these objectives, the policy describes several strategies and interventions. Setting up a welcoming regulatory environment that encourages private sector involvement and investment in renewable energy projects is an essential strategy. Such an initiative involves the formation of feed-in tariffs, net metering regulations, and other financial incentives to attract investors. The policy also stresses the role of capacity building and technology transfer, so that local workers can play a full part in this new sector. In addition, it includes plans for training technicians, engineers, and entrepreneurs, as well as setting up research centres to advance innovation in renewable energy facilities.

Furthermore, the policy emphasises that promoting energy efficiency and conservation work helps reduce total energy consumption requirements, thus increasing the effectiveness of renewable energies in all fields (Ministry of Energy 2021). It includes the implementation of standards and labelling programmes for energy efficiency, as well as the promotion of consumption-reducing projects in industry, buildings, and transportation. It acknowledges that public awareness and education are an integral part of promoting the adoption of renewable energy. Thus, it stresses the importance of public promotion activities, educational programmes, and the inclusion of sustainable energy topics in national school curricula to arouse interest and change people's attitudes towards environmentally friendly methods.

In general, Ghana's Renewable Energy Policy reflects the country's efforts to move towards a low-carbon and sustainable energy future. One of the strategic means identified by Ghana to help meet its national climate action targets and substantially reduce the country's dependence on fossil fuels, as well as mitigate climate change, is vigorously promoting the development and installation of renewable energy sources.

National Adaptation Plan

The NAP in Ghana is a strategic guide that seeks to strengthen the country's ability to resist climate change. It provides a guide to the identification and implementation of adaptation measures that will reduce vulnerability and enhance adaptive capacity at the national, regional, and local levels. The NAP's main goal is to integrate climate change adaptation with developmental planning, which means that sectoral policies, plans, and programmes should be given adequate consideration. The NAP thus endorses a multi-sectoral approach involving all stakeholders—not only government agencies, but also civil society organisations and the private sector.

The NAP process in Ghana consists of several stages. First, a comprehensive assessment of climate change impacts and vulnerability must be carried out to determine the sectors and regions that most urgently need adaptation intervention. The assessment should take into account such factors as climate projections, socioeconomic conditions, and existing adaptation. On this basis, adaptation options and strategies for each sector can be developed. This is necessary since, for instance, the agriculture sector differs from that of water resources, as coastal zones have differing needs with regard to health considerations. These approaches contain both short-term and long-term measures designed to strengthen adaptive capacity, cut risks, and promote sustainable development.

The NAP further stresses the need for capacity building and knowledge exchange to enable adaptation planning and implementation. It stimulates the establishment of a sound monitoring and evaluation framework to monitor progress, pinpoint problems, and assess the effectiveness of adaptation actions. Moreover, the NAP acknowledges that financing is required to underpin adaptive action. It calls for the mobilisation of both domestic and foreign financing, as well as the exploration of new types of financial arrangements, including PPPs, to finance climate actions in the country.

Ghana's NAP is in line with the country's development objectives and also meets international obligations, including those of the SDGs and the Paris Agreement. It underpins harmonised and consistent action, with climate change adaptation being integrated into national development planning and decision-making. Therefore, Ghana's NAP plays an important role in building up this country's resilience to climate change and achieving sustainable development. It is a strategic roadmap to identify and implement adaptation actions across intersectoral lines on the one hand, but it also mobilises financial resources for the effective use of those preparatory steps on the other.

Forest and Land Use Policy

The Forest and Land Use Policy in Ghana is an integral part of the country's national policies on climate change. It seeks to resolve problems arising from deforestation, forest degradation, and unsustainable land-use practices, which are major sources of GHG emissions. The policy also acknowledges the role of forests in helping to reduce climate change by sequestering carbon and its contribution to local livelihoods, as well as supporting biodiversity conservation and the delivery of ecosystem services. It also provides parameters for the sustainable management of forests and land. The overall objective is to lower deforestation while at the same time promoting the sustainable use of land.

Increasing forest cover through afforestation and reforestation is a principal objective of the Forest and Land Use Policy. This includes tree planting on degraded lands and the restoration of degenerated forests. The policy also calls for the sustainable management of existing forests to nurture their long-term conservation and carbon storage capabilities. Achieving these objectives calls for sound governance and institutional arrangements. One important aspect of this initiative is the establishment of a National Forest Authority to implement this policy and coordinate activities among government agencies, local communities, and private enterprises.

The Forest and Land Use Policy also acknowledges the rights and responsibilities of local communities in the management of forests. It emphasises the need for community involvement, traditional wisdom, and customary systems of land tenure in sustainable forest and farmland use. Access to community-based forest management approaches, such as community forests and joint venture forests, is encouraged. According to this policy, everyone should have a fair share of benefits and obligations. In addition, the policy seeks to address the drivers of deforestation and unsustainable land use. Agriculture expansion, illegal logging, mining, and infrastructure development have emerged as important drivers that require suitable regulations in force through adequate monitoring to ensure compliance. The policy also encourages sustainable agricultural practices, such as agroforestry and environmentally responsive land management, to relieve pressure on forests or help them adapt better to climate change.

Ghana's Forest and Land Use Policy is basically a comprehensive plan aimed at solving the problems of excessive deforestation, which threatens to devour much that remains wild in most African countries, including Ghana. In this way, the policy forms a firm foundation for Ghana's climate change mitigation and adaptation as well as biodiversity conservation efforts, with the ultimate aim of delivering sustainable forests.

These initiatives, among others, indicate the level of commitment Ghana holds to issues relating to climate change and sustainability, thereby positioning the country as a benchmark for other African countries in addressing climate issues holistically by mainstreaming climatic action into various sectors and national policy frameworks.

3 Challenges and Opportunities

3.1 Climate Financing Gaps in Ghana

Like many other African nations, Ghana is extremely susceptible to the effects of climate change. Climate-related problems include rising temperatures, unstable rainfall patterns, and the frequent occurrence of droughts, floods, and sea-level rises. These changes bring grave dangers to the nation's economy, food security, water resources, and overall development. Ghana needs massive financing to implement appropriate adaptation and mitigation measures to address climate change. However, despite the actions taken by governments and international organisations, there are still big holes in climate financing across the country.

In terms of domestic financing, there has been significant progress on Ghana's part in channelling climate finance from numerous sources. These include multilateral funds for tackling global warming; bilateral agreements with various countries like the United States Government and the Department for International Development (DFID) (the UK government agency responsible for development aid); and private investment, domestically called "venture capital," where investors invest primarily through the stock. The government has also formulated policies, strategies, and an institutional framework to attract climate finance into the country. In particular, the country has drawn funding from the GCF, the Adaptation Fund, and a number of bilateral climate finance channels. However, the existing gaps in the climate financing landscape remain despite these efforts. Current challenges include limited access to international climate funds, insufficient domestic resources, a lack of private sector engagement, and weak monitoring and evaluation systems.

Although resources are accessible to Ghana from international climate funds, the procedure for accessing these funds is still very complex and time consuming. Stringent requirements, complex application processes, and the limited capacity of the national institutions themselves hinder the effective use of available funds. As a result, many prospective projects and undertakings end up lacking the necessary financing. The problem is worsened by insufficient domestic resources. The overreliance on external funding is due to the fact that Ghana does not have abundant domestic resources for dealing with climate financing. The government's budget allotment for climate change-related activities is rarely enough to keep pace with the rising tide of adaptation and mitigation needs. This limited domestic resource base means that the country has difficulty carrying out climate projects.

Despite numerous government initiatives, including PPP in Ghana, participation of the private sector in climate finance remains low. The private sector is an important force for investment mobilisation and sustainable development. However, low awareness, insufficient understanding of the mechanisms related to climate finance, and perceived risks of climate-related projects prevent private-sector participation. This gap hinders the acquisition of further financial resources for climate-related endeavours. The current lack of adequate information for potential private investors is partly due to weak monitoring and evaluation systems for existing projects. To effectively track the impact of investments, the best monitoring and evaluation systems are critical for measuring whether finance produces results, as well as ensuring transparency and equitable accountability. Sadly, Ghana's current monitoring and evaluation systems for climate finance projects often leave much to be desired. This prevents the equitable assessment of project results and the fair allocation of resources.

To address these climate financing gaps in Ghana, various strategies and interventions can be implemented. First, boosting national institutions engaged in climate finance is necessary. Such an effort would include assistance with training and technical support for project proposal development, financial management, monitoring, and evaluation capabilities. Improving institutions will allow for more effective utilisation and access to climate financing resources. Other strategies include strengthening institutional capacity, streamlining access to international funds, mobilising domestic resources, and engaging with private companies, as well as improving monitoring and evaluation systems. Through the adoption of these strategies, Ghana stands a better chance of strengthening its resistance to climate change and attaining sustainable development.

3.1.1 Current Funding and Needs

In recent years, climate finance has been flowing steadily into Ghana, especially through international funding mechanisms and partnerships. The three largest providers of climate change funding to Ghana are the European Union (EU), the AfDB, and the United States Government. These funds predominantly targeted mitigation activities and were distributed across several projects in the country (CARE Climate Change 2021). Ghana has also received financing from the GCF to implement four projects in the north of the country. However, these funding sources are insufficient to address all of the climate change needs of the country (Statista 2023). An example of the climate related projects funded by the GCF in the Northern Ghana, is the Ghana Shea Landscape Emission Reductions Project and those based on women in agriculture. Furthermore, the AfDB has also played a major role under the ACCF. The ACCF was established in 2014 and has greatly offered assistance to African countries, including Ghana, with a current trust size of about USD 25.71 million.

With the vast requirements for climate finance funds, demonstrated by the country's vulnerability to climate change impacts, Ghana still needs more funding for mitigation and adaptation initiatives. The country requires high-level investment in sustainable agriculture, renewable energy, and infrastructure resilience. In addition, the determination exhibited by Ghana in its NDCs under the Paris Agreement requires huge financial injection, especially for the transition to a low-carbon economy. These financial needs also include the build-up of capacities in local institutions and communities for implementing and managing climate projects effectively.

There is still a gap between the present amount of funding and what is actually required. In spite of the essential contribution of international funds, they are unable to offer all the resources necessary for combating climate-poor conditions in Ghana. The reasons for this gap have been varied and include problems accessing international climate funds, insufficiently customised financing mechanisms, and the inconsistency of international funding with local priorities. In this regard, Ghana needs to upgrade its approaches to accessing and using climate finance. Such updates should include building capacity in institutions, establishing more PPPs, and developing unique financial mechanisms to address specific local requirements. In addition, the effective incorporation of climate finance into the broader development goals and prudent implementation of funded projects can go a long way in meeting Ghana's climate finance requirements.

3.1.2 Sources of Climate Finance and Their Limitations

Securing funds in relation to climate change mitigation and adaptation is not easy, especially among developing countries like Ghana. Different types of extant climate funds come with certain barriers and stringent conditions, as explained below.

International Climate Funds

Ghana accessed some international climate financing instruments, including the GCF, the Adaptation Fund, and the Global Environment Fund (GEF). These resources include grants, soft loans, and technical support for climate initiatives. Notably, getting such funding is not that simple, since there are strict conditions for eligibility, complicated procedures of application, and small capacities of local institutions in compliance with the necessary requirements. In addition, there are stiff competitions for these funds, making it difficult to avail sufficient resources for Ghana.

Bilateral and Multilateral Cooperation

Climate change funds are also supported in Ghana through bilateral and multilateral partnerships between developing countries and donor nations. Examples of bilateral cooperations include Ghana-German Climate Partnership (GGCP) that aims to support climate change mitigation and adaptation efforts in Ghana by focusing on renewable energy, energy efficiency, sustainable urban development, and climate-smart agriculture; and UK-Ghana Green Growth Programme that seeks to support Ghana's transition towards a low carbon and climate-resilient economy. In terms of multilateral cooperations, Ghana has engaged the GCF, which is a multilateral fund established to support developing countries in their efforts to combat climate change. The GCF provides financial resources to support climate adaptation and mitigation projects in Ghana. Similarly, Ghana has participated in the CIF, which is a multilateral initiative supporting climate-resilient and low carbon development projects. Ghana has accessed funding from the CIFs for various projects, including renewable energy and sustainable forestry. Such partnerships involve providing finances, transferring technologies, building capacities, and sharing knowledge. Nevertheless, these external funds remain woefully inadequate. For instance, UNFCCC's 2021 report pointed out that annual average of USD 830 million of climate finance flows in Ghana was tracked in 2019 and 2020. This is a meagre 5–9% of its required investment—estimated between USD 9.3–15.5 billion, underscoring the urgent necessity to enhance climate finance in order to accomplish Ghana's NDCs (Climate Policy Initiative 2021).

Domestic Public Finance

Aside the external funding, the Ghanaian government finances some climate change initiatives with funds from the national budget. In 2019 and 2020 for example, the public actors accounted for 87% of climate finance in Ghana (USD 722 million). Public climate finance came mainly from domestic budgets (USD 271 million) and Multilateral Development Financial Institutions (DFIs) (USD 248 million) in the form of grants and low-cost project debt. Other sources were international government (USD 82 million), multilateral climate funds (USD 34 million), bilateral DFIs

(USD 37 million), and others (USD 50 million) (Climate Policy Initiative 2021). Nevertheless, climate finance allocations are still inadequate, considering the estimated need of about 15.5 billion and urgency of climate crises. As a result, the government departments in charge of climate actions and policy implementation suffer from low capacity, poor budget utilisation, and general inefficiency.

Private Sector Investment

Scaling up climate finance in Ghana can only be done by encouraging private sector investment in climate-related projects. An analysis of the climate finance flows to Ghana in 2019/2020 revealed that the private finance remains largely elusive in Ghana, accounting for only 13% of overall climate finance (USD 106 million). Private finance was almost equally split between equity (45%) and debt (47%), with commercial FIs and corporations accounting for most private flows. In line with observed global trends, 88% of Ghana's private climate finance was invested in energy systems equally through debt and equity. International private finance constituted around 7% of overall private climate finance in 2019/2020, highlighting the opportunity for higher international climate-based investments in Ghana (Climate Policy Initiative 2021). To arouse the interest of the private sector to invest in climate actions, the government has instituted a number of policies, including fiscal incentives and PPP reforms. Even though some obstacles continue to exist, such as perceived high risks, weak financial access, and poor policies on private sector involvement, there is still a need to promote and encourage effective private investment into the sustainable energy sector in Ghana.

In general, various barriers limit Ghana's ability to obtain sufficient finance, even as it seeks more alternative avenues of climate finance. Eligibility-related impediments, complex processes of application, limited domestic public finance availability, and uncertain international cooperation, alongside insufficient private sector investments, are just some of these limitations. To address these limitations, institutions need to be strengthened, policy frameworks improved, and collaboration among various climate finance stakeholders in the country boosted.

3.2 Institutional Development and Governance

The manner in which Ghana deals with climate finance and investment, particularly with regard to institutional development and governance, involves a complex interaction of national policies, legislative frameworks, and international collaborations.

3.2.1 Policy Direction and Political Landscape

While Ghana has exhibited a commitment to combating climate change, its policy direction remains unclear. While the government of Ghana has enacted policies aimed at combating global warming and rolled out flagship programmes to promote green transition, the government's support for mining activities and fossil fuel extraction are still on the rise, indicating the existence of incoherence in policy frameworks Several factors may contribute to this discrepancy including economic considerations since Ghana relies heavily on revenues generated from natural resources which creates tension between pursuing economic growth and transitioning to greener alternatives; socio-economic development challenges like poverty, infrastructure development, and access to basic services; limited alternatives since transitioning to renewable energy sources and reducing reliance on fossil fuels often requires substantial investments in infrastructure, technology, and capacity building; and gap between policy formulation and effective implementation such as challenges in enforcement, monitoring, and regulation contributing to the continuation of environmentally harmful activities. Additionally, even though Ghana has enjoyed political stability over the past few decades, the discontinuity of public projects whenever there is a change in government has been a phenomenon of concern over the years. Historically, existing projects including climate change related initiatives are often affected by political changes, which distracts the free flow and effectiveness of the projects. For instance, the forthcoming 2024 elections might halt some ongoing initiatives due to the new administration's policies.

3.2.2 Legislative Frameworks and Targets

A decarbonisation target or strategy for the long term is non-existent in Ghana. With a strong legislative framework for renewable development and ambitious targets, the country has a low-carbon development strategy that extends through 2030. Ghana has implemented various legislative frameworks to address the effects of climate change including the National Climate Change Policy developed in 2010, the Renewable Energy Act (Act 832) enacted in 2011, the National Climate Change Adaptation Strategy (NCCAS) in 2016, the commitment to NDCs under the UNFCCC, incorporating climate change concerns into its efforts to achieve the SDGs, the Environmental Protection Agency (EPA) responsible for implementing and enforcing environmental policies, and the Ghana Climate Innovation Center (GCIC) established to support and nurture local innovation and businesses in the climate and green technology sector.

In terms of targets, Ghana has updated its NDC with more ambition across sectors and the inclusion of new greenhouse gases, Ghana raised its target to cut emissions by 64 $MtCO_2e$ by 2030. Ghana has committed to implementing unconditional actions that would result in 24.6 $MtCO_2e$, and conditional actions which have the potential to reduce emissions by 39.4 $MtCO_2e$ by 2030. The updated NDC lists 47 ways in which the country will mitigate and adapt to climate change, with each examined for its socioeconomic outcomes, job prospects, funding, number of beneficiaries and gender responsiveness. Through climate action, Ghana expects to create over one million jobs and avoid 2,900 deaths due to better air quality (UNFCCC 2022).

3.2.3 Institutional Capacity and Coordination

Accordingly, while Ghana has the institutional architecture to generate and coordinate climate finance, it faces obstacles in the mobilisation of sufficient resources for addressing climate-related issues. Climate change action coordinators for government institutions seem to be well-funded and staffed, a key element in any capacity-building process. However, the use of these structures for horizontal and vertical coordination on climate issues is not very effective.

3.2.4 Transparency and Public Awareness

Technical assistance is needed to enhance transparency and to review arrangements in climate policy. Although there have been efforts to sensitise the public on climate change issues, considerable effort is still needed. A nationally representative survey of Ghanaian adults conducted from August 1, 2019 to December 31, 2019, on knowledge, attitude, and adaptation to climate change in Ghana, revealed that that 43.9% of the respondents understood the meaning of climate change (Odonkor et al. 2020). This is an indication that global warning is gaining attention among the publics in Ghana. Although the idea of energy transition has been discussed, no concrete framework has been established for its intensive promotion.

3.2.5 International Engagement and Reporting

In a rare feat among developing countries, Ghana has shown its potential in international climate governance by presenting several GHG Inventory Reports to the UNFCCC. Ghana's efforts to present several GHG Inventory Reports to the UNFCCC demonstrate its commitment and potential in international climate governance. These reports provide valuable data on greenhouse gas emissions and removals within the country. Ghana's submission of these reports to the UNFCCC demonstrates its compliance with international reporting obligations and a willingness to be transparent in sharing its emissions data with the global community. The regular submission of these reports signals the country's commitment to monitoring and reporting its progress in addressing climate change. Even though a mere submission of the reports does not guarantee the success of the initiative, it is important to recognize that the submission of these reports is a positive step towards promoting international climate governance and transparency. Continued efforts to improve data quality, enhance stakeholder engagement, and utilize the reported information in decision-making processes will further enhance the success and effectiveness of Ghana's initiatives (Climate Action Tracker 2021).

3.2.6 Climate Finance Mobilisation and Projects

As an example of such an initiative, Ghana has participated in the Green GCF Readiness Programme with support from the UNDP and United Nations Environment Programme (UNEP), which aims to develop national capacities for planning for, accessing, and monitoring climate finance. Ghana is also exhibiting tremendous strides in the mobilisation and delivery of climate finance at scale, as the GCF has been a major source of funds for climate projects in this country. Examples of these projects are the Ghana Shea Landscape Emission Reductions Project and the AFAWA programme aimed at supporting climate-resilient agricultural practices in Ghana.

3.3 *Role of Government and Policy in Climate Action*

The government of Ghana remains a key player in climate actions, supporting some efforts related to climate change while also undertaking economic activities like fossil fuel extraction. Providing a clear policy direction for the transition to a zero-emissions society presents a challenge in balancing these aspects. However, the government has demonstrated its desire to amend Ghana's NDCs towards building resilience against climate change and achieving low-carbon development through bodies such as MESTI.

3.3.1 Political Commitment and Policy Direction

Mixed Messages and Political Landscape

Climate action by the government has been somewhat episodic. The government supports climate initiatives, but it also continues to back the extraction of fossil fuels. Climate action is not considered a compelling issue, although the two main political parties are aware of its necessity. Changing government policies could also prove risky to project implementation.

Nationally Determined Contributions (NDCs)

Ghana's NDCs outline the country's focus on minimising its GHG emissions and introducing climate adaptation measures to major sectors. Such measures include work in mass transit, infrastructure, land-use agriculture, energy, forest, and water resource management. Ghana submitted an updated NDC in 2021 and expects that implementing the 19 policy actions will achieve measurable targets by 2030, including absolute GHG emission reductions of 64 $MtCO_2e$, avoiding at least 2,900 premature deaths per year from improved air quality, and creating over one million green jobs that will benefit nearly 38 million people, with the majority being youth and women (UNFCCC 2022). The 13 adaptation measures are divided into seven unconditional and six conditional programmes of action. For the 34 mitigation measures, Ghana aims to implement nine unconditional programmes of action that would result in 8.5 $MtCO_2e$ of GHG reductions by 2025 and a further 24.6 $MtCO_2e$ by 2030, compared to the 2020–2030 cumulative emissions in a baseline scenario. Ghana also aims to adopt an additional 25 conditional programmes of action that have the potential to achieve 16.7 $MtCO_2e$ in reductions by 2025 and 39.4 $MtCO_2e$ by 2030, if financial support from the international and private sectors is made available to cover the full cost for implementation.

3.3.2 National Policies and Legislative Framework

National Climate Change Policy (NCCP)

Ghana's NCCP is a three-phased, all-inclusive climate change approach that focuses on adaptation, social development, and mitigation. It takes into consideration the vulnerability of its populations to climate change and attends to such strategic areas as agriculture, food security, disaster preparedness, natural resource management, and infrastructure development.

Renewable Energy Act and Legislative Gaps

While the Renewable Energy Act offers some legislative provisions for renewable energy development, Ghana does not have comprehensive climate-related legislation. The government lacks a long-term decarbonisation target or strategy, and the development of comprehensive climate legislation has not yet received any commitment.

3.3.3 Public Awareness and a Just Transition

Although Ghana's government is engaged in a media campaign to raise public awareness about climate-related issues, much teamwork remains to be done, since only a small percentage of the population knows about climate changes and their consequences. However, the government acknowledges this requirement and includes the "Just Transition"—greening the economy in a way that is as fair and inclusive as possible to everyone concerned, creating decent work opportunities and leaving no one behind—in its climate policy, while also involving the private sector in policy implementation.

Ghana's government leads climate action in Africa, demonstrating a clear line of vision through its NDCs and national policies. Nevertheless, improvements have to be made in terms of clearer policy directions, comprehensive climate legislation development, and increasing public awareness. The government plays a critical role in reconciling the ability to grow economically with low-carbon emissions, sustainable development, and the involvement of all stakeholders, including the private sector, in climate actions.

3.3.4 Effectiveness of Existing Institutions in Managing Climate Finance

Climate Finance Knowledge Hub (CFKH) in Ghana

This one-stop platform is vital for giving financial institutions and environment-friendly firms the knowledge and capabilities needed to secure funding for green technologies. Together with academia, it builds the capacities of Microfinance Institutions (MFIs), Micro, Small and Medium-sized Enterprises (MSMEs), and Technical Service Providers (TSPs) to enable them to compete for climate funds and innovate in the development of climate-smart products and services. The integrated e-Library of the CFKH provides a large number of resources, such as scientific and grey literature and research data in support of Climate-Smart Enterprises (CSEs) in Ghana.

Ministry of Finance's Climate Financing Division

This division was set up for improved coordination on a national scale and to ensure that Ghana is able to quicken its growth towards climate resilience by implementing her NDCs as well as meeting international obligations pertaining to climate change mitigation. Major progress has been made, such as ensuring adequate financial support for climate adaptation and mitigation interventions demonstrated through engagements with international partners who have pledged funding for programmes like the Ghana Shea Landscape Emission Reduction Project (GSLERP). Ghana's active role in climate financing mobilisation and its push towards a climate-resistant global financial architecture are reflected in these endeavours.

Government Policy and Climate Governance

The government's approach to combating climate change can be said to be somewhat contradictory because of its strong support of fossil-based fuels and extractive industries. These are some issues that influence the effectiveness of managing climate finance and help facilitate the shift towards a zero-emission society. Although Ghana has demonstrated some level of commitment to combating climate change, proper climate governance is still a low priority when it comes to government policies. An operational shortcoming is the presence of a suitable organisational structure for horizontal and vertical cooperation on climate change issues. The government has a hard time securing adequate climate financing because of the economic challenges associated with this endeavour, but if the coordinating institutions are good at managing their resources, capacity building and knowledge improvement will be easier to achieve.

Legislative and Strategic Framework

Ghana has no definitive long-term decarbonisation target or strategy, despite its low-carbon development strategy for 2030. The Renewable Energy Act creates an enabling legal framework for the development of renewables, but there is no full-fledged climate law. The lack of wider regulatory legislation will impede the effectiveness of climate finance management.

Transparency and Public Engagement

The fact that Ghana has regularly sent GHG Inventory Reports to the UNFCCC suggests that it is committed to climate change actions and resources. Nevertheless, the mechanisms to review the policies, although existent, are not yet fully functional and effective. Technical support for improving transparency and review mechanisms is needed. However, raising awareness about climate change must continue, although it takes only a few people to acknowledge climate change and its effects. As it embarks on developing its NCCP, the government has realised that the "Just Transition" should be enacted.

In a nutshell, there is a need to deal with issues of policy consistency, legislature, effective operation, and public involvement in the handling of climate finance in Ghana. Nevertheless, the current actions, as well as new advancements, suggest that stronger and more efficient climate finance is taking shape.

3.4 *Human Resources and Capacity Building*

The Ghana Microfinance Institutions Network (GHAMFIN), in collaboration with the Deutsche Gesellschaft für Internationale Zusammenarbeit (GIZ), established the CFKH in 2019. This e-learning platform focuses on specialised technical training and certification in climate finance. Its main focus is to ease the flow of cash in greening undertakings, which facilitates microfinance institutions and climate-smart enterprises' access to climate funds. In effect, this is a big boost to the efforts of financial service providers and MSMEs towards climate mitigation and adaptation and therefore allows them to confidently invest in climate-smart businesses.

3.4.1 Green Climate Fund Readiness Programme

In partnership with the UNDP and UNEP, this programme supports the building of capacities in national-level investment planning, access, and implementation of climate finance based on the GCF under a harmonised monitoring framework. The private sector and non-governmental stakeholders will also be developed by the initiative to increase access to climatic finances. Ghana has expressed its commitment to fighting climate change through the adoption of the NCCP (2014) and its willingness to join the global climatic agreement.

3.4.2 Challenges in Climate Finance and Capacity Building

Ghana continues to grapple with substantial challenges pertaining to the monitoring and evaluation of disbursed climate finance, despite the implementation of numerous initiatives seeking to create an efficient and transparent system. Several organisations within the country receive climate funds from various quarters and circumvent central coordinates, such as the MoF. Consequently, such a structure leads to poor government and donor coordination, resulting in duplications in climate change interventions and lack of accountability. An accurate understanding of climate information and capacity building is lacking in vulnerable populations, which also affects the adaptation process.

Challenges including coordination issues, distribution problems, and gaps in understanding still pose critical problems for human resources and capacity development. Ghana has taken steps to address capacity challenges in relation to climate finance and investment initiatives. The challenges must be met if Ghana is to meet its goal of climate change adaptation and mitigation.

3.4.3 Need for Skilled Workforces in Climate-Related Sectors

Different initiatives have reinforced the urgent demand for a knowledgeable labour force in Ghana to cope with climate change issues and capture prospects to enhance sustainability.

Climate Vulnerability and Economic Impact

The effects of climate change in Ghana have led to human development and economic vulnerability. Ghana is prone to floods, coastal erosions from rising sea levels, and soil erosion. The higher temperatures and unpredictable rainfall that the farmers are experiencing have also negatively resulted in reduced crop yields and labour productivity. This events further reaffirm the significance of having professionals who can engage in mitigating and adapting to climate change, integrated landscape management, climate-smart agriculture, and resilient infrastructure development.

Government Initiatives and Strategic Priorities

To address these challenges posed by global warming, and build a resilient and sustainable economy, the government of Ghana has identified a number of strategic priorities. These involve, for instance, climate-smart agriculture, sustainable cities, disaster-risk preparedness, forest resource management and conservation, clean energy transition, and modernised transport systems. An effective climate change response and sustainable development practices entail a specialised workforce in each of these areas.

Climate Change and Green Economy Learning Strategy (CCGELS)

In 2016, CCGELS was launched by MESTI, with technical support from the UNDP and UNITAR. The strategy was intended to increase the level of climate change education, awareness, and learning throughout Ghana. The initiative seeks to build national capacities in support of Ghana's intended nationally determined contribution (INDC) under the Paris Agreement. CCGELS points to the need for country-driven programmes with a view to strengthening the institutional capacity of good governance, science, innovation, and effective observation.

Climate Change Education in Higher Education

As an example of such an endeavour, the University of Ghana Business School provides a stringent 12-month Master of Science programme in climate change and sustainable development, replenishing Ghana and other nations with much-needed climate expertise. The emphasis on climate change scrutiny, reduction, and adaptation is important as it shows development in the realisation that masters-level instruction must be provided to address vital environmental issues.

National Climate Change Learning Strategy Development

This strategy, initiated in 2015, is anchored in the NCCP's key priority areas. It seeks to build the national education and training system towards actions for climate change learning. The Climate Change Learning Strategy highlighted the lack of sufficient human resources in this field, as only a small number of academics have researched the effects of climate change, even though there are climate change courses and programmes at universities. This stresses the importance of more integrated and organised education on climate change throughout the education system.

To combat climate change and achieve sustainable development, Ghana requires a highly skilled labour force in all fields pertaining to climate conditions. The CCGELS and specialised university programmes are good initiatives, but there is a need for broader systematic climate change education and training across all levels. This will help ensure that Ghana has the human resources needed to deal with its climate challenges and take advantage of resilient and sustainable development.

3.4.4 Current State and Potential Strategies for Capacity Development

Some of the current initiatives and strategies in the country are outlined below. The ultimate objective is to ensure the most prevalent capacity building and thereby enhance the capacities necessary for successful climate finance and investment.

Green Climate Fund (GCF) Readiness Programme

The GCF Readiness Programme is conducted in partnership with the UNDP and the UNEP to develop national capacity for planning, accessing, delivering, and monitoring climate finance from the GCF. The capacity of non-governmental organisations and the private sector to participate in climate financing procedures is also intended to be strengthened. This is a crucial first step towards enacting the spine of Ghana's climate action plan on reducing emissions and addressing the effects of climatic fluctuations.

Capacity Building Through the Africa Adaptation Programme (AAP)

Notably, the AAP has developed a substantial capacity for mainstreaming climate change adaptation (CCA) and disaster-risk reduction (DRR) into development planning in Ghana. Specifically, this programme has facilitated the training of high-ranking officers, mainstreamed climate change in the Functional Organisation Assessment Tool for budgeting, and integrated CCA and DRR into the Ghana Building Code. The AAP has also engaged the services of early warning experts to provide training on major issues related to meteorological information systems and climatic predictions for disaster preparedness.

Capacity Development for Accessing Climate Funds

Under the Paris Agreement, with respect to climate action investments, Ghana has developed its NDCs with respect to climate action investments. GCF training and sensitisation support enhanced knowledge regarding the funding process. Such efforts aimed to assist the primary players involved in coming up with quality proposals for funding requests. The initiative to promote quality grant proposal writing include partnering with GCF-accredited entities and national designated authorities in proposal submission through the MoF.

Potential Strategies for Further Development

Additional strategies may include increases in coverage of training programmes; diversification of programme content (regional and sector); strengthening private-sector involvement in climate finance; creating specialised curricula for tertiary or vocational education systems on the sustainable use of energy, renewable power generation, and mechanism development; and cross-generation exchanges at the village level between the Local Government Service (LGS) and community groups. Second, Ghana should work with other international bodies on different climate-related agreements for new investment and resources.

Ghana is already handling its climate finance and investment capacity. The evolving landscape means that there is increased political will to continue moving the climate agenda forward and to try scaling up such actions, as well as attempting to further anchor them in national development plans.

3.5 Integrating Climate Action with Other Sustainable Goals in Ghana

In Ghana, climate action is integrated with the pursuit of the SDGs in emphasising the importance of developing resilience and enhancing adaptive capacity to climate change risk and other disasters. The United Nations in Ghana buttressed this approach, as it resonates with the global call to end poverty and save the environment and climate for greater peace and prosperity for all.

Under the Climate Action Agenda (SDG 13), SDG targets for countries should cover strengthening resilience and adaptive capacity to climate-related hazards, integrating measures on climate change into national policies, raising levels of awareness and education about climate change issues, and promoting mechanisms that aim at effective planning for changes associated with the shift from fossil-based systems of energy production and consumption, including oil, natural gas and coal, to renewable energy sources like wind and solar, as well as lithium-ion batteries. The significance of private sector investment in Ghana's climate action plan is noteworthy. Ghana's NDC is aligned with the Paris Agreement, which details 31 climate actions that demand significant investment. In the 10-year period post 2020, Ghana needs USD 22.6 billion in investments from domestic and international public and private sources to finance these actions. USD 6.3 billion (28%) is expected to be mobilized from domestic sources whereas USD 16.3 billion (72%) will come from international support (The Climate and Development Knowledge Network (CDKN) 2017).

Without urgent action on climate change in Ghana, it is estimated that at least one million more people could fall into poverty due to climate-related disasters, and that income for poor households could be reduced by up to 40% by 2050 (World Bank 2022). The report maps out six priority directions for Ghana's climate-resilient and low-carbon development path. Key priorities include bringing innovative approaches to agriculture and environmental management, making cities more sustainable, stepping up disaster-risk preparedness, managing forest resources wisely, transitioning to clean energy, and modernising urban transport systems. The present value of the cost of climate action equals USD 2 billion per annum until 2050, around 2–3% of the total GDP from now to then. The imperative for the private sector to lead green growth has been highlighted, especially in sectors such as green building, renewable energy, and climate-smart agriculture. Financial tools like green and blue bonds, insurance, and financial protection mechanisms need to be considered to attract the private sector to invest in the green sector.

Moreover, there is a need in Ghana to address the social protection systems, expand financial inclusion, and develop skills for green jobs and livelihoods to mitigate the impacts on the poor. A low-carbon and climate-resilient path can turn challenges into opportunities, potentially leading to over USD 26 billion in economic benefits by 2040 (World Bank 2022).

Overall, Ghana's climate action integration into the achievement of other sustainable goals is a multimodal strategy that utilises policy integration, private sector investment, and the prioritisation of climate-resilient and low-carbon development pathways to promote inclusive growth while reducing the exposure of vulnerable populations to hazards associated with climatic change.

4 Conclusion

This chapter has highlighted issues related to climate finance and investment in Africa, focusing on Ghana as a specific case. A few major points emerged throughout the discussion. Specifically, this chapter has revealed where African climate finance and investment are today, what opportunities have arisen, and some of the challenges that stand in the way. It is clear that climate change poses a significant danger to the African continent's development and survival. These changes are of particular importance to these countries, especially increased temperatures, variable rainfall patterns, and rising sea levels. These changes immediately affect sectors such as agriculture, water resources, and infrastructure, reinforcing poverty, inequality, and food insecurity.

In response to these challenges, Ghana has realised the importance of climate finance and investment. The government has taken many steps to build an enabling climate finance environment by establishing various policies, strategies, and institutions. The formulation of the NCCP to provide strategic direction and coordinate issues of climate change in Ghana has had a significant impact on mobilising and channelling climate finance towards priority projects and programmes. In addition, international actors, from multilateral organisations to bilateral partners and private investors, have shown heightened interest in providing support for climate-related projects in this region. This external assistance has been invaluable, helping to bring together other human and material resources, as well as providing channels for the transfer of technology and further collaboration between local players and foreign firms.

Despite these encouraging developments, several obstacles remain. One of the main obstacles is that there are simply not enough financial resources available, either domestically or overseas, to ensure the success of this movement. Ghana is still limited in its ability to attract climate finance because of sub-optimal conditions, including weak institutional frameworks, insufficient data and information systems, and funders who do not have up-to-date knowledge about investment opportunities. In addition, a lack of coordination and coherence between different actors in climate finance and investment hinders the effective allocation of resources. Most importantly, a coordination mechanism or institution that can bring together government agencies, private sector actors, civil society organisations, and local communities is needed to strengthen the effect of climate financing.

Furthermore, the chapter emphasises that social and environmental safeguards must be considered in the climate finance domain. The investments must promote sustainable development, poverty reduction, gender equality, and the protection of ecosystems and biodiversity. Therefore, such funding requires sound monitoring and evaluation systems, as well as the involvement of local communities and disadvantaged groups in decision-making. In short, climate finance and investment in Ghana has significant potential, but also faces some challenges. Although great progress has been made in terms of mobilising resources and developing an enabling environment, much more still needs to be done. With international partners, the government must further strengthen institutions and improve data availability, as well as coordinate the relevant mechanisms. In addition, work should be done to foster sustainable investment in ways that are conducive to raising living standards and that remain respectful of local needs. Doing so will allow Ghana to effectively adapt to the impacts of climate change, soundly mitigate the occurrences of most climate change events, press forward in sustainable development, and fulfil its climate commitments.

References

Afghanaid (2023). COP28: Key takeaways from this year's climate change conference. https://www.afghanaid.org.uk/news/cop28-key-takeaways-from-this-years-climate-change-conference?gclid=Cj0KCQiAnfmsBhDfARIsAM7MKi1-luf1H0Z1IEL3yuatTqevO4Z420Zz_8hapcuRc1Kg5ZqxgjkTPsMaAi6BEALw_wcB

African Development Bank (AfDB) (2022). African Economic Outlook 2022: Supporting Climate Resilience and a Just Energy Transition in Africa. Available at https://www.afdb.org/en/documents/african-economic-outlook-2022

African Development Bank (AfDB) (2023). Africa Climate Change Fund. Available at https://www.afdb.org/en/topics-and-sectors/initiatives-partnerships/africa-climate-change-fund

African Forum and Network on Debt and Development (AFRODAD) (2023). Breaking the Cycle of Debt: Addressing the Reasons behind High Indebtedness in Africa and Recommendations for Sustainable Solutions. https://afrodad.org/breaking-the-cycle-of-debt-addressing-the-reasons-behind-high-indebtedness-in-africa-and-recommendations-for-sustainable-solutions/

African Union (AU) (2015). Agenda 2063: The Africa We Want, "A shared strategic framework for inclusive growth and sustainable development & a global strategy to optimize the use of

Africa's resources for the benefit of all Africans." Retrieved from https://au.int/sites/default/files/documents/33126-doc-framework_document_book.pdf

African Union (2013). Agenda 2063: The Africa We Want. Available at https://au.int/en/agenda2063/overview

AREI (2019). About the Africa Renewable Energy Initiative. Available at https://www.germanclimatefinance.de/files/2019/07/AREI-%E2%80%93-About-the-Africa-Renewable-Energy-Initiative.pdf

Barimalala, R., Kolstad, E. W., Parker, D. J., & Williams, D. A. (2023). Effects of the Congo Basin Rainforest on Rainfall Patterns. Report no. 12-2023, NORCE Climate and Environment.

Boko, M., I. Niang, A. Nyong, C. Vogel, A. Githeko, M. Medany, B. Osman-Elasha, R. Tabo and P. Yanda (2007). Africa Climate Change, 2007: Impacts, Adaptation and Vulnerability. Contribution of Working Group II to the Fourth Assessment Report of the Intergovernmental. https://www.ipcc.ch/site/assets/uploads/2018/02/ar4-wg2-chapter9-1.pdf

Britannica (2023). Climate of Africa - Factors influencing the African climate. Available at https://www.britannica.com/place/Africa/Conservation

CARE Climate Change (2021). Climate Finance Adaptation Study Report – Ghana. Available at: https://careclimatechange.org/wp-content/uploads/2021/01/Ghana-Climate-Adaptation-Finance-Tracking.pdf

Climate Action Tracker (2021). Climate Governance in Ghana. Retrieved from https://climateactiontracker.org/publications/climate-governance-in-ghana/

Climate and Clean Air Coalition (CCAC) (2023). CCAC Projects. Available at https://www.ccacoalition.org/partners/ghana#:~:text=Ghana%20committed%20to%20unconditionally%20lower,cost%20of%20implementing%20mitigation%20action

Climate Impact Partners (2023). Reforestation projects are critical to the health of our planet. https://www.climateimpact.com/explore-projects/nature-based-solutions-projects/reforestation/

Climate Policy Initiative (2021). Climate Finance in Ghana. Brief 2: Ghana Climate Finance Brief w/ Layout pp 2–11 https://www.climatepolicyinitiative.org/wp-content/uploads/2023/12/Climate-Finance-in-Ghana.pdf

Climate Watch (2021). What are Ghana's greenhouse gas emissions and emissions targets? https://www.climatewatchdata.org/countries/GHA?end_year=2020&source=Climate%20Watch&start_year=1990

Climate Watch (2023) World Resource Institute. Available at https://www.climatewatchdata.org/ghg-emissions?end_year=2020&start_year=1990

Cross, M. (Ed.). (2017). Knowledge and change in African Universities: Volume 1–Current debates. Springer.

Development Initiatives (2022). Climate adaptation finance to Africa: Key facts. Available at https://devinit.org/resources/climate-adaptation-finance-africa-key-facts/#note-source-o7O2tj2LX

Engel, U. (2023). The state of the Union. In Yearbook on the African Union Volume 3 (2022) (pp. 22–55). Brill.

EUMETSAT (2023). Monitoring tropical cyclones in the Indian Ocean - 2020–2022. Retrieved from https://www.eumetsat.int/monitoring-tropical-cyclones-indian-ocean-2020-present

Global Center on Adaptation (2023). Adaptation finance 'make or break' for Africa: Global Leaders Double Down on Calls for Increased Adaptation Funding. Available at https://gca.org/news/adaptation-finance-make-or-break-for-africa-global-leaders-double-down-on-calls-for-increased-adaptation-funding/

ICPAC (2021) 10 Climate Change impacts in East Africa you didn't know about. Available at https://medium.com/age-of-awareness/10-climate-change-impacts-in-east-africa-you-didnt-know-about-a952c8a20d6f

Intergovernmental Panel on Climate Change (IPCC) (2023). Regional fact sheet – Africa. Retrieved from https://www.ipcc.ch/report/ar6/wg1/downloads/factsheets/IPCC_AR6_WGI_Regional_Fact_Sheet_Africa.pdf

Intergovernmental Panel on Climate Change (IPCC) Reports (1997). The Regional Impacts of Climate Change: An Assessment of Vulnerability. Retrieved from https://archive.ipcc.ch/ipccreports/sres/regional/index.php?idp=30
International Organization for Migration (IOM) (2020). Migration in West and North Africa and across the Mediterranean: Trends, Risks, and Vulnerabilities. IOM, Geneva.
International Trade Administration (2023). Ghana - Country Commercial Guide, Oil and Gas. https://www.trade.gov/country-commercial-guides/ghana-oil-and-gas.
Leal Filho, W., Manolas, E., Azul, A. M., Azeiteiro, U. M., & McGhie, H. (2018). Handbook of Climate Change Communication: Vol. 2. Practice of Climate Change Communication. –2017.– 397 p.
MESTI (2021). Ghana: Updated Nationally Determined Contribution under the Paris Agreement (2020 – 2030) Environmental Protection Agency, Ministry of Environment, Science, Technology and Innovation, Accra.
Ministry of Energy (2021). Ghana National Energy Policy. Available at https://www.energymin.gov.gh/sites/default/files/2023-09/2021%20ENERGY%20POLICY.pdf
Ministry of Environment Science, Technology and Innovation (2013). Ghana National Climate Change Policy https://www.clientearth.org/media/p13faarf/national-climate-change-policy-ext-en.pdf
Odonkor, S. T., Dei, E. N., & Sallar, A. M. (2020). Knowledge, attitude, and adaptation to climate change in Ghana. *The Scientific World Journal, 2020.*
OECD Climate Change (2023). Climate Finance and the USD 100 Billion Goal. Retrieved from https://www.oecd.org/climate-change/finance-usd-100-billion-goal/#:~:text=At%20the%2015th%20Conference%20of,actions%20and%20transparency%20on%20implementation.
Onuoha, F. C., Dimnwobi, S. K., Okere, K. I., & Ekesiobi, C. (2023). Sustainability burden or boost? examining the effect of public debt on renewable energy consumption in Sub-Saharan Africa. Energy Sources, Part B: Economics, Planning, and Policy, 18(1), 2214917.
Reuters (2023). Comment: How high-integrity carbon markets can finance climate-smart economic growth in Africa by Tariye Gbadegesin. Industry Insight from Ethical Corporation Magazine, a part of Thomson Reuters.
Roxy, M.K. *et al.* (2020). Indian Ocean Warming. In: Krishnan, R., Sanjay, J., Gnanaseelan, C., Mujumdar, M., Kulkarni, A., Chakraborty, S. (eds) Assessment of Climate Change over the Indian Region. Springer, Singapore. https://doi.org/10.1007/978-981-15-4327-2_10
Sova CA, Chaudhury AS, Nelson WA, Nutsukpo DK, Zougmoré R. (2014). Climate Change Adaptation Policy in Ghana: Priorities for the Agriculture Sector. Working Paper No. 68. CGIAR Research Program on Climate Change, Agriculture and Food Security (CCAFS). Copenhagen, Denmark. Available online at: www.ccafs.cgiar.org
Statista (2023). Ghana: Share of economic sectors in the gross domestic product (GDP) from 2012 to 2022. https://www.statista.com/statistics/447524/share-of-economic-sectors-in-the-gdp-in-ghana/#:~:text=This%20statistic%20shows%20the%20share,sector%20contributed%20about%2042.03%20percent
The Africa Center for Strategic Studies (2022). Rising Sea Levels Besieging Africa's Booming Coastal Cities. Available at file:///C:/Users/user/Desktop/Data/africacenter.org-Rising%20Sea%20Levels%20Besieging%20Africas%20Booming%20Coastal%20Cities.pdf
The Africa NDC Hub, Report for COP27 (2022). Doubling Down on Delivering Africa's Climate Action Priorities - Policy recommendations from the Africa NDC Hub. Available at https://africandchub.org/sites/default/files/2022-12/ANDCH%20COP27%20Flagship%20Report_%20version_ENG_pdf
The Climate and Development Knowledge Network (CDKN) (2017). Budgeting for NDC action: initial lessons from four climate-vulnerable countries. Available at https://cdkn.org/sites/default/files/files/National-budgeting-for-NDCs_web.pdf
UN Climate Change News (27 October 2020). Climate Change Is an Increasing Threat to Africa. Available at https://unfccc.int/news/climate-change-is-an-increasing-threat-to-africa

UNDP Climate Promise (2023). For Africa to meet its climate goals, finance is essential. Retrieved from https://climatepromise.undp.org/news-and-stories/africa-meet-its-climate-goals-finance-essential
UNFCCC (2022). NDC Registry. Available at https://unfccc.int/NDCREG
United Nation (UN) (2017). Paris Agreement on climate change: One year later, how is Africa faring? Available at https://www.un.org/africarenewal/magazine/may-july-2017/paris-agreement-climate-change-one-year-later-how-africa-faring
United Nations (2015). SDG7 Energy Compact of the African Renewable Energy Initiative. https://www.un.org/sites/un2.un.org/files/arei_energy_compact_-_approved.pdf
United Nations Convention to Combat Desertification (UNCCD) (2007). Great Green Wall Initiative. Available at https://www.unccd.int/our-work/ggwi
United Nations Development Programme (UNDP) (2016). Africa Human Development Report 2016: Accelerating Gender Equality and Women's Empowerment in Africa. UNDP, New York.
United Nations Framework Convention on Climate Change (UNFCCC) (2020). Climate Change Is an Increasing Threat to Africa. Retrieved from https://unfccc.int/news/climate-change-is-an-increasing-threat-to-africa
United States Department of Agriculture (USDA) (2023). Ghana Climate Change Report. Available at https://apps.fas.usda.gov/newgainapi/api/Report/DownloadReportByFileName?fileName=Ghana%20Climate%20Change%20Report%20_Accra_Ghana_GH2023-0008.pdf
Weber, T., Haensler, A., Rechid, D., Pfeifer, S., Eggert, B., & Jacob, D. (2018). Analyzing regional climate change in Africa in a 1.5, 2, and 3 C global warming world. Earth's Future, 6(4), 643–655.
World Bank (2022). Ghana Can Turn Climate Challenges into Opportunities for Resilient and Sustainable Growth, says new World Bank Group Report. Available at https://www.worldbank.org/en/news/press-release/2022/11/01/ghana-can-turn-climate-challenges-into-opportunities-for-resilient-and-sustainable-growth-says-new-world-bank-group-report
World Bank Group (2023). The Big Push for Transformation through Climate and Development—Recommendations of the HighLevel Advisory Group on Sustainable and Inclusive Recovery and Growth. Washington, DC: World Bank. License: Creative Commons Attribution NonCommercial (CC BY-NC 3.0 IGO).

Climate Finance and Green Transition

Fei Wu, Qiang Ji, and Dayong Zhang

Abstract Given the strategic importance of enhancing China's commitment to address climate change through the development of renewable energy and the modernization of the energy structure, this chapter explores the impact of financial development on China's renewable energy growth, drawing from recent research by Ji and Zhang (2019). This study employs a time-series data and a novel systemic approach to examine the influences of stock market development, credit market growth, and the expansion of international investment on the growth of renewable energy in China over the past two decades. It shows the substantial contribution of the financial sector in reshaping China's energy landscape. Through a comparative analysis with the EU and US markets, it is revealed that China shares similarities with the EU market, particularly in the critical role played by financial development in promoting renewables, implying greater relevance of the EU's approach for China's trajectory in this context.

Keywords Climate finance · Green transition

1 Introduction

China heavily depends on fossil fuels, constituting approximately 90% of its overall energy consumption (refer to Fig. 1). The consumption of fossil fuels, especially coal, has been a major contributor to air pollution in China. The combustion of coal releases pollutants such as particulate matter, sulfur dioxide (SO_2), and nitrogen

F. Wu (✉) · D. Zhang
Research Institute of Economics and Management, Southwestern University of Finance and Economics, Chengdu 611130, China
e-mail: wufei@swufe.edu.cn

Q. Ji
Institutes of Science and Development, Chinese Academy of Sciences, Beijing 100190, China

School of Public Policy and Management, University of Chinese Academy of Sciences, Beijing 100049, China

F. Wu et al. (eds.), *Climate Finance*, Climate Change and Energy Transition,
https://doi.org/10.1007/978-981-97-3308-8_9

oxides (NOx), leading to degraded air quality, smog formation, and adverse health effects. Additionally, the heavy reliance on fossil fuels stands as a primary source of greenhouse gas emissions, exacerbating global climate change. According to data from the World Resource Institute (2012), China holds the position of the world's largest emitter of greenhouse gases, closely followed by the United States. The collective emissions from these two nations contribute over 30% to the global cumulative greenhouse gas emissions. This leadership in emissions highlights the crucial role China plays in the global efforts to mitigate climate change.

In response to mounting pressure due to potential global climate change, China and the United States signed a groundbreaking agreement on 12 November 2014. This agreement reflected a commitment to collaborative efforts aimed at curtailing greenhouse gas emissions. The significance of this agreement lies in the joint recognition of the responsibility these two major emitters bear in addressing the global climate crisis. Notably, China pledged to peak its greenhouse gas emissions by 2030, indicating a timeline for stabilizing and subsequently reducing its emissions. Additionally, the commitment includes increasing the proportion of energy derived from non-fossil fuel sources to approximately 20% by 2030. These targets signify a substantial shift towards cleaner and more sustainable energy practices. While China's commitment to peak emissions and transition towards non-fossil fuel sources is ambitious, questions persist regarding the effectiveness of policies and actions to achieve these goals without adversely impacting economic performance. Balancing environmental sustainability with economic growth remains a complex challenge, requiring careful policy planning, technological innovation, and international cooperation.

In addition to the environmental challenges posed by its heavy reliance on fossil fuels, China faces another significant challenge related to its economy's strong dependence on the global energy market. This dependency is particularly evident in China's reliance on the international crude oil market, which accounts for more than half of its overall energy consumption (Zhang et al. 2016a). The Chinese economy is

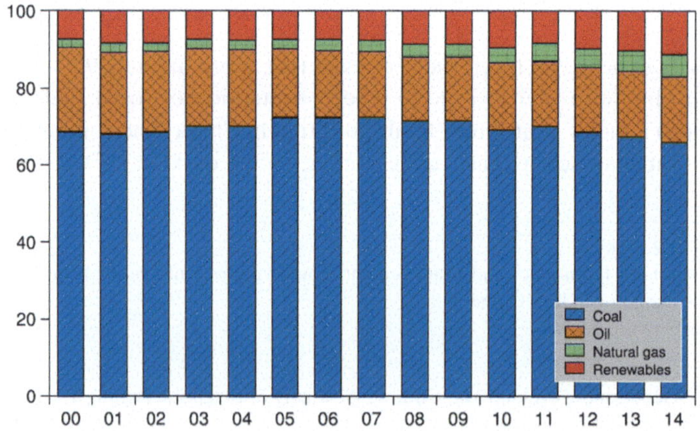

Fig. 1 Energy consumption structure in China between 2000 and 2014 (Ji and Zhang 2019)

vulnerable to instability in the international oil market, especially concerning recent fluctuations in prices and conflicts in the Middle East as well as between Russian and Ukraine. These price fluctuations and geopolitical risks can exert a notable influence on China's economic well-being. Given these challenges, concerns about energy security have gained prominence among policymakers in China. Ensuring a stable and secure energy supply is critical for sustaining economic growth and reducing vulnerability to external shocks. Policymakers must grapple with strategies to enhance energy security, diversify energy sources, and mitigate the impact of external market dynamics.

Faced with the dual challenges of meeting environmental responsibilities and ensuring energy security, Chinese authorities have proactively engaged in the exploration of strategies to transform the structure of energy production and consumption. The importance of the energy sector in achieving these goals has been explicitly highlighted since the presentation of the eleventh five-year plan (FYP) spanning 2006 to 2010. As China navigates the complexities of environmental sustainability and energy security, there has been a notable shift in focus towards enhancing energy efficiency and a growing emphasis on the development of renewable and clean energy sources. In a decisive move in 2005, the National People's Congress enacted the Renewable Energy Law, providing robust legislative support for the advancement of renewable energy. This legal framework marked a significant commitment to fostering the growth of clean energy sources, creating a conducive environment for investment, research, and development in the renewable energy sector.

The thirteenth Five-Year Plan (FYP) of China, covering the period from 2016 to 2020, represents a pivotal phase in the nation's strategic approach to energy development. This plan places a strong emphasis on advancing renewable energy as a fundamental element in upgrading China's energy structure. The primary goals are centered on fostering the development of renewable energy sources while concurrently promoting new technologies to enhance the efficiency and environmental sustainability of conventional energy sources still in use. The plan articulates a clear vision for the future of China's energy sector, aligning with broader global trends towards cleaner and more sustainable energy practices. The overarching goals of the thirteenth Five-Year Plan include restructuring the energy landscape, optimizing energy supply, fostering clean and low-carbon energy sources, and safeguarding national energy security. These goals align with broader global efforts to transition towards more sustainable and environmentally friendly energy systems. Under its guidance, the government is poised to extend support for initiatives in hydropower, wind, solar, and nuclear energy projects.

One of the key initiatives involves plans to install 60 gigawatts (GW) of hydropower capacity in the southwestern region of China. This strategic move leverages the abundant water resources in the region to harness clean and renewable energy. The establishment of a national new energy demonstration zone in Ningxia underscores the commitment to showcasing and advancing innovative energy technologies. This zone serves as a testing ground for new energy solutions, potentially including solar, wind, and other emerging technologies. It aims to demonstrate the viability and scalability of these solutions for wider adoption. In the eastern and southern regions of China, there are plans to expedite the development of distributed photovoltaic (PV) projects. This initiative contributes to the decentralization of power generation and encourages the use of clean energy sources. The thirteenth Five-Year Plan also places a specific focus on the development of wind power projects in coastal areas. Coastal regions often experience strong and consistent winds, making them ideal locations for wind power generation. The plan further outlines the implementation of planned nuclear energy projects, with the aim of achieving an installed capacity of 58GW. Additionally, during the thirteenth Five-Year Plan period, there is a commitment to having an additional 30GW of nuclear energy capacity under construction. By 2020, the thirteenth Five-Year Plan sets ambitious targets to reach a total installed capacity of 210GW for wind power and 110GW for solar power. These targets signal a substantial scaling up of renewable energy infrastructure, aiming to significantly increase the share of wind and solar power in the overall energy portfolio.

The transformation of China's energy structure is intricately tied to the regulatory landscape, legislative measures, and the overall policy environment. These factors play a pivotal role in shaping the direction and pace of development within the energy sector (Liu 2019). A crucial regulatory milestone in supporting the renewable energy sector in China was the introduction of the Renewable Energy Law (REL) in 2005. This legislative measure marked a significant advancement in the development of China's renewable energy sector. The REL established a comprehensive framework for promoting the utilization and development of renewable energy sources, providing a legal basis for fostering clean and sustainable energy practices. Research by Zhang et al. (2016b) indicates that the implementation of the REL marked a swift advancement in the development of China's renewable energy sector.

Over the years, China has consistently unveiled a series of additional policies aimed at advancing its energy structure. Liu (2019) conducts a comprehensive review of relevant policies in China, categorizing them into specialized and unspecialized rules. Both categories implicitly endorse the development of renewable energy, reflecting a multi-faceted and evolving policy landscape. Despite the positive strides facilitated by regulatory measures, the renewable energy sector in China faces challenges, with securing financing standing out as a primary obstacle. Zhang et al. (2013) emphasize the significance of financial support for renewable energy projects. Adequate funding is crucial for the successful implementation of projects, from the initial stages of research and development to the deployment of large-scale renewable energy infrastructure.

Statistics of over the past couple of decades show that China has achieved significant milestones in its renewable energy sector, marked by notable accomplishments and swift advancements. There is a commendable rise in the proportion of renewable energy, including hydro, wind, and nuclear power, in China's energy structure. In 2014, the proportion reached approximately 13.6%, reflecting a significant shift over the previous decade. This trend is indicative of the successful integration of renewable sources into the nation's energy mix, as depicted in Fig. 1 covering the period between 2000 and 2014. Concurrently, investments in renewable energy have witnessed substantial growth. According to the Global Trends in Renewable Energy

Investment reported by Bloomberg New Energy Finance in (2014), China's investment in renewable energy reached USD 59.6 billion in 2012. This propelled China to the status of the world's largest investor from 2013 onwards, underscoring the fervor exhibited by Chinese investors in advancing the renewable energy sector.

However, this enthusiasm has a flip side. While the sector has experienced remarkable growth, it has also witnessed instances of irrationality and overinvestment, as noted by some scholars (Zhang et al. 2016b, 2016c). Such tendencies can lead to resource wastage, foster unhealthy competition, and result in inefficiencies within the renewable energy sector. A notable example of the challenges faced by China's renewable energy sector is the boom and subsequent downturn in the solar photovoltaic (PV) industry in 2012. External shocks, including solar anti-dumping charges imposed by the European Union and the United States, led to severe repercussions. The industry faced disruptions, highlighting the vulnerability of overdependence on external markets and the need for strategic planning.

The renewable energy sector, as an emerging industry, carries inherent risks, requiring diverse sources of investment tailored to the unique characteristics of different projects. From smaller ventures to large-scale projects, the financing landscape is multifaceted, involving various mechanisms. Smaller ventures, especially those involving new and innovative technologies, may find venture capital or equity financing more suitable. On the other hand, larger-scale projects like nuclear energy endeavors often require substantial capital, making bank or debt financing more appropriate. The nuances of these financing needs are explored in detail by Zhang et al. (2016b), offering insights into the intricacies of funding mechanisms in the renewable energy sector. The realization of diverse financing needs within the renewable energy sector heavily depends on the backing of a well-established and robust financial system. A financial system that facilitates access to capital markets, provides efficient credit mechanisms, and supports risk mitigation is crucial for the successful development and deployment of renewable energy projects. The synergy between the financial system and the renewable energy sector is integral to fostering sustainable growth.

In navigating the dynamic intersection of financial development and the renewable energy sector in China, policymakers face critical questions that are pivotal in formulating informed strategies. These questions delve into the role of financial development, the significance of specific sectors within the financial domain, and the distinctions between China and other nations in terms of financial development. The study of Ji and Zhang (2019) addresses these queries through a systematic econometric methodology proposed by Diebold and Yilmaz (2009), offering quantitative insights derived from historical data. Their study seeks to answer the following research questions: To what extent does financial development contribute to the development of renewable energy in China? Which specific sectors within the financial domain hold greater significance in supporting renewable energy in China? What are the distinctions between China and other nations, such as the United States and the European Union, in terms of financial development for renewable energy?

The authors start with a broad examination of financial development in China and subsequently review pertinent literature to establish a theoretical framework elucidating the significance of financial development in the context of renewable energy development. A concise overview of the statistical method applied in this study is included in this chapter, followed by an introduction of the data incorporated into the econometric model and the rationale behind the selection of these variables. The findings in Ji and Zhang (2019) provide evidence that financial development plays a pivotal role, contributing to 42.42% of the overall variation in China's renewable energy growth. Notably, the study reveals that the capital market stands out as the most influential factor, closely followed by foreign investment. A comparative analysis with the European Union (EU) and the United States shows the relevance of the EU approach, suggesting that Chinese policymakers should scrutinize it more closely for potential insights.

2 An Overview of the Financial Market Development in China

This section provides a succinct overview of the evolution of financial markets in China during the last few decades, including the stock market, the banking sector, and foreign investment, with a focus on their contribution to developing renewable energy.

2.1 The Stock Market

Established in 1990 under the direct purview of the China Securities Regulatory Commission (CSRC), China proudly houses two prominent stock exchanges: the Shanghai Stock Exchange and the Shenzhen Stock Exchange. These financial institutions have grown to become global players, with their market capitalizations ranking fourth and seventh worldwide, respectively, as of the conclusion of December 2016, according to Bloomberg. At that juncture, the Shanghai and Shenzhen Stock Exchanges collectively accommodated a staggering 3,008 listed firms, amassing a formidable total market capitalization of RMB 53.1 trillion, as outlined by CSRC (Security market monthly report 2016). This data underscores the magnitude of the financial ecosystem fostered by these exchanges, attesting to their significance in the global financial landscape.

The stock market in China has undergone a transformative journey, evolving into a pivotal source of financing for domestic companies. Its role extends beyond mere market dynamics, playing a vital role in facilitating capital infusion, stimulating economic growth, and supporting the ambitions of burgeoning enterprises. The profound impact of these exchanges on China's economic landscape is evidenced by the aforementioned substantial market capitalization and the sheer number of listed firms, emphasizing their role as essential pillars of the nation's financial infrastructure. As China continues to stride confidently into the global economic arena, its stock exchanges stand as dynamic entities that not only reflect the vibrancy of the nation's financial sector but also serve as conduits for capital, fostering innovation, and contributing to the sustained development of the Chinese economy. The symbiotic relationship between the stock exchanges and the listed firms exemplifies the intricate interplay between finance and industry, further solidifying the stock market's position as a cornerstone of China's economic prowess.

The notion of renewable energy, though relatively novel in its inception, has rapidly evolved, and its progress has been significantly buoyed by the dynamic forces of the stock market. Figure 2 provides a comprehensive overview, showing the numbers of listed companies specializing in the four primary sources of renewable energy: solar power, wind power, nuclear power, and biomass. Within the biomass sector, 13 out of 17 firms went public after the turn of the millennium. This significant move resulted in the mobilization of substantial capital, with these companies collectively raising approximately RMB 8 billion through a series of initial public offerings (IPOs). Notably, the financial landscape underwent a discernible shift, with the average IPO scale experiencing a noteworthy surge from RMB 0.257 billion before 2008 to RMB 0.662 billion thereafter. This upward trajectory underscores the growing financial backing provided by stock markets to fuel the expansion and innovation within the realm of renewable energy.

The pivotal role of the stock market in the development of renewable energy, particularly in emerging markets, has become a subject of recent scholarly exploration. Liming (2009) contrasts financing channels for rural renewable energy development in China and India, highlighting the increasing significance of the stock market as a source of financing. Paramati et al. (2016) document a significant positive impact of stock market developments on clean energy adoption, based on data spanning the years 1991–2012 across 20 emerging market economies. Their findings

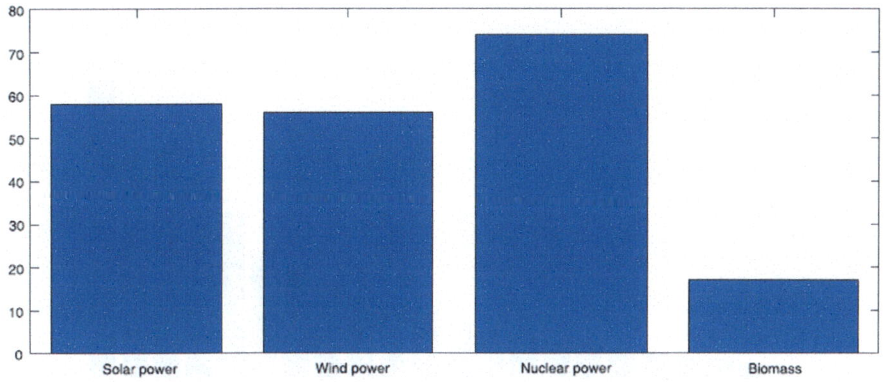

Fig. 2 Numbers of China's listed companies specializing in renewable energy (Ji and Zhang 2019)

confirm a significant positive impact of stock market developments on the broader adoption of renewable energy practices. This correlation highlights the instrumental role that financial markets play in fostering a conducive environment for the growth and integration of renewable energy solutions.

2.2 The Banking System

The banking sector stands as a venerable cornerstone within the framework of China's financial system, boasting a history that predates the emergence of the country's stock market. Its enduring legacy is deeply entrenched in China's economic evolution, playing a pivotal role in the nation's financial landscape. Figure 3 shows the trends of outstanding loans and growth rates of China's banking sector. Over the two decades spanning from 1995 to 2015, the volume of outstanding loans experienced a consistent upward trajectory, while the growth rate of loans exhibited fluctuations. Zhang and Wu (2012) argue that within the Chinese context, the banking sector has exerted a more profound and immediate impact on driving economic growth compared to the capital market. This perspective underscores the historical and contextual factors that have shaped China's financial development, emphasizing the central role played by traditional banking institutions in facilitating economic expansion. The sector's extensive reach into various facets of economic activity has positioned it as a linchpin for economic development and stability.

In China's banking sector, policy banks, notably the China Development Bank (CDB), stand as distinct institutions alongside commercial banks, collectively shaping the credit landscape and influencing the trajectory of the nation's economic development (For a comprehensive review of the historical development of China's

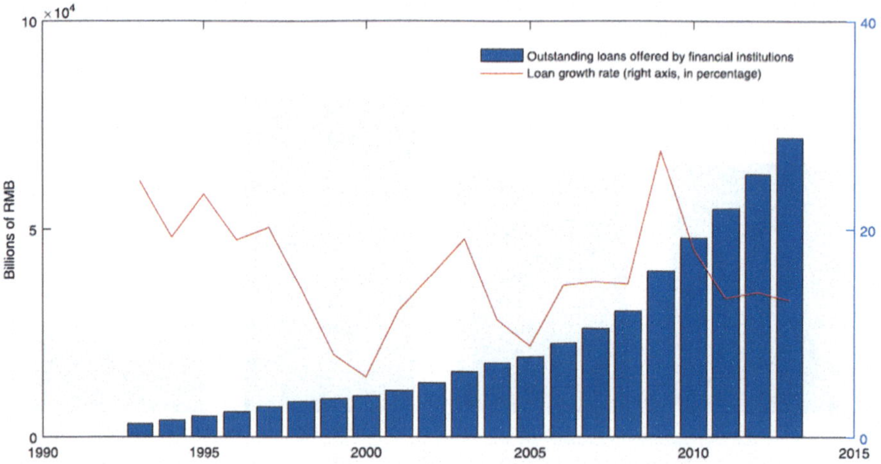

Fig. 3 Growth of domestic loans offered by banks in China (Ji and Zhang 2019)

banking system, please refer to Zhang et al. (2016d)). Policy banks in China occupy a unique position by specializing in the implementation of government policies geared toward strategic development. These institutions play a pivotal role in channelling financial resources to support significant infrastructure projects and initiatives in emerging sectors, notably in the realm of renewable energy. The CDB, for example, has extended over RMB 1.5 trillion in outstanding loans to green energy projects, with expectations of this figure continuing to ascend. An illustrative example of this commitment is evident in 2015 when the CDB allocated a substantial RMB 137.1 billion in loans expressly dedicated to renewable energy projects.

Concurrently, commercial banks have amplified their involvement in green development, aligning their strategies with China's overarching goals of sustainable growth and environmental stewardship. As of the conclusion of 2015, the cumulative outstanding loans from banks to green energy firms surpassed a noteworthy RMB 8 trillion. Among these, 21 major commercial banks contributed an impressive RMB 7 trillion, showcasing a concerted effort within the commercial banking sector to bolster renewable energy initiatives.

The dual financing channels inherent in China's banking sector have proven instrumental in providing substantial funding support to the burgeoning field of renewable energy development. This collaborative approach, involving both policy and commercial banks, reflects a nuanced synergy aimed at aligning financial resources with national objectives. The strategic role of policy banks in steering government-backed initiatives harmonizes with the agility and market-driven approach exhibited by commercial banks, creating a symbiotic relationship that fosters innovation and sustains momentum in the renewable energy sector. As China continues to position itself as a global leader in green development, the multifaceted contributions of both policy and commercial banks underscore the adaptability and resilience of the nation's banking sector.

Undoubtedly, securing loans from banks or tapping into the credit market remains a paramount source of financing for companies worldwide. Scholarly endeavors have sought to unravel the intricate connections between the credit market, energy dynamics, and sustainable development. Ziaei (2015), for instance, employs a Panel Vector Autoregressive (PVAR) model to study the relationships among the credit market, energy consumption, carbon emissions, and economic growth across a spectrum of 25 countries located in Europe, East Asia, and Oceania. He et al. (2019) investigate the impact of green credit on the advancement of the renewable energy sector in China. By examining data from 150 listed firms in China, they find a non-linear threshold effect between green credit and green development. This indicates that the relationship between financial support and sustainable development is not always linear; rather, it may reach critical thresholds that trigger transformative effects. From a global perspective to a specific focus on China, the research contributes to a growing body of knowledge that informs strategies for sustainable development.

2.3 International Investment

Since the initiation of the open-up policy in the late 1970s, the role of foreign capital has proven pivotal in propelling China's remarkable economic growth. Foreign Direct Investment (FDI) has become a primary driver, infusing the Chinese economy with essential elements such as capital, cutting-edge technology, specialized expertise, and various vital resources. This influx not only significantly bolsters China's international trade but also serves as a catalyst for fostering innovation, thereby exerting profound and far-reaching effects on the overall structural landscape of the economy. The symbiotic relationship between foreign investment and domestic economic dynamism underscores the transformative impact of globalization on China's economic trajectory.

Despite the recent deceleration in China's economic growth, particularly in the aftermath of the 2008 global financial crisis (as illustrated in Fig. 4), foreign capital remains a pivotal driving force in the country's economic landscape. Notably, this form of capital has undergone a significant shift towards emerging industries, placing a considerable emphasis on renewable energy. As outlined by the Ernst & Young Renewable Energy Country Attractiveness Index (Young 2016), China currently holds the second position globally, trailing only the United States. It is worth noting that potential policy shifts under the new US president could influence this ranking. China's commitment to advancing its renewable energy sector has positioned the nation to attract increased international investment in green projects. A noteworthy example is the burgeoning green bonds market in China, experiencing rapid expansion thanks to robust government support (Kidney and Oliver 2014). This trend positions China on the trajectory to become the preeminent destination for international investment in the renewable energy sector (Liu 2016). The confluence of policy initiatives and a burgeoning green economy underscores the resilience and adaptability of China's economic landscape in the face of global economic dynamics.

3 Literature Review

Due to the looming threat of global climate change driven by greenhouse gas (GHG) emissions, there is a growing global consensus advocating for the development of renewable energy as a means to curtail the reliance on fossil fuels. Despite the rapid growth of renewable energy (as noted in the International Energy Outlook (2013)), its share of total energy consumption remains relatively modest. A substantial body of recent literature has emerged to model the progression of renewable energy development (Ali et al. 2018; Brunnschweiler 2010; Omri and Nguyen 2014; Sadorsky 2009a, 2009b; Salim and Rafiq 2012; Zhao and Luo 2017). These studies seek to identify the drivers of renewable energy development and establish causal relationships between renewable energy development and a range of economic/financial variables, including economic growth, financial development, energy prices, emissions, etc.

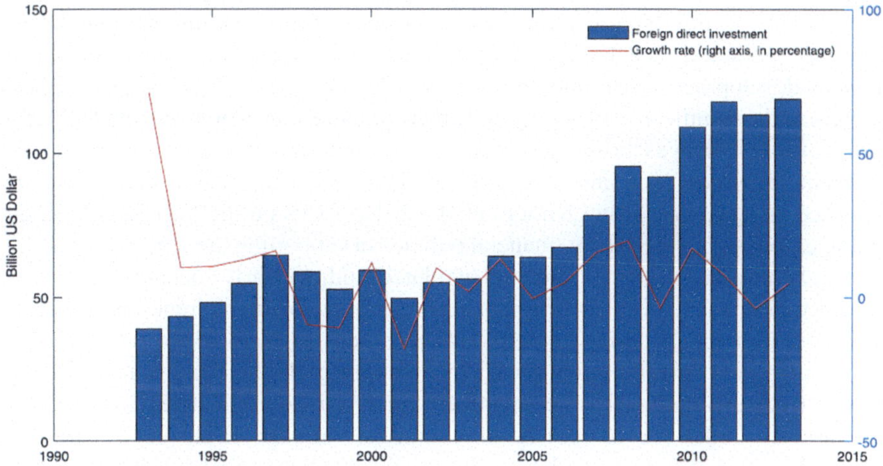

Fig. 4 Growth of foreign direct investment (FDI) in China (Ji and Zhang 2019)

For instance, Salim and Rafiq (2012) examine six major emerging economies, including China, to identify the factors influencing renewable energy consumption. Their empirical findings, derived from both panel-data and time-series models, indicate that income and pollutant emissions are the primary determinants of renewable energy consumption in China, with a bidirectional link between them in the short run. Their literature review shows that scholars typically approach this issue using either supply-side methods (Ma et al. 2008) or demand-side approaches (Sadorsky 2009a, 2009b). Supply-side studies employ production functions and examine technical changes, while demand-side analyses focus on variables such as emissions, energy prices, and income.

Apergis and Payne (Apergis and Payne 2010, 2012) employ panel time-series models to explore bidirectional causality between renewable energy consumption and economic growth, focusing on member countries of the Organization for Economic Cooperation and Development (OECD) (Apergis and Payne 2010) and a larger sample of 80 countries (Apergis and Payne 2012), respectively. In an extension of their work, Apergis and Payne (Apergis and Payne 2014) introduce a nonlinear smooth transition mechanism within the panel cointegration framework. Their empirical results, derived from annual data spanning 1980 to 2010 for seven Central American countries, indicate that emissions, energy prices, and economic growth significantly impact renewable energy consumption in the long run. Ohler and Fetters (Ohler and Fetters 2014) conduct a study covering 20 OECD countries from 1990 to 2008 and find bidirectional causality between renewable electricity generation and the growth of the gross domestic product (GDP), with the relationship contingent on the energy source.

The development of renewable energy faces constraints related to its financing sources. Despite substantial investments pouring into renewable energy projects in recent years (as noted by Bloomberg New Energy Finance (2014)), financing remains a significant concern, largely influenced by the state of financial infrastructure. This issue has sparked a recent wave of studies aimed at understanding the impact of financial development on the adoption of renewable energy. Creti and Nguyen (2018) emphasize the significance of energy and environmental considerations and highlight clear policy challenges in the post-Paris Agreement era. Among various factors, the financial effects or financial market implications of the Paris Agreement are identified as a primary issue. Kimura et al. (2016) focus on the East Asia Summit region, emphasizing the role of financial policies in supporting the renewable energy sector. Their findings and the collection of related studies clearly document the policy relevance of financial development in facilitating the transition to renewable energy.

Several individual studies have shifted their focus to examine the role of financial development in promoting clean development globally. For instance, Chang et al. (2016) explicitly take the financial sector into account when constructing a quantitative index for 16 East Asian countries. Paramati et al. (2016) find that the development of a stock market and foreign direct investment (FDI) can prompt emerging economies to adopt advanced technologies in clean energy production, subsequently increasing the proportion of clean energy use. The underlying concept is that stock market development facilitates both availability, that clean energy projects can acquire capital, and efficiency, that investors can attain higher risk-adjusted returns. Based on a panel of data spanning 1991–2012 for 20 emerging market economies, their model shows a significant positive impact from output, FDI inflows, and stock market development on the utilization of clean energy. Notably, these findings contrast with those of Lee (2013), who identifies no significant relationship between FDI inflows and clean energy consumption in the G20 countries.

Doytch and Narayan (2016) study the connection between Foreign Direct Investment (FDI) and energy demand through a detailed approach, by decomposing FDI inflows by sectors and investigating their impacts on renewable energy consumption. Employing a panel model encompassing 74 countries over the period from 1985 to 2012, the study shows that FDI plays a vital role in influencing the use of renewable energy. However, this role varies significantly across countries and industries. Omri et al. (2014) construct a dynamic simultaneous-equation model and document the presence of bidirectional causality between carbon emissions and FDI inflows. Ajmi et al. (2015) explore the relationships between carbon emissions, growth, and energy consumption in G7 countries (excluding Germany), with their findings supporting bidirectional causality in a time-varying form.

Kim and Park (2016) present further corroborating evidence of the significance of financial development in emissions reduction, particularly in influencing the adoption of renewable energy technology. Their empirical model incorporates measures of equity market and credit market development, employing a panel dataset encompassing 30 countries. The study reveals that the impact of financial development varies across different types of renewable energy; for instance, it proves more beneficial for solar PV compared to biomass and geothermal energy.

Recently, the role of financial development and other factors influencing reforms in China's energy consumption structure has attracted increasing interests from scholars. For instance, Liu and Li (2011) employ a Computable General Equilibrium

(CGE) model to illustrate that removing subsidies for coal or oil could contribute to improving China's energy consumption structure. Their simulation results indicate that a 3% reduction in coal subsidies could result in a 1.76% increase in the share of non-fossil fuel energy compared to the baseline scenario. Shahbaz et al. (2013) utilize various financial development measures, such as the inflow of FDI, stock market improvements, and banking activities, within an unrestricted error correction model. Their investigation aims to uncover the long-run relationship among financial development, growth, capital, trade, and energy use in China. The empirical results suggest that an uptick in energy demand is likely to follow financial development, potentially leading to increased emissions and energy dependence. The implication is that China should allocate more resources to invest in renewable energy and enhance energy efficiency in the long run.

In their examination of financial statement information from 106 listed renewable energy firms in China, Zhang et al. (2016b) identify the issue of overinvestment within these companies. This implies that when these firms have free cash flow, they are inclined to invest in projects that are less profitable. The findings suggest that managers of these firms may abuse their power and make irrational investment decisions. Moreover, the empirical results highlight the role of different financing channels in influencing the performance of these firms. The establishment and growth of a financial market play a crucial role in this context, emphasizing the necessity for proper regulation and sound mechanism design to ensure a healthy investment environment in the renewable energy sector.

In general, there has been a growing interest in the literature on the issues of developing renewable energy. While there is clear evidence of the role of financial development, these findings are predominantly derived from studies conducted across various countries. The work of Ji and Zhang (2019), in contrast, are specifically tailored to the market in China. Despite being a global leader in renewable energy investment, China's unique conditions are not thoroughly addressed in the cross-country studies. As previously mentioned, China is actively promoting further development in renewable energy and aspires to establish a green financial system (Force 2015). This raises crucial questions for policymakers: To what extent can financial development contribute to the advancement of renewable energy, and which facets of financial development are more influential? As of now, the existing literature has yet to provide definitive answers to these questions. While cross-country studies offer valuable insights into the determinants of renewable energy development, they fall short in addressing China's specific circumstances.

Another notable issue in the literature is that current research predominantly concentrates on either the demand side or the supply side, often overlooking the interplay of variables within the entire market system. In fact, all these variables tend to interact with one another. To address this concern, Ji and Zhang (2019) adopt a systemic approach, aligning with the goal to improve China's energy structure during the country's thirteenth Five-Year Plan (FYP) period. Various factors mentioned in the literature, encompassing both the demand and supply sides, are comprehensively incorporated into an unrestricted system in their study. By doing so, their work seeks to bridge the gap in the existing literature and furnish Chinese policymakers with vital information.

4 Methodology

The model employed in Ji and Zhang (2019) is based on the vector autoregressive model (VAR), which has been a powerful tool for examining interactions within a macroeconomic system since its introduction by Sims (1980). The VAR model allows all variables to be endogenous and incorporates them into a unified system, which offers a straightforward yet effective way of explicitly depicting the connections and interactions among economic factors.

Nevertheless, interpreting a VAR model can be intricate. The multitude of coefficients in a VAR model defies straightforward or standard explanation. Instead, methods like impulse response functions and variance decomposition are often employed to interpret the model. Both of these approaches are fundamentally forward-looking. An impulse response function reveals how the system reacts to specific shocks, while variance decomposition informs us about the extent to which the variation in one variable—measured by forecasting error—is accounted for by variables, including itself, within the system. On the basis of the variance decomposition approach, Diebold and Yilmaz (2009) introduce an intuitive method for interpreting the interconnections within a VAR system, which is then refined by the authors (Diebold and Yilmaz 2014).

Based on the approach of Diebold and Yilmaz (2009, 2014), Ji and Zhang (2019) construct a covariance-stationary K-variable VAR model, where K equals the number of selected variables (seven in this study). The model is estimated and then the forecasting error variance decomposition approach is applied. As the variance decomposition indicates the amount of information each variable contributes to the other variables in the autoregression, it is therefore possible to derive the information on: how much the variation in a given variable is explained by each of the other variables in the VAR model; how much information this variable gains from and contributes to the VAR system; pairwise relative contributions for all possible pairs of variables in the system. More technical explanation can be found in Ji and Zhang (2019). This approach basically enables the user to identify the information flow in the VAR system, as well as each variable's status of receiving or contributing information to the system. It also allows the identification of pairwise relationships in terms which variable acts as the driving force of the other, drawn on the intuition behind forecasting error variance decomposition.

5 Data and Variable Selection

The data utilized in Ji and Zhang (2019) span an annual frequency from 1992 to 2013, subject to the availability of stock market data in China, as official stock market data are not available prior to 1992. As discussed before, there are three major funding sources to support the needs of developing renewable energy in China: the stock market, the banking sector, and international capital. In accordance with these stylized facts, three indicators of financial development are employed to account for these funding channels, namely, the stock market development ("Stock"), which is the market capitalization of listed domestic companies as a percentage of GDP; the credit market development ("Credit"), which is measured by domestic credit provided by the financial sector as a percentage of GDP; and foreign investment ("FDI"), which is represented by FDI inflows as a percentage of GDP. The first two indicators represent the conditions for equity and debt financing, respectively, while the third indicator reflects the influence of international investment. Data of financial development are obtained from the CEInet Statistics Database and the National Bureau of Statistics in China.

To gauge the development of renewable energy and energy consumption structure, two variables are adopted by Ji and Zhang (2019). For their main analysis, the authors calculate the shares of renewable energy in total final energy consumption and use this percentage. This variable ("Renew01") reflects the general landscape of energy consumption in China and captures the overall trend in the growth of renewable energy. To check the robustness of their main results, another indicator ("Renew02") is adopted, which is the non-hydro renewable electricity net generation (in Billion KWh). The rationale is that hydropower holds the largest share and displays considerable difference from other forms of renewable energy. Upon excluding hydropower, the development trend of non-hydro renewables differs notably from the scenario of considering all renewables. This is evident in Fig. 5, which compares the change in the proportions of renewable energy over total energy consumption (left-hand panel) and the trend of net electricity generation from non-hydro renewable energy over the sample period. While the share of renewable energy in China's total energy consumption exhibits a substantial increase throughout the sample period (nearly doubling from 5.2% in 1993 to 10.2% in 2013), the net electricity generation from non-hydro renewable energy sources presents quite distinct patterns.

Furthermore, the right panel of Fig. 5 reveals a clear structural change after 2008, marked by a substantial surge in non-hydro renewable electricity generation. To address the potential influence of the structural change in the development of non-hydro renewables, the non-hydro renewable electricity net generation is used by Ji and Zhang (2019) to assess the robustness of the main results. The data of non-hydro renewable electricity net generation is obtained from the US Energy Information Administration (EIA) website.

Data source: CEInet Statistics Database and EIA for non-hydro renewable electricity.

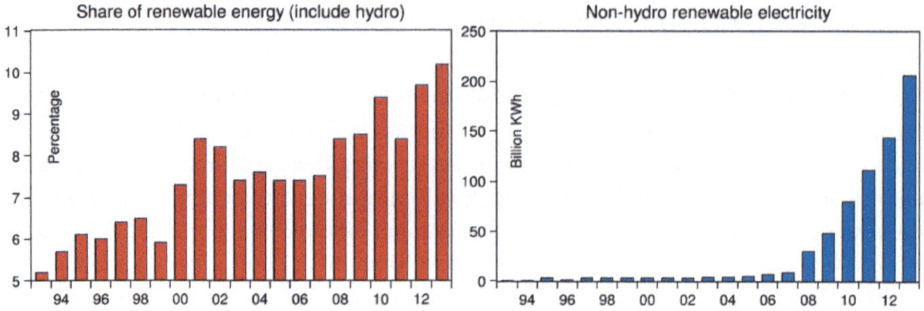

Fig. 5 Renewable energy development in China (Ji and Zhang 2019)

The selection of other variables for the construction of the VAR model generally follows the existing literature (Kim and Park 2016; Shahbaz et al. 2013). The variable GHG, which is the total greenhouse gas emissions (Mt of CO_2 or equivalent) gauges the level of environmental pressure, which tends to drive the adoption of renewable energy. The data of GHG are obtained from CAIT (2017). To address the impact from the fossil fuel side, the crude oil price variable ("Oil") is incorporated in the VAR model, which is Brent oil spot price in US dollars per barrel, with data obtained from the EIA website. To account for the influence of the macroeconomic condition, the authors follow the literature and add the economic growth variable (""Growth") to the model, which is the per capita GDP growth rate, with data collected from the National Bureau of Statistics in China.

To fulfill the stationary condition required by the VAR model (Diebold and Yilmaz 2009), all variables are transformed into growth rates. All the variables employed in the model exhibit positive mean growth rates, except for FDI inflows. The negative mean value for FDI inflows, being relative to GDP, may indicate that GDP experiences a more rapid growth rate than FDI inflows. The measure of growth in the non-hydro renewable energy sector displays significant variation, consistent with the observations in Fig. 5. Results from the KPSS unit root test confirm that all variables are stationary.

6 Empirical Results

6.1 The Contribution of Financial Development to Renewable Share

Ji and Zhang (2019) start with estimating the VAR model that incorporates seven variables, where the growth rate of renewable energy as a share of total energy consumption is used to represent the change in energy structure in China. The interactions within this system are visualized by plotting pairwise relative contributions between any two variables, shown in Fig. 6. An arrow from one variable pointing to another indicates that the former explains a greater portion of the variation in the latter than from the opposite direction. The authors mark the variable with the highest relative contribution to the system and its associated lines by red, and the variable with the lowest contribution by blue. This can also be interpreted as the blue-colored variable has the highest relative gain of information from the system.

Specifically, the red variable, stock market development, plays a crucial role in directing the information flow in the system. It contributes the most to the system in terms of net value and is net contributing to all the other variables in the system. By contrast, economic growth (marked in blue) exhibits the highest net gain from

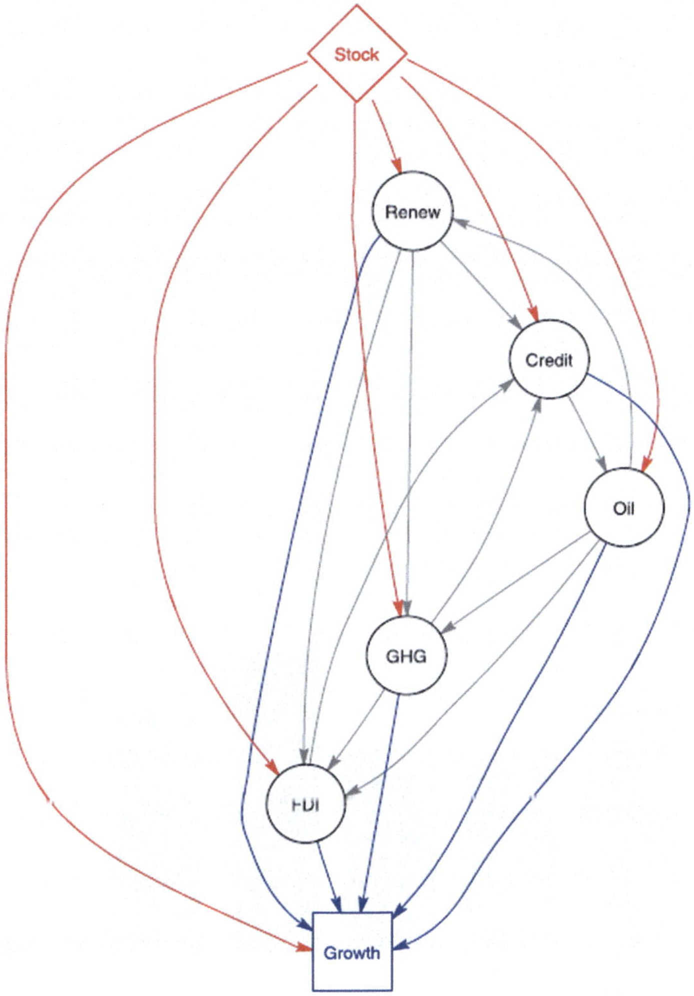

Fig. 6 Pairwise interactions in the VAR system (Ji and Zhang 2019)

the system, gaining relatively more than it contributes to all the other variables. In comparing the roles of three financial development measures, it is evident that stock market development plays a distinctive role as a net contributor to the shifts in the share of renewable energy within the overall energy consumption landscape. On the other hand, the development of the credit market and FDI appears to function as information receivers, susceptible to changes in the energy structure rather than actively leading these changes. Furthermore, changes in oil prices are identified as a net contributor to the development of renewable energy. Based on these observations, dynamics within the stock market, coupled with fluctuations in crude oil prices, can be used for predicting the tendency of renewable energy development. By closely monitoring these financial and commodity market dynamics, stakeholders and policymakers can potentially gain valuable foresight into the future trends and trajectories in the renewable energy sector, facilitating informed decision-making and strategic planning.

In terms of magnitudes of pairwise contributions, Ji and Zhang (2019) calculate the full-sample contribution of each variable to the system ("To") and how much each variable gains from the system ("From"). They then calculate a "Net" measure corresponding to the difference between To and From. The magnitudes of these measures show that the stock market development makes the highest net contribution to the system at 39.48%, while Growth gains the most from the system, with a net gain of 70.10%, consistent with the visualized information in Fig. 6 that stock market development is the top net contributor while economic growth is the top net receiver.

In terms of how much information the renewable energy share gains from the system and each of other variables, Ji and Zhang (2019) decompose its gain from each variable. Overall, the system (excluding renewable energy share itself) accounts for 79.23% of its variation. Comparing all the other factors, changes in oil prices contribute the most (19.60%) to the changes in renewable energy share, followed by the stock market development (16.25%) and then GHG (15.8%), generally consistent with existing evidence in the literature. Figure 7 visualizes these findings in a bar graph.

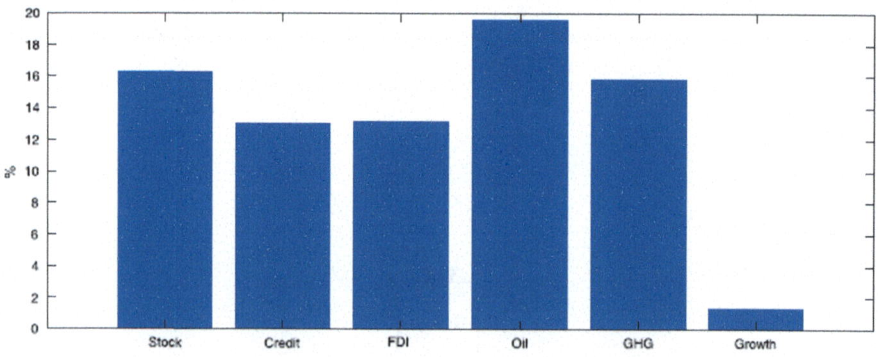

Fig. 7 Contributions to the variation of renewable energy share (Ji and Zhang 2019)

While Oil and GHG represent the influences stemming from the demand side on driving the development of renewable energy, the three financial development measures (Stock, Credit, and FDI) can be viewed as the supply-side factors. Collectively, the empirical results indicate that financial market development contributes 42.42% to the variation in China's renewable energy development over the past two decades, with the stock market contributing the most at 16.25%. In essence, the evolution of China's stock market emerges as a key explanatory factor accounting for a substantial portion of the fluctuations observed in renewable energy development, followed closely by international direct investment. These empirical findings send a distinct and crucial message to Chinese policymakers: bolstering financial development, with a specific emphasis on fortifying the stock market, is of paramount importance. Moreover, it underscores the imperative need to institute progressive financing policies specifically tailored to support the growth of renewable energy initiatives.

The robust statistical evidence presented in these findings lends substantial weight to recent initiatives in China aimed at establishing a green financial system. The empirical link between stock market dynamics and the trajectory of renewable energy development not only underscores the relevance of financial markets but also emphasizes their potential as powerful tools for steering and influencing the nation's sustainable energy future. In light of these results, there is a compelling case for policymakers to proactively foster an environment that not only encourages the growth of the stock market but also aligns it with the imperatives of renewable energy expansion. This strategic alignment can, in turn, propel China further towards its goals of sustainable development and environmental stewardship.

6.2 Robustness Check

To check the robustness of the main findings, Ji and Zhang (2019) use an alternative measure to capture the changes in China's energy structure, namely, the growth rate of non-hydro renewable electricity generation.

Expanding upon the earlier discussion, it is evident that hydropower stands out as a vital source of clean and renewable energy in China, yet its development unfolds with distinct features that distinguish it from other forms of renewable energy. First, there exists an inherent imbalance in its regional distribution, with a significant concentration in the southwestern part of the country. The challenge arises in transmitting electricity from these power-rich regions to the energy-demanding eastern regions, incurring substantial costs. Additionally, the development costs in these hydro-rich areas are escalating, contributing to the complexity of the hydroelectric landscape. Second, hydro projects typically manifest as large-scale endeavors, necessitating considerable state investment and involving protracted approval procedures that traverse various branches of the government. These complexities pose challenges to swift and streamlined development. Moreover, while hydropower undoubtedly addresses specific environmental concerns, it may simultaneously give rise to other environmental considerations.

Acknowledging these unique characteristics of hydropower, the trajectory of China's energy structure reform pivots towards non-hydropower alternatives. In fact, the period since 2008 has witnessed a noteworthy shift, with non-hydro renewable energy starting to assume a significant role in China's energy landscape. As illustrated in the right panel of Fig. 5, the non-hydro component of renewable energy has experienced a remarkable surge, signaling a strategic and conscious transition away from the challenges posed by hydropower towards a more diversified and sustainable energy future. This shift underscores a concerted effort to address the imbalances and complexities associated with hydropower, reinforcing the commitment to non-hydro alternatives as a more crucial direction for China's ongoing energy transformation.

Given the growing significance of non-hydro power in shaping the overall renewable energy landscape, there arises a critical need to assess the efficacy of our economic system, particularly when excluding hydropower from the equation. In achieve this purpose, Ji and Zhang (2019) construct a comparable seven-variable VAR model, substituting the growth rate of non-hydro renewable energy for the growth rate of the overall share of renewable energy in total energy consumption. The results of their analysis are depicted in Figs. 8 and 9, offering a comprehensive visual representation of the revised system. Figure 8 illustrates each variable's contribution to and gain from the system. Notable shifts emerge in comparison to the main analysis results. Despite these variations, the preeminence of stock market development persists as the foremost contributor to this refined system. This is evidenced by both its highest magnitudes of To and Net variables, affirming that stock market dynamics continue to wield substantial influence on information flow within the entire system. This persistence of stock market development's significance holds even when the hydro component is excluded from the renewable energy sector.

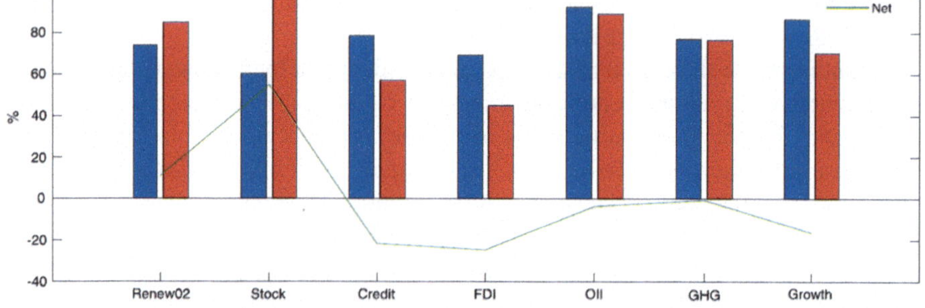

Fig. 8 Robustness check of the interactions within the VAR system (Ji and Zhang 2019)

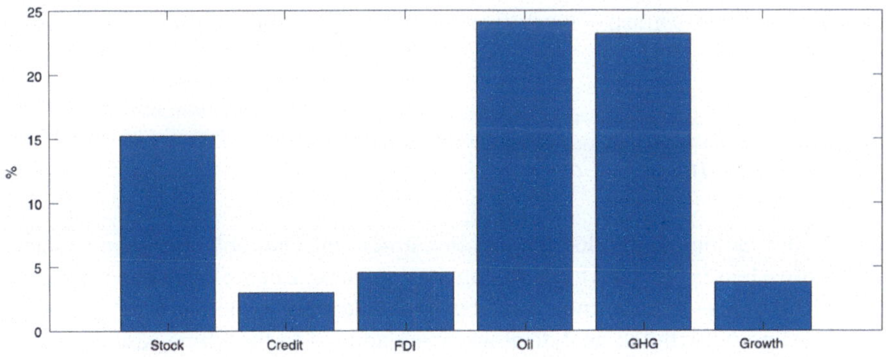

Fig. 9 Contributions to the variation of non-hydro renewable growth (Ji and Zhang 2019)

Such a finding implies that, irrespective of the specific composition of the renewable energy mix, the trajectory of stock market development remains a critical determinant, leading the informational dynamics within the system. Therefore, close attention to stock market dynamics not only enhances the ability to forecast the future development of the broader renewable energy sector but also proves instrumental in predicting trends specifically within the non-hydro renewables domain. This insight reinforces the enduring impact of financial markets on the renewable energy landscape, emphasizing their utility as predictive indicators for informed decision-making and strategic planning.

In a parallel vein, Ji and Zhang (2019) analyze the contributions made by the diverse variables to the variance in the growth of non-hydro renewable energy, as shown in Fig. 9. The results corroborate some of the patterns observed in the primary analysis, shown in Fig. 7. Akin to the main results, oil price changes remain the most significant contributor to the variation in the growth of non-hydro renewables. This underscores the enduring impact of oil price dynamics on the renewable energy landscape, even when focusing exclusively on non-hydro sources. A noteworthy departure from the primary results is observed in the second and third most influential contributors. In this robustness analysis, GHG emissions take precedence over stock market development, signifying an increased environmental influence on the growth of non-hydro renewables. This inversion suggests that, when isolating the development of non-hydro renewables, environmental pressures exert a more prominent role compared to the financing conditions emanating from equity markets.

Furthermore, when combining the contributions from Stock, Credit, and FDI, it is shown that financial market development still maintains a substantive role, contributing 22.74% to the variation in the growth of non-hydro renewables. Although this represents a slight reduction in magnitude compared to the main model, it underscores the enduring relevance of financial markets even in the context of a more focused analysis on non-hydro renewable energy. This nuanced understanding of the varied factors influencing the growth of non-hydro renewables contributes to a more comprehensive grasp of the intricate dynamics governing the renewable energy sector.

6.3 The US and EU Cases

In the examination of the adoption and investment in renewable energy, a valuable comparative lens is provided by assessing the experiences of the European Union and the United States—both acknowledged as global leaders in the realm of renewable energy. Aligning with the analytical approach applied to the China case discussed earlier, Ji and Zhang (2019) methodically assemble an identical set of variables for both the European Union and the United States, drawing from the World Bank's World Development Indicators (WDI) spanning the period from 1991 to 2012. This timeframe aligns closely with the scope of the former analysis on China. Notably, the sample period concludes in 2012 due to the end of available years of WDI data on renewable energy share and GHG emissions.

Using the VAR framework, the authors systematically calculate the contributions made by each variable to the variation in the share of renewables within each of the two markets. The results, shown in Fig. 10, offer a nuanced portrayal of the dynamic factors influencing the evolution of renewable energy adoption in these influential regions. This comparative analysis not only enriches our understanding of the distinctive trajectories of renewable energy development in the European Union and the United States but also provides valuable insights into the varied determinants shaping the renewable energy landscape on a global scale. Such a multifaceted perspective contributes to a more comprehensive comprehension of the intricate dynamics at play within the broader context of renewable energy adoption and investment.

The comparative analysis of the European Union and the United States reveals notable distinctions from the patterns observed in the Chinese market, particularly in the case of the United States. In the United States, the collective contribution of

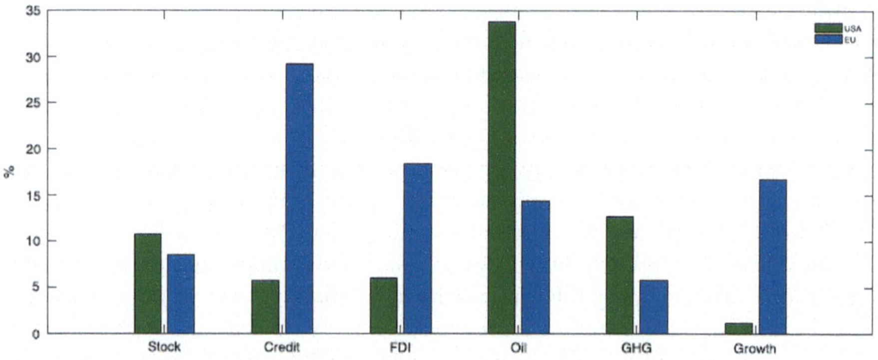

Fig. 10 Contributions to the variation of renewable share in the EU and US markets

financial market development to changes in the renewable energy share is comparatively modest at 22.57%. Intriguingly, oil price changes emerge as the predominant factor, accounting for approximately 33.78%, followed closely by GHG emissions. This suggests that, in the US market, the evolution of renewables is more influenced by information flows from the oil sector and environmental imperatives—namely, factors emanating from the demand side—relative to the supply side financing factors.

In stark contrast, financial factors wield a significantly more substantial influence on the renewable energy market in the European Union, where they collectively contribute a substantial 56.02% to changes in the renewable energy share. This echoes the earlier observation in the Chinese context, albeit with a noteworthy distinction: in the European Union, credit emerges as the primary contributor, whereas in China, it is the stock market. This difference underscores the varied financial dynamics at play in different global markets. Another intriguing distinction surfaces in the relative significance of economic growth. While making a marginal contribution in China, macroeconomic growth plays a more pronounced role in the EU context, contributing over 16.76% to the development of renewable energy. This variance implies the diverse determinants shaping the renewable energy landscape across these markets, highlighting the varied roles of economic, financial, and environmental factors in influencing the trajectory of renewable energy adoption and investment across markets.

Anticipating China's gradual progression toward trajectories observed in the two developed markets, the findings presented here imply that the European Union's model aligns more closely with China's trajectory than the US experience. This alignment is not entirely surprising, considering that the US has historically boasted the largest and most advanced financial markets for over a century. The prominence of financial market dynamics in the European Union, akin to the observed patterns in China, suggests a shared emphasis on the role of financial factors in influencing the development of renewable energy. On the other hand, while the United States is recognized for its abundant natural resources, both the European Union and China heavily rely on the international energy market and grapple with more pronounced energy constraints. This underscores the divergent energy landscapes these regions navigate, with the European Union and China navigating greater limitations and dependencies on global energy dynamics. The EU's model, which places a substantial emphasis on credit in influencing renewable energy development, may align more seamlessly with China's trajectory, reflecting a shared emphasis on financial factors in fostering sustainable energy transitions.

As China continues its trajectory of energy transformation, the experiences of these developed markets serve as valuable benchmarks, providing insights into the potential future evolution of China's renewable energy sector. The comparisons presented in this analysis of Ji and Zhang (2019) offer a glimpse into the complex interplay of financial, environmental, and economic factors that shape the renewable energy landscape in different global contexts.

7 Conclusion and Policy Implications

This chapter thoroughly reviews a study on China's renewable energy growth by Ji and Zhang (2019) and accordingly discusses the role of financial development during this course. The strategic significance of advancing China's commitment to combat climate change lies in the development of the renewable energy sector and the modernization of the energy structure. Policymakers and authorities have exerted considerable efforts to drive these initiatives forward. China's thirteenth Five-Year Plan (FYP) has reiterated the strategic significance of upgrading the country's energy structure, with concrete targets and strategies outlined to increase the proportion of renewable energy and encourage the production of clean energy. These initiatives underscore the Chinese government's commitment to emission reduction and pursuit of an environmentally sustainable trajectory for economic growth. Remarkable progress has been attained in the preceding two FYP periods, successfully meeting ambitious emissions reduction objectives despite substantial economic challenges.

However, venturing into renewable energy development is frequently fraught with risks and substantial initial costs. Policy interventions become imperative to cultivate a conducive atmosphere for the advancement of this sector. The financial landscape serves as a pivotal cornerstone in this endeavor. Currently, a critical impediment in China's energy revolution is the presence of financial constraints, intricately intertwined with the country's financial development. It is therefore crucial to consider to what extent financial development contributes to the progress of renewable energy in China, and identify the most important aspects of financial development in aiding the green transition and energy structural upgrading. The existing literature in China's proactive initiatives in establishing a green financial system has posited financial development as a crucial factor in renewable energy expansion.

Motivated by these studies, Ji and Zhang (2019) employ time-series data and a novel systemic approach to investigate the extent to which financial development has underpinned the growth of renewable energy in China over the last two decades. Three aspects of financial market development are considered in their study, namely, stock market development, credit market growth, and the expansion of international investment. The empirical findings highlight the substantial contribution of the financial sector to reshaping China's energy landscape. In totality, the development of the financial sector explains more than 40% of the variation in the changes observed in the renewable energy share. Notably, among these three financial variables, stock market development emerges as the most influential, consistent with the intuition that the development of an emerging sector often favors equity financing over debt financing due to inherent high risks. Employing the growth rate of non-hydro renewable electricity net generation as an alternative measure of renewable energy growth, the authors confirm the robustness of the above findings.

The empirical findings from the research carry significant policy implications. First, the results suggest the presence of a market mechanism in China that actively supports the transition towards green initiatives. Notably, the renewable energy sector stands to gain substantially from the overall progress of financial markets. The expansion of the stock market and reforms in credit markets can indirectly bolster the development of renewable energy by providing more efficient and cost-effective financing opportunities. Attracting international capital to invest in the renewable energy sector is identified as a crucial step in this direction.

Second, the study underscores the importance of targeted policy measures, particularly with a focus on the credit market. In comparison to the European Union, the role of the credit market in China is relatively weak. Although the establishment of a green financial system and related initiatives by major banks sends a clear signal to the market, there remains ambiguity regarding how the system can effectively support small or medium-sized enterprises (SMEs). These entities play an active and vital role in green development, emphasizing the need for specific policies catering to their unique challenges and contributions.

Third, the comparative analysis with the EU and US markets further reveals that China shares some similarities with the EU market in terms of the critical role financial development plays in promoting renewables. This stands in contrast to the distinct characteristics observed in the US case. The implication is that the EU's path may be more relevant to China, given their shared fundamental characteristics. Recognizing these similarities suggests that lessons and strategies from the EU's experience in advancing renewables may be more applicable and beneficial to China than those from the US market.

In conclusion, the empirical insights derived from the research conducted by Ji and Zhang (2019) underscore the critical need for policymakers in China to reinforce the role of the capital market and implement policies that actively support the burgeoning renewable energy sector. The significance of these findings extends beyond the immediate context, as they contribute statistical evidence advocating for the establishment of a robust green financial system within China. The emphasis on capital market strengthening and supportive policies emerges as a strategic imperative in the face of escalating global concerns regarding climate change and sustainable development. The research highlights the pivotal role that financial mechanisms can play in steering a country towards a greener and more sustainable trajectory.

While the empirical findings by Ji and Zhang (2019) are grounded in the context of China, their broader implications resonate across international boundaries, especially for economies in the developing world. The exploration of an optimal path for green transition is a shared global endeavor, and the generalizable nature of the findings offers valuable insights for policymakers in other developing economies. The transferability of these insights underscores the potential for cross-border collaboration and knowledge exchange in navigating the challenges and opportunities associated with sustainable development. As the world grapples with the imperative of mitigating climate change, studies of this nature serve as beacons, guiding policymakers towards evidence-based decisions that can shape a more sustainable and resilient future for nations around the world.

However, it is necessary to acknowledge the limitations in Ji and Zhang's (2019) study. The relatively small sample size and the specific empirical model employed introduce constraints on the generalizability of the results. Caution is warranted in interpreting numerical outcomes, as they may exhibit sensitivity to substantial variations in the variables. Future research endeavors in this domain should, therefore, aim to expand sample sizes and explore alternative empirical models to enhance the robustness and reliability of the findings.

References

Ajmi A N, Hammoudeh S, Nguyen D K, Sato J R. 2015. On the relationships between CO2 emissions, energy consumption and income: the importance of time variation. Energy Econ. 49, 629–638.

Ali, Q, Khan M T I, Khan M N I. 2018. Dynamics between financial development, tourism, sanitation, renewable energy, trade and total reserves in 19 Asia cooperation dialogue members. J. Clean. Prod. 2018 (179), 114–131.

Apergis N, Payne J E. 2010. Renewable energy consumption and economic growth: evidence from panel of OECD countries. Energy Policy 38, 656–660.

Apergis N, Payne J E. 2012. Renewable and non-renewable energy consumption-growth nexus: evidence from a panel error correction model. Energy Econ. 34, 733–738.

Apergis N, Payne J E. 2014. Renewable energy, output, CO2 emissions, and fossil fuel prices in Central America: evidence from a nonlinear panel smooth transition vector error correction model. Energy Econ. 42, 226–232.

Bloomberg New Energy Finance. 2014. Global Trends in Renewable Energy Investment, Report. Frankfurt School-UNEP Centre.

Brunnschweiler C N. 2010. Finance for renewable energy: an empirical analysis of developing and transition economies. Environ. Dev. Econ. 15 (3), 241–274.

CAIT Climate Data Explorer. 2017. Washington, DC: World Resources Institute. Available online at: http://cait.wri.org.

Chang Y, Fang Z, Li Y. 2016. Renewable energy policies in promoting financing and investment among the East Asia Summit countries: quantitative assessment and policy implications. Energy Policy 95, 427–436.

China Securities Regulatory Commission. 2016. Security market monthly report. November 2016.

Creti A, Nguyen D K. 2018. Energy and environment: transition models and new policy challenges in the post Paris Agreement. Energy Policy 122, 677–679.

Diebold F X, Yilmaz K. 2009. Measuring financial asset return and volatility spillovers, with application to global equity markets. Econ. J. 119, 158–171.

Diebold F X, Yilmaz K. 2014. On the network topology of variance decompositions: measuring the connectedness of financial firms. J. Econ. 182 (1), 119–134.

Doytch N, Narayan S. 2016. Does FDI influence renewable energy consumption? An analysis of sectoral FDI impact on renewable and non-renewable industrial energy consumption. Energy Econ. 54, 291–301.

Ernst & Young. 2016. Renewable energy country attractiveness index, October, 48.

GFT Force. 2015. Establishing China's green financial system, Report for the green finance task force. People's Bank of China and United Nations Environment Programme.

He L, Zhang L, Zhong Z, Wang D, Wang F. 2019. Green credit, renewable energy investment and green economy development: empirical analysis based on 150 listed companies of China. J. Clean. Prod. 208, 363–372.

International Energy Outlook. 2013. U.S. Department of Energy, Energy Information Administration. http://www.eia.gov/forecasts/ieo/.

Ji Q, Zhang D. 2019. How much does financial development contribute to renewable energy growth and upgrading of energy structure in China? Energy Econ. 128,114-124.

Kidney S, Oliver P. 2014. Greening China's Financial Markets. International Institute for Sustainable Development (IISD) (report).
Kim J, Park K. 2016. Financial development and deployment of renewable energy technologies. Energy Econ. 59, 238–250.
Kimura F, Kimura S, Chang Y, Li Y. 2016. Financing renewable energy in the developing countries of the East Asia Summit region: introduction. Energy Policy 95, 427–436.
Lee J W. 2013. The contribution of foreign direct investment to clean energy use, carbon emissions and economic growth. Energy Policy 55, 483–489.
Liming H. 2009. Financing rural renewable energy: a comparison between China and India. Renew. Sustain. Energy Rev. 13, 1096–1103.
Liu C. 2016. China on track to build world's largest green bond market. http://www.chinadaily.com.cn/business/2016-03/04/content-23746462.htm.
Liu J. 2019. China's renewable energy law and policy: a critical review. Renew. Sustain. Energy Rev. 99, 212–219.
Liu W, Li H. 2011. Improving energy consumption structure: a comprehensive assessment of fossil energy subsidies reform in China. Energy Policy 39, 4134–4143.
Liu P, Zhou Y, Zhou D K, Xue L. 2017. Energy performance contract models for the diffusion of green-manufacturing technologies in China: a stakeholder analysis from SMEs' perspective. Energy Policy 106, 59–67.
Ma H, Oxley L, Gibson J, Kim B. 2008. China's energy economy: technical change, factor demand and interfactor/interfuel substitution. Energy Econ. 30, 2167–2183.
Ohler A, Fetters I. 2014. The causal relationship between renewable electricity generation and GDP growth: a study of energy sources. Energy Econ. 43, 125–139.
Omri A, Nguyen D K. 2014. On the determinants of renewable energy consumption: international evidence. Energy 72, 554–560.
Omri A, Nguyen D K, Rault C. 2014. Causal interactions between CO2 emissions, FDI, and economic growth: evidence from dynamic simultaneous-equation models. Econ. Model. 42, 382–389.
Paramati S R, Ummalla M, Apergis N. 2016. The effect of foreign direct investment and stock market growth on clean energy use across a panel of emerging market economies. Energy Econ. 56, 29–41.
Sadorsky P. 2009. Renewable energy consumption, CO2 emissions and oil prices in the G7 Countries. Energy Econ. 31, 456–462.
Sadorsky P. 2009. Renewable energy consumption and income in emerging economies. Energy Policy 37, 4021–4028.
Salim R A, Rafiq S. 2012. Why do some emerging economies proactively accelerate the adoption of renewable energy? Energy Econ. 34, 1051–1057.
Shahbaz M, Khan S, Tahir M I. 2013. The dynamic links between energy consumption, economic growth, financial development and trade in China: fresh evidence from multivariate framework analysis. Energy Econ. 40, 8–21.
Sims C A. 1980. Macroeconomics and reality. Econometrica 48, 1–48.
World Resource Institute. 2012. http://www.wri.org/resources/charts-graphs/top-10-emitters-2012.
Zhang D, Wu Y. 2012. Household savings, the stock market, and economic growth in China. Emerg. Mark. Financ. Trade 48, 44–58.
Zhang S, Andrews-Speed P, Zhao X, He Y. 2013. Interactions between renewable energy policy and renewable energy industrial policy: a critical analysis of China's policy approach to renewable energies. Energy Policy 62, 342–353.
Zhang D, Cao H, Wei Y M. 2016. Identifying the determinants of energy intensity in China: a Bayesian averaging approach. Appl. Energy 168, 672–682.
Zhang D, Cao H, Zou P. 2016. Exuberance in China's renewable energy investment: rationality, capital structure and implications with firm level evidence. Energy Policy 95, 468–478.
Zhang D, Cao H, Dickinson D, Kutan A. 2016b. Free cash flows and overinvestment: further evidence from Chinese energy firms. Energy Econ. 58, 116–124.

Zhang D, Cai J, Dickinson D, Kutan A. 2016. Non-performing loans, moral hazard and regulation of the Chinese commercial banking system. J. Bank. Financ. 63, 48–60.
Zhao X, Luo D. 2017. Driving force of rising renewable energy in China: environment, regulation and employment. Renew. Sustain. Energy Rev. 68, 48–56.
Ziaei S M. 2015. Effects of financial development indicators on energy consumption and CO2 emission of European, East Asian and Oceania countries. Renew. Sustain. Energy Rev. 42, 752–759.

Climate Finance and Green Innovation

Xinrui Li, Xiuqin Wu, and Chin-Hsien Yu

Abstract Green innovation is the fundamental support and driving factor behind green development. It is an essential climate instrument with financial implications. This chapter introduces the relationship between climate finance and green innovation from a global perspective and further analyses the intrinsic mechanism and related economic consequences in the case of China.

Keywords Climate finance · Green innovation

1 Introduction to Green Innovation

Green innovation management is becoming increasingly important in practice and in academics. Green innovation is a combination of eco-friendly practices from the perspective of social responsibility and innovative practices from the perspective of economic growth (Schiederig et al. 2012). It can alleviate environmental problems and enhance environmental performance, as well as boost company competitiveness by lowering manufacturing costs and implementing differentiated operations. Ecological innovation, environmental innovation, and sustainable innovation are other terms for green innovation.

X. Li
School of Economics, Southwestern University of Finance and Economics, Chengdu 611130, China

X. Wu
School of Economics, Guizhou University of Finance and Economics, Guiyang 550025, China

C.-H. Yu (✉)
School of Public Administration, Southwestern University of Finance and Economics, Chengdu 611130, China
e-mail: evaniayu@gmail.com

F. Wu et al. (eds.), *Climate Finance*, Climate Change and Energy Transition,
https://doi.org/10.1007/978-981-97-3308-8_10

Green innovation is now defined in three ways. First, green innovation is perceived as lowering firms' environmental impacts. Through the invention, implementation, and introduction of new ideas, behaviours, products, and processes, green innovation helps lower a firm's environmental burden or accomplish environmentally specific sustainable development goals. The second is to view green innovation as the introduction of environmental performance, which involves creating new market areas, goods, services, and processes that are motivated by social, environmental, or sustainable challenges (Keeble and Lyon 2005). Third, green innovation is synonymous with environmental innovation or advances in environmental performance. It focuses on innovation along with environmental improvement trends and includes process innovation, product innovation, and organisational innovation. According to Rennings (2000), green innovation is defined as new ideas, new products, new services, new processes, or new management systems utilised to address environmental challenges. It includes technological advancements in energy saving, pollution prevention, pollution recycling, green product design, and corporate environmental management that are connected to green goods and green processes.

Green innovation is defined by the Organisation for Economic Co-operation and Development (OECD) as new creations or major improvements intentionally or unintentionally made by firms to products, processes, marketing methods, organisational structures, and institutional arrangements, resulting in differences with relevant peers, with the core principle of reducing negative impacts on the environment through product innovation, technological innovation, concept innovation, and system innovation (OECD 2008). Thus, the core principle of green innovation is innovation that can reduce negative impacts on the environment through product innovation, technological innovation, concept innovation, and system innovation.

Measuring green innovation is similar to measuring general innovation. Since environmental benefits are the essential difference between green innovation and general innovation, the indices of green innovation reflect this particularity. Table 1 shows the currently commonly used green innovation evaluation index system. Calel and Dechezleprêtre (2016) and Popp (2006) demonstrated that an investment in research and development (R&D) cannot definitively determine the kind of innovation because of the path-dependent impact of green technological innovation. In other words, investing more in production activities or R&D expenditures cannot directly reveal the results of innovation. Among them, the most widely used measuring approach is innovation output. Thus, this section primarily represents green innovation with patent-related data, as patents are commonly used as proxies for green innovation and development.

Table 1 Green innovation measurement indicators

Indicator	Sub-indicator
Innovation investment	Internal expenditures as a proportion of Gross Domestic Product (GDP)
	Expenditures for technology introduction by industrial firms
	Full-time equivalent of personnel
Innovation output	**Number of patent applications and authorisations**
	Total operating income of high-tech industries
	Technology market turnover
	Wastewater emissions
	Industrial sulphur dioxide emissions amount
Innovation Environment	Amount of industrial solid waste generated
	Revenue from sewage charges
	Total investment in environmental pollution control
	Resource tax

2 Theoretical Framework: Climate Finance and Green Innovation

2.1 Literature Review

2.1.1 Green Innovation

A wide body of research investigates the factors that determine both green innovation and development, with environmental restrictions receiving the greatest attention. The influence of government investment in research and development money on environmentally friendly innovation has also been advocated in this body of literature. A group of academics have also examined the importance of green finance, including, but not limited to, studies on technology transfer and tax subsidies (Tu et al. 2020; Leeuwen and Mohnen 2017).

A classic theoretical hypothesis about environmental regulations is the Porter hypothesis. Some studies testing the Porter hypothesis have found that strengthening environmental regulations will force companies to increase R&D expenditures (Río González 2009; Triguero et al. 2013). For instance, van Leeuwen and Mohnen (Leeuwen and Mohnen 2017) studied the impact of environmental regulations on ecological investment and innovation, finding that both existing and developing environmental policies significantly promote eco-innovations and eco-investments. Environmental regulatory measures also include energy restrictions, environmental protection legislation enforcement, government subsidies, and other forms of environmental control. For example, Berrone et al. (2013) and Li et al. (2017) discovered that government environmental regulations can encourage businesses to engage in green technology innovation. However, institutional pressure will encourage businesses to increase their investment in green innovation-related research and development, which will in turn encourage businesses to engage in green innovation activities.

Green credit policies reflect the incentive effect of green credit on clean investment through the comparative advantages of availability and convenience when companies obtain credit financing (Flammer 2021; Tang and Zhang 2020). Taking a green credit policy as an example, Liu et al. (2017) used a general equilibrium model to investigate the implications of the policy in the long run. They discovered that green credit policies are better at reducing investment in industries that use a lot of energy, but they are not as good at changing the structure of industrial production. Similarly, De Haas and Popov (Haas and Popov 2023) and Flammer (2021) provided evidence that green bond issuance and stock market development promote corporate green innovation from a global perspective. In addition, Li et al. (2018) explored how firms, banks, and governments utilise green loans for technical innovation and assessed the effectiveness of green loans and government subsidies in promoting cleaner manufacturing. They demonstrated that government-granted green loan subsidies can enhance environmental quality by reducing business energy emissions. According to research, subsidies not only enhance firms' propensity to develop technology but also raise their innovation risks (Xu and Xiao 2023). All these interventions are expected to tighten business financing limitations, encouraging decision makers to invest in intangible assets while lowering intangible assets.

Few studies have explored the role of finance in green innovation, despite its endowment advantages such as capital, which can solve problems such as a lack of behavioural incentives for microenterprises and an unfavourable policy environment. Unlike current command-based regulatory policies and green bonds, climate finance plays a role in ecological and environmental governance by guiding the allocation of funds.

2.1.2 Climate Finance and Green Development

To achieve a successful and just low-carbon transition, climate finance, especially mitigation finance, provides a large number of energy-related projects, such as low-carbon transport and renewable energy power plants (Buchner et al. 2019; UNFCCC 2020). Climate finance has effects on protecting the environment (Scandurra et al. 2017; Li et al. 2022; Lee et al. 2022), the economy (Carfora and Scandurra 2019), and the ability to adapt (Scandurra et al. 2020). Some studies have examined these effects from the point of view of programming implementation. For example, Scandurra et al. (2017) used a sample of 149 developing countries to test the relationship between climate funds and GHG emissions using a quantile regression model. Relatedly, Carfora and Scandurra (2019) used the propensity score matching method to conduct counterfactual analysis, with results showing that climate funds can help reduce greenhouse gas emissions and promote the development of renewable energy.

2.2 The Relationship Between Climate Finance and Green Innovation

2.2.1 Climate Finance and Low Carbon Development

To achieve the global objective of carbon neutrality, technological innovation serves as both the foundation and the key. Green technical innovation is the foundation of green development and the transformation of society into a more environmentally friendly society. Among the different types of climate policies, financial instruments are particularly important in providing financial support for low-carbon development and other solutions to climate shocks (Haas and Popov 2023; Li et al. 2022). To strike a balance between supporting developing countries in addressing climate change and achieving sustainable development, climate finance has emerged as an important climate instrument. As a climate tool with financial attributes, climate finance is an important means of supporting global sustainable development. The Paris Agreement reaffirms the importance of climate finance and focuses on the financial needs of developing countries (Castro and Betzold 2016). Climate finance is thus a potential avenue for promoting green innovations by means of executing diverse programmes, especially for low-carbon technology (Scandurra et al. 2017; Li et al. 2022).

As subsidy policies expire, investors allocate large amounts of mitigation climate finance to low-carbon and renewable energy industries. Specifically, climate finance has the ability to dynamically adjust the opportunity cost of environmental pollution through credit channels. This can result in an increase in clean investment, a reduction in pollution investment, and the achievement of the goal of using capital allocation to guide industrial clean transformation and green development. For example, the Brazilian government has begun to consider using local renewable resources to electrify remote communities. In some remote communities, renewable energy technologies have proven to be a more convenient and economical option than traditional power generation, meeting both climate goals and development needs (Owusu and Asumadu-Sarkodie 2016; Wang et al. 2018).

There are two perspectives from which the correlation between climate finance and low-carbon development can be interpreted. First, climate finance can provide the necessary capital and technology for low-carbon development. Since low-carbon technologies often have high initial investment costs and long payback periods, they require sufficient financial support to promote and apply them. Low-carbon technologies also require continuous innovation and improvement to improve efficiency and reduce costs, which, in turn, requires sufficient R&D investment and technology transfer. Climate finance can provide capital and technical support for low-carbon development through various means, such as grants, loans, subsidies, and insurance, thereby promoting the development and popularisation of low-carbon technologies.

Second, climate finance can provide the necessary incentives and constraints for low-carbon development. Since greenhouse gas emissions have the characteristics of global public goods—that is, emitters enjoy the benefits they bring but do not bear the losses they bring—there is a serious market failure problem. Policy intervention is necessary to achieve the optimal configuration of society and to address this problem. Climate finance can regulate the behaviour of greenhouse gas emitters through various methods, such as taxes, subsidies, quotas, and transactions, so that they can consider social welfare while considering their own interests. Climate finance can promote low-carbon development by providing positive incentives to encourage low-carbon behaviour or by imposing negative constraints to inhibit high-carbon behaviour.

Climate finance can use innovative financing tools, such as green bond funds and climate structural funds, to attract private investors with different risk appetites and investment periods to participate in low-carbon projects, thereby expanding the investor base and capital scale. The relationship between climate finance and green innovation can be reflected in the role of climate finance in low-carbon development to some extent, which is an important component of green development. This argument will be examined in Sect. 3 using global evidence.

2.2.2 The Role of Financing Constraints

According to Schumpeter's innovation theory, the availability of capital is a vital component in the process of technological progress. Unpredictability of returns, asymmetry of knowledge in the innovation process, high regulatory costs, etc. can pose innovative operations to severe external financing constraints. It is difficult for relevant businesses and projects to obtain long-term financial support under the traditional financial model because green innovation activities frequently have the characteristics of long return cycles, information asymmetry, and high risks. Additionally, these activities face serious maturity mismatches and investment constraints. This indicates that a greater amount of capital must be spent on green technology innovation to carry out breakthroughs that change the direction of the industry. As a result, firms may be more likely to have financial restrictions when attempting to implement green technology innovations. Therefore, it is necessary to supplement the process with special financial aid to address the environmental externalities connected to green technical technology innovation.

Some scholars have argued that financing constraints have a direct inhibitory effect on corporate technological innovation (Yu et al. 2021). When facing financial constraints, environmental protection companies may choose not to invest all the cash obtained through green credit into technological innovation. To overcome financial difficulties, companies may choose to invest some of the funds generated by green credits in high-return activities. Companies can use certain green credit funds to offset costs that must be reduced as financial conditions improve. However, companies with more financing constraints have higher external financing costs than companies with easy financing, and their investment–cash flow sensitivity is also greater. Green financing is particularly important for corporate investment in technological innovation.

Climate finance includes the allocation of financial resources in a manner that is ecologically responsible and based on the climatic context. The primary focus of climate finance is to invest in initiatives that are connected to the environment, particularly those related to the solution to climate change. Finance's capital allocation function enables the exertion of environmental governance and green development from the initial stage of the production process (Li et al. 2018). More specifically, climate finance has the potential to decrease investments in polluting projects and direct more funds to flow to environmentally friendly production processes and green industries. In terms of the impact of financial development on both macro and micro aspects, climate finance is not only conducive to the flow of money within the financial system from the pollution sector to the green sector but also to the attraction of large social capital flows into the green field. At the microscopic level, climate finance also provides an important impetus for local governments to increase their competitive advantage, accelerate energy savings and emissions reduction, and promote the green transition.

Climate finance can use the role of multilateral development banks and international financial institutions to establish a mixed financing structure, reduce private investors' risk exposure, and increase their return expectations through public sector policy intervention and risk sharing, thereby changing emerging economies. This indicates the risk–benefit characteristics of the overall climate transition. Therefore, through fund allocation among various types of industries, climate finance has the potential to alleviate financing constraints and promote the innovation of green technology. This assumption is confirmed in Sect. 4 through a case study of China.

3 Global Evidence: Climate Finance and Emission Reduction Efficiency

3.1 Introduction

To minimise global warming, the Intergovernmental Panel on Climate Change (IPCC) said that global yearly carbon emissions must be reduced by half by 2050. A combination of policy tools, such as carbon markets and technical innovation, is likely necessary to achieve the required emissions reductions. The Kyoto Protocol established the International Emissions Trading (IET), Joint Implementation (JI), and Clean Development Mechanism (CDM) formats, which serve as the primary foundations of the global carbon trading market (Michaelowa et al. 2019). Furthermore, international low-carbon technologies (LCT) are being used to reduce carbon dioxide emissions. These technologies include hydropower, wind power, photovoltaics, and renewable energy, with the goal of using energy more efficiently and making use of cleaner energy sources (Rai and Funkhouser 2015). Third, the Paris Agreement, established in 2015, employs National Determined Contributions (NDC) as the new compliance model. Protocol countries submit NDCs to the Paris Agreement to reduce global greenhouse gas emissions.

In general, climate finance refers to international capital flows for low-carbon and climate-resilient development (UNFCCC 2020; OECD 2011), which are primarily sourced from existing aid commitments and flows by bilateral agencies and multilateral funds (Xu and Xiao 2023). Developed countries and international multilateral organisations disburse multipurpose financial resources from developing countries through inclusive projects and programmes to combat climate change (Buchner et al. 2013). In this case, developing countries are the major recipients of climate finance. According to the purpose of funds, climate finance can be divided into mitigation finance and adaptation finance, which aim to reduce emissions and adapt to the adverse effects of climate shocks. Thus, climate finance provides a new framework for international climate action and a potential practice for low-carbon development. These capital flows have direct or indirect greenhouse gas mitigation or adaptation outcomes, which ultimately lead to the achievement of the net-zero carbon targets set by the Paris Agreement and the promotion of environmentally sustainable development (Castro and Betzold 2016; Oxfam 2020).

The implementation of climate finance involves the distribution of multipurpose assistance from donor countries to recipient developing nations with the aim of financing projects and programmes that deal with low emissions and environmental protection. Adaptation finance is a form of climate finance that helps people adjust to actual or expected climate change and its effects. By contrast, mitigation finance primarily focuses on reducing greenhouse gas emissions, such as by investing in renewable energy or reducing deforestation (Pickering et al. 2017).

The manufacturing processes of emerging nations are often accompanied by carbon emissions because developing countries are virtually always in the early phases of industrialisation (Shuai et al. 2017). To provide financial assistance to developing countries in supporting their efforts to prevent climate change and encouraging the development of green economies, climate finance helps them manage the trade-off between sustaining economic growth and reducing greenhouse gas emissions while also providing new incentives for low-carbon growth. It is critical to work out how to improve the efficiency of climate finance to effectively handle the rising severity of the climate change challenge.

3.2 Empirical Analysis

This section briefly examines international climate finance flows from 2000 to 2018 to determine whether climate finance is effective at lowering carbon emissions and fostering green development in recipient countries. The findings suggest that climate finance helps to reduce carbon emissions, with mitigation finance having a more notable effect than adaptation finance. Furthermore, climate finance has a greater negative impact on small island developing states (SIDS) and countries with higher economic growth. These results have important implications for green innovation and development.

Table 2 shows the results of the panel fixed-effect model. The coefficient of climate finance in column (1) is negative at the 5% significance level, which indicates that climate finance has a significant impact on reducing carbon dioxide emissions. This finding is consistent with Carfora and Scandurra (2019), who stated that climate funds have the potential to promote investment in renewable energy power production to minimise the excessive use of fossil energy, which in turn contributes to the reduction of greenhouse gas emissions. Investing in innovation also maximises the use of the little financial resources at hand and capitalises on the technological advancements occurring in developing countries. Thus, the basic results offer preliminary evidence that climate finance promotes the realisation of green development to some extent. In other words, funding and participation in collaborative research and development can be effective tools supplied through development assistance or technical collaboration. This is not unexpected, since climate finance can collect climate costs for high emitters through policies such as carbon pricing, thereby guiding private investment in projects with lower emissions. It can also provide data support and a scientific basis for carbon accounting and the international carbon market.

Based on the two different directions of climate finance goals, we divide overall climate finance into mitigation finance and adaptation finance to identify which portion of climate finance affects low-carbon development in recipient countries. Column (2) in Table 2 shows that the coefficients of mitigation finance are statistically significant and consistently negative, while adaptation finance seems to have no significant effect. In fact, mitigation finance is mostly linked to energy and electricity. This is because the goal of mitigation finance is to lower greenhouse gas (GHG) emissions and to focus on low carbon (Hallegatte and Rozenberg 2017). This can help balance the trade-off between low-carbon growth and economic growth (Buchner et al. 2019; Acheampong et al. 2021; Steckel et al. 2017). For example, some mitigation finance programmes can be used to assist ultra-supercritical coal-fired power facilities (Buchner et al. 2019). These plants may be more efficient and have lower life-cycle running costs than traditional pulverised coal. A new supercritical coal plant will still produce millions of tonnes of CO_2 every year for the next 30 years. Furthermore, climate finance can help governments replace new coal plants with highly efficient natural gas plants if the new facility emits less than half the carbon as a coal-powered business-as-usual option. In October 2021, the European Commission issued the world's largest green bond, raising a total of 12 billion euros for green and sustainable development investments. In the process of low-carbon development, green finance, such as climate finance, has become an important support.

The instruments of climate finance mainly consist of debt and grants. Grants are payments made in kind or cash to recipients for whom they are not legally obligated. Debt instruments stipulate that the principle and/or interest must be paid at some future date. Debt securities and loans are examples of debt instruments. Column (3) shows the results of different instruments for reducing emissions, in which climate finance in the form of grants has a more notable influence. Private capital may be mobilised via risk-mitigation tools, including insurance, guarantees, and local currency hedging. These tools, especially for grants, might be used by development

Table 2 Effects of climate finance on carbon dioxide emissions

Variable	CO_2 emissions		
	(1)	(2)	(3)
CF	−1.623** (0.827)		
MF		−0.942** (0.701)	
AF		6.083* (1.551)	
CF-GRANT			−1.225** (0.697)
CF-DEBT			−0.349 (1.106)
GDP	51.213*** (12.874)	47.532*** (12.057)	50.364*** (12.819)
FIN	0.220 (0.153)	0.204 (0.154)	0.209 (0.152)
POP	−58.221*** (19.420)	−74.515*** (22.294)	−58.955*** (19.333)
IND	1.324*** (0.450)	1.253*** (0.439)	1.303*** (0.463)
TRA	3.492 (8.440)	−1.587 (8.201)	4.534 (8.774)
Constant	607.024** (259.986)	856.277*** (300.708)	619.351** (259.185)
Year effect	Yes	Yes	Yes
Country effect	No	Yes	Yes
R-squared	0.924	0.925	0.924
Observations	1,246	1,249	1,249

Notes: Standard errors are in parentheses. *** $p < 0.01$, ** $p < 0.05$, and * $p < 0.1$. CF = the total amount of climate-related development finance received by the recipient countries in one year (log); MF = the total amount of mitigation-related development finance received by the recipient countries in one year (log); AF = the total amount of adaptation-related development finance received by the recipient countries in one year (log). Control variables include GDP (real GDP per capita), FIN (financial development), POP (the logarithm of total population), IND (the logarithm of industry, value added per worker), and TRA (trade openness)

partners, such as those for renewable energy and adaptation financing, where climate finance has been successful in raising capital but has not been able to attract private participation.

This section also investigates the heterogeneous effects on SIDs[1] due to differences in natural endowments, geographical locations, economic development, and social structure. On the one hand, these countries are the most vulnerable to climate change because of their locations, as well as their more serious social and economic problems. The majority of SIDS, being low-lying coastal nations, face a direct danger to their existence due to the increase in sea levels that may be attributed to global warming. On the other hand, the socio-economic features of SIDS enhance the problems of adapting to climate change and recovering from climatic catastrophes (Steckel et al. 2017). In addition, improving the situation of these countries is in line with the fundamental principles of climate justice and is conducive to the realisation of climate justice. Given that SIDS are particularly susceptible to the effects of climate change and that they have a relatively low degree of responsibility for climate change, the influence of climate finance on environmental performance might be different.

Table 3 reports the heterogeneity results for climate finance. For SIDS, climate finance, especially mitigation finance, remains strongly linked to improvements in low-carbon development. SIDS rely heavily on foreign aid due to their remoteness, isolation, and vulnerability to natural calamities (Scandurra et al. 2020; Niles and Lloyd 2013). The aid also assists in reducing their reliance on fossil fuels (Niles and Lloyd 2013; Anbumozhi et al. 2016). Due to their low financial resources and economic scale, SIDS often have more challenges in terms of generating local resources and depending on imported commodities. This, in turn, restricts the amount of financing available to decrease the risk of climate change and grow in a sustainable manner (Scandurra et al. 2020; Guillaumont 2010). Another possible explanation is the scale of climate finance. An assessment of climate finance flows as a percentage of GDP per capita reveals SIDS as larger recipients.

This is expected to be the case, since greater levels of economic growth led to better use of technology. Technology transfer and innovation take place within a complicated network of connections involving governments, firms, financiers, regulators, and others. Higher-income developing nations may look into alternative energy sources. In addition, a significant percentage of the money that is being spent on climate change mitigation is being utilised to assist countries with middle incomes in lowering their emissions, while nations with low incomes receive less of the benefits (Oxfam 2020). Additionally, climate finance promotes economic development, which in turn improves green development. This result is also in line with the findings of prior research (Shuai et al. 2017), which indicated that various levels of affluence play distinct roles in carbon emissions.

[1] Currently, 58 small island developing states (SIDS)—38 UN Members and 20 non-UN—are recognised by the United Nations Department of Economic and Social Affairs (UN-DESA). Our sample includes 28 small island countries that are developing countries for which data are available.

Table 3 Heterogeneity analysis: SIDS and non-SIDS

	CO_2 Emission		
	(1)	(2)	(3)
Panel A			
CF of non-SIDS	−15.444 (17.093)		
CF of SIDS	−10.440** (4.477)		
Panel B			
MF of non-SIDS		−16.782 (18.643)	
MF of SIDS		−16.800** (6.468)	
Panel C			
AF of non-SIDS			−27.073 (33.844)
AF of SIDS			−12.806* (6.678)
Controls	Yes	Yes	Yes
Observations	1,572	1,572	1,572
R-squared	0.947	0.947	0.947

Notes: Standard errors are in parentheses. *** $p<0.01$, ** $p<0.05$, and * $p<0.1$. CF = the total amount of climate-related development finance received by the recipient countries in one year (log); MF = the total amount of mitigation-related development finance received by the recipient countries in one year (log); AF = the total amount of adaptation-related development finance received by the recipient countries in one year (log). The control variables are the same as in Table 2

3.3 *Implications*

Technology is the core of the carbon peak carbon neutral policy, and finance is the material foundation. Climate-related investment and financing have been an important part of relevant policies since the world came together to control greenhouse gas emissions. From the perspective of innovation, as the current climate finance is mainly concentrated in the field of climate mitigation investment and financing, it is necessary to strengthen the innovation of climate adaptation investment and financing in the future, and find more and better solutions and practices to cope with climate challenges.

One of the primary uses of public climate finance is to support and invest in clean energy technologies. Continuous innovation is required to accomplish global low-carbon development, as are improved technology development and dissemination procedures. On the one hand, developed countries must considerably reduce their emissions. Conversely, the poorest and least developed countries must improve energy harvesting in a climate-friendly manner. Finally, the major emerging economies must change to a low-carbon development path that will allow for additional rapid economic expansion while slowing and eventually ending emissions rise. Without these modifications, neither technology transfer nor innovation would be possible.

While some of the mitigation technologies required for low-carbon development are available, most are more expensive than higher-polluting options. Government commitments to provide $10 billion per year by 2012 and $100 billion per year by 2020 in climate finance are required to support technology. Underdeveloped nations now need additional assistance to introduce these technologies. However, committed climate finance is insufficient to handle the entire challenge. Consequently, it should be spent in a way that reduces the cost of clean technology over time, thereby pushing widespread deployment and encouraging cost and performance improvements.

Energy efficiency solutions must also be widely available to slow the increase in energy demand while addressing energy access challenges by ensuring that new low-carbon generation meets the needs of more customers. Finally, completely new technologies that are still in the laboratory stage worldwide must be created and widely deployed, not only through the channel of climate finance. These advances in energy infrastructure will drive cost-effective, low-carbon development, with climate finance supporting and improving green innovation.

4 Case Study: Evidence from China

4.1 Green Innovation and Finance in China

The Chinese government has made significant progress in promoting green development. In recent years, the Chinese government has proposed the concept of green development to promote economic growth and development while ensuring that natural resource assets can continue to provide resources and environmental services that humans rely on for survival. Green patents refer to patents with green technology as the subject of invention (National Intellectual Property Administration, PRC). Compared with existing technologies, they should have the direct and obvious technical effects of reducing or stopping the consumption of natural resources and being environmentally friendly.

According to the "China Green Patent Statistical Report (2014–2017)" released by the Intellectual Property Office in 2018, China's green innovation activities are currently active, and the number of green patents has gradually increased. In this section, the development of green innovation in China is briefly introduced using green patent data.

Figure 1 depicts the number of patent applications related to green and low-carbon technologies. The green patent classification standards follow the green patent standards of the World Intellectual Property Office, and the databases are those of

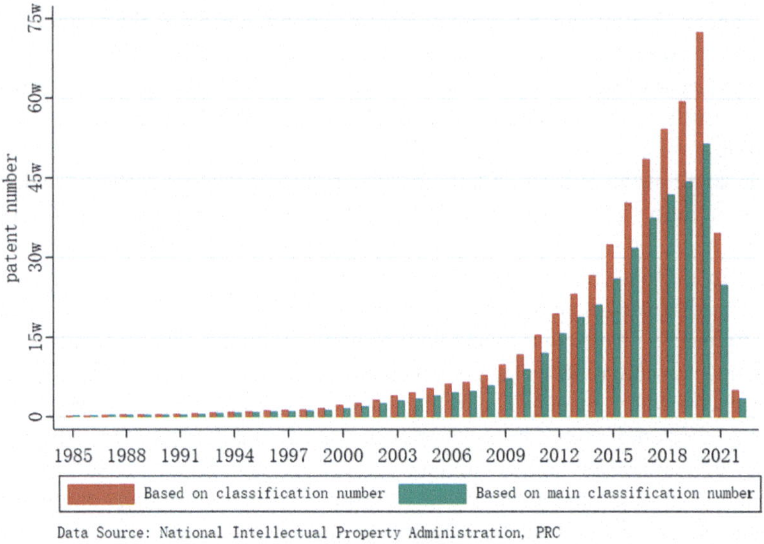

Fig. 1 The number of patent applications related to green and low-carbon technologies

the State Intellectual Property Office and Google Patent's patent statistics. Since the data after 2018 are partially missing, prior data are analysed. By the end of 2017, the number of valid green patents had reached 136,000. In terms of patent applications, from 2014 to 2017, the number of green patent applications reached 249,000, and the average annual growth rate was 3.7 percentage points higher than the overall average annual growth rate of China's invention patents.

Promoting green and low-carbon economic and social development is a key link to achieving high-quality development. From 2016 to 2021, the number of green and low-carbon patent authorisations in China has increased at an average annual rate of 6.5%, and innovation in green and low-carbon technologies has been active.[2] China has achieved rapid growth in patents in hydrogen energy, energy storage, and other technical fields. From 2016 to 2021, the number of patent authorisations issued by the State Intellectual Property Office grew the fastest in the field of hydrogen energy, with an average annual growth rate of 20.5%, and has achieved an average annual growth rate of more than double digits in the fields of energy storage technology, power-saving technology, and fuel-saving technology. China contributed more than 75% to the growth of global hydrogen energy and power-saving technology patent authorisations during this period.

This section also describes the development of green innovation in China from the perspective of spatial distribution. Figure 2 shows the distribution of patent applications related to green and low-carbon technologies in China in 2010 and 2020. Innovation in China has significant spatial dependence. The spatial concentration

[2] Based on information in a report of China National Intellectual Property Administration in 2022, https://www.gov.cn/xinwen/2022-12/28/content_5733989.htm#.

of innovative activities will effectively promote knowledge spillovers. Geographical media-based knowledge spillovers will significantly impact the distribution of innovative activities, thereby influencing broader economic patterns resulting from innovation. As a new concept of innovative development and a new model of technological innovation, green innovation inevitably has the spatial characteristics of traditional innovation. In view of China's development pattern of 'high in the east and low in the west,' the government should adapt to local conditions and adopt differentiated support policies to guide the coordinated and sustainable development of science, technology, and environment in different regions.

Several policy implications of the above regional differences can be proposed. First, the government should continue to encourage independent innovation in the eastern region and accelerate the pace of green and clean innovation. While maintaining sustained economic growth, the government should pay more attention to the improvement of environmental quality to promote innovation efficiency and develop to a higher and healthier level of innovation. Second, the government should actively promote the revitalisation and rise of the old industrial areas in the Northeast, give full play to the resource-rich advantages of the Northeast, increase scientific and technological innovation and personnel investment, and pay attention to the protection of the ecological environment. Finally, government support and innovative initiatives should be expanded in the central and western regions. To promote sustainable development in these regions, the government should guide and support the improvement of green innovation skills, with an emphasis on limiting environmental pollution in energy-dependent areas and enhancing the ecological environment.

Further, green development will inevitably lead to changes in China's overall economic pattern. Some studies show that green innovation has become an excellent way for relatively backward regions, such as the central and western regions, to catch up economically and narrow the gap between the east and the west. Therefore, studying the spatial pattern of green innovation can reveal the spatial agglomeration of green innovation in China, and the spatial path for the expansion and evolution of green innovation can be explored to coordinate the spatial balance of green innovation and promote the advancement of green innovation across the board.

Regarding climate finance, China's Ministry of Ecology and Environment[3] defines climate finance as investment and financing activities that guide and promote more funds to be invested in the field of addressing climate change to achieve nationally determined contributions and green and low-carbon development goals. Climate finance is an important part of green finance, and its scope of support includes both mitigation and adaptation to climate change. Mitigating climate change includes adjusting the industrial structure, optimising the energy structure, and increasing forests and grasslands. Adapting to climate change includes improving the adaptability of agriculture, water resources, forestry, and ecosystems.

---

[3] Source of information: https://english.mee.gov.cn/Resources/Reports/reports/202211/P020221110605466439270.pdf.

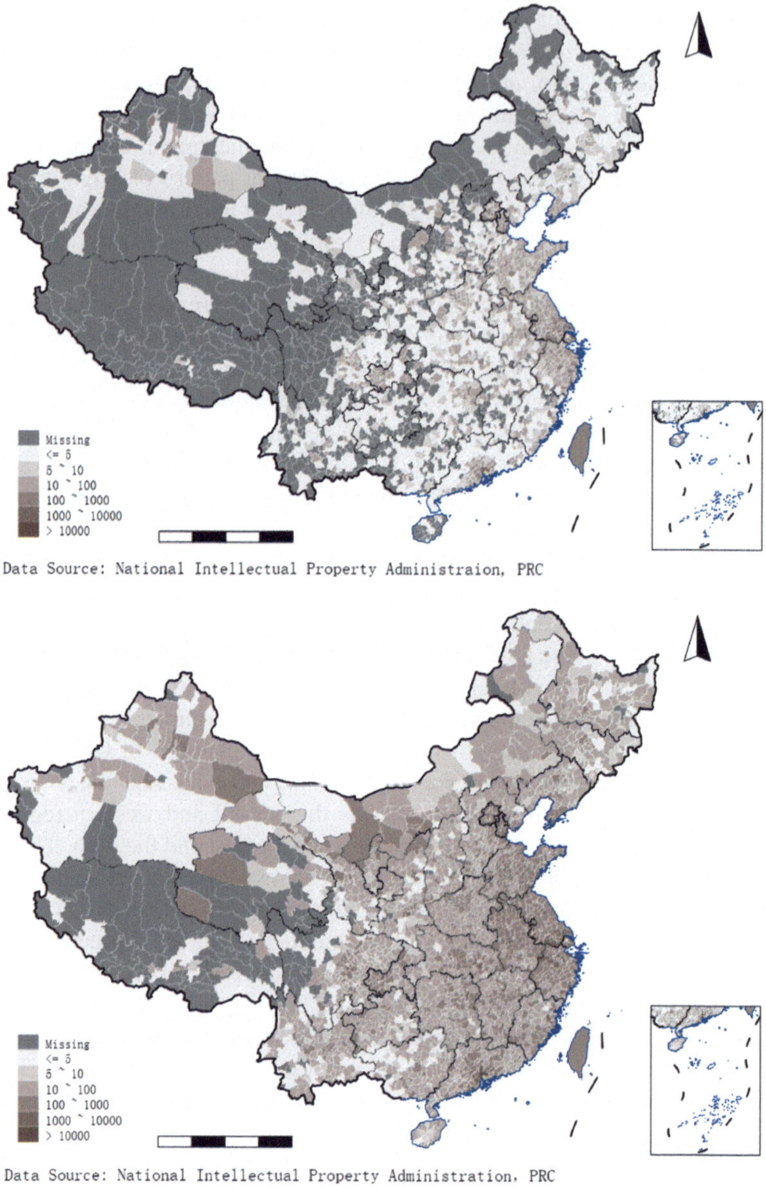

Fig. 2 The distribution of patent applications related to green and low-carbon technologies in 2010/2020

4.2 *Climate Finance and Financing Constraints*

4.2.1 Introduction

The Paris Agreement on the mitigation of climate change was signed by 195 participating nations at the United Nations Climate Change Conference in 2015 (COP 21, the Conference of the Parties). This agreement reached a consensus to keep the rise in global temperature well below 2 degrees Celsius compared to pre-industrial levels. Many nations have undertaken efforts to support the growth of green industry and green innovation to meet long-term climate objectives (Li et al. 2018; Acemoglu et al. 2016). As mentioned above, financing constraints restrict firms' capabilities to engage in environmentally friendly innovation. Access to funding resources may be a major impediment to their investments in green technologies (Andersen 2017). Financial limitations often restrict firms' green innovation due to its high degree of unpredictability and poor returns.

Compared to global climate finance, China only officially announced its official policies and guidance on climate finance in 2022. In August 2022, 23 localities were selected for the first batch of pilot projects for climate investment and financing. As of the end of June 2023, pilot localities had stockpiled nearly 2,000 climate-friendly projects involving nearly 2 trillion yuan, and the pilot work has achieved positive results.

However, a similar term, green finance, which is a wide term that encompasses investments and loans connected to promoting ecologically sustainable development (Green Finance Study Group (GFSG) 2016), has been widely used as a climate policy in China. Green finance, similar to climate finance, aims to create a favourable financial environment for promoting green growth. China has emerged as the top green investment destination around the globe as a result of the growing amount of investment in environmentally friendly industries. Recently, China announced its commitment to becoming carbon neutral by the year 2060, which will undoubtedly result in a significant investment in environmentally friendly projects and technologies (Polzin and Sanders 2020). Without policy support, it would have been impossible to realise previous successes, and achieving future goals also depends on such support.

The implementation of green finance strategies was specifically presented in addition to the implementation of comprehensive rules and administrative enforcements to assist green development. A pair of documents, titled "Opinions on Implementing Environmental Protection Policies and Rules and Preventing Credit Risks" and "Guiding Opinions on the Credit Work for Energy Conservation and Emission Reduction", were issued by the China Banking Regulatory Commission (CBRC) in 2007. The implementation of credit categorisation management in accordance with the environmental effects of projects is mandated by these rules, which advise financial institutions to limit or cease lending to sectors that fall into the "Two High and One Remaining" category. In addition, the CBRC published the "Green Credit Guidelines" in 2012, setting up the core framework of the green credit system and ensuring that resources are allocated to low-carbon, recycling, and ecological fields.

Since then, the CBRC has introduced additional green financing initiatives. Table 4 summarises a list of green financing policies.

Following these policies, China has made significant progress in green innovation. According to data from the "Report on Statistical Analysis of Green and Low-carbon Technology Patents Worldwide (2023)" of the Chinese National Intellectual Property Administration (CNIPA) (China National Intellectual Property Administration (CNIPA) 2023), between 2016 and 2022, 558,000 green and low-carbon technology patent applications were granted globally, of which 206,000 were granted by CNIPA, accounting for 36.8%. The green and low-carbon technology patents granted per year showed an average annual growth rate of 9.3%. China has become the major driving force behind the innovation of green and low-carbon technologies worldwide.

Challenges and problems still exist, even with these improvements. Green innovation, for example, is unevenly dispersed among firms. According to Fig. 3, at least 40% of all listed industrial firms do not have green patents. The most worrying factor here is that the proportion of these organisations has increased since 2018. The unequal distribution is primarily between state-owned enterprises (SOEs) and privately owned enterprises (POEs). As illustrated in Fig. 3, the emergence of zero green innovation firms can be linked to POEs. POEs may have greater financial constraints in R&D operations due to unequal loan disbursements from state-owned banks (Wu 2018). If funding constraints are a fundamental hurdle to green innovation, the poor performance of POEs demonstrates that they lack access to financing resources, even under current green finance standards.

It is essential for China to have a greater number of firms, particularly those in the private sector, participating in green innovation in order to meet its carbon aim by the year 2060. As a result, it is essential to evaluate whether the existing green financing strategy is effective in fostering green innovation and to determine how it operates. The financial system controlled by a major banking system is more likely to discriminate against the ownership of POEs compared to SOEs in China. This is also the case when compared to SOEs in China. Regarding receiving loans from banks, SOEs not only enjoy preferential access to credit, with longer loan periods and lower interest rates, but they also have to submit fewer guarantees. Therefore, the process of acquiring external finance is more challenging and expensive for POEs than it is for SOEs. As a result, it is essential to investigate whether the existing rules regarding green finance are biased against POEs. Such an examination is necessary if reducing financing limitations is the primary channel for increasing green innovation capacity.

4.2.2 Literature Review of Financial Constraints

Studies suggest that there is a strong correlation between innovation and the financial constraints of a firm. Gorodnichenko and Schnitzer (2013) documented that the ability for innovation is hindered by financial frictions. Using data collected from the Chinese manufacturing sector, Jin et al. (2019) further discovered an inverted U-shaped link between funding limitations and firm productivity. Along this line,

Table 4 Green finance policies in China since 2007

Policy	Institution and date	Significance
Guiding opinions on the credit work for energy conservation and emissions reduction	CBRC [2007] No.83 11/23/2007	(1) Implement different credit policies according to the energy-saving situation of firms and regions (2) Restrict credit for projects with a significant negative environmental impact (3) Incorporate credit for energy conservation and emission reduction into its regulatory assessment
Green credit guidelines	CBRC [2012] No 4 2/24/2012	(1) Offer a core framework of the green credit system (2) Clarify stipulations on policy boundaries, management methods, and assessment policies of energy-saving and environmental protection credit and green credit for banking financial institutions to ensure that credit funds are invested in low-carbon, recycling, and ecological fields
Supervisory guidelines for performance appraisal of banking financial institutions	CBRC [2012] No.34 6/12/2012	Incorporate green credit into the performance appraisal mechanism and put forward requirements for banks' green credit work and social responsibility
Opinions on green credit work	CBRC General Office [2013] No40 2/7/2013	Important guiding opinions on the subsequent green credit policy formulation have clarified and refined the specific requirements of green credit work
Green credit statistics system	CBRC General Office [2013] No 185 7/4/2013	Green credit statistics are conducted every six months for 21 major banks. The main contents are as follows: (1) the credit situation of banks involved in major risk firms, for example, backward production capacity, environment, and safety; (2) the green credit situation of banks
Key evaluation indicators for the implementation of green credit	CBRC General Office [2014] No 186 6/27/2014	(1) A specific indicator system under the framework of "Green Credit Guidelines." (2) Coverage: policy banks, state-owned commercial banks, joint-stock commercial banks, and postal savings banks
Energy efficiency credit guidelines	CBRC [2015] No. 2 1/13/2015 CBRC NDRC	(1) Clarify the scope and method of the "energy efficiency credit" business. The two credit methods are energy-saving project credits and contract energy management credits (2) Promote financial innovation and incentives and conduct asset securitisation pilots, green financial bonds, and innovations in guaranteed methods

(continued)

Table 4 (continued)

Policy	Institution and date	Significance
Guidance on building a green financial system	PBOC [2016] No.228 8/31/2016 PBOC MOF NDRC MEP CBRC CSRC CIRC	(1) Implements the requirements of the ecological civilisation construction in the financial field (2) Provides a leading document of the follow-up green financial policy
Notice on issuing the implementation plan for green bank evaluation (Trial Implementation)	CBA [2017] No.171 12/26/2017	Undertakes the green credit evaluation of the CBRC and aims at all kinds of banks
Notice on establishing a special statistical system for green loans	PBOC [2018] No.10 1/5/2018	Specifies the statistical calibre and method for quantitative indicators of green credit performance evaluation
Green credit performance evaluation scheme for banking depository financial institutions (Trial Implementation)	PBOC [2018] No.180 7/27/108	Marks whether the results of the green credit performance evaluation are included in the macro-prudential assessment of deposit financial institutions in the banking industry
Guidance catalogue for green industry	NDRC HZS [2019] No 293 2/24/2019	Standardises borders and unifies benchmarking

Note: (1) CBRC: China Banking Regulatory Commission; NDRC: National Development and Reform Commission; PBOC: The People's Bank of China; MOF: Ministry of Finance; MEP: Ministry of Environmental Protection; CSRC: China Securities Regulatory Commission; CIRC: China Insurance Regulatory Commission. (2) These polices are collected by the Natural Resources Defense Council (NRDC, 2019)[4]

[4] Source of information: http://www.nrdc.cn/Public/uploads/2019-07-15/5d2c1a4a26b1a.pdf.

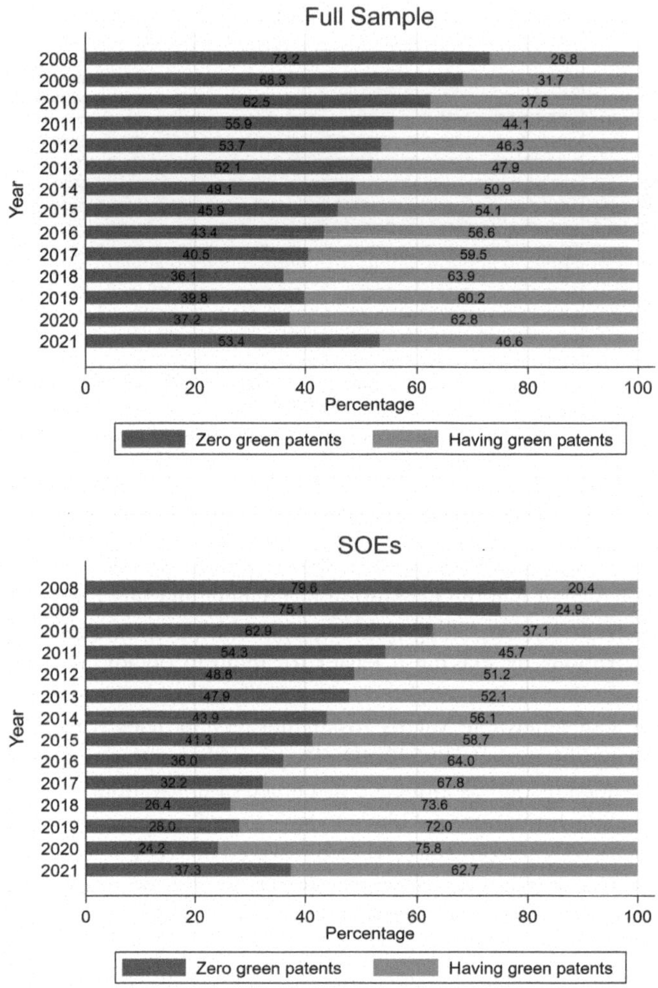

Fig. 3 Proportion of firms with green patents from 2008 to 2021

García-Quevedo et al. (2018) found that the limits imposed by funding have effects not only on the choices that firms make regarding innovation but also on the outcomes of innovation. However, Almeida et al. (2013) found that an increase in financial limitations would lead to increased innovation efficiency in firms because financing constraints might encourage firms to make optimum investment choices, which in turn improves capital efficiency (Aghion et al. 2012).

Fewer studies have focused on environmental innovation funding. Using survey data collected at the level of the European Union, Ghisetti et al. (2015) investigated the effects of financial barriers on the environmental innovations of small and medium

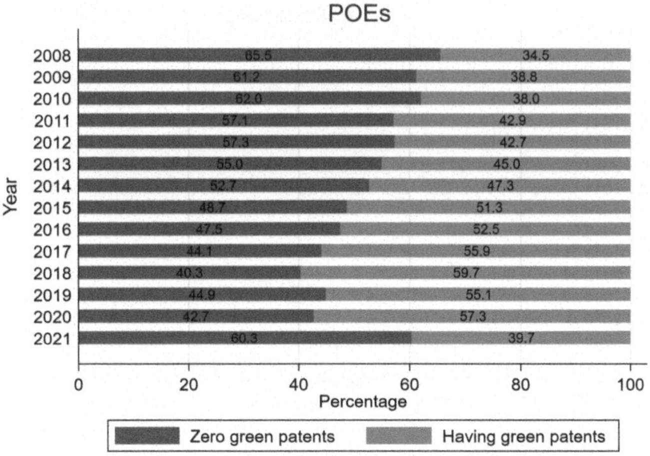

Fig. 3 (continued)

firms. They discovered that the perception of financial barriers hinders firms' environmental innovations, suggesting that firms should be encouraged to adopt environmental innovations by making it easier for them to obtain credit. Noailly and Smeets (2016) further investigated the role that financing constraints play in innovation activities in renewable versus fossil fuel technologies for 1,300 European companies during the period 1995–2009. They concluded that the constraints of a company's financial resources influence its choice of innovation.

Further, financial limitations are likely to have varied consequences for innovation across ownership. Megginson et al. (2014) discovered that SOEs can make substantial investments in research and development (R&D) to alleviate financial limitations. These constraints are loosened by implicit loan guarantees and access to state-owned banks that are provided by state ownership. In contrast, some studies believe that state ownership and political characteristics do not predominate in the private equity market, which leads to an increase in financing constraints. For instance, Bortolotti et al. (2019) discovered that state ownership affects investments in research and development by easing restrictions on financing and further limiting the inventive capacity of SOEs.

In addition, firms that are subject to government intervention tend to adopt conservative investment strategies and avoid investing in high-risk innovative projects (Tu et al. 2020; Andersen 2017; Amore et al. 2013; Mateut 2018). This is because innovation is typically time-consuming and has a high degree of uncertainty. In other words, it is believed that governmental intervention may have an effect on the limitations of finance. By using a sample of the United States from the 1980s to the 1990s, Amore et al. (2013) found that the deregulation policies implemented for interstate banks greatly boosted firms' innovative activities, especially those firms that were largely reliant on capital from outside sources. These policies have the potential to boost bank loans and encourage the growth of non-bank financial institutions. Similarly, Mateut (2018) found that the government's subsidy policy has the potential to greatly alleviate the funding limitations in countries that are not members of the European Union, considering that these nations are likely to have less established financial markets, and further stimulate innovative activities.

In summary, only a few studies have investigated the impact of financial constraints on green innovation, and even fewer have examined green innovation. The question of whether green finance policies are helpful in fostering green innovation remains ambiguous.

4.2.3 Empirical Analysis

This section describes the analysis of a dataset of listed Chinese firms from 2008 to 2021 to examine the relationship between financial constraints and green innovation. The information on green patenting is obtained from CNIPA, which is used as a proxy for the capabilities of firms in terms of green innovations. The data include patent numbers and individual patent claims. As an alternative measure of a company's commitment to environmentally friendly inventions, the green ratio—a comparison of the number of green patents to the overall number of patents—is computed.

Following Musso and Schiavo (2008), financing constraint (FC) is measured through a synthetic index developed from seven indicators: firm size (measured by total assets), profitability (measured by return on assets [ROA]), liquidity (measured by current assets over current liabilities, i.e., current ratio), cash flow-generating ability (measured by net cash flows from operating activities over current liabilities), solvency (measured by own funds over total liabilities), trade credit over total assets (measured by accounts payable over total assets), and net tangible asset ratio (measured by tangible assets over total assets).

A series of control variables is considered. A larger firm size and higher ROA indicate that a firm faces lower financing constraints. Liquidity and cash flow-generating ability mainly reflect a firm's ability to repay short-term debts. Solvency indicates the ability to repay long-term debts and reveals the stability of the financial structure and the affordability of its own funds to debts. The higher the proportion of accounts payable and net tangible assets in total assets, the higher the likelihood that a firm will carry out external financing.

Given that patent applicant information can help identify innovation classification (Amore and Bennedsen 2016) and that patents can be easily and accurately measured, green patent application data are used to assess a listed industrial firm's capability for green innovations. Patent data are accessible on the CNIPA website (http://www.sipo.gov.cn/), which contains all patent application information for invention patents, utility models, and design patents from the establishment of the Chinese patent system in 1985. The application number, application date, IPC classification, and applicants' names and addresses are all included in the patent application information (for further information, see Dang and Motohashi, 2015), and green patents are classed using the IPC Green Inventory categorisation. The analysis in this section solely evaluates invention patents and utility models to appropriately assess the capabilities of green inventions. CNIPA also provides information on the main independent claims. It is important to note that patents have an 18-month publication lag following filing. Hence, firm-year patent counts are based on the information of applicants' names and application dates, and patent counts can measure patent quantity.

As shown in Fig. 4, the number of green patents filed by SOEs is higher than that of POEs. Since the implementation of the Green Credit policy in 2012, the number of patents held by both POEs and SOEs has seen considerable growth.

Figure 5 shows how the average scores for the financial constraints have changed over time. The score of POEs was greater than that of SOEs at the beginning of the process; however, the gap between the two narrowed in 2005 as the score of POEs greatly decreased, while the score of SOEs significantly increased by a large amount. In 2004, the China Securities Regulatory Commission issued an order called "Interim Measures for the Stock Issuance and Listing Sponsorship System," which governed the issuing of new stocks and the disclosure quality of information of listed companies more stringently. Notably, green finance regulations have the potential to dramatically improve green innovation capabilities by removing the restrictions of funding that firms are now experiencing. According to the regulations that are now in place regarding green financing, POEs are less capable than SOEs of getting credits, which limits their capacity for green innovation.

Given that the method for issuing shares by SOEs is sometimes slow, convoluted, and costly, this rule has increased the financial constraints that SOEs confront. Furthermore, SOEs may have no incentive to issue additional stocks, as doing so

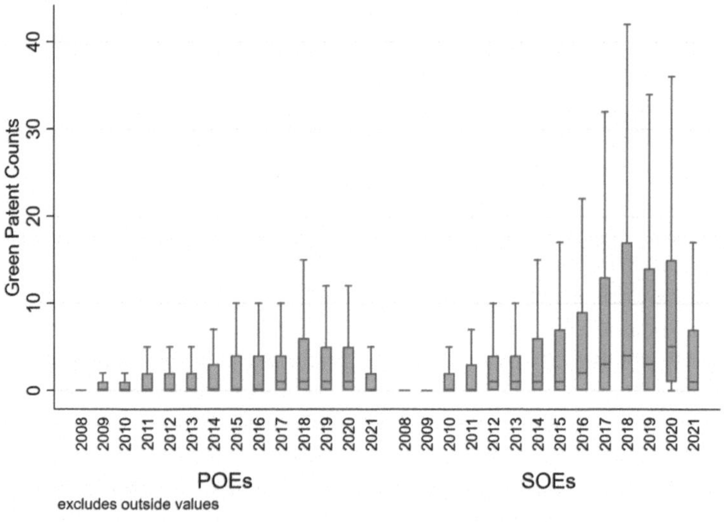

Fig. 4 Distributions of green patent counts for SOEs and POEs

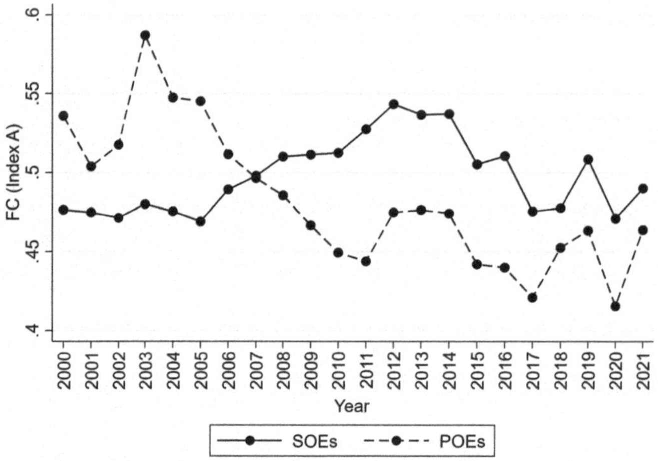

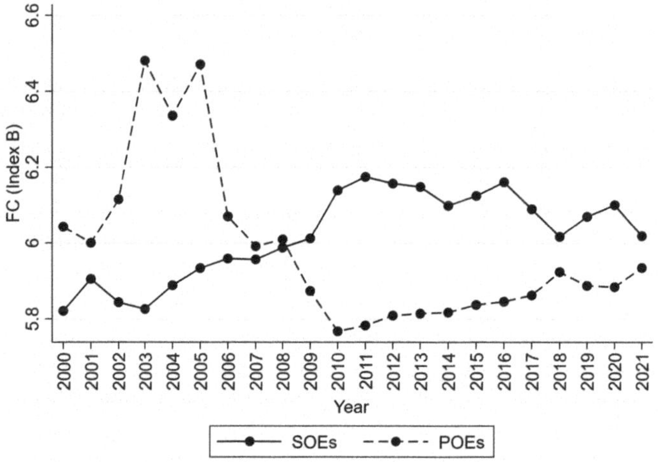

Fig. 5 Trends in average financing constraints for SOEs and POEs. *Note* FC (Index A) is constructed by taking the sum of the seven scaled values of each firm/year observation; we then obtain the aggregated index of 7–35, which is rescaled to a range of 1–10. FC (Index B) is constructed by taking the sum of the number of indicators on which the firm/year lies in the first quantile, and this has a range of 0–7

would result in a decrease in the number of state shares, which would result in a decrease in the state's control over the company (Xu and Wang 1999).

Table 5 reports the impact of financing constraints on green innovation, and all patent numbers are in natural logarithm form. The results reveal that financial limitations have a substantial negative relationship with green patent counts, which fall by

Table 5 Basic estimates

Variables	*ln* (Green Patents)	*ln* (Green Invention Patents)	*ln* (Green Utility Patents)
	(1)	(2)	(3)
Panel A: FC Index A			
FC Index A	−0.365*** (0.085)	−0.436*** (0.070)	−0.196*** (0.071)
Panel B: FC Index B			
FC Index B	−0.048*** (0.011)	−0.056*** (0.009)	−0.027*** (0.009)
Controls	Yes	Yes	Yes
Year fixed effect	Yes	Yes	Yes
City fixed effect	Yes	Yes	Yes
Observations	10,945	10,945	10,945

Note: FC (Index A) and FC (Index B) are one-year lagged terms. Control variables include firm size, age, SOE, ROA, cash flows, stock share, Herfindahl-Hirschman Index (HHI), city GDP, city population, and city industrial structure. Robust standard errors are in parentheses. ***, **, and * represent 1%, 5%, and 10% statistical significance levels, respectively.

36.5% when financing constraints rise by one score. Furthermore, we divide green patents into invention patents and utility patents, and the results show that financing constraints have a greater impact on green invention patents. This suggests that firm's capacity to get external funding limits their green innovation potential. A possible explanation is that investment in green activities is not only hazardous and expensive but also has a high failure rate, necessitating enough and reliable supporting financing.

Thus, greater difficulty in obtaining external finances suggests a larger level of uncertainty about funding sources, increasing the likelihood of failing creative efforts. Financing restrictions impede green innovation capabilities; thus, many companies use CDM programmes to support their emission reduction innovative efforts. Most emphasis in the CDM project design document (CDM-PDD) is placed on the application's goal of overcoming financial restrictions. Their projects are not very appealing to investors because they have a low internal rate of return. Even worse, they cannot get building money from a bank loan or pay for the project themselves.

To study the effectiveness of green finance regulations, further analyses are performed on whether financial limitations on green innovations differ over two time periods: 2008–2012 and 2013–2021. The findings are shown in Table 6. As illustrated in Panels A and B, compared to 2008–2012, financial constraints in 2013–2021 posed fewer limits for business green patents. Many green credit rules implemented between 2013 and 2021 made it simpler for firms to access green financing from commercial banks, thus easing firms' funding limitations for green innovations.

Table 7 examines the heterogeneous effects of green financing initiatives on SOEs and SOEs. The findings showed that during all periods, POEs were significantly more financed than SOEs. For example, if the funding limit for the index A assessment

Table 6 The effects of green finance policies

Variables	Full sample		
	(1)	(2)	(3)
	ln(Green patents)	*ln*(Green invention patents)	*ln*(Green utility patents)
Panel A: FC Index A			
FC Index A × Period 2008–2012	−0.662*** (0.175)	−0.440*** (0.136)	−0.551*** (0.143)
FC Index A × Period 2013–2021	−0.327*** (0.089)	−0.435*** (0.073)	−0.151** (0.074)
Panel B: FC Index B			
FC Index B × Period 2008–2012	−0.076*** (0.024)	−0.049*** (0.018)	−0.066*** (0.019)
FC Index B × Period 2013–2021	−0.045*** (0.012)	−0.057*** (0.010)	−0.023** (0.010)
Controls	Yes	Yes	Yes
Year fixed effect	Yes	Yes	Yes
City fixed effect	Yes	Yes	Yes
Observations	10,945	10,945	10,945

Note: Control variables are consistent with Table 5. Robust standard errors are in parentheses. ***, **, and * represent 1%, 5%, and 10% statistical significance levels, respectively

increased by one point, the number of patents of state-owned enterprises would hardly be affected, while POEs' patents would decline by 84.7 percent in 2008–2012 and 50.6 percent in 2013–2021. POEs seem to have benefited from the loosening of funding limits between 2013 and 2021. One probable reason is that since SOEs are frequently insured by the government, commercial banks are more ready to give additional loan money to them (Brandt and Li 2003). Green funding is not provided equitably to POEs, who have a relatively strong innovation capacity but are constrained by financial restrictions. With limited green financing sources, such credit discrimination makes POEs more likely to retain and grow production. A more conservative green innovation investment standard may limit green innovation.

Further, the findings in Panels A and B show that between 2013 and 2021, there were no significant restrictions to funding for SOE. Although POEs' green projects may be more promising and creative than SOEs' green projects, commercial banks are more willing to provide green credit funds for SOEs' green projects. This is because SOEs are backed by the government and have a lower risk of default, while private firms bear their own profits and losses and have a higher risk of failure. Commercial banks seek to provide financing to SOEs to obtain different green credit indicators while also providing guarantees for the SOEs' ROA. Compared with SOEs, it is still more difficult for POEs to obtain green credit funds from financial institutions, and financing restrictions on POEs have not eased the constraints on green innovation.

Table 7 Heterogeneous effects of green finance policies

Variables	SOEs			POEs		
	(1)	(2)	(3)	(4)	(5)	(6)
	ln(Green Patents)	*ln*(Green Invention Patents)	*ln*(Green Utility Patents)	*ln*(Green Patents)	*ln*(Green Invention Patents)	*ln*(Green Utility Patents)
Panel A: FC Index A						
FC Index A × Period 2008–2012	0.009	0.033	0.056	−0.847***	−0.558***	−0.775***
	(0.274)	(0.216)	(0.221)	(0.225)	(0.178)	(0.181)
FC Index A × Period 2013–2021	0.291*	−0.037	0.478***	−0.506***	-0.529***	−0.379***
	(0.163)	(0.144)	(0.134)	(0.107)	(0.085)	(0.090)
Panel B: FC Index B						
FC Index A × Period 2008–2012	0.004 (0.037)	0.010 (0.029)	0.002 (0.030)	−0.096*** (0.030)	−0.063*** (0.024)	−0.090*** (0.025)
FC Index A × Period 2013–2021	0.029 (0.022)	−0.005 (0.020)	0.046** (0.018)	−0.064*** (0.014)	−0.068*** (0.011)	−0.046*** (0.012)
Controls	Yes	Yes	Yes	Yes	Yes	Yes
Year fixed effect	Yes	Yes	Yes	Yes	Yes	Yes
City fixed effect	Yes	Yes	Yes	Yes	Yes	Yes
Observations	3,750	3,750	3,750	7,186	7,186	7,186

Note: Control variables are consistent with Table 5. Robust standard errors are in parentheses. ***, **, and * represent 1%, 5%, and 10% statistical significance levels, respectively

4.3 *Implications*

Financial constraints are one of the major obstacles to the development of green technology. Insufficient green technology innovation will lead to excessively high costs for green products and services, limiting the development of green production and consumption. In this case, the government should reduce the costs and prices of green production through large-scale green technology innovation, as well as promote the allocation of resources to green industries and production.

As for China, green innovation is critical to meeting the 2060 carbon neutrality objective, and it is necessary for the government to internalise the carbon neutrality aim when developing green financing policies. The government should foster green innovation while developing green financial policies and distributing financial resources to various types of firms. The government is also responsible for encouraging firms to consider climate change risks when investing in green innovation.

The findings discussed herein pose several policy implications. First, the government could establish regional green development funds to promote private companies' environmental governance and the growth of ecological and environmental protection industries. Second, the government should provide a framework for fully disclosing green project information, providing credible green credit evaluation indicators, and improving private company credit ratings. Furthermore, when lending to SOEs, the China Banking Regulatory Commission should encourage financial institutions to increase their appraisal of important corporate social responsibility metrics. Third, when evaluating financial institutions' green investment and financing performance, the central bank should consider the proportion of POEs investing in green projects rather than the amount of green credit. Fourth, POEs with funding needs should promptly disclose environmental information, undertake green assessments through qualified assessment agencies, and emphasise their own green features to lower the search costs of responsible investors. Finally, the China Banking Regulatory Commission should push financial institutions to disclose green credit investment and financing information and incorporate it into financial institutions' green credit performance assessments. This can ensure that a particular percentage of green funds are allocated to private firms, making it easier for relevant institutions to assess the benefits of green credit.

References

Acemoglu, D., Akcigit, U., Hanley, D., Kerr, W.R., 2016. Transition to clean technology. J. Polit. Econ. 124 (1), 52–104.

Acheampong, A. O., Erdiaw-Kwasie, M. O., Abunyewah, M., 2021. Does energy accessibility improve human development? Evidence from energy-poor regions. Energy Economics, 96, 105165.

Aghion, P., Askenazy, P., Berman, N., Cette, G., Eymard, L., 2012. Credit constraints and the cyclicality of RD investment: evidence from France. J. Eur. Econ. Assoc. 10 (5), 1001–1024. https://doi.org/https://doi.org/10.1111/j.1542-4774.2012.01093.x.
Almeida, H., Hsu, P.H., Li, D., 2013. Less is more: financial constraints and innovative efficiency. SSRN Electronic Publishing. https://ssrn.com/abstract=1831786.
Amore, M.D. and Bennedsen, M., 2016. Corporate governance and green innovation. Journal of Environmental Economics and Management, 75, pp.54-72.
Amore, M.D., Schneider, C., Zaldokas, A., 2013. Credit supply and corporate innovation. J. Financ. Econ. 109 (3), 835–855.
Anbumozhi, V., Kalirajan, K., Kimura, F. and Yao, X. eds., 2016. Investing on low-carbon energy systems: Implications for regional economic cooperation. Springer Singapore.
Andersen, D.C., 2017. Do credit constraints favor dirty production? Theory and plantlevel evidence. J. Environ. Econ. Manag. 84, 189–208.
Berrone, P., Fosfuri, A., Gelabert, L., Gomez-Mejia, L. R., 2013. Necessity as the mother of 'green' inventions: Institutional pressures and environmental innovations. Strateg. Manag. J., 34(8), 891–909.
Bortolotti, B., Fotak, V., Wolfe, B., 2019. Innovation at state owned firms. SSRN Electronic Publishing, 72. http://ssrn.com/abstract=3150280.
Brandt, L., Li, H., 2003. Bank discrimination in transition economies: ideology, information, or incentives? J. Comp. Econ. 31 (3), 387–413.
Buchner, B., Herve-Mignucci, M., Trabacchi, C., Wilkinson, J., Stadelmann, M., Boyd, R., et al., 2013. The global landscape of climate finance 2013. Climate Policy Initiative; Venice.
Buchner, B., Clark, A., Falconer, A., Macquarie, R., Meattle, C., Tolentino, R., Cooper, W., 2019. Global landscape of climate finance 2019. Climate Policy Initiative. https://climatepolicyinitiative.org/wp-content/uploads/2019/11/2019-Global-Landscape-ofClimate-Finance.pdf.
Calel, R. and Dechezleprêtre, A., 2016. Environmental policy and directed technological change: evidence from the European carbon market. Review of economics and statistics, 98(1), pp.173-191.
Carfora, A., Scandurra, G., 2019. The impact of climate funds on economic growth and their role in substituting fossil energy sources. Energy Policy, 129, 182–192.
Castro, P., Betzold, C., 2016. Climate Finance after the Paris Agreement: New directions or more of the same? https://doi.org/10.5167/UZH-137944.
China National Intellectual Property Administration (CNIPA), 2023. Report on Statistical Analysis of Green and Low-carbon Technology Patents Worldwide (2023). https://english.cnipa.gov.cn/art/2023/7/6/art_3262_186148.html.
De Haas, R., Popov, A., 2023. Finance and Green Growth. Econ J (London), 133(650), 637–668.
Del Río González, P., 2009. The empirical analysis of the determinants for environmental technological change: A research agenda. Ecol. Econ., 68(3), 861–878.
Flammer, C., 2021. Corporate green bonds. J. Financ. Econ., 142(2), 499–516.
García-Quevedo, J., Segarra-Blasco, A., Teruel, M., 2018. Financial constraints and the failure of innovation projects. Technol. Forecast. Soc. Change 127, 127–140.
Ghisetti, C., Mazzanti, M., Mancinelli, S., Zoli, M., 2015. Do financial constraints make the environment worse off? Understanding the effects of financial barriers on environmental innovations. SEEDS Working Papers, 0115.
Gorodnichenko, Y., Schnitzer, M., 2013. Financial constraints and innovation: why poor countries don't catch up. J. Eur. Econ. Assoc. 11 (5), 1115–1152.
Green Finance Study Group (GFSG), 2016. G20 Green Finance Synthesis Report. September. http://unepinquiry.org/wp-content/uploads/2016/09/Synthesis _Report_Full_EN.pdf.
Guillaumont, P., 2010. Assessing the economic vulnerability of small island developing states and the least developed countries. J. Dev. Stud. 46 (5), 828–854.
Hallegatte, S., Rozenberg, J. (2017). Climate change through a poverty lens. Nat. Clim. Chang., 7(4), 250–256.

Jin, M., Zhao, S., Kumbhakar, S.C., 2019. Financial constraints and firm productivity: evidence from Chinese manufacturing. Eur. J. Oper. Res. 275 (3), 1139–1156.

Keeble, J., Lyon, D. et al, 2005. Innovation High Ground: How Leading Companies are Using Sustainability Driven Innovation to Win Tomorrow's Customers. Arthur D. Little.

Lee, C.-C., Li, X., Yu, C.-H., Zhao, J., 2022. The contribution of climate finance toward environmental sustainability: New global evidence. Energy Econ., 111, 106072.

Li, D., Zheng, M., Cao, C., Chen, X., Ren, S., Huang, M., 2017. The impact of legitimacy pressure and corporate profitability on green innovation: Evidence from China top 100. J. Clean Prod., 141, 41–49.

Li, Z., Liao, G., Wang, Z., Huang, Z., 2018. Green loan and subsidy for promoting clean production innovation. J. Clean Prod., 187, 421–431.

Li, N., Shi, B., Wu, L., Kang, R., Gao, Q., 2022. Climate-Related Development Finance, Energy Structure Transformation and Carbon Emissions Reduction: An Analysis From the Perspective of Developing Countries. Front. Environ. Sci., 9.

Liu, J.-Y., Xia, Y., Fan, Y., Lin, S.-M., Wu, J., 2017. Assessment of a green credit policy aimed at energy-intensive industries in China based on a financial CGE model. J. Clean Prod., 163, 293–302.

Mateut, S., 2018. Subsidies, financial constraints and firm innovative activities in emerging economies. Small Bus. Econ. 50 (1), 131–162.

Megginson, W.L., Ullah, B., Wei, Z., 2014. State ownership, soft-budget constraints, and cash holdings: evidence from China's privatized firms. J. Bank. Finance 48 (48), 276–291.

Michaelowa, A., Shishlov, I., Brescia, D., 2019. Evolution of international carbon markets: lessons for the Paris Agreement. WIREs Clim. Change 10 (6), e613.

Musso, P., Schiavo, S., 2008. The impact of financial constraints on firm survival and growth. J. Evol. Econ. 18 (2), 135–149.

Niles, K. and Lloyd, B., 2013. Small Island Developing States (SIDS) & energy aid: Impacts on the energy sector in the Caribbean and Pacific. Energy for Sustainable Development, 17(5), pp.521-530.

Noailly, J., Smeets, R., 2016. Financing energy innovation: the role of financing constraints for directed technical change from fossil-fuel to renewable innovation. EIB Working Papers.

OECD, 2008. Environmental Innovation and Global Markets. Paris: Organization for Economic Cooperation and Development.

OECD, 2011. Handbook on the OECD-DEC Climate Markers. OECD, Paris.

Owusu, P. A., Asumadu-Sarkodie, S., 2016. A review of renewable energy sources, sustainability issues and climate change mitigation. Cogent Eng., 3(1), 1167990.

Oxfam. 2020. Climate Finance Shadow Report 2020. Assessing Progress Towards the $100 Billion Commitment. Available at: https://www.oxfam.org/en/research/climate-financeshadow-report-2020.

Pickering, J., Betzold, C., Skovgaard, J., 2017. Special issue: managing fragmentation and complexity in the emerging system of international climate finance. Int. Environ. Agreements 17, 1–16.

Polzin, F., Sanders, M., 2020. How to finance the transition to low-carbon energy in Europe? Energy Pol. 147, 111863.

Popp, D., 2006. International innovation and diffusion of air pollution control technologies: the effects of NOX and SO2 regulation in the US, Japan, and Germany. Journal of Environmental Economics and Management, 51(1), pp.46-71.

Rai, V., Funkhouser, E., 2015. Emerging insights on the dynamic drivers of international low-carbon technology transfer. Renew. Sust. Energ. Rev. 49, 350–364.

Rennings, K., 2000. Redefining innovation—Eco-innovation research and the contribution from ecological economics. Ecol. Econ., 32(2), 319–332.

Scandurra, G., Romano, A., Ronghi, M., Carfora, A., 2017. The effect of Climate Finance on Greenhouse Gas Emission: A Quantile Regression Approach. International Journal of Energy Economics and Policy, 7, 185–199.

Scandurra, G., Thomas, A., Passaro, R., Bencini, J., Carfora, A., 2020. Does climate finance reduce vulnerability in Small Island Developing States? An empirical investigation. J. Clean Prod., 256, 120330.

Schiederig, T., Tietze, F., Herstatt, C., 2012. Green innovation in technology and innovation management – an exploratory literature review. RD Management, 42(2), 180–192.

Shuai, C., Shen, L., Jiao, L., Wu, Y., Tan, Y., 2017. Identifying key impact factors on carbon emission: evidences from panel and time-series data of 125 countries from 1990 to 2011. Appl. Energy 187, 310–325.

Steckel, J. C., Jakob, M., Flachsland, C., Kornek, U., Lessmann, K., Edenhofer, O., 2017. From climate finance toward sustainable development finance. WIREs Climate Change, 8(1), e437.

Tang, D. Y., Zhang, Y., 2020. Do shareholders benefit from green bonds? J. Corp. Financ., 61, 101427.

Thomas, A., Theokritoff, E., 2021. Debt-for-climate swaps for small islands. Nat. Clim. Chang. 11, 889–891.

Triguero, A., Moreno-Mondéjar, L., Davia, M. A., 2013. Drivers of different types of eco-innovation in European SMEs. Ecol. Econ., 92, 25–33.

Tu, Q., Mo, J., Betz, R., Cui, L., Fan, Y., Liu, Y., 2020. Achieving grid parity of solar PV power in China- The role of Tradable Green Certificate. Energy Policy, 144, 111681.

UNFCCC, 2020. UNFCCC Standing Committee on Finance Fourth (2020) Biennial Assessment and Overview of Climate Finance Flows. United Nations Framework Convention on Climate Change (UNFCC).

Van Leeuwen, G., Mohnen, P., 2017. Revisiting the Porter hypothesis: An empirical analysis of green innovation for the Netherlands. Econ. Innov. New Technol., 26(1–2), 63–77.

Wang, Z., Danish, Zhang, B., Wang, B., 2018. Renewable energy consumption, economic growth and human development index in Pakistan: Evidence form simultaneous equation model. J. Clean Prod., 184, 1081–1090.

Wu, J., 2018. Financing constraints for RD in China: the role of state ownership. Appl. Econ. Lett. 26 (14), 1162–1166.

Xu, J., Xiao, H., 2023. The impact of government subsidies on the persistence of firm innovation: evidence from China. Appl. Econ. 44 (3).

Xu, X., Wang, Y., 1999. Ownership structure and corporate governance in Chinese stock companies. China Econ. Rev. 10, 75–98.

Yu, C.-H., Wu, X., Zhang, D., Chen, S., Zhao, J., 2021. Demand for green finance: Resolving financing constraints on green innovation in China. Energy Policy, 153, 112255.

Climate Finance: Policies and Regulations

Jingyan Huang and Kun Guo

Abstract This chapter aims to explore the issues related to climate finance policy and regulations; analyse the background, purpose, content and possible impacts and challenges of international climate finance policymaking; and then analyse the current climate finance regulatory system and give relevant cases. By gaining a deeper understanding of different countries' policies and regulatory measures, it will be possible to better understand the development of global climate finance and the related challenges.

Keywords Climate finance · Climate policy · Climate regulations · Transition policy

1 International Climate Finance Policy

With its growing severity, climate change has become one of the most critical concerns in the globe. Climate finance policy refers to the policy frameworks and measures formulated and implemented by national, regional or international organisations to combat climate change and promote the transition to a low-carbon economy (https://unfccc.int/topics/introduction-to-climate-finance). Climate finance policy and regulation are essential means for achieving climate goals and are important areas of global governance. To respond to climate change, various forces, such as governments, enterprises, social organisations and scholars, have been exploring and advancing climate finance policy and regulation. This chapter aims to explore those issues related to climate finance policy and regulation, analyse the background, purpose, content and possible impacts and challenges of international climate finance policymaking and then analyse the current climate finance regulatory system before

J. Huang
Sino-Danish College, University of Chinese Academy of Sciences, Beijing, China

K. Guo (✉)
School of Economics and Management, University of Chinese Academy of Sciences, Beijing, China
e-mail: guokun@ucas.ac.cn

F. Wu et al. (eds.), *Climate Finance*, Climate Change and Energy Transition,
https://doi.org/10.1007/978-981-97-3308-8_11

giving relevant cases. Gaining a deeper understanding of different countries' policies and regulatory measures will help in better understanding the development of global climate finance and the related challenges.

1.1 International Climate Conventions and Agreements

To mitigate the climate problem, governments have been actively taking countermeasures. The major international climate conventions and agreements include the United Nations Framework Convention on Climate Change (UNFCCC), the Kyoto Protocol and the Paris Agreement.

At the first World Climate Conference in 1979, climate change was first put on the agenda as an issue of concern. The United Nations Environment Programme (UNEP) and the World Meteorological Organization (WMO) established the Intergovernmental Panel on Climate Change (IPCC) in 1988, and in 1990, the IPCC published its first Climate Change Assessment Report (CCA Report), which provided the scientific basis for climate change. Based on this report, the United Nations General Assembly established the Intergovernmental Negotiating Committee (INC) in 1990 to negotiate a Framework Convention on Climate Change (UNFCCC), which was signed by 154 countries at the United Nations Conference on the Environment and Development (Rio Earth Summit) in 1992. The objective of the Convention was to stabilise the concentration of greenhouse gas at a level that would prevent dangerous human-induced climate change, and the contracting parties were called upon to achieve this objective within a time frame that would allow ecosystems to adapt naturally to climate change, ensure that food production is not threatened and promote sustainable economic development (United Nations 1992).

The Kyoto Protocol, which is complementary to the Convention, aimed to stabilise the level of greenhouse gases in the atmosphere at an appropriate level, thereby preventing drastic climate change from harming humankind (United Nations 1998). The Kyoto Protocol implemented the Convention by letting industrialised countries and economies in transition commit to limiting and reducing greenhouse gas (GHG) emissions in accordance with agreed targets. The Kyoto Protocol was adopted on 11 December 1997 and entered into force on 16 February 2005. The Kyoto Protocol binds only developed countries because they are primarily responsible for current atmospheric emissions of GHGs, and it imposed additional responsibilities on developed countries in accordance with the principle of 'common but different responsibilities and respective capabilities' (Miyamoto and Takeuchi 2019).

In response to climate change, 197 countries adopted the Paris Agreement at the 21st session of the Conference of the Parties (COP 21) on 12 December 2015 in Paris. The Agreement entered into force on 4 November 2016. The Paris Agreement was the second legally binding climate agreement of the Convention after the Kyoto Protocol (Reyseliani et al. 2022; Wirth 2017). The goal of the Agreement was to limit the increase of the global average temperature to less than 2°C above preindustrial

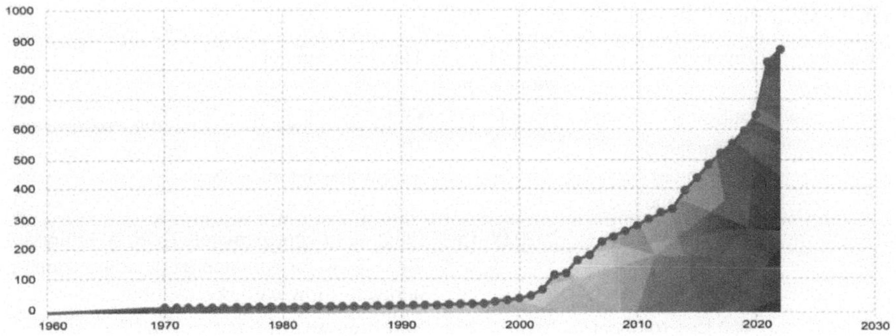

Fig. 1 Annual cumulative number of global climate finance policy instruments. *Data Source* PRI responsible investment regulation database, Data Extent: 1960–2022[1]

levels and to work towards limiting the temperature increase to 1.5°C above the preindustrial levels.

In addition to the above international climate conventions and agreements, the Copenhagen Accord, the Durban Accord, the Marrakesh Accords and others constitute a critical policy framework for the international community to address climate change (Chan et al. 2018; Dovie and Lwasa 2017).

Against this backdrop, many governments have introduced policies to help investors assess, manage and invest in climate risk. In 2021, the UN's Principles for Responsible Investment (PRI) identified a total of 225 new or revised policy instruments. Climate finance policies and regulations can support national policy objectives related to climate change and the Sustainable Development Goals (SDGs); enhance the resilience and stability of financial systems and economies; improve market efficiency by clarifying and calibrating the expectations of investors and companies; and increase the attractiveness of countries as investment destinations (Gomez-Echeverri 2018; Lamperti et al. 2020, 2021; Wall et al. 2019) (Fig. 1).

1.2 *The EU's Climate Finance Policy*

The EU is one of the world's largest economies in terms of greenhouse gas emissions. However, the EU stands as a staunch defender and adherent of the Paris Agreement and is one of the world's pioneering economics in proposing a carbon neutral programme. The EU's climate finance policy framework has laid out scientific and technological research and development programmes and adopted diversified fiscal and financial insurance measures (Table 1).

The European Commission's European Sustainable Investment Plan indicates that, between 2021 and 2030, the EU will mobilise at least 1 trillion euros to support

[1] The data for 2022 go up to 31 April 2022.

Table 1 Main climate finance policies of the EU

Category	Filenames	Time of publication	The main content
R&D layout	European Sustainable Investment Programme	2019.12.11	Mobilise at least EUR 1 trillion over the next 10 years to support the financing schemes of the European Green Deal
	The Innovation Fund	2020.06.15	Funding of approximately EUR 20 billion in 2020–2030 for commercial demonstration of innovative low-carbon technologies
	The Environment and Climate Action Programme of the 'LIFE Programme'	2018.10.25	Mobilisation of EUR 430.7 million to finance 142 new environment and climate action projects in six categories
	The R&D Tender of 'European Green Deal'	2020.09.22	Mobilise EUR 1 billion to tender for innovative research and development projects in 11 areas, including energy, construction, and transportation
	Supplementary Directives for the Operation of the Innovation Fund	2019.02.26	By 2030, applied innovation projects with broad technological representation and geographical coverage will be deployed
Finance, taxes and subsidies	Multi-Year Financial Framework (2021–2027)	2021.01.01	Put forward 10 fiscal and financial initiatives to invest at least EUR 108 billion in climate and environment over the next 7 years
	The Earth Planet Program	2017.12.12	Put forward 10 investment transformation initiatives to consolidate the EU's international leadership in combating climate change
	Energy Modernisation Fund	2020.07.09	Invest in energy system modernisation by allocating approximately EUR 14 billion from the carbon emissions trading system from 2021 to 2030
	Promoting a Climate-Neutral Economy: A Strategy for the Integration of the EU Energy System	2020.07.08	Revise the Energy Taxation Directive to align the taxation of industries with EU environmental and climate policies and phase out direct fossil fuel subsidies

(continued)

Table 1 (continued)

Category	Filenames	Time of publication	The main content
	Promoting a Climate-Neutral Economy: A Strategy for the Integration of the EU Energy System	2020.07.08	Extend the carbon emissions trading system to new sectors and provide more consistent carbon price signals among the energy sectors and member countries
Carbon emissions trading system and carbon price mechanism	'Fit for 55' Package	2021.07.14	Improve the carbon emissions trading system, taking fairness into account, and achieve a 61% reduction in emissions from industries covered by the carbon emissions trading system by 2030, compared with the level of 2005

Source Review and Enlightenment of the EU Carbon Neutrality Policy System

the European Green Deal. The EU will coordinate major scientific programmes such as the Innovation Fund and Horizon Europe to support the R&D and demonstration of low-carbon technologies in the following key industries: (1) clean energy and critical innovation technologies for a safe transition; (2) critical innovation technologies for industrial transformation; (3) key technologies for high-energy efficiency buildings; and (4) critical technologies for intelligent transportation (Wiesenthal et al. 2012).

Targeting a modern, clean economy and equitable society, the EU's multiannual financial framework for the year 2021 to 2027 and the European Sustainable Investment Plan have proposed seven fiscal and financial transformation measures (Manta 2020): (1) The European Regional Development Fund and the Cohesion Fund will raise at least 108 billion euros between 2021 and 2027 to support comprehensive demonstrations of renewable energy and low-carbon fuel production and consumption, financing for flagship projects in carbon–neutral industrial clusters, infrastructure construction and R&D vehicles' critical components. (2) Under the European Investment Plan, the European Investment Bank will develop a financial instrument for the efficient and energy-saving operation of buildings by using EU grants as guarantees to attract 10 billion euros in financing to improve the energy efficiency of buildings and lift 3.2 million households out of energy poverty. (3) The Connecting Europe Facility Plan will allocate at least 60% of its budget to support the construction of transport, energy and digital infrastructure. (4) The External Investment Plan will draw on 4.1 billion euros from the EU budget to attract up to 44 billion euros in additional investments. (5) The EU will take structural support actions for the coal and carbon-intensive regions. (6) Compared with 2014–2020, the LIFE Programme will increase its funding by 72% (reaching 5.4 billion euros), with more than 60% of the additional funding dedicated to achieving climate objectives. (7) The Common Agricultural Policy and Horizon Europe plan to allocate at least 40% and 35% of their budgets, respectively, to support the priorities of the European Green Deal.

Some proposals—A Clean Planet for All: A European Long-Term Strategic Vision for a Prosperous, Modern, Competitive and Climate-Neutral Economy and Promoting a Climate-Neutral Economy: The EU's Strategy for the Integration of Energy Systems—suggest revising the Energy Tax Directive, phasing out direct subsidies for fossil fuels and adjusting the tax standards for the transport sector, hence aligning taxes on energy, electricity, hydrogen production and hydrogen storage with the environmental and climate policies of the EU to avoid double taxation (EU 2018).

Five main features characterise the EU's climate finance policy:

(1) Increasing the commitment and policy intensity towards climate issues to gain initiative in climate cooperation with the United States. For instance, the EU proposed that developed countries would provide 100 billion euros annually in aid to developing countries and collaborate with the European Investment Bank within this framework.
(2) Launching the European Green Deal, setting a net zero greenhouse gas emissions target by 2050 to achieve climate neutrality, aiming to promote climate governance coordination within the EU and solidify its global leadership in climate governance.
(3) Developing sustainable finance policies, including the Sustainable Finance Classification Authority Act, the corporate sustainability disclosure directive and others, has aimed to capture the initiative in shaping international green finance regulations. These policies are intended to promote environmentally friendly investments within the financial industry and enhance resilience to climate change.
(4) Launching the Climate Adaptation Strategy proposes to increase adaptability to climate change and reduce the vulnerability associated with climate change. It calls for stricter requirements in some areas, such as industrial transformation, carbon pricing, the development of renewable energy sources and energy taxation.
(5) Achieving carbon neutrality through technological innovation, digital development and fiscal policy measures that promote carbon emission reduction in each sector and increase investment in new technologies.

The EU's climate finance policy promotes climate governance within the EU and leads the global climate governance process.

1.3 The United States' Climate Finance Policy

The United States is one of the main carbon emitters in the world. On 24 October 1992, the Energy Policy Act of 1992 enacted by the United States provided for the promotion of energy conservation, upgrading the efficiency of energy use and promoting the use of renewable energy, which was undoubtedly a positive signal to the negotiations on the Global Framework Convention on Climate Change. In December of that year, the United States promulgated the National Action Programme on Global

Climate Change to assess the greenhouse gas emissions of the United States and proposed government actions related to greenhouse gas emission reduction. However, the above 'no-regrets' measures and actions of the United States were not specifically designed to fulfil the Framework Convention on Climate Change but rather to 'address the issues of energy conservation and air pollution', with which the reduction of greenhouse gas emissions was regarded as a 'subsidiary dividend'.

Climate finance policy during the Obama administration continually sought change. First, he increased investment in the development of clean energy and promoted energy conservation and emission reduction activities. In early 2009, the Obama Administration introduced and Congress approved the American Recovery and Reinvestment Act of 2009 (Wilson 2012). A large amount of capital would be spent on clean energy development, energy efficiency upgrading, environmental protection and tax incentives to promote green initiatives. Second, it reduced oil consumption and promoted energy independence. Facing the sharp fluctuations in international oil prices and dangers of global climate change, the United States urgently needed to find new energy sources and increase its energy self-sufficiency rate and cleanliness. Third, the act helped determine the goal of reducing greenhouse gas emissions and establish a climate change response mechanism. Obama followed the Kyoto Protocol and set specific targets and timetables for greenhouse gas emission reduction for the United States in the form of total emission reductions, with a plan to reduce the United States' greenhouse gas emissions to its 1990 level by 2020 and, based on this, to reduce emissions by another 80% by 2050. Fourth, the act attached more importance to international climate cooperation and reshaped the United States' leadership in global climate governance. In 2008, the United States issued the Presidential Climate Action Plan for the first time and updated it every two years. The main contents include reducing carbon emissions through industrial regulation and actively taking responsibility for climate change in the world. The Presidential Climate Action Plan marked a transition of the United States' climate change policy from passive to active, from decentralised to centralised, and from fuzzy to clear, with the most representative initiative being the Clean Power Plan. The United States Environmental Protection Agency (EPA) first proposed the plan in June 2014, which set 2030 emission reduction targets for each state, allowed states to choose their emission reduction methods and gave states more freedom in carbon trading (Wilson 2012).

However, the Trump Administration reversed the Obama Administration's climate- and environmentally friendly policies, and the United States' position on climate change took a significant step backward (Daniels 2018). In March 2017, Trump signed an executive order announcing the indefinite suspension of the Clean Power Plan, which was designed to increase coal industry jobs, restore coal power plants and lower electricity prices. On 1 June 2017, the Trump Administration announced that the United States was withdrawing from the Paris Agreement, halting the implementation of its nationally owned contributions (NOCs) and its funding obligations, including contributions to the Green Climate Fund (GCF).

In late March 2021, Biden unveiled a $2 trillion infrastructure investment plan—the American Jobs Initiative—aimed at strengthening climate and clean infrastructure, including a $100 billion investment in the power grid and clean technology to help the United States decarbonise its electricity sector by 2035. To advance the implementation of the new emissions reduction targets, in November 2021, the Biden Administration launched the Long-Term Strategy for Moving Towards Net Zero Emissions by 2050, which provided a detailed long-term plan for the United States to achieve the ultimate goal of net zero emissions, set important nodes and milestones and specified the technological pathways that must be taken to achieve net zero emissions.

The United States has already introduced several laws related to environmental economics that contribute to the development of climate finance markets, such as the signing of the Inflation Reduction Act and enactment of the Climate Mobilisation Act. The New York Department of Financial Services (DFS) issued climate finance risk guidelines for New York–regulated banks and mortgage lenders to address the financial risks posed by climate change. The DFS also integrated climate risk into the governance frameworks, risk management processes and business strategies of financial institutions. In addition, the DFS joined the Network of Central Banks and Regulators for the Green Financial System (NGFS) and Sustainable Insurance Forum (SIF) to carry out international exchanges and cooperation in climate finance.

To promote the implementation of laws and policies related to green finance, the United States also established the Centre for Environmental Finance (CEF), the Environmental Advisory Board (EAB) and the Network of Environmental Finance Centres (NEFC). The CEF aims to provide creative and technical support to state-level local governments and the private sector in environmental finance cost management and green project management while also giving advice and evaluations of selecting systems, policies and trends related to environmental finance. The Environmental Finance Advisory Board (EFAB) can provide the financial industry with guidance on environmental finance tools to guide the actions of financial institutions. The Environmental Finance Centre Network (EFCN) provides training and education in environmental finance, management and technical support. In 2021, the United States issued two bills—the ESG Disclosure Simplification Act of 2021 and the Climate Risk Disclosure Act of 2021—that directed the SEC to engage in rule-making to harmonise standards for environmental, social and governance (ESG) disclosure requirements.

State governments have also actively enacted laws related to ecological and environmental protection as a way to promote the development of climate finance. Among them, California is at the forefront of environmental protection and green finance legislation. California enacted the Integrated Waste Management Ordinance in 1989 to promote the development of a circular economy. In 2006, the California Global Warming Solutions Act made California the first state in the United States to legally constrain itself to achieve its emissions reduction targets, while the Regulation on Control and Emissions Trading of Limiting the Total Amount of Carbon Dioxide Emissions in 2010 made the California government the first in the United States to use the free market to curb greenhouse gas emissions. In 2020, California officially launched the Climate-Smart Insurance Products Database, the first-ever consumer-facing inventory of green insurance policies, listing more than 400 green insurance products currently available to consumers and businesses.

Overall, the United States needs a top-level design for developing climate finance and a long-term strategy or roadmap for developing climate finance at the national level.

1.4 Climate and Financial Policy in the UK

As a world-leading financial service centre and sustainable development country, the UK is in a leading position in the development of global green finance, with a relatively complete climate financial system ranging from macro policy guidance to various market execution agencies (such as regulatory agencies, stock exchanges, financial institutions and so on) (Hafner et al. 2020). In terms of climate financial markets and products, the UK not only has its own unique innovation system, but it also aligns with internationally recognised standards and actively engages in strategic cooperation with countries around the world in climate investment and financing.

In 2019, the UK launched the *Green Finance Strategy* as the most important and comprehensive top-level design for green finance in the country; it combined private sector capital flows with clean, environmentally sustainable and resilient growth to ensure the UK's long-term competitiveness. The strategy mainly expounded on the development path of green finance from three aspects: domestic macro, micro and international cooperation. In macro terms, by reaching a consensus on clean development, clarifying responsibilities and advocating transparent mechanisms and overall planning, the government has been urged to mainstream climate and environmental factors as a financial and strategic priority. In micro terms, it mobilised private capital to promote clean and resilient growth by innovating green finance paths, encouraging green investment, emphasising market entry barriers and inclusiveness and establishing long-term stable development mechanisms. In terms of international cooperation, the main focus was to increase green finance innovation and stabilise the UK's leading position in the field of global green finance development. At the same time, under the guidance of the *Green Finance Strategy*, the *UK government Green Financing Framework* was launched in 2021, which mainly elaborated on the application methods of financing, the selection and evaluation framework of green projects, process management and reporting methods. It also echoed the International Capital Market Association (ICMA) *Green Bond Principles* of 2021, and the framework was combined with the UK's ongoing classification of environmentally sustainable economic activities ('UK Classification').

In addition to the top-level strategy, the UK has also continuously strengthened institutional construction in the field of climate finance, and these institutions have also signed numerous relevant agreements and policies. In 2019, the UK established the Green Finance Institute as a key policy recommendation for the industry-led Green Finance Working Group of the UK government. This institution not only participated in the formulation of the *Green Finance Strategy* throughout the process, but its subordinate Green Technology Advisory Group (GTAG) also provided independent advice to the government on implementing the UK Taxonomy in June 2021. In November 2020, several regulatory departments in the UK jointly published the *Roadmap to Mandatory Climate-Related Disclosure* in November 2020, announcing plans to achieve full-economy disclosure in accordance with the requirements of the Task Force on Climate-Related Financial Disclosures (TCFD) by 2025, with a significant number of mandatory requirements taking effect before 2023. In 2021, to further implement the UK's long-term commitment to achieving the net zero goal, the UK Treasury issued the *Financial Greening: Sustainable Investment Roadmap.* This roadmap was based on the Green Finance Strategy published by the UK government in 2019, and it formulated three stages for the UK to achieve financial greening: the information stage, the action stage and the transfer stage.

In terms of policies for various financial product segments, the UK has mainly covered a relatively comprehensive product and trading market in the form of various projects and plans. Among them, the most distinctive is the carbon market. Because of its previous affiliation with the EU, which is one of the most well-developed systems for the development of the global carbon market, the UK planned to rebuild a more advanced carbon market system after Brexit in 2020. At the same time, for establishing and regulating the UK carbon market, the government issued the *2020 Greenhouse Gas Emissions Trading Plan Order* in 2020, aiming to reshape the carbon trading system after Brexit. In addition, in terms of monitoring and disclosing ESG and environmental risks, the UK has implemented mandatory disclosure requirements, which were mostly in line with EU documents. For environmental stress testing in insurance, the Prudential Regulation Authority (PRA) of the UK specifically pointed out in the *2019 Insurance Stress Test* that banks should use their stress testing framework to assess the impact of climate-related risks on the UK's financial system.

The UK's climate finance policy is also reflected in taxation, mainly in the form of climate change tax and floor carbon tax. The Climate Change Levy was implemented in 2001, aiming to encourage energy efficiency and reduce energy use by increasing the effective price of energy to help the UK fulfil its commitments under the Kyoto Protocol and reduce greenhouse gas emissions. The tax was imposed on energy supply in industry, commerce, agriculture, local administration and some other services. The government could set different tax rates for different energy sources every year. In addition, preferential tax rates could be set for energy-intensive industries, and energy-intensive enterprises that have signed the CCA were eligible for a maximum 90% reduction in electricity tax rates. The UK launched the 'Floor Carbon Price' in 2013, a policy for power generation companies that imposed taxes on their energy use in the energy input link. This move was intended to improve the internalisation of climate change-related costs of electricity to encourage the reduction of carbon emissions.

1.5 Asia–Pacific Climate and Financial Policies

Investment in the climate finance sector in the Asia–Pacific region has mainly been driven by the Asian Development Bank (ADB) (Delina 2017). The ADB has formulated and promulgated a 2030 sustainable development strategy, which listed climate change and environmental issues as one of the seven priority areas for action. This strategy covered three aspects: improving climate change mitigation, enhancing climate and disaster resilience and strengthening environmental sustainability. The ADB's investment has had a positive impact in many areas. For example, the ADB's investment in renewable energy projects has helped some Asia–Pacific countries improve energy efficiency and reduce greenhouse gas emissions. The ADB has also provided technical assistance and training to help these countries implement climate change projects. In addition to investment, the ADB has also actively promoted policy formulation and dialogue. For example, they have cooperated with some countries to formulate and implement policies specific to their own climate change issues. Furthermore, the ADB also cooperates with other international financial institutions to promote sustainable development in the Asia–Pacific region. The ADB's climate finance policy aims to help the Asia–Pacific region achieve sustainable development, reduce dependence on fossil fuels, improve energy efficiency, reduce greenhouse gas emissions and adapt to the impact of climate change.

As representatives, China and Japan have promoted the construction of climate finance policies in the Asia–Pacific region, and South Korea has also established a corresponding climate finance policy system (McGee and Taplin 2009; Haites 2014).

China has adopted various policy measures in the field of climate finance to support responses to climate change and promote green development. The categories of China's climate finance policy instruments include 'hard law' and 'soft law'. Hard law is legally binding and mandatory, while soft law is not legally binding or has a weaker binding force than traditional law, such as guidelines from governmental departments intended to advise people and institutions on how something should be done or what something should be (Karlsson-Vinkhuyzen and Vihma 2009). In 2016, the People's Bank of China and seven other ministries jointly issued the *Guiding Opinions on Building a Green Financial System* (hereinafter referred to as the Guiding Opinions), which became the foundation and guiding document for China's development of green finance. The Guiding Opinions proposed a number of measures, including encouraging financial institutions to provide loans for green projects, supporting green enterprises in issuing green bonds, promoting environmental information disclosure and strengthening environmental risk management. Under the guidance of the *Guiding Opinions*, China has established a pilot zone for green financial reform and innovation, including nine places in six provinces (autonomous regions), including Zhejiang, Jiangxi, Guangdong, Guizhou, Gansu and Xinjiang, to explore new paths and models for the development of green finance through pilot projects in the pilot zone. At the same time, the Chinese government has issued a series of investment and financing policies to address climate change, including the *Notice on Carrying out the Pilot Work of Climate Investment and*

Financing, the *Pilot Work Plan for Climate Investment and Financing* and so on, aiming to guide and encourage financial institutions and social capital to increase investment in projects to address climate change.

Japan's climate finance policy mainly manifests in two ways: first, the Bank of Japan provides financial support for financial institutions to cope with climate change, and second, the Japanese government and financial institutions cooperate to launch new climate initiatives. First, the Bank of Japan released the *Strategy for Addressing Climate Change* on July 16, 2021, proposing a series of measures to address climate change. One important measure was to introduce new financial support measures to provide financial support for financial institutions to cope with climate change. Second, the Japanese government and financial institutions launched a new plan to provide funding for Japanese financial institutions that try to address climate change through investment and loans. In addition, the Bank of Japan has actively participated in international discussions on climate change, strengthened dialogue with financial institutions and established a 'Climate Change Response Collaborative Center' to build an internal organisational framework. The Japanese government has also formulated a series of policies aimed at the impact of climate change, such as developing stricter standards and regulations, limiting greenhouse gas emissions and promoting the development of renewable energy.

The South Korean government has adopted various policy measures in the field of climate finance to promote effective responses to climate change, such as participating in the International Green Finance Initiative, establishing a legal framework to support green finance, establishing green funds and encouraging financial institutions to participate in the International Green Finance Initiative. First, the South Korean government has actively participated in the International Green Finance Initiative. For example, the South Korean financial regulatory authority joined the Sustainable Stock Exchange Initiative, pledging to promote long-term sustainable investment, advance the disclosure of ESG information of listed companies and improve their ESG performance. In addition, the Industrial Bank of Korea joined the International Development Finance Club and the Bank of Korea joined the Central Bank and Regulatory Agency Green Finance Network (NGFS). The Financial Services Commission has also applied to join the NGFS to discuss and deal with issues related to climate- and environmental-related financial risks. Second, the South Korean government supports the development of green finance through establishing legal frameworks. For example, South Korea formulated the *Green Growth Basic Law* to provide legal support for green finance businesses; the *Tax Substitution System for Promoting Low-Carbon Green Growth* to help enterprises make green investments through tax policies. Third, the South Korean government has established green funds to promote sustainable development and reduce carbon emissions. For example, South Korea established a market-scale trading fund for voluntary greenhouse gas emission reduction to support greenhouse gas emission reduction projects. Finally, the South Korean government has also encouraged financial institutions to participate in the International Green Finance Initiative, such as the UNEP Financial Initiative, the United Nations PRI and so on. Some financial institutions in South Korea have also signed the Equator Principles, indicating that they attach importance to environmental and social impacts in project financing.

1.6 Comparison of International Climate and Financial Policies

The climate finance policies of the above countries and regions focus on four aspects: green investment, strengthening ESG integration and disclosure, promoting innovation and technological development and promoting international cooperation and standardisation. Together, these measures provide important support and impetus for addressing climate change and achieving the SDGs.

Promoting green investment: The countries jointly focus on encouraging financial institutions and investors to invest funds in sustainable development and green projects, such as renewable energy, energy efficiency improvement and clean technology. By guiding the flow of funds to a low-carbon economy and environmentally friendly projects, sustainable development can be promoted.

Strengthening ESG integration and disclosure: Financial institutions are required to consider ESG factors in investment decisions and risk management. Financial institutions need to integrate ESG standards and indicators to assess the sustainability performance and risks of enterprises, which can improve the sustainability of investment decisions. At the same time, enterprises must disclose ESG information to increase transparency and information alignment, promoting investors and stakeholders in evaluating the ESG performance of the company.

Promoting innovation and technological development: There are many policies encouraging green financial innovation and technological development to meet the needs of climate change and sustainable development. By providing fiscal and tax incentives, the government encourages advancements in clean technology and renewable energy, facilitating research and development as well as commercialisation.

Promoting international cooperation and standardisation: Providing a framework for international cooperation and standardisation can provide a platform for cooperation between different countries and regions. For example, the development and standardisation of green bond markets has facilitated cross-border capital flows and connectivity for green investment. Furthermore, through strengthened cooperation and knowledge sharing, the international community can collectively address the challenges of climate change and sustainable development.

However, there are still some differences in the specific content and implementation of climate finance policies in the EU, the UK, the United States and the Asia–Pacific region. These differences may stem from the legal, economic and social conditions in each region, as well as the priorities and positions of different governments, institutions and stakeholders.

The EU stands as a global leader in the fight against climate change, showcasing its commitment to sustainability through ambitious goals for carbon neutrality and sustainable development. At the heart of the EU's climate action strategy is its comprehensive climate finance policy, which aims to align financial practices with environmental objectives. This policy places a significant emphasis on promoting sustainable finance and green investment, marking a paradigm shift in the financial sector towards greater environmental responsibility. One of the key components of the EU's climate finance policy is the integration of ESG factors into financial decision-making processes. Financial institutions within the EU are required to adopt sustainable practices by incorporating ESG considerations and disclosing relevant information. This mandate is reinforced through regulations and directives, creating a regulatory framework that incentivizes responsible investment and lending practices. In tandem with the push for ESG integration, the EU actively promotes the development of green bonds and green finance markets.

Moreover, the UK, despite its departure from the EU, remains committed to promoting a low-carbon economy and sustainable finance. The UK government places a particular focus on building a green bond market as part of its broader strategy to mobilize funds for eco-friendly projects. Green bonds issued by the UK serve as a crucial financial tool, attracting investors keen on supporting initiatives aligned with environmental and sustainable development goals.

In the United States, climate finance policies exhibit a diverse landscape, with various governments at the state and city levels taking independent initiatives to address climate challenges. Many states and cities have recognized the urgency of climate action and, in response, have adopted their own financial policies to promote renewable energy development and implement measures to reduce emissions. At the state level, governments have been instrumental in formulating climate finance policies that align with regional priorities and challenges. These policies often include incentives, subsidies, and regulatory frameworks to encourage the adoption of renewable energy sources, such as solar and wind power. States may also implement carbon pricing mechanisms or cap-and-trade systems to incentivize emission reductions across different sectors. Cities, too, play a crucial role in shaping climate finance policies, particularly in densely populated urban areas. In addition to government-led efforts, financial institutions and investors in the United States are increasingly integrating ESG factors into their decision-making processes. Moreover, the private sector is witnessing a surge in sustainable finance, with investments directed toward projects and companies that adhere to ESG principles. This trend is not only driven by ethical considerations but also by the acknowledgment that environmentally conscious practices can contribute to long-term financial stability and resilience.

Climate finance policies in the Asia–Pacific region play a pivotal role in advancing environmental sustainability, with a primary focus on promoting green finance and sustainable development. These policies actively engage in fostering a transition towards a low-carbon economy by employing various strategies. One significant initiative involves the establishment and promotion of green bond markets. Moreover, the region's climate finance policies also emphasize the creation of green investment funds. By supporting initiatives such as sustainable agriculture, reforestation, and clean energy development, these funds contribute to both ecological well-being and long-term economic stability. In addition to financial mechanisms, climate finance policies in the Asia–Pacific region actively encourage corporate responsibility and transparency. Companies are urged to disclose ESG information, providing stakeholders with insights into their commitment to sustainability.

The Chinese government has demonstrated a proactive stance in addressing climate change by implementing a comprehensive set of measures within its climate finance policies. These initiatives operate on both regional and institutional levels, underscoring a commitment to promoting green and sustainable development while simultaneously enhancing risk management and supervision related to climate change (Wu 2023). At the regional level, China has strategically integrated climate finance policies into local governance structures, tailoring approaches to the unique challenges and opportunities within specific areas. By aligning climate finance measures with regional needs, the Chinese government aims to ensure that the impact is felt at the grassroots level, fostering community resilience and environmental sustainability. Institutionally, China has established frameworks and regulations to guide the implementation of climate finance policies. Additionally, there is a growing emphasis on incorporating climate risk management and supervision into financial institutions' practices, ensuring that investments consider and mitigate potential climate-related risks. Recognizing the significance of civil society in addressing climate change, the Chinese government encourages the active involvement of non-governmental organizations (NGOs) in climate change governance.

2 The System of Climate and Financial Regulations

2.1 The Composition of the Climate and Financial Regulatory System

Climate change is one of the most pressing challenges facing the world today, and its impact on human society and natural environment is profound. To address climate change, governments and international organisations are taking various measures, one of which is to establish a climate financial regulatory system. Climate financial regulation refers to the process of guiding and regulating financial institutions and market participants to consider climate risks and opportunities in financial activities through financial policies and rules and promoting low-carbon transformation and green development (Park and Kim 2020). Regulators use legal, economic and administrative means to supervise and manage those issues related to climate finance, including markets, instruments, institutions and other related issues.

From the perspective of system composition, climate financial regulation includes regulatory system, regulatory agencies, regulatory authority, regulatory scope, regulatory content and so on. From the perspective of market classification, the climate financial regulation system mainly includes financial regulation of bank credit, securities, insurance and so on. From the perspective of regulatory subjects, the climate financial regulation system consists of three levels: government regulation, market constraints and industry self-discipline. In terms of government regulation, it mainly involves aspects such as finance, taxation, trade, environment, and audit, which supervise climate investment and financing activities in accordance with relevant laws and regulations. In terms of market constraints, it mainly promotes financial institutions and enterprises to consciously carry out low-carbon transformation and green development through market-oriented means such as the carbon market and environmental liability insurance. Concerning industry self-discipline, the guidelines and standards strengthens information sharing, talent training, industry exchanges, financing promotion and risk prevention among members through the construction of industry organisations for climate investment and financing and cooperates with regulatory departments to do a good job in industry supervision.

The monitoring, reporting and verification (MRV) of climate finance, which defines the scope of climate funds, collects and reports climate finance data and evaluates the effectiveness of climate finance, is an important component of the construction of a climate finance regulatory system (https://primarysources.brillonline.com/browse/climate-change-and-law-collection/mrv-101-understanding-measurement-reporting-and-verification-of-climate-change-mitigation;cccc002020160020011). The MRV of climate finance can effectively supervise and report the sources, use and effectiveness of funds, on the one hand, while, on the other hand, it can make coordinated use of existing funds to fully play a positive role in addressing climate change and leverage more funds to flow into the field of climate change.

The Financial Stability Board and the Basel Committee have both established climate-related working groups to actively promote the regulation and disclosure of climate risks (Myklebust 2022). In December 2015, the Financial Stability Board established the TCFD, which aims to develop consistent and voluntary recommendations for climate-related financial disclosure. In February 2020, the Basel Committee established the Task Force on Climate-Related Financial Risks (TFCR), which is responsible for promoting the regulation of climate risks. The International Financial Reporting Standards Foundation (IFRS) established the International Sustainability Standards Board (ISSB) in 2021, which plans to launch an internationally accepted standard for climate-related regulatory reporting.

In addition, in December 2017, eight central banks, including the People's Bank of China, jointly initiated the establishment of the Central Bank and Regulatory Agency Green Finance Network (NGFS), aiming to promote the construction of climate finance systems in financial markets across the world, actively exploring the assessment and management of climate change risks; the organisation has become one of the most influential international green finance cooperation platforms (Dikau and Volz 2021). The International Association of Insurance Supervisors (IAIS) has also continued to provide guidance for insurance institutions' climate-related risk management practices (Prudential Regulation Authority 2021).

2.2 *Characteristics of a Climate Finance Regulatory System*

International organisations such as the World Bank, the International Monetary Fund and national financial regulators have conducted a great deal of research and practice around the regulation of the climate financial system. The current practice of climate risk management in the financial system is mainly centred on two objectives: to support the low-carbon transformation of the economy and to prevent financial risks caused by climate change. Among them, the former is essentially to address the causes of climate risk and reduce greenhouse gas emissions at the source by guiding the flow of capital to low-carbon industries through financial policy tools. The latter addresses the financial consequences of climate risks (physical and transition risks), that is, managing the various types of financial risks that may arise because of climate change.

Climate finance regulation is a cross-cutting regulation. Climate change involves multiple sectors, such as energy, transportation, agriculture and industry. Therefore, climate finance regulation needs to coordinate the policy objectives and actions of different sectors and institutions to form a unified regulatory framework. At the same time, climate finance regulations also need to cooperate with the international community and participate in global climate governance and financial regulation.

Climate finance regulation is dynamic regulation. The impacts of climate change are evolving, and our understanding of climate risks and opportunities is growing with the advancement of science and technology. Therefore, climate finance regulations need to be updated to meet the needs of different stages and scenarios. At the same time, climate finance regulations need to be flexible and innovative to cope with uncertainty and complexity.

Climate finance regulation is a comprehensive regulation. Climate finance regulation involves not only the stability and efficiency of financial markets, but also social equity and environmental protection. Therefore, climate finance regulation needs to consider the interests and impacts of multiple parties in a comprehensive manner and balance the various objectives and instruments to achieve a multiwin outcome. At the same time, climate finance regulations also need to be coordinated with other policy tools, such as taxes, subsidies, standards and so forth to form a policy mix conducive to climate action.

Therefore, the characteristics of the climate finance regulatory system include the following four points:

(1) Pluralism: The climate finance regulatory system consists of several parts, including government agencies, financial institutions and social organisations. These institutions play different roles in the regulatory process, forming a diversified regulatory system.
(2) Complexity: The climate financial regulatory system involves more fields and aspects, including finance, climate change, economy and others. The regulatory process needs to take these factors into account, and therefore the regulatory system can become more complex.

(3) Comprehensive: The climate financial regulatory system is not only concerned about financial risks, but also about the risks brought by climate change and interaction between the two, so it is necessary to comprehensively consider the factors of finance and climate change to carry out comprehensive regulation.
(4) International: The climate financial regulatory system needs to take into account international factors in the regulatory process, including international cooperation and international standards and, therefore, has a certain degree of internationalisation.

2.3 Development of the International Climate Finance Regulatory System

To cope with the impacts of climate change, governments, financial institutions and enterprises are adopting various measures, including reducing greenhouse gas emissions, improving energy efficiency, developing renewable energy, increasing green investments and so on. However, the implementation and effectiveness of these measures require corresponding regulatory and assessment mechanisms to ensure the transparency, sustainability and effectiveness of climate finance. This is where the importance of international climate finance regulations lies.

The history of international climate finance regulation can be traced back to the 1992 UNFCCC, the first global climate agreement aimed at 'preventing dangerous anthropogenic interference with the climate system that would jeopardize the well-being of humankind'. In 1997, the Kyoto Protocol further stipulated specific obligations for developed countries to reduce emissions, becoming the first global climate agreement and setting specific obligations for developed countries to reduce emissions and created three flexible mechanisms—the clean development mechanism (CDM), joint implementation (JI) and emissions trading (ET)—to facilitate the development of the carbon market. In 2015, the Paris Agreement set a global temperature rise target of 'well below 2°C, with a view to limiting it to 1.5°C' and required all parties to submit a Nationally Determined Contribution (NDC), indicating their action plan for mitigation and adaptation. The Paris Agreement also emphasised the important role of climate finance and calls for enhanced MRV of its sources, flows and impacts.

In addition to the UNFCCC and its related agreements, there are many other international organisations and initiatives involved in building and promoting climate finance regulation. For example, the World Bank Group (WBG) is one of the largest providers of climate finance, supporting countries' investments and innovations in low-carbon development, clean energy, energy efficiency and emission reduction through a number of programmes and instruments, such as the Multilateral Investment Fund (MIF), the Carbon Fund and the Energy Sector Management Assistance Program (ESMAP). The International Monetary Fund (IMF) is also actively promoting the reform and improvement of climate finance regulation, and it analyses and evaluates the progress and challenges of countries in climate-related fiscal policies, financial risk management and carbon pricing through its publications, such as the Fiscal Surveillance Report (FSR), the Global Financial Stability Report (GFSR) and the Country Reports. In addition, there are some multilateral or bilateral cooperation mechanisms, such as the Asian Infrastructure Investment Bank (AIIB), the European Bank for Reconstruction and Development (EBRD) and the China-France Climate Finance Working Group (CFWG), which also contribute to the coordination and innovation of climate finance regulation.

The international climate finance regulatory system is one of the important guarantees of the global response to climate change. The international climate finance regulatory system is mainly composed of the following three aspects:

(1) **Climate change policy**: Governments need to formulate corresponding climate change policies, clarify the development direction and goals of a low-carbon economy and provide guidance for financial regulation. The main relevant guiding documents for global climate regulation are the United Nations Framework Agreement on Climate Change, the Kyoto Protocol and the Paris Agreement. Countries have successively introduced relevant laws and regulations, which mainly include carbon trading certification laws, legal systems for carbon trading registration and settlement, legal systems for carbon trading contracts, carbon emission taxation systems, carbon labelling laws, carbon trade laws and so on.

    From the practices of various countries, incorporating climate factors into the traditional monetary policy framework is currently the main practice of climate risk management in the financial regulatory sector (Boyang Zhang et al., 2022). First, credit allocation policies guide financial institutions in supporting green industries and project financing. For example, the RBI has set up a 'Priority Industries List' to force commercial banks to allocate a fixed percentage of credit resources to the list of industries. Second, green quantitative easing, that is, the central bank directly buys green financial assets, such as the euro area (including the ECB and the euro area national central banks) asset purchase programme considering green bonds. The third is to incorporate sustainable investment criteria into the central bank's own portfolio management; for example, the French central bank pension fund will be excluded from coal investments. Fourth, climate considerations should be incorporated into central bank refinancing operational frameworks, such as collateral frameworks. Fifth is the implementation of differentiated reserve requirements. Overall, climate investments have positive externalities and can contribute to the overall welfare level of society in the long term. The purpose of monetary policy–related practices is precisely to try to reduce the production and consumption of carbon-intensive products and promote a low-carbon transition of the economy by promoting green financing and discouraging brown financing.

(2) **Climate change assessment**: The assessment of climate change is an important element of financial regulation and the impacts, risks and opportunities of climate change need to be assessed to develop appropriate responses. The Bank

of England published a comprehensive methodology in 2021, incorporating both physical and transformational risks into regular biennial scenario stress tests with the aim of testing climate risk across the financial system. The ECB similarly conducted a top-down climate stress test for the euro area in 2021, assessing physical and transition risks for banks and nonfinancial corporations over a 30-year time horizon. In recent years, financial regulators in various countries have actively carried out climate risk assessments and made considerable progress, also laying a solid foundation for climate risk management in the financial system.

(3) **Climate change finance**: Responding to climate change requires a large amount of financial support, so it is necessary to establish a corresponding climate change finance mechanism to ensure the effective input and use of funds. There are three main sources of international climate change funds: multilateral agencies, bilateral agencies and the private sector. The allocation of international climate change funds refers to the process of transferring funds from providers to recipients, including deciding on the objectives, criteria, conditions and procedures of the funds. The allocation of international climate change funds is influenced by a variety of factors, such as political, economic, social and cultural. Generally speaking, the allocation of international climate change funds should follow the following principles: effectiveness, efficiency, equity, transparency and accountability.

Regulatory systems for climate change finance vary but generally include the following three levels:

International level: The governing board or management committee of the funds is mainly responsible for formulating policies, standards and guidelines for the funds, as well as approving the projects and activities of the funds. The council or management committee is usually composed of a certain percentage of donors and beneficiaries of the fund to reflect the principles of balance and equity.

National level: The implementing agency of the fund is primarily responsible for implementing the projects and activities of the fund as well as monitoring and evaluating the effectiveness and impact of the fund. The executing agency is usually a national government department, agency or nongovernmental organisation accredited by the national government or the private sector.

Project level: The executing party of a project is primarily responsible for carrying out the specific tasks of the project and reporting on the progress and results of the project. Implementers are usually affiliates or partners of the implementing agency or third-party organisations selected or commissioned by the implementing agency.

Nevertheless, the regulation of international climate change finance still suffers from the problems of inconsistent regulatory standards, insufficient regulatory capacity, insufficient regulatory participation and unclear regulatory effects.

Overall, the international climate finance regulatory system requires the joint participation of governments, financial institutions, enterprises and all aspects of society to strengthen cooperation and jointly promote an effective response to global climate change.

In addition, although major countries around the world are actively exploring climate finance regulation, the lack of universally recognised concepts and frameworks has affected the effectiveness of financial support for low-carbon transitions. To accurately identify transition financial activities and support technological transformation, industrial upgrading, energy-saving and carbon reduction in high-carbon industries, the Climate Bonds Initiative (CBI) released the framework of the White Paper on Climate Bonds in 2020, which put forward five transition principles to avoid 'greenwashing', provided detailed explanations of credible transition objectives and pathways and strictly defined the transition activities as 'low carbon', 'low carbon' and 'high carbon'. It strictly framed the transition activities on a track consistent with the goals of the Paris Agreement and explicitly excluded activities unrelated to the transition path, thus squeezing the arbitrage space of 'whitewashing the transition'. The Climate Transition Finance Handbook issued by the ICMA and the Basic Guidelines on Climate Transition Finance in Japan have also defined the scope of transition finance, which is of great significance in guiding the financing of low-carbon transitions.

The development history of international climate finance regulation shows that climate finance is a complex system across fields, levels and subjects, which requires a comprehensive, unified and transparent international framework to guide and regulate the behaviour and responsibilities of all parties (Bhandary et al. 2021). However, international climate finance regulation currently faces many challenges and deficiencies, such as the lack of uniform definitions and standards, an effective information disclosure and verification mechanism and a fair distribution and benefit-sharing mechanism. These problems require enhanced communication and collaboration among governments, financial institutions and enterprises to jointly seek solutions. At the same time, more research and innovation is needed to improve the efficiency and effectiveness of climate finance regulation and to provide stronger support for addressing climate change.

3 Typical Cases

3.1 Enhancement and Standardisation of Climate-Related Disclosures for Investors by the U.S. Securities and Exchange Commission

On March 21, 2022, the SEC issued a proposal entitled 'Enhancement and Standardisation of Investor-Oriented Climate-Related Disclosure' (SEC Proposal) regarding amendments to the Securities Act, the Securities Exchange Act and Regulations Governing the Contents and Format of Non-Financial Disclosures (Regulation S-K) and Financial Disclosure Contents. The issuance of the SEC proposal reversed the situation where the disclosure of climate-related information in the United States lags behind EU and international standards and is regarded as a major policy adjustment by the Biden Administration to the Trump Administration's negative response to climate change, which will have a far-reaching impact on the disclosure of U.S.-listed companies (SEC.gov. 2022). The announcement focused on listed companies and investment organisations, requiring them to provide more accurate, transparent and comparable climate-related information to investors.

The SEC's 510-page proposal consisted of four sections: Introduction, Discussion, Invited Commentary and Economic Analysis, addressing climate-related disclosure from both nonfinancial and financial perspectives (Sharfman and Copland 2022).

The SEC requires public companies to provide the following climate-related information in their annual financial reports (Securities and Commission 2022):

- GHG emissions information: Listed companies are required to provide information on GHG emissions, sources of emissions and mitigation measures.
- Climate change risks: Listed companies need to assess and disclose the impact of climate change on their operations, finances and compliance, as well as the risks and opportunities they face.
- Climate governance information: Listed companies are required to provide information on the responsibilities, authorities and activities of the board of directors and its audit committee in relation to climate governance.
- Assurance of disclosure of relevant information: Listed companies need to provide assurance from the board of directors and its audit committee on the disclosure of climate-related information.

Specifically, the climate disclosure requirements are as follows: (1) There should be disclosure of the impact on financial statement line items, including extreme weather and other natural events (e.g., impairment losses, increased loss reserves), transformational activities (e.g., changes in asset salvage values or useful lives), and expenditures related to the mitigation of extreme weather and other natural risks and transformation activities if the amount of the impact exceeds 1% of the financial statement line item, for example, how extreme weather and other natural events and transformation activities affect the estimates and assumptions in financial statements? (2) The company should disclose how the public company's board of directors and management oversee climate-related risks, the risk management process, and the public company's response. (3) There should be other qualitative disclosures including the ways in which the impact on the business and its financial statements is or may be material, along with the ways in which it affects or may affect the listed company's 'strategy, business model and outlook'. It should be disclosed about the listed company's processes for identifying, assessing and managing climate-related risks and whether these processes are integrated into the listed company's broader risk management programme.

In addition, investment organisations are required to provide investors with the following climate-related information (Securities and Commission 2022):

- Climate-related information on portfolio companies: Investment institutions are required to provide information on GHG emissions, climate change risks and climate governance of their portfolio companies.
- Climate governance information of investment institutions: Investment institutions are required to provide information on their internal climate governance measures and policies as well as consider climate factors in their investment decisions.
- Assurance of relevant disclosures: Investment institutions are required to provide assurance from their boards of directors and audit committees on the disclosure of climate-related information.

The purpose of the announcement was to improve investors' understanding of climate-related risks and opportunities and to promote the sustainable development of the capital markets. At the same time, the announcement also required listed companies and investment institutions to take reasonable measures to ensure the accuracy, reliability and completeness of the climate-related information provided.

3.2 The UK Climate Change Act

The UK's Climate Change Act enacted in 2008 is an important step taken by the UK government to address the challenge of climate change (Bauer et al. 2012). The core objective of the Climate Change Act was to ensure that the UK would play an active role in adapting to and mitigating climate change. The most important of these objectives was to reduce greenhouse gas emissions to less than 80% of 1990 levels and develop plans for adapting to climate change. The key elements of the bill included the following (Dernbach and Kakade 2008):

- GHG reduction targets: Under the Act, the UK government set long-term targets for reducing greenhouse gas emissions. The initial target was to reduce GHG emissions by 80% by 2050 and set five-year carbon budget milestones.
- Budgets and plans: The Act required the government to set a carbon budget, which is the total amount of GHG emissions allowed over a specified period of time. The government was also required to publish regular climate change risk assessment reports and adaptation plans to address the impact of climate change.
- Independent Committee: The intent was to monitor the government's progress in addressing climate change, and in doing so, the bill created an independent body: the Committee on Climate Change. The Committee was given the responsibility for assessing and monitoring the government's carbon budget and action plan and advising the government and Parliament.
- Adaptation plans: In addition to reducing greenhouse gas emissions, the bill requires the government to develop plans to adapt to the risks and impacts of climate change. This includes the development of adaptation strategies and adaptation plans and ensuring that relevant departments take appropriate action in response to climate change.

The key aspect of the Climate Change Act was to bring the UK's climate objectives and government actions under legal constraints and ensure that the UK would take real action to mitigate climate change and adapt to its impacts. In addition, the Act provided a template for other countries to follow in developing similar climate policies and laws.

The UK was also the first country in the world to create a green economy policy bank (Owen et al. 2018). The UK Green Investment Bank (GIB) was set up by the UK government to promote renewable energy and a low-carbon economy. Established in 2012, the UK GIB was one of the UK government's key initiatives in tackling climate change and promoting sustainable development, with the aim of facilitating the transition to a low-carbon economy by investing in and supporting renewable energy, energy efficiency and other low-carbon projects. The UK GIB was initially funded by the UK government for initial construction, providing initial funding totalling approximately £3 billion. Subsequently, the institution has increased the amount of capital available for investment and expanded the coverage of green projects through issuing bonds and raising capital from private investors. To further promote green finance in the UK, the UK government privatised the GIB in 2017, selling it to the Macquarie Group, an Australian financial institution. At the same time, the UK government established a new national investment bank—the British Business Bank—to support broader economic development and innovation programmes.

3.3 China's Pilot Work Programme on Climate Investment and Financing

On December 23, 2021, China's Ministry of Ecology and Environment (MOE) and nine other ministries and commissions jointly released the Pilot Work Programme on Climate Investment and Financing. The Pilot Work Programme on Climate Investment and Financing was an important policy for promoting pilot work on climate investment and financing. The programme aimed to promote economic and social transformation towards green and low carbon by fostering and building the climate investment and financing market and guiding more funds into green and low-carbon projects related to addressing climate change. The programme specified the definition and scope of support for climate investment and financing, the objectives of the climate investment and financing pilot programme and eight key tasks. The programme emphasised the orderly development of carbon finance, the steady and orderly exploration of carbon financial services, including carbon funds, carbon asset pledge loans, carbon insurance and the strengthening of carbon accounting and information disclosure.

The programme specified the objective of the pilot: to promote the expansion of climate investment and financing through the exploration of innovative climate investment and financing models and standards while facilitating the inflow of capital to support the development of green and low-carbon projects. Here, climate investment and financing refer to investment and financing activities that guide and promote more capital in the field of addressing climate change to realise the national autonomous contribution target and the low-carbon development target, which is an important part of green finance (https://climate-laws.org/documents/climate-investment-and-financing-pilot-work-plan_6f3c?id=climate-investment-and-financing-pilot-work-plan_71d7). The scope supported in the programme included both mitigation and adaptation. Climate change mitigation included adjusting the industrial structure and actively developing strategic emerging industries; optimising the energy structure, vigorously developing nonfossil energy sources and implementing energy-saving and carbon-reducing renovation projects; carrying out pilot demonstrations of carbon capture, utilisation and sequestration; controlling greenhouse gas emissions from nonenergy activities, such as industry, agriculture and waste treatment; and increasing forests, grasslands and other carbon sinks. Adaptation to climate change included improving adaptive capacity in key areas such as agriculture, water resources, forestry and ecosystems, oceans, meteorology, disaster prevention, mitigation and relief; and strengthening basic capacity building for adaptation, accelerating infrastructure construction and improving scientific and technological capacity.

The programme proposed the following major tasks[2]:

- Identifying pilot areas: Select representative areas as pilots and explore locally appropriate climate investment and financing models through pilot work.
- Cultivate investment institutions: Encourage financial institutions and investment institutions to develop and promote financial products and services related to addressing climate change.
- Establish standards: Develop and promote standards and norms related to climate investment and financing, such as certification standards for green projects and environmental information disclosure requirements.
- Guiding funds: Guiding more capital into green and low-carbon projects to address climate change through the establishment of special funds and other means.
- Strengthening regulation: Establishing a sound regulatory mechanism for climate investment and financing to ensure that funds are utilised in accordance with norms and standards.
- Promoting experience: Promoting successful practices and models by summarising pilot experiences to promote the popularisation of climate investment and financing nationwide.

In addition, the programme also emphasised the importance and significance of the pilot work. By carrying out the pilot work, a climate investment and financing model suitable for China's national conditions can be explored in actual operations to promote the development of green finance and improve the ability to respond to

[2] Source: https://www.mee.gov.cn/xxgk2018/xxgk/xxgk05/202112/W020211224530353766483.pdf.

climate change. At the same time, it can also promote economic and social transformation towards green and low-carbon by guiding more capital into green and low-carbon projects.

References

Bauer, A., Feichtinger, J., Steurer, R. 2012. The governance of climate change adaptation in 10 OECD countries: Challenges and approaches. Journal of Environmental Policy & Planning 14(3): 279–304.

Bhandary, R.R., Gallagher, K.S., Zhang, F. 2021. Climate finance policy in practice: a review of the evidence. Climate Policy 21(4): 529–545.

Chan, G., Stavins, R., Ji, Z. 2018. International climate change policy. Annual Review of Resource Economics 10: 335–360.

Climate Change Laws of the World. Climate investment and financing pilot work plan. 2021. https://climate-laws.org/documents/climate-investment-and-financing-pilot-work-plan_6f3c?id=climate-investment-and-financing-pilot-work-plan_71d7

Daniels, B. 2018. Come hell and high water: Climate change policy in the age of Trump. FIU Law Review. 13: 65.

Delina, L. 2017. Multilateral development banking in a fragmented climate system: shifting priorities in energy finance at the Asian Development Bank. Int Environ Agreements 17(1): 73–88.

Dernbach, J.C., Kakade, S. 2008. Climate Change Law: An Introduction. Energy Law Journal. 29(1).

Dikau, S., Volz, U. 2021. Central bank mandates, sustainability objectives and the promotion of green finance. Ecological Economics 184: 107022.

Dovie, D.B.K., Lwasa, S. 2017. Correlating negotiation hotspot issues, Paris climate agreement and the international climate policy regime. Environmental Science & Policy 77: 1–8.

EU, A. 2018. Clean Planet for all, A European long-term strategic vision for a prosperous, modern, competitive and climate neutral economy. depth analysis in support of the commission communication com 773.

Gomez-Echeverri, L. 2018. Climate and development: enhancing impact through stronger linkages in the implementation of the Paris Agreement and the Sustainable Development Goals (SDGs). Philosophical Transactions of the Royal Society A: Mathematical, Physical and Engineering Sciences 376, 20160444.

Hafner, S., Jones, A., Anger-Kraavi, A., Pohl, J. 2020. Closing the green finance gap – A systems perspective. Environmental Innovation and Societal Transitions 34: 26–60.

Haites E. 2014. Aligning climate finance and development finance for Asia and the Pacific: Potential and prospects.

Karlsson-Vinkhuyzen, S.I., Vihma, A. 2009. Comparing the legitimacy and effectiveness of global hard and soft law: An analytical framework. Regulation & Governance 3(4): 400–420.

Lamperti, F., Dosi, G., Napoletano, M., Roventini, A., Sapio, A. 2020. Climate change and green transitions in an agent-based integrated assessment model. Technological Forecasting and Social Change 153, 119806.

Lamperti, F., Bosetti, V., Roventini, A., Tavoni, M., Treibich, T. 2021. Three green financial policies to address climate risks. Journal of Financial Stability 54, 100875.

Manta, O. 2020. Measures and Possible Support Solutions of the Sustainable European Economy in the Context of Actual Crises. European Journal of Marketing and Economics 3: 93–107.

McGee, J., Taplin, R. 2009. The role of the Asia Pacific Partnership in discursive contestation of the international climate regime. Int Environ Agreements 9(3): 213–238.

Miyamoto, M., Takeuchi, K. 2019. Climate agreement and technology diffusion: Impact of the Kyoto Protocol on international patent applications for renewable energy technologies. Energy Policy 129: 1331–1338.

MRV 101: Understanding measurement, reporting, and verification of climate change mitigation. https://primarysources.brillonline.com/browse/climate-change-and-law-collection/mrv-101-understanding-measurement-reporting-and-verification-of-climate-change-mitigation;cccc00 2020160020011

Myklebust, T. 2022. Climate-related financial risks: Considering an emerging framework for assessment and disclosure in a regulatory perspective. European Business Law Review 33(3).

Owen, R., Brennan, G., Lyon, F. 2018. Enabling investment for the transition to a low carbon economy: government policy to finance early stage green innovation. Current Opinion in Environmental Sustainability, Sustainability governance and transformation 2018(31): 137–145.

Park, H., Kim, J.D. 2020. Transition towards green banking: role of financial regulators and financial institutions. AJSSR 5(1): 5.

Prudential Regulation Authority. Climate change adaptation report: Climate-related financial risk management and the role of capital requirements. 2021.

Reyseliani, N., Hidayatno, A., Purwanto, W.W. 2022. Implication of the Paris agreement target on Indonesia electricity sector transition to 2050 using TIMES model. Energy Policy 169, 113184.

SEC.gov. SEC proposes rules to enhance and standardize climate-related disclosures for investors. 2022. https://www.sec.gov/news/press-release/2022-46

The U.S. Securities and Exchange Commission. The Enhancement and Standardization of Climate-Related Disclosures for Investors. 2022. https://www.sec.gov/2022.

Sharfman, B.S., Copland, J. 2022. Comment letter to the SEC on its proposed rule regarding climate-related risk disclosures. https://doi.org/https://doi.org/10.2139/ssrn.4139479

United Nations. United nation framework convention on climate change. 1992.

United Nations. Kyoto Protocol to the United Nations framework convention on climate change. 1998. https://unfccc.int/resource/docs/convkp/kpeng.pdf.

United Nations. Introduction to Climate Finance. https://unfccc.int/topics/introduction-to-climate-finance

Wall, R., Grafakos, S., Gianoli, A., Stavropoulos, S. 2019. Which policy instruments attract foreign direct investments in renewable energy? Climate Policy 19: 59–72.

Wiesenthal, T., Leduc, G., Haegeman, K., Schwarz, H.-G. 2012. Bottom-up estimation of industrial and public R&D investment by technology in support of policy-making: The case of selected low-carbon energy technologies. Research Policy 41: 116–131.

Wilson, D.J. 2012. Fiscal spending jobs multipliers: Evidence from the 2009 American Recovery and Reinvestment Act. American Economic Journal: Economic Policy 4: 251–282.

Wirth, D.A. 2017. The Paris Agreement as a new component of the UN climate regime. International Organisations Research Journal. https://papers.ssrn.com/abstract=3149823

Wu, S. 2023. A systematic review of climate policies in China: Evolution, effectiveness, and challenges. Environmental Impact Assessment Review 99, 107030.

SPRINGER NATURE

GPSR Compliance

The European Union's (EU) General Product Safety Regulation (GPSR) is a set of rules that requires consumer products to be safe and our obligations to ensure this.

If you have any concerns about our products, you can contact us on ProductSafety@springernature.com

In case Publisher is established outside the EU, the EU authorized representative is:

Springer Nature Customer Service Center GmbH
Europaplatz 3
69115 Heidelberg, Germany

The manufacturer's authorised representative in the EU is Springer Nature Customer Service Centre GmbH, Europaplatz 3, 69115 Heidelberg, Germany. If you have any concerns regarding our products, please contact ProductSafety@springernature.com

Printed and bound by CPI Group (UK) Ltd, Croydon, CR0 4YY
01/10/2026
02225863-0014